Public finance:

A normative theory

Public finance:

A normative theory

Richard W. Tresch
Boston College

1981

BUSINESS PUBLICATIONS, INC. Plano, Texas 75075
IRWIN-DORSEY LIMITED Georgetown, Ontario L7G 4B3

ISBN 0-256-02391-3
Library of Congress Catalog Card No.

Printed in the United States of America

1 2 3 4 5 6 7 8 9 0 MP 8 7 6 5 4 3 2 1

To
Alayne
Kimberly Sara
and
My Parents

Preface

Public Sector Economics: A Normative Theory evolved from the frustrations of teaching public expenditure and tax theory to graduate students in economics for a number of years without the benefit of an adequate textbook. Ours is a journals-oriented discipline, but pouring through article after article from a reading list is rough sledding for even very good students, especially in an area as broad and diverse as public sector economics. The text attempts to provide easier access to the literature by offering the graduate student a comprehensive and unified treatment of four major areas within the purview of public sector microeconomic analysis: public expenditure theory, tax theory, cost-benefit analysis, and fiscal federalism, emphasizing developments in the literature over the past ten years. While these areas were chosen primarily for the standard two-semester (three-quarter) Ph.D. field in public finance, the text is directly relevant to master's degree programs in economics, public administration, and urban and regional planning which stress quantitative economic analysis in general and cost-benefit analysis in particular. Upper-level undergraduates with strong quantitative backgrounds in constrained optimization techniques might also find the text useful, although it was written primarily with the graduate student in mind.

As its title suggests, the predominant theme of the text is normative theory, the optimal design of tax and expenditure policy. Positive theory, which considers the reactions to specific government policies, has an enormous literature of its own, and it was simply not possible to offer a comprehensive analysis of both normative and positive theory in one book. Positive aspects of government policy are hardly ignored, however. The entire section on cost-benefit analysis is designed to show how normative theory can be applied to real-world problems, and most chapters contain summaries of important contributions in the empirical literature.

Beyond the decision to focus on normative issues, the text reflects three principles of exposition that respond directly to the needs of the graduate student. First, the distinction between first-best and second-best analysis is carefully maintained throughout the text. Part II analyzes public expenditure and tax theory under the first-best assumptions of an underlying competitive market environment and unrestricted government policy responses to allocational and distributional problems. Until 10 or 15 years ago, the vast majority of public sector literature employed these assumptions, to the point where the first-best results can be considered the received doctrine. For instance, students with some undergraduate training in public finance will surely recognize many of the results, if not the methodology, contained in Part II. The public expenditure analysis covers externality theory, public goods, decreasing cost production, and the peak-load problem. The theory of taxation considers optimal income redistribution in a first-best environment, including the traditional principles of taxing according to benefits received and ability to pay, and the more recent notion of pareto-optimal redistributions.

Part III then reconsiders tax and expenditure theory under standard second-best assumptions such as legislated budget constraints and distorting taxation. First the tax analysis is expanded to include the allocational theory of taxation and tax incidence, both inherently second-best topics. The final chapters in Part III then rework many of the traditional results from public expenditure theory under second-best assumptions. Part III is especially responsive to the literature of the past decade, which has been predominantly concerned with second-best analysis. Second-best tax theory has long been part of the received doctrine, but it has been considerably sharpened and expanded during the past ten years. The second-best public expenditure analysis is really quite recent, however, and revolutionary.

Finally, the discussions of cost-benefit analysis and fiscal federalism in Parts IV and V are equally careful to distinguish between first-best and second-best assumptions.

The second principle is that a graduate text ought to do more than review the major theoretical and empirical results of its discipline. It should also emphasize how economists obtain these results, so that when the student confronts the professional literature it will be clear why a certain model was chosen to analyze a particular problem, and what properties the model has. Understanding the models commonly used to analyze public sector problems is a major goal of the text.

To this end, *Public Sector Economics* begins with a lengthy introduction (Part I) that extends well beyond the standard cursory presentation of market failure and pareto optimality as represented in the first chapter. Three additional chapters guide the student through a careful presentation of the main tools of public sector analysis, always stressing the general equilibrium approach used in all the best literature. These chapters set out full general equilibrium models of an economy defined first in terms of quantities and then in terms of prices, with careful explanations of each of their various elements, including social welfare functions, generalized production functions, various representations of market clearance and the distinctions between actual and compensated equilibria, expenditure functions, generalized profit functions, and so forth. Part I thus builds a solid, unifying foundation for the remainder of the text, because each public sector problem discussed in Parts II–V is analyzed, formally, as a particular modification of one of the basic general equilibrium models developed in Chapters 2 through 4.

For instance, every problem discussed in Part II utilizes a variation of the general equilibrium social welfare planning model developed in Chapter 2. The formal structure of the second-best analysis in Part III is only slightly more complex, using two or three versions of the general equilibrium market models developed in Chapter 4. These same models reappear throughout Parts

IV and V as well. Students familiar with general equilibrium modeling can skim much of the material in Part I, but others would be well advised to study the four introductory chapters in detail. They are central to the remainder of the text and, we believe, to most of the normative (and positive) theory in the professional literature.

Third, an entire section of the text has been devoted to cost-benefit analysis (Part IV), rather than a chapter or two as in most texts. The cost-benefit material is important in its own right for anyone concerned with policy, but it also serves to unify the theoretical concepts and results of the preceding three sections within a single conceptual framework. Rather than push forward with many new ideas, the cost-benefit chapters are written from the perspective of practical policy making. They emphasize the judgmental aspects of applied analysis and ask the student to reflect upon the relevance of tax and expenditure theory to policy making, which of necessity deals with problems that are much less well defined than the stylized models of the pure theory. Thus, Part IV serves as a bridge between theory and practice. In particular, it indicates how choices between first-best and second-best assumptions at each stage of a cost-benefit study will influence final policy recommendations.

The topics covered in the text are reasonably conventional within the confines of normative micro public sector analysis with, perhaps, two exceptions. First, the theory of fiscal federalism has been given an entire section of its own (Part V) despite the fact that it is not absolutely essential to a presentation of normative public sector theory. Federalism has generated enormous professional interest in the 1970s, and this body of literature is rather badly underrepresented in most public finance texts. We felt that graduate students in economics and related fields would welcome an extensive treatment of the federalism literature.

Second, the text makes one clean break with the traditional presentation of micro public sector theory in the area of taxation. Most public finance texts devote at least one chapter to each major U.S. tax, particularly the U.S. personal income tax, the U.S. social security tax, the U.S. corporate income tax, state sales taxes, and local property taxes. Rather than follow that taxonomic structure, the text concentrates on efficiency and equity principles that apply to all taxes. Actual U.S. tax policy is considered, but only by way of illustration as the principles are developed. Consequently, the chapters on taxation tend to be more theoretical and less institutional than the standard treatment. However, with the theoretical analysis in hand, students should be able to proceed comfortably to any one of the many excellent books that have been written on the individual taxes. In any event, we believe our general theoretical approach is more consistent with the recent thrust of normative tax analysis.

A few words on using the text will conclude these brief remarks. Our experience suggests that it is possible to cover material from all the chapters in two semesters (three quarters). Indeed, we hope the text is reasonably self-instructive, so that teachers will feel free to spend somewhat more class time on extensions and other topics of special interest.

The text can also be used for a one-semester course designed to give the student a broad introduction to public sector analysis. Chapters 1 and 2 from Part I and Chapters 6, 9, 10, 12, and 13 from Part II provide a reasonably comprehensive treatment of traditional first-best theory. Similarly, Chapters 3 and 4 from Part I, plus Chapters 14, 15, the second part of Chapter 16 on the many-person economy with linear technology, and 17 capture the essence of second-best analysis. A really ambitious course might also consider selected topics in cost-benefit analysis and/or fiscal federalism, time permitting.

ACKNOWLEDGMENTS

In 1966–67 Peter Diamond taught a remarkable seminar on government expenditure and tax theory to a small group of second-year graduate students at M.I.T. He found new and insightful ways to present the established first-best tax and expenditure results, and pushed far onto the frontiers of second-best theory, offering us material that was not to appear in the professional literature for years thereafter. By the mid 1970s Peter had published the ideas from the course that most interested him, leaving the remainder for others to discover independently. For those of us who went on to specialize in public sector economics, the notes from that seminar continue to provide a marvelous perspective on the mainstreams of the discipline.

Peter's influence on this text is inestimable, especially its first three parts. The numerous references to his published and unpublished work are testimony enough to that, but the entire structure of the first 22 chapters derives from that seminar of 15 years ago. Peter taught a systematic and unified approach to tax and expenditure theory that I have used in my own teaching and in writing the text. I hope he is pleased with the book, but at very least I have the pleasure of thanking publicly this exceptional scholar and teacher.

I am also deeply grateful to Robin Boadway of Queen's University and Liam Ebrill of Cornell University, both of whom carefully reviewed each chapter of the original manuscript. Their many insightful comments, criticisms, and suggestions have significantly improved the text.

My own students and colleagues at Boston College have been a constant source of inspiration and support. James Anderson, Marvin Kraus, Donald Richter, and John Riley helped me with specific sections of the text, but a listing of all the indirect contributors at Boston College would be many times longer.

Finally, I wish to thank Ms. Patricia Ryan, who typed the entire manuscript through all its revisions, an enormous task. Patty's dedication and efficiency were matched by her extreme good nature throughout, and I am most appreciative.

RICHARD W. TRESCH

Contents

Optimal Federalism and Grants-in-Aid: *The First-Best Policy Environment. Second-Best Policy Environment. Nonoptimal Distribution of Income.* The Growth of National Grants-in-Aid in the United States. The Baumol-Oates Model of Cost Disease: *Empirical Estimates of Local Public Service Growth. Tax Pressures and Fiscal Illusion.* Additional Design Characteristics of Grants-in-Aid: *Practical Issues in Grant Design. Alternative Design Criteria.* The Response to Grants-in-Aid: *The Theory of Grant Response. Empirical Evidence on U.S. Grants-in-Aid.*

I

Introduction: The content and methodology of public sector theory

1

Introduction—The content of normative public sector theory

The economic histories of all the advanced Western economies in the 20th century share one common trait, an enormous growth in the scope and influence of the government sector. Professional economic analysis of the public sector has reflected this growth, to the extent that no single treatise on public sector economics could possibly hope to capture the variety and richness of the literature on domestic economic policy, even at an introductory level. Consequently, we have chosen to limit the scope of this text in two ways. First, we will discuss only the microeconomic theory of the public sector relating to the issues of resource allocation and income distribution, as opposed to the macroeconomic theory of the public sector, or the theory of fiscal policy. Second, we will present only the normative theory of the public sector, what governments ought to be doing, as opposed to the positive theory, one which emphasizes the economic effects of existing governmental institutions and policies without necessarily judging their effectiveness in terms of some preconceived criteria. Of course, a complete separation of normative and positive theory is impossible. A normative analysis will naturally reflect upon how well existing government policies meet various normative objectives. In every chapter, though, our primary emphasis will be on the normative theory.

That a consistent normative theory of the public sector should have evolved at all from Western economic thought is perhaps surprising; but, in fact, virtually all Western public sector economists embrace the same set of policy norms, even though their political tastes may vary along the entire liberal-conservative spectrum. There is remarkable agreement on the problems the government ought to address and the appropriate course of government action. In a strictly technical sense, the consensus arises because economists have chosen, with only rare exceptions, one basic analytical model to describe all public sector economic problems. Given a common analytical framework, consensus is inevitable.

Chapter 1 describes in general terms the four fundamental issues that a normative analysis must confront, and shows how a particular set of values shared by virtually all Western economists has produced a common approach to these issues. Chapter 2 will present the formal structure of the basic general equilibrium model that has been most commonly used to develop normative public sector decision rules, showing how the value structure outlined in Chapter 1 has been incorporated into the formal model. Chapters 3 and 4 conclude a lengthy introduction to the theory of the public sector by describing some variations of the basic model that have proved useful for analyzing particular public sector problems. Students should have a firm grasp of this material before proceeding to the theory of the public sector, which begins in Part II.

TOWARD A NORMATIVE THEORY— THE FUNDAMENTAL ISSUES

Insofar as it relates to the economics of the public sector, normative analysis attempts to establish a set of policy guidelines in four broad areas:

1. The primary normative issue, upon which all others turn, is the question of *legitimacy:* In what areas of economic activity can the government properly become involved?

2. Once the appropriate sphere of government activity has been determined, the next question concerns the *decision rules* that the government ought to follow in each area. Taken together, these two questions comprise the heart of normative public sector theory, commonly referred to as the theory of government expenditures.

3. The theory of government expenditures in turn suggests a third normative question: How should the government finance these expenditures? Analysis of this question provides the basis for a comprehensive *normative theory of taxation* (or, more generally, a theory of government revenues), but the theory of taxation is not necessarily distinct from the theory of government expenditures. Frequently the decision rules for government expenditures describe not only the correct level of government expenditures in some area but also the corresponding means for financing the expenditures. When this occurs the theory of taxation is effectively subsumed within the theory of government expenditures. In other instances, however, expenditure theory does not specify a self-financing payment mechanism, in which case the theory of taxation becomes an interesting issue, per se. To give just one example, the government may be constrained to offer some services free of charge. If so, then normative theory must describe a separate set of criteria for raising the revenues to pay for these services.

4. The fourth, and final, normative issue is the *theory of fiscal federalism,* addressing the question: Which tasks should each government perform? A federalist system is a hierarchical collection of governments in which a citizen is, simultaneously, a constituent of more than one government, for example, the national-state-local structure in the United States, and similar arrangements in most other countries. The fundamental problem for a federalist structure is one of coordination, of sorting out the legitimate functions of government among the various governments within the system so that public policies do not work at cross-purposes with one another. Without proper coordination one can easily imagine potential conflicts arising, such as one government heavily taxing a person while another government is simultaneously trying to transfer

income to him, or one town actively promoting industrial development to the environmental detriment of neighboring towns.[1] The theory of fiscal federalism, then, accepts as given the normative rules for public expenditures and taxation established in response to the first three questions. It merely tries to ensure that these rules will be followed consistently throughout the entire fiscal structure.

Parts II–IV of the text develop the normative theories of public expenditures and taxation. Part V considers the special problems associated with a federalist system of government.

PHILOSOPHICAL UNDERPINNINGS

A normative analysis of the public sector necessarily begins with a statement of its philosophical foundations. Obviously a Marxist would answer the four fundamental questions differently from, say, Milton Friedman, who, rightly or wrongly, has been identified as the leading spokesman for 19th century economic liberalism. Moreover, a normative analysis of government policy would make little sense as a text unless there actually exists a fairly broad consensus regarding the appropriate philosophical foundations for public sector analysis.

In point of fact, there clearly is such a consensus in Western economic thought, if one judges solely by the sheer number of all published materials. Furthermore, this consensus is remarkably close to the views of the 19 century liberals, all the more surprising given the decided antigovernmental slant of liberal theory.

In the professional literature the government is hardly ever viewed as a competitor to the free market system. To the contrary, the competitive market economy is seen as the ideal economic system, so much so that competitive market failure is a necessary condition for public sector activity. Consequently, the answer to the fundamental question of public expenditure theory is that the government should perform only those functions which for some reason the competitive market cannot perform at all, or performs "sufficiently badly" to warrant public sector interference. Reasonable people may disagree, of course, on the meaning of "sufficiently badly," and just what this phrase implies in terms of legitimate government activity, but there also happens to be fairly close agreement on the list of legitimate government functions implied by the market failure criterion.

Belief in the competitive market system influences public sector theory well beyond the primary issue of legitimacy. Public sector analysis typically assumes that the government sector is operating within the context of an established market economy, one in which the private sector is perfectly competitive. If, in addition, it is assumed that there are no constraints limiting the form which government policies may take, the analysis is said to be *first best* in that the government can achieve the highest possible level of social well-being. These assumptions may seem unduly restrictive, but until the 1970s the vast majority

---

[1] For ease of expression, the masculine gender will be used in this text.

of public expenditure analysis assumed a first-best policy environment. Furthermore, most of the policy decision rules resulting from first-best analysis are so closely related to competitive market principles that they can be interpreted as follows: The government should do what the competitive market would have done if only the market could have acted.

Once constraints are added to the analysis, usually in the form of market imperfections or restrictions on permissible government policy responses, the analysis is said to be *second best*. Much of the recent literature on normative public sector theory has employed second-best assumptions. These studies have shown that most second-best decision rules tend not to have close competitive interpretations. One senses a certain disappointment on this score, as public sector economists have had to abandon the comforting market-oriented intuition of the first-best rules. Nonetheless, nearly all second-best analysis to date has posited the existence of a perfectly competitive market economy as the backdrop for government activity, with the occasional exception of an assumed monopolistic imperfection in one specific market. Thus, even second-best analysis retains close ties with the competitive market system.

THE PRINCIPLE OF CONSUMER SOVEREIGNTY

That public sector economics should be so closely related to competitive market principles hardly makes it unique within the profession. Many other fields of economic analysis share this feature as well, for example, consumer economics, industrial organization, and international trade. A partial explanation for this is simply that policy questions are so often studied within the context of a market economy. But more importantly, public sector economists embrace the same fundamental value judgment as do supporters of the free market system, the principle of *consumer sovereignty*: consumers (and producers) know best their own self-interests. With consumer sovereignty as the underlying principle, public policy pursues the same goal as the competitive market system, broadly speaking, the well-being of society expressed through the preferences of its individual citizens.

While this is hardly a startling revelation, it does have one remarkable implication for the normative theory of the public sector. To the extent possible the government *qua* government is supposed to be nonexistent, in the important sense that government officials are not permitted to interject their own preferences on policy issues into the analysis. There is, for example, no commonly accepted normative theory of government behavior, per se. Rather, the government's role is meant to be little more than that of an outside agent. The basic idea is that if the market system breaks down for some reason, the government is expected to design policies to set it back on track, but in doing so it must follow only the dictates of its citizens, again to the extent this is possible.

This particular feature of the normative theory renders it somewhat more distant from the positive theory than one might desire, since government administrators are constantly interjecting their own preferences into the decision-making process. But, at the same time, it is a source of richness and subtlety. A normative analysis based solely on the preferences of a government administrator would be little more than an exercise in the theory of consumer behavior. By forcing the government to consider only the preferences of its citizens, however, all sorts of interesting and difficult problems arise. For example, what is the government to do if individual preferences clash, as they inevitably will? Suppose one group of citizens wants more spending in a particular area, while another group wants less. How should the government resolve this conflict? Normative theory must provide answers to questions such as these. There are also nagging questions of a different nature. If the market system cannot solve a particular problem, acting as it does on individual preferences, why should the government be able to do any better, if all it has to work with are the same individual preferences? A strict libertarian economist might insist that government intervention can only be justified if markets fail *and* if it can be demonstrated conclusively that some *viable* government policy will actually improve upon the market results. Most economists, however, have been content to assign normative theory the lesser task of describing a *potential* improvement through government action. But this does raise the important issue of whether or not some normative policy prescription really is viable, and, if not, whether a different, viable, policy can actually improve social welfare. As one might expect, sometimes there are clear answers to questions such as these, sometimes not; but in any case it is the fundamental belief in the principle of consumer sovereignty that makes them compelling.

MARKET FAILURE

Since legitimacy for public action is defined in terms of market failure, it is natural to ask next in what sense markets fail. Of course the market system is entirely neutral with respect to society's well-being. Nonetheless, if conditions are "right," competitive markets will generate an allocation of resources that is *pareto optimal*, meaning that it is impossible to reallocate resources such that one consumer can be made better off without making at least one other consumer worse off. Given the belief in consumer sovereignty, pareto optimality expressed in terms of individual consumers is the natural definition of allocational efficiency.

The problem is that the conditions or assumptions underlying a perfectly functioning market system are far too strong. They typically will not hold in practice, and if they do not, then a public policy can be described that will be pareto superior to the free market allocation of resources. That is to say, public policy can reallocate resources so as to make at least one consumer better off without making any other consumer worse off. This principle underlies all normative policy prescriptions concerned with the allocation of resources. It establishes pareto optimality as the policy norm for all government activity concerned with resource allocation, and further implies that government intervention with free market allocations is legitimate if and only if one or more of these assumptions fails to hold.

To determine the subject matter of normative public sector theory, then, begin by considering the assumptions that would allow a free market economy to achieve a pareto-optimal allocation of resources. These "best" assumptions fall into two distinct groups. The first consists of a set of assumptions relating to the actual structure of individual markets within the market economy, which we shall designate as the "market assumptions." The second group contains a set of assumptions about consumers' preferences and production possibilities, which we shall designate as the "technical assumptions."

The market assumptions are necessary to assure that all markets are in fact perfectly competitive, so that each economic agent is a price taker. This will be the case if three assumptions hold:

a. There are large numbers of buyers and sellers in each market.
b. There is no product differentiation within each market.
c. All buyers and sellers in each market have access to all relevant market information.

The technical assumptions are required to assure that both consumption and production activities are "well behaved," meaning that competitive markets will actually generate a pareto-optimal allocation of resources. Consider the following set of technical assumptions:

1. Preferences are convex.
2. Consumption possibilities form a convex set.
3. No consumer is satiated.
4. Some consumer is not satiated.
5. Preferences are continuous.
6. Individual utility is a function of own consumption and own factor supplies.
7. Individual firm's production possibilities depend only upon own inputs and outputs.
8. Aggregate production possibilities are convex.

Debreu has shown that:[2]

a. If assumptions 1, 2, 3, 6, and 7 hold, a competitive equilibrium is a pareto optimum.
b. If assumptions 1, 2, 4, 5, 6, 7, and 8 hold, a pareto optimum can be achieved by a competitive equilibrium with the appropriate distribution of income.

Results (a) and (b) comprise the fundamental theorem of welfare economics. Assumptions 6 and 7 rule out the possibility of externalities in either consumption or production. Assumptions 1, 2, and 5 on individual preferences will be satisfied by the standard assumption of consumer theory, that utility functions are quasi concave, continuous, and twice differentiable. Assumptions 3 or 4 are commonly employed in economic analysis. Assumption 8 on aggregate

---

[2] Gerard Debreu, *The Theory of Value: An Axiomatic Analysis of Economic Equilibrium* (New York: John Wiley & Sons, Inc., 1959), chap. 6.

production possibilities implies constant or increasing opportunity costs, and will be satisfied if all individual firm's production functions are continuous, twice differentiable, and exhibit either decreasing or constant returns to scale. Assumption 8 rules out significant increasing returns to scale production, which would imply decreasing opportunity costs, or a production-possibility frontier convex to the origin.

Putting the market and technical assumptions together implies the following. If the three market assumptions hold so that all markets are perfectly competitive, and the combination of technical assumptions specified under (a) or (b) of the fundamental theorem in welfare economics hold as well, then a free market system will generate a pareto-optimal allocation of resources. If this were actually the case, the government sector would not be required to make any decisions with respect to the allocation of resources. Indeed it would not be permitted to do so, according to the normative theory.

PUBLIC POLICY AND THE DISTRIBUTION OF INCOME

If all the appropriate assumptions actually held, would there be anything at all for the government to do? The answer is yes, because societies have always shown concern for equity as well as efficiency in economic matters. A perfectly functioning market system can assure an efficient allocation of resources, but it cannot guarantee that the distribution of the goods and services will be socially acceptable. At any point in time, the market system takes the ownership of resources as a given, and if society deems the ownership pattern unjust, then it will probably find the distribution of goods and services produced by these resources unacceptable as well. Moreover there are no natural market mechanisms to correct for distributional imbalances should they occur, nothing analogous to the laws of supply and demand which, under the stringent conditions listed above, automatically search for pareto-optimal allocations. Thus, decisions concerning the distribution of income are the first order of business in public sector economics in the sense that even in the best of all worlds, with all the appropriate market and technical assumptions holding, the government will have to formulate some policy with respect to the distribution of income if society cares about equity. Of course society might simply choose to accept the market determined distribution, but this is still a distribution policy requiring collective choice, even though it involves no actual redistribution. Moreover no country has ever made this choice. At a minimum, then, a normative theory of the public sector must address the question of the optimal distribution of income.

Unfortunately, the notion of an optimal income distribution is an agonizingly difficult problem for the normative theory of the public sector, given that the fundamental value judgment is consumer sovereignty. By its very nature, any redistribution of income will violate the principle of consumer sovereignty, so long as the losers in the redistribution have not willingly parted with their incomes. We argued above that, to the extent possible, normative theory requires that public sector decisions be based entirely on consumers' preferences, and not those of government officials. This is simply not possible, however, with redistribution policy. The government must impose a set of preferences to resolve distributional issues. But if this is so, then a normative theory ideally should describe how these distributional preferences are to be formed. Unfortunately, normative analysis has never achieved this goal. Any number of suggestions has been proposed, but none has ever gained wide acceptance, nor is a consensus on distributional preferences ever likely to be achieved. If anything, modern welfare theory has suggested that interpersonal equity comparisons are essentially meaningless. In any event, there is currently no commonly accepted theoretical notion of an optimal distribution of income, certainly nothing comparable to the universal acceptance of pareto optimality as a guiding principle for allocational issues.

The lack of consensus on distributional norms turns out to be a severe problem for normative public sector theory, with implications far beyond the distribution question, per se. Because an economic system is a closed system in which all decisions are ultimately interrelated, any public policy decision made with respect to the distribution question will affect *all* public policy decisions relating to allocational issues as well. Thus the government cannot simply make a particular redistributional decision, for better or worse, and be done with it.

Public sector economics has never totally come to grips with this problem. Economists have all too often assumed away distributional problems in order to analyze more comfortable allocational issues, knowing full well that dichotomizing allocational and distributional policies is often not legitimate, and may produce normative policy prescriptions quite wide of the mark. Some of the more recent work in public sector theory has tried to incorporate distributional considerations directly into analyses primarily concerned with allocational issues, but even these studies usually make no attempt to justify particular distributional norms. Rather, the government's distributional preferences are simply taken as given, and normative policies are described with respect to these preferences. The spirit of the analysis is: "Have the government provide us with a set of distributional preferences, and we will tell it what it should do." Perhaps this is all economists can hope to do with the distribution question, but it is at least unsettling that policy decision rules depend so crucially upon the assumed pattern of distributional preferences.

THE PUBLIC SECTOR AND THE ALLOCATION
OF RESOURCES

As indicated above, the allocational issues in public sector economics follow directly from a breakdown in the assumptions necessary for a perfectly functioning market system. In reality, of course, neither the full set of market nor technical assumptions holds in practice, so there is broad scope for legitimate government activity. By tradition within the profession, the domestic microeconomic consequences of failures in the market assumptions typically fall within the domain of industrial organization or consumer economics. These fields analyze such problems as monopolistic behavior and imperfect information flows, along with the corresponding public policy responses such as antitrust and consumer-protection legislation. On the other hand, the microeconomic theory of the public sector, or public finance, has traditionally limited its concern to breakdowns in the technical assumptions,[3] concentrating primarily on the existence of externalities and increasing returns or decreasing cost production. This text will maintain that tradition.

Focusing on these two assumptions may seem overly restrictive, but Francis Bator has estimated[4] that about 97 percent of all government expenditures on goods and services in the United States, the exhaustive or resource-using expenditures, can be justified in terms of one or both of these conditions. Examples of U.S. government programs justified in terms of externalities would surely include defense, the space program, and related activities, which together comprise the overwhelming majority of exhaustive expenditures in the national budget; education, which accounts for nearly 40 percent of all state and local exhaustive expenditures; and many lesser items such as local public safety, the judicial system, and government-supported research and development programs. Public services exhibiting significant increasing returns-to-scale production include many types of public transportation (these services frequently generate externalities as well), the public utilities, many recreational facilities, and even television broadcasting, which may well be one of the purest examples of a decreasing cost service.

Table 1–1 lists expenditures and receipts for all U.S. governments, with expenditures cross-listed by functional category and National Income and Product Account. Two features of these data are especially noteworthy. First, the fact that most of the exhaustive or resource-using expenditures in the United States exhibit either externalities or increasing returns strongly suggests that the majority of U.S. citizens view the legitimacy issue exactly as put forth in this introductory chapter: public sector expenditures that take resources from the private sector can be justified only by a failure of the technical assumptions necessary for a perfectly functioning market system. Second, expenditures on goods and services accounted for only 32.9 percent of total federal government expenditures in fiscal 1980. The remainder were transfer payments which, while they obviously have allocational implications, can be thought of as primarily redistributive in their impact. As such, they can also be considered a response to market failure, namely the fundamental inability of the market system to guarantee an acceptable distribution of income. With the exception of interest payments on government debt, and possibly

---

[3] The theory of fiscal or stabilization policy, which attempts to design optimal expenditure and tax policies to promote macroeconomic goals, can be thought of as a response to imperfectly competitive market structures, particularly in the markets for labor. As such, it is certainly part of the theory of the public sector, but the text will consider only the microeconomic problems of resource allocation and optimal income distribution.

[4] Francis M. Bator, *The Question of Government Spending* (New York: Harper Bros. Publishers, 1960), p. 100.

Table 1–1

Expenditures and Receipts by Governments of the United States

1. The federal government

A. Expenditures (by function)
Fiscal year 1980 (estimates)

Category	Billions of Dollars	Percent of Total
Defense and defense related*	146.7	26.0
Energy, natural resources, environment	20.5	3.6
Agriculture	4.6	0.8
Commerce and housing credit	5.5	1.0
Transportation	19.6	3.5
Community and regional development	8.5	1.5
Education, training, employment, and social services	30.7	5.4
Health	56.6	10.0
Income security	190.9	33.9
Veterans' benefits and services	20.8	3.7
Justice administration and general government	9.4	1.7
General purpose fiscal assistance	8.7	1.5
Interest	63.3	11.2
Other	(−)22.2	(−)3.8
Total	563.6	100.0

A. Receipts

Source	Billions of Dollars	Percent of Total
Individual income taxes	238.7	45.6
Corporation income taxes	72.3	13.8
Social insurance taxes and contributions	162.2	31.0
Excise taxes	26.3	5.0
Estate and gift taxes	5.8	1.1
Customs duties	7.6	1.5
Other	10.9	2.0
Total	523.8	100.0

B. Expenditures (National Income and Product Account)
1980 (estimates)

Category	Billions of Dollars	Percent of Total
Purchase of goods and services	185.6	32.9
Transfers to persons and foreigners	235.1	41.7
Grants-in-aid to state, local governments	84.3	14.9
Net interest paid	49.2	8.7
Subsidies less current surplus of government enterprises	10.0	1.8
Total	564.2	100.0

II. State and local governments

A. General expenditures (by function)
(1976–1977)

Category	Billions of Dollars	Percent of Total
Education	102.8	37.5
Highways	23.1	8.4
Public welfare	35.9	13.1
Other†	112.5	41.0
Total	274.4	100.0

Table 1–1 *(continued)*

A. Receipts

Source	Billions of Dollars	Percent of Total
Property taxes	62.5	21.9
Sales and gross receipts taxes	60.6	21.2
Individual income taxes	29.2	10.2
Corporation net income taxes	9.2	3.2
Revenues from federal government	62.6	21.9
Other[‡]	61.7	21.6
Total	285.8	100.0

B. Expenditures (National Income and Product Account)
1979 (preliminary)

Category	Billions of Dollars	Percent of Total
Purchases of goods and services	309.8	93.9
Transfers to persons	36.3	11.0
Net interest paid	(−)9.5	(−)2.9
Subsidies less current surplus of government enterprises	(−)6.7	(−)2.0
Total	329.9	100.0

* Defense related includes international affairs, general science, and space technology.
† Includes health, hospitals, police, local fire protection, natural resources, sanitation, housing and urban renewal, local parks and recreation, general control, financial administration, interest on general debt, and unallocable expenditures.
‡ Includes licenses, other taxes and charges, and miscellaneous revenue sources.
Sources: *Economic Report of the President*, January 1980 (Washington, D.C.: U.S. Government Printing Office, 1980), tables B-69 (p. 285), B-73 (p. 289), B-74 (p. 290), B-75 (p. 291).

some grants-in-aid programs, these transfer payments are clearly a response to perceived distributional inequities.

METHODS OF PUBLIC SECTOR ANALYSIS

Free market principles not only influence the subject matter of public expenditure theory but they have also dictated a fairly standard approach to the analysis of allocational problems in terms of the kinds of questions one asks. The typical format is as follows. Suppose one of the technical assumptions does not hold, for example, that externalities are present in a given market. The first step is to determine the pareto-optimal conditions given that a technical assumption is violated. The pareto-optimal conditions are then compared to the conditions that the competitive market would generate if there were no government intervention. Naturally they will differ. The policy problem, then, involves designing a course of government action that will generate the pareto-optimal conditions. The government could always assume complete control of the market and simply dictate an appropriate allocation, but this is typically perceived as the policy option of last resort. Given the underlying belief in competitive markets, the initial quest is for a set of policy tools, usually tax and transfer schemes, that achieve the pareto-optimal conditions while permitting the continued operation of the offending market. If at all possible, in other words, the government should stand aside and simply guide the market system to the proper allocation of resources.

Along these same lines, public policy analysis has always been especially interested in the implications which a particular problem in one market has for all other markets. Can government intervention be limited to the one offending market, with decentralized competition maintained elsewhere, or must the government intervene in other markets as well? One hopes for the former.

The incentive to preserve the competitive market structure arises directly from the principle that the government should serve society primarily as an agent acting in direct response to the preferences of its citizens. A belief in consumer sovereignty implies not only that government interference be limited to demonstrated cases of market failure but also that it be the absolute minimum necessary to restore pareto optimality.

THE THEORY OF TAXATION

Most of the remarks thus far have been directed to the theory of public expenditures as opposed to the theory of taxation, because the former is logically prior to the latter. Public expenditure theory defines the legitimate areas of public concern as well as the permissible forms that policy may take. Moreover, as indicated above, public expenditure theory often contains its own theory of taxation in that the expenditure decision rules define a set of taxes and transfers necessary to guide the market system to a pareto optimum. The theory of taxation becomes interesting in its own right only when the expenditure decision rules indicate the need for specific government expenditures without simultaneously specifying how those expenditures are to be financed. When this occurs, however, the same principles that guide public expenditure analysis apply to the collection of tax revenues as well. In particular, taxes should promote society's microeconomic goals of allocational efficiency and distributional equity.

There is a natural tension, however, between tax policy and the goal of allocational efficiency. Most taxes create distortions in the market system by forcing suppliers and demanders to face different prices. These distortions, in turn, misallocate resources, thereby creating allocational inefficiency. Resource misallocation is not desirable, of course, but it is nonetheless an unavoidable cost of having to raise tax revenues. One goal of normative tax theory, then, is to describe how to design taxes that minimize these distortions for any given amount of revenue to be collected. Alternatively, if the government must use one of two or three specific kinds of taxes to raise revenue, normative tax theory should indicate which of these taxes creates the minimum amount of inefficiency. Questions such as these are part of the allocational theory of taxation and, just as with the allocational issues of public expenditure theory, the guiding principle is pareto optimality. According to the pareto criterion, the government should collect a given amount of revenue such that it could not raise the same amount of revenue with an alternative set of taxes that would improve at least one consumer's welfare without simultaneously lowering the welfare of any other consumer. If such pareto improvements are impossible, then tax policy satisfies the pareto criterion of allocational efficiency, even though it necessarily creates inefficiencies relative to a no-tax situation.

The second unavoidable effect of taxes is that they reduce some consumers' purchasing power, so that they necessarily become part of the government's redistributional program. Naturally one wants taxes that contribute to society's distributional goals, but there are two difficulties here. First, the redistributional theory of taxation suffers from all the indeterminacies of redistributional theory in general. Thus, while public sector economists generally agree on normative tax policy with respect to society's allocational goals, there is significant disagreement as to what constitutes good tax policy in a distributional sense. Second, there is a fundamental trade-off between efficiency and equity in taxation. Generally speaking, achieving greater redistribution requires levying higher tax rates on the "rich" but, as we shall discover, higher rates tend to increase inefficiency. In addition, taxing some good might be particularly desirable in terms of society's distributional goals, but highly undesirably on efficiency grounds, or vice versa. Understanding the nature of these kinds of trade-offs has always been a primary goal of normative tax theory.

GENERAL EQUILIBRIUM ANALYSIS

A final methodological point concerns the models used in public sector analysis. The only sound theoretical approach to public sector problems is general equilibrium analysis, which we will use exclusively throughout the text. Because of data and other resource restrictions, empirical analysis must frequently be partial in scope, but theoretical analysis suffers no such handicaps, nor should it. Specific instances of the pitfalls of theoretical partial equilibrium analysis abound in the public sector literature.

Examples favoring the general equilibrium approach are easy to come by. For instance, only general equilibrium analysis can determine whether or not a failure in one market requires corrective action in other markets as well. As another example, recent second-best general equilibrium analysis, in both expenditure and tax theory, has shown that market imperfections and constraints on government policy responses outside the area of immediate concern have a direct effect on optimal policy rules. Finally, the theory of taxation is much richer now that general equilibrium analysis has shown how assumptions about the disposition of tax revenues influence the allocational and distributional effects of any given tax. Partial analysis cannot possibly address any of these points with any subtlety.

CONCLUSION

Chapter 1 has discussed the predominant themes in the normative economic theory of the public sector, at least as that theory has evolved in Western economic thought. The five main points are as follows:

1. Government activity is justified strictly in terms of competitive market failure. In particular, the microeconomic theory of the public sector focuses on the problems created by externalities, decreasing cost production, and an unacceptable distribution of income, none of which can be resolved adequately by the free market system.
2. Consumer sovereignty is the underlying value judgment of normative public sector theory. This ties the theory closely to the free market system, since advocates of free markets also embrace the principle of consumer sovereignty.
3. Government policies should promote the microeconomic goals of allocational efficiency and distributional equity.
4. Belief in consumer sovereignty firmly establishes pareto optimality, defined in terms of individual consumers, as the guiding principle for all government policies designed to promote allocational efficiency. At the same time, however, it has been instrumental in preventing a consensus from forming on policy norms for distributional equity.
5. General equilibrium analysis is the only sound approach to a normative analysis of public sector economics.

The next three chapters will continue the introduction to public sector theory, with a twofold purpose in mind. On the one hand, they will present the specific general equilibrium models that have proven most useful for public sector analysis. In the process of developing these models, we hope to show how one can create fairly simple analytical descriptions of an entire economic system which have the following properties:

a. They incorporate the principle of consumer sovereignty.
b. They are flexible enough, despite their simplicity, to consider a wide range of policy problems.
c. They can capture all relevant market responses to particular government policies.

These three chapters will also compare and contrast the assumptions and methods of first-best and second-best analysis, a distinction that was merely alluded to in Chapter 1. Until the 1970s, public expenditure analysis was conducted almost exclusively within a first-best context. Tax theory, on the other hand, has long employed second-best assumptions, primarily because the allocational theory of taxation is inherently an exercise in the theory of the second best. However, most of the early tax analysis used misleading partial equilibrium models. Over the past ten years or so public sector economists have increasingly employed second-best general equilibrium models to analyze both tax and expenditure theory, with fairly dramatic results. Applying these models to tax issues has significantly sharpened and generalized the work of earlier tax theorists, and recent second-best public expenditure analysis has completely shattered the received doctrine of first-best expenditure theory. Therefore, understanding the distinctions between first-best and second-best general equilibrium analysis is crucial to achieving a full appreciation for existing public sector theory. These distinctions will be carefully developed in Chapters 2–4.

REFERENCES

Bator, Francis M. *The Question of Government Spending*. New York: Harper Bros. Publishers, 1960.

Debreu, Gerard. *The Theory of Value: An Axiomatic Analysis of Economic Equilibrium*. New York: John Wiley & Sons, Inc., 1959.

Economic Report of the President, January 1980. Washington, D.C.: U.S. Government Printing Office, 1980.

2

A useful general equilibrium
model for public sector analysis

Chapter 2 will develop an analytical model of an economy suitable for public sector analysis, and describe its main properties. For a model to be useful as a framework for public sector economics, it must possess four basic attributes. First, it must enumerate the preferences of every consumer and describe all the economy's underlying production relationships. That is, it must be a general equilibrium model of the economy. Second, it must be flexible enough to consider a broad spectrum of public sector problems, particularly those associated with externalities, decreasing cost production, income redistribution, and various issues in the theory of taxation. Third, it must be designed to highlight the two basic public policy norms, efficiency as embodied in the principle of pareto optimality, and interpersonal equity, the notion of a just distribution of purchasing power. Finally, it must be compatible with the operations of a market economy, since the text will discuss public sector decision making within the context of a market system.

In his 1954 article, "The Pure Theory of Public Expenditure,"[1] Paul Samuelson presented a model with exactly these attributes and used it to analyze a particular kind of externality problem, the existence of nonexclusive goods. Samuelson's model has since become the standard for virtually all neoclassical public sector analysis, for the simple reason that it has proved to be readily adaptable to the full range of public sector problems. Thus, as a prelude to the study of public sector economics it is absolutely essential that one understand the basic elements of the model, the properties of its solution, and certain variations of the model that public sector economists have found especially useful. These are the specific goals of Chapters 2–4.

A USEFUL GENERAL EQUILIBRIUM MODEL

As a starting point, it is useful to think of a general equilibrium model as an extension of the standard model of supply and demand for a single market,

---

[1] P. A. Samuelson, "The Pure Theory of Public Expenditure," *Review of Economics and Statistics*, November 1954. The following year Samuelson supplemented the mathematical analysis with a geometric presentation in P. A. Samuelson, "Diagrammatic Exposition of a Theory of Public Expenditure, *Review of Economics and Statistics*, November 1955. No articles have had any greater impact on public sector analysis.

applied to the economy as a whole. The basic elements are identical: a specification of the demand for goods and factors, a specification of the supply of goods and factors, and market clearance in all goods and factor markets.

There is one important difference, however. Single market models always specify supply and demand functions in terms of market prices since they are designed specifically to explain the behavior of prices as well as quantities. In their most general formulation, general equilibrium models are defined only in terms of the quantities of goods and factors demanded and supplied, using as their basic data individuals' preference functions and firms' production functions. Thus, they do not necessarily apply to market economies. A general equilibrium model can be specified in terms of prices and directly applied to a market economy, but this requires an additional set of specific assumptions concerning the market behavior of both consumers and producers (and the government in its dual role as consumer of some products and producer of others), exactly as is done in generating single market supply and demand functions. In order to avoid this additional complication at the outset, we will begin with the standard general equilibrium model of an economy defined in terms of quantities, without reference to a market economy. It can be thought of as a social welfare planning model in which an omniscient social planner dictates quantities to all consumers and producers. However, we will assume that all the technical assumptions necessary for a well-functioning competitive market system apply, and we will relate the solution of the model to standard competitive market behavior. This will provide a proper analytical foundation for introducing breakdowns in the technical assumptions one at a time in Part II, as we explore public expenditure and tax theory in the context of a competitive market economy. The model will also be useful immediately for analyzing the problem of achieving an optimal distribution of income, since that problem exists even if all the technical assumptions hold.

The Demand Side of the Model—Consumers' Preferences

As indicated in Chapter 1, individuals' preferences are the fundamental demand data for all normative public sector analysis. In general, they will be defined over all goods and services demanded, and all factors supplied.
Let:

X_{hg} = the demand for good g by person h. $h = 1, \ldots, H$
                                                      $g = 1, \ldots, G$

V_{hf} = the supply of factor f by person h. $h = 1, \ldots, H$
                                                      $f = 1, \ldots, F$

Define:

or
$$U^h = U^h(X_{h1}, \ldots, X_{hG}; V_{h1}, \ldots, V_{hF})$$

(2.1)
$$U^h = U^h(X_{hg}; V_{hf}) \qquad h = 1, \ldots, H$$

as the ordinal utility function for person h, assumed to be "well behaved."[2] By convention, factor supplies enter the utility function with a negative sign. For example, if X is the only good, and L, labor, the only factor, the utility of person h might be represented as

$$U = U^h(X_h; 24 - L_h)$$

where 24 represents the total hours in the day, and $(24 - L_h)$ is a "good," leisure.

The functions $U^h(\ )$ represent a complete description of individual preferences for the economy, defined over $H \cdot G$ individual good demands and $H \cdot F$ individual factor supplies.

The Supply Side of the Model—The Production Functions

The supply side of the model is completely described by the production functions relating factor inputs to the supply of goods and services. In order to remain fairly general at this point, define a separate production function for each output.

Let:

r_{gf} = factor f used in the production of good g. $g = 1, \ldots, G$
                                                              $f = 1, \ldots, F$

X^g = the aggregate amount of good g produced. $g = 1, \ldots, G$

Define:

$$X^g = \phi^g(r_{g1}, \ldots, r_{gF})$$

or

(2.2) $$X^g = \phi^g(r_{gf}) \qquad g = 1, \ldots, G$$

as the "well-behaved" production function relating the factor inputs to aggregate production of goods g.[3] The functions $\phi^g(\ )$ represent a complete description of the economy's production technology, defined over $G \cdot F$ individual inputs and G aggregate goods and services.

Market Clearance in the Aggregate

In a general equilibrium context, market clearance requires that markets for all goods and factors clear simultaneously. The demands for any one good by all consumers must equal the aggregate quantity of the good produced, and the sum of all supplies of a given factor by the consumers must equal the sum of the

---

[2] Utility functions are always assumed to be continuous, strictly quasiconcave, and twice differentiable, with all goods and factors infinitely divisible.

[3] All production functions are assumed to be continuous, twice differentiable, and well behaved in that their Hessians are negative definite, with all goods and factors infinitely divisible. Notice that our specification of production assumes away intermediate products.

demands for that factor by all the firms in the economy. Hence:

(2.3)   Goods markets: $\sum_{h=1}^{H} X_{hg} = X^g$ $g = 1, \ldots, G$

(2.4)   Factor markets: $\sum_{h=1}^{H} V_{hf} = \sum_{g=1}^{G} r_{gf}$ $f = 1, \ldots, F$

There are $G \cdot F$ market clearing equations.

Taken together, equations (2.1), (2.2), (2.3), and (2.4) provide a complete general equilibrium model of an economy.

THE PARETO-OPTIMAL CONDITIONS

Having specified consumers' preferences, production technology, and market clearance, the general equilibrium model is sufficiently detailed to determine the pareto-optimal or efficiency conditions for the economy as a whole. To see how this is done, recall that pareto optimally requires the existence of an allocation of resources such that no one consumer can be made better off by a reallocation of resources without simultaneously making at least one other consumer worse off. Pareto optimality thus defines a frontier, which can be represented in two-person utility space by the diagram in Figure 2–1, commonly called the utility-possibilities frontier.

A point such as A on the frontier satisfies pareto optimality in that movements from A require that the utility of at least one person must decrease. Conversely, all points under the frontier, such as point C, cannot be pareto optimal since it is possible to move in a northeast direction from C. Points such as B, beyond the frontier, are simply unattainable, given society's production technology, consumers' preferences with respect to supplying factors of production, and the requirements of market clearance.

FIGURE 2–1

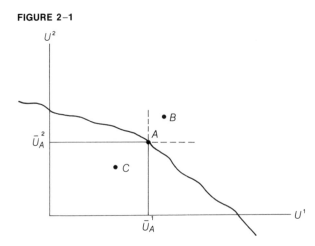

Since the locus of pareto-optimal allocations describes a frontier in utility space, all points on the frontier, such as A, have the following interpretation:

Given that person 2 is held at utility level $\bar{U}_A^2$, $\bar{U}_A^1$ is the maximum satisfaction attainable by person 1. Alternatively, given that person 1 is held at utility level $\bar{U}_A^1$, then $\bar{U}_A^2$ is the maximum utility attainable by person 2.

This suggests that the set of pareto-optimal allocations can be determined by solving the following problem algebraically:

Hold all but one person's utility constant, say, person 1. Maximize person 1's utility subject to the constraints that all other utilities are held constant, as well as the additional constraints implied by the G production functions and the $G \cdot F$ market clearance requirements. Formally:

$$\max_{(X_{hg};V_{hf};X^g;r_{gf})} U^1(X_{1g}; V_{1f})$$

$$\text{s.t.} \quad \bar{U}^h = U^h(X_{hg}; V_{hf}) \qquad h = 2, \ldots, H$$

$$X^g = \phi^g(r_{gf}) \qquad g = 1, \ldots, G$$

$$\sum_{h=1}^{H} X_{hg} = X^g \qquad g = 1, \ldots, G$$

$$\sum_{h=1}^{H} V_{hf} = \sum_{g=1}^{G} r_{gf} \qquad f = 1, \ldots, F$$

The pareto-optimal conditions will follow directly from the first-order conditions of this constrained optimization problem.

THE REDISTRIBUTION OF INCOME

While the model as it stands is sufficiently detailed to analyze conditions for allocational efficiency, it is entirely neutral with respect to the distribution question. The first-order conditions of the constrained optimum will solve for a single allocation of resources, but the constraints imposed upon utility levels $h = 2, \ldots, H$ are entirely arbitrary. Placing at least one of these consumers at a different utility level and solving again will determine a different allocation of resources, so long as the new constraints permit a feasible solution $(U^1(\ ) \geq 0)$. Since the utility constraints can be reset infinitely many times, solutions to the constrained optimum problem will admit to an infinity of feasible solutions, in general, all points on the utility-possibilities frontier. Unfortunately, the model as it stands will have no way of choosing a best allocation among these. According to the pareto criterion, they are all optimal. In this sense pareto optimality is an extremely weak criterion, really much too weak to finally resolve public sector issues. For instance, in terms of the pareto criterion, the following allocations are equivalent in a two-person economy: person 2 receives almost all the goods and services, and person 1 almost nothing; each person receives an equal allocation; person 1 receives almost all the goods and services, and person 2 almost nothing.

22

FIGURE 2–2

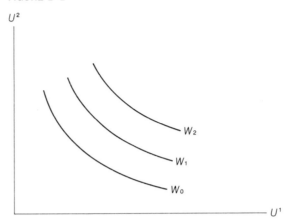

Societies typically will not be so neutral, however. They will almost certainly establish a set of equity norms and devise some method of ranking the possible outcomes according to these norms. Since most public sector economists believe economic analysis is properly concerned with distributional issues, they have seen fit to include a representation of distributional rankings in their models. The analytical device most frequently used for this purpose is the so-called Bergson-Samuelson individualistic social welfare function,[4] whose arguments are the individuals' utility functions. Write:

$$W = W[U^1(X_{1g}; V_{1f}), \ldots, U^H(X_{Hg}; V_{Hf})]$$

or

(2.5)
$$W = W[U^h(X_{hg}; V_{hf})]$$

The idea behind this social welfare function is that if society wants to resolve the distribution question, it must be able to determine at least a consistent ordinal ranking of the well-being of its individual members, analogous to the ordinal ranking of goods and factors implied by the utility index of an individual consumer. Graphically, $W(\ )$ generates a set of social indifference curves in $U^1 - U^2$ space, depicted by W_0, W_1, and W_2 in Figure 2–2, having most of the properties associated with the individual indifference curves.[5] If society can determine a consistent set of utility rankings, then it can select the distributionally best allocation among the infinity of pareto-optimal allocations. In

---

[4] After Abram Bergson and Paul Samuelson, who first described the function. Samuelson used this construct in his 1954 article, "The Pure Theory of Public Expenditure" referred to in footnote 1. Refer to Samuelson's lucid discussion of the social welfare function in P. A. Samuelson, *Foundations of Economic Analysis* New York: Atheneum Publishers, 1965), pp. 219–30. See also, A. Bergson, "A Reformulation of Certain Aspects of Welfare Economics," *Quarterly Journal of Economics*, 1938.

[5] In particular, the curves are everywhere convex to the origin, society is indifferent among the utility distributions along any one curve, higher numbered curves imply higher levels of social welfare, and no two indifference curves may intersect.

FIGURE 2–3

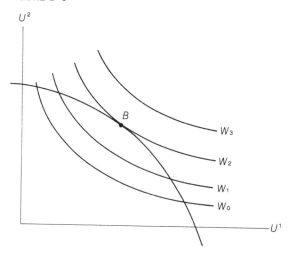

Figure 2–3, point B represents this best allocation, the point at which the utility-possibilities frontier attains the highest numbered social welfare indifference curve.[6] Frances Bator referred to this point as the "bliss point," a name that has stuck in the public sector literature.[7]

As originally formulated by Bergson and Samuelson, the social welfare function was meant to have two specific properties. First, it provides an *ordinal* ranking of social preferences with respect to the distribution of utility. This concept is somewhat tricky because the arguments of the social welfare function, unlike those of individual's utility functions, are ordinal. From consumer theory we know that monotonic transformations of an individual's utility function leave his goods demands and factor supplies unchanged. However, since these functions themselves are arguments of the social welfare function, arbitrary transformations of the individual's utility functions could easily change the implied social rankings. Samuelson and Bergson assumed that if such transformations occurred, the social welfare functions would itself change form to preserve the original rankings. Second, they felt the function should satisfy the pareto criterion, meaning that $\partial W/\partial U^h > 0$. This merely says that if one person's utility increases (decreases), all other utilities held constant, then social welfare must increase (decrease). Notice, however, that the rankings implied by $W(\ )$ are broader than those implied by the pareto criterion. The function $W(\ )$ can compare two allocations in which a movement from the first to the second increases some utilities while decreasing other's utilities. The pareto criterion

---

[6] Since continuity is not required of either $W(U^h)$ or the utility-possibilities frontier, B may not be a point of tangency.

[7] F. M. Bator, "Simple Analytics of Welfare Maximization," *American Economic Review*, March 1957.

cannot make this comparison. On the other hand, a pareto-superior reallocation will increase $W(\ )$ if $\partial W/\partial U^h > 0$.

In theoretical work it is often unnecessary to be more specific about the formulation of $W(\ )$. $\partial W/\partial U^h$ is simply understood to represent society's ethical judgment about the social marginal utility of person h, whatever that judgment may be. On the other hand, if one wishes to test the sensitivity of a normative policy rule to society's social welfare rankings, a specific parameterization of $W(\ )$ is essential. Many different functional forms appear in the literature, but the one suggested separately by Atkinson and Feldstein in 1973 is now used fairly extensively.[8] They define $W(\ )$ as

$$(2.6) \qquad W[U_h(\ )] = \left(\sum_{h=1}^{H} U_h^V \right)^{1/V} \qquad V \leq 1$$

where V is a constant reflecting society's aversion to inequality. $V = 1$ implies equal social marginal utilities, or complete indifference to inequality, the so-called utilitarian viewpoint. In effect, utilitarianism argues for ignoring distributional rankings altogether, and basing all social decisions on the straight sum of individual gains and losses from policy actions, individually perceived. It has a long standing in public sector economics and a fair number of current proponents, most notably Arnold Harberger.[9] At the other extreme, $V \to -\infty$ implies maximizing the utility of the worse-off individual, the so-called maximin criterion first proposed by John Rawls in 1971.[10] In between, increasingly

[8] A. Atkinson, "How Progressive Should the Income Tax Be?," in M. Parkin, ed., *Essays on Modern Economics* (London: Longman Group Ltd., 1973).

M. Feldstein, "On the Optimal Progressivity of the Income Tax," *Journal of Public Economics*, vol. 2, 1973. These specifications assume the government has chosen particular cardinal representations of the U_h on which to base its social welfare judgments.

[9] A. Harberger, "Three Basic Postulates for Applied Welfare Economics," *Journal of Economic Literature*, September 1971. Utilitarianism is Harberger's third postulate.

[10] J. Rawls, *A Theory of Justice* (Cambridge, Mass.: Harvard University Press, 1971). To see that $V \to -\infty$ implies the Rawls maximin criterion, differentiate W with respect to some U_j.

$$(2.6a) \qquad \frac{\partial W}{\partial U_j} = \frac{1}{V} \cdot \left(\sum_{h=1}^{H} U_h^V \right)^{(1/V-1)} \cdot VU_j^{(V-1)}$$

$$(2.6b) \qquad \frac{\partial W}{\partial U_j} = \frac{U_j^{(V-1)}}{\left(\sum_{h=1}^{H} U_h^V \right)^{\frac{V-1}{V}}} = \left[\frac{U_j}{\left(\sum_{h=1}^{H} U_h^V \right)^{1/V}} \right]^{(V-1)}$$

Dividing numerator and denominator inside the brackets by U_j and rearranging terms yields:

$$(2.6c) \qquad \frac{\partial W}{\partial U_j} = \frac{1}{\left[\sum_{h=1}^{H} \left(\frac{U_h}{U_j} \right)^V \right]^{(1-1/V)}}$$

Letting $V \to -\infty$ yields:

$$(2.6d) \qquad \frac{\partial W}{\partial U_j} = \frac{1}{\dfrac{1}{\left(\frac{U_1}{U_j} \right)^{\infty}} + \cdots + \dfrac{1}{\left(\frac{U_h}{U_j} \right)^{\infty}} + \cdots + 1 + \cdots + \dfrac{1}{\left(\frac{U_H}{U_j} \right)^{\infty}}}$$

larger negative values of V imply increasing aversion to extremes in the distribution of utility.[11] Hence, (2.6) is a particularly flexible functional form for examining the robustness of policy rules to distributional judgments.

LIMITATIONS OF SOCIAL WELFARE FUNCTIONS

While most public sector economists have accepted the Bergson-Samuelson individualistic social welfare function as a useful analytical device for representing a society's distributional norms, its significance for practical policy application is far from clear. There are any number of problems with representing distributional judgments in this way. In the first place, there are no obvious guidelines for determining any one particular social welfare function with its implied set of rankings. An appeal to consumer sovereignty is clearly insufficient, since it would require unanimous consent to arrive at a given set of social rankings, and unanimity would occur only by chance. So long as any one person disagrees with the social rankings, his consumer sovereignty will be violated, and someone is bound to disagree. Failing unanimity, one might think in terms of using a majority-rule democratic voting process to determine $W(\ )$, but Kenneth Arrow dealt that view a serious blow. He posited a set of five conditions that a social decision rule such as $W(\ )$ ought to satisfy, including nondictatorship, and proved that, in general, no such function could satisfy all five conditions simultaneously.[12] Of course, the rankings could simply be dictated by some government administrator or legislative body, but this is an uncomfortable resolution for a society otherwise committed to the principle of consumer sovereignty. What is worse, even a dictated specification of W may not be possible. Kemp and Ng have recently shown that under fairly general conditions, if the individual utility functions are ordinal, then a real valued social welfare function does not exist.[13] Their analysis suggests that any attempt to develop reasonable decision rules for ranking various resource allocations

---

If U_j is selected such that $U_j < U_h, j \neq h$, all variable terms in the denominator of (2.6d) go to zero in the limit, so that

$$(2.6e) \qquad \frac{\partial W}{\partial U_j} = 1$$

Selecting any other U_j implies that the denominator becomes large without limit. Hence

$$\frac{\partial W}{\partial U_j} = 0, \ U_j \neq \min_{(h)} U_h$$

[11] By inspection of (2.6c), the value of $\partial W/\partial U_j$ increases as V becomes increasingly negative, $U_j < U_h$, all $j \neq h$.

[12] Kenneth J. Arrow, *Social Choice and Individual Values* (New Haven, Conn.: Yale University Press, 1951).

[13] M. C. Kemp and Y-K Ng, "On the Existence of Social Welfare Functions, Social Orderings, and Social Decision Functions," *Economica*, February 1976. Refer also to the subsequent exchange between Kemp, Ng, and Samuelson in the February 1977 volume of *Economica*. P. A. Samuelson, "Reaffirming The Existence of 'Reasonable' Bergson-Samuelson Social Welfare Functions," *Economica*, February 1977; and M. C. Kemp and Y-K Ng, "More on Social Welfare Functions: The Incompatibility of Individualism and Ordinalism," *Economica*, February 1977.

by a set of equity norms will require both cardinality of individuals' preferences and direct interpersonal utility comparisons among individuals by the government. Students of welfare economics have long rejected both of these concepts.[14] Finally, even if one believes that governments do rank individuals along the lines suggested by an individualistic social welfare function, empirical analysis has never convincingly demonstrated what these rankings might be for any particular country.[15]

Despite these severe problems, we will follow the conventional practice of using the social welfare function to represent the distributional judgments of society. It is certainly reasonable to suppose that most societies do care about the distributional implications of their government's policies, and that government decision making ought to reflect this concern. Once these points are admitted, it would seem prudent to incorporate the social welfare function into a general equilibrium model that will be used to develop normative policy rules. It should be viewed, however, simply as an analytical device representing society's concern for distributive equity. The social welfare function in no way suggests what the distributional judgments should be, other than that they be consistent, individualistic, and satisfy the pareto criterion. The alternative of ignoring social welfare rankings entirely because we do not know what they are, or should be, would simplify the analysis, but if society really does care about equity, it would not produce a meaningful normative theory.[16]

MAXIMIZING SOCIAL WELFARE

Adding the social welfare function to the general equilibrium model significantly changes the nature of the model as a foundation for normative policy analysis. The policy objective becomes one of maximizing social welfare, as represented by the social welfare function, rather than simply tracing out the locus of pareto-optimal allocations. Moreover, all individual utilities are allowed to vary, so that the formal model is constrained only by the G production functions and the $G \cdot F$ market clearance equations. The first-order conditions of

---

[14] The classic reference is Ian Malcolm David Little, *A Critique of Welfare Economics* (Oxford, England: Oxford University Press, 1957).

[15] There have been numerous attempts, in various contexts, to estimate social welfare functions. One, by Burton Wiesbrod, will be discussed in Chapter 27 when we consider the role of distributional considerations in cost-benefit analysis. See B. A. Weisbrod, "Income Redistribution Effects and Benefit-Cost Analysis," in S. B. Chase, Jr., ed., *Problems in Public Expenditure Analysis* (Washington, D.C.: The Brookings Institution, 1968).

A more recent study by Christiansen and Jansen draws upon many-person second-best tax theory (Chapter 16) to estimate a social welfare function for Norway. See V. Christiansen and E. S. Jansen, "Implicit Social Preferences in the Norwegian System of Indirect Taxation," *Journal of Public Economics*, October 1978.

[16] The comments in this section barely scratch the surface of a voluminous literature on collectively determined decision rules. It is enough for our purposes to establish the central role of the social welfare function in normative public sector analysis. We would recommend D. Mueller, "Public Choice: A Survey," *Journal of Economic Literature*, June 1976, as a starting point for the student interested in the theory of social choice mechanisms.

the model will simultaneously determine the set of pareto-optimal and distributional conditions that bring society to the "bliss point," a single allocation and distribution of resources.

Analytically, social welfare maximization can be represented as follows:

$$\max_{(X_{hg};V_{hf};X^g;r_{gf})} W[U^h(X_{hg};V_{hf})]$$

$$\text{s.t.} \quad X^g = \phi^g(r_{gf}) \qquad\qquad g = 1,\ldots,G$$

$$\sum_{h=1}^{H} X_{hg} = X^g \qquad\qquad g = 1,\ldots,G$$

$$\sum_{h=1}^{H} V_{hf} = \sum_{g=1}^{G} r_{gf} \qquad f = 1,\ldots,F$$

Defining multipliers for each of the constraints and setting up the Lagrangian, the problem becomes:

$$\max_{(X_{hg};V_{hf};X^g;r_{gf})} L = W[U^h(X_{hg};V_{hf})] + \sum_{g=1}^{G} \mu_g[X^g - \phi^g(r_{gf})]$$

$$+ \sum_{g=1}^{G} \delta_g\left(\sum_{h=1}^{H} X_{hg} - X^g\right) + \sum_{f=1}^{F} \pi_f\left(\sum_{h=1}^{H} V_{hf} - \sum_{g=1}^{G} r_{gf}\right)$$

The Necessary Conditions for Social Welfare Maximization

The first-order conditions for this model are:

(2.7)
$$\frac{\partial L}{\partial X_{hg}} = \frac{\partial W}{\partial U^h}\frac{\partial U^h}{\partial X_{hg}} + \delta_g = 0 \qquad \begin{array}{l} h = 1,\ldots,H \\ g = 1,\ldots,G \end{array}$$

(2.8)
$$\frac{\partial L}{\partial V_{hf}} = \frac{\partial W}{\partial U^h}\frac{\partial U^h}{\partial V_{hf}} + \pi_f = 0 \qquad \begin{array}{l} h = 1,\ldots,H \\ f = 1,\ldots,F \end{array}$$

(2.9)
$$\frac{\partial L}{\partial X^g} = \mu_g - \delta_g = 0 \qquad g = 1,\ldots,G$$

(2.10)
$$\frac{\partial L}{\partial r_{gf}} = -\mu_g\frac{\partial \phi^g}{\partial r_{gf}} - \pi_f = 0 \qquad \begin{array}{l} g = 1,\ldots,G \\ f = 1,\ldots F \end{array}$$

and the constraints:

(2.11)
$$X^g = \phi^g(r_{gf}) \qquad g = 1,\ldots,G$$

(2.12)
$$X^g = \sum_{h=1}^{H} X_{hg} \qquad g = 1,\ldots,G$$

(2.13)
$$\sum_{h=1}^{H} V_{hf} = \sum_{g=1}^{G} r_{gf} \qquad f = 1,\ldots,F$$

There are $2H + 5G + 3F$ equations in all, which we assume will generate a unique solution to the $2H + 5G + 3F$ variables of the model, consisting of the $2H + 3G + 2F$ economic variables, X_{hg}, V_{hf}, X^g, r_{gf}, and $2G + F$ Lagrangian multipliers.[17]

The most striking feature of these equations for policy purposes is that the first $(HG + HF + G + GF)$ conditions can be combined into two distinct sets, one containing all the pareto-optimal efficiency conditions, and one containing the distributional requirements, which we will call the *interpersonal equity conditions*. Their distinguishing characteristic is that the pareto-optimal conditions do not contain any social welfare terms whereas the interpersonal equity conditions do. This makes intuitive sense considering that the pareto-optimal conditions describe how to achieve the allocations along the utility-possibilities frontier, and we know that they can be determined using a model that does not employ a social welfare function. On the other hand, the interpersonal equity conditions must of necessity involve the social welfare function since that function contains all relevant distributional information. It is also worth noting by way of introduction to policy analysis that the dichotomization of first-order conditions is not peculiar to this particular general equilibrium model. As we shall see, it applies as well to all general equilibrium models of public sector problems employing "first-best" assumptions. This feature is extremely important as a practical matter because it implies that the government can pursue its equity and efficiency goals with distinct sets of policy tools. We will return to these points later on in Chapter 3.

The *pareto-optimal conditions* themselves divide into three distinct sets: consumption relationships, production relationships, and interrelationships between production and consumption. To obtain the consumption relationships, standardize on any one person and consider the following pairs of first-order conditions:

1. Any two goods demanded by that person.
2. Any two factors supplied by that person.
3. Any one good demanded and any one factor supplied by that person.

Pairing the first-order conditions in this manner will eliminate any terms involving the social welfare function.

Since production does not involve the social welfare function, all pairs of production relationships will generate pareto-optimal conditions, including:

4. Any one factor used in the production of any two goods.
5. Any two factors used in the production of any one good.

---

[17] Existence of a unique solution is never guaranteed by simply matching the number of equations with the number of variables, but we do not want to consider the problem of existence in the text. Hence, existence of a unique solution for all maximization problems will be assumed throughout.

The interrelationships between production and consumption are derived by combining the first two sets of pairings. There are three relevant combinations:

6. The rate at which any one person is willing to trade any two goods (1) with their efficient rate of exchange in production (4).
7. The rate at which any one consumer is willing to substitute any two factors (2) with their efficient rate of exchange in production (5).
8. The rate at which any one consumer is willing to substitute any one good for any one factor (3) with their efficient rate of exchange in production (4).

Taken together, these eight pairings will generate all the conditions necessary for the economy to be on its utility-possibilities frontier. Should any one of them fail to hold, the omniscient planner can always find a reallocation of resources which will increase the utility of at least one person without making any other person worse off.

To derive the *interpersonal equity conditions* the first-order conditions must be paired in such a way as to retain the social welfare terms. Since these terms must involve the consumers, there are only two possible ways of doing this. Compare:

1. Any one good demanded by two different people, or
2. Any one factor supplied by two different people.

THE PARETO-OPTIMAL CONDITIONS

In order to demonstrate the derivation and interpretation of the pareto-optimal conditions we will consider the three conditions most commonly presented in microeconomic analysis, corresponding to the pairings in 1, 5, and 6 above. If all factors of production are supplied by consumers in absolutely fixed amounts, then these conditions, along with 4, are the only necessary conditions for a pareto-optimum. If factor supplies are not variable, the pairings 2, 3, 7, and 8 obviously have no meaning. In general, however, all eight conditions are necessary for overall economic efficiency.

Condition P1

Consider the first-order conditions for any two goods demanded by any one person, say X_{hg} and X_{hg*}.

$$(2.14) \qquad \frac{\partial L}{\partial X_{hg}} = \frac{\partial W}{\partial U^h} \frac{\partial U^h}{\partial X_{hg}} + \delta_g = 0$$

$$(2.15) \qquad \frac{2L}{\partial X_{hg*}} = \frac{\partial W}{\partial U^h} \frac{\partial U^h}{\partial X_{hg*}} + \delta_{g*} = 0$$

Dividing (2.14) by (2.15) yields:

(2.16)
$$\frac{\dfrac{\partial U^h}{\partial X_{hg}}}{\dfrac{\partial U^h}{\partial X_{hg^*}}} = \frac{\delta_g}{\delta_{g^*}} \qquad \begin{array}{l} \text{all } h = 1, \dots, H \\ \text{any } g, g^* = 1, \dots, G \end{array}$$

Notice that the social welfare term, $\partial W/\partial U^h$, cancels and the left-hand side is the familiar marginal rate of substitution, by person h, between goods g and g^*. Condition P1 (2.16) says that the marginal rate of substitution between any two goods must be the same for all people. To represent this geometrically, consider an economy with two people, persons 1 and 2, and two goods, X_g and X_{g^*}, as represented in Figure 2–4. This is the familiar Edgeworth box, in which the axes represent society's total production of X_g and X_{g^*}, respectively. Person 1's indifference curves are drawn with reference to the lower left-hand corner as the origin, and person 2's indifference curves are drawn with reference to the upper right-hand corner as the origin. The equality of marginal rates of substitution is represented by the "contract curve" AB, the locus of points at which the two sets of indifference curves are tangent. Any point along the contract curve is pareto efficient. Any allocation off the contract locus, such as C, is pareto inefficient in the sense that some other allocation exists which can make one or both people better off without making anyone else worse off. For example, suppose at C the slopes of the indifference curves are such that $MRS^1_{X_g,X_{g^*}} = 2$ and $MRS^2_{X_g,X_{g^*}} = 1.8$. If the planner forces person 1 to give 1.9 units of X_g to person 2 in exchange for 1 unit of X_{g^*}, person 1 is better off, since he is willing to exchange at a 2-for-1 ratio, by definition of the marginal rate of substitution. Person 2 will accept the 1.9-for-1 exchange as well, since he is willing to trade 1 unit of X_{g^*} for only 1.8 units of X_g in return. Obviously any (small) trade between the ratios 2:1 and 1.8:1, including the boundaries, will generate an allocation of the goods that is pareto superior to C (at the trade boundaries, only one person gains, but the other is no worse off). Only

FIGURE 2–4

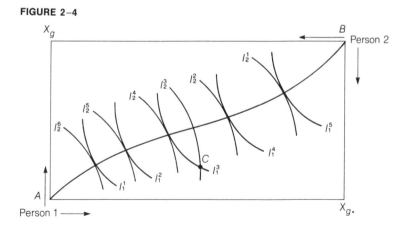

when the two MRS are equal is no such beneficial trade possible, which is true for any point along the contract curve. Note, finally, that the pareto criterion cannot rank points along the contract curve—they are all pareto optimal by condition P1.

Condition P5

Consider any two factors used in the production of any one good, say r_{gf} and r_{gf*}.

$$(2.17) \qquad \frac{\partial L}{\partial r_{gf}} = -\mu_g \frac{\partial \phi^g}{\partial r_{gf}} - \pi_f = 0$$

$$(2.18) \qquad \frac{\partial L}{\partial r_{gf*}} = -\mu_g \frac{\partial \phi^g}{\partial r_{gf*}} - \pi_{f*} = 0$$

Dividing (2.17) by (2.18) yields:

$$(2.19) \qquad \frac{\dfrac{\partial \phi^g}{\partial r_{gf}}}{\dfrac{\partial \phi^g}{\partial r_{gf*}}} = \frac{\pi_f}{\pi_{f*}} \qquad \begin{array}{l} \text{all } g = 1, \ldots, G \\ \text{any } f, f* = 1, \ldots, F \end{array}$$

The left-hand side is the technical rate of substitution of factors f and $f*$ in the production of good g.[18] Condition P5 (2.19) states that the technical rate of substitution between any two factors in the production of a good must be equal for all goods. The usual way of representing this condition geometrically is to think of the factors f and $f*$ as capital (K) and labor (L), respectively, and draw a production box analogous to the Edgeworth consumption box, as in Figure 2–5.

The axes represent society's total supply of capital and labor, a representation possible only under the assumption of fixed factor supplies. The isoquants $q_g^1, \ldots, q_g^5$ are drawn with reference to the lower left-hand corner as the origin, and the isoquants $q_{g*}^1, \ldots, q_{g*}^5$ with reference to the upper right-hand corner. As before, the contract locus of tangency points represents the pareto-optimal allocations of K and L between the two goods, X^g and X^{g*}, and all points off this locus are dominated according to the pareto criterion by some point on the locus. In this context the pareto criterion is defined in terms of production, but production efficiency is necessary for full pareto optimality defined in terms of individuals' utilities. If society can produce more of at least one good without sacrificing production of some other good, then simply by distributing the bonus someone can obviously be made better off without making anyone else worse off.

---

[18] Notice that the numerator and denominator of (2.19) equal the marginal products of factors f and $f*$, respectively, in the production of g. Hence, the technical rate of substitution between any two factors is the ratio of their marginal products.

FIGURE 2–5

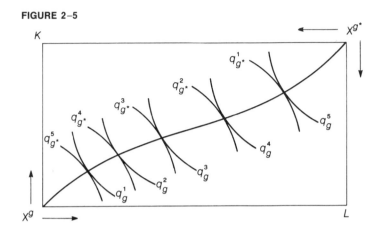

The contract locus in factor space in turn bears a point-to-point correspondence with the familiar production-possibilities frontier in goods space, depicted in Figure 2–6. If society is producing along the contract locus in factor space, it cannot realign its resources to produce more of one good without sacrificing some of the other good. But this is exactly what the production-possibilities frontier represents, the locus of pareto-efficient output allocations.

Condition P6

The rate at which consumers are willing to trade any one good for any other must equal their rate of exchange in (efficient) production.

The slope of the production-possibilities frontier in Figure 2–6 is the marginal rate of transformation (MRT) between the two goods, X^g and X^{g*}, in production, assuming efficient production. To derive the MRT algebraically, consider a single factor, f, switched from the production of good X^g to good X^{g*}. The

FIGURE 2–6

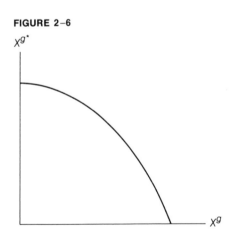

first-order conditions for r_{gf} and r_{g*f} are:

(2.20)
$$\frac{\partial L}{\partial r_{gf}} = -\mu_g \frac{\partial \phi^g}{\partial r_{gf}} - \pi_f = 0$$

(2.21)
$$\frac{\partial L}{\partial r_{g*f}} = -\mu_{g*} \frac{\partial \phi^{g*}}{\partial r_{g*f}} - \pi_f = 0$$

Rearranging terms:

(2.22)
$$-\mu_g \frac{\partial \phi^g}{\partial r_{gf}} = -\mu_{g*} \frac{\partial \phi^{g*}}{\partial r_{g*f}}$$

or

(2.23)
$$\frac{\dfrac{\partial \phi^{g*}}{\partial r_{g*f}}}{\dfrac{\partial \phi^g}{\partial r_{gf}}} = \frac{\mu_g}{\mu_{g*}} \qquad \begin{array}{l} \text{all } f = 1, \ldots, F \\ \text{any } g, g* = 1, \ldots, G \end{array}$$

The left-hand side of (2.23) is the marginal rate of transformation between X^g and X^{g*} obtained by switching factor f from good X^g to good X^{g*}. Since it holds for all factors switched between X^g and X^{g*}, it is simply *the* marginal rate of transformation between X^g and X^{g*}. It is also a statement of production condition (4), above.

The $MRT_{g*,g}$ must now be related to each consumer's $MRS^h_{g*,g}$. From the consumption condition, PI (2.16),

(2.24)
$$\frac{\dfrac{\partial U^h}{\partial X_{hg}}}{\dfrac{\partial U^h}{\partial X_{hg*}}} = \frac{\delta_g}{\delta_{g*}} = MRS^h_{g*,g} \qquad \begin{array}{l} \text{all } h, = 1, \ldots, H \\ \text{any } g*, g = 1, \ldots, G \end{array}$$

Consider, next, the first-order conditions with respect to X^g, the aggregate production of good g.

(2.25)
$$\frac{\partial L}{\partial X^g} = \mu_g - \delta_g = 0 \qquad g = 1, \ldots, G$$

Thus, $\mu_g = \delta_g$, all $g = 1, \ldots, G$, so that:

(2.26)
$$\frac{\dfrac{\partial U^h}{\partial X_{hg}}}{\dfrac{\partial U^h}{\partial X_{hg*}}} = \frac{\dfrac{\partial \phi^{g*}}{\partial r_{g*f}}}{\dfrac{\partial \phi^g}{\partial r_{gf}}} \qquad \text{any } g*, g = 1, \ldots, G$$

In other words,

(2.27)
$$MRS^h_{g*,g} = MRT_{g*,g} \qquad \text{any } g*, g = 1, \ldots, G$$

FIGURE 2–7

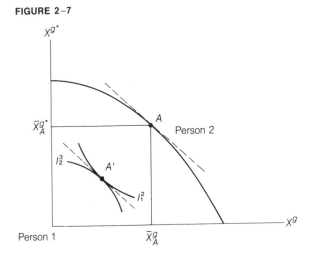

To picture this result, suppose society is at point A on the production-possibilities frontier in Figure 2–7. Let point A define the dimensions of an Edgeworth consumption box placed inside the frontier, consisting of $\bar{X}_A^{g^*}$ units of X^{g^*} and $\bar{X}_A^g$ units of X^g.

Condition P6 (2.25) says that society must distribute the total product at A between persons 1 and 2 such that the common MRS between the goods equals their MRT in production. Of all the pareto-efficient points on the consumption contract curve, society must choose A' giving person 1 (X_{1g^*}, X_{1g}), and person 2 the remainder.[19] Notice that while condition P6 has some distributional content, it is not a distributional rule in the sense of an interpersonal equity condition because it does not involve the social welfare function. The distribution $[(X_{1g}, X_{1g^*}), (\bar{X}_A^g - X_{1g}, \bar{X}_A^{g^*} - X_{1g^*})]$ is not determined by interpersonal utility comparisons.

Having satisfied P1, P5, and P6 simultaneously, A' defines a single point on the utility-possibilities frontier, point A'' in Figure 2–8, corresponding to A' in Figure 2–7. Thus, taken by themselves, conditions P1, P5, and P6 are consistent with an infinity of allocations.

If factor supplies are variable, attaining the utility-possibilities frontier requires satisfying four additional pareto-optimal conditions, corresponding to the pairings of first-order conditions 2, 3, 7, and 8. They are derived following the same procedures used to generate conditions P1, P4, P5, and P6, an exercise that will be left to the reader.

The conditions are as follows:

P2—the marginal rate of substitution between any two factors in supply must be equal for all people.

---

[19] There may be no point which satisfies (2.27) given A, or many points.

FIGURE 2–8

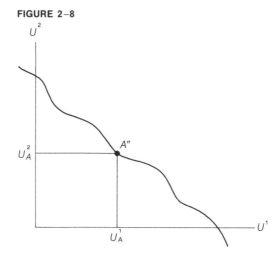

P3—the marginal rate of substitution between a good and a factor must be equal for all consumers.

P7—the common marginal rate of substitution between any two factors in supply must equal their common technical rate of substitution in the production of any good.

P8—the common marginal rate of substitution between any good demanded and any factor supplied must equal the marginal product of that factor in producing that good (or, the technical rate of substitution between the good and the factor in production).

PARETO OPTIMALITY AND PERFECT COMPETITION

The fundamental theorem of welfare economics states that if all the technical assumptions listed in Chapter 1 hold, then a perfectly competitive market system will generate all eight necessary conditions for full pareto optimality. A formal proof of the theorem requires mathematical techniques beyond the scope of this text, but an intuitive, heuristic argument illustrating the theorem is relatively straightforward. As with the derivation of the conditions themselves, we will illustrate this theorem with reference only to conditions P1, P5, and P6.

That condition P1 is satisfied in a competitive market economy follows immediately from the behavioral assumption that each consumer maximizes his utility function subject to a budget constraint, and the fact that in a perfectly competitive economy all consumers are price takers facing the same set of prices. Under these conditions a utility-maximizing consumer will set the marginal rate of substitution between any two goods equal to the ratio of their prices.[20] If all consumers do this, and each faces the same set of prices, then the marginal rate of substitution between any two goods will be equal for all consumers.

Similarly, condition P5 follows directly from the fact that profit-maximizing firms will produce any given output with the least-cost combination of factors of production. If a firm cannot influence factor prices, then it will cost minimize by producing such that the technical rate of substitution between any two of its factors equals the ratio of the factor prices.[21] If markets are perfectly competitive, then all firms will face the same set of factor prices. Consequently, the technical rate of substitution between any two factors will be equalized throughout the economy, as required by condition P5.

Condition P6 follows from the result that, in competitive markets, output price equals the marginal cost of production. If $P_g = MC_g$ and $P_{g*} = MC_{g*}$, then

(2.28)
$$\frac{P_g}{P_{g*}} = \frac{MC_g}{MC_{g*}} \qquad \text{any } g, g* = 1, \ldots, G$$

Each consumer (h) will set $MRS^h_{g*,g} = P_g/P_{g*}$. Moreover, assuming efficient production (that conditions P4 and P5 hold), the ratio of marginal costs between any two goods is equal to their marginal rate of transformation. MC_g gives the extra

---

[20] Formally, each consumer (h) will solve the following problem:

$$\max_{(X_{hg}; V_{hf})} \ U^h(X_{hg}; V_{hf})$$

$$\text{s.t.} \quad \sum_{g=1}^{G} P_g X_{hg} + \sum_{f=1}^{F} W_f V_{hf} = 0$$

where:

P_g = the price of the gth good.
W_f = the price of the fth factor.

The first-order conditions imply:

$$\frac{\dfrac{\partial U^h}{\partial X_{hg}}}{\dfrac{\partial U^h}{\partial X_{hg*}}} \equiv MRS^h_{g*,g} = P_g/P_{g*} \qquad \text{all } g*, g = 1, \ldots, G$$

[21] Formally, each firm (g) will solve the following problem:

$$\min_{(r_{gf})} \ \sum_{f=1}^{F} W_f r_{gf}$$

$$\text{s.t.} \quad X_g = \phi^g(r_{gf})$$

The first-order conditions imply:

$$\frac{\dfrac{\partial \phi^g}{\partial r_{gf}}}{\dfrac{\partial \phi^g}{\partial r_{gf*}}} \equiv TRS^g_{f*,f} = W_f/W_{f*} \qquad \text{all } f*, f = 1, \ldots, F$$

cost of (efficiently) producing an extra unit of X^g, and similarly for MC_{g*}. Hence, the ratio, MC_g/MC_{g*}, gives the rate at which $g*$ substitutes for g in production by transferring a dollar's worth of resources from g to $g*$, or vice versa.[22] Therefore, with marginal cost pricing in every market, $MRT_{g*,g} = P_g/P_{g*}$, and condition P6 is satisfied for all goods and services.

That perfectly competitive markets will also guarantee conditions P2, P3, P4, P7, and P8 can easily be shown by similar reasoning.

INTERPERSONAL EQUITY CONDITIONS

The competitive market system can generate the full set of pareto-optimal conditions, but no more. Like the pareto criterion itself, it is neutral with regard to points on the utility-possibilities frontier. If society is not neutral, clearly preferring some distributions of the economy's goods and services to others, it must create a governmental body to carry out its collective will with respect to the distribution. Moreover, if it is truly interested in the maximization of social welfare as represented by the Bergson-Samuelson social welfare function, the government must act according to the dictates of two additional sets of first-order conditions, the interpersonal equity conditions. As indicated above, the interpersonal equity conditions arise from pairings of the first-order conditions (2.7) and (2.8) that standardize on a single good or factor. Consider, for example, a single good demanded by two different people, say, X_{hg} and X_{h*g}. The first-order conditions are:

$$(2.29) \qquad \frac{\partial L}{\partial X_{hg}} = \frac{\partial W}{\partial U^h} \frac{\partial U^h}{\partial X_{hg}} + \delta_g = 0$$

$$(2.30) \qquad \frac{\partial L}{\partial X_{h*g}} = \frac{\partial W}{\partial U^{h*}} \frac{\partial U^{h*}}{\partial X_{h*g}} + \delta_g = 0$$

from which it follows that:

$$(2.31) \qquad \frac{\partial W}{\partial U^1} \frac{\partial U^1}{\partial X_{1g}} = \frac{\partial W}{\partial U^h} \frac{\partial U^h}{\partial X_{hg}} = \cdots = \frac{\partial W}{\partial U^{h*}} \frac{\partial U^{h*}}{\partial X_{h*g}} = \cdots$$

$$= \frac{\partial W}{\partial U^H} \frac{\partial U^H}{\partial X_{Hg}} = -\delta_g \qquad g = 1, \ldots, G$$

The terms $\partial W/\partial U^h \ \partial U^h/\partial X_{hg}$ indicate the marginal increase (decrease) in social welfare from a *ceteris paribus* unit increase (decrease) in person h's consumption of good g, consisting of the increase (decrease) in utility experienced directly by person h multiplied by the unit increase in social welfare per unit increase in person h's utility. Condition (2.31) says that interpersonal equity is

---

[22] That the marginal rate of transformation between g and $g*$ is also equal to the ratio of their marginal costs follows immediately from (2.23). Switch a dollar of factor f from $g*$ to g. The numerator and denominator measure the per dollar loss and gain in outputs $g*$ and g, respectively. Inverting each term gives the ratio of marginal costs.

achieved only if all goods are distributed such that, on the margin, social welfare is the same no matter who consumes the last unit of the good. A similar condition applies to all factor supplies as well.[23] By following this decision rule, and assuming the pareto-optimal conditions are satisfied, society in effect moves along the utility-possibilities frontier to the bliss point, which is distributionally the best of all possible pareto-optimal allocations.

Two extremely important policy implications of this rule should be emphasized. First, there are not really $(G + F)$ *independent* conditions, one for each good and factor. To the contrary, if the pareto-optimal conditions hold and society is able to satisfy the interpersonal equity condition for any one good g, then the condition is automatically satisfied for all other goods and factors. To see this, suppose interpersonal equity holds for good g, so that

$$(2.32) \qquad \frac{\partial W}{\partial U^h}\frac{\partial U^h}{\partial X_{hg}} = \frac{\partial W}{\partial U^{h*}}\frac{\partial U^{h*}}{\partial X_{h*g}} \qquad \text{any } h, h^* = 1, \ldots, H$$

If we also assume that pareto-optimal condition P1 holds,

$$(2.33) \qquad \frac{\dfrac{\partial U^h}{\partial X_{hg}}}{\dfrac{\partial U^h}{\partial X_{hg*}}} = \frac{\dfrac{\partial U^{h*}}{\partial X_{h*g}}}{\dfrac{\partial U^{h*}}{\partial X_{h*g*}}} \qquad \begin{array}{l} \text{any } h, h^* = 1, \ldots, H \\ \text{any } g, g^* = 1, \ldots, G \end{array}$$

or

$$(2.34) \qquad MRS^h_{g*,g} = MRS^{h*}_{g*,g} \qquad \text{any } h, h^* = 1, \ldots, H$$

Replace the social welfare terms in condition P1, maintaining the equality:

$$(2.35) \qquad \frac{\dfrac{\partial W}{\partial U^h}\dfrac{\partial U^h}{\partial X_{hg}}}{\dfrac{\partial W}{\partial U^h}\dfrac{\partial U^h}{\partial X_{hg*}}} = \frac{\dfrac{\partial W}{\partial U^{h*}}\dfrac{\partial U^h}{\partial X_{h*g}}}{\dfrac{\partial W}{\partial U^{h*}}\dfrac{\partial U^{h*}}{\partial X_{h*g*}}} \qquad \begin{array}{l} \text{any } h, h^* = 1, \ldots, H \\ \text{any } g, g^* = 1, \ldots, G \end{array}$$

But, from the interpersonal equity condition for good g, the numerators of the two ratios are equal. Therefore, the denominators are also equal, and interpersonal equity is satisfied for g^* as well. Since the choice of g^* was entirely

---

[23] From conditions (2.8),

$$\frac{\partial L}{\partial V_{hf}} = \frac{\partial W}{\partial U^h}\frac{\partial U^h}{\partial V_{hf}} + \pi_f = 0$$

$$\frac{\partial L}{\partial V_{h*f}} = \frac{\partial W}{\partial U^{h*}}\frac{\partial U^{h*}}{\partial V_{h*f}} + \pi_f = 0$$

Hence:

$$\frac{\partial W}{\partial U^h}\frac{\partial U^h}{\partial V_{hf}} = -\pi_f \qquad \begin{array}{l} \text{all } h = 1, \ldots, H \\ \text{any } f = 1, \ldots, F \end{array}$$

arbitrary, interpersonal equity must hold for all goods if it holds for the gth good.[24]

Thus, the government's task is much easier than it first appears to be. Difficult as it may be to satisfy any of the interpersonal equity conditions, at least they need be satisfied for only one good (or, alternatively, only one factor) in an otherwise competitive economy.

The second point relates to the actual policies required to satisfy these conditions. As noted in Chapter 1, the competitive market system is of no help. The interpersonal equity conditions will not hold in general when the economy achieves a competitive general equilibrium, and if they do not, there are no natural market forces that will work toward the necessary equality. The government must find some other means of satisfying the interpersonal equity conditions. By the same token, government redistributions must not undermine the considerable achievement of the competitive market system, namely, the attainment of full pareto optimality. If social welfare is to be maximized, the government must use the information contained in the social welfare function to move society *along* the utility-possibilities frontier to the bliss point. It cannot take society inside the frontier.

Only one form of redistribution will guarantee that the pareto-optimal conditions will continue to hold. The redistributions must be *lump sum*, meaning that the amount of a single good or factor redistributed among each consumer is invariant to the economic decisions of all consumers and producers. If the transfers satisfy the condition of invariance, they will not interfere with the operation of any goods or factor market, in the sense that all the eight pareto-optimal conditions can still be met. Indeed, this is but another way of defining a lump-sum tax or transfer.

Suppose, for example, that some consumer is required to pay a tax equal to his age. The tax is clearly invariant to all economic decisions. Furthermore, while the tax will lower that person's utility, he will still maximize utility by equating marginal rates of substitution to price ratios, as required by pareto optimality. On the other hand, a redistribution policy using as its policy tool a set of taxes and transfers that are not lump sum may satisfy the interpersonal equity conditions, but it must by definition violate one of the pareto-optimal conditions. As a result, society can no longer attain the bliss point. Suppose, for example, the government redistributes income using a set of taxes and transfers based on wage income. The wage tax (transfer) will certainly drive a wedge between the price of labor paid by the firms and the price of labor received by the consumers. Consequently, pareto-optimal conditions P7 and P8 cannot be fully satisfied.

Notice two qualities that lump-sum taxes and transfers *do not* possess. First, it is not true that lump-sum redistributions have no effect on economic activity.

---

[24] The F additional interpersonal equity conditions for the variable factor supplies will also be satisfied. This follows immediately from the subset of pareto-optimal conditions in P3 relating the marginal rate of substitution between good g and any factor f, and interpersonal equity for good g.

Any redistribution program can be expected, at very least, to shift individuals' demands for goods or supplies of factors, with obvious repercussions throughout the entire economy. Second, it is not true that lump-sum redistributions have no effect on the values of the marginal and technical rates of substitution, and marginal rates of transformation. Prices will change as demand (and factor supply) curves shift. Therefore, the value of some of the marginal rates of exchange will change as well, since consumers and producers equate these margins to relative prices. For instance, movement along the utility-possibilities frontier occasioned by the government's lump-sum redistribution policy can be expected to move society along its production-possibilities frontier. Since the marginal rate of transformation is the slope of this frontier, marginal rates of transformation will necessarily change if the frontier is anything but a straight line. Subsequently, all marginal rates of substitution will have to change as competitive market forces reestablish the pareto-optimal conditions. Thus, lump-sum redistributions only ensure that the pareto-optimal conditions continue to hold, not that they will hold at any particular value.

A lump-sum redistribution of one of the goods or factors, then, is the absolute minimum policy required of the government even in a world of perfect markets with all the technical assumptions of Chapter 1 holding, so long as society cares about the equity of its economic system.

One final point concerning the nature of lump-sum redistributions deserves mention. Economists typically refer to the redistributions as lump-sum redistributions of "income," often without elaborating further on the source of the "income." This can be confusing, however, because if more than one variable factor is being supplied by consumers, the meaning of "income" is ambiguous. Furthermore, the interpersonal equity conditions of social welfare maximization seem to suggest that physical quantities of some good or factor must be transferred, rather than a dollar value of "income." What, then, is the "income" that is being redistributed lump sum?

One possible interpretation is to assume that all consumers possess an initial endowment of some good, say, X^g, which is also produced and sold by some of the firms in the economy. Some consumers will want to consume their entire endowment of X^g and purchase additional quantities either from other consumers or the producers of X^g. Other consumers will consume only a part of their endowment and sell the rest. If the government redistributes the initial endowments the redistribution will clearly be lump sum. If it continues to redistribute until

(2.36)
$$\frac{\partial W}{\partial U^h} \frac{\partial U^h}{\partial X_{hg}} = -\delta_g \quad \text{all } h = 1, \ldots, H$$

it will have satisfied the interpersonal equity conditions for X^g. Assuming a competitive market system with all technical assumptions holding, full pareto optimality will also be maintained. Hence, the interpersonal equity conditions will be satisfied for all other goods and factors as well. Finally, by evaluating the endowments at either the pre- or post-transfer prices of X^g, one can speak of transferring a dollar value of "income," or purchasing power.[25]

Another common interpretation is to associate the "income" with some factor of production that consumers supply in absolutely fixed amounts. Transferring physical or dollar amounts of this resource is obviously lump sum, since by definition it is not a decision variable of any consumer. Moreover, these transfers will move society along its utility-possibilities frontier as those taxed lose utility and those receiving transfers gain utility. In effect, the government is satisfying the interpersonal equity conditions indirectly. Presumably there exists a redistribution of the fixed resource that will satisfy the interpersonal equity conditions for one of the variable goods or factors, say, X^g. But if $(\partial W/\partial U^h)(\partial U^h/\partial X_{hg}) = -\delta_g$, all $h = 1, \ldots, H$, and pareto optimality holds, then the interpersonal equity conditions will hold for *all* variable goods and factors. Thus, the existence of a fixed factor gives the government the leverage it needs to satisfy the interpersonal equity conditions, even though they are defined in terms of the variable goods and factors.

Finally, it may simply be assumed that the good or factor being transferred is serving as the numeraire, such that its price is equal to one at any general equilibrium. Nonmonetary competitive market economies determine pareto-optimal allocations of resources in terms of relative prices. The absolute price level is entirely arbitrary. Thus, it is always possible to single out a good or factor, set its price equal to one, and solve for the values of all other prices in terms of the one fixed price. If the numeraire good is chosen for redistribution, unit transfers of it are equivalent to unit transfers of purchasing power or "real" income.

POLICY IMPLICATIONS AND CONCLUSIONS

Chapter 2 was meant to be preliminary to an analysis of public policy, but the discussion of the interpersonal equity conditions and lump-sum redistributions produced a number of fundamental prepositions relating to the policy norm of distributive equity:

1. If society cares about distributive equity, it must establish a government to carry out its wishes. A perfectly functioning competitive market economy will generate an efficient (pareto-optimal) allocation of resources, but even the most perfect market system is neutral with respect to the question of equity.

2. The pursuit of equity can be represented analytically by a Bergson-Samuelson individualistic social welfare function, whose arguments are the utility functions of each individual in the society.

3. In the best of all worlds, with all the technical assumptions of a well-functioning market system holding, and perfectly competitive markets, distributive equity can be achieved by a set of lump-sum redistributions satisfying

---

[25] The same analysis could be applied to the endowment of a primary factor, such as land.

the first-order interpersonal equity conditions of social welfare maximization. Moreover, the interpersonal equity conditions represent a complete normative theory of income distribution in this setting. The normative question—What is the optimal distribution of resources?—has a remarkably simple answer. It is the distribution that satisfies the interpersonal equity conditions, given the distributional rankings implied by the underlying social welfare function. If some other distribution happens to exist, then the interpersonal equity conditions provide a complete normative policy prescription for achieving the optimal distribution. Nothing more need be said.

This striking result may seem relatively unimportant, in that few markets are perfectly competitive and many of the technical assumptions are frequently violated, but it is actually quite powerful. Our subsequent analysis will show that if the government has enough policy tools at its disposal to restore pareto optimality when faced with market imperfections and violations of the technical assumptions, and if it can redistribute resources in a lump-sum fashion, then it should use the lump-sum redistributions to satisfy the interpersonal equity conditions. This is a much stronger statement, and suggests the vital role of the interpersonal equity conditions in normative public sector theory.

It may well be, of course, that the requisite policy tools do not exist. Governments may not be able to restore pareto optimality, nor redistribute lump sum. If so, then the interpersonal equity conditions no longer provide a theory of optimal income distribution. We turn to this important point in Chapter 3.

REFERENCES

Arrow, Kenneth J. *Social Choice and Individual Values.* New Haven, Conn.: Yale University Press, 1951.

Atkinson, A. "How Progressive Should the Income Tax Be?" In *Essays on Modern Economics,* edited by M. Parkin, London: Longman Group Ltd., 1973.

Bator, F. M. "Simple Analytics of Welfare Maximization." *American Economic Review,* March 1957.

Bergson, A. "A Reformulation of Certain Aspects of Welfare Economics." *Quarterly Journal of Economics,* 1938.

Christiansen, V., and Jansen, E. S. "Implicit Social Preferences in the Norwegian System of Indirect Taxation." *Journal of Public Economics,* October 1978.

Feldstein, M. "On the Optimal Progressivity of the Income Tax." *Journal of Public Economics,* vol. 2, 1973.

Harberger, A. "Three Basic Postulates for Applied Welfare Economics." *Journal of Economic Literature,* September 1971.

Kemp, M. C. and Ng, Y-K. "More on Social Welfare Functions: The Incompatibility of Individualism and Ordinalism." *Economica,* February 1977.

————. "On the Existence of Social Welfare Functions, Social Orderings, and Social Decision Functions." *Economica,* February 1976.

Little, I. M. D. *A Critique of Welfare Economics.* Oxford, England: Oxford University Press, 1957.

Mueller, D. "Public Choice: A Survey." *Journal of Economic Literature,* June 1976.

Rawls, J. *A Theory of Justice.* Cambridge, Mass.: Harvard University Press, 1971.

Samuelson, P. A. "Diagrammatic Exposition of a Theory of Public Expenditure." *Review of Economics and Statistics,* November 1955.

————. *Foundations of Economic Analysis.* New York: Atheneum Publishers, 1965.

————. "Reaffirming the Existence of 'Reasonable' Bergson-Samuelson Social Welfare Functions." *Economica,* February 1977.

————. "The Pure Theory of Public Expenditure." *Review of Economics and Statistics,* November 1954.

Weisbrod, B. A. "Income Redistribution Effects and Benefit-Cost Analysis." In *Problems in Public Expenditure Analysis,* edited by S. B. Chase, Jr. Washington, D.C.: The Brookings Institution, 1968.

3

Lump-sum redistributions, first-best and second-best analysis

Are lump-sum redistributions a feasible policy tool for the government?

This may appear to be a relatively uninteresting question. One is tempted to answer, "probably not, but even if they are feasible it hardly matters. Few governments use lump-sum taxes and transfers. For instance, no major U.S. tax or transfer program is lump sum." All this is true, yet it is hard to imagine a more important question for normative public sector theory. It turns out that the answer has a dramatic impact on all normative policy prescriptions in every area of public sector analysis, whether it be concerned primarily with distributional questions or allocational issues. In public sector theory, lump-sum redistributions are a cutting edge between first-best and second-best analysis.

The issue is not so much one of the existence of lump-sum redistributions. Lump-sum tax and transfer programs are easy enough to describe. The age tax mentioned in Chapter 2 is an obvious example. Moreover, some countries actually do use tax and transfer programs that are essentially lump sum. In the 1972 U.S. presidential campaign, George McGovern proposed scrapping most of the existing U.S. welfare programs and replacing them with annual $1,000 transfer payments to each U.S. citizen. His proposal was soundly rejected, but other countries have long had demogrants of this nature (e.g., Canada, to the aged). It might be argued that decisions on family size are essentially economic and would influence the amount of transfer received. If so, then a demogrant is not strictly lump sum, although the legislation could easily be drafted such that only persons already living at the time of passage would receive the transfers. On the tax side, poll taxes have occasionally been used as revenue sources and they are certainly lump sum.

But the mere existence of such devices is not enough to render them feasible policy tools. The lump-sum taxes and transfers must be flexible enough so that they can be designed to satisfy the interpersonal equity conditions for social welfare maximization, and this is a very tall order indeed. To be effective, the taxes and transfers would almost certainly have to be related to consumption, or income, or wealth in order to distinguish the haves from the have nots, but then it is doubtful that they would be lump sum. Until a few years ago it was thought that income taxes were essentially lump sum, because empirical research was unable to discover any relationship between tax rates and either work effort or savings, implying that labor and financial capital were supplied in absolutely fixed amounts. However, more recent analysis, employing detailed micro data sets, suggests that both labor supply and savings behavior exhibit some price elasticity.[1] If so, taxes and transfers based on income will not be lump sum. It would appear, then, that assuming the government can pursue an optimal lump-sum redistribution policy is heroic in the extreme. Nonetheless, public sector economists have been quite willing to employ the assumption of feasible lump-sum redistributions in order to analyze allocational policy questions in a first-best framework.

FIRST-BEST ANALYSIS

First-best analysis simply means that the government has a sufficient set of policy tools, for whatever problems may exist, to restore the economy to the bliss point on its first-best utility-possibilities frontier. By the "first-best" utility-possibilities frontier, we mean the locus of pareto-optimal allocations constrained only by the economy's underlying production functions and market clearance.[2]

The required set of policy tools is broad indeed. If the analysis occurs within the context of a market economy, it is understood either that all markets are perfectly competitive or that the government can adjust behavior in noncompetitive markets to generate the perfectly competitive results. Faced with a breakdown in one of the technical assumptions discussed in Chapter 1, the government must be able to respond with a policy that restores first-best pareto optimality. As we shall discover in Part II, the required policy responses may be exceedingly complex, enough so that they have little hope of practical application. Finally, the government must employ optimal lump-sum redistributions in order to equalize marginal social utilities of income at the first-best bliss point.

It may seem odd that public sector economists have been so attracted to first-best analysis, given its stringent and unrealistic assumptions, but first-best analysis is really the only way to analyze, *ceteris paribus*, the particular allocation problems caused by breakdowns in the technical assumptions and by market imperfections, per se. Consider, first, the role of lump-sum redistributions in this regard.

If lump-sum redistributions are feasible, then the problem of social welfare maximization dichotomizes into separate efficiency and distributional problems, exactly as the model in Chapter 2 dichotomized into the pareto-optimal and interpersonal equity conditions. The intuition why this is so can readily be seen

---

[1] For an excellent review of recent empirical studies on labor supply and savings elasticities, see M. Boskin, "On Some Recent Econometric Research in Public Finance," *AEA Papers and Proceedings*, May 1976.

[2] If some factors or production are supplied in absolutely fixed amounts, they, too, will act as constraints on the set of attainable utility possibilities. The general equilibrium model of Chapter 2 assumed variable factor supplies so that, formally, consumers' disutility from supplying factors enters as an argument of the social welfare objective function rather than as a constraint.

in terms of concepts already developed. Suppose one of the technical assumptions in Chapter 1 fails, for example, that there exists a consumer externality, meaning that at least one person's utility depends on the goods demanded and/ or factors supplied by some other consumer(s). Suppose, further, that the government consists of an allocational agency charged with designing policies to correct for allocational problems such as externalities, and a distributional agency charged with creating an optimal distribution of income. If lump-sum redistributions are possible, the allocational agency can ignore the existence of a social welfare function and analyze the externality in the context of the first general equilibrium model presented in Chapter 2, the model in which one consumer's utility is maximized subject to the constraints of all other utilities held constant (and production and market clearance). This model is specifically designed to find the set of pareto-optimal allocations consistent with society's first-best utility-possibilities frontier given the presence of an externality or any other imperfection. All relevant structural elements of the policy necessary to correct for the externality will follow directly from the first-order conditions of this model. The allocational branch does not have to worry about social welfare because it knows that the distributional agency will be designing policies to ensure that social marginal utilities of income will be equalized along the first-best utility-possibilities frontier. In particular, it knows that any unwanted distributional consequences of the allocational policies will be fully offset by the distributional agency.

Suppose, instead, a single superagency concerns itself both with the externality and the original nonoptimal income distribution and develops a full model of social welfare maximization to analyze these two problems simultaneously. Since the first-order conditions of the model dichotomize, it would discover one set of pareto-optimal conditions that do not involve the social welfare rankings and one set of interpersonal equity conditions that equalize all social marginal utilities of income. These conditions would be identical with those developed independently by the separate agencies. Since the pareto-optimal conditions contain no social welfare terms, they must generate the first-best utility-possibilities frontier. No other result is consistent with social welfare maximization under first-best assumptions. Similarly, the interpersonal equity conditions must be identical to those developed by the independent distributional agency. Only one distribution, in general, is consistent with the bliss point.

Of course, at some point the two independent agencies would have to coordinate their efforts. Since an economy is a closed, interdependent system, all allocational disruptions will have distributional consequences, and vice versa. Consequently, the allocational branch cannot finally set its policies until it knows what the distributional branch has done, or is about to do, and vice versa. Continuing with the externality example, suppose the externality is a "bad" such as pollution, in that consumption by some of the people reduces the utility others receive from their own consumption (and factor supplies). Moreover, suppose the correct policy takes the form of a tax on the polluter (a reasonable supposition, as we shall discover in Chapter 6). By following the independent modeling process described above, the allocational branch will discover all the relevant *design* characteristics of the tax, such as what should be taxed and what parameters in the economy will determine the level of the tax rates, but the exact level of the tax rate will not be determined. As we have seen, the criterion of pareto optimality admits to an infinity of allocations, all of those on the utility-possibilities frontier. In principle, each allocation will have one particular tax rate associated with it, so that the final tax rate cannot be announced until the distributional agency announces its optimal redistributional policy, thereby selecting the allocation consistent with the bliss point. Turning the example around, the interpersonal equity conditions will tell the distributional agency all the relevant *design characteristics* of the optimal lump-sum redistributions, but the exact *levels* of all individual taxes and transfers will depend in part upon the gains and losses occasioned by the pollution tax. Thus, while it is possible analytically to distinguish between the design of allocation policies and the design of distributional policy, as first-best analysis does, the exact policies to be followed must be simultaneously determined. In formal terms, the pareto-optimal and interpersonal equity conditions are both necessary conditions for social welfare maximization. They must be solved simultaneously to determine a social welfare maximum.

Despite the ultimate interdependence of allocational and distributional policies, the first-best literature on public expenditure theory typically analyzes only efficiency problems inherent in the breakdown of the technical assumptions (or of market imperfections), ignoring completely the question of distributive equity. The analysis generally proceeds along the lines suggested in Chapter 1. First, the new pareto-optimal conditions are determined given that one of the technical assumptions fails. Then policies are described which will generate the correct pareto-optimal conditions. But predicting the effects of any government policy involves assumptions about the behavior of consumers and firms. How will they react to the policy? Public sector economists have most often chosen to analyze this question within the context of a competitive market economy, again primarily to retain a *ceteris paribus* framework. This has led them to consider two additional questions as well: (*a*) what allocation of resources will the competitive market generate in the absence of government intervention; and (*b*) can the government restore first-best pareto optimality while maintaining existing competitive markets, or is a complete government takeover of some activity absolutely necessary.

Distributional issues are ignored in the first-best literature, not because they are unimportant but rather because they are relatively uninteresting. As noted in the conclusion to Chapter 2, having said that the government should redistribute income lump sum to satisfy the interpersonal equity conditions necessary for social welfare maximization, there is nothing else to say. A breakdown in one of the technical assumptions may alter the form of the interpersonal conditions, but even so, they still have the interpretation that one good or factor should be redistributed to equalize the marginal social welfare from having any one person consume (supply) an extra unit of the good (or factor). On the other hand, the new pareto-optimal conditions will change significantly depending exactly on how the technical assumptions fail, both their form *and* interpretation. Small wonder, then, that first-best analysis tends to emphasize these conditions and often relegates the interpersonal equity conditions to a footnote, if they are mentioned at all. Knowing that the first-order conditions of a full model of social welfare maximization will dochotomize, there is no need to use the full model. A simple model highlighting the new first-best pareto-optimal conditions for the allocational problem at hand will be sufficient.

The first-best analysis in Part II of the text will be careful, however, to use the full model of social welfare maximization presented in Chapter 2 whenever the analysis requires a many-person economy. Carrying the social welfare function will serve to emphasize the importance of lump-sum redistributions to all first-best policy analysis.

First-best models have another remarkable property beyond the fact that the first-order conditions dichotomize into distinct sets of pareto-optimal and interpersonal equity conditions. The pareto-optimal conditions further dichotomize in the sense that a breakdown in one of the technical assumptions, or a market imperfection, will alter the pareto-optimal conditions for those goods and factors directly affected, but will leave unchanged the pareto-optimal conditions of all the unaffected goods and factors. This property makes the first-best assumptions especially attractive for *ceteris paribus* analysis of policy questions. For instance, the allocational problems created by an externality that is associated with a particular economic activity can be isolated from distributional considerations *and* from all other allocational issues within the economy.

A CONDENSED GENERAL EQUILIBRIUM MODEL

This property is also extremely useful in that it permits formal analysis with condensed versions of the standard general equilibrium model presented in Chapter 2. Condensations of the full general equilibrium are so common in the first-best literature that we will demonstrate how to reduce the model in a manner suitable for analyzing consumer externalities without actually considering a specific externality problem at this point. It is important to understand that these condensed models are appropriate general equilibrium representations of social welfare maximization, given the additional assumptions required to suppress parts of the full model.

When analyzing a consumer externality, carrying along the detailed production relationships of the model is not really necessary since we are primarily interested in the interrelationships among consumers, and we know that any changes in the pareto-optimal conditions on consumer behavior caused by the externality will not affect other pareto-optimal conditions or the interpretation of the interpersonal equity conditions. Thus, we will want to simplify the full model by de-emphasizing production as much as possible, while maintaining all its essential consumption elements. This can be accomplished with the following three modifications.

1. Define all goods and factors in terms of consumption by suppressing, notationally, the use of factors and the supply of goods by firms. Further, ignore the notational distinction between goods and factors, other than the convention that factors enter all utility and production relationships with a negative sign.

Let:

$$X_{hi} = \text{good } i \text{ consumed by or factor } i \text{ supplied by person } h.$$
$$i = 1, \ldots, N$$
$$h = 1, \ldots, H$$

so that there are N total goods and factors in the economy (instead of $G \cdot F$ as in the original model).

2. *Assume* production is efficient and can be represented implicitly as a production-possibilities frontier in terms of the aggregate amount of consumer goods produced and factors supplied.[3] Write:

(3.1)
$$F(X_1, \ldots, X_i, \ldots, X_N) = 0$$

where:

$X_i = $ the aggregate consumption (supply) of good (factor) i.

$F(\ ) = $ an implicit summary of all the relevant production relationships corresponding to the production-possibilities frontier in two-good space.

3. Finally, market clearance requires that

$$\sum_{h=1}^{H} X_{hi} = X_i \qquad i = 1, \ldots, N$$

These constraints can be incorporated directly into the production-possibilities frontier, obtaining:

(3.2)
$$F\left(\sum_{h=1}^{H} X_{h1}, \ldots, \sum_{h=1}^{H} X_{hi}, \ldots, \sum_{h=1}^{H} X_{hN}\right) = 0$$

or

$$F\left(\sum_{h=1}^{H} X_{hi}\right) = 0$$

---

[3] Unless otherwise stated, we will always assume that $F(\ )$ describes a regular (convex outwards) transformation surface for the economy. This in turn implies certain restrictions on the individual production functions. Kelvin Lancaster's *Mathematical Economics*, sects. 8.4 through 8.7, contains an excellent analysis of the necessary and sufficient conditions on the individual production functions for a regular transformation surface. Kelvin Lancaster, *Mathematical Economics* (New York: The MacMillan Co., 1968).

with the understanding that producers do not care who receives (supplies) an additional unit of a good (factor). That is,

(3.3)
$$\frac{\partial F}{\partial X_{hi}} = \frac{\partial F}{\partial X_i} \qquad \text{all } h = 1, \ldots, H$$

With these three changes, the social welfare maximization problem becomes extremely simple to represent formally:

$$\max_{(X_{hi})} W[U^h(X_{hi})]$$

$$\text{s.t.} \quad F\left(\sum_{h=1}^{H} X_{hi}\right) = 0$$

While this is a drastically condensed version of the original model, it is still perfectly valid as a general equilibrium model. Furthermore, it is sufficiently general to generate all relevant pareto-optimal conditions involving consumption, as well as the standard interpersonal equity conditions. As such it is ideal for analyzing consumer externalities, which essentially involve specifying which arguments enter whose utility functions.

To see that all the relevant first-order conditions remain, consider first the interpersonal equity conditions that are obtained from the first-order conditions with respect to any single good (or factor) consumed (supplied) by any two people, say X_{h1} and X_{j1}. Setting up the Lagrangian,

$$\max_{(X_{hi})} L = W[U^h(X_{hi})] + \lambda F\left(\sum_{h=1}^{H} X_{hi}\right)$$

and differentiating yields:

(3.4)
$$\frac{\partial L}{\partial X_{h1}} = \frac{\partial W}{\partial U^h} \frac{\partial U^h}{\partial X_{h1}} + \lambda F_1 = 0$$

(3.5)
$$\frac{\partial L}{\partial X_{j1}} = \frac{\partial W}{\partial U^j} \frac{\partial U^j}{\partial X_{j1}} + \lambda F_1 = 0$$

Therefore:

$$\frac{\partial W}{\partial U^h} \frac{\partial U^h}{\partial X_{h1}} = -\lambda F_1 \qquad \text{all } h = 1, \ldots, H$$

the same rule obtained in the more detailed model of Chapter 2.

To derive the consumption oriented pareto-optimal conditions, consider the first-order conditions with respect to two goods consumed by any one person (or two factors, or any one good and any one factor), say, X_{hi} and X_{hk}.

(3.6)
$$\frac{\partial L}{\partial X_{hi}} = \frac{\partial W}{\partial U^h} \frac{\partial U^h}{\partial X_{hi}} + \lambda F_i = 0$$

(3.7)
$$\frac{\partial L}{\partial X_{hk}} = \frac{\partial W}{\partial U^h} \frac{\partial U^h}{\partial X_{hk}} + \lambda F_k = 0$$

Rearranging, dividing, and simplifying,

(3.8)
$$\frac{\dfrac{\partial U^h}{\partial X_{hi}}}{\dfrac{\partial U^h}{\partial X_{hk}}} = \frac{F_i}{F_k} \qquad \begin{array}{l} \text{all } h = 1, \ldots, H \\ \text{any } i, k = 1, \ldots, N \end{array}$$

The ratio F_i/F_k gives the marginal rate of transformation (substitution) in production between goods (factors) i and k, and the left-hand side is their marginal rate of substitution in consumption. Hence, the single set of relationships, (3.8), reproduces pareto-optimal conditions P1, P2, P3, P6, P7, and P8 from the full model of Chapter 2. (Recall that i and k can be any two goods, any two factors, or any one good and any one factor.) Only the production efficiency conditions P4 and P5 cannot be reproduced with this model, but they are assumed to hold anyway whenever production is represented as one implicit production-possibilities frontier. In order to be on its production-possibilities frontier, production must occur on the contract locus in factor space. Thus, despite their simplicity, condensed versions of the standard model, such as this one, retain an enormous amount of analytical flexibility. As a result they have proven especially useful for analyzing public sector problems in a first-best framework. We will use them throughout Part II of the text.

SECOND-BEST ANALYSIS

Suppose, realistically, that lump-sum taxes and transfers are not available to the government, at least not with sufficient flexibility to generate the interpersonal equity conditions of the standard model. This changes the analysis rather drastically. To see why, consider two policy strategies, one designed to produce distributive equity, the other designed to restore first-best pareto optimality.

If the government chooses to redistribute income until social marginal utilities are equalized by using nonlump-sum taxes and transfers,[4] it will necessarily introduce distortions into the economy. In the context of a market economy, some consumers and/or producers will now face different prices for the same goods and/or factors. Since consumers and producers equate relative prices to their marginal rates of substitution and transformation, respectively, and since pareto optimality requires that $MRS = MRT$, some of the pareto-optimal conditions will no longer hold. The economy will be forced beneath its first-best utility-possibilities frontier.

Suppose, on the other hand, the government focuses only on allocational problems and chooses allocational policies designed to bring society to the utility-possibilities frontier.[5] Without simultaneously employing lump-sum

---

[4] Assume it is possible to equalize social marginal utilities without lump-sum redistributions. It may not be, given the available policy tools.

[5] Again, assume this is possible.

redistributions, however, the economy will not be at the bliss point, in general. The government may actually choose some policy mix designed to move the economy somewhat closer to full pareto optimality, and somewhat closer to distributive equity, but the point remains that removing the possibility of feasible lump-sum redistributions restricts the set of solutions available to the government, for example, to the shaded portion in Figure 3–1. The viable allocations and distributions may or may not include points on the first-best utility-possibilities frontier, but, importantly, they definitely exclude the bliss point. The policy problem now becomes one of finding the best policy option within this restricted set of opportunities. As such it is part of *second-best analysis*, defined as the analysis of optimal public sector policy given that the bliss point of first-best analysis is unattainable.

FIGURE 3-1

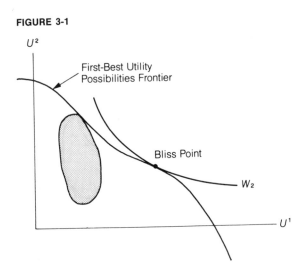

One immediate and very striking implication of second-best public expenditure analysis is that government policy should not necessarily try to keep society on its first-best utility-possibility frontier. Within the restricted set of policy alternatives, there may well be better points than those on the frontier. Assume, for example, that society is at point *A* in Figure 3–2 prior to government action, possibly because one of the technical assumptions of Chapter 1 has failed and the competitive market is therefore signaling the wrong allocation of resouces. If lump-sum redistributions were feasible and the world were otherwise first best, the government should design policies to restore full pareto optimality and redistribute lump sum to achieve the bliss point, point *D* in Figure 3–2. However, in a second-best environment without the option of lump-sum redistributions, the policy option which brings society to point *B* on the frontier is dominated by an alternative option that keeps society below the frontier, point *C*. Society's goal is still the maximization of social welfare,

FIGURE 3-2

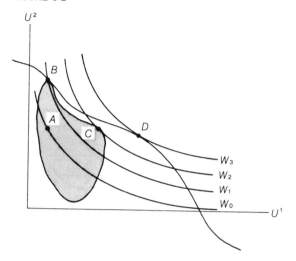

reaching the highest possible social indifference curve, but given the restricted set of available options, C is the maximum attainable level of social welfare. B is pareto efficient, C is not, but C's superior distributional attributes prove decisive. In a second-best environment, then, society's efficiency and equity norms are completely interrelated. In contrast with the first-best environment, they cannot be pursued with separate policy tools.

Second-best analysis has a number of other distinguishing characteristics. One definition of the second best has already been stated, the inability to attain the bliss point of the first-best environment. Alternatively, second-best analysis can be defined as the theory of optimal public sector policy given that additional constraints have been added to the first-best framework of social welfare maximization. As noted above, the first-best constraints consist solely of the underlying production relationships and market clearance.[6] The additional constraints will typically be restrictions on the permissible set of government policy tools, or maintained imperfections in the market environment in which the government operates. Any single additional binding constraint, or any combination of these constraints, renders the analysis second best.

Notice that we have been careful throughout this section to refer to the "first-best" utility-possibilities frontier, or the "first-best" bliss point. Given the existence of additional constraints it is always possible to derive a new utility-possibilities frontier and a new bliss point corresponding to the new restricted set of feasible allocations.

In terms of Figure 3–2, these would correspond to the outer boundary of the shaded portion and point C, respectively. In these terms the government can still be thought of as pursuing the distributionally best allocation among all

---

[6] And fixed factor supplies, if relevant. See footnote 2.

possible pareto-optimal allocations, exactly as in first-best analysis. While this is technically correct, it tends to obscure the important differences between first-best and second-best analyses, differences that can best be seen in terms of the set of attainable first-best allocations. In particular, the addition of a single binding constraints on the model of Chapter 2 renders the first-best bliss point unattainable, establishing the equivalence of the two definitions of second-best analysis.

Refusing to permit lump-sum redistributions is merely one of a large number of possible constraints on the feasible set of government policy tools. It is often one of the constraints chosen, because second-best analysis is basically an attempt to develop normative policy rules in more realistic policy environments, and denying the government feasible lump-sum redistributions is an obvious step toward realism. Beyond this, however, it is somewhat more difficult to generalize. The second-best literature has considered an enormous variety of additional constraints on available policy tools. This is hardly surprising since the set of potential constraints is virtually limitless, given the myriad of political realities and the staggering complexity of actual market economies. It is fair to say, however, that three kinds of policy restrictions have been most commonly employed in the literature (in addition to restrictions on lump-sum redistributions): the use of specific distorting taxes, the existence of legislated budget constraints on individual government agencies or on the government as a whole, and either the drafting of resources or the offer of certain government services at zero price.

a. Distorting Taxation

Actual taxes are most often *ad valorem* or per-unit taxes on either the buyers or suppliers of goods and factors, including sales and excise taxes on goods and services, income and payroll taxes on factors of production, and various kinds of wealth or property taxes. In addition, tax rates on income and wealth are often graduated, increasing with income (wealth). Since all these taxes introduce distortions into the economy, models which restrict the government to using one or more of them are necessarily second best. These models have had a monumental impact on public expenditure theory. The problems being analyzed are the same, primarily externalities and decreasing cost production, but by foregoing the possibility of lump-sum redistributions, the normative policy prescriptions become dramatically different. Models incorporating distorting taxation have also been extremely useful for studying the allocational theory of taxation, per se. Many questions that have no meaning in a first-best environment become interesting in a second-best environment, including: If the government must raise revenue using a single distorting tax, such as a particular sales or income tax, what are the costs to scociety? Are some taxes less costly, that is, less distorting than others, per dollar of revenue collected? If the government is free to vary a wide set of distorting taxes, what pattern of tax rates minimizes the resulting distortions while raising a required amount of revenue? Optimal taxes for solving problems such as externalities promote social welfare in a first-best environment. They cannot create distortions in the sense of welfare costs.

Analysis of the welfare costs of taxation has a long history dating back to the very beginnings of public sector economics. The allocational theory of taxation has always been a second-best analysis. The key change in tax theory over the past 15 years is not that assumptions with respect to tax instruments have become more realistic but rather that general equilibrium modeling techniques have increasingly replaced partial equilibrium analysis in studying these issues. The results have not been as dramatic as in public expenditure theory, but the allocational theory of taxation has been significantly sharpened and expanded by the recent second-best analysis.

b. Fixed Budget Constraints

Legislatures usually impose budgetary ceilings on individual government agencies that can be exceeded only by means of special supplemental appropriations. Frequently the budgets of entire governments are limited as well. In the United States, for instance, many state and local government administrations are required to submit annually balanced operating budgets. Even without this requirement, most state and local governments cannot routinely borrow in the national capital markets to cover annual operating deficits. Only the national government enjoys this privilege.

Imposing annual budget constraints is generally not a first-best strategy. Moreover, perfectly functioning capital markets would permit borrowing to finance worthwhile projects even if they could not be financed out of existing tax revenues. Faced with these constraints, however, government agencies may well be precluded from considering projects that would otherwise be worthwhile in a first-best environment. Thus, as a further step toward reality, researchers have incorporated annual budget constraints directly into their models to see how they affect traditional first-best policy rules. Once again, the new second-best policy prescriptions are often quite different from their first-best counterparts.

c. Drafting Resources or Giving Away Goods

Most goods and factors have a marginal opportunity cost associated with them. In a first-best world, their prices would reflect these costs, but governments sometimes choose to set prices well below opportunity costs, often at zero. The military draft is one example on the factor side. On the goods and services side, governments typically levy no charges for the side benefits of hydroelectric projects, such as flood control, recreational facilities, and irrigation. Not surprisingly, then, these pricing constraints have often been the focus of second-best analysis.

MARKET IMPERFECTIONS

Even if government policy tools are not directly restricted in any way, market imperfections will render the first-best bliss point unattainable. For example, markets containing monopolistic elements will generally not result in price equal to marginal cost, so that the pareto-optimal conditions will not hold for these goods and services. These market imperfections could be viewed as restrictions on government policy in the sense that the government is unable to correct the imperfections despite the theoretical existence of policies that would do so. In any case, a maintained market imperfection implies a second-best environment, and normative policy rules applicable to a perfectly competitive market environment will usually not be correct if monopoly elements are present.

In "The General Theory of the Second Best," Lipsey and Lancaster proved that if the first-best pareto-optimal conditions fail to hold for some goods and factors, then it is generally not optimal to pursue first-best pareto optimality for the other goods and factors. Their article now stands as a classic in public sector economics, and the Lipsey-Lancaster theorem is often referred to as *the* theorem of the second best.[7]

FURTHER IMPLICATIONS OF SECOND-BEST MODELING

Two further distinctions between first-best and second-best modeling are worth emphasizing in these introductory comments, both resulting from the feature that second-best general equilibrium models are basically first-best models modified by the addition of one or more constraints.

As noted earlier, the first-order conditions of first-best models dichotomize into one distinct set of efficiency or pareto-optimal conditions and one distinct set of distributional or interpersonal equity conditions. Moreover, the pareto-optimal conditions further dichotomize in the sense that changes in some of them occasioned by a breakdown in one of the technical assumptions will leave other pareto-optimal conditions unchanged. Second-best models typically do not dichotomize in either way. As a general rule, all the first-order conditions of a second-best model will contain both efficiency and equity considerations, especially if lump-sum distributions are not permitted. This is simply the formal counterpart to a point demonstrated earlier, that if the first-best bliss point is unattainable, the efficiency and equity norms are directly interrelated. This fact has been especially disheartening for normative analysis because it further limits the government's ability to honor the principle of consumer sovereignty. In a first-best environment the demand (factor supply) content of all allocational decision rules derives solely from individual's preferences, usually their marginal rates of substitution. The social welfare rankings

---

[7] R. G. Lipsey and K. Lancaster, "The General Theory of the Second Best," *Review of Economic Studies*, December 1956.

influence allocational decision rules only indirectly in that any redistribution can be expected to shift aggregate demands. Thus, in a very real sense, consumer sovereignty provides the basis for government intervention into the market economy, at least with respect to allocational problems. In a second-best environment, however, the allocational decision rules contain the social welfare rankings as well as terms representing individuals preferences, so that consumer sovereignty will be partially overridden even in allocational decision making. Moreover, given that there is nowhere near a consensus on how to form the social welfare rankings or what they should be, this implication of second-best analysis is doubly disturbing. It is no longer possible to isolate the uncertainties associated with the social welfare rankings into a single decision on optimal income distribution. What is worse, the social welfare terms contaminate *all* markets in general, even those which first-best analysis would leave entirely in the hands of the competitive market system.

Another discouraging difference is that second-best allocational decision rules generally do not have clear intuitive interpretations with obvious analogues to free market principles. First-best allocational decision rules often do, because they are usually just simple combinations of consumer's marginal rates of substitution and producers' marginal rates of transformation (technical rates of substitution for factors). Since competitive markets equate price ratios to these margins, a competitive market structure can always be described that will generate first-best pareto-optimal conditions of this type. This result is especially appealing if one believes in competitive markets, consumer sovereignty, and the least possible amount of government interference with the market system. In first-best analysis the government can often be viewed as a perfect imitator of perfectly competitive behavior.

There are two reasons why second-best allocational decision rules will not have competitive market interpretations. In the first place, terms from the additional constraints will naturally appear in the first-order conditions, with associated Lagrangian multipliers that tend to be unrelated to standard market concepts. Secondly, if lump-sum redistributions are forbidden, the decision rules will generally contain social welfare terms, as already noted, and these certainly have no competitive market analogue.

The thrust of these differences is that recent research in second-best public expenditure theory has offered the severest possible challenge to first-best orthodoxy. The newer second-best rules often bear no clear-cut relationship to their long standing first-best counterparts. Moreover, they tend to be less widely accepted as normative policy prescriptions. The problems associated with the presence of social welfare rankings have already been mentioned. But more than that, second-best optimal policy rules tend to be rather sensitive to modifications in constraints or additions of new constraints. Because the real world is obviously many times more constrained, more imperfect than any analytical model can hope to capture, this type of model sensitivity is also extremely troublesome. Finally, second-best policy environments tend to require much broader government intervention than first-best environments for any given set of problems requiring intervention.

SIMILARITIES BETWEEN FIRST-BEST AND
SECOND-BEST ANALYSIS

The numerous differences between first-best and second-best public expenditure analysis should not obscure the fact that, both methodologically and philosophically, the two approaches are virtually identical. The challenge to first-best orthodoxy is contained in the first-order conditions of second-best models. One would certainly not want to minimize the importance of this challenge, since the first-order conditions translate directly into normative policy rules. But second-best analysis hardly represents a methodological or philosophical break with first-best theory because in its attempt to be more realistic, all it does is attach some additional constraints to the basic first-best neoclassical general equilibrium model. This is hardly revolutionary. For instance, second-best analysis retains the fundamental notion that the government is interested in social welfare maximization, with social welfare indexed by means of an individualistic Bergson-Samuelson social welfare function. In principle, then, second-best analysis honors consumer sovereignty to the same degree as first-best analysis, even though its results are less clear-cut in this regard. Furthermore, second-best research has generally remained closely allied with the competitive market system, so much so that the following standard competitive market assumptions are commonplace in second-best models:

1. Consumers maximize utility subject to a budget constraint and have no control over any prices.
2. Private sector producers are decentralized, price-taking, profit maximizers, such that goods prices equal marginal costs and factor prices equal the value of marginal products.
3. If there is government production, the government buys and sells factors and outputs at the competitively determined private sector producer prices. This is often true *even if the second-best decision rules imply that a different set of "shadow" prices should be used to determine the optimal level of government production.*

There are two reasons why second-best analysis has emphasized competitive market behavior. The first turns on the *ceteris paribus* condition. Exploring the effects of particular market imperfections or policy restrictions on first-best public sector decision rules requires introducing them as constraints one at a time into an otherwise first-best model. If the analysis proceeds within the context of a market economy, this means that the parts of the market economy not specifically analyzed will have to be assumed competitive. As a result, second-best analysis to date has been much closer to a first-best perfectly competitive market environment than to highly imperfect real-world market economies. It is at best a small, hesitant step toward reality.

The second reason is also a matter of analytical convenience. The competitive market assumptions permit flexibility in model building, a feature that second-best analysis has frequently exploited. As noted in Chapter 2, general equilibrium models can always be defined in terms of quantities of goods and factors. The model developed in that chapter served as an example. By incorporating specific behavioral market assumptions, however, the model can be expressed directly in terms of prices, and the competitive assumptions happen to be the easiest ones to employ. For many second-best problems the price model has proven to be the most direct analytical approach.

To gain some preliminary intuition why this is so, consider the common second-best policy restriction that the government must use distorting taxation. Taxes create distortions by driving a wedge between the prices faced by different economic agents operating in a single market. If the general equilibrium model is already defined in terms of prices, the gross and net of tax prices (and the tax itself) can be incorporated directly into the model. Furthermore, all of the interesting allocational and distributional implications of the tax will follow directly from the first-order conditions of the price model. Proceeding in this way turns out to be far more convenient than beginning with a quantity model and reworking the first-order conditions using standard market assumptions to capture the effects of the taxes.

CONCLUSION

Chapter 3 has considered the differences and similarities between first-best and second-best policy analysis, paying particular attention to the role of lump-sum redistributions in distinguishing the two policy environments. The discussion ended with the point that whereas first-best analysis typically employs variations of the full social welfare maximization model developed in Chapter 2, whose arguments are quantities of goods and factors, second-best analysis frequently uses variations of this model defined in terms of prices. Chapter 4 will continue the point by discussing how standard competitive market assumptions can be used to replace each element of the basic general equilibrium model—the individual utility function, the production functions, and market clearance—with alternative analytical expressions defined in terms of prices. These expressions will complete the set of analytical tools needed for our study of public sector economics in the remainder of the text.

REFERENCES

Boskin, M.   "On Some Recent Econometric Research in Public Finance." *AEA Papers and Proceedings,* May 1976.

Lancaster, K.   *Mathematical Economics.* New York: The MacMillan Co., 1968.

————, and Lipsey, R. G.   "The General Theory of the Second Best." *Review of Economic Studies,* December 1956.

4

General equilibrium modeling specified in terms of prices

Chapter 4 will develop a variety of techniques for specifying general equilibrium models of social welfare maximization in terms of prices, techniques that are commonplace in the second-best literature. Specifying a complete general equilibrium model in terms of prices requires replacing each element of the standard model of Chapter 2 by a comparable relationship whose arguments are prices. All valid general equilibrium models contain demand relationships, supply relationships, and market clearance as their core, regardless of what other relationships might be added as constraints in a second-best analysis. Unlike Chapter 2, however, Chapter 4 will not build toward one particular specification. Converting the arguments in the model of Chapter 2 from quantities to prices requires highly specific assumptions about consumption and production behavior, and the structure of a general equilibrium price model will vary considerably depending upon the set of assumptions chosen. This is actually a welcome feature, since it gives the researcher some flexibility in choosing a model that is particularly well suited to the issue at hand. The second-best literature has exploited this flexibility. It has not chosen a single price model for its analytical framework to the same extent that first-best analysis has chosen the quantity model of Chapter 2.

Because of the many options available, Chapter 4 will concentrate on each element in the basic quantity model of social welfare maximization, developing a number of price specifications for its individual demand and production sectors, and the market clearance equations. The chapter will highlight why these particular specifications are the ones most frequently employed, and discuss their main analytical characteristics. We will also briefly consider how these individual elements can be combined into valid general equilibrium models. The various price models commonly used in second-best analysis appear to be quite different, so it is important to realize that they are all essentially general equilibrium representations of social welfare maximization under different assumptions about consumption and production behavior.

The analytical price constructs developed in Chapter 4 will be used extensively throughout Part III when we consider a number of public sector issues in a second-best policy environment. Consistent with the second-best literature, we will choose the general equilibrium model best suited to the particular issues being considered, rather than sticking with one model throughout. Switching models can be confusing, but with Chapter 4 as background, we should be able to focus on the policy issues involved without having to discuss in any great detail the particular general equilibrium model supporting the analysis.

Chapter 4 will also differ from Chapters 2 and 3 by distinguishing between one-person and many-person economies. As was noted in the last chapter, second-best decision rules in many-person economies generally contain both efficiency and distributional terms so that it is difficult to focus solely on the inefficiencies created by problems that are essentially allocational in nature, such as the existence of externalities. Thus, in order to gain insight into the purely allocational aspects of optimal policy rules, the second-best literature has often found it convenient to posit one-consumer economies, in which, of course, the distributional issues cannot arise. We will also use one-consumer models in Part III for this same purpose.

It will prove less confusing to discuss all aspects of one-consumer price modeling before considering many-person models, because some of the most useful one-person analytical constructs are inappropriate in a many-person context. This can be seen most easily once all the one-person relationships have been developed.

ONE-CONSUMER PRICE MODELS

The Demand Sector

In general equilibrium quantity models the consumer's utility function is the basic unit of demand (factor supply). If the consumer is placed in a competitive market context, it is universally assumed that he will maximize his utility function subject to a budget constraint defined over a fixed set of prices for all goods demanded and factors supplied. Given this assumption, there are a number of ways to express the consumer's preferences in terms of prices. The two most popular representations are the indirect utility function and the expenditure function.

The Indirect Utility Function.   The standard consumer problem, commonly referred to as the primal, can be represented as follows:

$$\max_{(X_i)} U(X_i)$$

$$\text{s.t.} \quad \sum_{i=1}^{N} q_i X_i = I$$

where:

X_i = the ith good demanded or factor supplied.

q_i = the price of good or factor i.

I = lump-sum income.

Three comments on the notation are in order:

1. For most purposes there is no need to distinguish, notationally, between goods and factors, except for the usual convention that factor supplies are measured negatively. The factors in X_i include only variable factor supplies.
2. I represents *lump-sum* income, as distinguished from income from variable factor supplies. It comes from sources such as gifts, lump-sum government transfer payments, pure economic profits received from production, or the income derived from a factor offered in absolutely fixed supply. If there are lump-sum taxes, I could be negative. In many second-best applications, I is set equal to zero, especially when lump-sum redistributions have been ruled out. This also rules out the other sources of I, such as pure economic profiits and income from fixed factors. If such income exists, it is often assumed to be taxed at a 100 percent rate.
3. Most second-best researchers have adopted the convention of using q for consumer prices and p for producer prices. The two will differ in the presence of distorting taxes. We will use this convention throughout the text.

The first-order conditions of the primal solve for the N goods demand and factor supply functions in terms of the prices and income.

$$(4.1) \qquad X_i = X_i(\vec{q}; I) \qquad i = 1, \ldots, N$$
$$\vec{q} = (q_1, \ldots, q_N)$$

The functions X_i are homogeneous of degree zero in prices and income (or prices, with $I \equiv 0$).

To form the *indirect utility function*, substitute these functions back into the utility function, creating an expression for utility in terms of prices and income:

$$(4.2) \qquad V^*(\vec{q}; I) = U[X_i(\vec{q}; I)]$$

$V^*(\vec{q}; I)$ contains all relevant information about a consumer's preferences, given the assumption of utility maximization in a competitive market context. Hence it can replace the ordinary utility function in any constrained welfare maximization problem defined in terms of prices and income. Rather than using $V^*(\ )$, however, it is often convenient to redefine the indirect utility function as

$$(4.3) \qquad V(\vec{q}; I) = -V^*(\vec{q}; I)$$

so that the partial derivatives $\partial V / \partial q_i$ are positive for goods and negative for factors. Unless otherwise stated, we will use $V(\ )$ rather than V^* throughout the text.

Finally, a result known as Roy's theorem, that $\partial V / \partial q_k = \lambda X_k$, all k, where λ equals the marginal utility of income, is a property of the indirect utility function used often in second-best public sector analysis. It is derived as follows:

From (4.2) and (4.3),

$$(4.4) \qquad \frac{\partial V}{\partial q_k} = -\frac{\partial V^*}{\partial q_k} = -\sum_{i=1}^{N} \frac{\partial U}{\partial X_i} \frac{\partial X_i}{\partial q_k}$$

Substituting $\partial U/\partial X_i = \lambda q_i$ from the primal yields:

(4.5)
$$\frac{\partial V}{\partial q_k} = -\lambda \sum_{i=1}^{N} q_i \frac{\partial X_i}{\partial q_k}$$

Next, differentiate the consumer's budget constraint with respect to q_k:

(4.6)
$$\frac{\partial\left(I - \sum_{i=1}^{N} q_i X_i\right)}{\partial q_k} = -X_k - \sum_{i=1}^{N} q_i \frac{\partial X_i}{\partial q_k} = 0$$

Thus:

(4.7)
$$\sum_{i=1}^{N} q_i \frac{\partial X_i}{\partial q_k} = -X_k$$

and, from (4.5),

(4.8)
$$\frac{\partial V}{\partial q_k} = \lambda X_k \qquad k = 1, \ldots, N$$

The Expenditure Function. The dual to the standard consumer problem of maximizing utility subject to a budget constraint is to minimize "expenditures" subject to utility being held constant.

Dual:

$$\min_{(X_i)} \sum_{i=1}^{N} q_i X_i$$

$$\text{s.t.} \quad U(X_i) = \bar{U}$$

"Expenditures" is understood to mean expenditures on all goods and services less income from all variable factors. The first-order conditions of the dual solve for goods demand and factor supply curves of the form:

(4.9)
$$X_i^c = X_i(\bar{q}; \bar{U}) \qquad i = 1, \ldots, N$$

These are compensated demand and supply curves, indicating the consumer's response to price changes given that utility is held constant. (By contrast, the ordinary market demand curves show responses to price changes given that lump-sum income is held constant.) The compensated functions X_i^c have a number of important properties:

a. The price derivatives $\partial X_i^c/\partial q_k$, $k = 1, \ldots, N$, are the Slutsky substitution terms in the Slutsky equation:

(4.10)
$$\left.\frac{\partial X_i^{\text{ord}}}{\partial q_k}\right|_{I=\bar{I}} = \left.\frac{\partial X_i^c}{\partial q_k}\right|_{U=\bar{U}} - X_k \left.\frac{\partial X_i^{\text{ord}}}{\partial I}\right|_{\bar{q}=\bar{q}}$$

Moreover, $\partial X_i^c/\partial q_i < 0$, all $i = 1, \ldots, N$, and $\partial X_i^c/\partial q_k = \partial X_k^c/\partial q_i$, all $k, i = 1, \ldots, N$.

b. Compensated demands and factor supplies are homogeneous of degree 0 in prices. Therefore, from Euler's theorem on homogeneous functions,

(4.11)
$$\sum_{k=1}^{N} q_k \frac{\partial X_i^c}{\partial q_k} = 0 \qquad \text{all } i = 1, \ldots, N$$

To form the expenditure function, replace the X_i of the objective function in the dual with the compensated supply and demand relationships (4.9) obtaining:

$$(4.12) \qquad M(\vec{q};\bar{U}) = \sum_{i=1}^{N} q_i X_i^c(\vec{q};\bar{U})$$

The function, M, is the consumer's *expenditure function*, defined solely in terms of prices and a constant utility level. Since the function is derived from the dual of the standard consumer problem, it is certainly a valid representation of consumer's preferences. Furthermore, the relationship between a primal problem and its dual guarantees that the numerical value of the expenditure function will equal the consumer's lump-sum income in the budget constraint, providing that $\bar{U}$ is the maximum utility level obtained from solving the standard utility maximization problem.

Two properties of the expenditure function are especially useful. First, the derivative of the expenditure function with respect to the kth price is the compensated demand (supply) for the kth good (factor). To see this, differentiate $M(\ )$ with respect to q_k:

$$(4.13) \qquad \frac{\partial M(\vec{q};\bar{U})}{\partial q_k} = \frac{\partial\left[\sum_{i=1}^{N} q_i X_i^c(\vec{q};\bar{U})\right]}{\partial q_k} = X_k^c + \sum_{i=1}^{N} q_i \frac{\partial X_i^c(\vec{q};\bar{U})}{\partial q_k}$$

From the first-order conditions of the primal:

$$(4.14) \qquad q_i = \frac{1}{\lambda} \cdot \frac{\partial U}{\partial X_i}$$

Therefore:

$$(4.15) \qquad \frac{\partial M(\vec{q};\bar{U})}{\partial q_k} = X_k^c + \frac{1}{\lambda} \sum_{i=1}^{N} \frac{\partial U}{\partial X_i} \frac{\partial X_i^c(\vec{q};\bar{U})}{\partial q_k}$$

But with utility held constant, the second term must be zero.

Hence:

$$(4.16) \qquad \frac{\partial M(q;\bar{U})}{\partial q_k} = X_k^c(\vec{q};\bar{U})$$

The second property follows immediately. The second derivative of the expenditure function is the first derivative of the compensated demand curve,

$$(4.17) \qquad \frac{\partial^2 M(\vec{q};\bar{U})}{\partial q_k \partial q_j} = \frac{\partial X_k^c(\vec{q};\bar{U})}{\partial q_j} = S_{kj}$$

the Slutsky substitution term.

Hicks' Compensating and Equivalent Variations

The expenditure function has proven to be an extremely useful analytical device in public sector theory, at least for one-consumer economies. As a general rule, government policies will change consumer prices and the lump-sum income

FIGURE 4-1

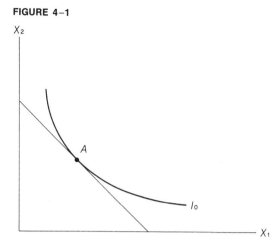

received by any one consumer. Economists are naturally interested in whether or not these changes have increased or decreased the consumer's welfare, and by how much. However, direct utility measures are not useful for this purpose because they require cardinality, the choice of a particular utility index, even though consumer's demands (and factor supplies) are invariant to monotonic transformations of the utility index. Rather, one wants an income measure of the gains and losses, invariant to monotonic transformations of the utility index, that is based on the notion of compensation, or indifference: How much lump-sum income (payment) is required to keep the consumer indifferent to the equilibria before and after the enactment of a particular government policy. The expenditure function provides the basis for this measure, since for *any* price vector $\check{q}$, $M(\check{q}; \bar{U})$ gives the lump-sum income necessary to keep the consumer at an arbitrarily selected utility level, $\bar{U}$. As such, it can be used to measure the lump-sum income required to compensate the consumer for the price and income changes occasioned by a set of government policies.

To relate the expenditure function to the standard treatment of income-compensation criteria in terms of consumer indifference curves, consider a two-good example in which all factor income is lump sum because of fixed factor supplies. Suppose that the consumer is originally in equilibrium at point A on I_0 in Figure 4–1, with relative prices q_1/q_2 indicated by the slope of the budget line tangent to I_0 at A. As the result of some government policy the price of X_2 increases, resulting in a new equilibrium at point B in Figure 4–2. (Assume the consumer's lump-sum income remains unchanged.)

The parallel distance between I_1 and I_0 gives an income measure of the welfare loss caused by this price increase. The distance is invariant to monotonic transformations of the utility index because the indifference curves are invariant to these transformations. In general, there are an infinity of possible income measures since the parallel distance between I_1 and I_0 will vary depending on the slope of the parallel lines used to measure the distance. So long as the same slope is chosen each time, however, comparability among alternative price

FIGURE 4–2

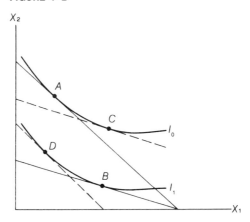

changes, or among different consumers, will be maintained. The two most popular, and natural, choices used to measure the parallel distance are the slopes corresponding to the initial and final price vectors, respectively.

In Figure 4–2, the parallel distance from B to C gives the additional lump-sum income necessary to compensate the consumer for the new set of prices, in the sense that he would then be indifferent to the new prices. This measure is called the Hicks Compensating Variation (HCV). The parallel distance from A to D gives the lump-sum income the consumer would be willing to sacrifice to maintain the old set of prices. This is called the Hicks Equivalent Variation (HEV).

The value of the expenditure function at the new price vector and the original utility level, $M(\vec{q}_1; \bar{U}^0)$, measures the lump-sum income necessary for indifference to the new price vector. Subtracting off the consumer's actual amount of lump-sum income, I^0, assumed unchanged in this example, gives the HCV.[1]

$$(4.18) \qquad HCV = M(\vec{q}_1; \bar{U}^0) - I^0$$

The expenditure function defined at the original set of prices and the new utility level, $M(\vec{q}_0, \bar{U}^1)$, measures the lump-sum income necessary for indifference to the new utility level but at the original price vector. Subtracting off the consumer's actual lump-sum income gives the HEV.[2]

$$(4.19) \qquad HEV = M(\vec{q}_0; \bar{U}^1) - I^0$$

---

[1] As defined in (4.18), the HCV is a loss measure. If, as in this example, goods prices should rise, then the income necessary to compensate the consumer will generally exceed the income actually available, and the HCV as written will be positive. Since the consumer is surely worse off, this positive value gives an income measure of his welfare loss. A welfare gain would be measured negatively. Some writers reverse the signs so that a gain is measured positively.

[2] Notice that if we considered instead the reverse situation, in which the price of X_2 fell and the consumer went from B to A, the (absolute) numerical value of the HCV above would be the HEV of the reverse situation and similarly for the HEV. Conceptually, however, they would each still be measured in the same way.

If, as in the more general case, both prices and lump-sum income change simultaneously, these two expressions have to be modified as follows. The Hicks Compensating Variation becomes

$$(4.20) \qquad HCV = M(\vec{q}_1; \bar{U}^0) - I^1$$

The HCV is the lump-sum income necessary to keep the consumer at the original utility level, given the new price vector, less the lump-sum income actually available at the *new* level, I^1. Alternatively, since $M(\vec{q}_0; \bar{U}^0) = I^0$, from the duality of the consumer problem,

$$(4.21) \qquad HCV = (I^0 - I^1) - [M(\vec{q}_0; \bar{U}^0) - M(\vec{q}_1; \bar{U}^0)]$$

Measured in terms of *changes* in lump-sum income, then, the consumer's gain or loss is his actual change in lump-sum income less the additional income required to keep him indifferent to the price changes, at the initial utility level.

Similarly, the HEV is now the income required to keep the consumer at the new utility level with the old price vector, less the income actually available in the initial situation.

$$(4.22) \qquad HEV = M(\vec{q}_0; \bar{U}^1) - I^0$$

Alternatively, since $M(\vec{q}_1; \bar{U}^1) = I^1$ from duality,

$$(4.23) \qquad HEV = (I^1 - I^0) - [M(\vec{q}_1; \bar{U}^1) - M(\vec{q}_0; \bar{U}^1)]$$

the actual change in lump-sum income less the additional income necessary to compensate the consumer, measured at the final utility level.

The change-in-income formulations (4.21) and (4.23) bear a direct relationship to areas under compensated demand curves. Consider the HCV as an example. The change in the value of the expenditure function can be written as a summation of integrals of first partial derivatives of the expenditure function.

$$(4.24) \qquad M(\vec{q}_0; \bar{U}^0) - M(\vec{q}_1; \bar{U}^0)$$

$$= \sum_{i=1}^{N} \int_{q_s^1}^{q_s^0} \frac{\partial M(q_1, \ldots, q_s, q_{s+1}, \ldots, q_N; \bar{U}^0)}{\partial q_s} dq_s$$

But, $\partial M(\vec{q}; \bar{U}^0)/\partial q_k = X_k^c$, the compensated demand for good k. Hence:

$$(4.25) \qquad M(\vec{q}_0; \bar{U}^0) - M(\vec{q}_1; \bar{U}^0) = \sum_{i=1}^{N} \int_{q_i^1}^{q_i^0} X_i^c dq_i$$

The right-hand side is the sum of areas under the compensated demand curves back to the price axis, as shown in Figure 4–3.

If q_0 were high enough so that quantity demanded was zero, then the shaded area would be the entire area behind X_k^c above the new equilibrium price q_k^1, an area commonly referred to as consumer's surplus.[3] Since the surplus is defined

---

[3] These same areas can be derived using the HEV and the demand curve, $X_k(\vec{q}; \bar{U}^1)$ assuming compensation at the new utility level, U^1.

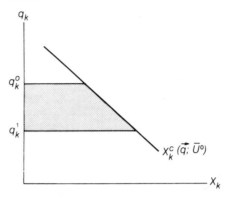

FIGURE 4-3

with reference to the compensated demand curve, it measures the value of X_k to the consumer as the amount he would be willing to pay for the opportunity to purchase X_k at price q_k^1.

The welfare measure (4.25) should be carefully distinguished from the welfare measure of price change given by the same areas behind the ordinary demand curves,

$$(4.26) \qquad A = \sum_{i=1}^{N} \int_{q_i^1}^{q_i^0} X_i^{\text{ord}}(\vec{q};\bar{I})dq_i$$

These areas, commonly referred to as Marshallian consumer surplus, differ from the areas in (4.25) in two important respects.[4] First, they are unrelated to the notion of indifference or compensation. Rather they belong to a broader class of welfare measures defined as money indexes of utility change, dU/λ, where λ is the marginal utility of income. To see this, totally differentiate the consumer's indirect utility function to obtain

$$(4.27) \qquad dV = \sum_{i=1}^{N} \frac{\partial V}{\partial q_i} dq_i$$

But $\partial V/\partial q_i = \lambda X_i$ (Roy's theorem). Therefore,

$$(4.28) \qquad dV = \lambda \sum_{i=1}^{N} X_i dq_i$$

or

$$(4.29) \qquad \frac{dV}{\lambda} = \frac{dU}{\lambda} = \sum_{i=1}^{N} X_i dq_i$$

---

[4] D. Richter, "Games Pythagoreans Play," *Public Finance Quarterly*, October 1977, contains a lucid discussion of various welfare change measures. The discussion in the text draws heavily from this paper.

Hence:

$$(4.30) \qquad \int_q \frac{dU}{\lambda} = \int_q \sum_{i=1}^{N} X_i dq_i$$

Finally, substituting the ordinary demands (factor supplies) for the X_i in (4.30) yields (4.26).

Notice that substituting the compensated demands (factor supplies) into (4.30) yields (4.25), so that the HCV (and HEV) is also a money index of utility change. But an important distinction is that it has a willingness-to-pay interpretation, whereas the Marshallian measure does not.

Second, the value of (4.25) is independent of the path of integration taken between the old and new prices, whereas the value of (4.26) is not. With income constant, a necessary and sufficient condition for path independence is $\partial X_i / \partial q_j = \partial X_j / \partial q_i$, all $i, j = 1, \ldots, N$.[5] Since all willingness-to-pay measures such as the HCV are based on compensated demands (factor supplies) whose partial price derivatives are symmetric, they necessarily satisfy the conditions for path independence. On the other hand, the Marshallian measure (4.26) will be path dependent, since the ordinary partial price derivatives are not symmetric, in general. Moreover, its value can be made arbitrarily large with a sutiable choice of paths between the old and new equilibrium.[6]

The issue of path independence is far from trivial. Since welfare change measures are essentially exercises in comparative statics, all such measures should depend only upon the value of prices (and income) at the old and new equilibria. The actual path taken between equilibria ought to be irrelevant. Thus, welfare measures based on indifference or willingness-to-pay notions have a legitimate claim of superiority over path dependent measures such as (4.26), despite the latter's interpretation as a money index of utility change, invariant to monotonic transformations of the utility index. This is unfortunate for policy purposes, however, since our econometric knowledge of ordinary demand (factor supply) relationships far exceeds our knowledge of compensated demand (factor supply) relationships.

Aggregate Production

In this section we will consider price representations of the aggregate production frontier rather than individual firm production functions. As noted in Chapter 2, many problems in first-best tax and expenditure theory can be analyzed without having to specify individual-firm production relationships. Assuming overall production efficiency so that the private sector is on its aggregate production-possibilities frontier is often sufficient. Not surprisingly,

---

[5] If income and all prices (except the numeraire) change, then the necessary and sufficient conditions include the condition that $\partial X_i / \partial I = 0$, all i except the numeraire. (With one good as numeraire, the condition on cross-price derivatives applies only to the nonnumeraire goods and factors.) These conditions imply that a necessary and sufficient condition for path independence with the ordinary demand curve is that all nonnumeraire income elasticities equal zero. This result follows immediately from the Slutsky equation, Ibid., p. 500.

[6] Ibid., pp. 501–2.

the same holds true for second-best analysis. Hence, it is extremely useful to define aggregate production possibilities in terms of prices. Should it be necessary to break down production by firms, the aggregate price constructs tend to carry over directly to the individual firm.

The key to deriving aggregate production relationships in terms of prices is the following. If aggregate production can be represented implicitly by an aggregate production-possibilities frontier, if all markets are perfectly competitive, and if all firms are profit maximizers, then aggregate production can be thought of as occurring within a single *price-taking* firm whose goal is the maximization of aggregate economic profits.[7]

Let:

Y_i = the ith good supplied or factor demanded by the single firm, with factors measured negatively.

P_i = the producer price of good i or factor i, assumed fixed.

$F^*(Y_1, \ldots, Y_N) = F^*(\vec{Y})$ = the aggregate production function for the economy.

The aggregate production analogue for the competitive market system is:

$$\max_{(Y_i)} \sum_{i=1}^{N} P_i Y_i$$

$$\text{s.t.} \quad F^*(\vec{Y}) = 0$$

with first-order conditions,

(4.31) $$P_i = \lambda F_i^* \qquad i = 1, \ldots, N\text{[8]}$$

and

(4.32) $$F^*(\vec{Y}) = 0$$

(4.31) and (4.32) can be solved for the N aggregate output supply and input demand functions,

(4.33) $$Y_i = Y_i(\vec{P}) \qquad i = 1, \ldots, N$$

each homogeneous of degree zero in the producer prices $\vec{P}$.[9] These supply and demand functions can then be used to generate two production relationships that are closely analogous to the consumer's indirect utility function and expenditure function, respectively.

---

[7] For the restrictions on individual firm's production functions that permit one to define a regular (convex to the origin) aggregate production transformation surface, consult K. Lancaster, *Mathematical Economics* (New York: The MacMillan Co., 1968), chap. 8, secs. 8.4–8.7. Also, see H. Varian, *Microeconomic Analysis* (New York: W. W. Norton Co., Inc., 1978), chap. 6, pp. 118–28.

[8] λ is the Lagrangian multiplier associated with the production function.

[9] If $F(\vec{Y})$ exhibits constant returns to scale, the relationships (4.33) will be correspondences rather than functions. Constant returns to scale, with fixed factor prices, implies constant long-run marginal output costs. Thus a "competitive" firm facing fixed output prices satisfies the $P = MC$ profit-maximizing condition at an infinity of outputs, and some outside mechanism must be posited to select an output for any given price. This is less of a problem for aggregate production, however, since the zero profit and supply-demand conditions will determine aggregate industry output.

The Production-Price Frontier

To derive the production analogue to the indirect utility function, replace the arguments of the aggregate production function with the supply and demand functions (4.33):

(4.34)
$$F(\vec{P}) = F^*[Y_i(\vec{P})] \equiv 0$$

$F(\vec{P})$, which we shall refer to as the production-price frontier, is defined solely in terms of producer prices and summarizes all relevant information about aggregate production in a competitive market economy, namely, the economy's underlying production possibilities and the aggregate supply and factor demand relationships from profit maximization.

The production-price frontier can be combined with the consumer's indirect utility function to form a complete general equilibrium representation for a one-consumer economy, defined in terms of prices. The only missing element is market clearance, which, in a market context, can be written as:

(4.35)
$$X_i(\vec{q}; I) = Y_i(\vec{P}) \qquad i = 1, \ldots, N^{10}$$

Incorporating the market clearance equations directly into the production-price frontier, the social welfare planning model of Chapter 2 for a competitive, decentralized economy can be represented as follows:

$$\max_{\vec{q}} \ V(\vec{q}; I)$$

$$\text{s.t.} \ F[X_i(\vec{q}; I)] = 0$$

This basic model can then be modified to incorporate a particular public sector problem. Because of its simplicity, it has proven to be an extremely popular model for analyzing policy issues under second-best assumptions.

The Profit Function

Another popular tool is the direct production analogue to the consumer's expenditure function. Instead of substituting the goods supply and input demand functions into the production frontier, they can be substituted back into the objective function of the profit maximization problem to obtain:

(4.36)
$$\pi(\vec{P}) = \sum_{i=1}^{N} P_i Y_i(\vec{P})$$

Analogous to the expenditure function, the *profit function*, $\pi(\vec{P})$, gives the pure lump-sum profits in the competitive economy for any given price vector,

---

[10] $\vec{q}$ will equal $\vec{P}$ in competitive markets unless distorting taxes drive a wedge between them. In that case, the two price vectors can be related by an additional set of equations such as:

$$\vec{q} = \vec{P} + \vec{t} \qquad \text{where } \vec{t} = (t_1, \ldots, t_N)$$

a vector of per-unit taxes.

$\check{P}$. It too incorporates all the relevant production information. In a competitive economy with variable factor supplies, pure economic profits will arise at a general equilibrium if aggregate production possibilities exhibit decreasing returns to scale. With constant returns to scale, pure profits are always identically equal to zero measured at the producer prices $\check{P}$ because competitive factor payments exhaust the revenues from selling the goods produced. As will be demonstrated in Chapter 9, perfect competition is incompatible with aggregate increasing returns to scale.

To see the relationship between profits and returns to scale, recall that the first-order conditions of aggregate profit maximization imply

$$(4.37) \qquad \frac{P_i}{P_j} = \frac{F_i^*}{F_j^*} \qquad \text{where } F_i^* = \frac{\partial F^*}{\partial Y_i}$$

Since $F^*(Y) = 0$, $F_i^*/F_j^* = -dY_j/dY_i$ from totally differentiating $F^*(\ )$ with respect to Y_j and Y_i. Hence,

$$(4.38) \qquad P_i = P_j \frac{dY_j}{dY_i} \qquad \text{or} \qquad P_j = \frac{P_i}{\dfrac{dY_j}{dY_i}}$$

If Y_i is an input and Y_j an output, equation (4.38) gives the familiar competitive result that the price of the input equals the value of its marginal product, or, equivalently, that output price equals marginal production costs. Throughout the text we will refer to the producer prices as the marginal cost prices, with the understanding that the reference is to goods supply prices and that there is aggregate private sector production efficiency.

Next, solve $F^*(\ )$ explicitly for output Y_j, writing

$$(4.39) \qquad Y_j = f(Y_1, \ldots, Y_{j-1}, Y_{j+1}, \ldots, Y_N)$$

Assuming $f(\ )$ is a homogeneous function, Euler's theorem says that

$$(4.40) \qquad \alpha Y_j = \sum_{i \neq j} f_i Y_i$$

where:

α is the degree of homogeneity.

But $P_i = f_i \cdot P_j$ from profit maximization. ($F_j^* \equiv 1$ in terms of equation (4.37)). Hence,

$$(4.41) \qquad \alpha Y_j = \sum_{i \neq j} \frac{P_i}{P_j} Y_i$$

or

$$(4.42) \qquad \alpha \cdot P_j Y_j = \sum_{i \neq j} P_i Y_i$$

With constant returns to scale, $\alpha = 1$, and there are zero pure economic profits. With decreasing returns to scale, $\alpha < 1$, so that $\sum_{i \neq j} P_i Y_i < P_j Y_j$. Producers in the aggregate make pure economic profits.

The profit function has another useful property analogous to the consumer's expenditure function. Its partial derivative with respect to the kth producer price is the kth aggregate supply (input demand) function, a result known as Hotelling's Lemma. To see this, differentiate $\pi(\vec{P})$ with respect to P_k to obtain

$$(4.43) \qquad \frac{\partial \pi(\vec{P})}{\partial P_k} = \frac{\partial \left[\sum\limits_{i=1}^{N} P_i Y_i(\vec{P}) \right]}{\partial P_k} = Y_k + \sum\limits_{i=1}^{N} P_i \frac{\partial Y_i(\vec{P})}{\partial P_k}$$

But from aggregate profit maximization,

$$P_i = -\lambda F_i^* \qquad i = 1, \dots, N$$

Therefore:

$$(4.44) \qquad \frac{\partial \pi(\vec{P})}{\partial P_k} = Y_k(\vec{P}) - \lambda \sum F_i^* \frac{\partial Y_i(\vec{P})}{\partial P_k}$$

However, $F^*(\vec{Y}) = 0$. Thus,

$$(4.45) \qquad \frac{\partial \pi(\vec{P})}{\partial P_k} = Y_k(\vec{P}) \qquad k = 1, \dots, N$$

Generalized HCV and HEV Welfare Measures

Since both the consumer's expenditure function and the profit function have values expressed as lump-sum income, it is natural to combine them into a general equilibrium measure of the welfare gain or less from price and income changes as the economy moves from one general equilibrium to another. Assuming no source of lump-sum income other than pure economic profits from production, an appropriate general equilibrium compensation welfare measure in a one-consumer economy with production is:

$$(4.46) \qquad L(\vec{q}, \vec{P}; \bar{U}) = M(\vec{q}; \bar{U}) - \pi(\vec{P})$$

where $\vec{q}$ and $\vec{P}$ refer to any given equilibrium level of consumer and producer prices, respectively, and $\bar{U}$ is an arbitrarily specified utility level. As written, (4.46) measures welfare loss,[11] defined as the lump-sum income required to maintain the consumer at $\bar{U}$, given $\vec{q}$, less the lump-sum income actually available from production, given $\vec{P}$.

Although our original discussion of income compensation measures ignored production, $L(\vec{q}, \vec{P}; \bar{U})$ compares directly with the earlier expressions because $\pi(\vec{P})$ merely specifies the source of lump-sum income available to the consumer. Therefore, if $(\vec{q}^0, \vec{P}^0)$ represents the vectors of consumer and producer prices at

---

[11] Suppose $\vec{q}$ rises to the consumer because of a tax. He will clearly be worse off. Hence, $L > 0$, since the income necessary to compensate for the new $\vec{q}$ will necessarily exceed the income actually available if he is worse off.

FIGURE 4-4

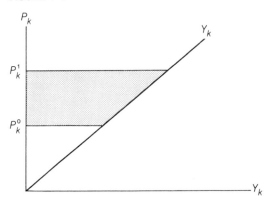

the initial situation and $(\vec{q}^1, \vec{P}^1)$ the corresponding vectors in the new general equilibrium then

(4.47) $$HCV = M(\vec{q}^1; \bar{U}^0) - \pi(\vec{P}^1) = L(\vec{q}^1, \vec{P}^1; \bar{U}^0)$$

The Hicks Compensating Variation is the lump-sum income necessary for indifference to the new vector of consumer prices, less the lump-sum income actually available from production. Furthermore, since $M(\vec{q}^0; \bar{U}^0) = \pi(\vec{P}^0)$ in a one-consumer economy with pure economic profits the only source of lump-sum income,[12]

(4.48) $$HCV = [M(\vec{q}^1; \bar{U}^0) - M(\vec{q}^0; \bar{U}^0)] - [\pi(\vec{P}^1) - \pi(\vec{P}^0)]$$
$$= L(\vec{q}^1, \vec{P}^1; \bar{U}^0)$$

Equation (4.48) measures welfare loss as the *change* in lump-sum income necessary to compensate the consumer for the change in prices, less the actual *change* in lump-sum income received from production. The first bracketed term has been interpreted as consumer surplus, or more generally, the sum of areas behind compensated demand curves (factor supply curves). Analogously, $\pi(\vec{P}^1) - \pi(\vec{P}^0)$ can be termed producer surplus, defined as a summation of areas behind *aggregate general equilibrium* supply (input demand) curves.

(4.49) $$\pi(\vec{P}^1) - \pi(\vec{P}^0) = \sum_{i=1}^{N} \int_{P_i^0}^{P_i^1} \frac{\partial \pi(\vec{P})}{\partial P_i} \, dP_i$$

(4.50) $$\pi(\vec{P}^1) - \pi(\vec{P}^0) = \sum_{i=1}^{N} \int_{P_i^0}^{P_i^1} Y_i dP_i [13]$$

The expression $\int_{P_k^0}^{P_k^1} Y_k dP_k$ measures the shaded area in Figure 4-4, the area behind the general equilibrium supply curve Y_k between prices P_k^0 and P_k^1.

---

[12] It is natural to assume the single consumer owns all production facilities and therefore receives any pure economic profits that may arise.

[13] Because $\partial Y_i / \partial P_j = \partial Y_j / \partial P_i$, producer's surplus is path independent. (There are no "income" terms associated with production.)

Thus the *HCV* with production combines both consumer's and producer's surpluses, properly measured in a general equilibrium framework.

Similarly,

(4.51) $$HEV = M(\vec{q}^0; \bar{U}^1) - \pi(\vec{P}^0) = L(\vec{q}^0, \vec{P}^0; \bar{U}^1)$$

or

(4.52) $$HEV = [M(\vec{q}^0; \bar{U}^1) - M(\vec{q}^1; \bar{U}^1)] - [\pi(\vec{P}^0) - \pi(\vec{P}^1)]$$

since $M(\vec{q}^1; \bar{U}^1) = \pi(\vec{P}^1)$ with profits from production as the only source of lump-sum income, returned to the consumer.

General Equilibrium Loss Minimization

The expression $L(\vec{q}, \vec{P}; \bar{U}) = M(\vec{q}; \bar{U}) - \pi(\vec{P})$ incorporates all relevant information about preferences and production in a one-consumer market economy. Only market clearance is missing for a complete general equilibrium specification.

It is tempting to posit the following as a legitimate general equilibrium social planning model for a competitive, decentralized economy, defined as a loss minimization problem:

$$\min_{(\vec{q}, \vec{P})} L(\vec{q}, \vec{P}; \bar{U}^0) = M(\vec{q}; \bar{U}^0) - \pi(\vec{P})$$

$$\text{s.t.} \quad X_i^c(\vec{q}; \bar{U}^0) = Y_i(\vec{P}) \quad i = 1, \ldots, N$$

Unfortunately the model is not legitimate as it stands.[14] The problem is that in a second-best environment $\vec{q} \neq \vec{P}$, in general, so that there will be some welfare loss in the economy (first-best pareto optimality requires that consumers and producers face identical prices, so the marginal rate of transformation between any two goods will equal their marginal rate of substitution). But the X_i^c's in the market clearance equations refer to compensated demands (factor supplies). If $\bar{U}^0$ is the nondistorted equilibrium, then market clearance cannot hold in terms of all goods and services. The economy cannot possibly produce the *compensated* equilibrium vector of goods and factors because if all the consumer's compensated demands (and factor supplies) were satisfied at the new vector of consumer prices, welfare loss would be zero, by definition. Thus, if we choose to specify compensation at the original nondistorted utility level, at best market clearance can hold in only $(N - 1)$ markets.

Therefore, when using loss minimization in second-best analysis, researchers usually let good 1 serve as an undistorted numeraire, with $q_1 \equiv P_1 \equiv 1$, and specify market clearance for the remaining goods. (The double normalization is possible because compensated demands (factor supplies) and actual goods

---

[14] See P. Diamond and D. McFadden, "Some Uses of the Expenditure Function in Public Finance," *Journal of Public Economics*, February 1974, for a complete discussion of the loss minimization technique. They cover all the points raised in this section, and then some.

supplies (factor demands) are homogeneous of degree zero in $\vec{q}$ and $\vec{P}$, respectively.) With these assumptions, the model can be recast into a valid representation of general equilibrium loss minimization, as follows:

$$\min_{(\vec{q},\vec{P})} L(\vec{q}, \vec{P}; \bar{U}^0) = M(\vec{q}; \bar{U}^0) - \pi(\vec{P})$$

$$\text{s.t.} \quad X_i(\vec{q}; \bar{U}^0) = Y_i(\vec{P}) \quad i = 2, \ldots, N$$

$$q_1 = 1$$

$$P_1 = 1$$

In this specification compensation is implicitly assumed to occur through good 1. That is, loss is understood to be the difference between the compensated demand for good 1 and the available supply of good 1, given that all other compensated demands and factor supplies are satisfied (market clearance holds for $i = 2, \ldots, N$). Thus, a formally equivalent problem is:[15]

$$\min_{(\vec{q},\vec{P})} L(\vec{q}, \vec{P}; \bar{U}^0) = M_1(\vec{q}; \bar{U}^0) - \pi_1(\vec{P}) = X_1^c(\vec{q}; \bar{U}^0) - Y_1(\vec{P})$$

$$\text{s.t.} \quad X_i^c(\vec{q}; \bar{U}^0) = Y_i(\vec{P}) \quad i = 2, \ldots, N$$

$$q_1 = 1$$

$$P_1 = 1$$

Loss minimization models are especially useful for second-best analysis precisely because they are specified in terms of compensated demand (and factor supply) curves. As we shall see, many second-best policy rules have a relatively simple and reasonably intuitive form when stated in terms of compensated demands, but are more difficult to express and understand in terms of ordinary demand curves. The loss-minimum approach provides a direct route to the simpler formulations. The alternative method of using a welfare maximization framework with the indirect utility function and production-price frontier solves for policy rules in terms of actual market equilibria and ordinary demand curves. The Slutsky equation must then be used to convert these rules into the more intuitive compensated versions.

Constant Opportunity Costs

To conclude the survey of production relationships, consider the simplest case of all, the assumption of linear (as opposed to general) production technology, or constant opportunity costs, depicted in Figure 4–5.

Linear production frontiers imply constant producer prices assuming production efficiency, a competitive market structure, and no "corner" solutions

---

[15] A formal proof of the equivalence between the two loss measures, $M_1(\vec{q}; \bar{U}^0) - \pi_1(\vec{P})$ and $M(\vec{q}; \bar{U}^0) - \pi(\vec{P})$, requires a fair amount of manipulation and will be left as an exercise for the reader. It involves differentiating the loss expressions and the market clearance equations, and exploiting the homogeneity properties of the M_i and π_i.

FIGURE 4–5

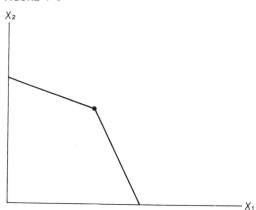

with resulting price indeterminancies. In the "relevant range" along a line segment on the frontier, all general equilibrium goods supply curves and factor demand curves are horizontal, as depicted in Figure 4–6, perfectly elastic at the equilibrium market prices.

The assumption of constant opportunity costs greatly simplifies general equilibrium models, for two reasons. In the first place, specifying a given vector of fixed producer prices summarizes *all* relevant production information since the producer price ratios equal the ratios of the constant marginal costs, and pure economic profits must be zero in a competitive equilibrium. Second, with supply (input demand) perfectly elastic in the relevant range, market clearance holds automatically for all goods and factors. Goods supplies (and factor demands) are assumed to adjust fully in response to changes in the consumer's goods demands (and factor supplies). Thus, a general equilibrium model need only consist of the indirect utility function or the expenditure function (pure profits must be zero) as the basic framework of analysis. Because of these

FIGURE 4–6

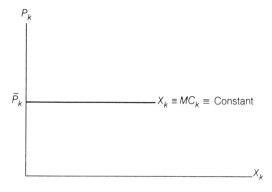

properties, the constant cost (linear technology) assumption is obviously quite useful if one is not particularly interested in exploring the production responses to government policies.

Market Clearance

In quantity models, market clearance guarantees that the demand and supply of goods and factors based on consumers' preferences match the supply and demand of goods and factors in production. The same is true for price models, but since it is supply and demand *schedules* that are equated in a price model, the market clearing equations also specify the relationships among individual market prices in equilibrium. For example, the set of N market clearance equations

$$(4.53) \qquad X_i(\vec{q}) = Y_i(\vec{P}) \qquad i = 1, \ldots, N$$

solves for the equilibrium vector of consumer prices, $\vec{q}$, given the equilibrium vector of producers prices, $\vec{P}$, or vice versa.

The preceding analysis of consumption and production relationships in general equilibrium price models has already developed three important points relating to the market clearance equations.

To summarize:

1. The full set of N market clearing equations (4.53) is applicable only to models describing actual market general equilibria and employing general production technologies, for instance, a model using the indirect utility function and the general production-price frontier.
2. Models of compensated equilibria, employing the expenditure and profit functions, require a set of market clearance equations of the form

$$X_i^c(\vec{q}; \overline{U}) = Y_i(\vec{P})$$

which relate $\vec{q}$ to $\vec{P}$ under the assumption that the consumer is compensated to remain at $\overline{U}$. Moreover, compensated market clearance can hold at most in only $(N - 1)$ markets. Compensation is assumed to occur in the uncleared market.
3. Models employing constant opportunity cost, linear production technologies do not have to specify market clearance at all. By assumption, production adjusts to demand at the fixed vector of producers' prices.

The only other point we wish to make concerns the relationship between market clearance, Walras' law, and competitive market behavior. Recall that Walras' law applies to general equilibrium models of actual market equilibria. It is usually stated as follows: If each economic agent is on his budget constraint (for producers this means profit maximizing) and all but one market is in equilibrium, the final market must also be in equilibrium. An alternative statement of Walras' law, one commonly used in second-best analysis, is this: If all but one economic agent is on his budget constraint (all firms profit maximizing), and all markets are cleared, then the last economic agent must also be on his budget constraint.[16]

The point of Walras' law is that one equation from the entire set of budget constraints and market clearance equations is redundant when solving for general equilibrium price vectors. Analytical general equilibrium models typically drop one of the market clearance equations, but the recent second-best literature has exploited the fact that dropping one of the budget constraints is also legitimate. In particular, second-best models using actual general equilibria within the welfare maximization framework typically choose between dropping an assumed government budget constraint that tax revenues must equal government expenditures, or one of the market clearance equations. Analytical constructs such as the indirect utility function and the production-price frontier implicitly assume that each consumer is on his individual budget constraint and that all firms are profit maximizing. For modeling purposes, then, the choice comes down to positing explicitly a government budget constraint and market clearance in all but one market, in accordance with the standard interpretation of Walras' law, or positing explicitly that all markets clear in accordance with the alternative interpretation. In the latter case, the government budget constraint need not enter the model explicitly. For example, the general equilibrium model presented on page 71 implicitly incorporates a government budget constraint. Walras' law guarantees it will hold in equilibrium.

MANY-PERSON GENERAL EQUILIBRIUM MODELS

Modeling distinctions between one-person and many-person models obviously center on the demand relationships. Aggregate production relationships will be the same in either model, and the adjustment required for market clearance is trivial. One-person market clearance equations of the form

$$(4.54) \qquad X_i(\vec{q}) = Y_i(\vec{P}) \qquad i = 1, \ldots, N$$

simply become

$$(4.55) \qquad \sum_{h=1}^{H} X_{hi}(\vec{q}) = Y_i(\vec{P}) \qquad i = 1, \ldots, N$$

in an H-person world, where $X_{hi} = $ demand (supply) for good (factor) i by person h.

As with the quantity models, the main problem for many-person price models involves specifying a set of social welfare rankings that will resolve distributional issues. The easiest way to do this, and the most popular, is to posit a Bergson-Samuelson social welfare function exactly as in the quantity models. The only difference in the price models is that the arguments of the social welfare function

---

[16] Diamond and Mirrlees discuss the alternative interpretation of Walras' law in P. Diamond and J. Mirrlees, "Optimal Taxation and Public Production" (Part I: Production Efficiency), *American Economic Review*, March 1971, pp. 14–15.

are the individual consumer's *indirect* utility functions. Because the indirect utility functions have prices and lump-sum income as arguments, so too will the social welfare function. The second-best literature commonly assumes a given distribution of lump-sum incomes, so that social welfare is represented as:

$$(4.56) \qquad W^*(\vec{q};\overline{I}^1,\dots,\overline{I}^H) = W[V^1(\vec{q};\overline{I}^1),\dots,V^H(\vec{q};\overline{I}^H)]$$
$$= W[V^h(\vec{q};\overline{I}^h)]$$

where:

$\vec{q}$ = the vector of consumer prices common to all consumers.

$\overline{I}^h$ = the fixed lump-sum income of person h.

This specification of social welfare is especially useful for all second-best analysis which assumes both that the government cannot redistribute income lump sum and that the original distribution is nonoptimal, meaning that the distribution does not satisfy the first-best interpersonal equity conditions. As was noted in Chapter 3, many second-best studies make these assumptions, with the implication that the social welfare rankings implied by W will be central to *all* policy problems, every bit as important as efficiency considerations.

The price specification of the Bergson-Samuelson social welfare function has a number of interesting properties worth analyzing in some detail at this point. Let us begin by differentiating social welfare with respect to one of the consumer prices, q_k.

$$(4.57) \qquad \frac{\partial W^*}{\partial q_k} = \sum_{h=1}^{H} \frac{\partial W}{\partial V^h} \frac{\partial V^h}{\partial q_k} \qquad k = 1,\dots,N$$

From Roy's theorem on individual indirect utility functions,

$$(4.58) \qquad \frac{\partial V^h}{\partial q_k} = \lambda^h X_{hk}$$

where:

λ^h = the marginal utility of lump-sum income for person h.

X_{hk} = the consumption of good k (supply of factor k) by person h.

Therefore:

$$(4.59) \qquad \frac{\partial W^*}{\partial q_k} = \sum_{h=1}^{H} \frac{\partial W}{\partial V^h} \cdot \lambda^h X_{hk}$$

Equation (4.58) says that the change in social welfare resulting from a marginal change in one of the consumer prices is a weighted summation of the individual's demands (supplies) of that good (factor), with the weights equal to the individual marginal *social* utilities. In turn, the marginal social utility for person h is the product of his own marginal utility of income, λ^h, and the marginal utility of social welfare with respect to his utility, $\partial W^*/\partial V^h$.

These individual social marginal utilities contain the same information as the social marginal utility terms from the quantity model of Chapter 2,

$$(4.60) \qquad \frac{\partial W}{\partial U^h} \frac{\partial U^h}{\partial X_{hk}} \qquad k = 1, \ldots, N$$

This can be seen directly by assuming that the kth good is the numeraire, with $q_k \equiv 1$. From the first-order conditions of the standard consumer model,

$$(4.61) \qquad \frac{\partial U^h}{\partial X_{hk}} = \lambda^h q_k = \lambda^h$$

Hence:

$$(4.62) \qquad \frac{\partial W}{\partial U^h} \frac{\partial U^h}{\partial X_{hk}} = \frac{\partial W}{\partial U^h} \cdot \lambda^h \equiv \frac{\partial W}{\partial V^h} \cdot \lambda^h$$

For the nonnumeraire goods $j \neq k$,

$$(4.63) \qquad \lambda^h = \frac{\dfrac{\partial U^h}{\partial X_{hj}}}{q_j}$$

illustrating the point discussed in Chapter 2 that these terms are really marginal social utilities of consumption, or purchasing power (*real* income).

One-Consumer Equivalence

Because the social welfare rankings pose such difficult problems for normative policy analysis, economists have long been interested in describing conditions under which many-person economies are analytically equivalent to one-consumer economies, that is, conditions under which changes in the distribution of income are irrelevant for policy purposes. The classic work in this regard is Samuelson's 1956 article "Social Indifference Curves,"[17] in which he described two sufficient conditions for ignoring the distributional implications of government policies. Recently Jerry Green has described a third sufficient condition.[18] The social welfare function (4.56) is especially convenient for analyzing these conditions.

a. Optimal Income Distribution. Suppose the first-best interpersonal equity conditions hold, either by accident or by means of optimal lump-sum redistributions by the government. Interpersonal equity implies:

$$(4.64) \qquad \frac{\partial W}{\partial U^h} \frac{\partial U^h}{\partial X_{hk}} = \frac{\partial W}{\partial U^j} \frac{\partial U^j}{\partial X_{jk}} \qquad \begin{matrix} \text{all } h, j = 1, \ldots, H \\ \text{all } k = 1, \ldots, N \end{matrix}$$

---

[17] P. A. Samuelson, "Social Indifference Curves," *Quarterly Journal of Economics*, February 1956.

[18] J. Green, "Two Models of Optimal Taxation and Pricing," *Oxford Economic Papers*, November 1975.

or, alternatively,

(4.65)
$$\frac{\partial W}{\partial V^h} \cdot \lambda^h = \frac{\partial W}{\partial V^j} \cdot \lambda^j \qquad \text{all } h, j = 1, \ldots, H$$

Let $\partial W / \partial U^h \cdot \lambda^h = \lambda$, where λ is defined as the common marginal social utility of real income.

Substituting this result into (4.59) yields:

(4.66)
$$\frac{\partial W^*}{\partial q_k} = \lambda \sum_{h=1}^{H} X_{hk} = \lambda \cdot X_k$$

where:

X_k = the aggregate demand for good k (supply of factor k).

Thus Roy's theorem holds in the aggregate. Furthermore, defining $I = \sum\limits_{h=1}^{H} I^h$, the total lump-sum income in the economy,

(4.67)
$$\frac{\partial W^*}{\partial I} = \sum_{h=1}^{H} \frac{\partial W}{\partial V^h} \frac{\partial V^h}{\partial I^h} \cdot \frac{\partial I^h}{\partial I} = \sum_{h=1}^{H} \frac{\partial W}{\partial V^h} \lambda^h \frac{\partial I^h}{\partial I}$$

$$= \lambda \sum_{h=1}^{H} \frac{\partial I^h}{\partial I} = \lambda$$

In other words, social welfare is independent of any change in the distribution of lump-sum income. This makes intuitive sense, because the interpersonal equity conditions guarantee that an additional dollar of lump-sum income will have the same effect on social welfare no matter who receives it. Hence, marginal changes in society's lump-sum income will always change W by λ, no matter whose income is changed. These results form the basis of a theorem proved by Samuelson in 1956, that if income is continuously and optimally redistributed, then there exists a standard indifference map in terms of aggregate quantities of consumers' goods (and factors), as depicted in Figure 4–7. The social indifference curves S_0, S_1, S_2 should be distinguished from the social welfare indiffer-

FIGURE 4–7

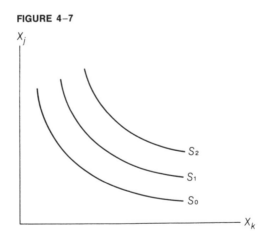

ence curves of Chapter 2, which were defined with respect to individual's utility functions.

The intuition behind the social indifference curves is that with continuous optimal redistributions, aggregate demands (factor supplies) will be uniquely determined by consumer prices and *aggregate* lump-sum income, just as an individual's indifference map, if consistent, will generate a uniquely determined set of individual demand and factor supply schedules defined over prices and the individual's income. This will generally not be true in the aggregate. Any exogenous shock to the economy, such as a new government policy, will, in general, affect consumer prices, aggregate lump-sum income, *and* the distribution of lump-sum income. Thus a set of exogenous shocks each generating identical changes in consumer prices and aggregate income could create different aggregate demands (and factor supplies) if they have differential effects on the distribution of income. If so, then a set of consistent social welfare indifference curves cannot exist. For example, a price change that increases the aggregate consumption of all goods, with aggregate factor supplies unchanged, may not increase social welfare if the distribution has simultaneously changed enough for the worse. But if more of everything is not necessarily better, then a consistent social ordering over aggregate quantities will not exist, in general. However, with optimal redistributions this anomaly cannot occur. More of everything will necessarily be better from society's viewpoint.

Optimal first-best redistributions, therefore, have the effect of dichotomizing normative policy rules into one set of efficiency rules devoid of social welfare rankings, and the single distributional rule equating social marginal utilities of income. The world may not be first-best because of additional constraints on the system, but it is equivalent to a one-person economy for policy purposes, in that policy rules developed in the context of a one-person economy will be the proper normative policy prescriptions for a many-person world.

b. Identical and Homothetic Preferences. Close inspection of equation (4.59) reveals a restriction on consumer preferences sufficient to generate a consistent set of social indifference curves in terms of aggregates even if the distribution of income is nonoptimal. Samuelson demonstrated this condition as well in his 1956 article. Multiply and divide (4.59) by X_k, the *aggregate* consumption (supply) of the kth good (factor), to obtain:

(4.68)
$$\frac{\partial W^*}{\partial q_k} = \sum_{h=1}^{H} \frac{\partial W}{\partial V^h} \lambda^h \left(\frac{X_{hk}}{X_k} \right) \cdot X_k \qquad k = 1, \ldots, N$$

Suppose it happened that:

(4.69)
$$\frac{X_{hk}}{X_k} = \frac{X_{hj}}{X_j} = \gamma^h \qquad \begin{array}{l} \text{all } k, j = 1, \ldots, N \\ \text{any } h = 1, \ldots, H \end{array}$$

With this restriction,

(4.70)
$$\sum_{h=1}^{H} \frac{\partial W}{\partial V^h} \lambda^h \frac{X_{hk}}{X_k} = \sum_{h=1}^{H} \frac{\partial W}{\partial V^h} \lambda^h \gamma^h = \theta \qquad \text{all } k = 1, \ldots, N$$

Therefore:

$$\frac{\partial W^*}{\partial q_k} = \theta X_k \qquad k = 1, \ldots, N \tag{4.71}$$

Roy's theorem again holds in the aggregate, a well-ordered social indifference map exists, and the many-person economy is equivalent to a one-person economy, regardless of the underlying distribution of income.

Restriction (4.69) says that each person's share of aggregate consumption (supply) must be the same for all goods (factors), although these shares may differ among individuals. It will be satisfied if all individuals' preferences are identical and homothetic. Homothetic preferences imply linear income-consumptions lines, or constant income elasticities equal to 1 for all goods (factors). Thus, $X_{hj} = k_{hj} \cdot X_{h1}$, all $j = 2, \ldots, N$. If, in addition, all preferences are identical, $k_{hj} = k_j$, all $h = 1, \ldots, H$. Consider the ratios of any individual's consumption to total consumption for good 1 and any other good (factor) j.

$$\frac{X_{h1}}{\displaystyle\sum_{h=1}^{H} X_{h1}} \quad \text{and} \quad \frac{X_{hj}}{\displaystyle\sum_{h=1}^{H} X_{hj}} \qquad j = 2, \ldots, N \tag{4.72}$$

Since $X_{hj} = k_j X_{h1}$,

$$\frac{X_{hj}}{X_j} = \frac{X_{hj}}{\displaystyle\sum_{h=1}^{H} X_{hj}} = \frac{k_j X_{h1}}{\displaystyle\sum_{h=1}^{H} k_j X_{h1}} = \frac{k_j X_{h1}}{k_j \displaystyle\sum_{h=1}^{H} X_{h1}} = \frac{X_{h1}}{X_1} \tag{4.73}$$

$$\text{all } j = 2, \ldots, N$$
$$\text{any } h = 1, \ldots, H$$

Hence, the ratio of individual consumption to total consumption is equal for all goods for any one person, as required.

The assumption of identical and homothetic preferences guarantees that changes in the distribution of income will have no effect on aggregate goods demands and factor supplies. With income elasticities constant and equal for all people, the percentage increases in demand (factor supplies) by the gainers in an income redistribution will be exactly offset by equal percentage decreases in demand (factor supplies) by the losers, no matter how much income is redistributed.

Martin Feldstein has labeled the term,

$$\sum_{h=1}^{H} \frac{\partial W}{\partial V^h} \lambda^h \frac{X_{hk}}{X_k} = \theta_k \qquad k = 1, \ldots, N \tag{4.74}$$

the *distributional coefficient* of aggregate X_k, a term now commonly used in the second-best literature.[19] The distributional coefficient combines the product

---

[19] M. Feldstein, "Distributional Equity and the Optimal Structure of Public Prices," *American Economic Review*, March 1972. Feldstein actually defined the term relative to a continuum of individual incomes, but the basic idea is identical.

of each person's marginal social ranking ($\partial W/\partial U^h \, \lambda^h$) and his proportion of total consumption X_{hk}/X_k. The assumption of identical and homothetic preferences has the further implication that the distributional coefficients of all goods are identical.

c. Green's Sufficient Condition. Jerry Green's third sufficient condition for assuming a one-person equivalent economy also follows directly from equation (4.59). If the covariance of $\partial W/\partial V^h \cdot \lambda^h$ with X_{hk}/X_k is identical to its covariance with X_{hj}/X_j, all $k, j = 1, \ldots, N$, then Roy's theorem will again hold in the aggregate, with all the same implications. What this would mean in economic terms is not clear, however.[20]

Unfortunately, none of the three sufficient conditions is a likely description of reality. Empirical research on individual consumption offers no support for the second condition, and many people will argue, reasonably, that the distribution of income is far from optimal. Whether or not Green's third condition holds is difficult to say, because it depends upon the social welfare terms $\partial W/\partial V^h$. Thus, it is virtually impossible to prove or disprove empirically. Given the uncertain philosophical and analytical foundations of the distributional rankings, this is a depressing conclusion for normative analysis. Positing one-consumer equivalent economies may provide some useful insights into the efficiency implications of a second-best policy environment, but the decision rules resulting from these models are not likely to have much normative policy significance.

The Expenditure Function in Many-Person Models

Up to this point we have been using the indirect utility functions to represent individual preferences in a many-person economy. It turns out this is really the only choice. The expenditure function is an extremely convenient and powerful analytical device in one-consumer models, but it is not especially useful in a many-person context. Of course, if any one of the three sufficient conditions holds guaranteeing the existence of an aggregate social indifference map, then the individual welfare measure

$$L(\vec{q}, \vec{p}; \bar{U}) = M(\vec{q}; \bar{U}) - \pi(\vec{p})$$

is valid in the aggregate. $M(q; \bar{U})$ is defined in terms of aggregate goods and factors. $\bar{U}$ implies that society is being held on one of its aggregate indifference curves. Furthermore, $\partial M/\partial q_k = X_k$, the aggregate compensated demand for (supply of) good (factor) k. The point is that if the many-person economy really is equivalent to a one-person economy, all analytical constructs and theorems applicable to a single consumer must necessarily apply in the many-consumer model, including the expenditure and loss functions.

Without this equivalence, however, the meaning of aggregate loss, or aggregate loss minimization, is unclear. Economists have long sought aggregate equivalents to one-person income-compensation criteria such as the HCV and

---

[20] Green, "Two Models of Optimal Taxation and Pricing."

the *HEV*, but so far the search is in vain. To see the problems with these aggregate compenation measures, define aggregate loss in the most natural way, as the simple sum of each individual's loss, individually perceived:

$$(4.75) \qquad L^A(\vec{q}, \vec{p}; \bar{U}) = \sum_{h=1}^{H} [M^h(\vec{q}; \bar{U}^h) - \pi^h(\vec{p})]$$

$$= \sum_{h=1}^{H} M^h(\vec{q}; \bar{U}^h) - \pi(\vec{p})$$

The expression $L^A(\ )$ measures the difference between the total lump-sum income necessary to keep each consumer on a given initial utility level and the available lump-sum income in the economy for any set of general equilibrium prices $(\vec{q}, \vec{p})$. Alternatively, aggregate gain is

$$G^A(\vec{q}, \vec{p}; \bar{U}) = \pi(\vec{p}) - \sum_{h=1}^{H} M^h(\vec{q}; \bar{U}^h)$$

The problem is this. $L^A(\ ) (G^A(\ ))$ accurately records each individual's perceived loss (gain), but it ignores the social rankings of these gains or losses. A dollar of loss (gain) is given equal weight on the margin $(=1)$ across all individuals. But this is generally inconsistent with the notion that society is interested in social welfare maximization. At nonoptimal income distributions individual losses (gains) would not receive equal weight.

Formally, one can ask: Will the following alternative general equilibrium models necessarily lead to the same normative decision rules if used as a basic framework for analyzing public sector problems?

a.
$$\min_{(\vec{q}, \vec{p})} L(\vec{q}, \vec{p}; \bar{U}) = \sum_{h=1}^{H} M(\vec{q}; \bar{U}^h) - \pi(\vec{p})$$

$$\text{s.t.} \quad \sum_{h=1}^{H} X_{hi}^c(\vec{q}; \bar{U}^h) = Y_i(\vec{p}) \qquad i = 2, \ldots, N$$

and

b.
$$\max_{(\vec{q})} W[V^h(\vec{q}; I^h)]$$

$$\text{s.t.} \quad F\left[\sum_{h=1}^{H} X_{hi}(\vec{q}; I^h)\right] = 0$$

The answer must certainly be no, in general, because the former excludes the social welfare rankings. Only in one-consumer equivalent economies will social welfare maximization and aggregate loss minimization generate identical policy rules.

The history of welfare economics records a long list of attempts to develop policy tests based on aggregate loss measures, all ending in failure. For instance, some years ago Scitovsky tried to develop a well-ordered social indifference map in terms of aggregate quantities, similar to the social indifference curves in Figure 4–7, with the property that each consumer maintained the same utility level along each social indifference curve. Samuelson showed that, in general, no such indifference map exists.[21] Hicks proposed the first of many analytical policy guidelines based on the notion of compensation, his compensating variation. According to Hicks, a policy should be undertaken if the gainers could compensate the losers and still have some income left over. In other words, $G^A(\vec{q}, \vec{P}; \bar{U}^0) \gtrless 0$ is a sufficient test for accepting or rejecting government policies. Clearly, however, unless compensation is actually paid, a policy could pass by this criterion and fail by the criterion that social welfare must increase, where social welfare is defined as $W = W[V^h(\vec{q}; I^h)]$. Imagine the following situation: (1) one person captures all the gains, (2) the other $(H\text{-}1)$ people lose, (3) the one gain exceeds the sum of the $(H\text{-}1)$ losses, (4) the social marginal utility of all $(H\text{-}1)$ losers is positive and large, and (5) the social marginal utility of the gainer is positive but extremely small. $G^A(\ )$ is positive by condition (3), but social welfare may well decrease given conditions (1), (2), (4), and (5). Similar contradictions can be demonstrated for all such aggregate compensation tests.

The economics profession has by now reached a consensus that if normative public sector theory is concerned with distributive equity, weighting dollars of loss (gain) equally across consumers is clearly illegitimate, unless one of the three sufficient conditions for one-consumer equivalence holds. Absent these conditions, social welfare maximization is the only appropriate theoretical framework for generating normative policy rules in a many-person world.

SUMMARY AND CONCLUSIONS

Chapter 4 considered a number of analytical constructs commonly used in the second-best literature to represent consumption and production behavior in terms of competitive consumer and producer prices, including: the indirect utility function, the expenditure function, the aggregate production-price frontier, the aggregate profit function, and the Bergson-Samuelson social welfare function specified in terms of consumer prices and the distribution of lump-sum income. The chapter also showed how the various production and consumption relationships can be combined, along with market clearance equations, into valid general equilibrium social welfare planning models for a competitive, decentralized economy. Distinctions were also made between actual versus compensated general equilibrium models and welfare maximization versus loss minimization approaches to policy analysis.

The analysis of Chapter 4 highlighted two important characteristics of second-best analysis:

1. Most second-best analysis to date occurs within the context of a competitive market economy. All the analytical tools developed in Chapter 4 depend upon perfectly competitive market behavior for their derivation. Thus, second-best policy analysis remains somewhat distant from real-world imperfections.

---

[21] Samuelson, "Social Indifference Curves."

2. Second-best literature often uses one-consumer models for analyzing allocational issues. These models may give some useful insights into the inefficiencies created by additional second-best constraints, but they are unlikely to produce useful normative policy rules. The conditions under which the effects of policy on the distribution of income can be ignored are so stringent that they are extremely unlikely to hold in practice, even approximately. Given the norm of distributive equity, society's social welfare rankings will almost always be policy relevant.

Chapter 4 completes the introduction to public sector analysis. Armed with the quantity model of Chapter 2 as an analytical framework for first-best analysis, and the various analytical constructs of Chapter 4 as convenient tools to apply in second-best contexts, we are ready to begin a comprehensive study of public expenditure and tax theory.

REFERENCES

Diamond, P., and McFadden, D. "Some Uses of the Expenditure Function in Public Finance." *Journal of Public Economics*, February 1974.

————, and Mirrlees, J. "Optimal Taxation and Public Production" (Part I: Production Efficiency). *American Economic Review*, March 1971.

Feldstein, M. "Distributional Equity and the Optimal Structure of Public Prices." *American Economic Review,* March 1972.

Green, J. "Two Models of Optimal Taxation and Pricing." *Oxford Economic Papers,* November 1975.

Lancaster, K. *Mathematical Economics.* New York: The MacMillan Co., 1968.

Richter, D. "Games Pythagoreans Play." *Public Finance Quarterly,* October 1977.

Samuelson, P. A. "Social Indifference Curves." *Quarterly Journal of Economics,* February 1956.

Varian, H. *Microeconomic Analysis.* New York: W. W. Norton & Co., Inc., 1978.

The theory of public expenditures and taxation—First-best analysis

Part II undertakes a first-best analysis of public expenditure and tax theory in the context of a market economy. Recall from the discussion in Chapter 3 that a first-best policy environment exists if the market economy is perfectly competitive and the government can use any policy tools necessary to restore full pareto optimality and achieve interpersonal equity. In other words, the government can bring the economy to the bliss point on its first-best utility-possibilities frontier.

The first-best policy environment may seem unduly restrictive, but it must be remembered that prior to the 1970s virtually all public expenditure analysis employed the first-best assumptions. The same is true of the large body of literature concerned with distributional issues in the theory of taxation. Only the allocational theory of taxation has consistently employed second-best assumptions from the very beginning of public sector economics. This occurred because the question of the welfare costs of taxation is inherently a second-best topic. As we shall discover in Part II, all interesting first-best efficiency issues relating to taxation are effectively subsumed within the optimal public expenditure decision rules. In a very real sense, then, Part II contains the received doctrine for the vast majority of public sector economics as reflected in all but the most recent texts. The second-best challenge to first-best orthodoxy has gained momentum only in the past ten years.

The general equilibrium model of social welfare maximization developed in Chapter 2 will serve as the analytical framework throughout Part II, modified only to the the extent necessary to describe the particular problem under consideration.

Chapters 5–8 consider the theory of externalities, with applications to U.S. policy. Chapters 9–11 analyze various issues in the theory of decreasing cost production, again with applications relating to U.S. experience. Chapters 12 and 13 conclude Part II with a discussion of taxation from a first-best perspective. Chapter 12 develops the first-best optimal tax rules, stressing their limitations as guidelines for actual tax policy. Chapter 13 discusses how the optimal rules have traditionally been modified so that they can serve as guidelines both for tax design and tax reform. By way of application, it also considers how well the U.S. federal personal income tax corresponds to the modified guidelines.

5

The problem of externalities—
An overview

Externalities can be defined as third-party effects, meaning that activity by a set of economic agents affects other economic agents, "third parties," not directly engaged in the activity. But this definition is insufficient for purposes of public policy analysis since virtually any (significant) economic activity can be expected to generate third-party effects. Because an economy is a closed, interdependent system, any given economic activity tends to cause repercussions throughout the entire economy. Yet not all economic activity requires public sector intervention.

Consider the following two examples of externalities: (a) A family living on a hillside builds an enormous fence around its property, more or less destroying the view of its neighbors; and (b) the demand for long-distance passenger travel shifts sharply and continuously toward the airplane, mostly at the expense of the railroads. Situation (b) will trigger a whole set of third-party effects as the economy works to accomodate the demand shift. Generally speaking, resources specific to air travel will gain, and those specific to rail will lose, signaling a shift of resources away from the railroads and toward the airlines. Since tastes presumably differ, and different people will now receive different incomes than before the shift to air travel, the whole pattern of demands for all goods and services will tend to shift, causing further changes in incomes and additional resource shifts to and from industries that may be totally unrelated to air or rail travel, and so on, endlessly. Yet the government need not necessarily intervene in this process. To the contrary, the very strength of the competitive market system is its ability to coordinate all these demand and resource shifts, while bringing the economy to a new, efficient equilibrium.

In situation (a), however, the third-party effects occur outside the normal market process. There is no natural market mechanism for recording the losses each neighbor suffers from the fence. Any redress they may seek would presumably occur through some kind of judicial proceeding.

There is a second crucial difference in these two examples. In situation (b), the demand shift per se has no affect on any of the fundamental *technical* relationships in the economy, either the consumers' utility functions or the producers' production functions. All third-party gains and losses accrue through changes in prices, both goods prices and factor prices. Some consumers will face new budget constraints and some firms new profit functions, with corresponding gains or losses, all caused by the competitive process of supply and demand, which continuously changes consumer and producer prices while searching for a new equilibrium. In situation (a), on the other hand, the neighbors lose not because prices have changed but because their utility functions have been altered. Each neighbor's ability to enjoy his own property has diminished because of the fence, independently of any price changes created by building the fence (of course, it is unlikely that prices would change in this case).

These two distinctions are the vital ones for public sector analysis. An externality, or third-party effect, requires government intervention to maintain efficiency if two conditions hold:

1. An activity by a set of economic agents enters ("alters") the utility functions of other consumers or the production functions of other producers not directly involved with the activity.
2. The gains and losses from these effects are not properly reflected in the competitive market system. In most cases, the second condition is redundant, since externalities satisfying the first condition are almost never handled properly by the competitive market system. Given the existence of externalities with these properties, a perfectly competitive market economy will no longer generate a pareto-optimal allocation of resources. Government intervention is required to keep society on its first-best utility-possibilities frontier.

Public sector economists struggled for years trying to pin-point these conditions. The puzzle was finally resolved in 1923 when Jacob Viner distinguished between pecuniary and technological externalities, terminology that persists in modern writing.[1] *Pecuniary externalities* refer to the pure-market price affects illustrated by situation (b), resulting directly from competitive market adjustments. They do not require public intervention to maintain pareto optimality. *Technological externalities* satisfy the two conditions necessary for government intervention.

A fair number of other, less crucial, distinctions also appear in the literature. For instance, public sector economists distinguish between *external economies* and *diseconomies*, the former referring to beneficial third-party effects, the latter to harmful third-party effects. Thus, one can speak of a "pecuniary external economy" or a "technological external diseconomy," and so forth. We will keep the distinction between economies and diseconomies in the text, but drop the pecuniary-technological distinction. Since our only concern is public policy, the term "externality" will always mean "technological externality."

The text will further distinguish between consumption, production, and consumption-production externalities as follows:

---

[1] J. Viner, "Cost Curves and Supply Curves," *Zeitschrift fur National-okonomie*, III, 1932, (reprinted in *American Economic Association Readings in Price Theory* [Chicago: Richard D. Irwin, Inc., 1952]). The conceptual distinction was first noted by Allyn Young in 1913, but without Viner's terminology. A. A. Young, "Pigou's Wealth and Welfare," *Quarterly Journal of Economics*, August 1913.

Consumption externality: Economic activity by some consumer enters (alters) the utility function of at least one other consumer but does not enter into (alter) any production relationships. Situation (a), above, would be an example of a consumer externality. Consumption of national defense is another, more important, example.

Production externality: Economic activity by some firm enters (alters) the production function of at least one other firm but does not enter (alter) the utility function of any consumer. One firm removing oil from a common pool situated under land owned by more than one firm would be an example. The rate at which any one firm extracts the oil will affect the degree to which all other firms can extract the oil.

Consumption-production externality: Activity by some consumer enters (alters) the production function of at least one firm or vice versa. Water pollution by a firm affecting both recreational and commercial fishing activities would be an example of a consumption-production externality.

These last three distinctions are useful analytically because they each generate different optimal policy rules. Chapters 6, 7, and 8 will consider each of them in turn, but with increasing brevity. Even though they require separate policy responses, the similarities among them are substantial enough to preclude a full treatment each time. Having analyzed one of them, the others can be dealt with using the same models and techniques, modified only slightly to capture the exact form of the externality. Finally, the text will make further distinctions within each class of externality when these distinctions have significant implications for public policy. We will begin with a comprehensive analysis of various kinds of consumption externalities in Chapter 6.

REFERENCES

Viner, J. "Cost Curves and Supply Curves." *Zeitschrift fur National-okonomie,* III, 1932. Reprinted in *American Economic Association Readings in Price Theory.* Chicago: Richard D. Irwin, 1952.

Young, A. A. "Pigou's Wealth and Welfare." *Quarterly Journal of Economics,* August 1913.

6

Consumption externalities

As indicated in Chapter 5, a consumption externality requires governmental intervention for economic efficiency whenever economic activity by some consumer enters (alters) the utility function of at least one other consumer and is not accounted for by the market system. The very definition itself suggests that the fundamental problem in analyzing consumption externalities is deciding exactly what activities enter whose utility functions and in precisely what form. In a strictly formal sense, the externality "game" is one of properly defining the arguments of each consumer's utility function, because once these arguments are set they will determine every relevant aspect of the externality, including the proper policy to be applied.

Because the emphasis here is on consumption interrelationships, it is useful to condense the standard general equilibrium model of Chapter 2 exactly as suggested in Chapter 2. That is:

1. Define all quantities in terms of consumption.

Let:

$$X_{ik} = \text{consumption of good } k \text{ (supply of factor } k) \text{ by person } i. \qquad \begin{aligned} k &= 1, \ldots, N \\ i &= 1, \ldots, H \end{aligned}$$

2. Assume production efficiency and write aggregate production as one implicit production-possibilities frontier:

(6.1) $$F(X_1, \ldots, X_N) = F(X_k) = 0$$

where:

X_k = aggregate consumption (supply) of good (factor) k.

3. Place the N market clearance relationships

(6.2) $$\sum_{i=1}^{H} X_{ik} = X_k \qquad k = 1, \ldots, N$$

directly into the production-possibilities frontier. Write:

(6.3) $$F\left(\sum_{i=1}^{H} X_{ik}\right) = 0$$

with the understanding that the producers do not care who consumes each good (supplies each factor). That is,

$$\frac{\partial F}{\partial X_{ik}} = \frac{\partial F}{\partial X_k} = F_k \qquad \begin{array}{l} \text{all } i = 1, \ldots, H \\ \text{any } k = 1, \ldots, N \end{array}$$

Thus, the basic model for analyzing all consumption externality problems in a first-best policy environment is:

$$\max_{(X_{ik})} W[U^h(\ )]$$

$$\text{s.t.} \quad F\left(\sum_{i=1}^{H} X_{ik}\right) = 0$$

where W is the individualistic social welfare function and the arguments of each person's utility function depend on the exact form of the externality being considered.

HOW BAD CAN EXTERNALITIES BE?

In defiance of all pedagogical custom, let us first consider the most difficult case and ask: At their worst, how bad can consumption externalities be? The worst possible situation imaginable would require a triple indexing of X, X_{ik}^j, $i = 1, \ldots, H$; $j = 1, \ldots, H$; and $k = 1, \ldots, N$, in which X_{ik}^j refers to the consumption (supply) of good (factor) k, by person i, affecting person j. That is, each person (h) worries about who consumes (supplies) what good (factor) and how it affects each person. Returning to the example of the fence in Chapter 5, each person in the neighborhood notes that person i built the fence (good k), and that it affects all people in the neighborhood differently. Thus, X_{ik}^j is different, conceptually, from X_{ik}^ℓ, $\ell \neq j$, and $\ell, j = 1, \ldots, H$ (assuming the neighborhood contains H people). It still refers to person i's fence, but person j and ℓ react differently to the fence and each person will take note of that difference. Had someone else built a fence, say, person m, then each person's utility would contain another H arguments, X_{mk}^j, $j = 1, \ldots, H$, and so forth. In the worst of all worlds, anything anyone did would affect everyone, and each person would take note of all these things. Hence, each utility function would contain all H^2N elements, X_{ik}^j, as arguments. This would surely be the worst possible consumption externality situation imaginable.

Fortunately, we can at least dispense with the superscript j without disservice to any realistic situation. While it may be that person i's fence affects all people in the neighborhood, and each differently, when any one person (h) considers the effects of the fence on himself and his neighbors, we can assume that the H separate effects dovetail into a single effect on person h's utility. Thus, person h's utility function will simply note that person i built a fence (good k), as opposed to someone else building a fence. At most, then, we need place $H \cdot N$ arguments, X_{ik}, in each person's utility function, writing

(6.4) $$U^h = U^h(X_{ik}) \qquad \begin{array}{l} \text{any } h = 1, \ldots, H \\ \text{all } \ i = 1, \ldots, H \\ \quad k = 1, \ldots, N \end{array}$$

to indicate that, in the worst of all worlds, each person (h) is affected by anyone's (i) consumption (supply) of any good (factor) k. The fact that person h considers the effects of some X_{ik} on all people is simply summarized as one effect on his utility, $U^h(X_{ik})$.

The general equilibrium model becomes:

$$\max_{(X_{ik})} W[U^h(X_{ik})]$$

$$\text{s.t.} \quad F\left(\sum_{i=1}^{H} X_{ik}\right) = 0$$

Notice that the goods (and factors) in this model are exclusive goods. X_{ik} means that person i physically consumes (supplies) an amount X_{ik} of good (factor) k, as indicated by the market clearance relationship $\sum_{i=1}^{H} X_{ik} = X_k$. X_{ik} enters into the utility function of all $(H - 1)$ other persons, but they are merely affected by X_{ik}, they do not physically consume it. Thus, there are $H \cdot (H - 1)$ *external* effects associated with the consumption (supply) of good (factor) k, and $H \cdot (H - 1) \cdot N$ total external effects, counting all N goods and factors in the worst of all possible worlds.

In the context of this model, a natural definition of a *pure public good (factor)* is:

(6.5) $$\frac{\partial U^h}{\partial X_{ik}} \neq 0 \qquad \text{all } i, h = 1, \ldots, H$$

If everyone is affected *on the margin* by anyone's consumption (supply) of good (factor) k, then it is a pure public good. The choice of marginal rather than total utility in the definition makes sense because, as we shall see, it is marginal utility (more accurately, marginal rates of substitution) which enter into pareto-optimal decision rules. Person h could be significantly affected by person i's consumption of good k in a total sense, but if the marginal affect is zero, then it turns out that person h's feelings will not matter for purposes of allocational efficiency. For the benefit of those somewhat familiar with the externality literature, we should also note that this definition differs from Samuelson's early definition of a pure public good which has gained fairly wide acceptance. Samuelson equated publicness to non exclusiveness, or jointness in consumption, meaning that if one person consumed the good (supplied the factor), then all could physically consume it (supply it). (For more on nonexclusive goods, refer to pages 107–21 of this text.) As noted above, however, in our model only person i consumes X_{ik}, only person j consumes X_{jk}, and so forth, and X_{ik} does not necessarily equal X_{jk}, for any $i, j = 1, \ldots, H$. Note, also that our definition of publicness says nothing about the signs of $\partial U^h/\partial X_{ik}$. For some h the derivative could be positive, for others negative, so long as $\partial U^h/\partial X_{ik}$ is never zero. The smoking of marijuana comes to mind as an example. Some people enjoy the fact that others indulge; other people dislike it.

Correspondingly, a pure private good (factor) is one for which

(6.6) $$\frac{\partial U^h}{\partial X_{ik}} = 0 \qquad i \neq h$$

Only person i is affected on the margin by his consumption (supply) of good (factor) k. As a general rule, we will write $U^h(X_{hk})$ to indicate that good (factor) k is a pure private good (factor) and $U^h(X_{ik})$ to indicate that a consumer externality exists that is *potentially* a pure public good. We say potentially because all the notation implies is that some person h is affected by at least one other person's consumption (supply) of good (factor) k as well as his own consumption of good k. It is not meant to imply that everyone is necessarily affected by each person's consumption of good (factor) k. $\partial U^h/\partial X_{ik}$ could equal zero for some i. All that is required for the existence of an externality is that one person's utility be a function of one other person's consumption (supply) of something.

THE WORST OF ALL WORLDS—ALL GOODS (FACTORS) PURE PUBLIC GOODS (FACTORS)

In the worst of all worlds, all goods (factors) are pure public goods (factors).[1] For policy purposes this is really a horrendous situation since the government can hardly interpret what the proper decision rules mean let alone have any hope of implementing them. The government's problem is:

$$\max_{(X_{ik})} W[U^h(X_{ik})]$$

$$\text{s.t.} \quad F\left(\sum_{i=1}^{H} X_{ik}\right) = 0$$

with the understanding that each utility function $U^h(\ )$ contains all $N \cdot H$ elements, $X_{ik}, i = 1, \ldots, H; k = 1, \ldots, N$.

Before proceeding, notice how deceptively similar this problem appears to social welfare maximization when there are only pure private goods. In our notation the pure private goods case would be represented as:

$$\max_{(X_{hk})} W[U^h(X_{hk})]$$

$$\text{s.t.} \quad F\left(\sum_{h=1}^{H} X_{hk}\right) = 0$$

In each case maximization occurs with respect to the N goods and factors consumed and supplied by each of H people. The difference is that in the worst of all worlds all arguments appear in each utility function, whereas in the pure private goods (factors) world only N arguments appear in each utility function. Moreover, the policy implications are enormously different. In the latter case the competitive market can achieve full pareto optimality. In the former case, the market will generally not achieve efficiency, and if not, the government is virtually powerless to act in an optimal manner.

---

[1] Ng provides an alternative model of this worst of all worlds in Y-K Ng, "The Paradox of Universal Externalities," *Journal of Economic Theory*, April 1975.

The problems for the government in the pure public goods case are self-evident upon examination of the first-order conditions for social welfare maximization, both the interpersonal equity conditions and the pareto-optimal conditions.

Interpersonal Equity Conditions

Recall that the interpersonal equity conditions are obtained by comparing the first-order conditions for any one good (factor) consumed (supplied) by any two people, say, X_{j1} and X_{i1}.

The first-order conditions are:[2]

$$(6.7) \qquad X_{j1}: \quad \sum_{h=1}^{H} \frac{\partial W}{\partial U^h} \frac{\partial U^h}{X_{j1}} = \lambda F_1$$

$$(6.8) \qquad X_{i1}: \quad \sum_{h=1}^{H} \frac{\partial W}{\partial U^h} \frac{\partial U^h}{\partial X_{i1}} = \lambda F_1$$

From conditions (6.7) and (6.8) it immediately follows that

$$(6.9) \qquad \sum_{h=1}^{H} \frac{\partial W}{\partial U^h} \frac{\partial U^h}{\partial X_{i1}} = \lambda F_1 \qquad \text{all } i = 1, \ldots, H$$

The interpretation of these conditions is identical with that of the standard model in Chapter 2 which contained only pure private goods: the government should redistribute good 1, lump sum, until social welfare is equalized on the margin across all individuals. This task is difficult in the best of times, but now it is extremely complex. When the government gives (takes) an extra unit of good (factor) 1 to (from) person i, it must know how *all* people will react to that transfer (tax) on the margin, not just how person i's utility is affected, and similarly for units transferred to or from any other person. Clearly, this is an impossible task, one the government could not even hope to approximate.

Pareto-Optimal Conditions

The pareto-optimal conditions also differ considerably from their counter-part in a world of pure private goods, both in form and interpretation. Recall that pareto-optimal conditions are obtained from the first-order conditions of any two goods consumed (factors supplied) by any one person, say, X_{ik} and X_{i1}.

The first-order conditions are:

$$(6.10) \qquad X_{ik}: \quad \sum_{h=1}^{H} \frac{\partial W}{\partial U^h} \frac{\partial U^h}{\partial X_{ik}} = \lambda F_k$$

$$(6.11) \qquad X_{i1}: \quad \sum_{h=1}^{H} \frac{\partial W}{\partial U^h} \frac{\partial U^h}{\partial X_{i1}} = \lambda F_1$$

---

[2] λ is the Lagrangian multiplier associated with the aggregate production frontier.

Dividing (6.10) by (6.11) yields:

(6.12)
$$\frac{\sum_{h=1}^{H} \frac{\partial W}{\partial U^h} \frac{\partial U^h}{\partial X_{ik}}}{\sum_{h=1}^{H} \frac{\partial W}{\partial U^h} \frac{\partial U^h}{\partial X_{i1}}} = \frac{F_k}{F_1} \qquad \begin{array}{l} \text{all } i = 1, \ldots, H \\ \text{any } k = 2, \ldots, N \end{array}$$

The right-hand side of (6.12) has a standard interpretation, the marginal rate of transformation in production (MRT) between goods (factors) k and 1. The left-hand side, however, has no natural interpretation. As written, it is a ratio of marginal impacts on social welfare from consuming (supplying) the two goods (factors), and there is no way to simplify the expression. In particular, the social welfare terms, $\partial W/\partial U^h$, do not cancel out, so that the rule is not really a pareto-optimal condition at all. Recall that pareto-optimal conditions do not contain social welfare terms. In this worst of all worlds, then, the model does not dichotomize into interpersonal equity and pareto-optimal conditions, the only exception we will encounter throughout all of Part II. All the decision rules are of the interpersonal equity type and can be achieved only by lump-sum redistributions of all the goods and factors, clearly a hopeless situation. Moreover, the competitive market system, which equates marginal rates of substitution in consumption to marginal rates of transformation, would be absolutely useless. Nothing short of a complete government takeover of the economy would be able to satisfy the first-order conditions for social welfare maximization.

THE EXISTENCE OF A PURE PRIVATE GOOD

Fortunately, the real world is not so riddled with consumption externalities. A large number of goods are truly pure private goods, or approximate pure privateness closely enough so that, in practice, a government would not bother intervening in their respective markets. To keep the discussion as general as possible, however, let us first assume there is only one pure private good in the economy, the first. Formally, $\partial U^h/\partial X_{i1} = 0, i \neq h$. The other $(N - 1)$ goods and factors remain pure public goods. As it turns out, only one private good is necessary to resurrect the dichotomy between the pareto-optimal and interpersonal equity conditions that normally exists in first-best analysis, and retain a role for the competitive market system in allocating all the goods and factors.

With a single private good, the social welfare maximization problem becomes:

$$\max_{(X_{ik};X_{h1})} \quad W[U^h(X_{ik}; X_{h1})]$$

$$\text{s.t.} \quad F\left(\sum_{i=1}^{H} X_{ik}; \sum_{h=1}^{H} X_{h1}\right) = 0$$

where:

$$k = 2, \ldots, N$$

Good 1 has been written separately to indicate specifically that it is purely private.

The Interpersonal Equity Conditions

Consider the interpersonal equity conditions with respect to good 1, the pure private good.

The *first-order conditions* are:

(6.13)
$$X_{h1}: \quad \frac{\partial W}{\partial U^h} \frac{\partial U^h}{\partial X_{h1}} = \lambda F_1$$

(6.14)
$$X_{i1}: \quad \frac{\partial W}{\partial U^i} \frac{\partial U^i}{\partial X_{i1}} = \lambda F_1$$

or

(6.15)
$$\frac{\partial W}{\partial U^h} \frac{\partial U^h}{\partial X_{h1}} = \lambda F_1 \qquad \text{all } h = 1, \ldots, H$$

(6.15) is identical to the interpersonal equity conditions in the standard model of Chapter 2. *We will assume the government can redistribute* X_1, *lump sum, to achieve this condition as part of its first-best policy strategy.*

The Pareto-Optimal Conditions

As above, consider the first-order conditions with respect to two goods (factors) consumed (supplied) by any one person, say, X_{ik} and X_{i1}. The choice of k is arbitrary, but it is important that good 1, the private good, be one of the two choices.

The *first-order conditions* are:

(6.16)
$$X_{ik}: \quad \sum_{h=1}^{H} \frac{\partial W}{\partial U^h} \frac{\partial U^h}{\partial X_{ik}} = \lambda F_k$$

(6.17)
$$X_{i1}: \quad \frac{\partial W}{\partial U^i} \frac{\partial U^i}{\partial X_{i1}} = \lambda F_1$$

Dividing (6.16) by (6.17) yields:

(6.18)
$$\frac{\displaystyle\sum_{h=1}^{H} \frac{\partial W}{\partial U^h} \frac{\partial U^h}{\partial X_{ik}}}{\displaystyle\frac{\partial W}{\partial U^i} \frac{\partial U^i}{\partial X_{i1}}} = \frac{F_k}{F_1}$$

Condition (6.18) can be simplified *if* the government has satisfied the interpersonal equity conditions for good 1. The left-hand side is a summation of social welfare terms over a common denominator, $\partial W/\partial U^i \, \partial U^i/\partial X_{i1}$. But if interpersonal equity holds,

(6.19)
$$\frac{\partial W}{\partial U^i} \frac{\partial U^i}{\partial X_{i1}} = \lambda F_1 \qquad \text{all } i = 1, \ldots, H$$

Thus, we can substitute for the denominator term by term, matching up the social welfare terms, and writing:

(6.20)
$$\sum_{h=1}^{H} \frac{\dfrac{\partial W}{\partial U^h} \dfrac{\partial U^h}{\partial X_{ik}}}{\dfrac{\partial W}{\partial U^h} \dfrac{\partial U^h}{\partial X_{h1}}} = \frac{F_k}{F_1} \qquad \begin{array}{l} \text{all } i = 1, \ldots, H \\ \text{any } k = 2, \ldots, N \end{array}$$

The social welfare indexes, $\partial W / \partial U^h$ cancel term by term, yielding:

(6.21)
$$\sum_{h=1}^{H} \frac{\dfrac{\partial U^h}{\partial X_{ik}}}{\dfrac{\partial U^h}{\partial X_{h1}}} = \frac{F_k}{F_1}$$

The left-hand side of (6.21) has a standard pareto-optimal interpretation, devoid of social welfare terms. It is a sum of marginal rates of substitution, each person's marginal rate of substitution between *his own consumption* of the pure private good and *person i's consumption* of good k. Thus, the rule can be written as:

(6.22)
$$\sum_{h=1}^{H} MRS^h_{X_{ik}, X_{h1}} = MRT_{k,1} \qquad \begin{array}{l} \text{all } i = 1, \ldots, H, \\ \text{any } k = 2, \ldots, N \end{array}$$

Note carefully that the ability to cancel the social welfare terms is not just a formal "trick." It implies correct policy action, the ability to redistribute lump sum in order to satisfy the interpersonal equity conditions. Without correct redistributions, the terms will not cancel and all the policy implications of the pareto-optimal conditions which we are about to discuss become irrelevant, since conditions (6.22) will not be the necessary conditions for a social welfare maximum. We will employ this cancellation technique repeatedly throughout the chapter, with the same policy implications understood each time. Without the ability to achieve correct lump-sum redistributions, none of the standard first-best policy prescriptions apply, even those ostensibly related only to allocational issues.[3] Finally, note that only good 1 need be redistributed lump sum, exactly as in the standard model of Chapter 2 which contained only pure private goods. If the government correctly redistributes good 1 and designs policies to achieve all the pareto-optimal conditions, then the interpersonal equity conditions will automatically apply to goods (and factors) $k = 2, \ldots, N$ as well. To see this, plug the social welfare terms back into the left-hand side of (6.21), obtaining (6.20). If (6.20) holds and the denominators are also equal to

---

[3] Notice that conditions (6.22) can be derived without reference to the social welfare function by solving the following problem: Maximize the utility of any one person, subject to holding the utilities of the remaining $(H - 1)$ people constant, and the production function and market clearance. But they will not be necessary conditions for a social welfare maximum in the absence of an optimal income distribution. The first-order conditions for externalities with a nonoptimal distribution are derived in Chapter 20.

λF_1 from interpersonal equity, then

$$(6.23) \qquad \sum_{h=1}^{H} \frac{\partial W}{\partial U^h} \frac{\partial U^h}{\partial X_{ik}} = \lambda F_k \qquad \begin{array}{l} \text{all } i = 1, \ldots, H, \\ \text{any } k = 2, \ldots, N \end{array}$$

as required by the interpersonal equity conditions for goods $k = 2, \ldots, N$.

The Pareto-Optimal Conditions — Policy Implications

Pareto-optimal rules for externality-generating exclusive goods that are combinations of marginal rates of substitution and marginal rates of transformation have two important properties:

a. The government can always achieve them by retaining decentralized competitive markets for each of the goods (factors) and levying a set of taxes that direct competitive behavior to the correct pareto-optimal conditions.
b. One can always describe a market structure with competitive prices that will achieve the correct pareto-optimal conditions without government intervention, although it is a much more complex market structure than normally exists. The point is that an externality problem can always be thought of as a problem of market failure, in the sense that the correct set of competitive markets simply does not exist.

Let us turn first to the problem of describing the proper set of taxes within a typical competitive market structure. Suppose the markets for goods (factors) $k = 2, \ldots, N$ are competitive. In the absence of government intervention, these markets will generate the conditions:

$$(6.24) \qquad MRS^h_{X_{hk}, X_{h1}} = MRT_{k,1} \qquad \begin{array}{l} \text{all } h = 1, \ldots, H \\ \text{any } k = 2, \ldots, N \end{array}$$

since both consumers and producers face the identical prices P_k and P_1 for goods (factors) k and 1, respectively. $MRS^h_{hk,h1}$ refers to person h's MRS between *his own consumption* of goods k and 1 (supply of factors k and 1). These are not the proper pareto-optimal conditions, but the government can exploit competitive market behavior in order to establish the proper set of corrective taxes. The government wants to generate the conditions (6.22).

Consider the decision by person i to consume (supply) good (factor) k, X_{ik}. His decision affects all other people, but for these people it is essentially a lump-sum event. Only person i decides the quantity X_{ik}; the others must accept it as a parameter. Thus, the government need only adjust person i's behavior, at least with respect to X_{ik}, as follows. Suppose that a competitive market already exists before government intervention so that $MRT_{k,1} = P_k/P_1$ from profit maximization. That is, the prices P_k and P_1 reflect the marginal costs of producing goods k and 1 (or values of marginal products if factors are involved). It will also be true that $MRS^i_{X_{ik}, X_{i1}} = P_k/P_1$ from utility maximization. The government does not want this, but it knows that if it establishes another set of prices for person i, say, P^i_k and P_1, then consumer i will set $MRS^i_{X_{ik}, X_{i1}} = P^i_k/P_1$, again from utility maximization. The goal, then, is to design a tax for person i, t_k^i, that simultaneously:

1. Drives a wedge between P_k^i/P_1 and P_k/P_1, such that:

(6.25)
$$\frac{P_k^i}{P_1} = \frac{P_k}{P_1} + \frac{t_k^i}{P_1}$$

2. Achieves the desired pareto-optimal condition,

$$\sum_{h=1}^{H} MRS_{X_{ik},X_{h1}}^h = MRT$$

Letting good 1 be the numeraire, so that $P_1 = 1$, the proper tax is $t_k^i = -\sum_{h \neq i} MRS_{X_{ik},X_{h1}}^h$, equal to the sum of the marginal effects on all others of person i's consumption (supply) of good (factor) k. With this tax, the price person i pays for good k, P_k^i/P_1, differs from the marginal cost or producers' price of k by exactly the summation of his marginal effects on all other consumers:

(6.26)
$$P_k^i = MRS_{X_{ik},X_{i1}}^i = MRT - \sum_{h \neq i} MRS_{X_{ik},X_{h1}}^h$$

Thus, the tax will establish the correct pareto-optimal condition on X_{ik}. Using the convention that the MRS between two goods is positive, if these side effects are beneficial (an external economy), then the "tax" t_k^i is negative, a subsidy, so that person i pays less than the marginal cost price of producing good k, and conversely if the side effects are harmful (external diseconomies). Moreover, the government can adjust the tax, at least in principle, to the desired level. Suppose at first the tax is zero, and X_{ik} generates external economies. Without benefit of the subsidy, person i consumes (supplies) too little of good (factor) k, and $t_k^i > -\sum_{h \neq i} MRS_{ik,h1}^h$. A subsidy to person i will lower t_k^i, increase X_{ik}, and thereby decrease the absolute value of each other person's $MRS_{X_{ik},X_{h1}}^h$. Thus, it is possible to find the t_k^i such that $t_k^i = -\sum_{h \neq i} MRS_{ik,h1}^h$, as required.

To allocate the aggregate amount of X_k correctly requires H separate taxes, t_k^i, $i = 1, \ldots, H$, one for each consumer (supplier) of X_k, determined exactly as above. Pareto optimality requires

$$\sum_{h=1}^{H} MRS_{X_{ik},X_{h1}}^h = MRT_{X_k,X_1} \qquad \text{all } i = 1, \ldots, H$$

The effects of the tax can also be considered in terms of supply and demand analysis with good 1 as the numeraire. The aggregate supply (demand) curve for good (factor) k has the usual interpretation. It is the horizontal summation of the marginal cost (value of marginal product) curves for each individual producer of k. The aggregate demand (supply) curve for good (factor) k is, similarly, the horizontal summation of each individual consumer's demand (supply) for good (factor) k, with this important difference. Before the individual curves are summed horizontally, they are each adjusted vertically downward (upward) by the amount of the tax (subsidy), t_k^i. Because of the way in which the taxes (subsidies) are defined, the vertical adjustment just equals, for person i, the value of $-\sum_{h \neq i} MRS^h_{X_{ik},X_{h1}}$ at each unit of X_{ik}, his marginal impact on all other people. Thus, the resulting individual demand curve for person i reflects the entire $\sum_{h=1}^{H} MRS^h_{X_{ik},X_{h1}}$, including person i's own MRS between goods k and 1. Since these adjusted curves are then summed *horizontally* to be equated with aggregate supply,

$$(6.27) \qquad \sum_{h=1}^{H} MRS^h_{X_{ik},X_{h1}} = MRT_{X_k,X_1} = P_k \qquad \text{all } i = 1, \ldots, H,$$

in aggregate equilibrium, as required for pareto optimality.

Designing the proper set of H taxes for any one pure public good is obviously a hopeless task. For *each* of the taxes the government must know $(H - 1)$ separate pieces of information, the $MRS^h_{ik,h1}$. The full set of H taxes, therefore, requires $H(H - 1)$ independent pieces of information, all of which may differ. In general, $MRS^h_{ik,h1} \neq MRS^j_{ik,j1}, j \neq h$. Finally, a world consisting of one pure private good and $(N - 1)$ pure public goods would require $H(N - 1)$ taxes and $H(H - 1)(N - 1)$ independent observations on the external marginal effects.

Of course it may happen that only a small subset of people is affected in this way by the consumption of some good, that is, the good is somewhere on the continuum between pure publicness and pure privateness. As is immediately obvious from the construction of the model, the pareto-optimal rule

$$\sum_h MRS^h_{ik,h1} = MRT_{k,1}$$

applies only to the subset of H people affected by person i's consumption of good k. The subset could number as few as two people (person i and one other), and pareto optimality would still be described by this rule. Furthermore, the subset of people whose consumption creates consumer externalities could number far fewer than H people.[4] There may only be one such person. As a practical matter, the government would only intervene if the subset of people affected by a particular externality were fairly large and/or the externalities generated in any one instance were deemed to be "substantial" in some sense. Very few goods (factors) are likely to meet this practical criterion. That is, most goods are certainly well toward the pole of pure privateness. All these considerations serve to mitigate the actual policy problems caused by consumption externalities. Nonetheless, if, for example, J people were affected by each of L goods as described by the model, then $J \cdot L$ taxes (subsidies) are required for allocative efficiency, a formidable task even if both J and L are "fairly small" relative to all the people and all the goods and factors in the economic system. If exclusive consumption activities give rise to external effects such that people care not only what the activity is but who is doing it, the inescapable conclusion is that

---

[4] For an analysis of externalities involving only a few affected parties, see R. H. Coase, "The Problem of Social Cost," *Journal of Law and Economics*, October 1960. Coase's article is an early classic in externality theory.

the government cannot reasonably be expected to find the proper set of corrective taxes even for one activity of this type, let alone for numerous activities. If examples such as the fence are prevalent (it obviously matters *who* builds the fence), the government's task is difficult indeed.

Externalities as Market Failure

The second property of pareto-optimal decision rules for exclusive activities that generate externalities is that they can always be achieved by competitive markets without government intervention, provided the proper markets exist. The "externality problem" can thus be viewed as a problem of nonexistence of markets.[5] Admittedly these market structures are often highly complex and not terribly realistic, but this particular relationship between externalities and market failure is worth discussing, if only to suggest possible alternative solutions to corrective taxes as a guideline to practical policy making when externalities affect only a few people.

Consider again person i's consumption of public good k, X_{ik}, from the model with only one pure private good, the first (for purposes of this discussion assume both X_k and X_1 are goods). The competitive market structure that would generate the pareto-optimal condition

$$\sum_{h=1}^{H} MRS^h_{X_{ik}, X_{h1}} = MRT_{X_k, X_1}$$

can be described as follows. (Once again, let good 1 be the numeraire, with $P_1 = 1$, for ease of exposition.) To supply good k, producers will insist on a price P_k equal to MRT_{X_k, X_1}. If consumer i wants to buy X_k, he will have to pay the producer this price. Suppose, however, that X_{ik} generates external economies for all other consumers. In this case both person i and all the others have a mutual interest in developing side markets to influence the final value of X_{ik}, the others because they would be willing to pay something to have person i increase his consumption of good k, and person i because he can extract side payments which effectively lower the price to him below the producer price, P_k.

Consider next the set of indifference curves for some person $h \neq i$, between X_{ik}, *person i's consumption* of good k, and X_{h1}, person h's *own consumption* of good 1, as shown in Figure 6–1. X_{ik} is a parameter for person h, but he determines his own consumption of good 1. Suppose their independent decisions place consumer h at point B on indifference curve I_1. The slope of I_1 at B is $MRS^h_{X_{ik}, X_{h1}}$. If these were two purely private goods both under the control of person h, then he would pay a competitive price for X_{ik} equal to $MRS^h_{X_{ik}, X_{h1}}$. Call this price P^h_{ik} (with $P_1 \equiv 1$). Suppose person h actually paid person i the competitive price $P^h_{ik} = MRS^h_{X_{ik}, X_{h1}}$, and all other consumers did likewise, having

[5] Kenneth Arrow argues for this view of the externality problem in K. J. Arrow, "The Organization of Economic Activity: Issues Pertinent to the Choice of Market versus Nonmarket Allocation," in R. H. Haveman and J. Margolis, eds., *Public Expenditure and Policy Analysis*, 2d ed. (Chicago: Rand McNally College Publishing Co., 1977).

FIGURE 6–1

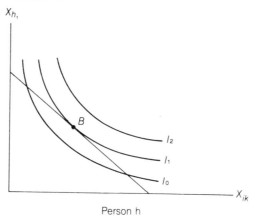

Person h

formed identical "competitive" side market relationships with person i. This set of competitive side markets could achieve the desired pareto-optimal condition. Person i would consider himself to be in equilibrium when

$$(6.28) \qquad P^i_{ik} + \sum_{h \neq i} P^h_{ik} = P_k$$

that is, when the price he is willing to pay for his own consumption of good k, equal to his own $MRS^i_{X_{ik}, X_{i1}}$, plus all the "competitive" side payments received from the $(H - 1)$ other consumers, just equaled the required supply price, P_k. But with

$$(6.29) \qquad P^h_{ik} = MRS^h_{X_{ik}, X_{h1}} \qquad \text{all } h = 1, \ldots, H$$

and

$$(6.30) \qquad P_k = MRT$$

this equilibrium would also satisfy the pareto-optimal condition

$$\sum_{h=1}^{H} MR\, S^h_{X_{ik} X_{h1}} = MRT_{k,1}$$

Notice that $(H - 1)$ "competitive" side markets are required just for person i's consumption of good k, plus the usual market between the producer and consumer i, or H markets in all. By a similar analysis, $H(H - 1)$ additional side markets would be necessary to allocate X_k correctly among all H consumers, $(H - 1)$ side markets for each of H consumers, a formidable set of markets indeed. Adding the H markets between the producers and each consumer, there would be H^2 markets in all. Furthermore, $H(H - 1)$ distinct side markets (H^2 total markets) are necessary for *each* pure public good.

The same analysis applies if the externality is a diseconomy (a "bad"), although the mutual gains come about indirectly. Achieving pareto optimality increases aggregate real income, which can then be redistributed to everyone's mutual gain. Each person i might miss this, however, and refuse to make "competitive" side payments equal to the marginal damage he is causing other people, since these payments have the all-too-obvious direct effect of lowering his utility, for which he might not be compensated when the additional real income is distributed.

Relating the problem of externalities to market failure in this way suggests why the market system breaks down in their presence even when it is mutually beneficial for people to form side markets. Normally, the existence of potential mutual gains from trade can be expected to promote markets. For these externalities, however, three particular difficulties undoubtedly hinder the development of the proper side markets. First, legal and/or political constraints may preclude formation of side markets, especially in the case of external diseconomies. Suppose industry in New York state is polluting Vermont air. Even if New Yorkers are convinced that side payments to Vermonters can increase the combined welfare of both states, they certainly have no guarantee that sufficient tax revenues (and other necessary income) will be transferred back to New York to make the potential gain for New Yorkers a real one. Without proper redistributions, New Yorkers may well be better off continuing to pollute, especially if most of the costs of pollution are borne by Vermonters because of prevailing westerly winds. These same circumstances will also create difficulties for government intervention in the form of corrective taxes as described in the previous section. Who will levy these taxes? Certainly not New York state, and Vermont cannot tax New York citizens for pollution damage. Moreover, the Constitution of the United States may well proscribe levying federal taxes on New York citizens based on damage caused to Vermont citizens. As will be argued in more detail in Part V, a federalist system of governments creates problems for any policy designed to correct for externalities whenever the externalities spill over jurisdictional lines.

Transactions costs can also be a severe hindrance to developing side markets. Suppose people benefit from other people's education, but differentially depending on just who is educated, for example, bright people verses dull people. Moreover, suppose people do not all benefit equally from any one person's education. In short, education may have the properties of a (virtually) pure public exclusive good, with many different marginal rates of substitution. If so, then the sheer number of side markets required to achieve an optimal amount of education for anyone is staggering (H is a very large number) and the costs of even trying to get everyone together are clearly prohibitive, meaning that they would almost surely offset any efficiency gains from achieving or even approaching pareto optimality. Put another way, normal competitive markets permit all consumers and producers to face the same price, an enormous advantage in terms of information requirements. Externalities of the type under consideration generally require negotiations and differential prices among all consumers in the market, a quantam jump in structural complexity. Small wonder, then, that such markets almost never form, even when the mutual gains, ignoring transactions costs, are obvious to all, such as for external economies.

Finally, mutually beneficial side payments might not obtain even if the externality were relatively simple, affecting only a few people, and none of the problems mentioned above existed. There remains the problem that the affected parties have an incentive not to reveal their true preferences. Suppose person i's consumption of good k generates an external economy for persons j and m. Despite the benefits he receives, person j might decide not to subsidize i's consumption, hoping instead that the other person, m, will do so. In the parlance of the literature, j desires to be a "free rider." Person m reasons similarly, and since no one wants to play the sucker, no side payments occur, despite the obvious gains to all. There exist various tax schema for avoiding the free-rider problem, but we will defer discussion of them until the next section on non-exclusive goods, since the relevation problem has been most closely associated with these goods. However, it could just as easily apply to exclusive goods.

NONEXCLUSIVE GOODS—THE SAMUELSON MODEL

Professor Samuelson was the first economist to analyze the problem of externalities using a formal general equilibrium model of social welfare maximization for his analytical framework. He developed and explained his model in the series of three articles mentioned in Chapter 2,[6] and it is safe to say that no other single work has been more influential to the development of public expenditure theory. For this reason alone, his model deserves special attention in any treatise on public sector economics. We will present it in some detail, since it also happens to be a useful vehicle for exploring a number of important issues, including:

a. Special problems created by nonexclusive goods. Samuelson chose the nonexclusive good for his example of an externality.
b. A method for introducing the government into the standard general equilibrium model, given that the government's preferences are not supposed to count, other than providing the social welfare function.
c. The important policy proposition that a competitive market system will correctly allocate pure private goods (and factors) even though some other goods (factors) generate externalities. This point could have been developed above by considering a model with two pure private goods. It will always hold providing the analysis uses first-best assumptions.
d. An initial presentation of the *benefits-received* principle of taxation, one of the two widely accepted normative criteria for judging whether or not a particular tax is equitable.

---

[6] P. A. Samuelson, "The Pure Theory of Public Expenditure," *Review of Economics and Statistics*, November 1954; P. A. Samuelson, "Diagrammatic Exposition of a Theory of Public Expenditure," *Review of Economics and Statistics*, November 1955; and P. A. Samuelson, "Aspects of Public Expenditure Theories," *Review of Economics and Statistics*, November 1958.

Nonexclusive Goods

A nonexclusive good (a service, really) has the property that if any one person consumes it, everyone necessarily *consumes* it in equal amounts. Nonexclusivity works both ways. If one person consumes the good, he cannot exclude others from consuming it. Additionally, if someone consumes the good, another individual within the domain of the good cannot exclude himself from consuming the good even if he should want to. Consumption is truly joint. These goods cause terrible problems for any society dedicated to competitive market principles and consumer sovereignty, but they are hardly *curiosa*. Defense and the exploration of outer space are two very important examples of nonexclusive goods.[7]

Because of the revelation problem, it is reasonable to assume that competitive markets will completely fail to allocate nonexclusive goods. If a consumer wants an exclusive good, he must purchase it, thereby revealing his preferences. But if a good is nonexclusive, the strategy of nonrevelation is a viable option. People have an incentive not to reveal their preferences, hoping that someone who wants the good will actually buy it. If someone does play the "sucker," all will immediately consume its services as "free riders." Under these conditions the government will surely be forced to consume the good in behalf of society for there to be any hope of achieving the proper allocation of resources to the good, and perhaps to have any of the good at all, *even though everyone might desire the services of the good*. This is why Samuelson labeled nonexclusive goods "public goods." As we shall see, these goods satisfy our own definition of public goods, which can also apply to exclusive goods as well, but in the externality literature Samuelson's equation of "publicness" with "nonexclusivity" (joint consumption) is the one most often employed.

Having decided that the government must consume the good, it is faced with two very important questions:

a. How much of the good should it consume?
b. How should people be taxed to pay for the government's purchases?

One can provide answers to both questions consistent with the standard criteria of consumer sovereignty, pareto optimality, and competitive market principles, but these answers depend upon consumers revealing their true preferences to the government. Unfortunately, consumers may well have no more incentive to relate their true preferences to the government than they did to the marketplace. In answer to question (b), therefore, the government seeks taxes that will force consumers to reveal their preferences.

---

[7] The terminology "nonexclusive" introduced by Samuelson is somewhat misleading in that some good might have the properties described above over a subset of individuals, yet not be available at all to still other people. Compare national defense with local police protection. Jointness of consumption is perhaps a more accurate description, leaving open the possibility that some consumers may be excluded. At this point, however, we will use nonexclusiveness and jointness in consumption interchangeably and assume the entire population is affected.

The Government in a General Equilibrium Model

In order to focus on the problems peculiar to nonexclusivity, assume that there is one nonexclusive good, the kth, and that all other $(N - 1)$ goods are pure private goods. Assume further that the market for nonexclusive goods is inoperative because of the free-rider problem, so that the government must decide how much of the good to consume and how to ask people to pay for it. The immediate problem, then, is to incorporate the government into the formal model of social welfare maximization.

One method of proceeding is to assume the government has a preference function for nonexclusive goods derived through some sort of political process, exactly the approach taken for the government's social welfare function. If this government preference function also includes the overall size of the private sector as one of its arguments, then the private sector defines the opportunity costs of public expenditures on the nonexclusive good, and finding the optimal amount of the "public" good becomes a simple exercise in consumer theory. The government would solve a problem of the general form:

$$\max_{\substack{\text{(public} \\ \text{expenditures,} \\ \text{private} \\ \text{sector)}}} G(\text{public expenditures, private sector})$$

$$\text{s.t.} \quad \text{Public expenditures} + \text{Private sector} = Y$$

where:

G = the government's preference function.

Y = total national product, to be split among the private and public sectors.

As was stressed in Chapter 1, however, the government is not supposed to interject its own preferences into the decision-making process. Rather, it is supposed to play the part of agent, acting solely upon consumers' preferences for its demand data whenever possible, that is, to honor the principle of consumer sovereignty. When faced with the distribution issue, it has no choice but to violate consumer sovereignty, so there must be some politically derived set of social welfare rankings establishing criteria for distributive equity. But such is not the case with allocational issues. Consumers do have preferences, and there is no reason why they cannot be honored, at least in principle. Thus, normative theory has rejected the construct of a distinct government preference function for nonexclusive goods, or, indeed, for any expenditures arising from strictly allocational considerations. Only consumers' demands enter the optimal normative policy rules.

The easiest analytical device for introducing government purchases into the standard general equilibrium model without creating a distinct government demand for these purchases is to create a fictitious individual, say, the first, to represent the government.[8] By fictitious we mean that $U^1(\vec{X}_1) \equiv 0$, where $\vec{X}_1$

---

[8] Peter Diamond first demonstrated this technique to us in a set of unpublished class notes.

is a vector of goverment purchases. The vector $\vec{X}_1$ will enter into the production-possibility frontier and market clearance—the goods themselves are real and use up scarce resources—but government preferences will never count, since $\partial U^1 / \partial X_{1k} \equiv 0$, any k. If good k is the only nonexclusive good, social welfare maximization can be represented analytically as:

$$\max_{(X_{1k}; X_{hj})} W[U^1(X_{1k}); U^h(X_{hj}; X_{1k})]$$

$$\text{s.t.} \quad F\left(\sum_{h=2}^{H} X_{hj}; X_{1k} \right) = 0$$

where:

X_{1k} = the nonexclusive good, purchased only by the government.

X_{hj} = good (factor) j consumed (supplied) by person h.

$\qquad h = 2, \ldots, H$

$\qquad j = 1, \ldots, k-1, k+1, \ldots, N$

U^1 = the (fictitious) preference function of the government.

Notice that even though only the government purchases good k, X_{1k} enters into each person's utility function, since everyone automatically consumes the entire services of this nonexclusive goods. When exclusive goods generate externalities, there is a distinct difference between the services it provides privately to each individual who purchases it and the flow of external "services" received by other consumers in the form of external economies or diseconomies. Think once again of the fence. The person who built the fence receives a flow of services that are distinct from the "services" bestowed upon his neighbors. With nonexclusive goods, however, there is no such distinction. Whatever services are available to the purchaser, these identical services are automatically available to all others, whether they want the services or not. It is possible, however, to have an exclusive good, say, good k, which for some reason is purchased only by the first (real) individual and which generates externalities for all other consumers. In this case the model would have the identical formal structure to the model for the nonexclusive good k, with identical first-order conditions. Thus, even though nonexclusive goods have a distinctive interpretation and economic implications that are often quite different from exclusive goods that generate externalities, we should expect that the decision rules will be identical to those already developed in the context of exclusive goods. Indeed, this is the case.

Consider, first, the *interpersonal equity conditions*. Take the first-order conditions with respect to X_{h1} and X_{21}, obtaining:

(6.31) $$X_{h1}: \quad \frac{\partial W}{\partial U^h} \frac{\partial U^h}{\partial X_{h1}} = \lambda F_1$$

(6.32) $$X_{21}: \quad \frac{\partial W}{\partial U^2} \frac{\partial U^2}{\partial X_{21}} = \lambda F_1$$

Consequently,

(6.33)
$$\frac{\partial W}{\partial U^h} \frac{\partial U^h}{\partial X_{h1}} = \lambda F_1 \qquad \text{all } h = 2, \ldots, H$$

Once again, lump-sum redistributions are required to reach the bliss point.

The *pareto-optimal conditions* are obtained somewhat differently in this model. We have to compare the government's purchase of good k, X_{1k}, with any other consumer's purchase of any private good, say, X_{j1}.

The first-order conditions are:

(6.34)
$$X_{1k}: \sum_{h=2}^{H} \frac{\partial W}{\partial U^h} \frac{\partial U^h}{\partial X_{1k}} = \lambda F_k$$

(Recall that $\partial U^1/\partial X_{1k} \equiv 0$.)

(6.35)
$$X_{j1}: \frac{\partial W}{\partial U^j} \frac{\partial U^j}{\partial X_{j1}} = \lambda F_1$$

Dividing (6.34) by (6.35),

(6.36)
$$\frac{\displaystyle\sum_{h=2}^{H} \frac{\partial W}{\partial U^h} \frac{\partial U^h}{\partial X_{1k}}}{\dfrac{\partial W}{\partial U^j} \dfrac{\partial U^j}{\partial X_{j1}}} = \frac{F_k}{F_1} = MRT_{X_k, X_1}$$

But if the government has correctly redistributed good 1 such that the interpersonal equity conditions hold, then

$$\frac{\partial W}{\partial U^j} \frac{\partial U^j}{\partial X_{j1}} = \quad , \qquad \text{all } j = 2, \ldots, H.$$

Selectively substituting for the denominators in each term on the left-hand side of (6.36) and canceling $\partial W/\partial U^h$ term by term, yields:

(6.37)
$$\sum_{h=2}^{H} \left(\frac{\dfrac{\partial U^h}{\partial X_{1k}}}{\dfrac{\partial U^h}{\partial X_{h1}}} \right) = MRT_{X_k, X_1}$$

or

(6.38)
$$\sum_{h=2}^{H} MRS^h_{X_{1k}, X_{h1}} = MRT_{X_k, X_1}$$

Condition (6.38) gives the familiar result that the sum of each person's marginal rates of substitution between the nonexclusive good and good (factor) 1 equals the marginal rate of transformation between X_k and X_1 in production. Samuelson was the first to demonstrate formally the summation rule for externalities. Subsequent research showed that this same rule applies to exclusive goods as well, a fact already demonstrated above.

Competitive Determination of All Private Goods and Factors

Before discussing the government's prospects of satisfying the pareto-optimal conditions, consider the proposition that in a first-best policy environment, pure private goods and factors can be allocated efficiently by the competitive market system despite the presence of externalities elsewhere in the economy. To see this, consider the pareto-optimal conditions for any two pure private goods (or factors). Compare, for example, the first-order conditions for X_{h1} and X_{hm}, two goods (factors) consumed (supplied) by person h.

The first-order conditions are:

$$(6.39) \qquad X_{h1}: \quad \frac{\partial W}{\partial U^h} \frac{\partial U^h}{\partial X_{h1}} = \lambda F_1$$

$$(6.40) \qquad X_{hm}: \quad \frac{\partial W}{\partial U^h} \frac{\partial U^h}{\partial X_{hm}} = \lambda F_m$$

Dividing (6.39) by (6.40),

$$(6.41) \qquad \frac{\dfrac{\partial U^h}{\partial X_{h1}}}{\dfrac{\partial U^h}{\partial X_{hm}}} = \frac{F_1}{F_m} \qquad \begin{array}{l} \text{all } h = 2, \ldots, H \\ \text{any } 1, m \neq k \end{array}$$

or

$$(6.42) \qquad MRS^h_{X_1, X_m} = MRT_{X_1, X_m}$$

These are the standard pareto-optimal conditions for private goods developed in Chapter 2 which will be generated by competitive markets for 1 and m, a point also demonstrated in Chapter 2. Therefore, the existence of nonexclusive goods does not upset the competitive allocations of the other pure private goods, at least with first-best assumptions. That this property could have been demonstrated just as easily in the model of exclusive goods that generate externalities should be obvious from the structural similarities of the two models developed in this chapter.

Government Policy Problems

Knowing that it should purchase a nonexclusive good to the point at which $\sum_{h=2}^{H} MRS^h_{X_{1k}, X_{h1}} = MRT_{X_k, X_1}$ may not be very helpful to the government in practice, since it still has the vexing problem of determining each person's MRS under the handicap of nonrevelation. The problem is not that a MRS is a special theoretical construct which cannot be observed in practice. For pure private goods its value is easily determined. Assuming rational behavior, the marginal rate of substitution between any two goods for any consumer simply equals the price ratio of the two goods. Rather, the problem is nonexclusivity, nonrevelation, per se. Unfortunately, competitive market analogues are of little help. The government cannot simply set a tax (price), ask each consumer how

FIGURE 6–2

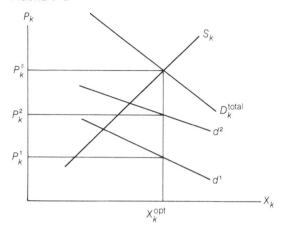

much he would be willing to buy at that price, and compare quantities demanded with quantities supplied at the producer price to check for equilibrium. If consumers thought they might actually have to buy the stated amounts at the going price, they might well hide their preferences. But even if nonrevelation were not a problem, this competitive process would not generate the pareto-optimal quantity in any case because the market analogue is reversed for nonexclusive goods. In terms of standard supply and demand concepts, the proper method of reaching equilibrium is for the government to call out an output, ask each consumer how much he would be willing to pay for the last unit of the good, add each consumer price, and compare the aggregate consumer price with the producer (marginal cost) price to determine if an equilibrium has been achieved.

Every consumer presumably has a demand curve for the nonexclusive good even if he won't reveal it. Just as with the externality portion of exclusive goods, these demand curves must be added vertically, not horizontally, to arrive at aggregate demand. (There is no further horizontal summation, however, since the quantity selected by the government *is* the aggregate quantity.) The quantity at which the vertical summation of individual demand curves intersects the supply curve satisfies the pareto-optimal condition (6.38).

This reversed competitive process is depicted in Figure 6–2 for the two-person case. In the diagram:

1. d^1 and d^2 are the individual's demand curves for X_k, reflecting their respective $MRS^i_{k,1}$ at every X_k, with good 1 the numeraire.
2. D^{total}_k is the vertical summation of d^1 and d^2.
3. S_k is a normal supply curve for X_k, reflecting the $MRT_{k,1}(MC_k)$ at every X_k, with good 1 the numeraire.
4. P^s_k is the producers' supply price at X^{opt}_k.
5. $P^2_k = MRS^2_{X_k,X_{21}}$ at X^{opt}_k (assuming $P_1 = 1$).
6. $P^1_k = MRS^1_{X_k,X_{11}}$ at X^{opt}_k.

At X_k^{opt},

(6.43) $$P_k^s = P_k^1 + P_k^2$$

or

(6.44) $$MRT_{X_k, X_1} = MRS_{X_k, X_{11}}^1 + MRS_{X_k, X_{21}}^2$$

Thinking in terms of defense, if the last weapon system costs \$20 billion, and in the aggregate consumers are willing to pay \$20 billion based on their marginal rates of substitution, the defense budget is in equilibrium.

Thus, it is possible to describe a competitive analogue for establishing equilibrium for nonexclusive goods. But this is not terribly useful in practice, since consumers have little incentive to reveal their demand prices at each quantity. The government has little choice but to select a quantity and hope that its choice is correct without benefit of the normal market signals to aid its judgement.

Payment for the Public Good

In strictly formal terms, the question: "How should people be taxed to pay for a nonexclusive good such as defense?" can be viewed as uninteresting. The allocational issue involves the government selecting a given quantity of the good and hoping that the pareto-optimal condition is satisfied. Suppose it is. The government's output choice is a lump-sum event from each consumer's point of view, and since the government is not interfering in any other market, the pareto-optimal conditions for all other goods and factors will hold as well. In order to preserve these conditions, all the government need do is raise taxes on a lump-sum basis. There is an infinity of choices, such as a head tax based on age scaled upward or downward until sufficient revenues have been collected. Of course, any given tax will shift people's demands for the nonexclusive good, simply because their incomes will have changed, thus dictating a new output choice to satisfy the pareto-optimal condition for the nonexclusive good. But any pattern of lump-sum taxes will permit all the pareto-optimal conditions to hold by the definition of a lump-sum tax. The "only" allocational problem for the government remains selecting the correct output for the chosen tax. Furthermore, all adverse distributional consequences of a particular tax will be fully offset by the lump-sum redistributions that satisfy the interpersonal equity conditions. In this sense, then, the tax question is uninteresting.

Nonetheless, public sector economists have expressed considerable interest in the payments mechanism, for two reasons. In the first place, citizens may not accept any pattern of lump-sum taxation to pay for these goods, especially if there is no strong consensus regarding the social welfare function. They may well insist that the taxes satisfy commonly accepted notions of distributional justice, that they be fair as well as efficient. Second, it would be extremely helpful if the tax system induced people to reveal their true preferences for the nonexclusive good. If the free-rider problem can be avoided, the government will have removed the principal barrier toward achieving the pareto-optimal allocation. Should these taxes also be deemed equitable, so much the better. Let us consider the question of equity first.

The Benefits-Received Principle of Taxation

Although there are no equity standards agreed to by all people, two general principles of fair taxation have gained remarkably wide acceptance in Western economic thought. Taxes are deemed fair if they are related to the *benefits received* from public goods and services, or if they are closely related to each person's *ability to pay*.

The *benefits-received principle of taxation* is meant to apply to all resource-using public expenditures, such as nonexclusive goods. Its rationale is based on the following argument:

> The government is engaged in allocational activities only because one of the technical assumptions underlying a well-functioning market system fails to hold and the competitive market system is signaling an incorrect allocation of resources. Since the government is merely substituting for the competitive market system in these instances, taxes raised to finance these activities should imitate the *quid-pro-quo* aspect of market prices. Competitive markets in effect extract payments from consumers and producers reflecting the benefits received from their market transactions. Thus, taxes should reflect the benefits received from government services.

The benefits-received principle is obviously limited to the allocational, or resource using, part of the government's budget. Transfer payments designed to achieve distributional goals cannot possibly be financed in accordance with this principle. Consequently, public sector economists have adopted a second practical guideline for equitable taxation, the *ability-to-pay* criterion, first proposed by Adam Smith.[9] It simply states that taxes raised to support distributional programs should be related to each person's ability to pay. It is also used as the default option for allocational expenditures when, for some reason, taxes cannot easily be related to benefits received. Since the overall distributional impact of a tax-transfer program depends as much on the manner in which taxes are raised as on the pattern of transfer payments, the ability-to-pay principle is obviously closely related to society's distributional norms. It will be discussed in detail in Chapters 12 and 13. Our present goal is to consider fair tax schemes designed to finance expenditures on nonexclusive goods, for which the benefits-received principle is meant to apply.

Saying that taxes should be related to the benefits received from public expenditures is still too general for policy purposes, for it begs the obvious question of exactly what benefits should be used: total?, average?, marginal?, and so forth. There is less agreement on this subsidiary question than on the general principle itself, but one can make an excellent case for choosing marginal benefits as the fairest tax base. If society firmly believes in competitive market principles and views the government as an agent merely substituting for the market in any of these allocational areas, then a tax system that duplicates competitive

---

[9] Adam Smith, *The Wealth of Nations*, ed. E. Cannan (New York: G. P. Putnam's Sons, 1904), vol. II, p. 310. The ability-to-pay doctrine is also closely associated with John Stuart Mill. See John Stuart Mill, *Principles of Political Economy*, ed. W. J. Ashley (London: Longmans Green & Co., Ltd., 1921).

pricing principles ought to be considered fair by that society. Of course, competitive prices equal marginal benefits, more accurately consumers' (producers') marginal rates of substitution (marginal rates of transformation) between any two goods (factors). If taxes also equal marginal rates of substitution, then they truly become pseudo competitive prices. It hardly matters whether one labels them taxes or prices.

Following this competitive interpretation of the benefits-received principle, the government ideally should levy a set of H differential taxes to pay for the nonexclusive good, equal to each person's marginal rate of substitution between the good and a private (numeraire) good at the quantity selected by the government. In terms of Figure 6–2, person 2 would pay a tax $t_k^2 = P_k^2$, and person 1 a tax $t_k^1 = P_k^1$. In equilibrium, these taxes would add exactly to the supply price P_k, equal to the marginal cost of producing X_k at the equilibrium output. Taxing or pricing in this way is know as Lindahl pricing, after the Swedish economist Eric Lindahl, who first proposed this method of taxation.[10] Lindahl prices have the dual properties of preserving allocational efficiency *and* satisfying widely held notions of tax equity because of their direct correspondence with competitive market pricing. Notice, further, that these taxes are exactly equivalent to the optimal taxes for externality-generating exclusive goods. Those taxes (subsidies) *had* to be directly related to marginal damage (benefit) in order to achieve pareto optimality. In fact, interpreting benefits received as *marginal* benefits received is required for most allocation problems. Lindahl prices are not necessary for achieving pareto optimality with nonexclusive goods, but they do happen to support the efficient allocation. Their basic appeal remains one of equity, that they represent a competitive interpretation of the benefits-received principle of taxation.

One might well ask how Lindahl prices can be said to imitate competitive pricing, since everyone faces the same price in the market system, whereas Lindahl prices may differ for each person. The answer lies in the peculiar way in which nonexclusive goods must be marketed, described above. For normal markets, in which price is the common parameter faced by all consumers, each person is allowed to buy different quantities, but in doing so everyone will reach a point at which price equals his marginal rate of substitution, assuming the numeraire good is the basis of comparison. Hence, in equilibrium, marginal rates of substitution will be equal for all consumers, but quantities purchased will differ, in general. Recall that the situation is reversed for the nonexclusive good. Everyone is forced to consume the same quantity. Since people's tastes differ, so too will their marginal rates of substitution at that quantity, implying that the price (tax) each pays will differ as well. The normative competitive pricing principle common to both situations is that price should equal a con-

---

[10] E. Lindahl, *Die Gerechtigkeit der Besteverung*, Lund, 1919, reprinted (in part) in R. A. Musgrave and A. T. Peacock, eds., *Classics in the Theory of Public Finance* (New York-London, 1958). See also subsequent developments in L. Johansen, "Some Notes on the Lindahl Theory of Determination of Public Expenditures," *International Economic Review*, September 1963; and P.A. Samuelson, "Pure Theory of Public Expenditures and Taxation," in J. Margolis and H. Guitton, eds., *Public Economics* (New York: St. Martin's Press, 1969).

FIGURE 6–3

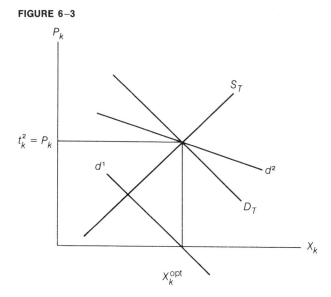

sumer's marginal rate of substitution as the proper reflection of his willingness to pay on the margin. The properties of the good being marketed will determine whether or not a single price satisfies this principle.

It should be noted that virtually any set of differential taxes is consistent with competitive pricing applied to nonexclusive goods. Returning to the two-person example in Figure 6–2, it might well be that at the equilibrium quantity person 1 values the marginal unit at zero, as in Figure 6–3. If the quantity X_k^{opt} really is pareto optimal, then $t_k^2 = P_k$ as drawn, and person 2 would pay for the good in its entirety. Person 1 would pay nothing, even though in a total or average sense he benefits from having the good, as evidenced by his willingness to pay positive prices for inframarginal units of the good. In fact, depending on the slopes of d^1 and d^2, person 1 may actually be willing to pay more for X_k on a unit-by-unit basis than person 2, even though his marginal evaluation of the good is zero. Thus, a tax schema based on marginal benefits can produce strikingly different results from one based on total or average benefits received.

It could also happen that at the optimum, person 1 believes the government has purchased too much X_k, so that from his point of view the marginal units actually do harm. If this were true, then $t_k^1 < 0$, and $t_k^2 > P_k$, as shown in Figure 6–4. Person 2 pays *more* per unit than competitive producers require to supply the good, and subsidizes person 1 for the harm caused him on the margin at the equilibrium. Notice that these particular subsidies have nothing whatsoever to do with standard distributional issues. They simply reflect taxes set equal to marginal rates of substitution.

This situation is hardly an anomaly—it almost certainly applies to defense spending, at least in the United States. Some people believe the defense budget is much too large and causes them positive harm, at least on the margin. Others

FIGURE 6–4

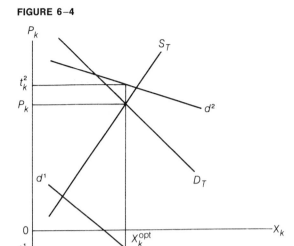

would just as clearly be willing to accept an increase in their current tax burdens if the additional revenues were spent on defense. In the late 1960s some people refused to pay their federal income taxes in protest against the war in Vietnam. Their protest highlighted one of the problems peculiar to nonexclusive goods. If a consumer does not want an exclusive good, he may simply refuse to buy it. This choice does not exist for the nonexclusive goods, but at the very least these protesters felt entirely justified in not paying to support the U.S. effort in Vietnam. On the whole, these people were probably not staunch believers in competitive market principles, yet these principles supported their protest rather well. One wonders how much of a subsidy would have been required to offset the harm done to them, and whether the war effort really was pareto optimal. Some of these people obviously had extremely negative marginal rates of substitution. In principle, even a relatively few negative marginal rates of substitution could generate an $X_k^{opt} \approx 0$ according to the pareto-optimal rule, if they were extremely negative. Of course, the war protest turned on other moral issues. The purely economic competitive market principle was hardly, if ever, used, but it certainly could have been.

At the other extreme, many who wanted an even stronger U.S. commitment undoubtedly believed very strongly in competitive pricing principles. Would they have been willing to pay the Lindahl subsidy consistent with these principles? Probably not, the point being that the commitment to a competitive market interpretation of the benefits-received principle might not necessarily be very strong, despite the logic of its underlying rationale. It can easily be overridden by other moral principles, such as the principle that everyone ought to support the country in time of U.S. military involvement. Even on more narrow economic grounds, people's commitments to various ethical principles might well become confused. For instance, people may simply reject the notion of differential payments for goods commonly consumed. Equal payment for equal consumption might well appeal to many people's sense of equity, even though this criterion bears no close relationship to competitive market pricing principles in which marginal benefit, not consumption, is what counts. Moreover, an appeal to pure economic theory cannot resolve these confusions. Recall that *any* payment schema for nonexclusive goods is consistent with pareto optimality, so long as it is lump sum. A benefits-received principle consistent with competitive market principles is required in other contexts, but not here.[11]

Preference Revelation and Taxation

In 1971 Edward Clarke achieved a significant theoretical breakthrough by describing a set of taxes that would, in principle, avoid the "free-rider" problem with nonexclusive goods.[12] His schema of necessity breaks with the competitive pricing model which, as we have seen, offers no incentive for people to reveal their preferences. Rather, his taxes are based on the preferences of all others in society, as follows.

Suppose the nonexclusive good, k, is competitively supplied at constant cost, with $P_k = MC_k$. Without loss of generality, set $P_k \equiv \$1$. The government begins by assigning arbitrary tax shares t_h to each person, with $\sum_{h=1}^{H} t_h = 1$, and asks everyone to reveal his demand curve for the public good, d_k^h. Ordinarily, the intersection of the horizontal price line, $\$1$, and the vertical summation of the individual d_k^h would determine the optimal quantity of the public good, but the government has no assurance that the consumers have revealed their true preferences. Hence, the government proceeds as follows. Consider person i. All demand curves except person i's are summed vertically, and the government selects the quantity given by the intersection of this new aggregate demand curve and $(\$1 - t_i)$, the combined tax share of the other $(H - 1)$ individuals. This initial selection is depicted in Figure 6–5, as quantity X_k^A, with

AD = the vertical summation of all H announced demand curves.

$AD - d_i$ = the vertical summation of all but person i's demand curve.

$\$1 - t_i$ = the assigned tax share of the other $(H - 1)$ individuals combined.

---

[11] The entire discussion of Lindahl pricing as a benefits-received tax points out that, strictly speaking, the benefits-received principle has no real standing *as an equity principle* in the formal neoclassical model of social welfare maximization. All equity considerations in the formal model are contained in the social welfare function, which bears no relationship at all to any benefits-received tax, including Lindahl prices. (We are grateful to Robin Boadway for emphasizing this point.) Nonetheless, benefits received as an equity principle was well established in the public sector literature prior to the advent of the formal neoclassical model.

[12] E. H. Clarke, "Multipart Pricing of Public Goods," *Public Choice*, Fall 1971; and Edward Clarke, "Multipart Pricing of Public Goods: An Example," in S. Mushkin, ed., *Public Prices for Public Products* (Washington, D.C.: Urban Institute, 1972). The discussion in the text closely follows the presentation of "Clarke taxes" by Tideman and Tullock in T. N. Tideman and G. Tullock, "A New and Superior Process for Making Social Choices," *Journal of Political Economy*, December 1976. By now, a number of preference revelation mechanisms have appeared in the literature. For an alternative tax schema applicable to many public goods simultaneously, see T. Groves and M. Loeb, "Incentives and Public Inputs," *Journal of Public Economics*, August 1975.

FIGURE 6-5

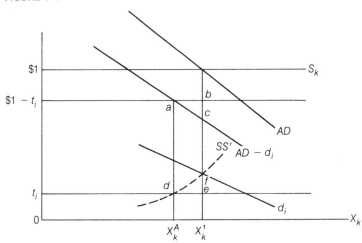

Person i is then given the following choice. He can accept X_k^A, with a total tax payment $t_i \cdot X_k^A$. Alternatively, the government will increase (decrease) the amount of X_k, providing person i pays an additional "Clarke tax" (receives an additional Clarke subsidy) equal to the amount required to make all the other consumers indifferent to the change. For instance, should person i vote an increase to X_k^1, his Clarke tax would be equal to the triangle abc. Generally, his Clarke taxes or subsidies are given by the areas between SS' and t_i, the mirror image of the areas between $(AD - d_i)$ and ($\$1 - t_i$). Hence, area $def =$ area abc. Unless d_i is horizontal at t_i, person i will always choose the Clarke tax (subsidy) *and* reveal his true preferences. As drawn in Figure 6–5, if d_i is his true demand curve, person i will choose X_k^1 and pay the Clarke tax def, in addition to the assigned tax share $t_i \cdot X_k^1$. Any other choice will reduce the net benefits from consuming X_k. If d_i were false, it would pay the consumer to select the intersection of the true d_i and SS' and pay the corresponding Clarke tax (receive the corresponding Clarke subsidy) along with the assigned tax share. Hence, self-interest dictates true revelation of preferences, and what holds for person i holds for all. Once each individual is confronted with the same choice, the adjusted X_k^1 in Figure 6–5 will correspond to the true pareto optimum.

Notice that the Clarke tax schema bears no necessary relationship to Lindahl prices, or any other tax schema that might be deemed equitable, since the assignment of initial tax shares is entirely arbitrary. However, Tideman and Tullock argue that Clarke taxes could be made consistent with Lindahl prices by letting one citizen assign the tax shares under the following condition: the assignor pays a penalty equal to some proportion of aggregate Clarke taxes.[13] Presumably this person would have an incentive to minimize Clarke taxes,

---

[13] Tideman and Tullock, "A New and Superior Process for Making Social Choices," p. 1156.

which implies reassigning taxes shares as closely as possible to each person's true marginal evaluation. In the best of all worlds, then, people reveal their true preferences by means of the Clarke tax schema, the government chooses the true pareto-optimal allocation of X_k, and tax payments correspond to Lindahl pricing, the competitive interpretation of the benefits-received principle of taxation.

Of course, it is extremely doubtful that any government could administer the Clarke schema even approximately over a large population. The computational requirements are obviously enormous. And even if it could, Tideman and Tullock note that each individual Clarke tax is likely to be quite small, enough so that many people might actually abstain from voting for a new allocation. Moreover, they also show how coalitions might form to undermine its revelation properties.[14] One must conclude that Clarke taxes do not resolve the free-rider problem as a practical matter.[15]

AGGREGATE EXTERNALITIES

Thus far we have considered two kinds of externalities, each of which is likely to cause severe practical problems for a government commited to applying standard neoclassical policy norms: externalities arising from exclusive goods for which the identify of each individual consumer matters, and nonexclusive goods. Fortunately, a number of important externalities have a special form much more amenable to corrective public policy action. Consider the example of highway congestion. An additional car on a congested highway generates an external diseconomy to anyone driving on the highway because it adds to the total number of vehicles on the road, to the *total* amount of congestion. But no one should care who is actually driving the additional car. This is an example of an *aggregate externality*, meaning that the external effect depends only upon the aggregate level of some exclusive economic activity. The identity of the individuals constituting the aggregate is irrelevant. An individual's consumption matters only in that a *ceteris paribus* change in each level of individual consumption will change *aggregate* consumption. In terms of the congestion example, if X_{ik} = person i's use of a particular highway, we can write:

$$(6.45) \quad C = C\left(\sum_{i=1}^{H} X_{ik}\right) = C(X_k) \quad \frac{\partial C}{\partial X_{ik}} = \frac{\partial C}{\partial X_k} \quad \text{all } i = 1, \ldots, H$$

where:

C = congestion on the highway.

X_k = aggregate use of the highway at any given time.

---

[14] Ibid, pp. 1156–58.

[15] On the other hand, Johansen argues that the free-rider problem is overblown anyway, in that elected representatives have numerous political incentives to reveal their preferences. L. Johansen, "The Theory of Public Goods: Misplaced Emphasis?," *Journal of Public Economics*, February 1977.

The condition $\partial C/\partial X_{ik} = \partial C/\partial X_k$ implies that unit changes in any person's consumption has an identical effect on total congestion. If consumers only care about the aggregate level of congestion, then they will each have a utility function of the form:

$$(6.46) \qquad U^h = U^{*h}[X_{hn}; X_{hk}; C(X_k)] = U^h\left(X_{hn}; X_{hk}; \sum_{i=1}^{H} X_{ik}\right)$$

where:

$X_{hn} =$ good (factor) n consumed (supplied) by person h, $n = 1, \ldots, k-1, k+1, \ldots, N$, each assumed to be a pure private good (factor).

$X_{hk} =$ use of the highway by person h.

C and X_k as above.

$U^h(\ )$ has the following properties:

$$(6.47) \qquad \frac{\partial U^{*h}}{\partial X_{ik}} = \frac{\partial U^h}{\partial X_k} \qquad i \neq h$$

$$(6.48) \qquad \frac{\partial U^{*h}}{\partial X_{ik}} = \frac{\partial U^h}{\partial X_{hk}} + \frac{\partial U^h}{\partial X_k} \qquad i = h$$

If anyone but person h uses the road, his utility is affected simply because aggregate road use increases, thus increasing congestion. When person h uses the road, however, there are two distinct effects. On the one hand, he is adding to the congestion exactly as any other driver would, and with the same consequences for his utility. On the other hand, person h has some private reason for choosing to be on the road that is totally unrelated to the congestion problem. He may or may not consciously understand that his choice to drive on the road necessarily contributes to the congestion and thereby lowers his utility, a point we will return to below. But he certainly views his own use of the road differently from anyone else's use of the road. This is why the derivative of U^h with respect to X_{hk} has two separate terms. Note, finally, that congestion must be a function of aggregate road use, not a general function of individual road use such as $C^* = C^*(X_{1k}, \ldots, X_{ik}, \ldots, X_{Hk})$. With this more general formulation, $\partial U^{*h}/\partial X_{ik} \neq \partial U^{*h}/\partial X_{jk}$, $i \neq j$, and we are back in a situation of externalities in which the individual consumer matters.

Congestion is not the only example of an aggregate externality by any means. Virtually all pollution externalities affecting consumers, whether caused by other consumers or by producers, can be though of as aggregate externalities arising from some exclusive economic activity. Smog, noise pollution, and industrial air and water pollution all share this property, one that is extremely important for policy purposes. If an externality does have an aggregate formulation, it can usually be corrected by a single tax levied on each person in the externality-causing activity. The government need not design a set of H taxes, one specific to each individual. The single tax solution depends upon one additional behavioral assumption, that when an individual engages in the activity for his own personal reasons, he ignores the effect of his activity on the aggregate externality. This is certainly plausible.

To derive the single tax case, consider social welfare maximization when a single exclusive good (factor) k gives rise to an aggregate externality affecting all other consumers. Assume all other $(N - 1)$ goods and factors are purely private. The government's problem becomes:

$$\max_{(X_{hn}; X_{ik})} W\left[U^h\left(X_{hn}; X_{hk}; \sum_{i=1}^{H} X_{ik} \right) \right]$$

$$\text{s.t.} \quad F\left(\sum_{h=1}^{H} X_{hn}; \sum_{i=1}^{H} X_{ik} \right) = 0$$

where:

$$n = 1, \ldots, k - 1, k + 1, \ldots, N.$$

Interpersonal Equity Conditions

As always in first-best analysis, we will need the interpersonal equity conditions as a prerequisite to obtaining the pareto-optimal conditions. Consider the first-order conditions with respect to two different people's consumption (supply) of good 1, say, X_{h1} and X_{j1}.

The first-order conditions are:

(6.49)
$$X_{h1}: \quad \frac{\partial W}{\partial U^h} \frac{\partial U^h}{\partial X_{h1}} = \lambda F_1$$

(6.50)
$$X_{j1}: \quad \frac{\partial W}{\partial U^j} \frac{\partial U^j}{\partial X_{j1}} = \lambda F_1$$

Thus,

(6.51)
$$\frac{\partial W}{\partial U^i} \frac{\partial U^i}{\partial X_{i1}} = \quad \text{all } i = 1, \ldots, H$$

the standard result.

Pareto-Optimal Conditions

Compare the first-order conditions for person i's consumption of the externality good (factor), k, and his consumption of any other good (factor), say, good 1 (X_{i1}).

The first-order conditions are:

(6.52)
$$X_{ik}: \quad \frac{\partial W}{\partial U^i} \frac{\partial U^i}{\partial X_{ik}} + \sum_{h=1}^{H} \frac{\partial W}{\partial U^h} \frac{\partial U^h}{\partial X_{ik}} = \lambda F_k$$

(6.53)
$$X_{i1}: \quad \frac{\partial W}{\partial U^i} \frac{\partial U^i}{\partial X_{i1}} = \lambda F_1$$

Condition (6.52) for X_{ik} reflects the fact that person i receives personal enjoyment from good (factor) k (the first term) and that his consumption affects everyone, *including himself*, through the externality (second term). Because the externality is of the aggregate form, condition (6.52) can be rewritten

$$(6.54) \qquad X_{ik}: \quad \frac{\partial W}{\partial U^i} \frac{\partial U^i}{\partial X_{ik}} + \sum_{h=1}^{H} \frac{\partial W}{\partial U^h} \frac{\partial U^h}{\partial X_k} = \lambda F_k$$

where:

$$X_k = \sum_{i=1}^{H} X_{ik}$$

Next follow the usual procedure for obtaining the pareto-optimal conditions by dividing (6.54) by (6.53) to obtain:

$$(6.55) \qquad \frac{\dfrac{\partial W}{\partial U^i} \dfrac{\partial U^i}{\partial X_{ik}} + \displaystyle\sum_{h=1}^{H} \dfrac{\partial W}{\partial U^h} \dfrac{\partial U^h}{\partial X_k}}{\dfrac{\partial W}{\partial U^i} \dfrac{\partial U^i}{\partial X_{i1}}} = \frac{F_k}{F_1} \qquad i = 1, \ldots, H$$

Assuming the interpersonal equity conditions have been achieved for good (factor) 1, separating the left-hand side of (6.55) into $(H + 1)$ terms, selectively substituting the interpersonal equity conditions term by term, and canceling the social welfare derivatives $\partial W/\partial U^h$ in each term, yields:

$$(6.56) \qquad \frac{\dfrac{\partial U^i}{\partial X_{ik}}}{\dfrac{\partial U^i}{\partial X_{i1}}} + \sum_{h=1}^{H} \left(\frac{\dfrac{\partial U^h}{\partial X_k}}{\dfrac{\partial U^h}{\partial X_{h1}}} \right) = \frac{F_k}{F_1} \qquad i = 1, \ldots, H$$

Condition (6.56) can be rewritten as:

$$(6.57) \qquad MRS^i_{X_{ik}, X_{i1}} + \sum_{h=1}^{H} MRS^h_{X_k, X_{h1}} = MRT_{X_k, X_1} \qquad i = 1, \ldots, H$$

Pareto optimality requires that the marginal rate of transformation between goods (factors) k and 1 be equal to each person's marginal rate of substitution between his personal use of k and good 1, plus the summation of everyone's (his own included) marginal rate of substitution between the externality and good 1. Bringing all the externality terms over to the right-hand side,

$$(6.58) \qquad MRS^i_{X_{ik}, X_{i1}} = MRT_{X_k, X_1} - \sum_{h=1}^{H} MRS_{X_k, X_{h1}} \qquad i = 1, \ldots, H$$

Notice that the right-hand side of (6.58) is independent of i. That is, each consumer's "personal use" marginal rate of substitution differs from the marginal rate of transformation by the same amount, the summation of all marginal external effects. This differs significantly from the result when the externality depended upon who consumed good k. In that case, pareto optimality required:

(6.59)
$$\sum_{h=1}^{H} MRS^h_{X_{ik},X_{h1}} = MRT_{X_k,X_1}$$

or

(6.60)
$$MRS^i_{X_{ik},X_{i1}} = MRT_{X_k,X_1} - \sum_{h \neq i} MRS^h_{X_{ik},X_{h1}}$$

Hence, the personal use marginal rates of substitution differ from the marginal rate of transformation by a variable amount, depending upon whose personal use is being considered. Consequently, H taxes were required to correctly allocate good k, one for each consumer.

On the other hand, in the aggregate case only a single tax is necessary. Let good (factor) 1 be the numeraire, $P_1 \equiv 1$. Faced with a producer price P_k, the producers will set $P_k = MRT_{X_k,X_1}$ by profit maximization. Faced with a consumer price q_k, each consumer will set $MRS^i_{X_{ik},X_{i1}} = q_k$, $i = 1, \ldots, H$, if he ignores the marginal external effect of his consumption (supply). To achieve pareto optimality, then, place a unit tax, t_k, on each consumer equal to $-\sum_{h=1}^{H} MRS^h_{X_k,X_{h1}}$, the sum of the marginal external effects. With the unit tax, and assuming utility and profit maximization,

(6.61)
$$q_k = P_k + t_k$$

and

(6.62)
$$MRS^i_{X_{ik},X_{i1}} = MRT_{X_k,X_1} - \sum_{h=1}^{H} MRS^h_{X_k,X_{h1}}$$

as required. If the external effects are diseconomies, $t_k > 0$, and vice versa, following the convention that $MRS > 0$ for goods, < 0 for bads.

The single externality tax is commonly referred to as a Pigovian tax, after the British economist A. C. Pigou, who first proposed it as a pareto-optimal solution to an externality problem.[16] Notice, however, that the single tax is correct only under two conditions: (a) that the externality has a simple, aggregate formulation; and (b) that consumers ignore all external effects when maximizing utility. The behavioral assumption is crucial because if any consumer considers so much as a single external effect, the Pigovian tax will no longer be pareto optimal. Suppose, for example, that consumer i considers both the direct personal effect and the indirect externality effect on himself when deciding how much of good k to consume. He will equate the gross of tax price, q_k, to $MRS^i_{X_{ik},X_{i1}} + MRS^i_{X_k,X_{i1}}$, and the single tax scheme breaks down. The government would need an additional tax for each consumer who considered external effects in this way, and the aggregate externality would be just as difficult to correct as externalities for which individual identities mattered.

---

[16] A. C. Pigou, *The Economics of Welfare*, 4th ed. (London: MacMillan & Co., Ltd., 1932), part II, chap. XI (p. 224 in the 1950 reprint).

FIGURE 6–6

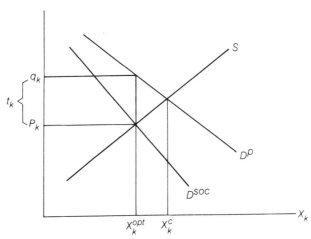

The aggregate externality case is easy to represent with standard supply and demand analysis. In Figure 6–6, S is a normal supply curve for X_k. D^p is the "private" aggregate demand curve, obtained by horizontal summation of the individuals' personal use demand curves reflecting their personal use marginal rates of substitution. D^{soc} is the true "social" demand curve equal, at every X_k, to D^p plus the (negative) aggregate marginal external effects, $\sum_{h=1}^{H} MRS^h_{X_k, X_{h1}}$. The Pigovian tax forces consumers off D^p onto D^{soc}, establishing the pareto-optimal equilibrium at the intersection of D^{soc} and S. Figure 6–6 highlights an important property of the tax, that it must equal the sum of the marginal external effects $(-\sum_{h=1}^{H} MRS^h_{X_k, X_{h1}})$ *at the optimal level of* X_k. Setting the tax equal to the aggregate marginal damage in the initial situation, presumably X_k^c, the competitive equilibrium without the tax, is not correct.

Given that only a single tax is necessary, there is at least some hope that the government can reach (approximately) the correct tax even if its initial choice is incorrect, although finding t_k^{opt} is hardly a trivial problem. The effectiveness of any trial and error solution will depend upon four factors: the exact nature of the trial and error process used, the government's ability to assess aggregate marginal damages, the shape of the marginal damage function ($\sum_{h=1}^{H} MRS^h_{X_k, X_{h1}}$, the difference between D^p and D^{soc} at each X_k), and the stability of the competitive market being taxed. For example, if the curves S, D^{priv}, and D^{soc} of Figure 6–7 describe the competitive market and the marginal damages for some actual market, then the following trial and error process is stable and will generate t_k^{opt} in the limit:[17] The government sets an initial tax equal to the

[17] See M. Kraus and H. Mohring, "The Role of Pollutee Taxes in Externality Problems," *Economica*, May 1975; and W. J. Baumol, "On Taxation and the Control of Externalities," *American Economic Review*, June 1972, for further discussion of the suitability of sequential pollution taxes in determining a global optimum.

FIGURE 6-7

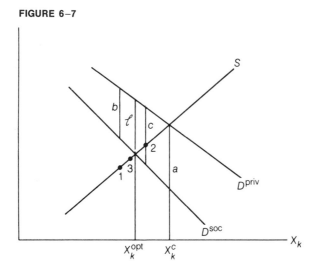

marginal damages at the no-tax competitive equilibrium and recomputes the tax to equal marginal damages at each successive equilibrium. The resulting pattern of equilibria converge to X_k^{opt}, as shown in Figure 6-7.

The tax, t_k, is initially set at a, equal to the marginal damages at X^c. With $t_k = a > t_k^{opt}$, the market overshoots X^{opt}, establishing a new equilibrium at 1 on S. The marginal damages have been reduced to b, however, so t_k is adjusted to equal b. This tax overshoots X^{opt} in the opposite direction, bringing the economy to 2 on S. Readjusting the tax to equal c, the new higher marginal damages, brings the economy to 3 on S, and so forth. The trial and error process is clearly approaching X^{opt}, with $t_k = \ell$ in the limit.

Most markets with externalities are undoubtedly similar to the one described here in that they are stable and exhibit marginal damages positively related to the level of economic activity. Hence, it is reasonable to assume that simple trial and error processes will generate results that are at least approximately optimal for a broad range of aggregate externalities.[18] As always, though, there is the usual caveat of all first-best analysis. If the government cannot achieve the interpersonal equity conditions by means of lump-sum redistributions of income, and there is no reason to suppose that it can, then a tax equal to $-\sum_{h=1}^{H} MRS_{X_k, X_{h1}}^h$ may not be consistent with the (constrained) social optimum. We will return to this point in Chapter 20, which discusses externality theory in a second-best framework.

TAXONOMIES OF EXTERNALITIES: A POSTSCRIPT

Externalities are found in such a wide variety of activities and take so many different forms that a number of public sector economists have suggested various

---

[18] There are other means besides taxes for achieving the optimum. We will consider some of the alternatives in Chapter 7 within the context of a production externality.

taxonomies for classifying the innumerable cases into a few broad prototypes, each with its own general characteristics and policy implications.[19] No one taxonomy will encompass every possible externality, but the idea is to capture most of the "important" cases with some degree of generality. Chapter 6 has its own implicit taxonomy, a three-way classification consisting of nonexclusive or jointly consumed goods, aggregate externalities arising from some exclusive activity, and individualized externalities, also arising from some exclusive activity.[20] In our view, these categories do cover most important externalities, especially since the third acts as a residual flexible enough to model the vast majority of cases. The basic point on modeling externalities that we made in the introductory remarks of this chapter bears repeating: Once one specifies which activities enter whose utility functions (production functions), there is nothing more to be done other than parameterizing the model and computing its first-order conditions. The individualized externality model admits almost all possible specifications. Our particular taxonomy also serves to highlight an extremely important policy implication: Unless an externality satisfies the conditions of the aggregate case, the government will have great difficulty designing policies consistent with first-best pareto optimality.

Despite these advantages, our taxonomy is somewhat deficient in that it accepts the characteristics of each externality as a technological datum rather than an economic decision variable.[21] In particular, it cannot neatly categorize an important set of activities in which the people affected by the externality themselves determine the number of people to be affected in order to maximize the utility received from the externality. James Buchanan first described this type of activity with reference to private clubs.[22] Hence, they have come to be known as "club goods." The idea is that membership in a club permits one access to a Samuelsonian jointly consumed good, the services provided by the club. Therefore, one decision the members must make is the optimal level of services to be jointly provided. The solution depends on the standard $\Sigma MRS = MRT$ rule. At the same time, however, the current members must also decide

---

[19] See, for example, M. Kamien, N. Schwartz, and D. Roberts, "Exclusion, Externalities, and Public Goods," *Journal of Public Economics*, vol. 2, 1973; and A. DeSerpa, "Congestion, Pollution, and Impure Public Goods, *Public Finance*, no: 1–2, 1978.

Kamien et. al., distinguish three characteristics of consumption externalities as policy relevant: (a) the appearance of some activity in someone else's utility function; (b) a parameter indicating the degree to which each person reacts to others' consumption; and (c) a parameter indicating the degree to which each person is excluded from others' consumption activities, with exclusion using up scarce resources. That is, the exclusion parameter enters society's aggregate production function.

DeSerpa believes it is most useful to determine whether or not experiencing an externality is separable from the activity generating the externality. He suggests a three way classification along these lines: (a) purely inseparable (driving-congestion), (b) purely separable (pollution), and (c) discretely inseparable (waiting in line—no externality without participation, purely inseparable with participation).

[20] There is also, of course, the additional cross-classification of consumption, production, and consumption-production externalities given in Chapter 5 which, presumably, everyone would accept. It is inherent in the definition of a technological externality that some activity enters directly into some other utility or production function.

[21] We are grateful to Liam Ebrill for calling our attention to this point.

[22] J. Buchanan, "An Economic Theory of Clubs," *Economica*, February 1965.

how large the total membership should be. Unlike the pure Samuelsonian good, they have the ability to exclude other people from consuming the joint services. That is to say, they can determine the extent of the externality and will presumably do so on the basis of standard economic calculations, equating the benefits and costs on the margin of adding new members. The benefits accrue in the form of cost spreading. Each member contributes a smaller portion of total service costs as new members are added. The costs take the form of increased congestion which reduces the marginal value of any given service level. Obviously, our model of the Samuelsonian public good would have to be modified somewhat to include the membership or exclusion decision.

If private clubs were the only example of this type of externality, "club goods" would not be of much interest, but, in fact, many locally provided public services—police, fire protection—exhibit precisely these attributes. Consequently, they have played a central role in the economic theory of fiscal federalism, the subject of Part V in the text. To avoid duplication, we will defer a formal analysis of these goods until Chapter 29.

REFERENCES

Arrow, K. J. "The Organization of Economic Activity: Issues Pertinent to the Choice of Market versus Nonmarket Allocation." In *Public Expenditure and Policy Analysis*, 2d ed., edited by R. H. Haveman and J. Margolis. Chicago: Rand McNally College Publishing Co., 1977.

Baumol, W. J. "On Taxation and the Control of Externalities." *American Economics Review*, June 1972.

Buchanan, J. "An Economic Theory of Clubs." *Economica*, February 1965.

Clarke, E. H. "Multipart Pricing of Public Goods." *Public Choice*, Fall 1971.

————. "Multipart Pricing of Public Goods: An Example." In *Public Prices for Public Products*, edited by S. Mushkin. Washington, D.C.: Urban Institute, 1972.

Coase, R. H. "The Problem of Social Cost." *Journal of Law and Economics*, October 1960.

DeSerpa, A. "Congestion, Pollution, and Impure Public Goods. *Public Finance*, no: 1-2, 1978.

Groves, T., and Loeb, M. "Incentives and Public Inputs." *Journal of Public Economics*, August 1975.

Johansen, L. "Some Notes on the Lindahl Theory of Determination of Public Expenditures." *International Economic Review*, September 1963.

————. "The Theory of Public Goods: Misplaced Emphasis?" *Journal of Public Economics*, February 1977.

Kamien, M.; Schwartz, N.; and Roberts, D. "Exclusion, Externalities, and Public Goods." *Journal of Public Economics*, vol. 2, 1973.

Kraus, M., and Mohring, H. "The Role of Pollutee Taxes in Externality Problems." *Economica,* May 1975.

Lindahl, E. Die Gerechtigkeit der Besteverung, Lund, 1919. Reprinted, in part, in *Classics in the Theory of Public Finance,* edited by R. A. Masgrave and A. T. Peacock. New York–London, 1958.

Mill, J. S. *Principles of Political Economy.* Edited by W. J. Ashley. London: Longmans Green & Co., Ltd., 1921.

Ng, Y-K. "The Paradox of Universal Externalities." *Journal of Economic Theory,* April 1975.

Pigou, A. C. *The Economics of Welfare.* 4th ed., London: MacMillan & Co., Ltd., 1932.

Samuelson, P. A. "Aspects of Public Expenditure Theories." *Review of Economics and Statistics,* November 1958.

————. "Diagrammatic Exposition of a Theory of Public Expenditure." *Review of Economics and Statistics,* November 1955.

————. "Pure Theory of Public Expenditures and Taxation." In *Public Economics,* edited by H. Guitton and J. Margolis. New York: St. Martin's Press, 1969.

————. "The Pure Theory of Public Expenditure." *Review of Economics and Statistics,* November 1954.

Smith, A. *The Wealth of Nations.* Vol. II. Edited by E. Cannan. New York: G. P. Putnam's Sons, 1904.

Tideman, T. N., and Tullock, G. "A New and Superior Process for Making Social Choices." *Journal of Political Economy,* December 1976.

7

Production externalities

A production externality requiring public sector intervention exists whenever production activity by some firm directly enters into (or "alters") the production function of at least one other firm, and this effect is not captured in the marketplace. Having analyzed various consumption externality models in some detail, there is no need for a detailed treatment of production externalities. The definition of a production externality is obviously exactly analogous to that of consumption externalities. It is not surprising, then, that the production models and the resulting pareto-optimal decision rules are virtually identical with their consumption counterparts, with the roles of consumption and production naturally reversed. In particular, there are these important similarities:

1. Pareto-optimal decision rules for consumption externalities involve equating marginal rates of transformation in production to summations of marginal rates of substitution in consumption. For production externalities, summations of marginal rates of transformation in production equate to marginal rates of substitution in consumption.
2. In both instances, the government can usually achieve pareto optimality by retaining decentralized markets and taxing (subsidizing) the externality-generating activity;
3. We saw with consumption externalities that public policy becomes extremely complex if it matters who actually consumes the externality-generating good, since the government must design a set of H corrective taxes, one for each of H people consuming the good. On the other hand, if only aggregate consumption matters for the external effect, a single tax paid by all consumers will suffice for pareto optimality. The same distinction holds true for production externalities as well.

Because of these similarities, Chapter 7 will analyze only the aggregate production externalities model. The aggregate model is by far the one most widely used in policy applications, and it provides a simple analytical framework for considering a number of policy implications that could have been discussed in the preceding chapter but are especially intuitive in a production framework. Most of the policy examples in Chapter 7 will center on pollution control since industrial pollution is a particularly appropriate and important application of the aggregate production externalities model. Having analyzed the aggregate case and noted its similarities with aggregate consumption externalities, the reader should have no difficulty modeling other types of production externalities and noting the similarities with their consumption counterparts.

THE BASIC ANALYTICAL MODEL FOR PRODUCTION EXTERNALITIES

The analysis of consumption externalities used a condensed version of the general equilibrium model in Chapter 2 for its analytical framework, of the form:

$$\max_{(X_{ik})} W[U^h(X_{ik})]$$

$$\text{s.t.} \quad F\left(\sum_{i=1}^{H} X_{ik}\right) = 0$$

where X_{ik} was defined as the consumption of good k by person i. The way in which the X_{ik} entered each person's utility function determined the appropriate policy response by the government. Production externalities can also be analyzed with a condensed version of the full general model, the only difference being that the model must highlight possible interdependencies in production rather than in consumption. To achieve this, we will ignore once again any notational distinction between goods and factors but define the arguments, X, in terms of production.

Let:

$$X_{ji} = \text{good (factor) } i \text{ supplied (demanded) by firm } j, \qquad j = 1, \ldots, J$$
$$\text{factors measured negatively.} \qquad\qquad\qquad\qquad\quad i = 1, \ldots, N$$

There are J firms and N goods and factors. Since we are now interested in production interrelationships, writing production as a single production-possibilities frontier is no longer useful. The model must retain the individual-firm production relationships from Chapter 2, which we will represent here implicitly as

$$(7.1) \qquad\qquad\qquad f^k(X_{ji}) = 0 \qquad k = 1, \ldots, J$$

This would be the most general formulation, allowing for the worst possibility that each of the J production relationships has $J \cdot N$ arguments, the production (use) of any of the N goods (factors) by any of the J firms in the economy. It also permits each good and factor to be produced, although this is not necessary. k need not be indexed from $1, \ldots, N$.

Analogous with consumption externalities, it is natural to define a pure public good (factor) as one for which

$$(7.2) \qquad\qquad\qquad \frac{\partial f^k}{\partial X_{ji}} \equiv f^k_{ji} \neq 0 \qquad \text{all } k, j = 1, \ldots, J$$

That is, production (use) of good (factor) i affects all production relationships on the margin no matter where activity i occurs. Similarly, a pure private good (factor) is one for which

(7.3)
$$\frac{\partial f^k}{\partial X_{ji}} \equiv f^k_{ji} = 0 \quad k \neq j$$

Firm k's use or production of i affects only itself on the margin. Production with private goods and factors can be represented notationally as $f^k(x_{ki}) = 0$, analogous with the notation of Chapter 6.

Relative to the full model of Chapter 2, the condensation occurs in the demand sector of the model. Interrelationships among consumers are irrelevant to the study of production externalities, so that it is no longer necessary to retain a many-consumer economy along with the social welfare function to resolve distributional questions. These could be retained, to be sure, but the existence of production externalities will not alter any of the pareto-optimal consumption conditions or the interpersonal equity social welfare conditions derived in Chapter 2. No loss of generality occurs, then, by assuming a one-consumer-equivalent economy in which the consumer supplies all factors of production and receives all the produced goods and services, providing it is understood that one-consumer equivalence arises because the government is optimally redistributing lump sum to satisfy the interpersonal equity conditions of social welfare maximization. Without this assumption (or one of the restrictions on preferences discussed in Chapter 4 that are sufficient for one-consumer equivalence) the pareto-optimal conditions developed in this chapter would literally apply only to a one-consumer economy. They would not have much normative policy significance.

With this understanding, the demand sector of the model can be represented as:

(7.4)
$$U(X_1, \ldots, X_i, \ldots, X_N) = U(X_i)$$

where:

X_i = aggregate production of (demand for) good (factor) i.

Finally, market clearance implies:

(7.5)
$$X_i = \sum_{j=1}^{J} X_{ji} \quad i = 1, \ldots, N$$

Equation (7.5) can be incorporated directly into the utility function as:

(7.6)
$$U\left(\sum_{j=1}^{J} X_{ji}\right)$$

with

$$\frac{\partial U}{\partial X_{ji}} = \frac{\partial U}{\partial X_i} \quad \begin{array}{l} j = 1, \ldots, J \\ \text{all } i = 1, \ldots, N \end{array}$$

Condition (7.6) implies that consumers should not care where production activity occurs.

Thus, the complete general model for analyzing production externalities is:

$$\max_{(X_{ji})} U\left(\sum_{j=1}^{J} X_{ji}\right)$$

$$\text{s.t.} \quad f^k(X_{ji}) = 0 \qquad k = 1, \ldots, J$$

AGGREGATE PRODUCTION EXTERNALITIES

To provide a fairly relevant context for the analysis of the aggregate externality case, suppose all firms are located around a lake and that they all use the water as a coolant for their production processes. Using the water in this manner heats it up, so that each firm returns the water to the lake at a higher temperature than it originally received the water. Naturally, the hotter the water, the less effective it is as a cooling agent. The heat, then, is the source of a technological production externality (a diseconomy), because each firm's production function is directly affected. Moreover, suppose the firms do not care who is heating the water, they merely react to the increased temperature of the water, which is in turn a function only of the total amount of water used by all the firms as a cooling agent. Thus, the heat pollution is an example of an aggregate externality.[1]

To model this example, let factor i be water and assume that all other goods and factors are purely private. The production relationships in this case are:

$$(7.7) \qquad f^{*k}(X_{kn}; X_{ki}; H) = 0 \qquad \begin{aligned} n &= 1, \ldots, i-1, i+1, \ldots, N \\ k &= 1, \ldots, J \end{aligned}$$

and

$$(7.8) \qquad H = H\left(\sum_{j=1}^{J} X_{ji}\right)$$

where:

H = heat.

Substituting H into f^{*k} yields:

$$(7.9) \qquad f^k\left(X_{kn}; X_{ki}; \sum_{j=1}^{J} X_{ji}\right) = 0 \qquad k = 1, \ldots, J$$

These production relationships distinguish between each firm's private use of water as a coolant, represented by the argument X_{ki}, and the external effect

---

[1] Notice that if the firms were situated along a river, as is often the case, the aggregate model would not apply. The firm furthest upstream would be unaffected by how any of the remaining firms use the water; the second firm would be affected only by the first firm's use of the water; and so on, so that it matters to each firm who uses the water. Unfortunately the aggregate model may not be as generally applicable for industrial pollution as it is for pollution affecting consumers. To the extent this is so, corrective public policy action becomes much more difficult to implement, as we have seen with consumption externalities.

of the heat, represented by the argument $\sum_{j=1}^{J} X_{ji}$. Thus,

$$(7.10) \qquad \frac{\partial f^{*k}}{\partial X_{ji}} = \frac{\partial f^{k}}{\partial X_{i}} \qquad j \neq k$$

$$(7.11) \qquad \frac{\partial f^{*k}}{\partial X_{ji}} = \frac{\partial f^{k}}{\partial X_{ji}} + \frac{\partial f^{k}}{\partial X_{i}} \qquad j = k$$

That is, if firm k uses water, its production function is twice affected on the margin, once by the cooling effect of the water and once by the increased heat to which it contributes. When some other firm uses water, firm k is affected only because the water temperature has increased.

Combining (7.6) and (7.9) the complete model of social welfare maximization is:

$$\max_{(X_{jn}; X_{ji})} U\left(\sum_{j=1}^{J} X_{ji} \right)$$

$$\text{s.t.} \quad f^{k}\left(X_{kn}; X_{ki}; \sum_{j=1}^{J} X_{ji} \right) \qquad \begin{array}{l} n = 1, \ldots, i-1, i+1, \ldots, N \\ k, j = 1, \ldots, J \end{array}$$

Supplying Lagrangian multipliers, λ^{k}, for each of the production functions, the Lagrangian is:

$$\max_{(X_{jn}; X_{ji})} L = U\left(\sum_{j=1}^{J} X_{ji} \right) + \sum_{k=1}^{J} \lambda^{k} f^{k}\left(X_{kn}; X_{ki}; \sum_{j=1}^{J} X_{ji} \right)$$

The First-Order Conditions—Pareto Optimality

In production models of this type, with one-consumer economics, there are only pareto-optimal conditions, which are derived by considering any two activities by any one firm. Let us first establish the important result that the presence of production externalities in some markets implies intervention only in those markets. The perfectly competitive allocation is correct for all other activities. To see this, consider goods (factors) m and 1 supplied (demanded) by firm j, X_{jm} and X_{j1}, $m \neq i$.

The first-order conditions are:

$$(7.12) \qquad X_{jm}: \frac{\partial U}{\partial X_{m}} = -\lambda^{j} \frac{\partial f^{j}}{\partial X_{jm}} \qquad \begin{array}{l} \text{all } j = 1, \ldots, J \\ \text{any } m \neq i \end{array}$$

$$(7.13) \qquad X_{j1}: \frac{\partial U}{\partial X_{1}} = -\lambda^{j} \frac{\partial f^{j}}{\partial X_{j1}} \qquad \text{all } j = 1, \ldots, J$$

Dividing (7.12) by (7.13):

$$(7.14) \qquad \frac{\dfrac{\partial U}{\partial X_{m}}}{\dfrac{\partial U}{\partial X_{i}}} = \frac{\dfrac{\partial f^{j}}{\partial X_{jm}}}{\dfrac{\partial f^{j}}{\partial X_{j1}}} \equiv \frac{f^{j}_{jm}}{f^{j}_{j1}} \qquad \text{all } j = 1, \ldots, J$$

This is the standard competitive result, that the marginal rate of substitution in consumption between two goods or factors equals their marginal rate of transformation in production no matter where produced. Since 1 and m can be goods or factors, conditions (7.14) reproduce pareto-optimal conditions P4–P8 from the full model of Chapter 2.[2]

To derive the pareto-optimal rules for factor i (water), which generates the aggregate externality, consider the use of water by firm j and its supply of good 1, X_{ji} and X_{j1}, respectively (assume X_1 is a good for purposes of interpretation). The first-order conditions are:

$$(7.16) \qquad X_{ji}: \quad \frac{\partial U}{\partial X_i} = -\lambda^j \frac{\partial f^j}{\partial X_{ji}} - \sum_{k=1}^{J} \lambda^k \frac{\partial f^k}{\partial X_i} = -\lambda^j f^j_{ji} - \sum_{k=1}^{J} \lambda^k f^k_i$$

$$(7.17) \qquad X_{j1}: \quad \frac{\partial U}{\partial X_1} = -\lambda^j \frac{\partial f^j}{\partial X_{j1}} = \lambda^j f^j_{j1} \qquad j = 1, \ldots, J$$

Dividing (7.16) by (7.17):

$$(7.18) \qquad \frac{\dfrac{\partial U}{\partial X_i}}{\dfrac{\partial U}{\partial X_1}} = \frac{\lambda^j f^j_{ji} + \displaystyle\sum_{k=1}^{J} \lambda^k f^k_i}{\lambda^j f^j_{j1}}$$

The left-hand side has a standard interpretation as the marginal rate of substitution between the consumption of good 1 and the supply of factor i (water). To interpret the right-hand side, the λ^k multipliers must be removed. To do this, note that

$$(7.19) \qquad \frac{\partial U}{\partial X_{j1}} = \lambda^j f^j_{j1} \qquad \text{all } j = 1, \ldots, J$$

from the first-order conditions. (7.19) says that the marginal "kick" to utility from the production of good 1 must be the same no matter which firm produces it, a condition which holds if production is pareto optimal, as it will be with a perfectly competitive market for good 1. Using this result, the right-hand side can be cleared of the λ^k terms by separating the right-hand side into $J + 1$ terms, making the appropriate substitution for $\lambda^j f^j_{j1}$ in the denominator, and canceling the λ's term by term. This procedure is exactly analogous to the one

---

[2] It will be useful at this point to comment on the various possible interpretations of the production derivatives. Differentiating $f^j(\ ) = 0$ with respect to X_{j1} and X_{jm} yields:

$$(7.15) \qquad \frac{f^j_{jm}}{f^j_{j1}} = -\frac{dX_{j1}}{dX_{jm}}\bigg|_{\text{all other goods and factors constant}}$$

If both m and 1 are goods, the ratio is a marginal rate of transformation. If both are factors, it is a technical rate of substitution between the factors in production. Finally, if 1 is a good and m a factor, the ratio is the marginal product of factor m in producing good 1 (recall that factors are measured negatively). Thus, while we will speak generally of the ratio as a marginal rate of transformation throughout Chapter 7, we will switch to one of the other interpretations if a specific example warrants it.

used to simplify expressions for consumer externalities, but with this important difference. For the consumer case, the procedure was legitimate only under the assumption that the proper lump-sum redistributions were carried out to satisfy the interpersonal equity conditions of social welfare. In the production case, all that is necessary is pareto optimality for the pure private goods, which the competitive market will generate without any government policy action.

Having applied this procedure, the first-order conditions become:

$$(7.20) \qquad \frac{\frac{\partial U}{\partial X_i}}{\frac{\partial U}{\partial X_1}} = \frac{f_{ji}^j}{f_{j1}^j} + \sum_{k=1}^{J} \left(\frac{f_i^k}{f_{k1}^k} \right) \qquad \text{all } j = 1, \dots, J$$

The marginal rate of substitution between good 1 and factor i in consumption must equal, for each firm, the private use marginal product of factor i in the production of good 1 (the coolant property of the water) and the additional aggregate marginal effect that increased use of factor i has on the production of good 1 through the externality (the adverse effects on all firms production of good 1 due to increased water temperature). For firm k, the ratio $f_i^k/f_{k1}^k = -dX_{k1}/dH$, the (negative) marginal product of heat on its production of good 1. These two effects combined are the true social marginal product of factor i in the production of good 1. For purposes of further discussion, rewrite the condition (7.20) as

$$(7.21) \qquad MRS_{i,1} = MP_{ji,j1}^j + \sum_{k=1}^{J} MP_{i,k1}^k \qquad j = 1, \dots, J$$

Consistent with our analysis of an aggregate consumption externality, suppose each firm considers only the cooling properties of water when deciding how much to use. It ignores the external heat affect, not only on all others but on itself. If this is so, then the government can achieve pareto-optimal condition (7.21) by retaining a decentralized market for factor i and setting a unit tax on the use of i, equal to the sum of its external effects on the margin. Define consumer prices q_i and q_1, producer prices p_i and q_1, and a tax, t_i, such that

$$(7.22) \qquad \frac{q_i}{q_1} = \frac{p_i}{q_1} + \frac{t_i}{q_1}$$

If the market for good 1 is competitive, its consumer and producer prices will be identical in equilibrium. The consumer will equate $q_i/q_1 = MRS_{i,1}$. Each firm will equate $p_i/q_1 = MP_{ji,j1}^j$, or $p_i = MP_{ji,j1}^j \cdot q_1$, the familiar competitive result that firms equate the price of an input to the value of its marginal product. This assumes, of course, that each firm ignores the external effects of using factor i. Without any government intervention, $p_i = q_i$, and the $MRS_{i,1}$ would equal the private marginal product for each firm in equilibrium. To achieve the correct pareto-optimal conditions, the government must set $t_i = (\sum_{k=1}^{J} MP_{i,k1}^k) \cdot q_1$, equating the tax rate to the marginal value of the external effects. With this tax, and competitive behavior,

$$(7.23) \qquad \frac{q_i}{q_1} - \frac{t_i}{q_1} = MRS_{i,1} - \sum_{k=1}^{J} MP^k_{i,k1} = \frac{p_i}{q_1} = MP^j_{ji,j1} \qquad j = 1, \ldots, J$$

or

$$(7.24) \qquad MRS_{i,1} = MP^j_{ji,j1} + \sum_{k=1}^{J} MP^k_{i,k1} \qquad j = 1, \ldots, J$$

as required for pareto optimality.

A single Pigovian tax will suffice since the aggregate marginal damage is equal no matter which firm increases its use of factor i. The divergence between the marginal rate of substitution and the marginal external effects, $MRS_{i,1} - \sum_{k=1}^{J} MP^k_{i,k1}$ from equation (7.21), is independent of j. The only difference from the consumer externality is that the tax equals the value of the marginal external effects rather than the negative of this value, simply because the firm is paying the tax. If the marginal external effect is adverse as in the heat example, the tax is negative (each marginal product $MP^k_{i,k1}$ is negative) since in the new equilibrium, the producer price p_i must exceed the consumer supply price q_i. Conversely, for external economies each firm is subsidized in amount equal to the aggregate marginal external benefit of the activity. With the single tax then, the consumer's marginal rate of substitution is correctly equated to the full social marginal product of factor i in the production of good 1.

Note, finally, that the production model has been written in its most general form. Realistically, any source of pollution will affect only a small subset of firms in the economy. In terms of the general model, this simply means that in the summation of the external effects, $MP^k_{i,k1} = 0$, most k.

Geometric Interpretations

Three equivalent geometric interpretations have been commonly used in the literature to depict aggregate production externalities, especially in the context of industrial pollution. The most straightforward representation is in terms of the factor market for i (water) since this is where the external effect actually occurs.

In Figure 7–1, factor demand curve D^{priv} is the horizontal summation of each firm's private demand curve for i, equal to the firm's common private-use marginal product between good 1 and water (assuming $q_1 = p_1 = 1$, with good 1 the numeraire). The supply curve S represents consumers' marginal rate of substitution between i and 1. Without government intervention, the market clears at (X^c_i, p_c) with $q_c = MRS_i = MP^j_{ji,j1} = p_c$. The curve D^{soc} represents the true social value of marginal product between 1 and i, differing from D^{priv} at each level of input by a vertical distance equal to the external aggregate marginal damage ($\sum_{k=1}^{J} MP^k_{i,k1}$). The optimum quantity of i occurs at the intersection of D^{soc} and S, the point at which the social marginal product equals the marginal rate of substitution. If a tax is levied on the use of factor i exactly equal to the aggregate external marginal damage at the optimum, X^{opt}, then the decentralized

FIGURE 7-1

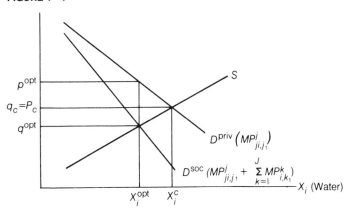

market will select X^{opt}, with producer and consumer prices p^{opt} and q^{opt}, respectively, and $q^{opt} = p^{opt} - t_i$.

An alternative supply-demand interpretation focuses on the market for good 1 (no longer assumed to be the numeraire). Figure 7-2 is meant to represent the idea that production of goods generating external diseconomies should be reduced relative to the no-intervention competitive equilibrium, X_1^c. The supply curve S is the horizontal summation of each firm's private marginal cost ($q_i/MP_{ji,j1}^j$). S^{soc} represents the true social marginal cost of producing good 1, equal to

$$\left(\frac{q_i}{MP_{ji,j1}^j + \displaystyle\sum_{k=1}^{J} MP_{i,k1}^k} = \frac{q_i}{MP_{i,1}^{soc}} \right)$$

Since $\sum_{k=1}^{J} MP_{i,k1}^k < 0$ for external diseconomies, S^{soc} lies above S^{priv}, as drawn. D is the standard aggregate demand for good 1. In equilibrium, the

FIGURE 7-2

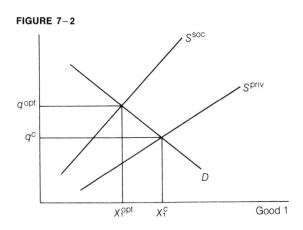

FIGURE 7-3

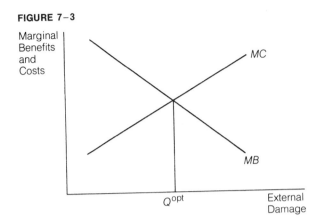

price q_1 should reflect the social marginal cost of producing good 1, as it does at (X_1^{opt}, q^{opt}) and not the private marginal cost, as at (X_1^c, q^c). This is equivalent to saying that input prices must equal the value of the social marginal products, not the value of private marginal products.

Extreme care must be taken with this geometric interpretation, however, for two reasons. First, output effects in the presence of externalities are not as straightforward as this partial equilibrium diagram might suggest. Baumol and Oates have demonstrated that with combined production and consumption externalities, which may well exist with industrial pollution, the conditions required to guarantee output reductions for activities which generate external diseconomies are fairly restrictive.[3] Second, the diagram appears to suggest that a tax on good 1 equal to the divergence between private and social marginal cost at the optimum X^{opt} will generate a pareto-optimal allocation of resources. This is generally not true, as will be demonstrated below. A single tax must be on the direct source of the externality to generate the pareto-optimal conditions, in this case on the use of factor i.

A final geometric interpretation, especially common in pollution analysis, says that the external damage should be reduced until the marginal benefits from reducing the damage just equal the marginal costs of the reduction.

In Figure 7–3, Q^{opt} represents the optimal amount of external damage. It is a useful device for showing that, in general, zero damage (pollution) is typically not the pareto-optimal solution. This diagram can be directly related to Figure 7–1 in the following manner. The marginal benefit of reducing external

[3] W. J. Baumol and W. Oates, *The Theory of Environmental Policy* (Englewood Cliffs, N.J.: Prentice-Hall, Inc., 1975), chap. 7. For a similar comprehensive analysis with consumer externalities, see P. A. Diamond and J. Mirrlees, "Aggregate Production with Consumer Externalities," *Quarterly Journal of Economics*, February 1973; and E. Sadka, "A Note on Aggregate Production with Consumer Externalities," *Journal of Public Economics*, February 1978. The earliest recognition of possible output anomalies with externalities is generally credited to Buchanan and Kafolgis in J. Buchanan and M. Kafolgis, "A Note on Public Goods Supply," *American Economic Review*, June 1963.

damage is simply the negative of the marginal cost of increasing the external damage. In Figure 7–1, this marginal cost is $\sum_{k=1}^{J} MP_{i,k1}^k$, the value of the reduction in output of good 1 through the externality caused by a marginal increase in factor i (assuming $q_1 = 1$, the numeraire). Thus, the MB curve of Figure 7–3 equals the vertical distance between D^{priv} and D^{soc} in Figure 7–1. The marginal cost of reducing damage is an opportunity cost, equal, at each factor input, to the marginal private value of factor i in production of good 1 (D^{priv} in Figure 7–1), less the value at which consumers are willing the supply factor i (curve S in Figure 7–1). Hence, the MC curve in Figure 7–3 equals the divergence between curves D^{priv} and S in Figure 7–1. Q^{opt} in Figure 7–3 thus corresponds to X^{opt} in Figure 7–1. $MB = MC$ in terms of damage reduction when the divergence between D^{priv} and D^{soc} equals the divergence between D^{priv} and S in the market for factor i.

ALTERNATIVE SOLUTIONS TO PRODUCTION EXTERNALITIES[4]

Levying a unit tax on an externality causing activity equal in value to its aggregate marginal external effects is a direct and intuitive policy prescription, but is not the only choice open to the government. Depending upon institutional and political constraints, the government may want to consider some alternative solution. This section will analyze a number of admissible alternatives, and highlight some common pitfalls, solutions that have a certain intuitive appeal at first pass but which are not able to achieve the correct pareto-optimal conditions.

Alternative Tax Policies

A unit tax (subsidy) on the externality-generating activity essentially works by changing the vector of relative prices in the economy from that which would obtain in a no-intervention competitive situation to the set of relative prices necessary to support the pareto optimum. In all nonmonetary general equilibrium models, only relative prices determine the allocation of resources, whether or not externalities are present. This implies that any set of absolute prices that maintain the unique vector of pareto-optimum relative prices is an admissible solution to the externality problem. There are an infinity of these, *including a vector in which the externality-generating activity is not taxed*, but simply retains its pre-policy value. An interesting problem, then, is to find the set of taxes (and subsidies) which generates the pareto-optimal allocation given that, for some reason, the externality causing activity cannot be taxed.

To derive the alternative taxes, recall the full set of pareto-optimal conditions for an aggregate externality generated by factor i, with all other goods and

---

[4] The analysis in this section relies heavily on a series of models developed by Holtermann in S. Holtermann, "Alternative Tax Systems to Correct for Externalities, and the Efficiency of Paying Compensation," *Economica*, February 1976.

factors purely private:

$$(7.25) \qquad \frac{U_m}{U_1} = \frac{f^j_{jm}}{f^j_{j1}} \qquad \begin{array}{l} m = 2, \ldots, i-1, i+1, \ldots, N \\ j = 1, \ldots, J \end{array}$$

$$(7.26) \qquad \frac{U_i}{U_1} = \frac{f^j_{ji}}{f^j_{j1}} + \sum_{k=1}^{J} \left(\frac{f^k_i}{f^k_{k1}} \right) \qquad j = 1, \ldots, J$$

We know that a single unit tax on factor i,

$$t_i = \sum_{k=1}^{J} \left(\frac{f^k_i}{f^k_{k1}} \right) \cdot q_1$$

will achieve the pareto optimum. Suppose, instead, the government levies unit taxes (subsidies) on all goods and factors, including factor i, such that $q_m - t_m = p_m, m = 1, \ldots, N$. Faced with these new producer prices, each profit-maximizing competitive firm will satisfy the following conditions:

$$(7.27) \ (q_m - t_m) = \left(\frac{f^j_{jm}}{f^j_{j1}} \right) \cdot (q_1 - t_1) \qquad \begin{array}{l} m = 2, \ldots, i-1, i+1, \ldots, N \\ j = 1, \ldots, J \end{array}$$

$$(7.28) \qquad (q_i - t_i) = \left(\frac{f^j_{ji}}{f^j_{j1}} \right) \cdot (q_1 - t_1) \qquad j = 1, \ldots, J$$

The consumers meanwhile will equate

$$(7.29) \qquad \frac{U_m}{U_1} = \frac{q_m}{q_1} \qquad m = 1, \ldots, N$$

Arbitrarily set $t_1 = a$. To satisfy the pareto-optimal conditions for the private goods and factors, the government must set

$$(7.30) \qquad t_m = a \cdot \left(\frac{f^j_{jm}}{f^j_{j1}} \right) \qquad m = 2, \ldots, i-1, i+1, \ldots, N$$

To see that these are the required taxes, substitute for t_m and t_1 in (7.27) to obtain

$$(7.31) \qquad \left[q_m - a \left(\frac{f^j_{jm}}{f^j_{j1}} \right) \right] = \frac{f^j_{jm}}{f^j_{j1}} (q_1 - a)$$

Hence,

$$(7.32) \qquad q_m = \left(\frac{f^j_{jm}}{f^j_{j1}} \right) \cdot q_1$$

and

$$(7.33) \qquad \frac{q_m}{q_1} = \frac{U_m}{U_1} = \frac{f^j_{jm}}{f^j_{j1}} \qquad m = 2, \ldots, i-1, i+1, \ldots, N$$

as required.

To satisfy the pareto-optimal conditions for factor i, set:

$$(7.34) \qquad t_i = a\left(\frac{f^j_{ji}}{f^j_{j1}}\right) + \sum_{k=1}^{J}\left(\frac{f^k_i}{f^k_{k1}}\right) \cdot q_1$$

Substituting t_i and t_1 into (7.28), and rearranging terms, yields:

$$(7.35) \qquad q_i = \left[\left(\frac{f^j_{ji}}{f^j_{j1}}\right) + \sum_{k=1}^{J}\left(\frac{f^k_i}{f^k_{k1}}\right)\right] \cdot q_1$$

as required. For any given a, then, the vector of taxes described by (7.30) and (7.34) will generate the pareto-optimum allocation in the presence of this particular externality. A similar exercise will obviously provide an alternative vector of taxes for any other form of production externality.

Since the value of a is arbitrary, it can be chosen to highlight a number of interesting cases. For example, $a = 0$ produces the single Pigovian tax on factor i. At the other extreme, a can be chosen such that the externality-generating activity is untaxed. Set:

$$(7.36) \qquad a = -\left(\frac{f^j_{j1}}{f^j_{ji}}\right) \cdot \sum_{k=1}^{J}\left(\frac{f^k_i}{f^k_{k1}}\right) \cdot q_1$$

Substituting (7.36) into (7.34)

$$(7.37) \qquad t_i = \left[-\left(\frac{f^j_{j1}}{f^j_{ji}}\right) \cdot \sum_{k=1}^{J}\left(\frac{f^k_i}{f^k_{k1}}\right) \cdot q_1\right]\left(\frac{f^j_{ji}}{f^j_{j1}}\right) + \sum_{k=1}^{J}\left(\frac{f^k_i}{f^k_{k1}}\right) \cdot q_1 = 0$$

Unfortunately, leaving the externality-generating activity untaxed necessitates a complex set of taxes, or subsidies, on all other goods and factors, in general. Substituting (7.36) into (7.30) yields:

$$(7.38) \qquad t_m = a \cdot \left(\frac{f^j_{jm}}{f^j_{j1}}\right) \equiv -\left(\frac{f^j_{jm}}{f^j_{j1}}\right) \cdot \left(\frac{f^j_{j1}}{f^j_{ji}}\right) \cdot \sum_{k=1}^{J}\left(\frac{f^k_i}{f^k_{k1}}\right) \cdot q_1$$

$$m = 2, \ldots, i = 1, i + 1, \ldots, N$$

Notice that these alternative taxes (subsidies) properly reflect the value of the externality. Rewrite t_1 as:

$$(7.39) \qquad t_1 = -\left(\frac{\partial i}{\partial 1}\right)_j \left[\sum_{k=1}^{J}\left(\frac{\partial 1}{\partial i}\right)_k\right] \cdot q_1,$$

and t_m as:

$$(7.40) \qquad t_m = -\left(\frac{\partial 1}{\partial m}\right)_j\left(\frac{\partial i}{\partial 1}\right)_j\left[\sum_{k=1}^{J}\left(\frac{\partial 1}{\partial i}\right)_k\right] \cdot q_1$$

where:

$$\left(\frac{\partial i}{\partial 1}\right)_j = \frac{f^j_{j1}}{f^j_{ji}}, \text{ and so forth.}$$

t_1 measures the reduction in profits throughout the economy, arising solely from the externality, resulting from a unit increase in X_{j1}. Firm j's decision to increase good 1 increases its use of factor i (1st term) which because of the externality reduces the level of good 1 in all firms, including j (2d term). Multiplying these effects by q_1 evaluates their revenue implications by the consumers' opportunity value of good 1. Similarly, t_m measures the reduction in profits throughout the economy, due solely to the external effects, caused by a unit increase in good (factor) m[5].

The direct policy implication of this exercise can be summarized as follows: If the government chooses not to tax the externality-generating activity, it must tax (or subsidize) all other goods and factors that bear a *direct* relationship to this activity through the individual firms' production functions. In the general model under consideration, this means literally all other goods and factors in the economy. With other simple externalities the subset of alternative taxes (subsidies) may not be too large (see below), but there is certainly a general presumption to attack the problem directly rather than indirectly. An equally important corollary is that it is generally not correct to substitute for the single tax on the externality-causing factor of production either a single tax (subsidy) on the output of firms using this factor or a single subsidy (tax) on some other factor that can substitute for the externality factor in the firms' production processes. For instance, if electric generating plants heat water to the detriment of other firms, do not simply tax the plants' outputs of electricity in lieu of taxing their use of water. This result was suggested above in the section on geometric interpretations. Similarly, do not subsidize the plants to cool the water before reentering it into the environment in lieu of taxing their use of water. Regardless of the intuitive appeal of these simple alternatives, they cannot achieve the pareto optimum. Formally, if factor c represents a factor that cools water, it is obvious from (7.25) and (7.26) that a subsidy to c, with $t_m = 0$, $m = 1, \ldots, c - 1, c + 1, \ldots, N$ cannot possibly achieve the pareto-optimal conditions. No value of a is consistent with this solution. Intuitively, a subsidy for coolants offers no incentive to reduce water use in the first place, so that the generating plants will use too much water and too much coolant. Furthermore, if other firms not involved in the externality use the coolant for some purpose, they will not face the same price for this resource as do the generating plants, because they are not subsidized. Hence, additional pareto-optimal conditions will fail as well.

Internalizing the Externality

Tax policy is not necessary to the solution of externalities. Suppose a single conglomerate owned all the firms affected by a particular externality. In terms of our general model, this would include every single firm in the economy,

---

[5] Firm j's decision to increase m changes good 1, other things equal (1st term), which changes its use of factor i (2d term). This, in turn, changes the level of good 1 in all firms because of the externality (3d term), which is then evaluated at q_1.

but in real life examples externalities will be much less pervasive. If one firm does own all affected firms, then its own internal profit-maximizing decision-making process will correctly account for the externality without any need of government intervention. Our model may be unduly general, but it can be used to illustrate this point quite effectively.

The single firm would solve the following problem: allocate the goods and factors among all production sites to maximize joint profits. Formally,

$$\max_{(X_{kn})} \sum_{k=1}^{J} \sum_{n=1}^{N} P_n X_{kn}$$

$$\text{s.t.} \quad f^k\left(X_{kn}; \sum_{j=1}^{J} X_{ji}\right) = 0$$

The first-order conditions for this problem are:

(7.41)
$$P_n = -\lambda^k f_{kn}^k \qquad n \neq i, k = 1, \ldots, J$$

(7.42)
$$P_i = -\lambda^k f_{ki}^k - \sum_{j=1}^{J} \lambda^j f_i^j \qquad k = 1, \ldots, J$$

It follows immediately that

(7.43)
$$\frac{P_n}{P_1} = \frac{f_{kn}^k}{f_{k1}^k} \qquad n \neq i, k = 1, \ldots, J$$

and

(7.44)
$$\frac{P_i}{P_1} = \left(\frac{f_{ki}^k}{f_{k1}^k}\right) + \sum_{k=1}^{J} \left(\frac{f_i^k}{f_{k1}^k}\right) \qquad k = 1, \ldots, J$$

If all markets are perfectly competitive, and there are no taxes, then:

$$q_n = p_n \qquad n = 1, \ldots, N$$

Thus, from utility and profit maximization,

(7.45)
$$\frac{q_n}{q_1} = \frac{U_n}{U_1} = \frac{f_{kn}^k}{f_{k1}^k} = \frac{P_n}{P_1} \qquad \begin{aligned} n \neq i \\ k = 1, \ldots, J \end{aligned}$$

and

(7.46)
$$\frac{q_i}{q_1} = \frac{U_i}{U_1} = \left(\frac{f_{ki}^k}{f_{k1}^k}\right) + \sum_{k=1}^{N} \left(\frac{f_i^k}{f_{k1}^k}\right) = \frac{p_i}{P_1} \qquad k = 1, \ldots, J$$

the required pareto-optimal conditions.

This example illustrates two important principles. The first is simply an analytical point. To determine the pareto-optimal conditions for any situation involving only production externalities, it is not necessary to develop a full general equilibrium model. All one need assume is that society is trying to maximize total profits in the economy at fixed producer prices, subject to all the production constraints. A number of researchers have exploited this property and ignored the demand side entirely. This can be misleading, however, because it is not possible to solve for the optimum prices, p_n, without specifying consumer preferences as well. Hence, all profit-maximizing specifications implicitly assume that the prices in the objective profit function are set equal to their values at the full pareto optimum.

The second principle is that *some* decision making unit has to "internalize" an externality in order to achieve pareto optimality. This is a fundamental prerequisite for any public policy designed to correct for externalities, whatever type they may be. With respect to production externalities, if the firms cannot or will not internalize the externalities by themselves, then the government must force society to "see" the correct pattern of interrelationships by setting the taxes (and subsidies) outlined above. In practice, however, effective internalization may be difficult to achieve, no matter how it is attempted. As will be discussed in detail in Part V, one of the main problems with a federalist system with national, state, and local governments is that the jurisdictional boundaries of any one government seldom correspond to the pattern of externalities present in the economy. This is particularly true for most forms of air and water pollution. Individual state and local governments often cannot internalize all the external effects simply because many of the affected citizens are not within their jurisdictions. The national government could theoretically internalize all externalities, but it seldom has the flexibility to offer variable policy solutions tailored to specific local pockets of external effects, especially if the externalities cut across lower level jurisdictions. This jurisdictional dilemma may well go a long way toward explaining why the United States has never been able to mount an effective antipollution policy.

Additional Policy Considerations

There are a number of additional policy considerations that can best be analyzed in the context of a simpler and probably more realistic model, in which only one firm is the source of the externality. Imagine a situation in which firm 1 produces a by-product, call it z_1, which enters the production function of all other firms in the economy but which is a decision variable only for the first firm. Assume, further, that z_1 has no effect on consumers, and that all other goods and factors are purely private. In this model, the production functions can be represented as:

(7.47)
$$f^1(X_{1n}; z_1)$$

(7.48)
$$f^j(X_{jn}; z_1) \qquad \begin{aligned} n &= 1, \ldots, N \\ j &= 2, \ldots, J \end{aligned}$$

The government's problem is:

$$\max_{(X_{1n}; X_{jn}; z_1)} U\left(\sum_{j=1}^{N} X_{jn} \right)$$

$$\text{s.t.} \quad \begin{aligned} f^1(X_{1n}; z_1) &= 0 \\ f^j(X_{jn}; z_1) &= 0 \end{aligned}$$

with the corresponding Lagrangian:

$$\max_{(X_{1n};X_{jn};z_1)} L = U\left(\sum_{j=1}^{N} X_{jn}\right) + \lambda^1 f^1(X_{1n};z_1) + \sum_{j=2}^{J} \lambda^j f^j(X_{jn};z_1)$$

$$j = 2, \ldots, J$$
$$n = 1, \ldots, N$$

The first-order conditions for this problem are:

(7.49)
$$U_n = \lambda^j f^j_{jn} = \lambda^1 f^1_{1n} \qquad n = 1, \ldots, N$$
$$j = 2, \ldots, J$$

(7.50)
$$\lambda^1 f^1_{z_1} + \sum_{j=2}^{J} \lambda^j f^j_{z_1} = 0$$

Alternatively,

(7.51)
$$\frac{U_n}{U_1} = \frac{f^j_{jn}}{f^j_{j1}} = \frac{f^1_{1n}}{f^1_{11}} \qquad n = 1, \ldots, N$$
$$j = 2, \ldots, J$$

and

(7.52)
$$\frac{f^1_{z_1}}{f^1_{11}} + \sum_{j=2}^{J} \left(\frac{f^j_{z_1}}{f^j_{j1}}\right) = 0$$

(7.52) follows from the fact that $\lambda^j f^j_{j1} = \lambda^1 f^1_{11} = U_1 \neq 0$, $j = 2, \ldots, J$, which can then be used to remove the Lagrangian multipliers from (7.50).

Following the same line of argument as with the aggregate externality in the original more general model, a number of important policy implications can easily be demonstrated. The first two will be left as an exercise for the reader.

1.   The government can achieve pareto optimality by setting a unit tax on firm 1's production of z_1, such that

$$t_z = -\sum_{j=2}^{J} \left(\frac{f^j_{z_1}}{f^j_{j1}}\right) \cdot q_1$$

equal to the value of the marginal external effect from producing z_1. All other goods and factors are untaxed.

2.   Alternatively, the government can achieve pareto optimality with the following set of taxes *on firm 1*:

(7.53)
$$t^1_1 = a = \left(\frac{f^1_{11}}{f^1_{z_1}}\right) \cdot \sum_{j=2}^{J} \left(\frac{f^j_{z_1}}{f^j_{j1}}\right) \cdot q_1$$

$$t^1_n = -a\left(\frac{f^1_{1n}}{f^1_{11}}\right) \qquad n = 2, \ldots, N$$

$$t^1_z = 0$$

There is no need to levy any taxes on firms $j = 2, \ldots, J$. This clarifies a point alluded to above, that in lieu of taxing the source of the externality directly, the government need tax (or subsidize) only those goods and factors which directly substitute for the externality-causing activity in production. Since z_1 is not a decision variable for firms $j = 2, \ldots, J$, their production of the other goods and factors can be left untaxed.

3. In the context of the original model it was shown that a single tax on an output or a substitute factor would not achieve pareto optimality. In terms of the current model, a similar point is that the government cannot merely subsidize (tax) firms $j = 2, \ldots, J$ for the damage (gain) caused by firm 1's production of z_1. No matter what form the subsidy (tax) may take, if firm 1 is not taxed appropriately, society cannot possibly satisfy the pareto-optimal condition (7.52). Firm 1, if untaxed, will produce z_1 until $f_{z_1}^1/f_{11}^1 = 0$, contrary to the requirements of pareto optimality. Furthermore, if the government chooses to subsidize the other firms by means of a unit subsidy (tax) of any of the other firm's outputs or inputs, or any other type of subsidy that changes their first-order profit-maximizing conditions, then a subset of conditions (7.51) must fail as well. Firms $j = 2, \ldots, J$ and firm 1 will face different prices for at least one of the N goods and factors. Consequently,

$$\frac{f_{jn}^j}{f_{j1}^j} \neq \frac{f_{1n}^1}{f_{11}^1}$$

for some n and j, contrary to the pareto-optimal conditions.

4. This leads directly to a fourth point. Suppose the government taxes z_1 correctly (assume the externality is a diseconomy for purposes of further discussion) in accordance with (1), above. If it wishes the government can use the tax revenues to compensate some or all of the remaining firms $j = 2, \ldots, J$, the "victims" of the externality, but it must do so in a lump-sum fashion. z_1 is a lump-sum event from the point of view of the other firms, so too must be the payment, or some of the pareto-optimal conditions (7.51) will fail to hold.

5. With respect to the policy of taxing z_1, the government need not place a unit tax on the entire production of z_1. It can instead tax the production of z_1 only above some arbitrary minimal level $\bar{z}$, perhaps, using the pollution example again, a level judged to be harmless. Alternatively, it can subsidize firm 1 for reducing t_1 below some other arbitrary level, $\bar{\bar{z}}_1$, perhaps the level of z_1 at the untaxed, pre-policy, competitive equilibrium. The objective profit function for firm 1 with each of these alternatives is:

(7.54) a. $\displaystyle\sum_{n=1}^{N} p_n X_{1n} - t_z z_1$

(7.55) b. $\displaystyle\sum_{n=1}^{N} p_n X_{1n} - t_z(z_1 - \bar{z}_1)$

(7.56) c. $\displaystyle\sum_{n=1}^{N} p_n X_{1n} + s_z(\bar{\bar{z}}_1 - z_1)$

where:

$s_z = $ a unit subsidy.

FIGURE 7-4

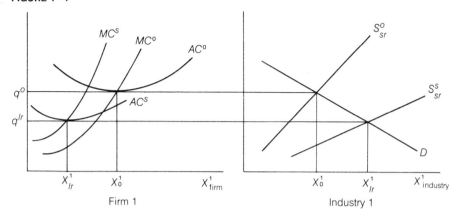

Firm 1   Industry 1

They will all lead to the same first-order conditions if firm 1 maximizes any one of them subject to its production constraint $f^1(x_{ln}; z_1) = 0$. Since we know objective function (a) will generate the proper pareto-optimal conditions if

$$t_z = - \sum_{j=2}^{J} \left(\frac{f^j_{z_1}}{f^j_{j1}} \right)$$

so too must (b) and (c) so long as

$$s_z = t_z = - \sum_{j=2}^{J} \left(\frac{f^j_{z_1}}{f^j_{j1}} \right)$$

$\overline{z}_1, \overline{\overline{z}}_1, t_z$, and s_z in (b) and (c) are all parameters fixed by the government. Thus, the terms $t_z \cdot \overline{z}_1$ and $s_z \cdot \overline{\overline{z}}_1$ cannot affect the first-order conditions for profit maximization.

Policy options (b) and (c) may cause problems in the long run if the government is not careful, however—a point first demonstrated by Baumol and Oates in their book *The Theory of Environmental Policy*.[6] Consider the subsidy, option (c). In the unlikely event that $\overline{\overline{z}}_1$ happens to equal the value of z_1 at the full pareto optimum, firm 1 will receive no net subsidy and no problem can arise. But one would expect $\overline{\overline{z}}_1$ to be set at a value greater than z_1^{opt}, in which case firm 1 will actually receive a subsidy. If so, and the economy were at a zero-profit competitive equilibrium before the subsidy, other firms will now have an incentive to enter the industry represented by firm 1 in order to receive the same subsidy. In effect what policy (c) does is raise the marginal costs of firm 1 by an amount related to the unit subsidy s_z, while simultaneously *lowering* its average costs because of the lump-sum subsidy, $s_k\overline{\overline{z}}_1$. The average cost effect will occur so long as $\overline{\overline{z}}_1 > z_1^{opt}$. The situation is depicted in Figure 7-4. To interpret the diagram, think of good 1 as the output of firm 1, and that

---

[6] Baumol and Oates, *The Theory of Environmental Policy*, chap. 12.

a large number of such firms comprise industry 1. The original no tax (subsidy) long-run equilibrium for the industry is at (q_0, X_0^1), with each firm contributing output equal to X_0^1.

With policy (c), each firm's marginal costs shift upward from MC^0 to MC^s, but their average costs fall from AC^0 to AC^s because, net, they are subsidized by amount $s_k \cdot (\bar{\bar{z}}_1 - z_1)$. The new long-run equilibrium is at X_{lr}^1. Each firm's production has decreased from X_0^1 to X_{lr}^1, but entry of new firms causes industry output to rise. As a result, total production of z_1 may actually rise, surely an unwanted result.

The problem is that a subsidy given only to the existing producers in industry 1 is not truly a lump-sum subsidy for the economy as a whole *in the long run*, if other firms have the option of entering the industry. As discussed in Chapter 2, a lump-sum payment (receipt) must have the property that economic decisions cannot alter the size of the payment (receipt). Thus, to make these subsidies truly lump sum in the long run, they must either be offered to all firms whether or not they actually enter the first industry, or given only to the *original* firms in the industry and not to new entrants. Since governments are probably not going to do either of these, the safest policy is simply a unit tax on the full amount of z_1, policy option (a).

Strictly speaking, the Baumol-Oates subsidy problem cannot arise in the model as presented above because of our implicit assumption that only firm 1 can produce z_1. Hence, the other firms $j = 2, \ldots, J$ are not even potential entrants into industry 1. On the other hand, one can imagine a different model in which firms $j = 2, \ldots, J$ can produce z_1 in the long run, but given the going market prices $(P_1, \ldots, P_N)$, and the form of the $(J - 1)$ relationships, $f^j(\ )$, they choose not to produce z_1, at least not without a subsidy. This is the type of model Baumol and Oates have in mind.

Policy option (b) also fails if the alternative Baumol-Oates model really applies in the long run. Policy (b) raises average costs so long as $z_1^{opt} > \bar{z}_1$, but not by the same amount as a tax on the full amount of z_1. If type 1 firms can become other kinds of firms, not enough of them will exit industry 1 in the long run. In effect, the term $t_z \cdot \bar{z}_1$ acts as a locational subsidy and will not be consistent with pareto optimality.

In any case, the original conclusion still stands: The safest policy is a straight unit tax on the full amount of z_1. With this policy it does not matter which of the two models actually applies. It is always pareto optimal.

6. If z_1 is an external economy (research and development, perhaps) and the number of beneficiaries is small, the government may decide to let firm 1 treat z_1 as a private resource and market it, providing of course that firm 1 can exclude the external services associated with z_1 from nonpurchasers (research and development may actually be a bad example in this respect). Otherwise a free-rider problem is likely.

The pareto-optimal marketing of z_1 follows directly the marketing examples given for consumption externalities. The only requirement is that each firm $j = 2, \ldots, J$ pay firm 1 a "competitive" price, equal to the value of z_1 to firm

j on the margin. Suppose each firm j pays firm 1 a price

(7.57)
$$P^j_{z_1} = (-) \frac{f^j_{z_1}}{f^j_{11}} \cdot q_1 \qquad j = 2, \ldots, J$$

The required pareto-optimal condition is:[7]

(7.58)
$$\frac{f^1_{z_1}}{f^1_{11}} + \sum_{j=2}^{J} \frac{f^j_{z_1}}{f^j_{j1}} = 0$$

Faced with prices $p^j_{z_1}$, firm 1 will solve the following problem:

$$\max \sum_{n=1}^{N} p_n X_{1n} + z_1 \cdot \sum_{j=2}^{J} p^j_{z_1}$$

$$\text{s.t.} \quad f^1(X_{1n}; z_1) = 0$$

The first-order conditions are:

(7.59)
$$p_n = -\lambda f^1_{1n} \qquad n = 1, \ldots, N$$

and

(7.60)
$$\sum_{j=2}^{J} p^j_{z_1} = -\lambda f^1_{z_1}$$

Alternatively, dividing (7.60) by the first equation in (7.59),

(7.61)
$$\sum_{j=2}^{J} \left(\frac{p^j_{z_1}}{p_1} \right) = \frac{f^1_{z_1}}{f^1_{11}}$$

But if $p^j_{z_1} = -f^j_{z_1}/f^j_{j1} \cdot q_1, j = 2, \ldots, J$, and $p_1 = q_1$, then:

(7.62)
$$-\sum_{j=2}^{J} \left(\frac{f^j_{z_1}}{f^j_{j1}} \right) = \frac{f^1_{z_1}}{f^1_{11}}$$

as required for pareto optimality. Of course it is highly doubtful that such an optimal market solution will naturally arise. But if there are only a few firms interested in obtaining z_1, a market solution may well be an acceptable practical alternative to a government subsidy to firm 1. Our analysis has ignored both the administrative costs associated with government programs and the costs of market transactions, but it may be that the administrative costs of operating and monitoring a subsidy program are considerable, enough so that an approximately optimal market solution is pareto superior.

CONCLUDING COMMENTS—THE PROBLEMS OF NONCONVEX PRODUCTION POSSIBILITIES

The analysis in Chapter 7 has assumed that aggregate production possibilities are strictly convex. This is a crucial assumption, for without it there

---

[7] For purposes of interpretation it may be helpful to think of X_1 as a resource, such as labor, used by all firms.

FIGURE 7-5

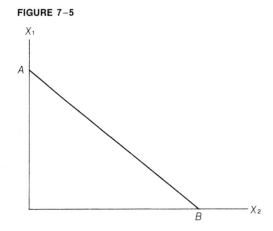

is no guarantee that the tax policies and their equivalents offered as a means of achieving pareto optimality are more than locally optimal. They may not represent a global optimum. Unfortunately, production externalities themselves can generate significant nonconvexities, so that the problem is a very real one.[8]

It would be premature to analyze in any detail the problems created by nonconvex production possibilities (increasing returns—decreasing costs), since the general theoretical treatment of nonconvexities appears in Chapter 9. But the crux of the problem can be seen with reference to a simple two-good, one-factor economy.

Suppose that goods X_1 and X_2 are produced with linear technology by a single factor of production, L (labor). If there are no externalities, the production-possibilities frontier will be a straight line reflecting constant opportunity costs, as depicted in Figure 7–5. If, however, X_2 generates an external diseconomy for X_1, production of X_2 will imply lower quantities of X_1 than are available on AB, *except at the endpoints.* Hence, assuming the frontier is continuous, it must contain nonconvex segments near the endpoints, as depicted in Figure 7–6.

To see the local-global problem, suppose society initially ignores the externality, thereby underestimating the true costs of producing X_2, and achieves an equilibrium at D on indifference curve I_0 in Figure 7–6. Opportunity costs are incorrectly measured by the slope of the line segment EF, equal to the slope of the linear frontier AB (dotted line). A Pigovian tax forces society to see the true, higher opportunity costs and a new equilibrium obtains at point T, on indifference curve I_1, with less production of X_2. However, given the nonconvexities there *may* be an even better allocation. For instance, in Figure

---

[8] See Baumol and Oates, *The Theory of Environmental Policy*, chap. 8 for an excellent detailed analysis of the nonconvexity issue and the important distinction between local and global solutions to externality problems.

FIGURE 7–6

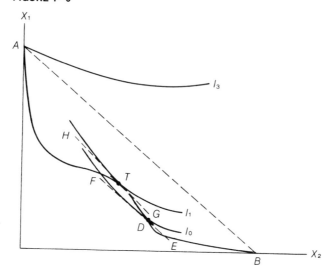

7–6 the endpoint A, with no production of X_2, places society on its highest possible indifference curve, I_3. Thus, while T represents a *local* improvement over D, A is the *global* optimum, and the Pigovian tax cannot possibly achieve it. A similar demonstration applies to the case of external economies.

Rather than pursue this analysis any further, we will simply assume that the local optimum is the global optimum and turn to a brief critique of recent U.S. antipollution policy in Chapter 8 as an application of the principles established in Chapters 6 and 7.

REFERENCES

Baumol, W. J., and Oates, W. *The Theory of Environmental Policy.* Englewood Cliffs, N.J.: Prentice-Hall, Inc., 1975.

Buchanan, J., and Kafolgis, M. "A Note on Public Goods Supply." *American Economic Review,* June 1963.

Diamond, P., and Mirrlees, J. "Aggregate Production with Consumer Externalities." *Quarterly Journal of Economics,* February 1973.

Holtermann, S. "Alternative Tax Systems to Correct for Externalities, and the Efficiency of Paying Compensation." *Economica,* February 1976.

Sadka, E. "A Note on Aggregate Production with Consumer Externalities." *Journal of Public Economics,* February 1978.

8

Some reflections on U.S. antipollution policy—
An application of externality theory

THE LINES OF ATTACK

During the past ten years or so the federal government of the United States has been waging an all-out war on air and water pollution, an effort noteworthy not only both because of its variety and intensity but also because it ignores almost entirely the theoretical considerations of the previous two chapters.

The national government became directly involved in the fight against water pollution in 1956 with the passage of the Federal Water Pollution Control Act of 1956. This legislation established a two-pronged attack against water pollution, consisting of:

a. Identifying and regulating sources of industrial water pollution.
b. Subsidizing construction of municipal waste treatment plants.

The federal initiatives against air pollution came later, with the passage of The Clean Air Act of 1963. As originally drafted it was only concerned with identifying and regulating stationary (i.e., industrial) sources of air pollution, but a subsequent amendment in 1965 established guidelines for reducing automobile emissions that were to take effect for new vehicles produced in 1968. The four policies—(1) regulation of industrial water pollution; (2) regulation of industrial air pollution; (3) automobile emissions standards; and (4) municipal waste treatment subsidies—constitute the bulk of the national government's antipollution campaign to this day.[1]

Regulation of Industrial Water Pollution

The Water Pollution Control Act accomplished very little during its first 16 years despite numerous amendments designed to enhance its effectiveness. The federal government engaged in various studies of industrial pollution and recommended actions against individual polluters, but the responsibility of regulating polluters was left to the states. In truth, the states seldom acted.

---

[1] For an excellent summary of these four programs, see E. Mills, *The Economics of Environmental Quality* (New York: W. W. Norton Co, Inc., 1978), chap. 7. We will only briefly sketch their salient characteristics.

154

Federal initiatives began in earnest in the 1970s with the establishment of the Environmental Protection Agency and passage of the 1972 amendments, which gave to the EPA the responsibility of issuing permits to all industrial polluters. The 1972 amendments required the EPA to determine the "best practicable discharge control technology" for each polluter and insist that the polluter install that technology by 1977 in order to continue to receive a permit. Moreover, by 1983 each polluter was required to install the "best available technology economically feasible" in order to receive a permit, such technology also to be determined by the EPA. The amendments called for the complete elimination of discharges into navigable waters by 1985.[2]

Regulation of Industrial Air Pollution

The early years of the Clear Air Act closely paralleled those of the Water Pollution Control Act, with numerous studies but little effective action against polluters. The federal initiatives vastly increased under the amendments of 1970, which gave the EPA responsibility for establishing ambient air standards over defined regions throughout the country and ensuring that all new stationary sources installed the "best adequately demonstrated control technology." It was not clear whether such technologies would be subjected to any cost or benefit tests since there was no mention of costs or benefits in the guidelines.[3]

Automobile Emissions Standards

The 1965 automobile emissions standards were also ineffective, so the 1970 amendments to the Clear Air Act tried to strengthen them as well. The amendments required that cars produced in 1975 must emit 10 percent or less of the hydrocarbons and carbon monoxide allowed in the previous standards. The 1976 models had to meet a similar emission standard for nitrous oxide.[4] By the mid-70s all new cars were equipped with emission control devices but they fell far short of the original standards. Out of sympathy to the oil embargo and rising gasoline and oil prices, Congress granted the auto industry delays in meeting interim standards in 1973, 1974, and 1975.[5] Still further extensions were granted on August 8, 1977.[6]

Municipal Waste Treatment

Much as with the other programs, municipal waste treatment subsidies remained extremely small throughout the 1950s and 1960s. Appropriations

---

[2] Ibid., pp. 186–87.

[3] Ibid., p. 142.

[4] Ibid., p. 192.

[5] See Ibid., pp. 209–14, for a history of the delays.

[6] E. Seskin, "Automobile Air Pollution Policy," *Current Issues in U.S. Environment Policy*, Resources for the Future, ed. P. Portney (Baltimore, Md.; John Hopkins University Press, 1978), p. 77.

TABLE 8–1
Appropriations of Municipal Waste Treatment Grants

Fiscal year	1957	1960	1965	1970	1975	1977–82
Appropriation ($ millions)	50	46	90	800	4,000	24,500

Sources: E. Mills, *The Economics of Environmental Quality* (New York: W. W. Norton & Co., Inc., 1978), p. 188; and A. Myrick Freeman, III, "Air and Water Pollution Policy," ed. P. Portney, *Current Issues in U.S. Environmental Policy*, Resources for the Future (Baltimore, Md.: Johns Hopkins University Press, 1978), p. 61.

increased significantly during the 1970s, although President Nixon tried at first to impound the funds, arguing that the subsidies were inconsistent with macroeconomic policy goals. The 1972 amendments to the Water Pollution Control Act increased the federal share of construction costs to 75 percent[7], and the 1977 amendments assured a continued high level of appropriations through 1982. The appropriations are summarized in Table 8–1. It is also noteworthy that the federal grants subsidize construction costs only, not maintenance or operating costs. Nor are they in any way related to the amount of pollution abatement that actually takes place.

These programs clearly bear little relationship to the theory of externalities developed in Chapters 6 and 7. None of them involves taxing the pollution at its source, the most direct and obvious solution to the problem. Further, none of them corresponds well to any of the acceptable policy alternatives offered in lieu of a direct tax. What makes this all the more surprising is that other countries have had considerable success with tax policy, most notably the West Germans in the Ruhr River Valley Basin. Yet, despite these successful precedents and the dictates of externality theory, the United States has largely chosen the route of direct regulation and waste treatment, continuing a basic policy strategy that has been employed time and again throughout its history at all levels of government with little notable success. Granted, the war on pollution is now being waged on a larger scale than ever before, with significantly greater initiatives by the national government. In previous efforts the state and local governments had been the chief regulators. Perhaps the change in jurisdiction and scale will have a telling effect this time, but one cannot be overly confident. Political considerations aside, the state and local governments still retain primary responsibility for three of the programs, and these policies generally make little economic sense.

PRELIMINARY THEORETICAL CONSIDERATIONS

Before undertaking a critique of U.S. antipollution policy, it will be useful to develop an analytical framework for considering a combined consumption-production externality, defined as an externality in which some production (consumption) activity enters the utility function (production function) of at least one consumer (producer). The externality may affect other producers

---

[7] Mills, *The Economics of Environmental Quality*, pp. 187–88.

(consumers) as well. Some instances of pollution are essentially pure consumption externalities, for example, smog created by automobile emissions. Others qualify as pure production externalities, such as the destruction of commercial fishing grounds through dumping of industrial wastes. But many important examples of industrial pollution obviously affect consumers, perhaps more so than other producers. The dumping of industrial wastes into waterways destroys recreational uses of the water as well as commercial fishing. The most important external diseconomy of industrial air pollution may be to people's health. These are clearly examples of consumption-production externalities, and they require a broader analytical perspective than was provided in either of the two proceeding chapters.

Unfortunately, even a simple example of a consumption-production externality necessitates a fairly complex analytical model. To keep the analytics as simple and intuitive as possible, we will consider the general case of a single aggregate consumption-production externality, in which the aggregate use of one factor of production enters into each person's utility function and all firm's production functions, with all other goods and factors purely private. This will permit a direct comparison of results with our previous analysis of aggregate consumption and production externalities in Chapters 6 and 7. As it turns out, the policy rules are virtually identical. A single Pigovian tax on the externality-generating factor will achieve a pareto optimum. The only difference is that the tax will now be based on both the consumers' marginal rates of substitution and the producers' marginal rates of transformation with respect to the aggregate external effects. All private goods and factors can continue to be allocated in competitive markets without government interference.

Analysis of consumption-production externalities is inherently complex because capturing the extent of the external effects requires the full general equilibrium model of Chapter 2, or its equivalent. Condensing the model as we have previously would hide essential aspects of the externality. Thus, the notational requirements alone are formidable, but having worked through the general equilibrium model of Chapter 2 and the pure consumption and production-externality models of Chapters 6 and 7, the analysis of consumption-production externalities should be reasonably straightforward and predictable.

Following the notation of Chapter 2,

Let:

X_{hg} = consumption of good g by person h. $g = 1, \ldots, G$
                                                                 $h = 1, \ldots, H$

V_{hf} = factor f supplied by consumer h (measured negatively).
                                                                 $f = 1, \ldots, F$
                                                                 $h = 1, \ldots, H$

r_{gf} = factor f used in the production of good g. $g = 1, \ldots, G$
                                                                 $f = 1, \ldots, F$

X^g = the aggregate output of good g. $g = 1, \ldots, G$

Assume that the *aggregate* quantity of factor i (e.g., water) used in production enters the utility functions of all consumers and all firms in the economy because its use gives rise to pollution which affects all agents.

Let:

$$(8.1) \qquad X^g = \phi^{*g}(r_{gf}; r_{gi}; P) = \phi^g\left(r_{gf}; r_{gi}; \sum_{g=1}^{G} r_{gi}\right)$$

$$g = 1, \ldots, G$$
$$f = 1, \ldots, i-1, i+1, \ldots, F$$

$$(8.2) \qquad U^h = U^{*h}(X_{hg}; V_{hf}; P) = U^h\left(X_{hg}; V_{hf}; \sum_{g=1}^{G} r_{gi}\right)$$

$$h = 1, \ldots, H$$
$$g = 1, \ldots, G$$
$$f = 1, \ldots, F$$

where

$\phi^g(\ ) = $ the production function for X^g.

$U^h(\ ) = $ the utility function for person h.

$P = P(\sum_{g=1}^{G} r_{gi}) = $ pollution as a function of all firms' use of factor i.

Notice that each production relationship, $\phi^g(\ )$, incorporates each firms "personal use" of factor i, (r_{gi}), as well as the pollution externality $(\sum_{g=1}^{G} r_{gi})$. The usual conditions for aggregate externalities apply:

$$(8.3) \qquad \frac{\partial \phi^{*g}}{\partial r_{ji}} = \frac{\partial \phi^g}{\partial \left(\sum_{g=1}^{G} r_{gi}\right)} \qquad j \neq g$$

$$(8.4) \qquad \frac{\partial \phi^{*g}}{\partial r_{ji}} = \frac{\partial \phi^g}{\partial r_{ji}} + \frac{\partial \phi^g}{\partial \left(\sum_{g=1}^{G} r_{gi}\right)} \qquad j = g$$

$$(8.5) \qquad \frac{\partial U^h}{\partial r_{gi}} = \frac{\partial U^h}{\partial \left(\sum_{g=1}^{G} r_{gi}\right)} \qquad g = 1, \ldots, G$$

Society's problem is to maximize social welfare subject to the production constraints and market clearance:

$$\max_{(X_{hg}, V_{hf}, X^g, r_{gf})} W\left[U^h\left(X_{hg}; V_{hf}; \sum_{g=1}^{G} r_{gi}\right)\right]$$

$$\text{s.t.} \qquad X^g = \phi^g\left(r_{gf}; r_{gi}; \sum_{g=1}^{G} r_{gi}\right)$$

$$\sum_{h=1}^{H} X_{hg} = X^g \qquad g = 1, \ldots, G$$

$$\sum_{h=1}^{H} V_{hf} = \sum_{g=1}^{G} r_{gf} \qquad f = 1, \ldots, F$$

where:

W = the social welfare function.

Defining multipliers for each constraint, the Lagrangian for this problem is:

$$\max_{(X_{hg};V_{hf};X^g;r_{gf})} L = W\left[U^h\left(X_{hg};V_{hf};\sum_{g=1}^{G} r_{gi}\right)\right]$$

$$+ \sum_{g=1}^{G} \delta^g\left(X^g - \phi^g\left(r_{gf};r_{gi};\sum_{g=1}^{G} r_{gi}\right)\right)$$

$$+ \sum_{g=1}^{G} \mu^g\left(X^g - \sum_{h=1}^{H} X_{hg}\right)$$

$$+ \sum_{f=1}^{F} \pi_f\left(\sum_{h=1}^{H} V_{hf} - \sum_{g=1}^{G} r_{gf}\right)$$

Except for the terms $\sum_{g=1}^{G} r_{gi}$ this model is identical to that of Chapter 2. By inspection the first-order conditions will be identical for all arguments except the r_{gi}, $g = 1, \ldots, G$, leading to the exact same set of pareto-optimal conditions and interpersonal equity conditions applying to all the other goods and factors, in both production and in consumption. Moreover, we know that competitive markets will generate the pareto-optimal conditions in each case, and that lump-sum redistribution of one of the goods, say, X^1, is necessary for interpersonal equity. Thus, the combined consumption-production pollution externalities do not affect the marketing of the purely private goods and factors, or the policy rules for optimal redistributions, exactly the result obtained in the pure consumption and production-externality models. All one need do, then, is examine the pareto-optimal conditions for each firm's use of factor i.

To derive these conditions consider the first-order conditions for a single firm's use of factor i and 1, say, r_{gi} and r_{g1}.

The first-order conditions are:

(8.6)
$$r_{gi}: \quad \frac{\partial L}{\partial r_{gi}} = \sum_{h=1}^{H} \frac{\partial W}{\partial U^h} \frac{\partial U^h}{\partial\left(\sum\limits_{g=1}^{G} r_{gi}\right)} - \delta^g \frac{\partial \phi^g}{\partial r_{gi}}$$

$$- \sum_{g=1}^{G} \delta^g \frac{\partial \phi^g}{\partial\left(\sum\limits_{g=1}^{G} r_{gi}\right)} - \pi_i = 0$$

$$g = 1, \ldots, G$$

(8.7)
$$r_{g1}: \quad \frac{\partial L}{\partial r_{g1}} = -\delta^g \frac{\partial \phi^g}{\partial r_{g1}} - \pi_1 = 0 \qquad g = 1, \ldots, G$$

Dividing (8.6) by (8.7) and substituting for the appropriate term $\partial\phi^g/\partial r_{g1}$ in the denominator yields:

$$(8.8) \quad \frac{\sum\limits_{h=1}^{H} \dfrac{\partial W}{\partial U^h} \dfrac{\partial U^h}{\partial \left(\sum\limits_{g=1}^{G} r_{gi}\right)}}{-\delta^g \dfrac{\partial \phi^g}{\partial r_{g1}}} + \frac{\dfrac{\partial \phi^g}{\partial r_{gi}}}{\dfrac{\partial \phi^g}{\partial r_{g1}}} + \sum\limits_{g=1}^{G} \left[\frac{\dfrac{\partial \phi^g}{\partial \left(\sum\limits_{g=1}^{G} r_{gi}\right)}}{\dfrac{\partial \phi^g}{\partial r_{g1}}} \right] = \frac{\pi_i}{\pi_1}$$

$$g = 1, \ldots, G$$

To simplify this expression further, consider the first-order conditions with respect to V_{hi} and V_{h1}, any consumer's supply of factors i and 1.

$$(8.9) \quad V_{hi}: \quad \frac{\partial L}{\partial V_{hi}} = \frac{\partial W}{\partial U^h} \frac{\partial U^h}{\partial V_{hi}} + \pi_i = 0$$

$$(8.10) \quad V_{h1}: \quad \frac{\partial L}{\partial V_{h1}} = \frac{\partial W}{\partial U^h} \frac{\partial U^h}{\partial V_{h1}} + \pi_1 = 0$$

Hence,

$$(8.11) \quad \frac{\pi_i}{\pi_1} = \frac{\dfrac{\partial U^h}{\partial V_{hi}}}{\dfrac{\partial U^h}{\partial V_{h1}}} \quad h = 1, \ldots, H,$$

and, from (8.7) and (8.10),

$$(8.12) \quad \pi_1 = -\delta^g \frac{\partial \phi^g}{\partial r_{g1}} = -\frac{\partial W}{\partial U^h} \frac{\partial U^h}{\partial V_{h1}} \quad \begin{array}{l} g = 1, \ldots, G \\ h = 1, \ldots, H \end{array}$$

Substituting (8.12) and (8.11) into (8.8) yields:

$$(8.13) \quad \frac{\sum\limits_{h=1}^{H} \dfrac{\partial W}{\partial U^h} \dfrac{\partial U^h}{\partial \left(\sum\limits_{g=1}^{G} r_{gi}\right)}}{-\dfrac{\partial W}{\partial U^h} \dfrac{\partial U^h}{\partial V_{h1}}} + \frac{\dfrac{\partial \phi^g}{\partial r_{gi}}}{\dfrac{\partial \phi^g}{\partial r_{g1}}} + \sum\limits_{g=1}^{G} \left[\frac{\dfrac{\partial \phi^g}{\partial \left(\sum\limits_{g=1}^{G} r_{gi}\right)}}{\dfrac{\partial \phi^g}{\partial r_{g1}}} \right] = \frac{\dfrac{\partial U^h}{\partial V_{hi}}}{\dfrac{\partial U^h}{\partial V_{h1}}}$$

$$\begin{array}{l} g = 1, \ldots, G \\ h = 1, \ldots, H \end{array}$$

But if interpersonal equity holds, then,

$$(8.14) \quad \frac{\partial W}{\partial U^h} \frac{\partial U^h}{\partial V_{h1}} = \quad \text{all } h = 1, \ldots, H$$

Appropriately substituting (8.14) in the denominator of the first term of (8.13) and canceling the social welfare derivatives term-by-term yields:

$$(8.15) \quad -\sum_{h=1}^{H} \left[\frac{\frac{\partial U^h}{\partial (\sum r_{gi})}}{\frac{\partial U^h}{\partial V_{h1}}} \right] \frac{\frac{\partial \phi^g}{\partial r_{gi}}}{\frac{\partial \phi^g}{\partial r_{g1}}} + \sum_{g=1}^{G} \left[\frac{\frac{\partial \phi^g}{\partial (\sum r_{gi})}}{\frac{\partial \phi^g}{\partial r_{g1}}} \right] = \frac{\frac{\partial U^h}{\partial V_{hi}}}{\frac{\partial U^h}{\partial V_{h1}}}$$

$$g = 1, \ldots, G$$
$$h = 1, \ldots, H$$

Rearranging terms:

$$(8.16) \quad \frac{\frac{\partial U^h}{\partial V_{hi}}}{\frac{\partial U^h}{\partial V_{h1}}} - \frac{\frac{\partial \phi^g}{\partial r_{gi}}}{\frac{\partial \phi^g}{\partial r_{g1}}} = + \sum_{g=1}^{G} \left[\frac{\frac{\partial \phi^g}{\partial (\sum r_{gi})}}{\frac{\partial \phi^g}{\partial r_{g1}}} \right] - \sum_{h=1}^{H} \left[\frac{\frac{\partial U^h}{\partial (\sum r_{gi})}}{\frac{\partial U^h}{\partial V_{h1}}} \right]$$

$$g = 1, \ldots, G$$
$$h = 1, \ldots, H$$

(8.16) says that the private marginal rates of substitution between factors *i* and 1 in supply and in use differ by an amount equal to the combined external effects of the use of factor *i* expressed in terms of factor 1, no matter which firm uses factor *i* nor which consumer supplies factor *i*. Thus, despite the awkward notational requirements, the result is completely analogous to the results for aggregate consumption or production externalities. Without the externality, the private marginal rates of substitution between factors *i* and 1 in use and supply should be equal, as would be the case with a competitive market. Given the externality this equality no longer holds, but as always with aggregate externalities, their divergence is independent of which consumer is supplying the factors or which firm is using them. In other words, the right-hand side of (8.16) is independent of *g* or *h*. To correct for the externality, therefore, all the government need do is set a single tax on the use of factor *i*, paid by the firms, set at a value equal to the value of the marginal damage (gain) at the optimum:[8]

$$(8.17) \quad \frac{t_i}{q_1} = \left[+ \sum_{g=1}^{G} \left(\frac{\frac{\partial \phi^g}{\partial (\sum r_{gi})}}{\frac{\partial \phi^g}{\partial r_{g1}}} \right) - \sum_{h=1}^{H} \left(\frac{\frac{\partial U^h}{\partial (\sum r_{gi})}}{\frac{\partial U^h}{\partial V_{h1}}} \right) \right]$$

Consumers will set

$$\frac{q_i}{q_1} = \frac{\frac{\partial U^h}{\partial V_{hi}}}{\frac{\partial U^h}{\partial V_{h1}}},$$

---

[8] Alternatively, the government could set the tax on the supply of factor *i*. So long as all agents on one side of a market pay the same tax rate, it doesn't matter which side of the market is taxed. A downward shift in the factor demand curve, or an upward shift in the factor supply curve will produce an identical general equilibrium.

and producers will set

$$\frac{p_i}{q_1} = \frac{\dfrac{\partial \phi^g}{\partial r_{gi}}}{\dfrac{\partial \phi^g}{\partial r_{g1}}},$$

assuming they ignore the effect of the externality when purchasing r_{gi}. Since $q_1 = p_1$ with X^1 marketed competitively, and

$$(8.18) \qquad \frac{q_i}{q_1} = \frac{p_i + t_i}{q_1}$$

this tax will generate the pareto-optimum conditions (8.16). The solution is depicted in Figure 8–1 using standard supply and demand analysis for factor i, with $q = 1$, the numeraire.

S represents the horizontal summation of each consumers MRS in supply, the terms $\partial U^h / \partial V_{hi} / \partial U^h / \partial V_{h1}$. Similarly, D^{priv} represents the horizontal summation of each firms private use MRT, the terms $\partial \phi^g / \partial r_{gi} / \partial \phi^g / \partial r_{g1}$. D^{soc} corrects D^{priv} by vertically subtracting the marginal external diseconomy at every aggregate r_i.

At the optimum, the difference between the private MRS and MRT, represented by the vertical distance $D^{\text{priv}} - S$, just equals the value of the marginal external effects,

$$+ \sum_{g=1}^{G} \left(\frac{\dfrac{\partial \phi^g}{\partial (\sum r_{gi})}}{\dfrac{\partial \phi^g}{\partial r_{g1}}} \right) - \sum_{h=1}^{H} \left[\frac{\dfrac{\partial U^h}{\partial (\sum r_{gi})}}{\dfrac{\partial U^h}{\partial V_{h1}}} \right]$$

represented by $D^{\text{priv}} - D^{\text{soc}}$. Thus, the only difference with a combined externality is in the terms reflecting the extent of the marginal damage, which now

FIGURE 8–1

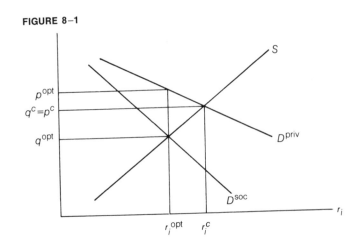

incorporate both consumption and production. Otherwise the analysis is identical to that of the simpler models, not only for aggregate externalities but for other forms of externalities as well, as could easily be verified.

Finally, the same alternative solutions are open to the government should it choose not to levy a direct tax on the source of the externality, a point which could also be easily verified. Qualitatively, then, the existence of combined production-consumption externalities alters none of the insights gained from analyzing the simpler production and consumption externality models.

A second preliminary consideration is that societies cannot be expected to find the full social optimum solution to pollution externalities, a point argued effectively by Baumol and Oates in their *Theory of Environmental Policy*.[9] Consider again Figure 7–3, in which the problem of pollution for society is depicted as finding the optimum amount of pollution, that point at which the additional opportunity costs of reducing pollution just equal the additional benefits. The primary problem is that no one really knows what the marginal benefits are to society of additional pollution reduction, especially if consumers are affected by the pollution. There are at least four problems with determining these benefits. First, there remain serious gaps in our basic scientific knowledge of the effects of various pollutants. Which pollutants are truly carcinogens? What concentrations of these pollutants are safe for humans, or animals? Firm answers to questions such as these must await further scientific research. Second, even if the effects of these pollutants were known, the costs of pollution (benefits of less pollution) involve among other things increased human sickness and possibly loss of life. Providing the proper dollar valuation for these phenomena is bound to be difficult and controversial even for the simplest cases.[10] Third, the government must aggregate each person's individual measure of loss to arrive at the aggregate marginal damage on which the tax is to be levied, without benefit of normal markets in which people are forced to reveal their preferences. Finally, the government must measure the marginal benefits at the optimum, not at the original pre-intervention equilibrium. In terms of Figure 8–1, the tax should equal the divergence between D^{priv} and D^{soc} at r_i^{opt}, not at r_i^c. Even if the marginal (benefits) at r_i^c were known with reasonable accuracy, their value at r_i^{opt} may well be subject to great uncertainty, especially if r_i^{opt} is far from r_i^c. (A trial and error process may discover r_i^{opt}, however, a point discussed in Chapter 7.

Given all these difficulties, governments typically adopt a "standards" approach for pollution in which they somewhat arbitrarily select a specified level of pollution as the desired level and design policies to meet the standard.

The legislation for the Clean Air and Water Pollution Control Acts suggests that the United States has chosen zero or near-zero pollution for its standard, a

[9] W. J. Baumol and W. Oates, *The Theory of Environmental Policy* (Englewood Cliffs, N.J.: Prentice-Hall, Inc., 1975), chap. 10. The model they use to analyze environmental pollution contains a combined consumption-production aggregate externality and is therefore similar to the model analyzed here.

[10] Professor Broome has some interesting thoughts on the problems of evaluating the loss of life, in J. Broome, "Trying to Value a Life," *Journal of Public Economics*, February 1978. See our discussion in Chapter 26.

level undoubtedly well below the true social optimum. Nonetheless, whatever standard is selected, the rational goal becomes trying to achieve this standard at minimum opportunity cost to society. In an otherwise first-best world, alternative antipollution strategies would naturally be evaluated strictly in terms of the cost criterion, since any unwanted redistributional effects of a given policy could be offset by lump-sum redistributions.

Minimizing the opportunity costs of achieving a given pollution standard is formally equivalent to maximizing social welfare subject to the additional constraint that the standard is satisfied, since the opportunity costs are simply losses in social welfare. As such, the analysis is second best, but we will consider it here because of its relevance to pollution externalities and the fact that the solution to the constrained social welfare optimum problem is also a single tax, whose properties are virtually identical to the unconstrained tax. Thus, the insights gained from considering the full social optimum problem carry over to the actual problem most societies try to solve, and any proposed solution can be usefully compared with the tax solution as the correct one from a strictly economic viewpoint.

To analyze the constrained social welfare optimum, let us continue with the same aggregate consumption-production externality as above, in which

$$\text{Pollution } (P) = P\left(\sum_{g=1}^{G} r_{gi} \right) \tag{8.19}$$

Assume the government arbitrarily wants pollution set at a given level, $\bar{P}$. Since P is solely a function of $\sum_{g=1}^{G} r_{gi}$, we can reinterpret the constraint to be

$$\bar{R}_i = \sum_{g=1}^{G} r_{gi} \tag{8.20}$$

where $\bar{R}_i$ is the permissible level of total use of factor i, corresponding to pollution level $\bar{P}$. Writing the constraint in terms of $\bar{R}_i$ avoids having to introduce P explicitly into the analysis. Further, we will assume this is the only additional constraint in an otherwise first-best policy environment.

Formally, the only difference between the full social optimum problem and the constrained social welfare problem is the constraint itself. Modifying the original problem, then, the government's problem becomes

$$\max_{(X_{hg}; V_{hf}; X^g; r_{gf})} W[U^h(X_{hg}; V_{hf}; \sum_{g=1}^{G} r_{gi})$$

$$\text{s.t.} \quad X^g = \phi^g\left(r_{gf}; r_{gi}; \sum_{g=1}^{G} r_{gi} \right) \quad g = 1, \ldots, G$$

$$\sum_{h=1}^{H} X_{hg} = X^g \quad g = 1, \ldots, G$$

$$\sum_{h=1}^{H} V_{hf} = \sum_{g=1}^{G} r_{gf} \quad f = 1, \ldots, F$$

$$\bar{R}_i = \sum_{g=1}^{G} r_{gi}$$

With the corresponding Lagrangian:

$$
\max_{(X_{hg};V_{hf};X^g;r_{gf})} L = W\left[U^h\left(X_{hg}; V_{hf}; \sum_{g=1}^{G} r_{gi} \right) \right]
$$

$$
+ \sum_{g=1}^{G} \delta^g \left[X^g - \phi^g\left(r_{gf}; r_{gi}; \sum_{g=1}^{G} r_{gi} \right) \right]
$$

$$
+ \sum_{g=1}^{G} \mu^g\left(X^g - \sum_{h=1}^{H} X_{hg} \right) + \sum_{f=1}^{F} \pi_f\left(\sum_{h=1}^{H} V_{hf} - \sum_{g=1}^{G} r_{gf} \right)
$$

$$
+ \lambda\left(\bar{R}_i - \sum_{g=1}^{G} r_{gi} \right)
$$

By inspection, the first-order conditions for all purely private goods and factors will be identical to those of the unconstrained model. Hence we know immediately that the government need not interfere in any market except that for factor i. Similarly, the interpersonal equity conditions will remain unchanged since they are unaffected by r_{gi}. Finally, the first-order condition for the r_{gi} will obviously differ from (8.6) by only the single term $-\lambda$, the multiplier applied to the additional constraint. Hence,

$$
(8.21) \quad \frac{\partial L}{\partial r_{gi}} = \sum_{h=1}^{H} \frac{\partial W}{\partial U^h}\frac{\partial U^h}{\partial (\sum r_{gi})} - \delta^g \frac{\partial \phi^g}{\partial r_{gi}} - \sum_{g=1}^{G} \delta^g \frac{\partial \phi^g}{\partial (\sum r_{gi})} - \pi_i - \lambda = 0
$$

$$
g = 1, \ldots, G
$$

Following the same steps to the pareto-optimal conditions as above, involving the first-order conditions for r_{g1}, V_{hi}, V_{h1} and the interpersonal equity conditions, we obtain:

$$
(8.22) \quad -\frac{\dfrac{\partial U^h}{\partial V_{hi}}}{\dfrac{\partial U^h}{\partial V_{h1}}} + \frac{\dfrac{\partial \phi^g}{\partial r_{gi}}}{\dfrac{\partial \phi^g}{\partial r_{g1}}} - \sum_{h=1}^{H}\left[\frac{\dfrac{\partial U^h}{\partial (\sum r_{gi})}}{\dfrac{\partial U^h}{\partial V_{h1}}}\right] + \sum_{g=1}^{G}\left[\frac{\dfrac{\partial \phi^g}{\partial (\sum r_{gi})}}{\dfrac{\partial \phi^g}{\partial r_{g1}}}\right] - \frac{\lambda}{\pi_1} = 0
$$

$$
g = 1, \ldots, G
$$
$$
h = 1, \ldots, H
$$

which differs from (8.16) only by the presence of the term λ/π_1. As before, the first two terms represent the private marginal rates of substitution between factors i and 1 in supply and use, respectively. The third and fourth terms give the marginal social costs of the externality due to aggregate changes in the supply and use of factor 1 caused by unit increases in the use of factor i by any firm. The final term is an additional marginal social cost arising from imposing the resource constraint on the solution. (The division by π_1 merely expresses the loss of social welfare in terms of good 1, since $\pi_1 = -\partial W/\partial U^h \ \partial U^h/\partial V_{h1}$, $h = 1, \ldots, H$, from the first-order conditions for V_{h1}.) Terms three through five, then, give the full marginal cost of any firm using factor i.

As before, each consumer will set

$$\frac{\dfrac{\partial U^h}{\partial V_{hi}}}{\dfrac{\partial U^h}{\partial V_{h1}}} = \frac{q_i}{q_1}$$

faced with consumer prices g_i and g_1. Similarly each competitive firm will set

$$\frac{p_i}{q_1} = \left(\frac{\dfrac{\partial \phi^g}{\partial r_{gi}}}{\dfrac{\partial \phi^g}{\partial r_{g1}}} \right)$$

if it ignores the external effects of its purchases. To achieve the new pareto optimum, then, the government must set a tax on each firm's use of factor i, such that

(8.23)
$$\frac{t_i}{q_1} = - \sum_{h=1}^{H} \left[\frac{\dfrac{\partial U^h}{\partial (\sum r_{gi})}}{\dfrac{\partial U^h}{\partial V_{h1}}} \right] + \sum_{g=1}^{G} \left[\frac{\dfrac{\partial \phi^g}{\partial (\sum r_{gi})}}{\dfrac{\partial \phi^g}{\partial r_{g1}}} \right] - \frac{\lambda}{\pi_1}$$

Only the single tax is necessary, because the private marginal rates of substitution between i and 1 in supply and use is identical for each consumer and each firm (the right-hand side of (8.23) is independent of g and h). Furthermore, unlike designing a tax to achieve the full social optimum, finding the proper level of tax is relatively simple. All the government need do is experiment with various tax levels until the aggregate constraint is satisfied. Once this occurs, the tax will automatically equal the full marginal social costs at the constraint $\bar{R}_i$, as required for pareto optimality. Put another way, in (8.23) all values are measured at the constraint level $\bar{R}_i$. Thus, once the tax finds the constraint, (8.23) is automatically satisfied.

To fully appreciate this point, compare the new result to the full social optimum, which required that

(8.24)
$$\frac{\dfrac{\partial U^h}{\partial V_{hi}}}{\dfrac{\partial U^h}{\partial V_{h1}}} - \frac{\dfrac{\partial \phi^g}{\partial r_{gi}}}{\dfrac{\partial \phi^g}{\partial r_{g1}}} = - \sum_{h=1}^{H} \left[\frac{\dfrac{\partial U^h}{\partial (\sum r_{gi})}}{\dfrac{\partial U^h}{\partial V_{h1}}} \right] + \sum_{g=1}^{G} \left[\frac{\dfrac{\partial \phi^g}{\partial (\sum r_{gi})}}{\dfrac{\partial \phi^g}{\partial r_{g1}}} \right]$$

and a tax such that

(8.25)
$$t_i = - \sum_{h=1}^{H} \left[\frac{\dfrac{\partial U^h}{\partial (\sum r_{gi})}}{\dfrac{\partial U^h}{\partial V_{h1}}} \right] + \sum_{g=1}^{G} \left[\frac{\dfrac{\partial \phi^g}{\partial (\sum r_{gi})}}{\dfrac{\partial \phi^g}{\partial r_{g1}}} \right]$$

all terms evaluated at the full social optimum.

FIGURE 8–2

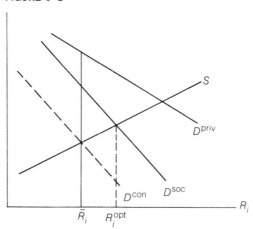

The only difference is that the new tax contains an additional term, λ/π_1, reflecting the additional marginal social costs of imposing the constraint. If by chance $\bar{R}_i = R_i^{opt}$, where R_i^{opt} is the full social optimum, then the two taxes are identical. λ measures the marginal gain to social welfare of relaxing the constraint. Hence, λ must equal 0 if $\bar{R}_i = R_i^{opt}$, since relaxing the constraint at the optimum cannot increase social welfare. However, if $\bar{R}_i < R_i^{opt}$ so that the constraint is binding, λ will be positive, representing the additional marginal social costs of the incorrect standard.

In Figure 8–2, if the government wants to achieve $\bar{R}_i$, it must set a tax equal to the difference between D^{priv} and S at $\bar{R}_i$, that is, equal to

$$
\left(\frac{\dfrac{\partial U^h}{\partial V_{hi}}}{\dfrac{\partial U^h}{\partial V_{h1}}} - \frac{\dfrac{\partial \phi^g}{\partial r_{gi}}}{\dfrac{\partial \phi^g}{\partial r_{g1}}} \right)
$$

measured at $\bar{R}_i$. The externality costs are measured by the vertical distance between D^{priv} and D_1^{soc} exactly as in Figure 8–1 (equal at each r_i) to

$$
- \sum_{h=1}^{H} \left[\frac{\dfrac{\partial U^h}{\partial (\sum r_{gi})}}{\dfrac{\partial U^h}{\partial V_{h1}}} \right] + \sum_{g=1}^{G} \left[\frac{\dfrac{\partial \phi^g}{\partial \left(\sum\limits_{g=1}^{G} r_{gi} \right)}}{\dfrac{\partial \phi^g}{\partial r_{g1}}} \right]
$$

The additional distance between D^{soc} and S at $\bar{R}_i$ is a measure of λ/π_1, the marginal constraint cost.[11] Notice that λ/π_1 is in effect a residual cost, such that if the tax does find $\bar{R}_i$, then it will automatically represent the full marginal

---

[11] Alternatively, the distance between D^{priv} and S measures the full marginal opportunity costs of reducing R_i to $\bar{R}_i$. The marginal benefit of the pollution reduction is $D^{priv} - D^{soc}$ at $\bar{R}_1$. Hence the distance $D^{soc} - S$ measures the net cost of the constraint.

social costs of using resource i as required for pareto optimality of the constrained problem. The diagram also indicates that these constraint costs will be zero only if $\bar{R}_i = R_i^{opt}$.

The final point is that this tax must minimize the opportunity costs of achieving the resource constraint. This could be demonstrated by setting up a cost minimization problem but that is not necessary. Since the tax satisfies the pareto-optimal conditions of the constrained social welfare maximization problem, it must be cost minimizing in a production sense. If production were inefficient, a reallocation of resources could increase outputs without additional resources and the bonus could be used to increase social welfare. But this contradicts the fact that social welfare is maximized given the arbitrary standard. $\bar{R}_i$ may be an awful choice, far from the optimum, but given that society chose it, taxing the use of resource i until $\bar{R}_i$ is met is the least cost way of achieving the standard $\bar{R}_i$.

THE ADVANTAGES OF TAXATION

It should be intuitively clear by now why direct taxation of the source of pollution is welfare optimizing (cost minimizing). First, if the tax is designed correctly, it forces the user of a polluting activity to consider the full social costs of his decision. Furthermore, the tax is easy to design if society uses a standards approach. Secondly, it permits each firm (consumer) to respond as flexibly as possible to these social costs. Using production as the source of the externality for purposes of illustration, the tax will raise the costs for each polluting firm of producing any given bundle of outputs. Each firm will react by trying to minimize these additional costs. If no substitutions are possible, then the firm will simply continue producing as before and pay the tax, or go out of business. Generally, though, factor substitutions are possible and each firm will try to find the best new combination of factors for producing any given output at minimum cost. For some firms this may mean using other factors more intensively at the expense of the polluting factor. Others may introduce a new factor to remove the pollution as it occurs. Since each firm is seeking its own least-cost solution, society's costs of reaching the standard will be minimized in the aggregate, providing of course that the tax properly reflects the social marginal costs of using the polluting factor. [12] This is the essence of the matter.

U.S. POLICIES AGAIN

Automobile Emissions Control Equipment

The policies chosen by the United States generally lack these advantages. Consider first the automobile emissions control policy which requires that all cars be equipped with particular antipollution devices. There are at least two glaring deficiencies with this solution. First, automobile emissions create

---

[12] Production possibilities must also remain convex in the presence of the externality. Refer to the discussion of this point at the end of Chapter 7.

problems only in the large urban areas where traffic is highly concentrated, and even then the effects vary depending on prevailing atmospheric conditions. Requiring that people who drive in cities only infrequently or not at all reduce their automobile pollution to the same extent as predominately city drivers cannot possibly be close to the optimum. From an economic point of view, a policy of taxing people only for city driving would appear to be preferable. Secondly, the equipment approach lacks the flexibility of a tax policy. It essentially assumes that such equipment is the least-cost method of reaching a given standard, an assumption which may be far from true. A tax based on where people drive and the amount of pollutants emitted from their automobile is the policy suggested by externality theory. Whether such a tax can actually be administered is an important question, but its obvious economic advantages warrant its careful consideration as an alternative to the present policy.

Direct Regulation of Industrial Pollution

Direct regulation of industrial pollution, the approach of both the Clean Air Act and the Water Pollution Control Act is also seriously flawed relative to a tax policy. In principle, regulation can be equivalent to the tax for any given standard, but only if it duplicates the exact pattern of resource use and production occasioned by the tax. But this is clearly an impossible task. More than likely the regulation will take the form of simple rules that are decidedly worse than the tax. For example, suppose society wants a 50 percent reduction in some form of industrial pollution. The preferred solution is to tax the source of the pollution until, *in the aggregate*, pollution is reduced by 50 percent. If direct regulation is used instead, the government may have little choice legally than to dictate a 50 percent reduction of pollution by each polluter. This is essentially the approach taken by the Environmental Protection Agency for both air and water pollution. If enforced, it will achieve the desired aggregate reduction to be sure, but at opportunity costs far in excess of the tax policy. In general each polluter will not reduce pollution by 50 percent with the tax. Faced with the tax those firms that can readily substitute other factors for the polluting factor may well reduce their pollution much more than 50 percent. On the other hand, some company with little or no substitution possibilities producing a highly desirable (i.e., profitable) product may simply pay the tax and continue as before. In the aggregate the tax achieves the 50 percent reduction, but with great variation among firms. This is exactly what must happen to minimize the costs of the 50 percent reduction. Under the 50 percent regulatory scheme, on the other hand, those firms which can substitute at relatively low cost will stop at 50 percent reduction, whereas the highly profitable firms with limited substitution possibilities will have to reduce output by nearly 50 percent to meet the requirement, at great loss to society in terms of opportunity costs.

A second problem with regulation, stressed by Edwin Mills,[13] is that the incentive structure is backwards. With the tax firms have an incentive to make

---

[13] E. Mills, "Economic Incentives in Air-Pollution Control," in M. I. Goldman, ed., *Controlling Pollution: The Economics of a Cleaner America*, (Englewood Cliffs, N.J.: Prentice-Hall, Inc., 1967).

the best substitutions possible to minimize their tax burdens. With regulation there is a clear market incentive to cheat, since the polluting activity is still priced at its original value, well below its true social marginal costs. This is especially true of water and air pollution, since these resources are often free. Moreover, it is up to government prosecuters to bring suit, and under U.S. law they bear the burden of proof. Whether or not a judicial system of threat and punishment will deter cheating is an open question, but with such a simple tax as an alternative, there is no need to beg the issue. In point of fact, individual state regulations have never had much effect in the United States, probably because the firms could offer the counterthreat of moving if prosecuted. The recent federal laws may be more effective deterrents to cheating in this respect, but it is still the responsibility of the individual states to bring suit against the polluters. One must remain skeptical.

Direct regulation makes some sense as a standby weapon for short-term emergencies. If air pollution becomes extremely dangerous due to unusual atmospheric conditions, a temporary ban on automobiles may be the only effective short-term solution. Also, if the United States seriously pursues the goal of zero pollution, then society will be indifferent to the tax versus regulation. The only way to achieve zero pollution in the aggregate is for each polluter to stop polluting entirely. The zero pollution target is almost certainly unattainable, however, and indeed the laws contain the marvelously vague standards of "best adequately demonstrated technology" (air pollution) and "best available technology economically feasible" (water pollution). One wonders how the EPA will ever be able to determine these for each industrial polluter, and whether their determinations will ever stand up in the courts. What, for example, does "economically feasible" mean—no reduction in profits? In any event, the standard of zero discharges into navigable waters is certainly unreachable by 1985. It will undoubtedly be pushed back, much as the automobile emissions standards were continually relaxed during the 1970s. If the desired reduction is reevaluated to be less than 100 percent, it is difficult to see any good economic reason for choosing regulation over the tax approach as the basic antipollution strategy, especially for industrial pollution.

Municipal Waste Treatment Facilities

Subsidizing waste treatment facilities to clean up pollution is certainly a policy worth considering. Suppose someone invented a method for cleaning up vast amounts of water pollution for only a few pennies. Clearly an antipollution policy would want to make liberal, perhaps exclusive, use of this technology. In general, any such technology is attractive so long as it is "cheap enough," but whether or not the government should subsidize the use of cleaning facilities is a complex question, depending on the exact form of the externality, available policy options, and the nature of waste treatment technology.

To keep the analysis of waste treatment relatively simple, let us return to the one-source production-externality model of Chapter 7 in which firm 1 produces a substance, Z_1, that enters into all firms production functions, including its own. Call Z_1 a pollutant. To focus on the treatment issue, assume that Z_1 is positively related to firm 1's use of factor i, say, water, and negatively related to its use of another factor, k, say, cleanser. That is:

$$(8.26) \qquad Z_1 = g(X_{1i}; X_{1k}) \qquad \frac{\partial g}{\partial X_{1i}} > 0 \qquad \frac{\partial g}{\partial X_{1k}} < 0$$

There are N purely private goods and factors produced by the J firms in addition to Z_1. Therefore,

Let:

$$X_{jn} = \text{good (factor) } n \text{ produced (used) by firms } j.$$
$$j = 1, \ldots, J$$
$$n = 1, \ldots, N$$

$(8.27) \qquad f^j(X_{jn}; Z_1) = $ the production function of firm j, with Z_1 a control variable only for firm 1

$$j = 1, \ldots, H$$

and

$$(8.28) \qquad U\left(\sum_{j=1}^{J} X_{jn} \right) = \text{the utility function of the single consumer, incorporating the } N \text{ market clearance equations}$$

Since this is a straight production externality, the consumer is unconcerned with the production of Z_1. The government's problem is

$$\max_{(X_{jn}; Z_1)} U\left(\sum_{j=1}^{J} X_{jn} \right)$$

$$\text{s.t.} \quad f^j(X_{jn}; Z_1) \quad j = 1, \ldots, J$$
$$Z_1 = g(X_{1i}; X_{1k})$$

with corresponding Lagrangian:

$$\max_{(X_{jn}; Z_1)} L = U\left(\sum_{j=1}^{J} X_{jn} \right) + \sum_{j=1}^{J} \lambda^j f^j(X_{jn}; Z_1) + \mu[Z_1 - g(X_{1i}; X_{1k})]$$

The first-order conditions are:

$$(8.29) \qquad \frac{\partial L}{\partial X_{jm}} = \frac{\partial U}{\partial X_m} + \lambda^j \frac{\partial f^j}{\partial X_{jm}} = 0 \qquad \begin{matrix} j = 1, \ldots, J \\ m \neq i, k \end{matrix}$$

$$(8.30) \qquad \frac{\partial L}{\partial X_{ji}} = \frac{\partial U}{\partial X_i} + \lambda^j \frac{\partial f^j}{\partial X_{ji}} = 0 \qquad j = 2, \ldots, J$$

$$(8.31) \qquad \frac{\partial L}{\partial X_{jk}} = \frac{\partial U}{\partial X_k} + \lambda^j \frac{\partial f^j}{\partial X_{jk}} = 0 \qquad j = 2, \ldots, J$$

$$(8.32) \qquad \frac{\partial L}{\partial X_{1i}} = \frac{\partial U}{\partial X_i} + \lambda^1 \frac{\partial f^1}{\partial X_{1i}} - \mu \frac{\partial g}{\partial X_{1i}} = 0$$

$$(8.33) \qquad \frac{\partial L}{\partial X_{1k}} = \frac{\partial U}{\partial X_k} + \lambda^1 \frac{\partial f^1}{\partial X_{1k}} - \mu \frac{\partial g}{\partial X_{1k}} = 0$$

$$(8.34) \qquad \frac{\partial L}{\partial Z_1} = \lambda^1 \frac{\partial f^1}{\partial Z_1} + \sum_{j=2}^{J} \lambda^j \frac{\partial f^j}{\partial Z_1} + \mu = 0$$

From conditions (8.29), (8.30), and (8.31), it follows immediately that

$$(8.35) \qquad \frac{\dfrac{\partial U}{\partial X_m}}{\dfrac{\partial U}{\partial X_1}} = \frac{\dfrac{\partial f^j}{\partial X_{jm}}}{\dfrac{\partial f^j}{\partial X_{j1}}} \qquad \begin{array}{l} j = 1, \ldots, J \\ m \neq i, k \end{array}$$

$$(8.36) \qquad \frac{\dfrac{\partial U}{\partial X_i}}{\dfrac{\partial U}{\partial X_1}} = \frac{\dfrac{\partial f^j}{\partial X_{ji}}}{\dfrac{\partial f^j}{\partial X_{j1}}} \qquad j = 2, \ldots, J$$

$$(8.37) \qquad \frac{\dfrac{\partial U}{\partial X_k}}{\dfrac{\partial U}{\partial X_1}} = \frac{\dfrac{\partial f^j}{\partial X_{jk}}}{\dfrac{\partial f^j}{\partial X_{j1}}} \qquad j = 2, \ldots, J$$

The government should not interfere in the competitive markets for any good or factor other than to i or k; nor should it interfere with the purchases of factors i and k by firms $2, \ldots, J$. To obtain the pareto-optimal conditions for firm 1's purchase of i and k, substitute for μ from (8.34) into (8.32) and (8.33) and use the fact that $\partial U / \partial X_{j1} = -\lambda^j \partial f^j / \partial X_{j1}, j = 1, \ldots, J$, selectively substituting for firm j term by term in denominators, to obtain:

$$(8.38) \qquad \frac{\partial U}{\partial X_i} + \lambda^1 \frac{\partial f^1}{\partial X_{1i}} + \left(\lambda^1 \frac{\partial f^1}{\partial Z_1} + \sum_{j=2}^{J} \lambda^j \frac{\partial f^j}{\partial Z_1} \right) \frac{\partial g}{\partial X_{1i}} = 0$$

$$(8.39) \qquad \frac{\partial U}{\partial X_k} + \lambda^1 \frac{\partial f^1}{\partial X_{1k}} + \left(\lambda^1 \frac{\partial f^1}{\partial Z_1} + \sum_{j=2}^{J} \lambda^j \frac{\partial f^j}{\partial Z_1} \right) \frac{\partial g}{\partial X_{1k}} = 0$$

$$(8.40) \qquad \frac{\dfrac{\partial U}{\partial X_i}}{\dfrac{\partial U}{\partial X_1}} = \left(\frac{\dfrac{\partial f^1}{\partial X_{1i}}}{\dfrac{\partial f^1}{\partial X_{11}}} \right) + \left[\left(\frac{\dfrac{\partial f^1}{\partial Z_1}}{\dfrac{\partial f^1}{\partial X_{11}}} \right) + \sum_{j=2}^{J} \left(\frac{\dfrac{\partial f^j}{\partial Z_1}}{\dfrac{\partial f^j}{\partial X_{j1}}} \right) \right] \cdot \frac{\partial g}{\partial X_{1i}}$$

$$(8.41) \qquad \frac{\dfrac{\partial U}{\partial X_k}}{\dfrac{\partial U}{\partial X_1}} = \left(\frac{\dfrac{\partial f^1}{\partial X_{1k}}}{\dfrac{\partial f^1}{\partial X_{11}}} \right) + \left[\left(\frac{\dfrac{\partial f^1}{\partial Z_1}}{\dfrac{\partial f^1}{\partial X_{11}}} \right) + \sum_{j=2}^{J} \left(\frac{\dfrac{\partial f^j}{\partial Z_1}}{\dfrac{\partial f^j}{\partial X_{j1}}} \right) \right] \cdot \frac{\partial g}{\partial X_{1k}}$$

Following the usual argument, the government can achieve the first-order conditions if it taxes firm 1's use of resource i and *simultaneously* subsidizes its use of resource k, such that

(8.42)
$$t_i = \left[\left(\frac{\frac{\partial f^1}{\partial Z_1}}{\frac{\partial f^1}{\partial X_{11}}}\right) + \sum_{j=2}^{J} \left(\frac{\frac{\partial f^j}{\partial Z_1}}{\frac{\partial f^j}{\partial X_{j1}}}\right)\right] \cdot \frac{\partial g}{\partial X_{1i}} \cdot q_1$$

(8.43)
$$s_k = \left[\left(\frac{\frac{\partial f^1}{\partial Z_1}}{\frac{\partial f^1}{\partial X_{11}}}\right) + \sum_{j=2}^{J} \left(\frac{\frac{\partial f^j}{\partial Z_1}}{\frac{\partial f^j}{\partial X_{j1}}}\right)\right] \cdot \frac{\partial g}{\partial X_{1k}} \cdot q_1$$

t_i and s_k measure, respectively, the social marginal value of firm 1 using an additional unit of factors i and k. For example, the right-hand side of (8.42) can be interpreted as:

(8.44)
$$-\frac{\Delta X_1}{\Delta Z_1} \cdot \frac{\Delta Z_1}{\Delta X_{1i}} \cdot q_1$$

or the marginal values of X_1 by all firms because of the increase in Z_1 occasioned by a unit increase in X_{1i}. Similarly, s_k gives the value of the marginal increase in X_1 by all firms due to a unit increase in X_{1k}. If the function g contained numerous other factors besides X_{1i} and X_{1k}, one could easily show that firm 1's use of all these factors would have to be taxed or subsidized. Thus, subsidizing the cleaning agent makes sense only if all other factors directly related to the pollutant are taxed (subsidized) as well.

There is an alternative, and simpler, policy for the government, however. It can choose to tax the pollutant Z_1 directly, leaving *all* other goods and factors untaxed no matter who uses them, including the first firm. To see this, consider the reaction of firm 1 to a tax, t_z, on Z_1. It will solve the following problem:

$$\max_{(X_{1n};Z_1)} \sum_{n=1}^{N} q_n X_{1n} + t_Z \cdot Z_1$$

$$\text{s.t.} \quad f^1(X_{1n}; Z_1) = 0$$
$$Z_1 = g(X_{1i}, X_{1k})$$

The Lagrangian is:

$$\max_{(X_{1n};Z_1)} L = \sum_{n=1}^{N} q_n X_{1n} + t_Z Z_1 + \lambda[f^1(X_{1n}; Z_1)]$$
$$+ \mu[Z_1 - g(X_{1i}, X_{ik})]$$

The first-order conditions are:

(8.45)
$$q_n + \lambda \frac{\partial f^1}{\partial X_{1n}} = 0 \qquad n \neq i, k$$

(8.46)
$$q_i + \lambda \frac{\partial f^1}{\partial X_{1i}} - \mu \frac{\partial g}{\partial X_{1i}} = 0$$

(8.47)
$$q_k + \lambda \frac{\partial f^1}{\partial X_{1k}} - \mu \frac{\partial g}{\partial X_{1k}} = 0$$

(8.48)
$$t_z + \lambda \frac{\partial f^1}{\partial Z_1} + \mu = 0$$

From (8.45):

(8.49)
$$\frac{q_n}{q_1} = \frac{\dfrac{\partial f^1}{\partial X_{1n}}}{\dfrac{\partial f^1}{\partial X_{11}}} \qquad n \neq i, k \text{ as required for pareto optimality}$$

As we discovered, there is no need to tax these goods and factors. Next, substitute for μ from (8.48) into (8.46) and (8.47) to obtain:

(8.50)
$$q_i + \lambda \frac{\partial f^1}{\partial X_{1i}} + \left(t_z + \lambda \frac{\partial f^1}{\partial Z_1}\right) \cdot \frac{\partial g}{\partial X_{1i}} = 0$$

(8.51)
$$q_k + \lambda \frac{\partial f^1}{\partial X_{ik}} + \left(t_z + \lambda \frac{\partial f^1}{\partial Z_1}\right) \cdot \frac{\partial g}{\partial X_{1k}} = 0$$

But from (8.45), $q_1 = -\lambda \, \partial f^1/\partial X_{11}$. Therefore,

(8.52)
$$\frac{q_i}{q_1} = \left(\frac{\dfrac{\partial f^1}{\partial X_{1i}}}{\dfrac{\partial f^1}{\partial X_{11}}}\right) + \left[\frac{t_z}{q_1} + \left(\frac{\dfrac{\partial f^1}{\partial Z_1}}{\dfrac{\partial f^1}{\partial X_{11}}}\right)\right] \cdot \frac{\partial g}{\partial X_{1i}}$$

(8.53)
$$\frac{q_k}{q_1} = \left(\frac{\dfrac{\partial f^1}{\partial X_{1k}}}{\dfrac{\partial f^1}{\partial X_{11}}}\right) + \left[\frac{t_z}{q_1} + \left(\frac{\dfrac{\partial f^1}{\partial Z_1}}{\dfrac{\partial f^1}{\partial X_{11}}}\right)\right] \cdot \frac{\partial g}{\partial X_{1k}}$$

If (a)

$$t_z = q_1 \cdot \sum_{j=2}^{J} \left(\frac{\dfrac{\partial f^j}{\partial Z_1}}{\dfrac{\partial f^j}{\partial X_{j1}}}\right)$$

the value of the marginal external effects of firm 1's use of Z_1; and (b) factors i and k are untaxed (unsubsidized) so that the consumer and firm 1 face the same prices for the factors, q_i and q_k, then the pareto-optimal conditions (8.40) and (8.41) will obtain.

These alternative solutions demonstrate a number of points with specific reference to waste treatment that were developed in the more general context of Chapter 7:

1. If the government taxes the pollutant directly, there is no need to tax or subsidize anything else, including waste treatment. Waste treatment may well be a "cheap" solution to the pollution problem, but the firms will discover this for themselves in response to the pollution tax. Waste treatment now has value to the firm in that it reduces the tax payments by reducing the quantity of the pollutant, Z_1. Consider equation (8.53) once again. The firm will equate

$$\frac{q_k}{q_1} = \frac{\dfrac{\partial f^1}{\partial X_{1k}}}{\dfrac{\partial f^1}{\partial X_{11}}} + \frac{\dfrac{\partial f^1}{\partial Z_1}}{\dfrac{\partial f^1}{\partial X_{11}}} \cdot \frac{\partial g}{\partial X_{1k}}$$

without the tax. The additional incentive to use X_{1k}, the cleansing agent, arises from the terms $t_z/q_1 \cdot \partial g/\partial X_{1k}$, which gives the reduction in tax revenues per unit increase in X_{1k}, expressed in terms of good 1. With t_z equal to the marginal external effects of Z_1, this is exactly the extra incentive society desires. No further inducement is necessary.

2. Waste treatment becomes attractive only if the government cannot tax the pollutant directly, but then all factors related to the pollutant must either be taxed or subsidized. All these factors in effect become sources of externality working through the untaxed pollutant. If using an additional unit of water (X_{1i}) affects all firms, so, too, does an additional unit of cleanser (X_{1k}). This example demonstrates the proposition developed in the preceding chapter using a more general model: If the externality is not taxed, then the government must tax (subsidize) all other goods and factors directly related to the externality. Here the only factors directly related to Z_1 are X_{1i} and X_{1k}.

3. Suppose each of the other firms could use the cleansing agent X_k to reduce the amount of Z_1 it receives from firm 1. This would require a modification in the model as it now stands, since the level of Z_1 is assumed to be a parameter for firms $2, \ldots, J$. Without actually solving this model, it should be clear from the theory developed in Chapter 7 that the government cannot achieve pareto optimality simply by subsidizing $X_{jk}, j = 2, \ldots, J$. Any pareto-optimal solution must involve some set of taxes (subsidies) on firm 1, the source of the externality. Unfortunately the waste treatment grants suffer exactly this defect. Suppose municipality 2 is situated downstream from municipality 1. If municipality 1 dumps untreated sewage into the stream at its downstream border, it has no obvious incentive to build a facility. Town 2 may well accept the federal funds to clean up its water, but this solution cannot be pareto optimal since it does nothing to retard the pollution at its source. Given that localities must pay 25 percent of the cost, it is small wonder that many localities have chosen not to build the facilities.

4. Large waste treatment facilities subsidized by the government make sense, even given direct taxation of the pollutant, if waste treatment exhibits significant economies of scale or decreasing unit costs. This is an entirely separate issue from the externality point and will be analyzed in Chapter 9. The crux of the matter is that each individual polluter should not be using resources

for waste treatment at high unit costs when larger facilities can be operated at much lower unit costs. In fact, waste treatment does exhibit scale economies. Nonetheless, the federal grant program which leaves the option of building up to each individual municipality will not necessarily provide the proper amount of waste treatment. Nor should polluters be untaxed in the first place.

CONCLUDING COMMENTS

One of the most effective antipollution campaigns occurred in West Germany's Ruhr River Basin, a system of five rivers on which a significant portion of West Germany's heavy industry is located.[14] West Germany created a separate jurisdictional body to regulate the basin, decided the quality of water it wanted for each of the rivers, and used a combination of taxes on polluters and waste treatment facilities to achieve the new pollution standards. While the program may not have been pareto optimal—taxes, for example, were based on average and not marginal damage levels—the results were dramatic nonetheless. The standards were achieved fairly rapidly, and the taxes did induce firms to substitute other resources for water. On average, West German firms on the Ruhr River use far less water than their U.S. counterparts.[15] Water apparently is highly substitutable in production, a fact which makes the U.S. reluctance to tax polluters all the more incomprehensible. Most economists would agree, we believe, that the federal antipollution campaign is much more costly/less effective than it need be. The assumptions of first-best analysis may be highly restrictive, but the theoretical economic evidence against the four major U.S. antipollution programs is nonetheless fairly overwhelming.

REFERENCES

Baumol, W. J., and Oates, W. *The Theory of Environmental Policy,* Englewood Cliffs, N.J.: Prentice-Hall, Inc., 1975.

Broome, J. "Trying to Value a Life." *Journal of Public Economics,* February 1978.

Freeman, III, A. Myrick. "Air and Water Pollution Policy." In *Current Issues in U.S. Environmental Policy,* Resources for the Future, edited by P. Portney. Baltimore, Md.: Johns Hopkins University Press, 1978.

Goldman, M. I. "Pollution: The Mess Around Us." In *Controlling Pollution: The Economics of a Cleaner America,* edited by M. I. Goldman. Englewood Cliffs, N.J.: Prentice-Hall, Inc., 1967.

Kneese, A. Y. "Water Quality Management by Regional Authorities in the Ruhr Area." In *Controlling Pollution: The Economics of a Cleaner*

---

[14] For an excellent overview and analysis of the water quality management program on the Ruhr, see A. Y. Kneese, "Water Quality Management by Regional Authorities in the Ruhr Area," in M. I. Goldman, ed., *Controlling Pollution.*

[15] For instance, steel production on the Ruhr uses 2.6 cubic yards of water per ton on average, whereas the industry average worldwide is 130 cubic yards per ton. M. I. Goldman, "Polution: The Mess Around Us," in M. I. Goldman, ed., *Controlling Pollution,* p. 36.

America, edited by M. I. Goldman. Englewood Cliffs, N.J., Prentice-Hall, Inc., 1967.

Mills, E. S. "Economic Incentives in Air-Pollution Control." In *Controlling Pollution: The Economics of a Cleaner America,* edited by M. I. Goldman. Englewood Cliffs, N.J.: Prentice-Hall, Inc., 1967.

―――. *The Economics of Environmental Quality.* New York: W. W. Norton & Co., Inc., 1978.

Seskin, E. "Automobile Air Pollution Policy." In *Current Issues in U.S. Environmental Policy,* Resources for the Future, edited by P. Portney. Baltimore, Md.: Johns Hopkins University Press, 1978.

9

The theory of decreasing cost production

Production of some goods and services exhibits significant decreasing costs or increasing returns to scale,[1] meaning that unit or average costs for an individual firm continue to fall up to a significant proportion of total market demand. Whenever this occurs, government intervention will almost certainly be required to ensure a social welfare optimum. Public sector economics has traditionally concerned itself only with the extreme case, in which a single firm's average costs decline all the way to total market demand. Since a single firm can supply the entire industry output, this has been called the "natural monopoly." The problems created by less extreme instances of decreasing cost production, which lead to oligopolistic market structures, have traditionally been covered in courses on industrial organization. In keeping with this tradition, Chapter 9 will analyze only the natural monopoly so that "decreasing costs" mean decreasing unit costs up to total market demand.

Decreasing cost production requires government intervention in a market economy for the simple reason that it is totally incompatible with a competitive market structure. Decreasing cost industries cannot possibly have a competitive structure, with large numbers of price-taking firms. Moreover, even if the competitive structure were possible, it would not be desirable. In order to capture the benefits of increasing returns production, the entire output must be produced by a single firm. This is why decreasing cost industries are referred to as "natural monopolies" and why they necessarily violate the technological assumption of well-behaved production required for a well-functioning competitive market system.

Decreasing cost industries are not all that rare. They typically occur in the production of services rather than products, in particular, for those services requiring relatively large setup costs, after which large numbers of users can be serviced with relatively low marginal costs. The combination of high start-up costs and low marginal costs causes unit costs to decline even as the number of users becomes large. Services having these attributes include many forms of transportation, especially highways and rail transit; the "public utilities," such as telephone service, electricity, water, and sewage; some recreational facilities such as beaches and parks; television; and first-class mail delivery. Television

---

[1] See Appendix at end of this Chapter.

is perhaps the clearest example among these. It requires considerable resources to produce, transmit, and receive any one television program, but once the program is produced, and the transmitting and receiving facilities are in place, the costs of having another viewer turn on his set is nil. Since the number of viewers is the relevant unit of output, average costs will decrease continuously as the number of viewers increases. Marginal costs are undoubtedly greater than zero for each of the other services, but they are nonetheless relatively insignificant compared with the fixed costs of establishing the service.[2]

Chapter 9 will explore the pareto-optimal conditions for efficient production with decreasing cost industries, indicating why the competitive market system cannot achieve them, and considering the pricing and investment rules implied by the efficiency conditions. The pricing rules imitate standard competitive principles and are therefore relatively straightforward. The investment rules are far from standard, however. Investment in decreasing cost industries has a lumpy all-or-none aspect to it that is absent in the usual marginal investment analysis applied to the small competitive firm. Furthermore, profitability is not necessarily a reliable investment guideline for decreasing cost services. Nor are there necessarily any substitute criteria that can be readily applied in practice. As a result, investment decisions for these industries are frequently among the most difficult decisions the government has to make, even under the somewhat sterile assumptions of first-best theory.

Chapter 10 will review actual U.S. policy with respect to these decreasing cost services. It turns out that governments in the United States generally have not adopted the first-best price and investment decision rules for decreasing cost services. Rather, they tend to prefer some form of average cost pricing and the standard private-sector profitability criteria for investment decisions, neither of which is pareto optimal. Chapter 10 will consider why average cost pricing and profitability are so popular and analyze their properties relative to the first-best decision rules.

Chapter 11 will conclude the discussion of decreasing cost industries with an analysis of the so-called "peak-load problem" which arises whenever two conditions exist. First, demand must be highly variable over the relevant demand cycle, such that at times demand for the service is well below the capacity of the system, while at other times demand is at "peak load" and straining against capacity, meaning either that it can only be satisfied at greatly increased marginal costs, or that it cannot be satisfied at all, at least not at the going market price. There may be an absolute capacity constraint on the system. Second, it must not be possible to inventory off-peak production in order to satisfy demand at the peak.

The peak-load phenomenon is fairly common, and certainly not restricted to decreasing cost industries. In fact, most of the literature on the peak-load

---

[2] It is true that marginal costs can rise significantly at the point of congestion for those services, such as highways and recreational facilities, that can become congested, but congestion is an example of an externality. It is unrelated to the phenomenon of significant scale economies or decreasing costs.

problem assumes constant or decreasing returns-to-scale production. Nonetheless, it is appropriate to consider this problem as part of the analysis of decreasing costs since nearly all of these industries satisfy both of the conditions for the peak-load phenomenon, and both pricing and investment rules change considerably with variable demand. Fortunately, the main results obtained with the assumptions of constant or increasing cost production carry over virtually intact to the decreasing cost case.

DECREASING COSTS IN GENERAL EQUILIBRIUM ANALYSIS

The general equilibrium model of Chapter 2 is many times more complex than it need be to analyze decreasing costs. The problems created by a decreasing cost firm are directly related to the particular form of its production function, nothing more. Unlike the externality problem there is no need to model explicitly the interrelationships among either consumers or producers. Thus, the demand side of the model can be adequately represented by a single consumer. Were the model to include many consumers and a social welfare function, the first-order conditions would merely reproduce the interpersonal equity conditions and the pareto-optimal consumption conditions of the full model in Chapter 2. Similarly, positing many "well-behaved" firms will merely reproduce the standard pareto-optimal production conditions for those firms. Hence, a single producer will also suffice so long as its production exhibits increasing returns to scale. Finally, there is no need to carry along N goods and factors. A one-good, one-factor economy is all that is necessary. Consequently, a general equilibrium model consisting of one person, with one source of (decreasing cost) production, at which a single output is produced by means of a single input is sufficiently general to capture both the nature of the decreasing cost problem and the decision rules necessary to ensure full pareto optimality. Keeping the model this simple has the additional advantage of permitting a two-dimensional geometric analysis, a welcome relief from the notational complexities of the various externality models.

Therefore, let us assume:

1. A single consumer with utility function

(9.1) $$U(X, L)$$

where:

$X =$ the single output.

$L =$ labor, the only factor of production.

By the usual convention, L enters $U(\ )$ with a negative sign. The indifference curves corresponding to $U(X, L)$ are represented in Figure 9–1.

2. Production of X using L occurs according to the production relationship

(9.2) $$X = f(L)$$

represented in Figure 9–2, with $\partial F/\partial L \equiv f' > 0$, $\partial^2 F/\partial L^2 \equiv f'' > 0$ and $f(0) = 0$.

FIGURE 9–1

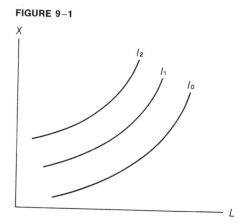

FIGURE 9–2

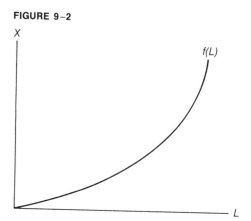

Thus, f is a homogeneous function exhibiting increasing returns to scale. As shown in the Appendix at the end of this chapter, X must also have continuously declining average costs.

3. Prices P_X and P_L, common to both the consumer and producer.

Notice that market clearance automatically holds in this model since it is understood that the consumer supplies all the input used by the firm, consumes all the output produced by the firm, and receives (pays) all pure economic profits (losses) arising from production at prices P_X and P_L.

The Pareto-Optimal Conditions

Society's problem is the standard one:

$$\max_{(X,L)} U(X,L)$$

$$\text{s.t.} \quad X = f(L)$$

Because the model is so simple, the pareto-optimal conditions can be derived by substituting the production function into the utility function and solving the unconstrained maximum:

$$\max_{(L)} U(f(L); L)$$

The first-order conditions are:

(9.3)

$$U_X f' + U_L = 0$$

or

(9.4)

$$U_X f' = -U_L$$

Condition (9.4) gives the standard result that labor should be used to produce X until the marginal utility of X just equals the marginal disutility of further work.

DECREASING COSTS AND COMPETITIVE MARKETS

Even if the second-order conditions for a welfare maximum are satisfied, a competitive industry cannot achieve condition (9.4). A price-taking competitive firm would solve the following problem:

$$\max_{(L)} P_X f(L) - P_L L$$

The first-order conditions are:

(9.5)

$$P_X f' - P_L = 0$$

or

(9.6) $$P_X f' = P_L \qquad \text{alternatively, } P_X = P_L / f' \equiv MC_X$$

As usual, condition (9.6) says that the competitive firm will hire labor until the value of labor's marginal product just equals the price of labor, or supply X until price equals marginal costs.

On the surface this result would appear to satisfy the full pareto-optimal conditions. We know that the consumer will maximize utility by equating

(9.7)

$$\frac{U_X}{P_X} = \frac{-U_L}{P_L}$$

or

(9.8)

$$P_X = -\frac{U_X}{U_L} \cdot P_L$$

Substituting for P_X in (9.6) yields:

(9.9)

$$-\frac{U_X}{U_L} \cdot P_L \cdot f' = P_L$$

FIGURE 9-3
Utility Maximum

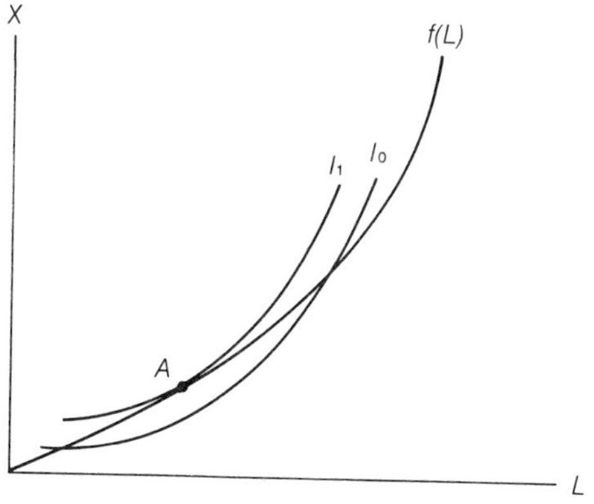

or

(9.10)
$$U_X f' = -U_L$$

the pareto-optimal condition (9.4).

With increasing returns-to-scale production, however, the second-order conditions cannot be ignored, since both the indifference curves and the production function have the same general curvature. To ensure that condition (9.4) represents a utility maximum, the derivative of (9.4) with respect to L must be less than zero. Thus,

(9.11)
$$\frac{d\left(f' + \dfrac{U_L}{U_X}\right)}{dL} < 0$$

or

(9.12)
$$\frac{df'}{dL} + \frac{d\left(\dfrac{U_L}{U_X}\right)}{dL} < 0 \qquad \text{(Note: } U_L < 0\text{)}$$

Equation (9.12) implies that the curvature of the indifference curves for X and L must be greater than the curvature of the production function. If the reverse is true, (9.4) represents a utility *minimum* along the production frontier. Refer to Figures 9-3 and 9-4.

While competitive behavior appears to be pareto optimal, the problem is that setting the price of labor equal to its marginal revenue product is *not* a profit maximum position for a decreasing cost firm. Since $Pf'' > 0$, the second-order conditions will always fail to hold for the competitive firm. Thus, condition (9.6) gives a profit-*minimizing* condition, not a profit-maximizing one. The perfectly competitive, decreasing marginal cost firm would maximize profits by increasing output indefinitely. The situation is depicted in Figure 9-5.

FIGURE 9–4
Utility Minimum

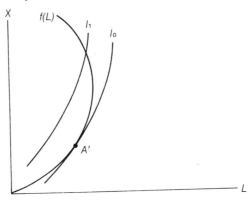

FIGURE 9–5

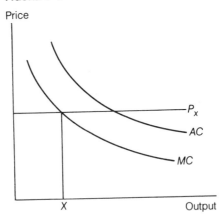

Since marginal costs, P_L/f', decline continuously,[3] the firm loses on every unit up to X, but that is the output given by (9–6). Marginal profits begin at $X + 1$ and increase as X increases. Ultimately the industry will consist of a single firm producing the entire market demand.

Competition and decreasing costs are incompatible in still another sense. Even if the government were able to subsidize the losses suffered by each firm producing at X in Figure 9–5, society would not want this solution. To exploit the scale economies one firm has to become the entire industry, hence a "natural monopoly."

---

[3] $d(P_L/f') = -P_L f''/(f')^2 < 0$. Strictly speaking, marginal costs could be constant or rising since decreasing costs refers to decreasing unit costs. But since $MC < AC$ when AC are declining, any $P = MC$ "equilibrium" will imply losses for the competitive firm.

THE PRICING RULE

Economic efficiency requires that the full pareto-optimal condition (9.4) holds. But this implies that the monopoly firm must set price equal to marginal cost, since only if $P_X = P_L/f' = MC$ will $U_X f' = -U_L$. Referring to Figure 9-6, the monopolist must produce at X_{opt}, the point at which market demand and marginal cost intersect. There are two problems with this solution, however. First, the unregulated monopolist will not select X_{opt}, but X_m, where $MR = MC$, and $P_m > P_x$. Thus, the government must either force the monopolist to select (P_x, X_{opt}), or take over the industry. Secondly, a regulated monopolist (or the government), if forced to produce at $P_x = MC$, will make perpetual losses, with $AC > MC$. Since the monopolist must cover his full costs in the long run, he will have to be subsidized by an amount equal to $X_{opt}(AC - MC)$. Moreover, the subsidy must not create inefficiencies elsewhere in the economy. It must be lump sum. In this simple economy the consumer would transfer the required income to the firm. Such a transfer is possible, because the excess of the consumer's earned income over his expenditures, $P_L \cdot L - P_X X$, exactly matches the firm's deficit. In a many-person economy this transfer becomes part of the interpersonal equity conditions, the only difference being that the taxes collected must be sufficient to cover both the transfers to other individuals and the transfers to decreasing cost firms.

FIGURE 9-6

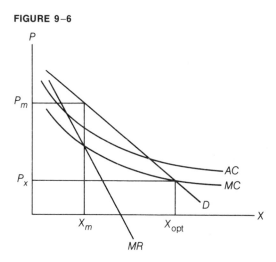

INVESTMENT RULES

When confronted with decreasing cost production, society must make a fundamental investment decision that does not present itself in "normal" industry situations. If the firm is forced to price optimally at $P = MC$ it cannot cover the opportunity costs of investing in that industry. Of course, the lump-sum subsidy it receives will always permit the firm to cover opportunity costs,

FIGURE 9–7

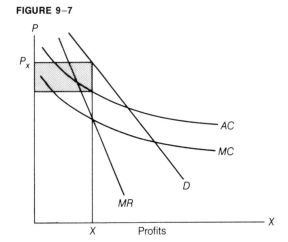

but this in itself is not especially helpful since profits (losses) are still not performing their customary function as a signal for investment. Society is, instead, presented with a unique all or none decision: Is providing the service at $P = MC$, with subsidy, preferable to not having the service at all? This is obviously quite different from the standard investment question, in which the present value formula is used to determine the profitability of a marginal increment to the capital stock evaluated at current (expected) market prices.

As it turns out, one can usefully distinguish two cases, which we shall refer to as the "easy" case and the "hard" case, depending on whether or not a profit maximizing monopolist could at least break even *if* allowed to do so.[4]

a. The Easy Case. Suppose we know that demand is sufficiently high so that a monopolist, if allowed to act as a monopolist, could *at least* break even by charging a single price for its product. This would certainly apply to most public utilities, urban highways, television, and many recreation services. In other words, the market demand curve is at least tangent to the firm's AC curve, as in Figures 9–7 and 9–8.

We will show that if (at least) break-even production is possible, the service should be produced. Potential profitability is thus a sufficient condition for having the service. However, price must be set at marginal costs, with a lump-sum subsidy to cover the resulting losses at that price. The monopolist must not be allowed to capture these potential profits.

---

[4] Since capital is suppressed in the simple geometric analysis, we are implicitly assuming that the capital stock is optimal for any given X, that is, that AC and MC are minimum long-run costs. The all-or-none test is an additional question, asking whether or not first-best optimal production and pricing is preferred to having no service at all. We should also note that the essentials of our analysis of the all-or-none test can be found in P. Diamond and D. McFadden, "Some Uses of the Expenditure Function in Public Finance, "*Journal of Public Economics*, February 1974.

FIGURE 9–8

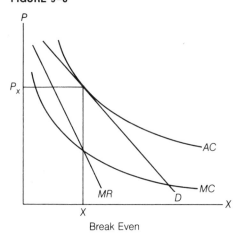

Break Even

b. The Hard Case. Unfortunately, the ability to break even is not a necessary condition for providing the service. Suppose demand is everywhere below *AC*, as in Figure 9–9, such that there is no single price at which a profit maximizing monopolist could break even. Clearly no private firm unless heavily subsidized would be interested in this market. However, society may be interested in having the government provide the service, once again, at the intersection of price and marginal cost. But notice that even potential profitability is not a useful investment guideline for this case. As we shall discover, the necessary conditions involve other criteria which do not have close market analogues.

The hard case is not merely a theoretical *curiosum*. Many, if not most, rural highways would certainly fall into this category, and possibly a fair number of recreational facilities as well, wilderness areas and the like. It is also likely that

FIGURE 9–9

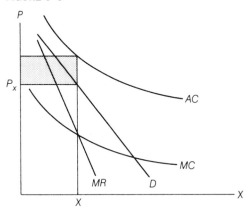

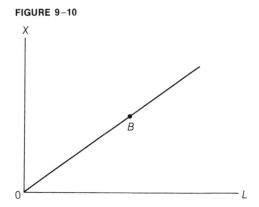

FIGURE 9–10

rail transit systems are examples of the hard case. Despite a history of continual real fare increases, rail transit deficits continue to grow in most U.S. cities. It may be that no single fare would cover full rail transit costs.

The Sufficient Conditions—The Easy Case

Let us first establish the sufficient conditions for decreasing cost production.

Proposition: If a profit-maximizing monopolist can at least break even by charging a single price, society should produce the good, but at $P = MC$, with lump-sum transfers to cover the resulting deficit.

A geometric proof will suffice, providing we use the consumer's indifference map and the production-possibilities frontier in $(X–L)$ space. The demand curve–average cost diagrams are useful for illustrating certain points, but illegitimate as a representation of general equilibrium. Their use requires ill-conceived notions of consumer's surplus.[5]

The first step in the proof is to characterize break-even production in $(X–L)$ space. Suppose a monopolist produces at some point such as B in Figure 9–10 and sets relative prices P_L/P_X equal to the slope of the ray from the origin through B. The monopolist would just break even, since at any point along the ray,

(9.13) $$X = P_L/P_X \cdot L \qquad \text{or} \qquad P_X X = P_L L$$

This example is *not* to suggest a monopolist would actually do this, but only to depict the limiting, break-even, $P = AC$ case.

Similarly, if the consumer faces relative prices P_L/P_X, he will be at an equilibrium such as B, in Figure 9–11. A ray from the origin through B with slope $P_L/P_X = k$, also serves as the consumer's budget line with no lump-sum taxes or transfers.

---

[5] The geometric proofs of the necessary and sufficient conditions were demonstrated to us by Peter Diamond in his graduate Public Finance class at MIT. See, also, P. Diamond and D. McFadden, "Some Uses of the Expenditure Function in Public Finance," especially for the "hard case."

FIGURE 9–11

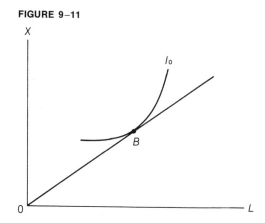

FIGURE 9–12

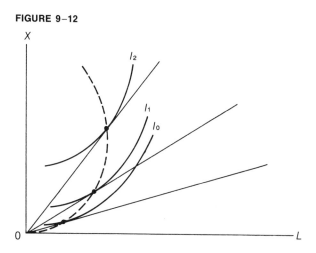

We can trace out a price-consumption line for the consumer by varying the slope of the ray through the origin, as in Figures 9–12 and 9–13. Thus a point on the price-consumption locus can represent an actual general equilibrium solution for the economy, in which the consumer is in equilibrium, and the firm is breaking even. This general equilibrium will be feasible if the price-consumption locus intersects the production-possibilities frontier, such as at point B in Figure 9–14. Of course, production is not pareto optimal at B. The slope of the production-possibilities frontier at B is the marginal product of labor. Let it equal a. Hence, $MC_B \equiv P_L/a < P_X$, since P_L/P_X = slope of the ray from the origin through B, the average product of labor. On the other hand, point B is still preferred to the origin, the point of zero production. This follows because the consumer is in equilibrium at B, so that the indifference curve on which point B lies is tangent to the ray through the origin. Hence, B must lie above the indifference curve that passes through the origin, establishing the

FIGURE 9–13

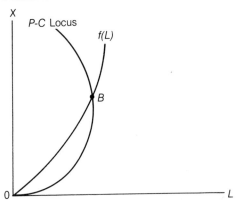

FIGURE 9–14

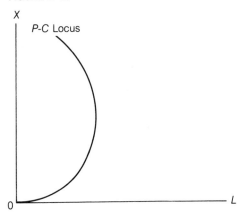

proposition that feasibility of break-even production is a sufficient condition for having the service.

Society can benefit most from the service by producing at point A in Figure 9–15, at which the production-possibilities frontier is just tangent to one of the consumer's indifference curves.

For A to be a general market equilibrium, P_L/P_X must be set equal to the slope of the production-possibilities frontier at A, so that $P_X = MC_X \equiv P_L/f'$. This price ratio, however, is the slope of a ray intersecting the L axis at point b, not the origin. Thus, the ray can be a budget line for the consumer only if the consumer first surrenders b units of labor lump sum, so that

$$(9.14) \qquad P_X X - P_L \cdot L = -P_L \cdot b$$

Similarly, with $P_X = MC_X$ at A, the firm makes pure economic losses equal to $P_L \cdot b$, since the ray is also the firm's profit line. Hence, with the lump-sum transfer of $P_L \cdot b$, and marginal cost pricing, the firm covers its full costs and the consumer attains his highest possible indifference curve.

FIGURE 9–15

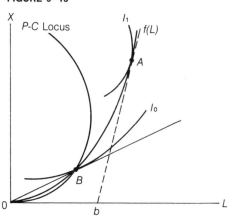

The Necessary Conditions—The Hard Case

The existence of a break-even production point such as B in Figure 9–15 implies the existence of a preferred pareto-optimal point such as A, but a pareto-optimal point A preferred to zero production does not imply B. Suppose the price-consumption line lies everywhere above the pp frontier (except at the origin), as in Figure 9–16.

Since the P-C locus defined all possible break-even general equilibrium points, break-even production is clearly not feasible. This corresponds, in $(P_X$–$X)$ space, to the situation in which the demand curve for X is everywhere below the AC curve. Yet society may still prefer production at $P_X = MC$. The key now is the indifference curve passing through the origin. If it lies everywhere above the production-possibilities frontier as in Figure 9–17, society should not produce X. The consumer prefers zero production to any of the available

FIGURE 9–16

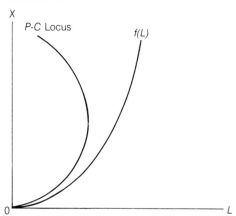

FIGURE 9–17

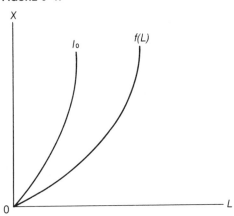

FIGURE 9–18

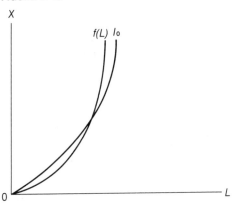

FIGURE 9–19

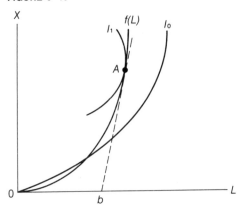

choices. If it crosses the pp frontier as in Figure 9–18, then there will exist a
higher indifference curve tangent to the frontier. Society should produce at the
tangency point A in Figure 9–19, set $P_X = MC_X$, and transfer b units of labor
lump sum from the consumer to the firm, exactly as above.

Notice that even potential profitability is no guideline in this, the hard case.
Even if the firm were allowed to maximize profits it could not so much as break
even by setting a single price. The government must rely on alternative willingness-to-pay lump-sum income measures of welfare, such as Hicks Compensating
Variation (HCV), to determine whether production is worthwhile. Given the
enormous popularity of the HCV in the public sector literature, the application
of the HCV to the decreasing cost problem is worth pursuing in some detail.

Consider the indifference curve through the origin, I_0, in Figure 9–20.

FIGURE 9–20

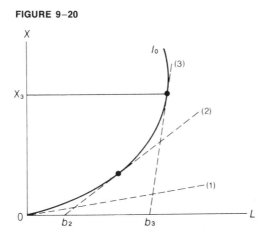

The tangency lines (1), (2), and (3) represent budget lines for the consumer,
in which the ratio of prices P_L/P_X equals the slope of the corresponding line and
the consumer first sacrifices, lump sum, 0, 0–b_2, and 0–b_3 units of labor, respectively. For example, P_X is so high (relative to P_L, assumed constant) on budget
line (1) that the consumer purchases no X. As P_X drops until, say, budget line
(3) applies, the consumer will purchase X_3. Moreover, since utility is being held
constant along I_0, the distance 0–b_3 can be interpreted as the lump-sum income
(in terms of labor) the consumer is willing to pay for the opportunity to purchase
X at the reduced price (equal to $P_L/$(slope of (3))). The income sacrificed keeps
utility constant by exactly offsetting the utility gains resulting from the reduction in P_X. Hence, 0–b_3 is the HCV for this P_X, measured relative to a P_X so
high that demand is zero. Furthermore, X_3 is a point on the consumer's compensated demand curve for X, compensated to equal the utility level represented
by I_0.

The HCV can then be compared with the actual amount of income the consumer must sacrifice for feasible decreasing cost production. Consider Figure
9–21. At point A on I_1, with marginal cost pricing, the firm requires 0–b units

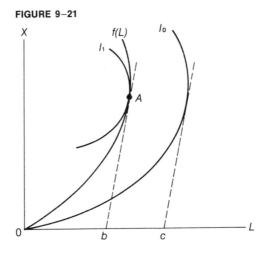

FIGURE 9–21

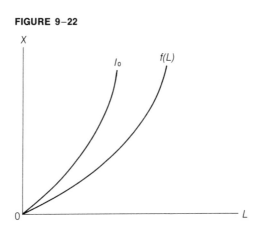

FIGURE 9–22

of L to break even, but at those prices the HCV is $0-c$. The consumer would clearly be willing to pay $0-b$, and society should provide the service. Alternatively, in Figure 9–22, with I_0 everywhere above the pp frontier, the consumer would never be willing to sacrifice the lump-sum income required for the firm to cover its cost with marginal cost pricing. Hence, the service should not be provided. In summary, then, the necessary condition for providing the service involves a direct comparison between the consumer's HCV, at $P_X = MC_X$, and the utility level with zero production, and the firm's deficit at the marginal cost price. This test can also be represented in (P_X-X) space, an interpretation worth analyzing since it appears in many sources, especially intermediate level texts.

Consider the market for X as represented by the demand and cost curves in Figure 9–23. The necessary condition is often stated as follows: If the area EP_XA exceeds the fixed cost subsidy, P_XABC, then society should operate the service at X. These tests use Marshallian consumer surplus as the measure

FIGURE 9–23

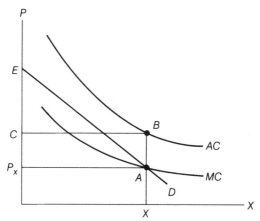

of benefit which has no willingness-to-pay interpretation. But if the demand curve is the compensated demand curve and only P_X varies, then these rules are equivalent to our preceeding discussion.

To see this, suppose the government is considering whether or not to operate a new, decreasing cost industry at $P = MC$. Should the government decide not to produce, the consumer remains at the status quo, call it A, with utility level $= U^A$. Should the government produce X, the consumer is in situation B, at utility level U^B. The question is whether $U^B \gtrless U^A$. The expenditure function provides the answer since

$$U^B > U^A$$

$$iff\ M(\vec{P}; U^B) > M(\vec{P}; U^A) \quad \text{for any price vector, } \vec{P}$$

That is, for any price vector $\vec{P}$, situation B costs more if it represents greater utility.[6]

To see how the expenditure function generates the all-or-none tests described above, assume

(9.15) $$M(\vec{P}^A; U^A) = -T_A$$

or

(9.16) $$\sum_i P_i^A X_i^A \bigg|_{comp} = -T_A$$

Note that T_A could well be 0. It measures lump-sum income from taxes, transfers, fixed factors, and pure economic profits. With no decreasing cost production, and all income earned income, it is reasonable to assume $T_A = 0$, although not necessary.

---

[6] The sufficient condition follows directly from the assumption of nonsatiation, which implies a positive marginal utility of income. The necessary condition follows from the fact that well-behaved indifference curves cannot cross. Thus, given two market situations with identical prices, the one with higher income must create higher utility.

Situation B will require an additional subsidy, bringing the total to T^B. Therefore, let

(9.17)
$$M(\vec{P}^B; U^B) = -T^B$$

Evaluating the expenditure functions at $\vec{P} = \vec{P}^B$, the new prices,[7]

(9.18)
$$U^B > U^A \quad \textit{iff} \quad M(\vec{P}^B; U^B) > M(\vec{P}^B; U^A)$$

(9.19)
$$\textit{iff} \quad -T^B > M(\vec{P}^B; U^A)$$

or

(9.20)
$$\textit{iff} \quad T^B < -M(\vec{P}^B; U^A)$$

But

(9.21)
$$-T^A = M(\vec{P}^A; U^A)$$

Thus,

$$U^B > U^A \quad \textit{iff}$$

(9.22)
$$T^B - T^A < M(\vec{P}^A; U^A) - M(\vec{P}^B; U^A)$$

The left-hand side of (9.22) is the additional lump-sum subsidy required for the new process to cover its fixed costs. It corresponds to distance $0-b$ in Figure 9–21. The right-hand side gives the income the consumer is willing to sacrifice to face prices $\vec{P}^B$ as opposed to $\vec{P}^A$. Thus, it corresponds to distance $0-c$ in Figure 9–21. As we saw in Chapter 4, the right-hand side also represents a summation of areas under compensated demand (supply) curves.[8]

(9.23)
$$M(\vec{P}^A; U^A) - M(\vec{P}^B; U^A) = \sum_{i=1}^{N} \int_{P_i^B}^{P_i^A} X_i^C dP$$

If the new product is the first good and it is "small," so that prices P_i, $i \geqq 2$ remain unchanged, then

(9.24)
$$M(\vec{P}^A; U^A) - M(\vec{P}^B; U^A) = \int_{P_1^B}^{P_1^A} X_1^C dP_1$$

where P_1^A is the price at which the demand curve intersects the price axis, and P_1^B is the marginal cost price. Hence, the area defined by (9.24) is $EP_X A$ in Figure 9–23, providing D refers to the compensated demand curve.

Marshallian Consumer's Surplus and Hicks Compensating Variation

Needless to say, the hard case is bound to be extremely difficult for the policy maker. Operating the service at any single price will generate losses, and justifying its continued operation in the face of these losses requires knowing

---

[7] The expenditure functions could also be evaluated at $\vec{P}^A$ which would involve Hicks Equivalent Variation rather than Hicks Compensating Variation.

[8] Since the X_i are compensated demand (factor supply) curves, the order of integration makes no difference.

an income measure, the Hicks Compensating Variation (HCV), that is certainly not easy to come by. Econometric knowledge to date has supplied precious little information on the compensated demands for any consumer goods. At best the policy maker may know the aggregate market demand curve, although even this is extremely unlikely. The all-or-none test requires knowing the demand relationship over the entire range of prices, from $P = MC$ up to a price high enough to preclude any demand for the service. But econometric analysis will typically provide information on just a portion of the curve estimated over a relatively narrow range of historical prices. In some instances there may be reasonably ways to extrapolate the estimated relationship back to the price axis, but even so one is left with the actual demand curve, not the compensated demand curve.

Suppose the actual demand curve is known with a reasonable degree of certainty. Can it provide any useful measures of the total benefits of the service? The answer depends upon what one is willing to assume. A frequent ploy is the assume away income effects so that the actual and compensated demand curves are one and the same. In this case, Marshallian consumer surplus and the HCV are identical. But this is hardly an attractive assumption. Almost all goods have some income elasticity of demand, and for services such as the public utilities and recreational facilities it is likely to be considerable. The higher the income elasticity of demand, the more these two benefit measures will diverge.

Robert Willig has recently provided an enormous dose of optimism by suggesting that assuming away income effects may not be necessary, since Marshallian consumer surplus is likely to be an extremely close approximation of the HCV, even for fairly large income elasticities. Specifically, he has proven that, *for a single price change*[9]

$$(9.25) \qquad \frac{C - A}{A} \approx \frac{\eta A}{2M^0}$$

where:

C = Hicks Compensating Variation due to the price change.
A = Marshallian consumer surplus.
η = the income elasticity of demand.
M^0 = income in the original, no service, situation.

As Willig points out, if the surplus (A) is 5 percent of total income (M^0), even with an income elasticity (η) as high as .8, the error in using A for C is approximately 2 percent, well within the range of demand estimation error. Hence, this approximation formula would appear to be a significant step forward toward practical application, but it is not without its problems.

In the first place, the assumption of a single price change is crucial to Willig's proof. If more than one price changes so that (9.23) applies, the Marshallian

---

[9] R. D. Willig, "Consumer's Surplus Without Apology," *American Economic Review*, September 1976.

measure will not be path dependent, a point discussed at length in Chapter 4. Unfortunately, for large projects such as mass transit, highway, or public utility investments, the single price change assumption is highly suspect.

Second, Willig's formula applies only to the individual demand curves of a single consumer and not to aggregate demand. Whether or not it can be used in the aggregate depends on the validity of the first-best assumption that the government has transferred income lump sum to satisfy the interpersonal equity conditions of social welfare. If so, then the many consumer economy is equivalent to a one-consumer economy in that there exists a consistent set of social indifference curves expressed in terms of aggregate quantities of goods and services (and factors).[10] If income has not been optimally redistributed, however, Willig's formula does not apply in the aggregate, nor has he been able to develop a many-person counterpart. Of course, the HCV computed from aggregate demand estimates is not correct either. An aggregate HCV-type measure requires weighting the individual measures by factors based in part on each person's social marginal utility of income, a point that will be developed at length in the second-best analysis of Part III. Suffice it to say here that the perceived benefits to people with high social marginal utilities of income will carry more weight in the aggregate than the perceived benefits of those with low social marginal utilities of income, where perceived benefits are given by the individual's HCV's. In a first-best world, marginal social utilities of income are equalized, so that the distribution issue cannot arise.

Despite these problems, Willig's approximation formula stands as an important empirical contribution to the first-best analysis of decreasing cost industries (and first-best cost-benefit analysis generally). Whether or not one considers income to be optimally distributed is surely a matter of personal taste, but if the policy analyst is willing to assume that it is, Willig has provided a useful alternative to the questionable practice of assuming away income effects when estimating willingness-to-pay measures of price changes.

DECREASING COSTS AND PUBLIC GOODS

We conclude Chapter 9 with a brief discussion of the relationship between decreasing cost services and public goods, a point of some confusion in the professional literature. Decreasing cost goods with zero (or approximately zero) marginal costs are sometimes referred to as "public goods" because any one person's consumption of the good will not diminish the quantity available for others to consume.[11] The uncongested highway, bridge, or tunnel, national wildlife preserves, and television viewing are all reasonably good examples.

---

[10] Alternatively, one can assume that all preferences are identical and homothetic. Refer to the discussion of one-consumer equivalence in Chapter 4.

[11] Francis Bator describes "publicness" in this manner in *The Question of Government Spending*: "There are activities, however, where the additional cost of extra use are literally zero. The economist labels the output of such activities 'public'." (p. 94). F. M. Bator, *The Question of Government Spending* (New York: Harper Bros. Publishers, 1960). (See pp. 90–98 for an extended discussion of zero marginal cost, decreasing cost services, especially pp. 94 and 96.)

Yet referring to these services as "public goods" because marginal costs are (approximately) zero is extremely misleading. Samuelson coined the phrase "public good" for a particular kind of externality-generating activity, the non-exclusive good. In Chapters 6 and 7 we suggested an alternative definition that could also be applied to exclusive goods, providing the externalities generated by their consumption (production) are all pervasive. The point is that the term ought properly be reserved for certain kinds of externalities, and not brought into the realm of decreasing cost theory. To apply it as well to decreasing costs, even when marginal costs equal zero, is bound to create confusion, because the pareto-optimal rules for externality-generating activities differ substantially from their decreasing cost counterparts. For example, consumption externalities create pareto-optimal rules of the form $\sum MRS = MRT$. Decreasing cost services, on the other hand, follow the normal competitive rules, $MRS = MRT$, for pareto optimality. Furthermore, the marginal production costs of externality-type "public goods" need not be zero. The marginal costs for weapons systems, for one example, are obviously considerable.

To see that these two rules imply two distinct allocative mechanisms, compare the pareto-optimal allocations of an externality-type "public good" and a decreasing cost service in a two-person economy given that:

1. The marginal costs of providing each good are zero at every output.
2. The individual demand curves for each good are identical. These relationships are shown in Figure 9–24.

If marginal costs (MRT) are zero for the decreasing cost good, then each person should be allowed to consume the good until his personal MRS is zero. The aggregate demand curve, $D^{\text{total}(DC)}$, is the *horizontal* summation of d_1 and d_2, and the optimum quantity is X_{DC}^{opt}, the point at which $D^{\text{total}(DC)}$ intersects the X axis. If marginal costs (MRT) are zero for the externality-type "public good,"

FIGURE 9–24

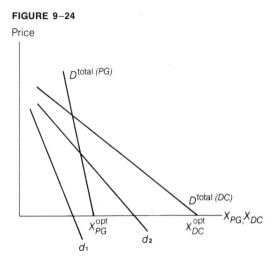

then the proper allocation occurs when $MRS^1 + MRS^2 = 0$. The aggregate demand curve, $D^{total(PG)}$ is the *vertical* summation of d_1 and d_2, and the optimum quantity is X_{PG}^{opt}, the point at which $D^{total(PG)}$ intersects the X axis.

Finally, the decreasing cost good can be marketed more or less normally in that each consumer should face the same price ($=0$). Of course the government does have to ensure that the fixed costs are covered with a lump-sum subsidy, but this is true of any properly marketed decreasing cost service, even those with nonzero marginal costs. On the other hand, "marketing" the externality-type public good requires a complex set of side markets and separate prices for each of the consumers. Thus, the statements "consumption by one implies consumption by all" (or "consumption by anyone affects everyone"), and "any one person's consumption does not diminish the quantity available to anyone else" are hardly equivalent statements. Indeed the second statement implies nothing more than zero marginal costs (MRT).

In our view, then, the appellation "public good" should be reserved for instances of pervasive externalities, more or less as Samuelson originally intended. If the term is also used to characterize zero marginal cost decreasing cost services it loses its particular analytical significance. It may as well refer to any good requiring government intervention, since there is no analytical reason to distinguish between zero- and nonzero marginal cost decreasing cost services.

REFERENCES

Bator, F. M. *The Question of Government Spending.* New York: Harper Bros. Publishers, 1960.

Diamond, P. A. and McFadden, D. "Some Uses of the Expenditure Function in Public Finance." *Journal of Public Economics,* February 1974.

Willig, R. D. "Consumer's Surplus Without Apology." *American Economic Review,* September 1976.

APPENDIX

RETURNS TO SCALE, HOMOGENEITY, AND DECREASING COSTS

Since increasing returns to scale imply decreasing average costs, the two terms will be used interchangeably throughout the text. To see that the former implies the latter, consider the homogeneous production function:

(9A.1) $$Y = f(X_1, \ldots, X_N) = f(X_i)$$

where:

$X_i = $ input i.
$Y = $ output.

By the definition of homogeneous functions,

(9A.2) $$\alpha^\beta Y = f(\alpha \cdot X_i)$$

Increasing returns to scale implies that $\beta > 1$, or a scalar increase (decrease) in each of the factors generates a more-than-proportionate increase (decrease) in output. Furthermore, if the production function is homogeneous of degree β, then the marginal production functions, $\partial Y/\partial X_k \equiv f_k(X_i)$ are homogeneous of degree $\beta - 1$. This follows immediately by differentiating $\alpha^\beta Y = \alpha^\beta f(X_i) = f(\alpha X_i)$ with respect to X_k:

(9A.3) $$\alpha^\beta f_k(X_i) = \frac{\partial f(\alpha X_i)}{\partial X_k} = \alpha f_k(\alpha X_i)$$

Hence:

(9A.4) $$\alpha^{\beta-1} f_k = f_k(\alpha \ X_i) \qquad k = 1, \ldots, N$$

To minimize production costs for any given output, the firm will solve the following problem:

$$\min_{(X_i)} \sum P_i X_i$$

$$\text{s.t.} \quad Y = f(X_i)$$

The first-order conditions imply:

(9A.5) $$\frac{P_i}{P_1} = \frac{f_i(X_i)}{f_1(X_i)} \qquad i = 2, \ldots, N$$

or that the ratio of factor prices equals the technical rate of substitution of the factors in production. Suppose the firm increases (decreases) its use of all factors X_i by the scalar α. Since $f_i(\alpha X_i) = \alpha^{\beta-1} f_i(X_i)$, this scalar increase (decrease) will continue to satisfy the first-order conditions:

(9A.6) $$\frac{f_i(\alpha X_i)}{f_1(\alpha X_i)} = \frac{\alpha^{\beta-1} f_i(X_i)}{\alpha^{\beta-1} f_1(X_i)} = \frac{f_i(X_i)}{f_1(X_i)} = \frac{P_i}{P_1}$$

Hence, if a vector of inputs $\vec{X}_i^*$ minimizes cost, so too will any vector $\alpha \vec{X}_i^*$.

But if all inputs are increased by the scalar α, total costs will increase by α, and output will increase by a factor α^β. Thus, the total cost function must be of the form

(9A.7) $$TC = kY^{1/\beta}$$

since $k \cdot (\alpha^\beta Y)^{1/\beta} = \alpha \cdot k \cdot Y^{1/\beta} = \alpha \cdot TC$. Finally,

(9A.8) $$AC = TC/Y = k \cdot Y^{(1/\beta - 1)} = k \cdot Y^{(1-\beta/\beta)}$$

Differentiating

(9A.9) $$\frac{\partial AC}{\partial Y} = \left(\frac{1-\beta}{\beta}\right) k \cdot Y^{(1-\beta/\beta-1)} < 0 \qquad \beta > 1$$

Hence, average costs decline continuously as output increases with increasing returns to scale.

10

Reflections on U.S. policy with respect to decreasing cost services: Equity and efficiency aspects

Suppose a decreasing cost service satisfies the requirements of the "easy case," that a profit-maximizing monopolist could at least break even. There will then be three obvious policy choices for the government, each depicted in Figure 10–1. The simplest option is to preserve free enterprise, offer the natural monopoly to a private owner, and let him act as a profit-maximizing monopolist. Presumably the monopolist will produce output X_m at which $MR = MC$ and set price equal to P_m. At (P_m, X_m) he will make pure profits of $(P_m - AC) \cdot X_m$. The other two choices involve government intervention, either in the form of a direct government takeover of the service or private ownership with government regulation. In either case, the government can choose to follow the dictates of first-best theory, charge the marginal cost price, and subsidize the operation out of general tax revenues in amount $(AC - MC) \cdot X_{opt}$; or charge a price equal to average costs, in which case no additional subsidy is required.

FIGURE 10–1

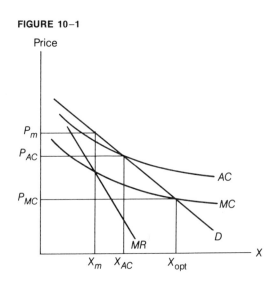

U.S. governments at all levels have overwhelmingly adopted the average cost pricing strategy, or some close approximation to it, whether or not the service is publicly or privately owned. This may seem surprising given the general support for free enterprise in the United States, or the persuasive first-best theoretical arguments favoring marginal cost pricing with government intervention, but exceptions to average cost pricing for decreasing cost services are relatively rare. For example, fees for recreational facilities such as beaches and parks are usually set to cover full costs. Tolls on urban highways, bridges, and tunnels are often designed to cover the full costs of the entire network of transportation facilities under the jurisdiction of local transportation authorities. The federal gasoline tax was originally established to defray the expenses of constructing the Interstate Highway System. Similarly, state gasoline tax rates are determined primarily by the anticipated expenses of state highway departments. Public utility rates are generally designed to cover all expenses including a fair rate of return to the private investors. Admittedly, unless the "fair return" equals the opportunity cost of capital services this is not strictly average cost pricing, but its philosophy is more or less identical. One can think of the utility regulatory commissions as building a pseudo average cost curve that includes the "fair" rate of return and setting rates equal to these pseudo average costs. In the few instances where governments choose not to average cost price, they usually offer the services at no charge. One thinks immediately of some national and state parks and beaches, and of over-the-air commercial television. Since the marginal cost of these services is likely to be near zero, where the quantity axis defines the number of users or viewers, these can be thought of as examples of optimal pricing, so long as the service remains uncongested.

A key question, then, is why average cost pricing is so predominant in the United States. What are its perceived advantages, and to what extent are these perceptions reasonable?

In our view, the United States accepts the average cost option as a reasonable compromise between the other natural policy alternatives on both equity and efficiency grounds. We would also hazard a guess that equity issues are the more compelling to the general public, but efficiency arguments are at least considered in most public deliberations on price setting. Chapter 10 will explore the equity and efficiency arguments for and against average cost pricing relative to the other alternatives. The point is not to attack the average cost pricing philosophy, although economic theory would reject it. It obviously has great appeal. We merely want to speculate on the sources of its appeal and analyze the extent to which its attractions are reasonable and the extent to which they are misguided, and perhaps even a little dangerous.

EQUITY CONSIDERATIONS

The interesting equity issue concerns the choice between average cost pricing and marginal cost pricing. We accept it as axiomatic that U.S. citizens will not willingly permit a private owner to "exploit" a natural monopoly and earn monopoly profits. Public dissatisfaction in the United States over price increases that are ostensibly justified by cost increases is often severe. One can well imagine the public's outrage over a charge of profiteering at the public's expense. Perhaps the outstanding example of the government hedging against profiteering occurs in defense contracting.[1] Complex weapon systems continually experience significant cost overruns, one of the most obvious reasons being that the government negotiates cost-plus-fixed-fee contracts through the research and development stages of the production cycle, so that there is little incentive to hold down cost. An equally obvious solution is to insist on fixed-fee contracts from the beginning, but given initial uncertainties over cost and quality parameters the government has been willing to use them only sparingly. Apparently the federal government considers the risk of huge profits (and huge losses) for its few large weapons suppliers less acceptable than the cost overruns, despite incessant public disfavor with the latter. The defense contractors are probably not decreasing cost industries, but the same principle undoubtedly applies to the decreasing cost services as well. The risk of profiteering is probably sufficient to rule out the private monopoly option. One might argue that a natural monopoly would not fully exploit its monopoly power knowing that excessive profits would not be tolerated. For example, while ticket prices are usually raised for important sporting events (e.g., baseball's World Series, football's Super Bowl), public pressure clearly keeps owners from setting even higher, market-clearing prices. In any case, average cost pricing avoids the issue, at least in principle. As a practical matter, it is questionable whether a monopoly such as a public utility can be effectively regulated to avoid all monopoly profit.

The more subtle question is why governments favor average cost over marginal cost pricing, despite the obvious efficiency advantages of the latter. We believe the answer lies in the public's conception of the benefits-received principle of taxation or prices, a principle which was first discussed in Chapter 6 in the context of paying for nonexclusive goods.

Recall that the benefits-received principle is an equity principle[2] which, broadly interpreted, states that each consumer should pay for a public service in direct proportion to the benefits he receives. A natural corollary is that those who receive no benefits should not have to pay for the service. Suppose the government chooses the marginal cost pricing option for the decreasing cost services. This creates problems in terms of the benefits-received principle, since the government will have to subsidize the service out of general tax revenues. Once it does this, however, there is no guarantee that consumers will pay the

---

[1] The classic references on defense contracting are M. Peck and F. Scherer, *The Weapons Acquisition Process: An Economic Analysis* (Boston, Mass.: Division of Research, Graduate School of Business Administration, Harvard University, 1962); and F. Scherer, *The Weapons Acquisition Process: Economic Incentives* (Boston, Mass.: Division of Research, Graduate School of Business Administration, Harvard University, 1964).

[2] Recall also from the discussion of Chapter 6 that the benefits-received principle is not a valid equity principle within the formal neoclassical model, despite its long standing within the profession.

full costs of the service in proportion to their use of the service. Moreover, some nonusers may end up paying some of the cost out of general taxes. As indicated in Chapter 6, the benefits-received principle begs the issue of which benefits payments ought to be related to. But given that decreasing cost services are exclusive, so that nonusers can easily be distinguished from users, and intensive users distinguished from nonintensive users, one could reasonably argue that average cost pricing satisfies the intent of the benefits-received principle, whereas marginal cost pricing does not. If people adopt this point of view, and believe that the equity gains from average cost pricing outweigh its efficiency losses relative to marginal cost pricing, then average cost pricing is entirely reasonable.

An economist can easily attack this position by appealing to first-best theoretical principles, but it is not at all clear that the general public will find the economic case very compelling. To review the results of Chapters 6 and 9, the economic argument runs as follows. The benefits-received principle is meant to be applied to all exhaustive or resource using government expenditures, those undertaken to correct for misallocations of resources within a competitive market system. Its primary justification as an equity principle is that it imitates the *quid-pro-quo* payment mechanism of the free market system. But it has the additional goal of supporting an efficient allocation of resources, exactly as competitive prices do in markets for which all the technical and market assumptions hold. Without this additional function the principle defeats the very purpose of government intervention in the first place.

For public goods there was an infinity of payment schemes that preserved pareto optimality, but for decreasing cost services this is not so. Only if the benefits principle is interpreted to mean marginal cost pricing will its efficiency function be upheld. Marginal cost pricing is, of course, also consistent with the equity criterion that it should imitate competitive pricing. Each person is allowed to consume the good until price equals MRS (assume the other good is the numeraire), which in turn is equated to the MRT in production. According to this interpretation, then, payment is related to use only to the point at which price covers marginal cost.

While it is true that the benefits-received principle so interpreted will not cover the full costs of decreasing cost services, this is irrelevant. According to first-best theory, payment of the required subsidy through lump-sum taxes depends only upon the social welfare function, specifically the interpersonal equity conditions of social welfare maximization. It has nothing to do with use or nonuse of the service. Those people who ultimately support these services through the subsidies are simply those who originally have relatively low social marginal utilities of income. Conversely, people whose use of the service is implicitly subsidized by the set of taxes and transfers receive implicit subsidies only because of their social welfare ranking.

To clarify this point further, suppose a decreasing cost service were paid for by an efficient two-part tariff consisting of a marginal cost price for actual use and a one-time, lump-sum fee collected from all actual and potential users of the service.[3] Superficially this seems desirable since the users pay the full costs.[4] But the "Distribution Bureau" will effectively override the lump-sum payments if they do not square with the interpersonal equity conditions. Suppose, for example, that only poor people use rail transit and that the interpersonal equity conditions require net redistribution from the rich to the poor. The lump-sum user fees will drive the social marginal utilities further apart, but the Bureau can easily offset this by taking even more income from the rich and transferring it to the poor, until social marginal utilities are equalized. The poor users appear to be paying for the service, but in fact the rich do, precisely because they are rich. In social welfare maximization the interpersonal equity conditions will always take precedence.

The marginal cost interpretation of the benefits-received principle may be consistent with first-best principles, but the general public is not likely to accept it, especially its equity implications. Subsidizing a public utility out of general revenues would undoubtedly be most unpopular, even though it would permit lower rates for use of the service. Consider the following situation. Each year the state of Massachusetts contributes tens of millions of dollars to cover the deficits of Boston's Metropolitan Bay Transit Authority. According to the first-best interpersonal equity conditions it is at least possible that people out-outside of Boston should pay for the transit deficits, but these subsidies are extremely unpopular. In short, we are quite prepared to admit that an average cost interpretation of the benefits-received principle squares best with the public's notion of equity in these matters. First-best theory to the contrary, economists should perhaps concede that average cost pricing has certain appealing equity properties.

EFFICIENCY CONSIDERATIONS

The efficiency advantages of marginal cost pricing in a first-best environment are, of course, unambiguous, since the marginal cost price is pareto optimal. But at least the "easy case" service will pass a gross efficiency test if priced at average cost, since we showed that operating the service at the break-even output is preferable to having no service at all. However, if average cost pricing is applied to the "hard case," society risks having the service fail even this gross efficiency test.

It is, of course, impossible to apply strict average cost pricing in the "hard case" because demand is everywhere below-average costs. But in lieu of covering the full costs, the public may insist on minimizing the deficit as the "next-best" alternative, on the grounds that if the users cannot cover the full costs of the service they at least should pay for as much of the costs as possible. Minimizing

---

[3] The one-time fee must be collected from potential users or an economic choice to use or not use the service would dictate the amount of payment, contrary to the notion of lump sum. We saw this same problem when considering subsidies for nonpolluting behavior in Chapter 7.

[4] Potential but not actual users can be thought of as purchasing an option to use the service which, if they pay the fee, must have value to them.

FIGURE 10–2

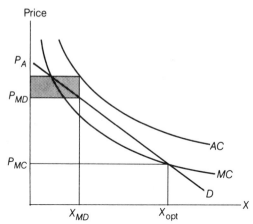

the deficit may not be a harmless extension of the average cost principle, however.

Suppose the situation is as represented in Figure 10–2, with (P_{MD}, X_{MD}) the price and output combination that minimizes the deficit, and the shaded portion equal to the minimum deficit. The problem is that although the service may be worthwhile if priced at marginal costs and operated at X_{opt}, it may well fail the all-or-none necessary condition at (P_{MD}, X_{MD}). That is, it is possible for the Hicks Compensating Variation from P_A to P_{MC} to exceed the lump-sum subsidy required to cover the deficit at X_{opt}, while the HCV from P_A to P_{MD} fails to cover the deficit at X_{MD}. The mere potential for satisfying the all-or-none test at the optimum is not enough. Unless society actually operates the service at a level sufficient to pass this test, it is simply wasting resources. Clearly, minimizing the deficit is not the same principle as maximizing the difference between total benefits, as measured by the HCV + total revenues,[5] and total costs.

Rail transit in a number of urban areas could well be an outstanding example of this phenomenon, although we do not know enough about either transit demand or costs to say for sure. Despite numerous fare increases designed specifically to eliminate deficits (presumably demand is inelastic in the relevant range), the deficits persist and, predictably, ridership diminishes. Quite possibly rail transit is an example of the "hard case" in that no single fare will avoid deficits. Moreover, if ridership continues to decline in response to the fare increases, the transit system may finally not be worth operating.

Public officials are always under pressure to discontinue or curtail any service which incurs losses simply because it incurs losses. The public will almost certainly reject a policy of lower fares and even larger deficits, yet this may be the only way in which transit service can pass an all-or-none test. At the

---

[5] For purposes of this discussion, assume zero income effects, so $D^{actual} = D^{compensated}$

same time, the perception that running no trains at all is preferable to running near-empty trains at prices well in excess of marginal costs may well be accurate. This is but another instance of the policy difficulties inherent in "hard case" decreasing cost services.

AVERAGE COST VERSUS MONOPOLY PRICING: THE AVERCH-JOHNSON EFFECT

The most interesting efficiency issue for decreasing cost services is the presumed efficiency gains of average cost pricing over unregulated monopoly pricing. As indicated above, both these options necessarily imply efficiency losses relative to marginal cost pricing in an otherwise first-best environment.

One might presume, looking at Figure 10–1, that average cost pricing is more efficient than monopoly pricing because output and prices are closer to their optimum values. Once again, however, these partial equilibrium diagrams can be misleading. In this case they mask important relationships in the factor markets. An unregulated monopolist will hire factors efficiently, assuming competitive factor markets. A regulated monopolist may not do so, depending on the exact form of the regulation, and it is possible that the welfare costs of these factor market inefficiencies will swamp the efficiency gains induced by increasing output.

The public utilities, with their special form of price regulation, have been analyzed more intensively than any other decreasing cost service, and it was here that the potential for factor market inefficiencies was first discovered. In 1962 Averch and Johnson proved that utility regulation caused firms to become excessively capital intensive. Subsequent analysis by numerous authors has demonstrated that because of this "Averch-Johnson effect," utility regulation may not increase social welfare relative to unregulated monopoly even if the utility's output increases in response to regulation.[6] Since public utility regulation is not precisely average cost pricing, the utility effects of government regulation in other decreasing cost services may not be so ambiguous. Nonetheless, the public utilities are important enough to warrant a brief analysis of the Averch-Johnson effect here.

As indicated in the introductory remarks to this chapter, public utility regulation is essentially a two-step process. First, the regulatory commissions establish an allowable or "fair" rate of return to capital. Then, analyzing recent and projected data on costs and demand, they establish a rate or price for the service that will generate this "fair" return to capital. The process may not work so well in practice given the usual uncertainties associated with demand and cost estimation and the fact that the commissions meet only infrequently, but assume for purposes of analysis that the regulators are able to force the fair rate of return on the utility.[7]

---

[6] H. Averch and L. Johnson, "Behavior of the Firm under Regulatory Constraint," *American Economic Review*, December 1962.

[7] A good general reference on U.S. regulatory policies is P. W. MacAvoy, ed., *The Crisis of The Regulatory Commissions* (New York: W. W. Norton & Co., Inc., 1970), parts I, II, and VII.

It is worth noting that an analysis of the Averch-Johnson effect leads us into the realm of second-best theory, since the regulated fair rate of return is an addition to the first-best constraints of production functions and market clearance. However, our analysis is intended as an exercise in positive rather than normative theory. We merely want to establish the effects of existing regulatory practice in an otherwise first-best environment, rather than develop a theory of optimal regulation.[8]

In order to analyze the welfare effects of public utility regulation the general equilibrium model of Chapter 9 has to be expanded to include a second factor of production, capital, but that is all. Therefore, rewrite the single consumer's utility function as

$$U = U(X, K, L)$$

and the single decreasing cost production function as

$$X = f(K, L)$$

where:

X = the consumer good.

L = labor, measured negatively in the utility function.

K = capital, also measured negatively in the utility function.

Market clearance is implicit, as before. Further, define the following prices:

P_X = the price of good X.

P_L = the price of L.

P_K = the opportunity cost of capital services, the return necessary to keep capital in the industry.

r = the allowable "fair" rate of return to capital in the production of X.

For the regulation to be effective, r must be set such that

(10.1)
$$R_{\max} > r \geqq P_K$$

where:

$R_{\max}$ = the unregulated monopolist's maximum possible rate of return to capital.

Whether it is effective or not, the rate-of-return constraint can be represented as

(10.2)
$$P_X \cdot X - P_L \cdot L \leqq r \cdot K$$

or

(10.3)
$$P_X \cdot X - P_L \cdot L - r \cdot K \leqq 0$$

---

[8] Chapter 21 discusses the average cost pricing philosophy in the context of a multiproduct firm, a second-best problem first described by Boiteux. We placed it in Part III because the Boiteux analysis does have normative content.

(10.3) says that the total returns to capital must be no greater than the allowable returns. Notice that the regulatory constraint is defined in terms of the returns to capital and *not* pure economic profits, $(P_X \cdot X - P_L \cdot L - P_K \cdot K)$, which the firm is assumed to maximize. In the analysis to follow, we will usually assume that the firm always earns the maximum allowable return, so that the constraint (10.3) holds as an equality.

Constrained Profit Maximization

Before turning directly to the effect of the allowable return constraint on utility, consider first how a profit-maximizing monopolist will react to the constraint.

The monopolist will solve the following problem:

$$\max_{(X,K,L)} P_X \cdot X - P_L \cdot L - P_K \cdot K$$

$$\text{s.t.} \quad X = f(K,L)$$
$$P_X \cdot X - P_L \cdot L - r \cdot K = 0$$

Substituting the production function into the objective function and returns constraint, noting that P_X is a function of output for a monopolist, and assuming the constraint is binding, the problem becomes:

$$\max_{(K,L)} P[f(K,L)] \cdot f(K,L) - P_L \cdot L - P_K \cdot K$$

$$\text{s.t.} \quad P[f(K,L)] \cdot f(K,L) - P_L \cdot L - r \cdot K = 0$$

with the corresponding Langrangian:

$$\max_{(K,L)} = P[f(K,L)] \cdot f(K,L) - P_L \cdot L - P_K \cdot K$$
$$- \lambda(P[f(K,L)] \cdot f(K,L) - P_L \cdot L - r \cdot K)$$

The first-order conditions are, after rearranging terms:

(10.4) $K: \quad (P + P'f) \cdot f_K - P_K - \lambda[(P + P'f)f_K - r] = 0$

(10.5) $L: \quad (P + P'f) \cdot f_L - P_L - \lambda[(P + P'f)f_L - P_L] = 0$

(10.6)   Constraint: $\quad P[f(K,L)] \cdot f(K,L) - P_L \cdot L - r \cdot K = 0$

where:

$$(P + P'f) = \frac{\partial(P_X \cdot X)}{\partial X} = MR_X$$

$$f_K = \frac{\partial f}{\partial K}$$

$$f_L = \frac{\partial f}{\partial L}$$

There are four possibilities depending on the value of r set by the regulatory commission.

1. $r > R_{max}$.

The commission could set the allowable return greater than the maximum return attainable by the unregulated monopolist, either because it is especially generous to the industry or because the industry has very little monopoly power to exploit in any case. If this happens the constraint is not binding and λ is zero. Hence, from (10.4) and (10.5),

(10.7) $$(P + P'f)f_K = P_K$$

(10.8) $$(P + P'f)f_L = P_L$$

so that

(10.9) $$\frac{f_K}{f_L} = \frac{P_K}{P_L}$$

Notice that by equating the price of each factor to its marginal revenue product ($MR_X \cdot f_K$ and $MR_X \cdot f_L$, respectively) the monopolist hires factors efficiently. This follows because the consumer will equate

(10.10) $$\frac{P_K}{P_L} = \frac{U_K}{U_L}$$

Therefore,

(10.11) $$\frac{f_K}{f_L} = \frac{U_K}{U_L}$$

as required for pareto optimality. In other words, if the only inefficiency in an otherwise competitive economy is the existence of monopoly power for some goods and services, the economy will still operate on its production-possibilities frontier. The efficiency loss results from being on the wrong portion of the frontier, because $P_X > MR_X = MC_X$, with too little production of the monopolist's output and too much output from the competitive sectors.

2. $r < P_K$.

If a regulatory commission sets the allowable return below the opportunity cost of capital, the industry will presumably shut down. Consequently, regulators may be biased to set r considerably in excess of P_K.

3. $r = P_K$.

If the allowable return exactly equals the opportunity cost of capital there are a number of possibilities. (10.4) and (10.5) become:

(10.12) $$[(P + P'f)f_K - P_K] \cdot (1 - \lambda) = 0$$

(10.13) $$[(P + P'f)f_L - P_L] \cdot (1 - \lambda) = 0$$

both of which are satisfied so long as $\lambda = 1$. Hence, this is a degenerate case, since any combination of K and L satisfying (10.6) is equally attractive to the monopolist. No matter what it does, it can only earn the opportunity level of returns $P_K \cdot K$.

Baumol and Klevorick have proven that[9]

$$0 \leq \lambda \leq 1 \tag{10.14}$$

with λ assuming its boundary values in the extreme cases of $r > R_{max}$ and $r = P_K$, respectively. The proof is somewhat tedious and will not be reproduced here, but this result is crucial to all further results of this section.

4. $R_{max} > r > P_K$, as intended.

In the effective constraint range, (10.4) and (10.5) become:

$$(1 - \lambda)[(P + P'f)f_K] = P_K - \lambda r \tag{10.15}$$

$$(1 - \lambda)[(P + P'f)f_L] = P_L(1 - \lambda) \tag{10.16}$$

Dividing (10.15) by (10.16) and simplifying yields:

$$\frac{f_K}{f_L} = \frac{P_K - \lambda r}{P_L(1 - \lambda)} = \frac{P_K(1 - \lambda) - \lambda(r - P_K)}{P_L(1 - \lambda)} = \frac{P_K}{P_L} - \frac{\lambda(r - P_K)}{P_L(1 - \lambda)} \tag{10.17}$$

Since $r > P_K$ and $0 < \lambda < 1$, the second term on the right-hand side of (10.17) is positive. Therefore,

$$\frac{f_K}{f_L} < \frac{P_K}{P_L} = \frac{U_K}{U_L} \tag{10.18}$$

Capital and labor are no longer hired efficiently. Moreover, since $f_K/f_L < P_K/P_L$, the firm will hire more capital and less labor for any given output relative to the efficient combinations of K and L. This is the Averch-Johnson effect, illustrated in Figure 10–3.

The solid line is an isocost line with slope P_K/P_L. The efficient combination for producing quantity X_0 given prices P_K and P_L is point $A(L_e, K_e)$. With the regulatory constraint the firm moves to a point such as $B(L_c, K_c)$, at which the technical rate of substitution f_K/f_L is less than the ratio of factor prices.

The particular form of the regulatory constraint gives the firm an extra incentive to hire capital in that adding capital increases the allowable returns $r \cdot K$, whereas hiring additional labor confers no such advantage. In fact, the regulatory constraint does not alter the decision rule for hiring labor. From (10.16), $(P + P'f)f_L = P_L$, exactly as in the unregulated case. Of course, as the amount of capital varies from its optimum so too will the actual amount of labor hired, but the marginal decision rule for hiring labor remains unchanged.

---

[9] Our analysis of the Averch-Johnson effect relies heavily on two sources, a set of unpublished class notes by Peter Diamond of M.I.T. and W. J. Baumol and A. Klevorick, "Input Choices and Rate of Return Regulation: An Overview of the Discussion," *The Bell Journal of Economics and Management Science*, Autumn 1970. Their proof of (10.14) can be found on pp. 166–68.

FIGURE 10–3

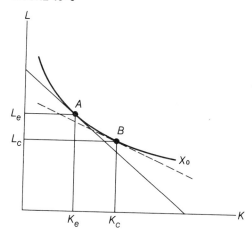

Producing inefficiently reduces the maximum possible returns for the industry but this is irrelevant so long as the fair returns are less than the maximum. The goal is simply to increase profits as much as possible within the confines of the constraint. According to Averch and Johnson this phenomenon may explain why Bell Telephone offered telegraph services in competition with Western Union in the 1950s even though its telegraph operation was yielding only a 2.6 percent return on capital (in 1955). Since the demand for telephone service is price inelastic, Bell Telephone could add the capital from its telegraph operation to its overall rate base and capture the increased allowable returns from its telephone customers. This may also explain why some utilities have been relatively unconcerned with price increases from their suppliers. Higher prices for capital equipment also increase the capital base for computing allowable returns.[10]

The Effects of Regulation on Utility

Deriving the effects of regulation on the consumer's utility is hardly a straightforward exercise. We must calculate the total change in utility with respect to changes in the fair rate of return, dU/dr, for values of r in the constraint range, given both the first-order conditions from constrained profit maximization of the firm and utility maximization of the consumers. That is, the calculated change in utility must be consistent with a full general equilibrium market solution for the economy.

Begin with the consumer's utility function, $U(X, K, L) = U[f(K, L), K, L]$ and recall that the last two arguments K and L enter with a negative sign as

---

[10] Averch and Johnson, "Behavior of the Firm under Regulatory Constraint," pp. 1057–65.

factor supplies. Totally differentiating U with respect to r yields:

$$(10.19) \qquad \frac{dU}{dr} = U_X \left(f_K \frac{dK}{dr} + f_L \frac{dL}{dr} \right) - U_K \frac{dK}{dr} - U_L \frac{dL}{dr}$$

From utility maximization in a market economy,[11]

$$(10.20) \qquad \frac{U_X}{P_X} = \frac{U_L}{P_L} = \frac{U_K}{P_K}$$

Using (10.20) to substitute for U_K and U_L in (10.19), and multiplying and dividing the first term in (10.19) by P_X, yields:

$$(10.21) \qquad \frac{dU}{dr} = \frac{U_X}{P_X} \left(P_X f_K \frac{dK}{dr} + P_X f_L \frac{dL}{dr} \right) - \frac{U_X}{P_X} P_K \frac{dK}{dr} - \frac{U_X}{P_X} P_L \frac{dL}{dr}$$

Factoring out U_X/P_X and rearranging terms,

$$(10.22) \qquad \frac{dU}{dr} = \frac{U_X}{P_X} \left[(P_X f_K - P_K) \frac{dK}{dr} + (P_X f_L - P_L) \frac{dL}{dr} \right]$$

The profit maximizing regulated firm will satisfy conditions (10.4) and (10.5) above. From (10.5)

$$(10.23) \qquad P_X f_L - P_L = - P' f f_L$$

From (10.4), after addition and subtracting of λP_K and rearranging terms,

$$(10.24) \qquad (1 - \lambda)[(P + P'f)f_K - P_K] = \lambda(P_K - r)$$

Hence,

$$(10.25) \qquad P_X f_K - P_K = \frac{\lambda}{(1 - \lambda)} (P_K - r) - P' f f_K$$

Substituting (10.23) and (10.25) into (10.22) yields:

$$(10.26) \qquad \frac{dU}{dr} = \frac{U_X}{P_X} \left[\left(\frac{\lambda}{(1 - \lambda)} (P_K - r) - P' f f_K \right) \frac{dK}{dr} - P' f f_L \frac{dL}{dr} \right]$$

But

$$(10.27) \qquad \frac{dX}{dr} = f_X \frac{dX}{dr} + f_L \frac{dL}{dr}$$

from the production function. Therefore, (10.26) simplifies to

$$(10.28) \qquad \frac{dU}{dr} = \frac{U_X}{P_X} \left[\frac{\lambda}{(1 - \lambda)} (P_K - r) \frac{dK}{dr} - (P'f) \frac{dX}{dr} \right]$$

The final step involves signing dK/dr and dX/dr, since we know that $\lambda/(1 - \lambda) > 0$; $(P_K - r) < 0$; $P' < 0$; and $f > 0$.

---

[11] K and L also enter negatively in the consumer's budget constraint, $P_X X + P_L L + P_K K = 0$, so that there are no negative signs in the ratios of first-order conditions.

The sign of dK/dr can be determined by totally differentiating the first-order conditions for constrained profit maximization, equations (10.4)–(10.6). As it turns out, differentiating the constraint equation (10.6) is all that is required. From (10.6)

$$(10.29) \qquad P \cdot \left(f_K \frac{dK}{dr} + f_L \frac{dL}{dr} \right) + f \cdot P' \cdot \left(f_K \frac{dK}{dr} + f_L \frac{dL}{dr} \right)$$
$$- P_L \frac{dL}{dr} - K - r \frac{dK}{dr} = 0$$

Rearranging terms,

$$(10.30) \qquad [(P + P'f)f_K - r]\frac{dK}{dr} + [(P + P'f)f_L - P_L)]\frac{dL}{dr} - K = 0$$

But from (10.5), $(P + P'f)f_L - P_L = 0$. Therefore,

$$(10.31) \qquad [(P + P'f)f_K - r]\frac{dK}{dr} - K = 0$$

Next, add and subtract r in equation (10.4) and rearrange terms to obtain:

$$(10.32) \qquad [(P + P'f)f_K - r](1 - \lambda) - P_K + r = 0$$

or

$$(10.33) \qquad [(P + P'f)f_K - r] = \frac{(P_K - r)}{(1 - \lambda)}$$

Substituting (10.33) into (10.31) yields:

$$(10.34) \qquad \frac{(P_K - r)}{(1 - \lambda)}\frac{dK}{dr} - K = 0$$

Hence,

$$(10.35) \qquad \frac{dK}{dr} = \frac{K(1 - \lambda)}{(P_K - r)} < 0$$

with $r > P_K$ and $0 < \lambda < 1$ in the effective constraint range. dK/dr, then, is unambiguously negative throughout the constraint range. The lower the regulatory commission sets the fair rate of return, the more capital the firm will use. It is tempting to conclude that dX/dr must also be negative. But

$$(10.36) \qquad \frac{dX}{dr} = f_K \frac{dK}{dr} + f_L \frac{dL}{dr}$$

and depending on the production relationship between K and L, dL/dr could be positive. However, Baumol and Klevorick show that unless capital is a regressive factor of production for the unregulated monopolist (a rise in P_K leads to a rise in unregulated output), dX/dr and dK/dr will have the same sign.[12] Since regressivity is unlikely, we will assume $dX/dr < 0$.

---

[12] Baumol and Klevorick, "Input Choices and Rate of Return Regulation," p. 176–78.

Returning to equation (10.28), with dX/dr, $dK/dr < 0$, the sign of dU/dr is indeterminant. The first of the bracketed terms is positive, indicating the utility decreasing consequences of the Averch-Johnson effect, but the second term is negative (including the initial minus sign), reflecting the utility increasing effects of a regulated increase in output. Thus, there is no guarantee that this particular form of regulation increases social welfare.

Despite these ambiguous findings, there are two sources of optimism for believers in regulation, one theoretical, one quasi-empirical. At the purely theoretical level, the change in utility is unambiguously positive as r is lowered to the upper boundary of the constraint range, that is, to the point at which the monopolist is first effectively constrained. This follows because $\lambda \to 0$ at the upper boundary which, from (10.28), implies $dU/dr < 0$.

Empirical Analysis

This result may not be worth much, but recently Callen, Mathewson, and Mohring have provided some interesting empirical evidence suggesting that the welfare increasing output effect will dominate the welfare decreasing Averch-Johnson effect for a wide range of reasonable demand and production parameters.[13] Specifically, they posit a simple economy of the kind we have been assuming with a constant elasticity aggregate demand function $P = A \cdot Q^{-e}$, where $1/e$ is the price elasticity of demand, and a generalized Cobb-Douglas production function of the form $Q^B = K^\alpha L^{1-\alpha}$, where $1/B$ is the degree of homogeneity. Hence, $B < 1$ implies increasing returns to scale. Factor supplies are assumed fixed. Having specified demand, production, and factor supplies they are able to compute the unregulated and regulated general equilibria for many different values of r in the constraint range. They then compare the percentage change in social benefits as a result of regulation, using the expression,

(10.37)
$$\Delta SB = \frac{W^{**} - W^*}{R(Q^*)}$$

where:

W^{**} = the social benefits at the regulated equilibrium.

W^* = the social benefits at the unregulated equilibrium.

$R(Q)$ = the market value of the monopolist's output at Q.

Q^* = output at the unregulated equilibrium.

Social benefits for a particular output $\bar{Q}$ are computed as the area under the demand curve up to $\bar{Q}$ less the total costs of producing $\bar{Q}$. This commonly used measure of total benefits is called social surplus, equal to the sum of producers' and consumer's surplus. It is discussed at length in the Appendix to Chapter 11.

---

[13] J. Callen, G. Mathewson, and H. Mohring, "The Benefits and Costs of Rate of Return Regulation," *American Economic Review*, June 1976.

Two very striking general conclusions emerge from their analysis. They found that for most values of the demand and production parameters (1) the optimal fair rate of return is much closer to the opportunity cost of capital than to the unregulated return; and (2) the welfare gains from optimal regulation are substantial, with values of ΔSB frequently in excess of .5. Moreover, even nonoptimal r's often yield significant welfare gains. They compute the optimal r as the one which maximizes their measure of social benefits given the firm's reaction to the returns constraint.

They also compute the social benefits for marginal cost pricing and true average cost pricing and conclude that "at least for combinations of parameter values which reflect capital intensive production processes [high α] with substantial scale economy [low β], rate-of-return regulation could capture a substantial share of the benefits derivable from setting price equal to average or (except when the elasticity of demand is large) even marginal cost."[14] These results are especially encouraging given the wide range of parameter values they were able to test for and the fact that constant elasticity demand formulations have generally given acceptable econometric results in consumer demand analysis.

SUMMARY AND CONCLUSIONS

Our brief reflections on the decided U.S. preference for average cost pricing of decreasing cost services were somewhat speculative, but they tend to be less critical of this practice than the professional literature generally. The usual arguments in favor of marginal cost pricing with lump-sum subsidy were summarized and found to be airtight in terms of first-best theoretical principles. But the equity arguments for average cost pricing are at least reasonable, and there is some evidence to suggest that the efficiency costs relative to marginal cost pricing may not be terribly large. The "hard case" decreasing cost services stand out as the only notable possible exception.

A final point on average cost pricing deserves attention. Some writers are especially critical of average cost pricing because it creates no incentives for least-cost production. So long as demand is inelastic, a monopolist forced to average cost price can always cover any production inefficiencies simply by raising his price. Thus, whether he is inefficient or not, his returns are the same (the degenerate case $r = P_K$, above).

Neil Singer's excellent undergraduate test, *Public Microeconomics*, is a case in point. Speaking on general principles for regulating monopolies, Singer says:

> It is hard to overstate the harm done by the policy of setting the regulated price equal to average cost .... If a monopolist is guaranteed a return of, say, 8 percent on his invested capital regardless of how efficiently he uses factors of production, then his incentive for using factors in the most productive ways disappears.[15]

[14] Ibid., p. 290.
[15] N. M. Singer, *Public Microeconomics* (Boston, Mass.: Little, Brown and Co., 1972), p. 75.

The real problem in the decreasing cost case, however, is not the average cost price, but simply the lack of potential competitors. Suppose the firm were forced to marginal cost price, with a subsidy to cover the shortfall of revenues from full costs. This is the pareto-optimal solution assuming the firm produces at *least* marginal costs. But without competitors there is no special incentive to be factor efficient here either. If this pricing policy is to be pareto optimal in practice, the regulator must know the firm's best or lowest total cost curve, force price to equal the resultant best marginal costs, and subsidize only the shortfall of revenues from lowest total costs. This is a tall order, but if the regulatory commission can do this it can force price to equal the minimum possible average costs as well if it so desires, without creating any extra disincentives for least-cost production relative to the marginal cost option. For example, there is no reason for the Averch-Johnson effect to occur with true average cost pricing. It arises from a particular method of regulating the utilities which is philosophically akin to average cost pricing but not identical to it.

Singer recognizes this point when speaking specifically of decreasing cost services, citing lack of competition as a major source of cost inefficiency. However, his general comments against average cost pricing apparently still apply.[16] We would suggest that lack of potential competition is the *only* source of this particular kind of cost inefficiency relative to marginal cost pricing.

REFERENCES

Averch, H., and Johnson, L. "Behavior of the Firm under Regulatory Constraint." *American Economic Review,* December 1962.

Baumol, W. J., and Klevorick, A. "Input Choices and Rate of Return Regulation: An Overview of the Discussion." *The Bell Journal of Economics and Management Science,* Autumn 1970.

Callen, J.; Mathewson, G.; and Mohring, H. "The Benefits and Costs of Rate of Return Regulation." *American Economic Review,* June 1976.

Kahn, A. *The Economics of Regulation: Principles and Institutions,* vol. I (*Economic Principles*), vol. II (*Institutional Issues*). New York: John Wiley & Sons, Inc., 1970, vol. I, 1971, vol. II.

MacAvoy, P. W., ed. *The Crisis of the Regulatory Commissions.* New York: W. W. Norton & Co., Inc., 1970.

---

[16] Ibid., pp. 76, 79. There are a number of other interesting issues relating to the public utilities which we have ignored. The theory of decreasing cost production straddles a number of disciplines, including public finance, industrial organization, and transportation economics. Most public finance texts cover the rudiments of the theory, as we have done, and leave the details for other courses. For instance, two extremely interesting and timely questions in public utility analysis are price discrimination, in which the utility subsidizes one set of customers at the expense of other customers, and cream skimming, in which outside competitors enter the most profitable components of a multipart operation (e.g. intracity, business-to-business phone service). These issues are typically covered in texts on industrial organization, of which we would strongly recommend A. Kahn, *The Economics of Regulation: Principles and Institutions*, vol. I (*Economic Principles*), vol. II (*Institutional Issues*), (New York: John Wiley & Sons, Inc., 1970, vol. I, 1971, vol. II).

Peck, M., and Scherer, F. *The Weapons Acquisition Process: An Economic Analysis.* Boston, Mass.: Division of Research, Graduate School of Business Administration, Harvard University, 1962.

Scherer, F. *The Weapons Acquisition Process: Economic Incentives.* Boston, Mass.: Division of Research, Graduate School of Business Administration, Harvard University, 1964.

Singer, N. M. *Public Microeconomics.* Boston, Mass.: Little, Brown and Co., 1972

11

The peak-load problem

Most of the important decreasing cost services—the public utilities, all forms of transportation, many recreational facilities—experience highly variable demands over the course of their relevant demand cycles. At times, demand is well below the capacity to supply the services, the "off peak." At other times, demand is straining at capacity, meaning either that there is some absolute design capacity for the service which demand exceeds at some predetermined price or that demand can be satisfied only at much higher marginal costs than some predetermined norm. This is the so-called "peak-load" demand. In addition to variable demand, it is impossible to inventory production of these services at the off peak to satisfy peak users. Services with these two characteristics are said to experience a peak-load problem.

Two aspects of the development of the peak-load problem in the professional literature deserve attention at the outset. First, until the mid-1970s virtually all economists adopted the notion that peak use occurs at the absolute maximum output or design capacity of the system, to the point where this can now be identified as the "traditional" view of the peak load.[1] In 1976, however, Panzar sharply attacked the traditional viewpoint, proving that if production follows standard neoclassical properties, a cost-minimizing firm would never produce at full capacity. In particular, suppose production is characterized as follows:

$$(11.1) \qquad q_t = f(X_t; k)$$

where:

q_t = output in time t.

X_t = a vector of variable inputs at time t.

k = an input (e.g., capital) fixed in the short run, used in all periods, and defining the capacity of the system.

---

[1] We would recommend the following references on the peak-load problem as traditionally defined: O. Williamson, "Peak-Load Pricing and Optimal Capacity," *American Economic Review*, September 1966; J. Dreze, "Some Post-War Contributions of French Economists to Theory and Public Policy," *American Economic Review*, June 1964 (supplement); I. Pressman, "A Mathematical Formulation of the Peak-Load Pricing Problem," *The Bell Journal of Economics and Management Science*, Autumn 1970; and H. Mohring, "The Peak-Load Problem with Increasing Returns and Pricing Constraints," *American Economic Review*, September 1970.

The Williamson and Dreze articles provide some useful geometric interpretations. The other two articles are more mathematical.

The standard neoclassical properties are that (a) $f(X_t; k)$ is continuously differentiable and quasi concave; (b) $f_k = \partial f / \partial k > 0$; and (c) $f(0; k) = f(X_t; 0) = 0$ (production requires some of all inputs).

In addition, let:

$$(11.2) \qquad h(k) = \max_{(X_t)} f(X_t; k)$$

represent the maximum capacity of the system.

Panzar was able to prove that a cost-minimizing firm whose technology satisfies properties (a)–(c) would not attain $h(k)$, in general, regardless of the intensity of demand in any period. The intuition behind this result is simply that producing $h(k)$ requires employing costly variable factors (X_t) until their marginal products are zero, which is clearly not a cost-minimizing strategy. Panzar also showed that the traditional notion of peak production at maximum capacity results from imposing fixed factor proportions on $f(\ )$, or

$$(11.3) \qquad f(X_t; k) = \min\left(\frac{X_t}{a}; k\right)$$

with

$$(11.4) \qquad h(k) = k$$

Taken together, these two assumptions imply a total cost function of the form

$$(11.5) \qquad TC = \gamma \cdot \sum_{t=1}^{T} q_t + \delta \cdot \max_{(t)} q_t$$

which characterizes all of the traditional literature.[2]

Despite Panzar's criticisms, we will adopt assumptions (11.3) and (11.4) in this chapter in keeping with the traditional formulation. The results of this model have a number of interesting characteristics which are well established in public sector analysis. Differences with the "neoclassical" results will be highlighted throughout the chapter.

A second aspect of the traditional literature worth noting merely reiterates our introductory comments to Chapter 9, that there is no necessary connection between decreasing cost production and the peak-load problem. The literature has exploited this fact, because by adopting assumptions (11.3) and (11.4) researchers have necessarily been assuming long-run constant returns to scale. We do the same and simply indicate how the results must be modified with increasing returns to scale.

---

[2] J. Panzar, "A Neoclassical Approach to Peak-Load Pricing," *The Bell Journal of Economics*, Autumn 1976. Refer also to A. Marino, "Peak-Load Pricing in a Neoclassical Model with Bounds on Variable Input Utilization," *The Bell Journal of Economics*, Spring 1978, which attempts to resurrect some of the traditional results with more flexible technologies.

THE PEAK-LOAD PROBLEM: AN ANALYTICAL FRAMEWORK

There are two key theoretical issues associated with the peak-load problem: (1) faced with variable demands, how should firms price to maintain pareto optimality?, and (2) what is the pareto-optimal level of capacity? An analysis of these questions must make explicit two distinctions at the outset, one related to cost and one related to demand, and take care that costs and demands are measured in the same units of time.

The cost distinction is simply the usual one between the short run and long run, in which the short-run costs include all operating costs not specifically associated with the factor that defines the capacity of the system, usually some type of capital. Capacity is assumed fixed in the short run. Long-run costs include the costs of the factors associated with capacity, as well as the other factors that are variable in the short run. The distinction between short run and long run is often blurred in economic analysis. For example, all previous modeling in Chapter 2–10 has implicitly been assuming the long run since all factors were variable for any producer. But the peak-load problem requires the existence of a given capacity, that is, a short run, to have any meaning.[3]

FIGURE 11–1

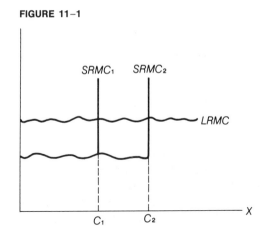

As a first step toward developing some intuition into the peak-load problem consider the representation of a short-run and long-run marginal costs in Figure 11–1. (As in all of economic theory it is the marginal costs that matter.) The pattern of short-run marginal costs is irrelevant up to capacity. What matters is that at capacity they are indeterminate, a vertical line, consistent with the notion that there is some absolute maximum capacity for the system, corresponding to equation (11.2). Thus, for capacity C_1, $SRMC_1$ may follow any given path up to C_1, depending upon factor prices and the production

---

[3] Even if there is no ultimate capacity constraint, but rather just sharply rising marginal costs beyond some level of production, these costs are understood to be short-run marginal costs.

function. At C_1, however, $SRMC_1$ necessarily becomes vertical. If more capacity is added to the system, to level C_2, then short-run marginal costs continue beyond C_1, once again determined by factor prices and the production function, until C_2, at which point they again become vertical, and so forth. The pattern of $LRMC$ depends entirely upon factor prices and the production function. By definition, there is no capacity constraint in the long run. For the time being assume capacity can be added (subtracted) in infinitely divisible units so that long-run marginal costs are defined for all levels of output, exactly as shown in Figure 11–1. Notice also that $LRMC$ are drawn above the variable portions of the various $SRMC$ curves. This is reasonable, since $LRMC$ include all the costs associated with the short run plus the marginal costs of capacity.

For ease of exposition, we will initially assume constant returns-to-scale production, with constant long-run and short-run marginal costs, as shown in Figure 11–2.

FIGURE 11–2

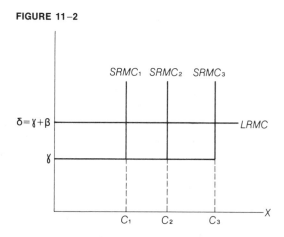

Figure 11–2 is consistent with equation (11.5), in which the short-run marginal operating costs equal γ for all values of X, and the long-run marginal costs are δ for all X, equal to the sum of the marginal operating costs, γ, and the marginal capacity costs, β. β measures the opportunity or rental value of the capital services offered by an additional unit of capacity.[4]

The obvious demand distinction is between peak and off-peak demand. For a given level of capacity, $\bar{C}$, the peak and off-peak are defined as follows in the "traditional" model: let $X^D = X^D(P)$ represent the demand for X. Determine the quantity demanded when $P = \gamma$, the short-run marginal costs. If $X^D_\gamma = X^D(\gamma) \leq \bar{C}$, demand is said to be off-peak. If $X^D_\gamma = X^D(\gamma) > \bar{C}$, demand is said to be peak. That is, the short-run marginal cost price defines the reference price at which capacity either can (off-peak) or cannot (peak) satisfy the quantity

---

[4] At this point we are also assuming that defined short-run marginal costs, γ, are unaffected by changes in capacity.

FIGURE 11-3

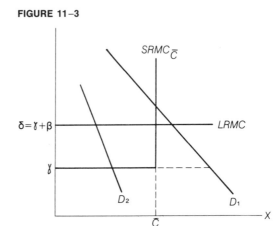

demanded. According to this definition, D_2 is an off-peak demand and D_1 a peak demand in Figure 11-3, given that capacity equals $\bar{C}$.

Finally, to ensure commensurability, we will assume all demands and costs are measured over the smallest unit of time for which demand fluctuations are relevant, defined as the demand (or cost) *period*. The full demand (cost) *cycle* refers to the unit of time over which the entire pattern of individual period fluctuations tends to recur. Given these definitions, the demand cycle is necessarily split into periods of equal length. So, for instance, if one hour defines the minimum unit of time for which fluctuations in electricity demand are relevant, and a full day defines a natural cycle, then there are 24 relevant demand and cost periods, some peak, some off-peak. In Figure 11-3, with two demand periods represented, it is understood that each period occurs for exactly one half of the full cycle.[5]

THE PEAK-LOAD PROBLEM: INTUITIVE ANALYSIS

An intuitive discussion of the peak-load problem will be helpful before undertaking the formal general equilibrium analysis since a general equilibrium model detailed enough to capture the pareto-optimal pricing and investment rules given a variable pattern of demands is fairly complex, even when stripped to the bare essentials. Thus, the formal model should be easier to comprehend with some anticipation of the results.

It turns out that both the pricing and investment rules are closely related to standard competitive principles. Consider, for example, the pricing rules for

---

[5] This time-period accounting convention follows Dreze, "Some Post-War Contributions of French Economists." Williamson, "Peak-Load Pricing and Optimal Capacity," defines demands and costs relative to the entire cycle. Naturally, they each arrive at the same pricing and investment rules. So long as cost and demand are commensurate, the accounting procedure employed cannot affect the results.

FIGURE 11–4

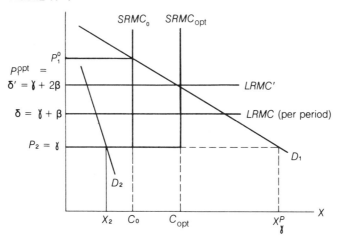

the variable demand market depicted in Figure 11–4, with capacity initially equal to C_0, D_2 the off-peak demand, and D_1 the peak demand. We know that pareto optimality requires marginal cost pricing in a first-best policy environment, and the same holds true here. The only question is whether price should equal short- or long-run marginal cost. Based on our knowledge of how competitive markets work, the answer must be short-run marginal costs. Price *always* equals short-run marginal cost because at any given time the short-run costs define the opportunity costs of producing more (or less) of the product. Only in long-run equilibrium, when firms have adjusted their plant size to continuing market conditions and new (old) firms have entered (exited) the industry, will price also equal long-run marginal costs. Applying the short-run marginal cost pricing principle to the peak-load problem implies that P_2, the off-peak price, should equal γ, the short-run marginal costs, and that P_1, the peak price, should equal P_1^0, the price at which the quantity demanded at the peak just equals capacity output. Thus, variable demands imply variable prices.

The off-peak price is obviously a straightforward application of short-run marginal cost pricing. The peak price is somewhat more subtle, but a moment's reflection will indicate that the optimum price must be such as to price quantity demanded to capacity. Only this price ensures that all those who place the highest value on each successive unit of X up to C_0 end up buying the product. By contrast, if P_1 were maintained at γ (or set at any level below P_1^0), there would be excess demand (equal to $X_\gamma^P - C_0$ with $P_1 = \gamma$). If free trading were possible, those willing to pay at least P_1^0 for any unit could always induce those who received the product on a first-come basis but who do not value all the units at P_1^0 to surrender some product at a price at least equal to P_1^0. Since these trades are mutually beneficial, they must be pareto superior to the original excess demand situation. The pareto optimum would occur when all such mutually beneficial trades had been exhausted. With price set equal to P_1^0, however, the pareto optimum is obtained directly. To summarize the pricing rules:

Off-peak: Set price equal to short-run marginal costs.

Peak: Set price such that the quantity demanded equals the given capacity.

Similar intuitive reasoning based on competitive behavior will also discover the correct investment rule determining the optimal level of capacity. In the long run a competitive firm varies all its factors until the marginal costs are equal among all factors, and in turn equal to price. Recall the first-order conditions for least cost (competitive) production,

$$(11.6) \qquad P_G = \frac{P_f}{MP_f} \qquad \text{all } f = 1, \ldots, F$$

where:

P_G = price of output.

P_f = price of factor f.

MP_f = the marginal product of factor f.

These are long-run marginal costs since all factors are being varied. Price also equals short-run marginal costs measured at the long-run equilibrium, since some of these factors are variable in the short run as well as the long run. When applying these principles to the peak-load problem, however, it is clear that the equation of short- and long-run marginal costs can occur only in the peak demand period. Marginal changes in capacity have no value to off-peak users. Hence the off-peak price, P_2, should remain at measured $SRMC$, γ, whether capacity equals C_0, or C_{opt} in Figure 11–4, or any value such that D_2 remains an off-peak demand ($D_2(\gamma) < \bar{C}$). This further implies that peak users should pay the *entire* costs associated with marginal additions to capacity, that is, marginal capacity costs defined over the entire cycle. Since β measures only the per period marginal capacity costs, the relevant long-run marginal costs for peak users are $\gamma + 2\beta$, or $LRMC'$ in Figure 11–4. Thus C_{opt} occurs where peak demand and $LRMC'$ intersect, at which point $P_1^{opt} = LRMC' = SRMC_{opt}$, consistent with competitive pricing *and* investment rules.

Notice, finally, that with constant returns production total revenues will equal total costs over the demand cycle at the optimum:

$$(11.7) \qquad TR = P_1^{opt} \cdot C_{opt} + P_2 \cdot X_2$$

and

$$(11.8) \qquad TC = (\gamma + 2\beta)C_{opt} + \gamma \cdot X_2$$

with $P_1^{opt} = \gamma + 2\beta$; $_2 = \gamma$

Hence the equation of total revenues and costs could be used as an alternative test for optimal capacity, but only with constant returns to scale. Unfortunately, one would expect increasing returns in most public sector applications, for which $TR < TC$ at the optimum. Nonetheless, the equation of price with long-run marginal costs defined as above will occur at the optimum, whatever behavior production might exhibit (assuming infinitely divisible capacity).

A GENERAL EQUILIBRIUM MODEL OF THE PEAK-LOAD PROBLEM

Having gained an intuitive feel for the pareto-optimal pricing and investment rules, we can proceed with a full general equilibrium analysis of the peak-load problem. It should be noted at the outset that the addition of a capacity constraint for one of the goods does not render the analysis second best, since the constraint is nothing more than a property of one of the production functions in the economy. It in no way limits the policy options available to the government, nor does it imply noncompetitive behavior. Therefore, this constraint is entirely consistent with the usual first-best assumptions.

The peak-load problem can be analyzed with an extremely condensed version of the full general equilibrium model of Chapter 2, but it cannot be quite as simple as the model used in Chapter 9. Positing a one-consumer equivalent economy is once again sufficient, but the peak-load problem requires some additional detail in the production sector of the model, which in turn necessitates a set of market-clearing equations. At very least there must be three goods, each with its own production functions: one representing peak-load output of the service in question; one representing the service's off-peak output; and one other good which can be thought of either as a Hicksian composite good or a single good selected at random from the full set of all other goods and services which need not be specified explicitly in the formal model. Whichever interpretation is chosen, this other good serves as the source of opportunity cost for employing resources in the variable demand sector of the economy. The model also requires at least two factors of production, one of which is directly related to capacity in the variable demand sector, to distinguish separate short- and long-run equilibria.

With these considerations in mind,

Let:

X_1 = the quantity of the variable demand service during peak demand.

X_2 = the quantity of the variable demand sector during off-peak demand.

X_3 = an additional good or service produced in the economy.

L_i = labor used in the production of good i, $i = 1, 3$.

K_1 = capital used in the production of goods 1 and 2, shared equally by the goods.

K_3 = capital used in the production of good 3.

$f^1(L_1, K_1)$ = the production function for good 1.

$f^2(L_2, K_1)$ = the production function for good 2.

$f^3(L_3, K_3)$ = the production function for good 3.

$$U = U(X_1, X_2, X_3; L_1 + L_2 + L_3; K_1 + K_3) = \text{the utility}$$
function of the consumer, with market clearance for
each factor included directly in the utility function, for
example:

$$L_{\text{supply}} = L_1 + L_2 + L_3$$
$$K_{\text{supply}} = K_1 + K_3$$

By the usual conventions, factors L and K enter utility negatively, and

$$\frac{\partial U}{\partial L_i} = \frac{\partial U}{\partial L} \quad i = 1, 3 \qquad \frac{\partial U}{\partial K_i} = \frac{\partial U}{\partial K} \quad i = 1 \text{ and } 3$$

That is, the consumer does not care which firms buy his labor and capital services.

$C = $ capacity in the variable demand sector.

$C(K_1) = $ the functional relationship between capacity and capital in the variable demand sector.

$X_1 = C$ defines the capacity constraint on X_1—notice that only X_1 can be a peak demand in this model.

With these basic elements the economy's problem is:[6]

$$\max_{(X_1, X_2, X_3; L_1, L_2, L_3; K_1, K_3; C)} U(X_1, X_2, X_3; L_1 + L_2 + L_3; K_1 + K_3)$$

s.t.
$$X_1 = f^1(L_1, K_1)$$
$$X_2 = f^2(L_2, K_1)$$
$$X_3 = f^3(L_3, K_3)$$
$$X_1 = C$$
$$C = C(K_1)$$

with the corresponding Lagrangian:

$$\max_{(X_1, X_2, X_3; L_1, L_2, L_3; K_1, K_3; C)} L = U(X_1, X_2, X_3; L_1 + L_2 + L_3; K_1 + K_3)$$
$$+ \lambda_1[X^1 - f^1(L_1, K_1)] + \lambda_2[X^2 - f^2(L_2, K_1)]$$
$$+ \lambda_3[X^3 - f^3(L_3, K_3)]$$
$$+ \lambda_4(X_1 - C) + \lambda_5[C - C(K_1)]$$

The nine first-order conditions are:

(11.9) $\qquad X_1: \quad U_{X_1} + \lambda_1 + \lambda_4 = 0$

(11.10) $\qquad X_2: \quad U_{X_2} + \lambda_2 = 0$

---

[6] Notice that the constraints $X_1 = C$ and $C = C(K_1)$ are consistent with equation (11.4) and, if binding, implicitly impose equation (11.3) on f^1 and f^2, given cost minimizing production behavior.

(11.11) $\qquad X_3: \quad U_{X_3} + \lambda_3 = 0$

(11.12) $\qquad L_1: \quad U_{L_1} - \lambda_1 f^1_{L_1} = 0$

(11.13) $\qquad L_2: \quad U_{L_2} - \lambda_2 f^2_{L_2} = 0$

(11.14) $\qquad L_3: \quad U_{L_3} - \lambda_3 f^3_{L_3} = 0$

(11.15) $\qquad K_1: \quad U_{K_1} - \lambda_1 f^1_{K_1} - \lambda_2 f^2_{K_1} - \lambda_5 \dfrac{\partial C}{\partial K_1} = 0$

(11.16) $\qquad K_3: \quad U_{K_3} - \lambda_3 f^3_{K_3} = 0$

(11.17) $\qquad C: \quad -\lambda_4 + \lambda_5 = 0$

where:

$$U_{X_i} \equiv \frac{\partial U}{\partial X_i} \qquad i = 1, 3$$

$$f^i_{L_i} \equiv \frac{\partial f^i}{\partial L_i} \qquad i = 1, 3$$

$$f^j_{K_i} \equiv \frac{\partial f^j}{\partial K_i} \qquad j = 1, 3; i = 1 \text{ and } 3$$

Since the consumer is indifferent to whom he supplies factors,

(11.18) $$U_{K_1} = U_{K_3}$$

and

(11.19) $$U_{L_1} = U_{L_2} = U_{L_3}$$

Therefore, from (11.12), (11.13), and (11.14),

(11.20) $$\lambda_1 f^1_{L_1} = \lambda_2 f^2_{L_2} = \lambda_3 f^3_{L_3}$$

and from (11.15) and (11.16),

(11.21) $$\lambda_3 f^3_{K_3} = \lambda_1 f^1_{K_1} + \lambda_2 f^2_{K_1} + \lambda_5 \frac{\partial C}{\partial K_1}$$

But $\lambda_4 = \lambda_5$ from (11.17). Thus, (11.21) can be rewritten as

(11.22) $$\lambda_3 f^3_{K_3} = \lambda_1 f^1_{K_1} + \lambda_2 f^2_{K_1} + \lambda_4 \frac{\partial C}{\partial K_1}$$

Furthermore, there can be only one price for capital, P_K, and one price for labor, P_L, in any market equilibrium because the consumer is indifferent in supply. If different factor prices prevailed temporarily in the different industries, the consumer would switch his supply from low-priced to high-priced industries until the factor prices were equalized. This market result is crucial to all that follows.

Capacity Constraint Not Binding

We know that without a binding capacity constraint the model will generate all the standard results of competitive price theory. It will prove useful to begin by analyzing this case as a basis for comparing the peak-load results when capacity is binding.

The value of λ_4, the Lagrangian multiplier associated with the capacity constraint, reflects whether or not the constraint is binding. λ_4 measures the increase in utility resulting from a unit relaxation of the capacity constraint. But if the constraint is not binding, relaxing the constraint cannot change utility. Hence, $\lambda_4 = 0$. Moreover, if $\lambda_4 = 0$, then $\lambda_5 = 0$ from (11.17). Using these results and defining prices $P_K, P_L, P_{X_1}, P_{X_2}, P_{X_3}$, the standard competitive results can easily be derived.[7]

Pareto-Optimality—Goods and Factors

Consider first the pareto-optimal conditions between the three goods and labor. Dividing (11.9) by (11.12),

$$(11.23) \qquad \frac{-U_{X_1}}{U_{L_1}} = \frac{1}{f^1_{L_1}}$$

Dividing (11.10) by (11.13),

$$(11.24) \qquad \frac{-U_{X_2}}{U_{L_2}} = \frac{1}{f^2_{L_2}}$$

Dividing (11.11) by (11.14),

$$(11.25) \qquad \frac{-U_{X_3}}{U_{L_3}} = \frac{1}{f^3_{L_3}}$$

With competitive markets the consumer will set:

$$(11.26) \qquad \frac{-U_{X_i}}{U_{L_i}} = \frac{P_{X_i}}{P_L} \qquad i = 1, 3$$

and each firm will set:

$$(11.27) \qquad \frac{P_{X_i}}{P_L} = \frac{1}{f^i_{L_i}} \qquad i = 1, 3$$

Alternatively,

$$(11.27a) \qquad P_{X_i} \cdot f^i_{L_i} = P_L \qquad \text{(Price of labor = Value of labor's marginal product in } X_i)$$

$$(11.27b) \qquad P_{X_i} = \frac{P_L}{f^i_{L_i}} \qquad \text{(Price of } X_i = SRMC_{X_i})$$

Together, (11.26) and (11.27) (or (11.27a), (11.27b)) imply the pareto-optimal conditions (11.23)–(11.25).

---

[7] Since K_1 is available for both X_1 and X_2, P_K corresponds to a two-period price (equal to 2β with reference to our earlier intuitive analysis).

Next consider the pareto-optimal conditions between goods and capital. Divide (11.15) by (11.9) to obtain:

(11.28)
$$\frac{-U_{K_1}}{U_{X_1}} = f^1_{K_1} + \frac{\lambda_2}{\lambda_1} f^2_{K_1}$$

Divide (11.15) by (11.10) to obtain:

(11.29)
$$\frac{-U_{K_1}}{U_{X_2}} = \frac{\lambda_1}{\lambda_2} f^1_{K_1} + f^2_{K_1}$$

Finally, dividing (11.16) by (11.11) yields:

(11.30)
$$\frac{-U_{K_3}}{U_{X_3}} = f^3_{K_3}$$

The consumer will set:

(11.31)
$$\frac{-U_{K_3}}{U_{X_3}} = \frac{P_K}{P_{X_3}}$$

Competitive firm 3 will equate:

(11.32)
$$\frac{P_K}{P_{X_3}} = f^3_{K_3}$$

Alternatively,

(11.32a)
$$P_K = P_{X_3} \cdot f^3_{K_3} = VMP^{X_3}_{K_3}$$

or

(11.32b)
$$P_{X_3} = \frac{P_K}{f^3_{K_3}} = LRMC_{K_3}$$

(11.31) and (11.32) ((11.32a) or (11.32b)) imply (11.30), the pareto-optimal conditions between X_3 and K_3. Moreover, from (11.32b) and (11.27b), firm 3 will equate $SRMC_{L_3}$ and $LRMC_{K_3}$ in equilibrium, both equal to P_{X_3}.

Turning to K_1, the consumer will equate:

(11.33)
$$\frac{-U_{K_1}}{U_{X_1}} = \frac{P_K}{P_{X_1}}$$

and

(11.34)
$$\frac{-U_{K_i}}{U_{X_2}} = \frac{P_K}{P_{X_2}}$$

Also, from (11.9) and (11.10).

(11.35)
$$\frac{U_{X_1}}{U_{X_2}} = \frac{\lambda_1}{\lambda_2} = \frac{P_{X_1}}{P_{X_2}}$$

Producers in the variable demand sector will equate

(11.36)
$$\frac{P_K}{P_{X_1}} = f^1_{K_1} + \frac{P_{X_2}}{P_{X_1}} f^2_{K_1}$$

or

(11.37)
$$\frac{P_K}{P_{X_2}} = \frac{P_{X_1}}{P_{X_2}} f^1_{K_1} + f^2_{K_1}$$

Alternatively,

(11.38) $$P_K = P_{X_1} f^1_{K_1} + P_{X_2} f^2_{K_1}$$

Equation (11.38) says the competitive firm will hire K_1 until its price equals the value of its marginal product, the sum of its marginal values in producing X_1 and X_2. Moreover, hiring K_1 in this way satisfies pareto optimality, since equations (11.33)–(11.37) imply conditions (11.28) and (11.29).

Finally, relate the use of capital to its effects on short-run marginal costs in each industry. Dividing (11.32a) by (11.27a) for X_3 yields:

(11.39) $$\frac{P_K}{P_L} = \frac{f^3_{K_3}}{f^3_{L_3}}$$

which can be written as

(11.40) $$P_K = \frac{P_L}{f^3_{L_3}} \cdot \left(\frac{\partial X_3}{\partial K_3}\right) = SRMC_{X_3} \cdot \frac{\partial X_3}{\partial K_3} = \frac{\partial SRTC}{\partial X_3} \cdot \frac{\partial X_3}{\partial K_3} = \frac{\partial SRTC}{\partial K_3}$$

where:

$SRTC \equiv$ short-run total costs.

Equation (11.40) says capital should be employed up to the point where the cost of the last unit, P_K, just equals the savings in short-run (operating) total cost from employing the last unit. This is the standard investment rule for the optimal plant size of a competitive firm.

The same rule applies to the variable demand firm. Dividing (11.38) by (11.27a) for X_1 yields:

(11.41) $$\frac{P_K}{P_L} = \frac{P_{X_1} f^1_{K_1} + P_{X_2} f^2_{K_1}}{P_{X_1} f^1_{L_1}}$$

But $P_{X_1} f^1_{L_1} = P_{X_2} f^2_{L_2}$. Therefore,

(11.42) $$\frac{P_K}{P_L} = \frac{f^1_{K_1}}{f^1_{L_1}} + \frac{f^2_{K_1}}{f^2_{L_2}}$$

which can be rewritten as

(11.43) $$P_K = \frac{P_L}{f^1_{L_1}} \cdot \frac{\partial X_1}{\partial K_1} + \frac{P_L}{f^2_{L_2}} \cdot \frac{\partial X_2}{\partial K_1} = SRMC_{X_1} \cdot \frac{\partial X_1}{\partial K_1} + SRMC_{X_2} \frac{\partial X_2}{\partial K_1}$$

$$= \frac{\partial SRTC_{X_1}}{\partial K_1} + \frac{\partial SRTC_{X_2}}{\partial K_1}$$

Again, capital should be hired until its extra costs (P_K) just equal the savings in short-run (operating) total costs from all products combined. These are nothing more than the standard investment rules for a multioutput firm. Hence, both the pricing and investment rules for a variable demand firm are identical in structure to those of a standard two product firm, providing the capacity "problem" at the peak merely involves increased short-run marginal costs and not an absolute capacity constraint. Since there is no restriction that $f^1(L_1, K_1) = f^2(L_2, K_1)$, the increasing short-run marginal cost version of the peak-load demand problem is implicit in this formulation of the model. Summarizing the main results for pareto optimality:

Pricing Rules[8]

Variable Demand Sector

(1) $P_{X_1} = SRMC_{X_1}$

(2) $P_{X_2} = SRMC_{X_2}$

Other Goods

(3) $P_{X_3} = SRMC_{X_3}$

Investment Rules

Variable Demand Good

(4) Increase capacity until the extra capacity costs just equal the combined reduction in short-run operating costs for both peak and off-peak demand periods.

(5) If the capacity constraint is not binding, or the peak-load "problem" merely refers to rapidly increased marginal costs to satisfy peak use, and the market for the good is competitive, there is no need for government intervention. The standard competitive results will generate pareto optimality.

Other Goods

(6) The existence of a variable demand firm has no effect on the pareto-optimal conditions for a single demand firm. Competitive markets for all other goods will generate the pareto-optimal conditions.

Capacity Constraint Binding

With the capacity constraint binding two results differ from the unconstrained case, the pricing rules for X_1, the peak demand, and the investment rules for K_1, the source of the capacity constraint.

Pricing Rules. The price of each good continues to equal its short-run marginal cost, exactly as expected. In fact, the pricing rules for X_2 and X_3 are identical to the unconstrained case. Equations (11.23)–(11.27) continue to apply to both X_2 and X_3 since the first-order conditions (11.10), (11.11), (11.13), and (11.14) are unchanged by the constraint. Thus, setting

(11.44)
$$P_{X_i} = \frac{P_L}{f_{L_i}} = SRMC_{X_i} \qquad i = 2, 3$$

will generate the pareto-optimal conditions, exactly as before. In terms of the peak-load problem, the off-peak price should cover only short-run marginal

---

[8] Panzar also shows that (a) if the production technology exhibits decreasing returns to scale in the short run, $P_{X_1} \cdot X_1 > P_L \cdot L_1$ and $P_{X_2} \cdot X_2 > P_2 \cdot L_2$, so that all users contribute to capacity costs, $P_K \cdot K$; and (b) under the assumption of strict short-run concavity, implying rising $SRMC_{1,2}$, P_{X_1} and P_{X_2} will be directly and monotonically related to X_1 and X_2, respectively. Panzar, "A Neoclassical Approach to Peak-Load Pricing," pp. 525–26.

costs. This point is important because with a capacity constraint long-run and short-run marginal costs will generally be unequal at the optimal level of capacity.

The pricing rule for X_1 is more complicated with the capacity constraint. The short-run involves comparing the first-order conditions for X_1 with L_1. Dividing (11.9) by (11.12) yields:

(11.45)
$$\frac{-U_{X_1}}{U_L} = \frac{\lambda_1 + \lambda_4}{\lambda_1 f_{L_1}^1} = \frac{1}{f_{L_1}^1} + \frac{\lambda_4}{\lambda_1 f_{L_1}^1}$$

the pareto-optimal condition. Since the consumer will set $-U_{X_1}/U_L = P_{X_1}/P_L$, the producer must satisfy

(11.46)
$$\frac{P_{X_1}}{P_L} = \frac{\lambda_1 + \lambda_4}{\lambda_1 f_{L_1}^1}$$

or

(11.47)
$$P_{X_1} = \frac{P_L}{f_{L_1}^1} + \frac{P_L \lambda_4}{\lambda_1 f_{L_1}^1}$$

$P_L/f_{L_1}^1$ is the short-run marginal cost as traditionally defined in the variable range of output before the constraint is binding. (11.47) says price must exceed these marginal costs by the amount $P_L \lambda_4/\lambda_1 f_{L_1}^1$ to achieve pareto optimality. As it turns out, P_{X_1} must equal the value at which the peak-load quantity demanded equals capacity. To see this, consider equation (11.46). From (11.45), the right-hand side of (11.46) equals the consumers MRS between X_1 and L_1. Furthermore, $X_1 = C$ with the constraint binding. Thus, with labor as the numeraire ($P_L \equiv 1$), P_{X_1} must equal the point on the demand curve at which demand and capacity intersect. Returning to equation (11.47), the term $P_L \cdot \lambda_4/\lambda_1 f_{L_1}^1$ must therefore equal the distance between the defined short-run marginal costs at capacity ($P_L/f_{L_1}^1$) and the point at which demand intersects capacity, the distance ($P_{X_1} - \gamma$) in Figure 11–5.

This distance is frequently referred to as the *quasi rent* for X_1. To give the term more intuitive appeal, note that $\lambda_1 f_{L_1}^1 = U_{L_1}$ from (11.12), and that λ_4 gives the increase in utility due to a marginal increase in capacity, $\partial U/\partial C$.

FIGURE 11–5

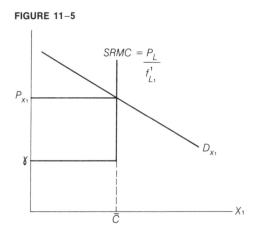

Therefore,

$$(11.48) \qquad \frac{P_L \lambda_4}{\lambda_1 f_L^1} = P_L \frac{\dfrac{\partial U}{\partial C}}{\dfrac{\partial U}{\partial L_1}} = -P_L \frac{dL_1}{dC} \bigg|_{U = \bar{U}}$$

The quasi rent measures the value of the additional labor the consumer is willing to supply to have another unit of capacity for X_1. Also,

$$(11.49) \qquad \frac{P_L}{f_{L_1}^1} = P_L \frac{\lambda_1}{U_L} = P_L \frac{\dfrac{\partial U}{\partial X_1}}{\dfrac{\partial U}{\partial L_1}} = -P_L \frac{dL_1}{dX_1} \bigg|_{U = \bar{U}}$$

Thus, P_X in its entirety measures $-P_L \, dL/dX_1 |_{U=U}$, the value of labor the consumer is willing to supply to have an additional unit of final product, X_1.

The Investment Rules. The investment rules for X_3 are identical to the unconstrained case. Conditions (11.30)–(11.32), (11.39), and (11.40) continue to apply.

The investment rules for K_1 are significantly altered, however. Dividing (11.15) by (11.12),

$$(11.50) \qquad \frac{U_{K_1}}{U_{L_1}} = \frac{\lambda_1 f_{K_1}^1 + \lambda_2 f_{K_1}^2 + \lambda_5 \dfrac{\partial C}{\partial K_1}}{\lambda_1 f_{L_1}^1}$$

Recalling that $\lambda_1 f_{L_1}^1 = \lambda_2 f_{L_2}^2$, and $\lambda_5 = \lambda_4$, (11.50) becomes:

$$(11.51) \qquad \frac{U_{K_1}}{U_{L_1}} = \frac{f_{K_1}^1}{f_{L_1}^1} + \frac{f_{K_1}^2}{f_{L_2}^2} + \frac{\lambda_4}{\lambda_1 f_{L_1}^1} \frac{\partial C}{\partial K_1}$$

the pareto-optimum condition between labor and capital used in the production of X_1. From consumer maximization, $P_K/P_L = U_{K_1}/U_{L_1}$. Thus, for pareto optimality the firm must equate

$$(11.52) \qquad \frac{P_K}{P_L} = \frac{f_{K_1}^1}{f_{L_1}^1} + \frac{f_{K_1}^2}{f_{L_2}^2} + \frac{\lambda_4}{\lambda_1 f_{L_1}^1} \cdot \frac{\partial C}{\partial K_1}$$

Alternatively,

$$(11.53) \qquad P_K = \frac{P_L}{f_{L_1}^1} \cdot \frac{\partial X_1}{\partial K_1} + \frac{P_L}{f_{L_2}^2} \cdot \frac{\partial X_2}{\partial K_1} + P_L \frac{\lambda_4}{\lambda_1 f_{L_1}^1} \cdot \frac{\partial C}{\partial K_1}$$

which can be rewritten as

$$(11.54) \qquad P_K = \frac{\partial SRTC_{X_1}}{\partial K_1} + \frac{\partial SRTC_{X_2}}{\partial K_1} + (P_{X_1} - SRMC_{X_1}) \frac{\partial C}{\partial K_1}$$

or

$$(11.55) \qquad (P_{X_1} - SRMC_{X_1}) \frac{\partial C}{\partial K_1} = P_K - \frac{\partial SRTC_{X_1}}{\partial K_1} - \frac{\partial SRTC_{X_2}}{\partial K_1}$$

The left-hand side of (11.55) is the marginal quasi rent resulting from an additional unit of K_1. The right-hand side gives the marginal capital costs for K_1, equal to the direct costs, P_K, less the savings in short-run total costs for both X_1 and X_2 resulting from a marginal increase in capital. Compare this result with equation (11.43) for the unconstrained case, in which capital is hired until the direct costs on the margin just equal the savings in short-run total costs, or, in other words, until the marginal capital costs are zero. In the constrained case, marginal capital costs remain positive at the optimum, equal to the amount by which the price of X exceeds the variable component of short-run marginal costs. Thus, short- and long-run marginal costs are equal only in the indeterminant (vertical) range of $SRMC$. The optimal capacity (as opposed to K_1) is represented in Figure 11-6. Notice that Figure 11-6 implicitly assumes $\partial SRTC / \partial K_1 = 0$, in which case $P_K =$ marginal capital costs $= (P_{X_1} - SRMC_{X_1}) =$ quasi rents at the optimum.

FIGURE 11-6

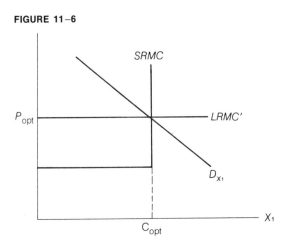

The identical analysis could have been carried out by starting with the first-order conditions for K_1 and X_2. This will be left as an exercise for the reader.

Note, finally, that combining these results with the investment rule for K_3 determines the general equilibrium allocation of capital between sectors.

$$(11.56) \quad P_K = \frac{\partial SRTC_3}{\partial K_3} = \frac{\partial SRTC_1}{\partial K_1} + \frac{\partial SRTC_2}{\partial K_1} + (P_{X_1} - SRMC_{X_1}) \frac{\partial C}{\partial K_1}$$

For all unconstrained sectors the direct marginal capital costs (P_K) equals the savings in short-run costs. Only in the constrained sector is there an additional quasi rent term. These conditions will be satisfied if all unconstrained sectors are competitive and the variable demand sector follows the short-run marginal cost pricing and investment rules (11.47) and (11.55).

To summarize the pareto-optimal rules in like manner to the unconstrained case:

Pricing Rules

Variable Demand Sector

(1)′ X_1 = set price such that the quantity demanded equals capacity.

(2)′ $P_{X_2} = SRMC_{X_2}$

Other Goods

(3)′ $P_{X_3} = SRMC_{X_3}$

Investment Rules

Variable Demand Sector

(4)′ Increase capacity until the quasi rents from additional capacity $(P_{X_1} - SRMC_{X_1})$ at the peak demand just equal the marginal capacity costs, defined as P_K less the savings in short-run total costs for both off-peak and peak demand periods resulting from an additional unit of capacity. Notice that the off-peak demand period enters into the investment decision only if the short-run costs of supplying off-peak demand are related to capacity. Off-peak demand is otherwise irrelevant.[9]

Other Goods

(5)′ The investment rules for unconstrained firms are unaltered by the existence of capacity constraints somewhere in the economy.

Implications for Government Policy

(6)′ Government intervention into either sector is unnecessary so long as they are both competitive. This point has already been demonstrated for the single demand sector. The proof for the variable demand sector is as follows. The variable demand firm will solve the following profit-maximization problem:

$$\max_{(L_1, L_2, K_1, C)} \quad P_{X_1} f^1(L_1, K_1) + P_{X_2} f^2(L_2, K_1) - P_L(L_1 + L_2) - P_K K_1$$

$$\text{s.t.} \quad f^1(L_1, K_1) = C$$

$$C = C(K_1)$$

with corresponding Lagrangian:

$$\max_{(L_1, L_2, K_1, C)} \quad L = P_{X_1} f^1(L_1, K_1) + P_{X_2} f^2(L_2, K_1) - P_L(L_1 + L_2)$$

$$- P_K K_1 + \theta_1 [f^1(L_1, K_1) - C] + \theta_2 [C - C(K_1)]$$

The first-order conditions are:

(11.57) L_1: $P_{X_1} f^1_{L_1} - P_L + \theta_1 f^1_{L_1} = 0$

(11.58) L_2: $P_{X_2} f^2_{L_2} - P_L = 0$

(11.59) K_1: $P_{X_1} f^1_{K_1} + P_{X_2} f^2_{K_1} - P_K + \theta_1 f^1_{K_1} - \theta_2 \dfrac{\partial C}{\partial K_1} = 0$

(11.60) C: $-\theta_1 + \theta_2 = 0$

---

[9] Compare this with the "neoclassical" result, page 233, footnote 8.

From (11.57),

$$(11.61) \quad P_{X_1} = \frac{P_L}{f^1_{L_1}} - \theta_1 = SRMC_{X_1} + \frac{\partial \pi}{\partial C} = SRMC_{X_1} + \left(\begin{matrix}\text{quasi rents of addi-}\\\text{tional capacity}\end{matrix}\right)$$

where:

π = profits.

$\theta_1 = -\dfrac{\partial \pi}{\partial C}$ from the definition of a Lagrangian multiplier.

Substituting (11.58), (11.60), and (11.61) into (11.59), and solving for P_K yields:

$$(11.62) \quad P_K = \left(\frac{P_L}{f^1_{L_1}} - \theta_1\right) f^1_{K_1} + \frac{P_L}{f^2_{L_2}} f^2_{K_1} + \theta_1 f^1_{K_1} - \theta_1 \frac{\partial C}{\partial K_1}$$

Noting that $\theta_1 = -\partial \pi / \partial C$, $P_L / f^1_{L_1} = SRMC_{X_1}$ up to C, and $P_L / f^2_{L_2} = SRMC_{X_2}$, (11.62) becomes:

$$(11.63) \quad P_K = SRMC_{X_1} \frac{\partial X_1}{\partial K_1} + SRMC_{X_2} \cdot \frac{\partial X_2}{\partial K_1} + \frac{\partial \pi}{\partial C} \cdot \frac{\partial C}{\partial K_1}$$

Noting that $\partial \pi / \partial C = (P_{X_1} - SRMC_{X_1})$ and rearranging terms yields:

$$(11.64) \quad \left(P_K - \frac{\partial SRTC_{X_1}}{\partial K_1} - \frac{\partial SRTC_{X_2}}{\partial K_1}\right) = (P_{X_1} - SRMC_{X_1}) \frac{\partial C}{\partial K_1}$$

$$= \text{(quasi rent of additional capital)}$$

identical to equation (11.55).

The general equilibrium model has therefore generated all the results predicted by our intuitive analysis of the traditional peak-load problem using standard competitive market principles. The model proved to be somewhat cumbersome because it required specifying three goods, two factors, and a capacity constraint. The Appendix to this chapter presents a greatly simplified partial equilibrium analysis of the traditional peak-load problem using the concept of social surplus maximization, where social surplus is defined as the difference between Marshallian consumer surplus and total production costs. The social surplus model is widely used in first-best public sector analysis both because of its relative simplicity and also because it generates correct decision rules despite using Marshallian consumer surplus as the measure of social benefits. Of course, one can never be certain such shortcuts are appropriate until verified by a legitimate model, which is why we choose the more cumbersome approach for the main body of the text.

SPECIAL ASPECTS OF THE PEAK-LOAD PROBLEM

Having developed a full general equilibrium analysis of the peak-load problem in its simplest form, it will be relatively easy to consider four complications that often appear in practical applications.

Interdependent Demands

The demands for peak and off-peak use often bear a substitute relationship to one another. Since the product is identical in both periods except for the actual timing of its consumption, peak users will often shift some of their demand to the off-peak as the price spread between peak and off-peak service increases, and vice versa. Fortunately, these substitution effects require no adjustments whatsoever to the pricing and investment rules developed above. While the intuitive analysis implicitly assumed the demands were independent, there were no such restrictions on demand in the formal general equilibrium model. The demands for each of the goods, X_1, X_2, and X_3, as well as the supplies of K and L will in general be functions of all the prices, and any lump-sum income or taxes that may exist within the system. Hence, whether or not all the prices actually appear in the consumer's demand and factor supply functions, all the pricing and investment rules resulting from the model continue to apply. This is not meant to imply that these substitution effects are of no practical importance, however. They most certainly are. In the first place, society will be able to save some resources it would otherwise use to supply capacity if the peak-load demand curve shifts in as a result of the peak-off-peak price differential. This makes it especially imperative to charge the proper price at the peak. In addition, as prices change with changes in capacity, the substitution effects may increase the tendency for demand periods to change status, meaning that a former peak demand becomes an off-peak demand, and vice versa. These shifts make it that much more difficult for the government to find the optimal pattern of prices, but this is only a practical consideration. So long as the peak and off-peak demands are correctly defined, with the proper price and investment rules applied, these shifts impose no additional theoretical problems.

Multiple Peak and Off-Peak Demands

In practice there may be numerous well-defined peak and off-peak demand periods. The general equilibrium model would have to be extended to cover these additional periods, with separate goods and production functions defined for each period. But it is not really necessary to redo the entire model. The structure of the modified model and its resulting first-order conditions are readily discernible.

Briefly, the formal model would change in two ways. Each new demand period, whether peak or off-peak, would require an additional production function of the form:

$$X_i = f^i(L_i, K_1) \qquad i = 4, 5, \ldots, N$$

where:

X_i = the ith demand period for the service.
L_i = labor used to produce the service in period i.

K_1 remains common to the production of service in all periods. Second, the peak demands would require additional constraints of the form

$$X_k = C \qquad k = \text{an index of peak demand.}$$

A moment's reflection would indicate that the modified general equilibrium model yields the following conclusions:

1.   There would be no change in the pricing and investment rules for the pareto-optimal production of the "other" goods and services in the economy, represented by X_3. None of its first-order conditions will be modified.

2.   Off-peak prices will continue to equal short-run marginal costs in the relevant range. Equations identical to (11.10), (11.13), (11.26), and (11.27) will apply to every off-peak demand.

3.   Each peak-load demand should be priced such that quantity demanded equals the given capacity. That is, each peak load should earn a quasi rent relative to short-run marginal costs in the variable range. Equations identical, or similar, to (11.9), (11.12), and (11.45) through (11.49) will apply to each peak-load demand, all with identical interpretations. The price of X at any peak should reflect the value of labor the consumer is willing to supply to have an additional unit of X_1 for any given capacity during each peak period.

4.   The investment rule for optimal capacity will be expanded to include all demand periods. Optimal capacity occurs when the *sum* of the quasi rents for all peak demand periods just equals the marginal capacity costs of additional capacity. Marginal capacity costs will now be defined as P_K less the sum of the savings in short-run marginal costs in all time periods (peak *and* off-peak) resulting from an additional unit of K_1.

Equations (11.51) and (11.52) will be modified to include marginal costs from all the demand periods as follows:

$$(11.65) \qquad \frac{U_{K_1}}{U_{L_1}} = \sum_{\text{all periods}} \frac{f^i_{K_1}}{f^i_{L_1}} + \sum_{\substack{\text{peak demand} \\ \text{periods}}} \frac{\lambda_k}{\lambda_j f^j_{L_j}} \cdot \frac{\partial C}{\partial K_1}$$

$$(11.66) \qquad \frac{P_K}{P_L} = \sum_{\text{all periods}} \frac{f^i_{K_1}}{f^i_{L_1}} + \sum_{\substack{\text{peak demand} \\ \text{periods}}} \frac{\lambda_k}{\lambda_j f^j_{L_j}} \cdot \frac{\partial C}{\partial K_1}$$

where:

   k, j are both indexed over the corresponding peak demand periods. That is, $k = 1, j = 1$ refer to peak demand in period 1.

Therefore, (11.55) will become:

$$(11.67) \qquad \sum_{\substack{\text{peak demand} \\ \text{periods}}} (P_{X_i} - SRMC_{X_i}) \frac{\partial C}{\partial K_1} = P_K - \sum_{\text{all periods}} \frac{\partial SRTC_{X_i}}{\partial K_1}$$

the modified investment rule stated above. As noted above, when capacity is expanded (contracted) toward the optimum, some periods that were formerly peak (off-peak) demands may well become off-peaks (peaks). All this means is that some terms on the left-hand side of (11.67) will become zero. Once again, this presents no theoretical problems, although it may lead to practical difficulties.

Demand Periods of Different Lengths

Suppose the demand for a public utility such as electricity exhibits the following pattern:

1. A two-hour peak in the early morning and a second two-hour peak of equal intensity in the early evening.
2. An equal, and substantially lower, demand over the remaining 20 hours of the day, the off-peak.[10]

Hence, demand is at a uniform peak for one sixth of the demand cycle, and a uniform off-peak for five sixths of the cycle.

The peak-load literature suggests two methods of accounting for demands of unequal duration. Following Dreze, we define two hours as the relevant demand period, with costs defined accordingly, such that the demand cycle consists of 12 distinct periods, 2 peak and 10 off-peak. The other possibility, following Williamson, is to define costs on a per day (cycle) basis and consider two distinct demand periods, one peak and one off-peak, with weights of one sixth and five sixths, respectively. Either accounting convention is appropriate, since demands and costs are commensurate in each case, and they both correctly account for the duration as well as the intensity of peak demand. (Refer to the Williamson article, "Peak-Load Pricing and Optimal Capacity," for a demonstration of the weighting technique.)

Indivisible Capacity

Additions to capacity in small increments may not be possible. Ideally society wants the firm to satisfy equation (11.55) (or (11.67)), but its only choices may be to stop short of the optimum, at which point the quasi rents from peak demand exceed the marginal capital costs, or make a large addition to capacity that will drive the quasi rents below marginal capital costs. The situation is depicted in Figure 11–7 for constant returns to scale. C_{opt} is the desired level of capacity, but the nearest choices open to the firm are C_0 and C_1, where C_1 is the minimum possible increment to C_0. At C_0 quasi rents $(P_{X_1}^0 - \gamma) > 2\beta$; at C_1, $(P_{X_1}^1 - \gamma) < 2\beta$, where β = the marginal capacity costs per period.

Deciding whether or not the increment from C_0 to C_1 is worthwhile requires the same all-or-none test developed for the "hard case" decreasing cost service. Taking C_0 as the origin, the test is whether the benefits of lowering P_{X_1} from $P_{X_1}^0$ to $P_{X_1}^1$ exceed the additional total costs at C_1 relative to C_0. These costs are just the area under $LRMC'$ from C_0 to C_1. The benefits can be measured in a

---

[10] The demand for electricity undoubtedly fluctuates more throughout the day than represented in this example, but the assumed pattern is sufficient for illustrating the treatment of unequal peak and off-peak periods of demand.

FIGURE 11–7

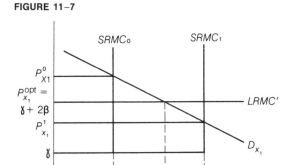

number of ways. One measure developed in Chapter 9 was total consumer expenditures on the new output equal to $P^1_{X_1}(C_1 - C_0)$, plus the Hicks Compensating Variation for the price change, the area behind the compensated demand for X_1 between $P^0_{X_1}$ and $P^1_{X_1}$, with C_0 taken as the axis. Demand is compensated at the original utility level represented by output C_0.

This test applies whether the industry exhibits increasing, decreasing, or constant long-run average costs. The all-or-none test in Chapter 9 had to be performed because the industry was a "hard case" decreasing cost industry. Here the test is required because capacity is lumpy and price will not exactly equal *LRMC* at the optimum. Of course, if the revenues from both the peak and off-peak services fall short of total costs for any level of capacity because long-run average costs are decreasing, then a broader all-or-none test is required comparing C_{opt} with zero production. Moreover, decreasing cost firms are not likely to operate at design capacity at any period, so that prices will equal measured short-run marginal costs in every period, in line with Panzar's "neoclassical" model.

THE WELFARE COSTS OF NONOPTIMAL PRICING AND INVESTMENT RULES—SOME EMPIRICAL EVIDENCE

Decreasing cost services in the United States are seldom priced in accordance with first-best peak-load theory. As indicated in Chapter 10, the usual policy is to charge a single price throughout the demand cycle sufficient to cover the full average costs of providing the service. These average cost prices, in addition to their other drawbacks, tend to encourage too much demand during the peak and too little demand during the off peak. There are a few exceptions to uniform prices. Variable time-of-day pricing is occasionally used by the public utilities and on urban transportation facilities, but the transportation examples are perverse. Variable pricing consists of discounts to commuters during the rush hour!

Investment strategies for these services are more diverse, but given that prices are usually nonoptimal, there is a strong presumption against the existence of optimal capacities for any of these services. Since optimal pricing is a prerequisite for the optimal investment rules, optimal capacities will be discovered only by chance.

Reliable econometric evidence on the welfare cost of ignoring peak-load pricing and investment rules is virtually non existent for the decreasing cost services. Recently, however, Professors Kraus, Pinfold, and Mohring have offered some "quasi-empirical" evidence on highway transportation which strongly suggests that peak-load tolls are far below their first-best optimum values.[11] This is hardly surprising, but their study also indicates that the welfare costs of actual user charges relative to optimal prices are probably rather small. Their analysis also suggests that highway capacity is far from optimal and that this does generate significant welfare losses.

Their analysis is similar in spirit to the Callen, Mathewson, Mohring study of public utility regulation referred to in Chapter 10. They posit specific utility and production functions within the context of a simple general equilibrium model and use these functions as a basis for developing welfare loss measures for various nonoptimal pricing and investment policies. This type of quasi-empirical analysis is useful for analyzing the sensitivity of welfare losses to a wide range of "reasonable" demand and cost parameters,[12] in order to place upper and lower bounds on expected welfare losses. If these bounds are fairly close together, then the study provides useful information on welfare costs in lieu of econometric evidence on actual demand and cost functions.

Their general equilibrium model is approximately as complex as the model used in this chapter. There are three goods, consisting of one-mile freeway trips per person in both the peak and off-peak periods during the day, and a Hicksian composite good representing the rest of the economy. For the demand side of the model they assume there are I identical consumers, each of which has an initial endowment of resources that can be transformed into any of the goods, and a *CES* utility function of the form $U = [\varepsilon e_i(X_i + \beta_i)^{\delta}]^{1/\delta}$, where δ, e_i, and β_i are parameters. They chose this particular form because it generates integrable demand functions. Since they also assume that the government can tax and transfer the resource endowment lump sum to satisfy the interpersonal equity conditions of an egalitarian social welfare function, their economy is equivalent to a one-consumer economy, and the aggregate demand functions will yield legitimate willingness-to-pay measures of welfare loss. The particular loss measure they employ is the Hicks Equivalent Variation in moving from the first-best optimal price vector to various nonoptimal alternatives.

---

[11] M. Kraus, H. Mohring, and T. Pinfold, "The Welfare Costs of Non-Optimal Pricing and Investment Policies for Freeway Transportation," *American Economic Review*, September 1976.

[12] In their model "reasonable" means essentially that the peak and off-peak price and income demand elasticities are roughly consistent with those presented in the highway literature, and that their general equilibrium solutions for peak and off-peak travel are roughly equivalent to the observed pattern of travel on freeways in the Minneapolis–St. Paul metropolitan area.

As with most quasi-empirical studies the utility functions are chosen primarily on the basis of analytical convenience. What makes their analysis compelling are the specific cost relationships they use for the supply side of the model (they posit cost functions rather than production functions). There are two distinct sources of costs, the long-run capacity costs associated with building and/or expanding the freeways and the short-run costs to the consumer of driving on the freeways. The bulk of the short-run costs are the opportunity costs of travel time spent on a one-mile trip. After an intensive search of the relevant highway literature, Kraus, et al. determined that reasonable long- and short-run cost functions were:

(11.68)
$$K = d + ek$$

and

(11.69)
$$SRAVC_j = 3.67 + V[1 + X_j/\alpha \cdot k]^{2.5}$$

where:

K = dollars spent on capacity.

k = capacity of a one-mile stretch of freeway measured in annual person-trips.

d, e = parameters whose values depend on the location of the road. Rural roads are considerably cheaper than roads near the central business district.

V = value of travel time.

$SRAVC_j$ = short-run variable costs, all internal to the consumer.

X_j/α = annual rate of one-mile trips, X_j, during period j, where j = peak, off-peak.

Two properties of these cost functions deserve attention. First, the parameter d is positive. Hence, average capacity costs are uniformly decreasing. Secondly, short-run variable costs, $(X_j \cdot SRAVC_j)$, increase at an increasing rate with X_j. Thus, marginal costs are higher at the peak than the off-peak as required for the peak-load problem.

Having specified these particular utility and cost functions, and the resource endowment, Kraus et al. then find the first-order conditions for a first-best welfare optimum and solve for the resulting optimal prices and capacity. As expected, the optimal prices equal short-run marginal costs, and optimal k occurs when the marginal (total) capacity costs just equal the excess of total revenues over short-run total costs. Since they posit decreasing average capital costs $(d > 0)$, the consumers also pay a lump-sum tax to cover the difference between average and marginal (unit) capital costs at the optimum.

The only unusual feature of their model is the definition of price. When the consumer uses the road he necessarily "pays" $SRAVC_j$, but none of this is received by the government to cover highway costs. Thus, to arrive at the correct price, the government must add a toll in each period equal to the difference between $SRAVC_j$ and $SRMC_j$. The toll revenues are then compared with marginal capacity costs to determine the optimal level of capacity.

Governments in the United States use one of two methods to finance nearly all highway construction. Some roads are toll roads, for which the tolls cover the capital costs. Kraus et al. call this the "pure deficit" toll. Other roads are freeways paid for out of gasoline and other excise taxes. These taxes essentially act as additional fixed charges to the consumer per mile trip, approximately 13 cents, whether the trip occurs at the peak or off-peak. Kraus et al. call this the "single" toll. In either case, the effective "price" to the consumer is his personal $SRAVC_j$ plus the respective toll. Notice that consumer "prices" are actually higher at the peak with either of these tolls, since $SRAVC_{peak} > SRAVC_{off-peak}$, but the differential between the peak and off-peak is not as great as it would be with $SRMC$ pricing. These two full prices, then, are the ones compared with the optimal prices.

Their analysis yields four main conclusions:

(1)   The "single" toll (of about .6¢ per person-mile) is just about right for peak use on an efficiently designed rural road, but only 7–15% of its optimum value on an urban road near a CBD, if time is valued at $2.50/hour. If time is valued at $4.00/hour, the proper urban peak-load toll would be equivalent to a tax of [$1–$2.20] per gallon of gasoline. Thus, in urban areas the peak load prices are way too low.

(2)   Despite the wide divergence between actual and optimum peak load prices, the welfare costs of the actual prices are very low in either their "pure-deficit" or "single toll" variants. The Hicks equilibrating variation is only [4%–2.3%] of total optimum trip expenditures for a wide range of demand parameters. Given that the model ignores both the additional administrative costs of instituting optimal prices, and the distortions caused by general taxes that would actually be used to cover the capital deficits, the authors conclude it not be worthwhile to change to a system of optimal tolls.

(3)   Their model yields optimum peak-load road use that is usually much less than 90% of capacity in the urban centers for most values of the demand and cost parameters. Given that actual road use appears to exceed 90% of capacity during urban rush hours, their model strongly suggests that actual capacity is too low. This may be of some consequence, because

(4)   Welfare losses are much more sensitive to non-optimal capacity than to non-optimal prices. If highway capacity is constrained to be only 50% of its optimum value, the welfare losses range from [15–30%] of trip expenditures at the optimum. Of course the model also ignores all external diseconomies of highway travel such as air pollution. Had these been included optimal capacity may well have been reduced considerably.

Sensitivity analyses of this kind can only be suggestive, but the Kraus-Mohring-Pinfold model is the most comprehensive empirical test of first-best peak-load pricing theory currently available. Whether these results are representative for nonhighway services is problematic, especially given their conclusion that highway capacity is far too low. Ordinarily, with prices set below the optimum during the peak, one would tend to expect overinvestment in capacity. Moreover, because travel time increases during the rush hour, the effective price to the consumer is higher at the peak than the off-peak. The pricing policies of other services, for which price is actually uniform throughout the demand cycle, may create larger percentage welfare losses. Nonetheless, their conclusion that nonoptimal pricing does not create significant welfare losses is striking.

REFERENCES

Dreze, J. "Some Post-War Contributions of French Economists to Theory and Public Policy." *American Economic Review,* June 1964 supplement).

Kraus, M.; Mohring, H.; and Pinfold, T. "The Welfare Costs of Nonoptimal Pricing and Investment Policies for Freeway Transportation." *American Economic Review,* September 1976.

Marino, A. "Peak-load Pricing in a Neoclassical Model with Bounds on Variable Input Utilization." *The Bell Journal of Economics,* Spring 1978.

Mohring, H. "The Peak-load Problem with Increasing Returns and Pricing Constraints." *American Economic Review,* September 1970.

Panzar, J. "A Neoclassical Approach to Peak-load Pricing." *The Bell Journal of Economics,* Autumn 1976.

Pressman, I. "A Mathematical Formulation of the Peak-load Pricing Problem." *The Bell Journal of Economics and Management Science,* Autumn 1970.

Williamson, O. "Peak-load Pricing and Optimal Capacity." *American Economic Review,* September 1966.

APPENDIX

SOCIAL SURPLUS MAXIMIZATION APPLIED TO THE PEAK-LOAD PROBLEM[1]

Although it is not a legitimate measure of social welfare except under highly restrictive assumptions, social surplus maximization has had a long and fruitful history in the theory of the public sector. Because of this, a text on public sector economics would be remiss if it did not demonstrate the technique at least once. This Appendix will apply it to the "traditional" peak-load problem.

Social surplus maximization is a partial equilibrium technique employing market demand and cost functions instead of the utility and production functions of standard first-best general equilibrium analysis. The basic idea is this. Suppose there is some good X whose value to society is to be optimized. Turning first to the supply of X, it is assumed that all producers of X are competitive and hire factors of production efficiently. Under these conditions there exists

[1] This Appendix relies heavily on the geometric analysis in Williamson and Dreze. We would also like to thank John Riley of UCLA for his comments and suggestions. O. Williamson, "Peak-Load Pricing and Optimal Capacity," *American Economic Review,* September 1966; and J. Dreze, "Some Post-War Contributions of French Economists to Theory and Public Policy," *American Economic Review,* June 1964 (supplement).

a least total cost curve for X, $C = C(X)$, which can be used in place of the production function to summarize all relevant production parameters. This is perfectly legitimate. The problem with social surplus maximization arises on the demand side of the model.

Instead of working with individuals' utility functions, social surplus maximization simply posits the aggregate market demand curve for X, $P_X = P(X)$, written in the Marshallian manner with price as the dependent variable. The net social benefits for any given value of X are then represented as:

$$(11A.1) \qquad\qquad SB = \int_0^X P(X)dX_i - C(X)$$

the entire area under the aggregate demand curve to X less the total costs of producing X. Notice that the area under the demand curve equals the sum of aggregate Marshallian consumer's surplus for X and the actual revenues paid by the consumer to the firm. It is meant to represent the total dollar benefits from consuming any quantity X. Subtracting off the costs of producing X gives the net social benefits, or "social surplus."

SB is clearly inappropriate as a measure of social benefits. We know that Marshallian consumer's surplus is not a legitimate willingness-to-pay measure of individual benefits unless there are zero income effects (refer to the discussion of these measures in Chapter 4). Even if it were appropriate, aggregating individual benefits and working with the aggregate demand curve implicitly assumes that the interpersonal equity conditions hold.[2] Hence, the technique can be thought of as a subset of first-best theory, if indeed it can be classified as part of any legitimate set of economic theory. The benefits measure is further restrictive in that aggregate demand for X is specified solely as a function of its own price.[3] Finally, social surplus is a partial equilibrium concept. In effect, it exploits the well-known result of first-best general equilibrium models that problems in one market do not alter the pareto-optimal decision rules in other markets.

With all these theoretical limitations, why is the measure so popular? There are basically two reasons. First, even though SB is generally meaningless as a measure of social welfare it usually yields the proper first-best policy rules. First-best pareto optimal require marginal cost pricing. But this is precisely the decision rule given by social surplus. Maximizing SB with respect to X involves finding the X for which $\partial SB/\partial X = 0$. $\partial C(X)/\partial X$ obviously equals the marginal cost of producing X. Less obviously,

$$(11A.2) \qquad\qquad \frac{\partial \int_0^X P(X)dX_i}{\partial X} = P(X)$$

A mathematical proof of (11A.2) requires rather sophisticated techniques and will not be reproduced here, but the intuition behind the result is clear. (11A.2)

---

[2] Alternatively, it requires severe restrictions on the underlying utility functions. Once again, refer to Chapter 4 for a discussion of the sufficient conditions for one-consumer equivalence.

[3] This assumption can be relaxed, but it greatly complicates the analysis.

FIGURE 11A–1

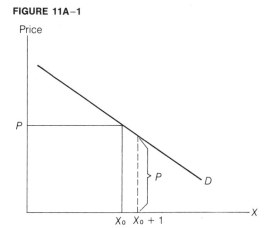

says that marginal change in X, at any X, will change the area under the demand curve by $P_X(X)$, in the limit. Referring to Figure 11A–1 the increased area from X_0 to $X_0 + 1$ is clearly best approximated in the limit by a rectangle of dimensions $1 \times P$. Hence, $\partial SB/\partial X = P_X - MC_X = 0$, the usual first-best result. Carrying the intuition further, even though the area under the demand curve is meaningless as a measure of *total* benefits, the value of an *additional* unit of X is properly measured by P_X. Along the demand curve $P_X = MRS^h_{X,\text{numeraire}}$, all consumers $h = 1, \ldots, H$, so that P_X is an appropriate marginal willingness-to-pay measure of benefits.

Given that social surplus maximization can usually be counted on to generate the correct pareto-optimal pricing rules in a first-best policy environment, its popularity is secured by the fact that it is many times simpler than even an extremely condensed version of the full general equilibrium model of Chapter 2. For instance, it took a fair amount of manipulation to derive the price and investment rules for the peak-load problem in Chapter 11, even though the general equilibrium model was stripped to its bare essentials. The social surplus model can achieve the same results in just a few steps, and with slightly more generality in certain respects.

THE SOCIAL SURPLUS MODEL OF
THE PEAK-LOAD PROBLEM

To capture the essence of the peak-load problem using the social surplus approach assume:

1. N demand subperiods of equal length.
2. N aggregate demand curves

$$p^i = p^i(X^i) \qquad i = 1, \ldots, N$$

where p^i, X^i = price and output in period i, respectively.

3. Total short-run operating costs in each period are a function of output in that period and of overall capacity. Define:

$$C^i = C^i(X^i, Y) \qquad i = 1, \ldots, N$$

where C^i = total short-run operating costs in period i, and Y = total capacity.

4. Capacity costs are a function of total capacity

$$C = C^0(Y)$$

5. N capacity constraints.

$$X^i \leq Y; Y - X^i \geq 0 \qquad i = 1, \ldots, N$$

The problem is to maximize social surplus with respect to the X^i and Y, subject to the capacity constraints. Total benefits are defined as the sum of areas under the individual period Marshallian demand curves $P^i(X^i)$, taken to the quantity axis. Total costs include operating costs in each period plus the capacity costs. Formally:

$$\max_{(X^i, Y)} SB = \sum_{i=1}^{N} \int_0^{X^i} P^i(X^i) dX^i - \sum_{i=1}^{N} C^i(X^i, Y) - C^0(Y)$$

$$\text{s.t.} \qquad (Y - X^i) \geq 0 \qquad i = 1, \ldots, N$$

Defining multipliers for each of the capacity constraints, the Lagrangian is:

$$\max_{(X^i, Y)} L = \sum_{i=1}^{N} \int_0^{X^i} P^i(X^i) dX^i - \sum_{i=1}^{N} C^i(X^i, Y) - C^0(Y)$$

$$+ \sum_{i=1}^{N} \lambda^i(Y - X^i)$$

The $(N + 1)$ first-order conditions with respect to X^i and Y are:

(11A.3) $\qquad X^i: \quad P^i(X^i) - \dfrac{\partial C^i}{\partial X^i} - \lambda^i = 0 \qquad i = 1, \ldots, N$

(11A.4) $\qquad Y: \quad - \sum_{i=1}^{N} \dfrac{\partial C^i}{\partial Y} - \dfrac{\partial C^0}{\partial Y} + \sum_{i=1}^{N} \lambda^i = 0$

The four main results for the peak-load problem follow directly from these conditions.

The off-peak price:

1. If the capacity constraint is not binding in some period, say the jth, then $X^j < Y$ and $\lambda^j = 0$. But if $\lambda^j = 0$, it follows from (11A.3) that

(11A.5) $\qquad\qquad P^j(X^j) = \dfrac{\partial C^j}{\partial X^j} = SRMC_j$

This is the usual off-peak pricing rule, corresponding to equation (11.27b).

The peak price:

2. If the capacity constraint is binding period j, then $\lambda^j > 0$, and from (11A.3),

(11A.6)
$$P^j(X^j) = \frac{\partial C^j}{\partial X^j} + \lambda^j$$

P^j is exactly as pictured in Figure 11A–2, the price at which peak demand and short-run marginal cost intersect. As a Lagrangian multiplier, λ^j measures the gains to social surplus in the jth market resulting from a unit relaxation of the capacity constraint. But if capacity is increased by 1 unit, so too is X_j. Peak quantity demanded will increase by 1 unit, leading to a gain of exactly $P_j - \gamma$. P_j is the value of a unit increase in total benefits from which the short-run marginal costs γ must be subtracted to arrive at the gain in net social benefits. The increased capacity costs are spread over all N markets.[4] Hence, they are insignificant so far as the jth market is concerned. (11A.6) is therefore equivalent to (11.47).

FIGURE 11A–2

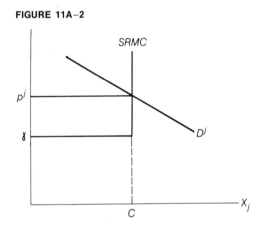

The investment rules for optimal capacity:

3. To arrive at the proper investment decision rule sum the N first-order conditions (11A–3) to obtain

(11A.7)
$$\sum_{i=1}^{N} P^i(X^i) - \sum_{i=1}^{N} \frac{\partial C^i}{\partial X^i} = \sum_i \lambda^i$$

But, from (11A–4),

(11A.8)
$$\sum_{i=1}^{N} \frac{\partial C^i}{\partial Y} + \frac{\partial C^0}{\partial Y} = \sum_{i=1}^{N} \lambda^i$$

---

[4] With reference to the intuitive analysis in Chapter 11, $\partial C^0/\partial Y = N \cdot \beta$.

Therefore:

(11A.9)
$$\sum_{i=1}^{N}\left[P^i(X^i) - \frac{\partial C^i}{\partial X^i}\right] = \sum_{i=1}^{N}\frac{\partial C^i}{\partial Y} + \frac{\partial C^0}{\partial Y}$$

(11A.9) says expand capacity until the combined quasi rents at the peaks are just equal to marginal capacity costs. Off-peak periods become relevant only in that marginal costs vary with capacity (presumably they are lowered). But price in those periods still does not contribute to capacity costs, since

$$P^j(X^j) > \frac{\partial C^j}{\partial X^j}$$

only when the capacity constraint is binding. Hence, (11A–9) conveys the same information as equation (11.67).

Investment rules, no capacity constraints:

4. If there are no capacity constraints, then $\lambda^i = 0$, $i = 1, \ldots, N$, and the first-order condition (11A.4) becomes:

(11A.10)
$$-\sum \frac{\partial C^i}{\partial Y} = \frac{\partial C^0}{\partial Y}$$

This is the usual long-run rule for optimal plant size: expand capacity until the extra capacity costs just equal the combined savings in operating costs from expanding capacity. It is equivalent to equation (11.43).

The simplicity of social surplus maximization is striking when compared with the general equilibrium approach to the peak-load problem in Chapter 11. But it must be remembered that it takes careful general equilibrium modeling to establish the validity of this technique for any given problem. Social surplus maximization is not foolproof. For example, it will not yield valid all-or-none tests for decreasing cost services, or lumpy additions to capacity, because these decision rules are not expressed in terms of marginals. They require valid willingness-to-pay measures for discrete price changes.

REFERENCES

Dreze, J.   "Some Post-War Contributions of French Economists to Theory and Public Policy." *American Economic Review*, June 1964 (supplement).

Williamson, O.   "Peak-Load Pricing and Optimal Capacity." *American Economic Review*, September 1966.

12

The first-best theory of taxation

REVIEW OF THE THEORY

Taxes are an integral part of first-best public policy, but having analyzed the first-best theory of public expenditures, there is no need to develop a separate first-best theory of taxation. This reason is that public expenditure theory, in addition to answering the two fundamental questions of normative public sector theory—what are the legitimate areas of government sector intervention and what decision rules should the government follow in each area—simultaneously provides a complete normative theory of taxation, a theory delineating the welfare enhancing possibilities of taxation. Public expenditure decision rules often require specific kinds of taxes. Whenever this occurs, these taxes promote society's equity and efficiency norms, that is, they support society's quest for a social welfare maximum, the first-best bliss point. Beyond that, however, there is no role for tax policy in a first-best policy environment, at least not at a purely theoretical level.

There are, for example, no interesting efficiency questions independent of public expenditure theory. Either the expenditure theory describes some particular tax necessary to achieve a pareto-optimal allocation of resources, or it does not. If not, then there is no further role for taxation in promoting economic efficiency. To give some examples, we found that exclusive goods which generate either consumption or production externalities can be allocated correctly with a set of taxes (subsidies) equal to the marginal damage (benefits) resulting from the externality. In this case first-best expenditure and tax theory are synonymous. Similarly, decreasing cost services require marginal cost pricing for pareto optimality. Whether one refers to those prices as "prices," "fees," "tolls," or "taxes" hardly matters. First-best charges for these services can always be thought of as taxes set according to the competitive interpretation of the benefits-received principle of taxation, the only interpretation consistent with economic efficiency. One can, of course, analyze the efficiency costs of distorting taxation, but this is inherently a second-best exercise.

At times public expenditure theory requires certain government expenditures without specifying exactly how to collect the revenues to finance these expenditures. The leading examples are Samuelsonian nonexclusive public goods and the deficits of decreasing cost services when prices (taxes) are set equal to marginal costs. The only efficiency criterion is that the taxes be lump sum to avoid creating distortions elsewhere in the economy. But any pattern of lump-sum taxation will preserve allocative efficiency in these areas.

The problem of how to collect lump-sum taxes has also been "solved," of course. The answer is to apply society's equity norms as represented by the interpersonal utility rankings implicit in an individualistic social welfare function. Specifically, taxes (transfers) for these purposes should be consistent with the interpersonal equity conditions of social welfare maximization,

$$\frac{\partial W}{\partial U^h} \frac{\partial U^h}{\partial I^h} = \qquad \text{all } h = 1, \ldots, H$$

where I^h can loosely be thought of as lump-sum income.[1] Whether the interpersonal equity conditions are viewed as part of first-best expenditure theory or first-best tax theory depends upon one's personal taste. In either case, they are the sole distributional criterion for taxation (and transfer) in a first-best policy environment representing, simultaneously, a complete theory of optimal income distribution and thus of optimal income redistribution through lump-sum taxation and transfer.

Therefore, having considered the tax and transfer implications of both the pareto-optimal and interpersonal equity conditions of first-best social welfare maximization, there is nothing more to add concerning tax policy on a purely theoretical level.

PARETO-OPTIMAL REDISTRIBUTION

In 1969 Hochman and Rodgers attempted to extend the first-best theory of taxation by suggesting that general lump-sum taxes and transfers ought to be determined by a set of pareto-optimal conditions as well as the standard interpersonal conditions.[2] They argued that it is entirely reasonable to suppose individuals have preferences concerning the proper distribution of income independently from society's social welfare rankings collectively determined through the political process. It is clear, for instance, that people's behavior is sometimes motivated either by altruism or envy. But this suggests that individual utility is a function of the distribution of income as well as the usual goods and factors, which further implies that the optimal distribution will be determined in part by a set of pareto-optimal conditions. In effect, the distribution of income becomes another consumer externality.

The easiest way to model the notion of pareto-optimal redistributions is to imagine a simple exchange economy in which each individual, h, has an

---

[1] More precisely it is a good or factor (presumably the numeraire) singled out for taxation and transfer.

[2] H. Hochman and J. Rodgers, "Pareto-Optimal Redistributions," *American Economic Review*, September 1969. Also, R. Goldfarb, "Pareto Optimal Redistribution: Comment," *American Economic Review*, December 1970.

endowment of two goods and/or factors, Y_h and Z_h. The total supply of Y and Z is assumed fixed, equal to $\sum_{h=1}^{H} Y_h$ and $\sum_{h=1}^{H} Z_h$, respectively.[3]

Suppose each person's utility is a function of his consumption of Y and Z, and the distribution of Y among all members in society. That is:

$$U^h = U^h(Y_h, Z_h, X)$$

where:

$X = X(\vec{Y}_h)$ represents the distribution of Y among all H individuals.

Society's problem is to allocate Y_h and Z_h to maximize social welfare, subject to the total fixed endowment of Y and Z. Formally,

$$\max_{(Y_h, Z_h)} \ W[U^h(Y_h, Z_h, X(Y_1, \ldots, Y_H))]$$

$$\text{s.t.} \quad \sum_{h=1}^{H} Y_h = \bar{Y}$$

$$\sum_{h=1}^{H} Z_h = \bar{Z}$$

with the corresponding Lagrangian:

$$\max_{(Y_h, Z_h)} \ L = W[U^h(Y_h, Z_h, X(Y_1, \ldots, Y_H))] + \theta \left(\bar{Y} - \sum_{h=1}^{H} Y_h \right)$$

$$+ \delta \left(\bar{Z} - \sum_{h=1}^{H} Z_h \right)$$

The first-order conditions with respect to the Y_i and Z_i are:

$$(12.1) \qquad Y_i: \quad \frac{\partial W}{\partial U^i} \frac{\partial U^i}{\partial Y_i} + \sum_{h=1}^{H} \frac{\partial W}{\partial U^h} \frac{\partial U^h}{\partial X} \frac{\partial X}{\partial Y_i} - \theta = 0 \qquad i = 1, \ldots, H$$

$$(12.2) \qquad Z_i: \quad \frac{\partial W}{\partial U^i} \frac{\partial U^i}{\partial Z_i} - \delta = 0 \qquad i = 1, \ldots, H$$

To derive the pareto-optimal conditions, consider goods (factors) Z and Y consumed (supplied) by person i. Dividing (12.1) by (12.2) yields

$$(12.3) \qquad \frac{\dfrac{\partial W}{\partial U^i} \dfrac{\partial U^i}{\partial Y_i} + \sum_{h=1}^{H} \dfrac{\partial W}{\partial U^h} \dfrac{\partial U^h}{\partial X} \dfrac{\partial X}{\partial Y_i}}{\dfrac{\partial W}{\partial U^i} \dfrac{\partial U^i}{\partial Z_i}} = \frac{\theta}{\delta} \qquad i = 1, \ldots, H$$

To remove the social welfare terms, assume the government has redistributed the Z_i lump sum to satisfy the interpersonal equity conditions (12.2). Making the appropriate term-by-term substitutions from (12.2) into (12.3) and canceling

---

[3] Since we are concerned with distributional rules, there is no need to model production. Production could be included but it would not affect the distributional decision rules.

the social welfare terms, exactly as we did with consumer externalities in Chapter 6 yields:

$$(12.4) \qquad \left(\frac{\frac{\partial U^i}{\partial Y_i}}{\frac{\partial U^i}{\partial Z_i}}\right) + \sum_{h=1}^{H} \left(\frac{\frac{\partial U^h}{\partial X}\frac{\partial X}{\partial Y_i}}{\frac{\partial U^h}{\partial Z_h}}\right) = \frac{\theta}{\delta} \qquad i = 1, \ldots, H$$

The left-hand side of (12.4) has the standard form for a consumer externality. In particular, (12.4) says that the government should equate each person's personal-use marginal rate of substitution between Y and Z, plus the sum of everyone's marginal rate of substitution between Z and the distributional parameter X. These rules are virtually identical to the pareto-optimal rules for allocating exclusive pure public goods, and can be achieved either by direct government redistributions of the Y_i, or, assuming competitive behavior, by a set of H personalized taxes on good (factor) Y,

$$(12.5) \qquad t_i = \sum_{h=1}^{H} \left(\frac{\frac{\partial U^h}{\partial X}\frac{\partial X}{\partial Y_i}}{\frac{\partial U^h}{\partial Z_h}}\right)$$

As always with pure public goods, the government's task is formidable, but it can be eased somewhat if one assumes, as the literature usually does, that only a subset of people, the "rich," are concerned with the distribution of income because only they can affect it. Formally,

$$(12.6) \qquad \frac{\partial U^r}{\partial X} \neq 0 \qquad r = \text{subset of the rich.}$$

$$\frac{\partial U^p}{\partial X} = 0 \qquad p = \text{subset of the poor.}$$

To be concrete, suppose there is only a single rich person (1) and a single poor person (2) and that conditions (12.6) hold. The pareto-optimal conditions (12.4) become:

$$(12.7a) \qquad \left(\frac{\frac{\partial U^1}{\partial Y_1}}{\frac{\partial U^1}{\partial Z_1}}\right) + \left(\frac{\frac{\partial U^1}{\partial X}\frac{\partial X}{\partial Y_1}}{\frac{\partial U^1}{\partial Z_1}}\right) = \frac{\theta}{\delta}$$

$$(12.7b) \qquad \left(\frac{\frac{\partial U^2}{\partial Y_2}}{\frac{\partial U^2}{\partial Z_2}}\right) + \left(\frac{\frac{\partial U^1}{\partial X}\frac{\partial X}{\partial Y_2}}{\frac{\partial U^1}{\partial Z_1}}\right) = \frac{\theta}{\delta}$$

Combining (12.7a) and (12.7b),

$$
(12.8) \qquad \left(\frac{\frac{\partial U^1}{\partial Y_1}}{\frac{\partial U^1}{\partial Z_1}}\right) + \left[\left(\frac{\frac{\partial U^1}{\partial X}\frac{\partial X}{\partial Y_1}}{\frac{\partial U^1}{\partial Z_1}}\right)\left(\frac{\frac{\partial U^1}{\partial X}\frac{\partial X}{\partial Y_2}}{\frac{\partial U^1}{\partial Z_1}}\right)\right] = \left(\frac{\frac{\partial U^2}{\partial Y_2}}{\frac{\partial U^2}{\partial Z_2}}\right)
$$

Condition (12.8) can be satisfied by a single redistribution of Y_1 ($= -Y_2$) from person 1 to person 2, or a single tax on person 1, until person 2's own MRS_{Y_2,Z_2} just equals the total MRS_{Y_1,Z_1} for person 1, consisting of person 1's own personal-use MRS_{Y_1,Z_1} and his view of the combined marginal effects of his loss of Y_1 through the distribution parameter. In a real-world application, the government would undoubtedly consider only few representative groups and assume that preferences within each group concerning the distribution of income were identical.

It is difficult to know how to react to this extension of first-best tax theory. The notion that people judge the distribution of income as individuals independently from society's social rankings is certainly appealing. Moreover to the extent they do, it is true that the distribution becomes a consumer externality, and pareto-optimal redistributions are necessary conditions for social welfare maximization. Of course, it is extremely unlikely any government will ever be able to satisfy these conditions, although the same could be said of any exclusive activity generating fairly pervasive external effects. The major drawback to pareto-optimal redistributions, however, is that they do not preclude an additional set of redistributions, the usual ones necessary to satisfy the interpersonal equity conditions. There are an infinity of pareto-optimal redistributions, one for each original distribution of income. Pareto-optimal redistributions help bring society to its utility-possibilities frontier, but society still has to find the best point on this frontier by applying the interpersonal equity conditions. In effect, society has to determine whose feelings concerning the distribution of income are to count the most. Moreover, the distribution required for interpersonal equity could easily swamp those required for pareto optimality. This would tend to happen whenever social marginal utilities at some initial distribution were widely divergent. For example, if society gives very low social weights to the rich and very high weights to the poor at the initial distribution of income, the government will redistribute large amounts of income from the rich to the poor to satisfy the interpersonal equity conditions. Once this occurs, the additional adjustments required by the pareto-optimal formula are likely to be minuscule by comparison.

The reasoning behind pareto-optimal redistributions is sound, but we believe first-best public sector theory is best served by letting the interpersonal equity conditions stand as the single distributional rule. Positing a social welfare function implies that its rankings were derived through accepted political channels, at least for democratic societies. Any one individual may disagree with the terms of this particular kind of social contract but, as a good citizen, he must be willing to abide by it, and not expect the government to act on his own preferences with respect to the distribution. Pareto-optimal redistributions are most compelling when no social welfare rankings have been agreed to, but then first-best theory remains incomplete. It accepts an infinity of allocations and distributions as social equals, all those consistent with pareto optimality. In our view, a normative theory concerned with distributional equity should not be this accommodating. It must describe optimal policies rules as if society has agreed upon a set of equity norms, whether or not this is so.

PARETO-OPTIMAL REDISTRIBUTIONS—EMPIRICAL EVIDENCE

Whether the United States actually tries to achieve a pareto-optimal redistribution is certainly debatable, but two recent empirical studies have lent some credence to the theory. Orr and Zimmerman independently tested models attempting to explain payments under Aid for Dependent Children, the largest single welfare program in the United States.[4] Both their models are based on the concept of pareto-optimal redistributions, and the results in each case are quite favorable to the theory.

In developing their empirical models, both authors assume that (a) there are two sets of people, one rich and one poor; (b) the rich effectively control the political process so that they alone decide how much income will be redistributed to the poor; (c) dollars of transfer payments are distributed equally among all the poor, with the costs shared equally by all the rich; and finally, (d) each rich person has a utility function of the form:

(12.9) $$U^i = U^i(Y_i; \vec{Y}_p) \qquad i \in R, \text{ the rich}$$

where:

$\vec{Y}_p =$ the vector of incomes of all the poor people, $p = 1, \ldots, P$.
$Y_i =$ the income of rich person i.

Assumptions (b) and (d) capture the fundamental tenet of pareto-optimal redistribution theory, that rich people will voluntarily offer some of their income to the poor. However, assumption (c) may preclude finding an actual first-best pareto-optimal redistribution since that will generally require unequal sharing of the costs and benefits.

In order to derive a testable model the authors then determine the optimal amount of transfer under these assumptions. Let B represent a dollar of income transferred to each poor person. From the point of view of a rich person, the

---

[4] L. Orr, "Income Transfers as a Public Good: An Application to AFDC," *American Economic Review*, June 1976; and D. Zimmerman, "On the Relationship between Public Good Theory and Expenditure Determinant Studies," *National Tax Journal*, June 1975.

optimal level of B occurs when $\partial U^i / \partial B = 0$, or

(12.10) $$\frac{\partial U^i}{\partial B} = \frac{\partial U^i}{\partial Y_i} \frac{\partial Y_i}{\partial T_i} \frac{\partial T_i}{\partial B} + \sum_{p=1}^{P} \frac{\partial U^i}{\partial Y_p} \frac{\partial Y_p}{\partial B} = 0 \qquad i \in R$$

where:

$$\frac{\partial Y_p}{\partial B} \equiv 1$$

$$\frac{\partial Y_i}{\partial T_i} \equiv -1$$

With equal sharing of the tax burden:

(12.11) $$\frac{\partial T_i}{\partial B} = \frac{P}{R} \qquad \begin{array}{l} P = \text{number of poor.} \\ R = \text{number of rich.} \end{array}$$

Thus, (12.10) becomes:

(12.12) $$-\frac{\partial U^i}{\partial Y_i}\left(\frac{P}{R}\right) = \sum_{p=1}^{P} \frac{\partial U^i}{\partial Y_p} \qquad i \in R$$

The right-hand side of (12.12) is the marginal benefit to (rich) taxpayer i of transferring a dollar to each poor person. The left-hand side is person i's marginal costs, the loss in utility per dollar of income transferred multiplied by his share of the costs. Notice that each rich person should prefer a government transfer program in which all rich people are required to share the costs to private charity. Acting on his own, the marginal costs to person i of transferring \$1 to all poor people are $-\partial U^i / \partial Y_i \cdot P$. Moreover, income redistribution is similar to the Samuelsonian-type nonexclusive public good. If any one rich person makes a transfer, all rich people benefit. Hence, without a government program the free-rider problem is likely to occur, with too little income redistributed, even though each rich person is willing to redistribute.

Equation (12.12) implies a number of testable hypotheses for any transfer program such as $AFDC$. Transfer payments per person will be greater:

1. The higher the income of the "rich" taxpayers. Higher Y_i implies lower $\partial U^i / \partial Y_i$ which lowers the marginal cost of transfers.
2. The lower is P/R. The ratio of poor to rich acts as a price to the rich for transferring income. The lower the ratio the lower the price.
3. The larger is P. Increasing the absolute number of poor presumably increases the marginal benefits of transferring income more than it increases the marginal costs. One more poor person increases marginal benefits by $\partial U^h / \partial Y_{P+1}$. Marginal costs increase by

(12.13) $$\frac{\partial\left(\dfrac{P}{R}\right)}{\partial P} = \frac{\partial\left(\dfrac{P}{T-P}\right)}{\partial P} = \frac{(T-P)+P}{(T-P)^2} = \frac{T}{(T-P)^2}$$

where:

$$T = P + R = \text{total population}.$$

assuming total population constant. If $P \ll T$, the increase in marginal costs will be small.

4. The more altruistic the rich are, that is, the higher $\partial U^i / \partial Y_p$, $p = 1, \ldots, P$.
5. The higher the federal share of state AFDC payments on the margin. AFDC is a combined state-federal program in which each state determines the amount of aid and the federal government reimburses the state for part of the payments, the actual percentage depending on the state's income and the amount of aid given per recipient. This feature requires a simple modification of equation (12.12). Suffice it to say that an increase in the federal share lowers the marginal costs of transfers to the poor within any given state.

Using a sample of annual observations from all 50 states and the District of Columbia from 1963 to 1972, and an appropriate set of explanatory variables, Orr was able to generate empirical support for all five hypotheses. Zimmerman's study was somewhat less ambitious. He had data for 1971 only and used a reduced set of explanatory variables, but his results were consistent with both the first and second hypotheses. Moreover, the elasticities he reported were remarkably close to Orr's. His income elasticity was .61; Orr's, .65 (in the first half of Orr's sample period). Zimmerman's "price" elasticity (the ratio of rich to poor) was .24, Orr reported price elasticities of $-.12$ and $-.23$. The former applied to the ratio of poor to rich, the latter to the federal matching percentage.[5]

While the Orr-Zimmerman studies support the view that some narrowing of income differentials in the United States confers external economies on the rich, they obviously do not prove that AFDC payments are motivated by pareto-efficiency considerations. Each of Orr's five hypotheses is equally compatible with the interpersonal equity view of income redistribution given a suitable choice of the social welfare weights. But the fact that the authors' empirical estimates are consistent with all aspects of the pareto-redistribution theory is noteworthy just the same, all the more so since previous researchers who used the federal matching discounts as price variables to explain AFDC payments, without benefit of the pareto theory, were generally unable to obtain significant, negative price elasticities.[6] Thus, even if one believes, as we do, that the notion of pareto-optimal redistributions adds little of substance to first-best public sector theory, its power in explaining the large AFDC transfer program in the United States cannot be denied.

---

[5] Zimmerman used the ratio of rich to poor for his explanatory variable whereas Orr used the ratio of poor to rich. Both results have the expected sign. In Orr's formulation, the federal matching share and the ratio of poor to rich should have the same elasticity. That they were fairly close is encouraging.

[6] Tresch, for instance, often found extremely low negative and even *positive* price elasticities in his study of public assistance payments. R. Tresch, "State Governments and the Welfare System: An Econometric Analysis," *Southern Economic Journal*, July 1975.

REFERENCES

Goldfarb, R. "Pareto Optimal Redistribution: Comment." *American Economic Review,* December 1970.

Hochman, H., and Rodgers, J. "Pareto-Optimal Redistributions." *American Economic Review*, September 1969.

Orr, L. "Income Transfers as a Public Good: An Application to AFDC." *American Economic Review*, June 1976.

Tresch, R. "State Governments and the Welfare System: An Econometric Analysis." *Southern Economic Journal*, July 1975.

Zimmerman, D. "On the Relationship between Public Good Theory and Expenditure Determinant Studies." *National Tax Journal*, June 1975.

13

First-best principles of taxation—
Toward application

Even though the first-best theory of taxation describes taxes for financing every conceivable type of public expenditure, policymakers will often find it difficult, if not impossible, to apply first-best principles when designing taxes. Only occasionally is the translation from theory to practice relatively straightforward. We argued in Chapter 6 that the government should be able to approximate the first-best tax for aggregate externalities reasonably well. Similarly, it ought to be possible to set taxes (prices) for decreasing cost services roughly equal to short-run marginal costs. Unfortunately, however, it is all too easy to describe other situations for which the proper set of taxes is unlikely to obtain even to a rough order of approximation. For example, the pareto-optimal conditions for individualized externalities require a hopelessly complex set of taxes, and the government may have great difficulty finding acceptable taxes to finance nonexclusive goods.

The preceding examples all relate to the pareto-optimal conditions of first-best social welfare maximization. As difficult as they may be to apply, the problems they create for tax design pale in comparison with the first-best interpersonal equity conditions. It is one thing to posit a social welfare function as an analytical representation of society's interpersonal equity valuations, but tax designers would need to know the exact form of this function. Yet no one knows what the social welfare rankings are, nor what they should be. Given our fundamental ignorance here, guidelines of the form

$$(13.1) \qquad \frac{\partial W}{\partial U^h} \frac{\partial U^h}{\partial X_{hi}} = \frac{\partial W}{\partial U^j} \frac{\partial U^j}{\partial X_{ji}} \qquad \begin{array}{l} \text{all } h, j = 1, \ldots, H \\ \text{all } i = 1, \ldots, N \end{array}$$

are hardly guidelines at all for the policymakers. At best they can only be broadly suggestive.

As it turns out, the standard theoretical principles underlying tax design are not derived from a strict interpretation of first-best tax theory. They were developed long before first-best principles were clarified by the work of Samuelson and others over the past 25 years, and given the problems associated with applying first-best principles, they have not been supplanted by the recent theoretical developments. There are, and always have been, two accepted principles of tax design: (1) taxes may be collected on the basis of *benefits received* from the public expenditures they finance, or (2) taxes may be collected on the basis of each individual's *ability to pay*. One can think of these as second-level theoretical principles created specifically as guidelines for practical tax design. They are intended to be only roughly consistent with first-best (and second-best) neoclassical public sector theory

The *benefits-received principle* is meant to apply to all exhaustive or resource-using expenditures, those undertaken because of breakdowns in the technical (and market) assumptions underlying a well-functioning market system. As such it has two purposes, to assist in the restoration of efficiency and to satisfy society's notion of equitable taxation.[1] We argued in Chapters 6 and 10 that a competitive interpretation of the benefits-received doctrine is consistent with both goals and corresponds exactly with the pareto-optimal conditions of first-best theory. But it has never been clear that the benefits-received doctrine was ever intended to correspond perfectly with first-best theoretical principles. Chapter 6 discussed how a strict competitive interpretation of the benefits-received principle applied to a Samuelson nonexclusive good such as defense might require side payments that many people would have difficulty accepting as equitable, even though they basically support the benefits-received principle. And Chapter 10 considered the enormous appeal of average cost pricing for decreasing cost services, a noncompetitive, nonoptimal "tax" mechanism that is nonetheless broadly consistent with the notion of payments according to benefits received. Quite clearly, the competitive, first-best interpretation of the benefits-received principle has not predominated in designing taxes or prices for these services.

These points have been discussed in detail in the preceding chapters. We would only add here that the benefits-received principle would surely take precedence over the ability-to-pay principle when either could be applied. A society believing in consumer sovereignty and competitive markets would naturally prefer that all government expenditures be financed on a benefits-received basis. But this is clearly impossible so long as one of society's goals is distributive equity. Transfer payments obviously cannot be financed by the benefits-received principle, even if the transfers result from a pareto-optimal redistribution. The principal beneficiaries of pareto-optimal redistributions are presumably the transfer recipients, not the altruistic taxpayers. Hence, one additional notion of tax equity is required to complete even a second-level normative theory of tax design. In first-best theory, the interpersonal equity conditions provide the missing link; in tax design theory the ability-to-pay principle served as the additional norm, applicable to the financing of all transfer payments. It also serves as a default option when the benefits-received principle is difficult to apply, such as in the financing of nonexclusive goods.

Chapter 13 will focus on the ability-to-pay principle, indicating how one proceeds from the principle to actual tax policy, and analyzing the U.S. federal

---

[1] Recall, however, that it has no particular standing as an equity principle in the formal neoclassical model.

personal income tax as an application. The relationship between ability to pay as conventionally interpreted and the interpersonal equity conditions of first-best theory will also be considered.

ABILITY TO PAY: THEORETICAL CONSIDERATIONS

The ability-to-pay principle has been in existence since the very beginning of modern public sector economics, having first been proposed by Adam Smith.[2] Smith argued that all general taxes not subject to the benefits-received criterion ought to be collected according to the taxpayers' abilities to pay. John Stuart Mill also argued for taxation based on equity notions rather than benefits received. He believed everyone should be asked to sacrifice equally to the commonwealth. They should not expect a *quid-pro-quo* from the government, in direct contrast to taxes paid according to benefits received.[3]

Taxation according to ability to pay has since gained virtual unanimous acceptance as an equity norm for tax design, but its application requires specifying exactly how people should be asked to sacrifice.[4] To this end two subprinciples have evolved which have also gained widespread acceptance, *horizontal equity* and *vertical equity*. *Horizontal equity* says that equals should be treated equally. Two people judged to have equal ability to sacrifice should bear the same tax burden. *Vertical equity* permits unequal treatment of unequals; that is, two people with unequal abilities to sacrifice can properly expect to suffer unequal tax burdens. One could hardly quibble with either subprinciple, but even they remain deficient as guidelines for tax design. Each begs an important and difficult question. For horizontal equity, the key question is the definition of equality. In applying the vertical equity criterion, society must decide just how unequally unequals can be treated. As might be expected, consensus begins to fall away in answering these two questions, although a conventional "neoclassical" wisdom did evolve early on in the professional literature, one that has only recently been seriously challenged by neoclassical economists. Before presenting the conventional resolution to these issues, however, two theoretical points should be stressed.

The first point is that the ability-to-pay principle of equitable taxation, along with its subprinciples of horizontal and vertical equity, can be interpreted in such a way as to be wholly consistent with the interpersonal equity conditions of first-best social welfare maximization. The interpersonal equity conditions will always satisfy horizontal equity so long as "equals" are defined as any two people with identical preferences, abilities, opportunity sets, and marginal social utilities, $\partial W/\partial U^h$. Two taxpayers equal in these four dimensions would obviously pay the same tax in the process of satisfying the interpersonal equity

---

[2] Adam Smith, *The Wealth of Nations*, ed. E. Cannan (New York: G. P. Putnam's Sons, 1904), vol. II, pp. 300–310.

[3] John Stuart Mill, *Principles of Political Economy*, ed. W. J. Ashley (London: Longmans, Green Co., Ltd., 1921), p. 804.

[4] For an excellent history of the development of ability-to-pay principles, see R. A. Musgrave, *The Theory of Public Finance* (New York: McGraw-Hill Book Co., 1959), chap. 5.

conditions. Moreover, the interpersonal equity conditions are necessarily consistent with the principle of vertical equity as well. Any two people differing in at least one of the four dimensions listed above will generally pay different taxes in the process of satisfying the interpersonal equity conditions, even though they do not indicate what the exact pattern of tax payments will be.

The second point is that the historical development of the ability-to-pay doctrine can properly be considered as part of first-best theory. Ability to pay as a sacrifice principle relates specifically to the goal of distributive equity. Second-best tax theory is concerned, first and foremost, with the efficiency costs of distorting taxation. In a many-person second-best environment, efficiency considerations must be tempered by the relative inequities imposed by alternative distorting taxes so that second-best theory has an interest in ability-to-pay principles, but the principles themselves have nothing whatsoever to do with questions of efficiency. Hence, ability to pay can be analyzed most conveniently in a first-best policy environment, one in which efficiency and equity issues are separable. This is precisely what happened in the professional literature.

Careful distinctions between first-best and second-best analysis are a fairly recent phenomenon, but it is clear that early ability-to-pay theorists were implicitly assuming a first-best environment. We have two clues on this. First, the ability-to-pay literature generally ignores efficiency considerations altogether. This would be impossible in a second-best framework. A second clue is that ability-to-pay theory has traditionally equated tax payments with tax burdens. This, too, implies a first-best environment, for reasons which can only be sketched at this point in the text.

Tax incidence theory, the subject matter of Chapter 17, distinguishes the burden of a tax—who sacrifices as a result of the tax—from the impact of a tax—who physically pays the tax to the government. We were careful above when defining horizontal and vertical equity to refer to "tax burdens." The traditional definitions use "tax payments," as follows:

Horizontal equity: equals should pay equal taxes.

Vertical equity: unequals should pay unequal taxes.

The difference is significant. Tax incidence theory shows that under certain conditions in a first-best policy environment, lump-sum tax payments are an appropriate measure of individual welfare losses, or "burdens," using standard willingness-to-pay criteria such as Hick's Compensating or Equivalent Variations. With distorting taxes, however, the tax payments are never entirely accurate measures of welfare loss. These points are fairly subtle and will be discussed in detail in Chapter 17. What matters here in terms of the ability-to-pay principles is that equal tax payments may yield unequal burdens with distorting taxes simply because of the resulting distortions. Alternatively, unequal tax payments may entail equal sacrifices. Hence, once the possibility of distorting taxation is recognized, horizontal and vertical equity must be more broadly defined in terms of "tax burdens," as we have done. Conversely, equating tax payments with tax burdens must imply both a first-best policy environment *and* lump-sum taxation.

In order to focus strictly on the equity issues involved with the ability-to-pay doctrine we will adopt a first-best framework and equate tax payments with tax burdens. This is at best an uneasy convenience, however. The problem is that the conventional wisdom on ability to pay has chosen for its "ideal" tax base one that is almost certainly not lump sum, so that it is impossible to ignore distortions entirely. Furthermore, the federal personal income tax, which we have chosen to illustrate the application of ability to pay, contains a number of second-best distortions which can only be understood in terms of the broader interpretation of horizontal and vertical equity. Thus, we will occasionally stray from the first-best assumptions.

APPLYING HORIZONTAL AND VERTICAL EQUITY— THE CONVENTIONAL WISDOM

The search for horizontal and vertical equity begins with the definition of the tax base. Since taxes are collected by applying a rate structure to a tax base, the only way of guaranteeing that two equals pay the same tax and two unequals pay different taxes is if the tax base itself is the defining characteristic of equality. Finding the proper tax base is all that matters for horizontal equity. Vertical equity requires specifying the rate structure as well to determine exactly how unequally unequals are to be treated.

Horizontal Equity

There will never be unanimous agreement on an ideal tax base, but until recently neoclassical economists had come to agree that income, properly defined, is the best tax base for the purpose of satisfying horizontal equity. This conclusion was based on a three-part argument: (1) The first principle of tax design is that people ultimately bear the burden of any tax no matter what is actually taxed. For example, corporate income taxes and sales taxes are levied on business firms in the United States, but the fact that a business firm pays $X million in taxes is of little consequence. In terms of tax equity the interesting questions are which people finally bear the burden of these taxes, the consumers of the final product, the labor employed by the firm, the stockholders of the firm, third parties not directly associated with the firm, and so forth. Social welfare, after all, is directly related to individuals' utility functions, not to production relationships, and any tax will eventually burden people either as consumers or as suppliers of factors, or both. (2) The second point is that individuals ultimately sacrifice utility when they pay general taxes, so that the ideal tax base would be individual utility levels. (3) This is impossible, of course, so that the final part of the argument is that, in lieu of taxing utility, the tax base should be the best possible surrogate for individual utility.

Haig-Simons Income. These three principles of tax design are agreed to by virtually all neoclassical economists. The only disagreement comes in selecting the best possible surrogate. The conventional wisdom says that income serves best in this capacity where income is defined as the individual's increase in purchasing power during the tax year. Using standard national income accounting terminology, income as accretion in purchasing power can be defined as

> *Income* ≡ personal income plus the change in the value of assets existing as of the beginning of the tax year, or capital gains,[5]

a measure commonly referred to as the Haig-Simons definition of income after Professors Haig and Simons, who first proposed it independently in the 1920s and 1930s. It has also been labeled the Comprehensive Tax Base.

In terms of horizontal equity, then, two people with identical amounts of Haig-Simons income are equals by definition and should pay the same tax. Similarly, two people with different amounts of Haig-Simons income are unequal and should pay different taxes by the principle of vertical equity, how much different depending on how the rate structure varies with income.

It is understood that all components of Haig-Simons income are equivalent. In particular, neither the sources nor uses of income should affect the amount of tax paid, so that distinctions of the following kind are all irrelevant:

Sources of income:

1. Whether income is derived from personal income or capital gains.
2. Whether personal income is earned (wages, rents, etc.) or unearned (transfer payments).
3. Whether earned income derives from labor, capital, or land.

Uses of income:

4. Whether income is consumed or saved. Both consumption and savings increase utility. In terms of tax policy the only relevant consideration is the increase in purchasing power, whether realized currently or postponed through savings.
5. Within capital gains, whether a gain is "realized" by selling an asset or simply "accrues" on paper. Allowing gains to accrue is merely one particular form of savings. Also, capital losses should be fully offset against other income.
6. The pattern of consumption is also irrelevant, since all consumption decisions are viewed as voluntary and thereby utility increasing. This includes items such as private charity and tax payments to other governments. The only exceptions are expenditures necessary for earning income in the first place, so-called business expenses. Presumably income used in this

---

[5] Notice that the Haig-Simons definition uses personal rather than disposable income since the former includes personal income taxes which are originally part of the tax base. The classic references are H. C. Simons, *Personal Income Taxation*, (Chicago: University of Chicago Press, 1938); and R. M. Haig, "The Concept of Income: Economic and Legal Aspects," in R. M. Haig, ed., *The Federal Income Tax*, (New York: Columbia University Press, 1921).

manner does not represent an accretion in utility-increasing purchasing power.

7. Finally, accretions in purchasing power matter, not accumulated purchasing power. Wealth in any form is not an appropriate tax base. Of course, any tax base other than Haig-Simons income is tautologically inappropriate if Haig-Simons income is accepted as the correct base. Thus, the Haig-Simons criterion automatically precludes such general taxes as sales taxes, gift and estate (inheritance) taxes, all personal property taxes, selective excise taxes (except when required by the benefits-received principle), and separate taxation of specific sources of income, such as the payroll (social security) tax and the corporate income tax.

Criticisms of Haig-Simons Income. The Haig-Simons income measure is certainly a reasonable interpretation of the ability-to-pay doctrine, especially since it bears a distinct intellectual kinship to the interpersonal equity conditions of social welfare maximization through its relationship to individual utility. But being only a surrogate utility measure it is also open to fairly easy criticism.

For example, intellectual kinship to the interpersonal equity conditions is more likely to appeal to neoclassical economists than to economists from other persuasions. Marxists, for example, would surely opt for differential treatment of wage and profit income. As another example, Nicholas Kaldor once proposed an expenditure tax on the grounds that the distinction between consumption and saving is meaningful. According to Kaldor, when individuals consume they use up scarce resources for their own personal satisfaction, to the sacrifice of others' well-being. Savings, on the other hand, is a personal form of sacrifice that permits an increase in the stock of capital to the potential future benefit of all citizens. Therefore, society can properly discriminate against consumption in taxation even if taxes are based on a sacrifice principle, providing sacrifice is viewed from a social rather than an individual perspective.[6]

Neoclassical support for an expenditures tax has grown in recent years, but not for the reasons it appeals to Kaldor. The "new" neoclassical position is that Haig-Simons income is flawed because it relates only to a single year, whereas the entire thrust of consumer theory over the past 20 years has been to view consumer decisions as occurring within the context of an entire lifetime. But if lifetime utility is the relevant standard of equality, then annual consumption expenditures (including bequests) are likely to be a better surrogate for utility than income, especially annual income. According to the long-run point of view, two people with identical patterns of lifetime consumption plus bequests can most reasonably be said to have enjoyed the same level of utility over their lifetimes. If their consumption expenditures are taxed annually, they will also pay the same amount in lifetime taxes, consistent with the principle of horizontal equity. If annual income is the tax base, however, their tax payments may easily differ depending on their streams of earnings and borrowings. An obvious corollary in terms of vertical equity is that unequal lifetime consumption

---

[6] N. Kaldor, *An Expenditure Tax*, (London: George Allen & Unwin, Ltd., 1955).

patterns imply unequal utility and can be taxed unequally. Again, an annual tax on consumption can accomplish this, whereas an annual income tax may not.[7]

Even ignoring the lifetime argument, the Haig-Simons income measure may simply not be a very good surrogate for utility, despite its relationship to purchasing power. Only if people have identical tastes, equal abilities, and equal opportunities in the marketplace is income (or consumption) a perfect surrogate for utility. Under these conditions, two people with identical Haig-Simons income will enjoy the same level of utility and should be taxed equally. However, people obviously differ considerably in each of these dimensions, in which case the correlation between income (consumption) and utility is much less certain. To cite some obvious examples, if two people place widely different values on their leisure time yet earn the same income, their levels of satisfaction are likely to be quite different. Alternatively, if one of two people with identical tastes and abilities is forced to take a relatively unattractive job because of discrimination, then the fact that they earn equal (unequal) incomes is no guarantee that they enjoy equal (unequal) levels of satisfaction.

It is difficult to know how to react to this particular criticism. The Haig-Simons criterion is obviously flawed, but so too will be any alternative proposal so long as tastes, abilities, and opportunities in the marketplace differ among individuals. As a general rule, the same conditions that make Haig-Simons income a perfect surrogate for utility apply to all other surrogate measures as well. Hence, given that these conditions do not hold in practice, it may well be futile to search for a better tax base. In our view, which is decidedly neoclassical, the most compelling alternative to Haig-Simons income is the expenditure base, as the best approximation to utility over an individual's lifetime. But even this is flawed when set against the neoclassical standard of the interpersonal equity conditions from social welfare maximization.

The neoclassical view of the ability-to-pay principle has crystalized as follows, whether in a lifetime context or not: given that people differ in tastes, abilities, and opportunities, horizontal equity requires that if two people have the same level of utility before taxes they should have the same level of utility after taxes. This is consistent with our earlier definition of horizontal equity in terms of tax burdens. In 1976 Professor Feldstein specifically stated that as *the* ability-to-pay criterion for tax design.[8] In doing so he was merely reaffirming the second point in the chain of reasoning leading from the general principle of horizontal and vertical equity to the definition of a tax base, that the notion of personal sacrifice makes sense only when defined in terms of utility.

The fundamental issue is whether the ability-to-pay principle thus defined is a useful addition to neoclassical tax theory. On the one hand, it is not necessarily consistent with the interpersonal equity conditions of social welfare maximization which are, presumably, *the* neoclassical statement of distributive equity. Admittedly, the interpersonal equity conditions are seriously flawed as guidelines for tax design, but so long as people differ in terms of preferences or

---

[7] See M. Feldstein, "On the Theory of Tax Reform," *Journal of Public Economics*, July–August 1976 (International Seminar in Public Economics and Tax Theory), especially pp. 87–89.

[8] Feldstein, "On the Theory of Tax Reform," p. 83.

abilities or opportunities, it is not clear that the Feldstein criterion is any more useful to the policymaker. It would appear, therefore, that neoclassical theorists have developed a competing principle of distributive equity to no useful purpose. One might just as well ask: Does using Haig-Simons income (or anything else) as the tax base, with a given rate structure, reasonably approximate the interpersonal equity conditions of social welfare maximization?

To be concrete, let us compare the interpersonal equity conditions and the Feldstein ability-to-pay criterion within the context of a two-person, two-good exchange economy, with fixed endowments of the two goods. Let X_{ij} = consumption of good j by person i, $i, j = 1, 2$. The first-order conditions for a social welfare maximum in this economy are:

$$(13.2) \qquad Pareto\ optimality: \quad \frac{\dfrac{\partial U^1}{\partial X_{11}}}{\dfrac{\partial U^1}{\partial X_{12}}} = \frac{\dfrac{\partial U^2}{\partial X_{21}}}{\dfrac{\partial U^2}{\partial X_{22}}}$$

$$(13.3) \qquad Interpersonal\ equity: \quad \frac{\partial W}{\partial U^1}\frac{\partial U^1}{\partial X_{11}} = \frac{\partial W}{\partial U^2}\frac{\partial U^2}{\partial X_{21}}$$

$$\frac{\partial W}{\partial U^1}\frac{\partial U^1}{\partial X_{12}} = \frac{\partial W}{\partial U^2}\frac{\partial U^2}{\partial X_{22}}$$

If the two people have unequal social welfare weights, $\partial W/\partial U^1 \neq \partial W/\partial U^2$, evaluated at equal utility levels, the Feldstein "equal utility before tax–equal utility after tax" criterion will clearly be inconsistent with (13.3) in general. Suppose, however, that the social welfare weights are equal so that (13.3) becomes

$$(13.4) \qquad \frac{\partial U^1}{\partial X_{11}} = \frac{\partial U^2}{\partial X_{21}}$$

$$\frac{\partial U^1}{\partial X_{12}} = \frac{\partial U^2}{\partial X_{22}}$$

Even (13.4) differs from the Feldstein criterion if people's tastes and initial endowments are unequal.

If the two consumers happen to enjoy the same level of utility at an initial pareto-optimum before the government redistributes one of the goods to satisfy the interpersonal equity conditions, there is no guarantee they will enjoy equal utility levels after the socially optimum tax and transfer has been effected. The following simple model provides a counter example:

Let:

$$U^1 = X_{11}(3 + X_{12}) + 27$$
$$U^2 = \tfrac{1}{2} \cdot X_{21}(1 + 2X_{22})$$
$$X_{11} + X_{12} = 10$$
$$X_{21} + X_{22} = 10$$

The reader can verify that an initial equal utility pareto-optimum occurs at:

	X_1	X_2
Person 1	(4,	2.4)
Person 2	(6,	7.6)

The social welfare optimum, satisfying both (13.2) and (13.4), occurs at:

	X_1	X_2
Person 1	(5,	15/4)
Person 2	(5,	25/4)

with unequal utilities. The difference, of course, is that interpersonal equity requires equal aftertax *marginal* utilities, whereas the Feldstein criterion requires equal aftertax utility levels. Even ignoring differences in social welfare weights, these two rules will be consistent only if preferences are identical.

The unsettling conclusion to all this is that if the interpersonal equity conditions are the true neoclassical standard for judging general tax policies, and preferences and endowments (abilities, opportunities) differ, there is no single tax base that can be used to define equality, even on a theoretical level. Suppose the government arbitrarily selects any one good or factor to redistribute lump sum. Under the given assumptions, two nonidentical people could conceivably consume (supply) the same quantity of the good (factor) in the pretax equilibrium. If so, they would sacrifice the same amount of the good (factor) if it were chosen as the tax base, whereas the interpersonal equity conditions would generally require unequal sacrifices. In short, no simple rules can turn nonidentical people into equals for the purposes of ability-to-pay taxation.

Conversely, if people were identical across all relevant attributes, then any number of equality measures would be consistent with interpersonal equity, including Haig-Simons income, total consumption, and any one of the goods consumed or factors supplied by an individual consumer, since identical consumers will consume (supply) an identical bundle of goods (factor supplies). This is not worth much, of course, since if all people were identical there would be no need for redistributive taxation. General taxes would still be necessary to cover decreasing cost deficits, but the government could confidently take equal amounts of any one good or factor from everyone.

Thus the Haig-Simons income measure is no more or less susceptible to criticism than any other surrogate attempting to describe two identical individuals, if the interpersonal equity conditions of social welfare maximization are taken as the correct ability-to-pay criteria. Of course, one can always reject these conditions as the equity norm, but it is not clear why neoclassical theory should do so, nor is it clear what other standard should replace interpersonal equity. Yet without agreement on a theoretical standard, debate over alternative surrogate tax bases cannot be meaningful. Tax design becomes solely a matter of personal taste. Perhaps this is all it can be, in which case it is still fair to say that most neoclassical economists accept Haig-Simons income as the best tax base among the feasible alternatives, with consumption the only serious challenger. One clear indication of this preference is that economists invariably use Haig-Simons income as the basis for judging the progressivity or regressivity of *any* tax, whether it taxes income or not. Taxes are said to be *progressive* if the ratio of tax collections to income rises as income rises and *regressive* if the ratio declines. If the ratio is invariant to income, the tax is said to be *proportional.*[9] Most economists regard these ratios as the best single "quick-and-dirty" measure of the distributional impact of a tax. The fact that they tend to use Haig-Simons income in the denominator is telling in our view.[10]

Vertical Equity

So far the discussion has centered on the choice of a tax base, the first step toward achieving both horizontal and vertical equity. But achieving vertical equity requires an additional step, the specification of a rate structure to be applied to the base. Once this is done, the exact manner in which unequals are to be treated unequally will have been determined.

It is difficult to expand very much on the few introductory comments made at the beginning of this chapter. Assuming that the interpersonal equity conditions are the ultimate standard for tax equity, they will determine the proper rate structure to apply to whatever good or factor the government decides to tax and transfer lump sum. Unfortunately, no one rate structure stands out as an obvious candidate, for the same uncertainty exists here as with the choice of the tax base. Indeed, if interpersonal equity is the accepted norm, then one can view the problem of tax design strictly in terms of defining the rate structure. According to this point of view, the choice of a tax base is irrelevant in that any one of the goods or factors can be singled out for tax and transfer. Thus, to achieve interpersonal equity the government can select a good (or factor) arbitrarily and then determine the rate structure to be applied to this good (factor) that produces the exact pattern of taxes and transfers (negative rates) implied by the interpersonal equity conditions. As a practical matter this may not be a fruitful approach, however. As noted above, the interpersonal equity conditions may imply that two people who consume (supply) the good (factor) equally in the pretax situation should pay taxes at a different rate, whereas practical tax design will undoubtedly require that the same rate be applied to

---

[9] For distorting taxes, an income measure of tax burden would be substituted for tax collections.

[10] For instance, in their comprehensive study of the U.S. tax system, Pechman and Okner define progressivity and regressivity exactly as we have and calculate effective tax rates using an approximation to Haig-Simons income in the denominator. They note that their definition of income "... corresponds closely to an economist's comprehensive definition of income ... this concept includes transfer payments and capital gains accrued during the year (whether realized or not) ... indirect business taxes, as well as direct taxes, are included in income" (p. 2). J. Pechman and B. Okner, *Who Bears the Tax Burden?* (Washington, D.C.: The Brookings Institution, 1974).

equal quantities of the chosen tax base. When these problems arise, one can either fault the selection of the tax base or the rate structure applied to an arbitrarily chosen base.

For the purposes of further discussion, suppose that a correct (or at least satisfactory) tax base has been discovered. Can anything useful then be said about an appropriate, or "satisfactory," rate structure in a first-best environment? As a general rule economists are fairly pessimistic—there is certainly no conventional support for any particular rate structure comparable to that which exists for the Haig-Simons income tax base. There are a number of reasons for this. In the first place, a wide variety of rate structures, whether they imply progressive, regressive, or proportional taxation, will simultaneously satisfy the vertical equity criterion of unequal treatment of unequals, and redistribute "income" from wealthier individuals to poorer individuals. For example, a tax structure that applies a 10 percent rate to a Haig-Simons income of $50,000 and a 5 percent rate to incomes of $200,000 is regressive, but it collects more tax from the wealthier individuals, in broad concordance with the ability-to-pay doctrine. Thus, neither the interpersonal equity conditions nor the ability-to-pay doctrine usefully limit the choice of potential rate structures, in general. However, pushing the analysis somewhat further, if it is agreed that interpersonal equity requires transfers from the rich to the poor as a rough guideline, then it is tempting to argue for a progressive or graduated rate structure along the following lines. Suppose we assume that all social welfare weights are equal so that interpersonal equity becomes $\partial U^h/\partial X_{hi} = $, all $h = 1, \ldots, H$, where X_i is the good or factor transferred lump sum. If one assumes diminishing marginal utility in X_{hi}, then the tax structure that will equalize marginal utilities would appear to be progressive. To see this, suppose there are three identical subsets of consumers, whose pretax marginal utilities are, respectively:

$$(13.5) \qquad \frac{\partial U^1}{\partial X_{1i}} = 10 \qquad \frac{\partial U^2}{\partial X_{2i}} = 9 \qquad \frac{\partial U^3}{\partial X_{3i}} = 8$$

with:

$X_{3i} > X_{2i} > X_{1i}$ because of diminishing marginal utility.

If the government wants to collect a given amount of tax revenue for redistribution to other, poorer groups, then interpersonal equity requires that the government tax people in group 3 until either (a) their marginal utility rises to 9 or (b) the required tax revenue has been collected. If (a) applies, then the government taxes both groups 2 and 3 until (c) their marginal utility rises to 10 or (d) the required tax revenue has been collected. If (c) applies, then the government taxes all three groups, maintaining equality on the margin, until the revenue requirement has been satisfied. This pattern of tax collections certainly seems to be progressive.

There are several problems with this argument, however. First, the assumption of diminishing marginal utility is neither a necessary nor sufficient condition for diminishing marginal rates of substitution, the condition for a well-behaved consumer indifference map. Even if marginal utility is diminishing with one utility index, there exists an admissible monotonic transformation of the utility function which will leave demands (and factor supplies) unchanged and lead to constant or even increasing marginal utility for one good. That is, given a utility index $\phi(X)$ and its transformation $F[\phi(X)]$, $F' > 0$,

(13.6)
$$\frac{\partial^2 F[\phi(X)]}{\partial X_i^2} = F' \frac{\partial^2 \phi}{\partial X_i^2} + \frac{\partial \phi}{\partial X} F'' > 0$$

is consistent with $\partial^2 \phi / \partial X_i^2 < 0$ for $F'' > 0$. Needless to say, economists are skeptical of any arguments based on cardinal utility measures.

Second, even if the government picks one cardinal representation of the utility index satisfying diminishing marginal utility for each person for purposes of establishing the various taxes, the tax program described above may not be progressive. Using a simple general equilibrium model with one good and one factor, Sadka was able to show that lump-sum taxes consistent with either a maximin or utilitarian social welfare function would not necessarily be progressive, where factor income is used as the basis of comparison. Whether the taxes are progressive or not turns on a number of parameters, including the elasticity of the consumers' indifference curves between the factor and the good, third derivatives of the utility function, and the like. Certainly no conclusions can be drawn a priori.[11]

Finally, different kinds of social welfare functions than Sadka analyzed, with widely differing social marginal utilities, could easily imply proportional or even regressive taxation. $(\partial W / \partial U^h)(\partial U^h / \partial X_{hi})$, $h = 1, \ldots, H$ are the decisive terms, not $\partial U^h / \partial X_{hi}$.[12]

In terms of actual U.S. tax policy, the evidence on rate structure is mixed. On paper at least, the federal personal income tax is highly progressive, with a graduated rate structure ranging from 14 percent to 60 percent, although it turns out to be much less progressive in fact. The federal corporate tax taxes small corporations at lower rates than large corporations. Some state income taxes are also mildly progressive. But many U.S. taxes employ a single rate, so that whether or not the tax is progressive depends upon the elasticity of its tax base with respect to Haig-Simons income (assuming that the tax payments are an accurate measure of tax burden, which as we have indicated, is often not a good assumption). One could argue that the federal rates accurately reflect society's view of the proper rate structure in that the states and localities avoid graduated structures not on equity grounds but simply because they fear competition from other jurisdictions. Nor can they live with highly variable tax collections. Progressive rates increase the variance of revenues because the collections are more sensitive to any given change in the tax base. The problem for the state and local governments is on the down side. States and localities

---

[11] E. Sadka, "On Progressive Taxation," *American Economic Review*, December 1976.

[12] Musgrave, *The Theory of Public Finance*, chap. 5, contains an excellent analysis of the relationships between the rate structure, various equity interpretations of sacrifice, and individuals' utility schedules.

have particular difficulties adjusting to revenue shortfalls because they cannot routinely issue debt to cover operating deficits.

All this is pure conjecture, of course. In a more concrete vein, Pechman and Okner have estimated that the overall U.S. tax structure is roughly proportional. But since this is the net result of a large variety of taxes, some of which are mildly progressive, some mildly regressive, and still others virtually proportional, it would be hasty to conclude on the basis of their study that U.S. citizens prefer proportional taxation.[13]

REFLECTIONS ON THE HAIG-SIMONS CRITERION IN PRACTICE—THE FEDERAL PERSONAL INCOME TAXES

Despite its appeal to public sector economists, the Haig-Simons income measure has not fared well in practice in the United States. Only the personal income taxes pay so much as lip service to the Haig-Simons criterion, yet no government in the United States uses the personal income tax for the majority of its tax collections. U.S. state and local governments rely primarily on sales and property taxes, respectively, neither of which is valid according to the Haig-Simons criterion. State sales taxes may appear to be consistent with the proposal that consumption expenditures serve as the tax base, but in practice these taxes exclude broad classes of expenditures from taxation, and they usually tax all included items at one fixed rate. What expenditure tax proponents have in mind is a tax computed and paid annually by the consumer exactly as the federal income tax is, except that it would exclude savings from the tax base. If the tax base were computed in this manner, a graduated rate schedule could readily be applied to expenditures, removing the stigma from sales taxes that they tend to be regressive.

The federal personal income tax is the single largest tax in the United States, but it still does not comprise the majority of federal tax collections. The bulk of federal revenues comes from a variety of taxes, including the corporation income tax, a payroll tax, various excise taxes, and estate taxes, all of which are illegitimate under the Haig-Simons criterion. Furthermore, taxable income under the federal personal income tax is considerably smaller than Haig-Simons income.[14] Nonetheless, it at least pays lip service to conventional ability-to-pay principles.

Recall that according to the Haig-Simons criterion, the federal income tax base should include personal income and capital gains on assets held from the beginning of the tax year, without regard to the sources or uses of income. In fact, the tax base falls far short of this. Regarding the capital gains portion of income, gains should be taxed as they accrue and at the same rate applied to personal income. Moreover, capital losses should be fully offset against other income since they represent equal dollar decreases in purchasing power. Finally,

---

[13] Pechman and Okner, *Who Bears the Tax Burden?*, p. 10.

[14] Since many state income taxes use the federal definition of taxable income they too fail to satisfy the Haig-Simons criterion.

the tax base should reflect increases in real purchasing power only. Increases in income arising solely from inflation should not be taxed. If money income is used as the tax base, then at least all sources of income should be treated equally with respect to the effects of inflation on purchasing power.

Capital gains taxation is deficient on all counts. Capital gains are taxed on a realized basis only, that is, when the asset is actually sold, and then only at half of the rate applied to personal income. The ability to offset losses against income is limited to offsets against capital gains. Finally, the tax base is defined in terms of money income with no adjustments for the effects of inflation on purchasing power. As a result, capital and wage income are treated differentially with respect to their real increases in purchasing power.

The personal income portion of the tax base is also far removed from the Haig-Simons ideal. According to Pechman, the tax base includes only 49.7 percent of total personal income, on average.[15] The discrepancy results from a variety of sources, to be discussed below.

We do not intend to engage in a comprehensive analysis of the federal income tax in this text. The interested reader can find detailed critiques of this tax in a number of excellent texts. We would especially recommend Joseph Pechman's *Federal Tax Policy* or Richard Goode's *The Individual Income Tax*. In addition, Peter Diamond's article, "Inflation and the Comprehensive Tax Base," contains an excellent analysis of the capital gains provisions.[16] The remainder of Chapter 13 will simply offer a selection of the key issues relating to capital gains and personal income taxation.

The Inflationary Bias against Income from Capital[17]

The U.S. tax codes were written for a noninflationary economy. This, in itself, has created a source of horizontal inequity now that the U.S. economy has developed a decided inflationary bias, simply because inflation causes money asset income to grow more rapidly than money wage income. Consequently, equal growth in money income from these two sources reflects unequal growth in real purchasing power, so that equal taxation implies unequal treatment, in violation of horizontal equity.[18] The inequity is compounded by the graduated rate schedule, since asset income's artifically expanded tax base will also be taxed at higher rates.

To see how the differential inflation effect arises, suppose an economy has been experiencing inflation since time $t = 0$. Define the accumulated inflation

---

[15] J. Pechman, *Federal Tax Policy*, 3d ed. (Washington, D.C.: The Brookings Institution, 1977), table B-5, p. 326. This figure is for 1974. According to Pechman's table B-5 the percentage rose steadily from 37.3 percent in 1950 to 52.1 percent in 1969, and then declined slightly and leveled off during the 1970s.

[16] R. Goode, *The Individual Income Tax*, rev. ed. (Washington, D.C.: The Brookings Institution, 1976); and P. Diamond, "Inflation and the Comprehensive Tax Base," *Journal of Public Economics*, August 1975.

[17] The analysis in this section follows Diamond, "Inflation and the Comprehensive Tax Base," pp. 228–30.

[18] Vertical equity is also necessarily violated by this phenomenon.

to time t as

(13.7)
$$I(t) = \exp \int_0^t i(s)ds$$

where:

$i(t)$ = the instantaneous rate of inflation at time t.

Assume further that inflation is fully anticipated so that $i(t)$ represents both the actual and expected rate of inflation. If $W(t)$ represents wage income at time t without inflation, then

(13.8)
$$W'(t) = W(t) \cdot I(t)$$

is wage income with inflation.

Let $Y(t)$ represent income from capital in the absence of inflation.

(13.9)
$$Y(t) = r(t) \cdot V(t)$$

where:

$r(t)$ = the real rate of return.

$V(t)$ = the value of an asset without inflation.

The bias arises because expected inflation affects income from capital in two ways. It increases *both* the value of assets *and* the rate of return on assets. Let:

(13.10)
$$V'(t) = V(t) \cdot I(t)$$

represent the value of assets with inflation, and

(13.11)
$$n(t) = r(t) + i(t)$$

represent the nominal rate of return. Hence,

(13.12)
$$Y'(t) = n(t) \cdot V'(t) = [r(t) + i(t)]V(t) \cdot I(t)$$

where:

$Y'(t)$ = income from capital with inflation.

Dividing (13.12) by (13.8), using (13.9) and (13.10), and rearranging terms yields:

(13.13)
$$\frac{Y'(t)}{W'(t)} = \frac{(r(t) + i(t)) \cdot V(t) \cdot I(t)}{W(t) \cdot I(t)} = \frac{Y(t)}{W(t)} + \frac{i(t)V'(t)}{W'(t)} > \frac{Y(t)}{W(t)}$$

Therefore, capital income grows more rapidly then wage income simply because of the inflation factor. If the tax base is money income, capital income will be overly taxed. By inspection of the right-hand side of (13.13), the inflationary bias can be removed by subtracting from money asset income the expected rate of inflation times the value of assets with inflation ($i(t) \cdot V'(t)$) before applying the tax rates.

The inflation adjustment should be applied to all sources of capital income, but the nature of the adjustment will vary depending upon the particular form of the asset. For example, if the income derives from an interest-bearing asset, the taxable income should include only the percentage of interest payments resulting from the real rate of return. That is, if $Y'(t) = (r(t) + i(t)) \cdot V'(t)$, then

$$(13.14) \qquad Y'(t) - i(t) \cdot V'(t) = r(t)V'(t)$$

But,

$$(13.15) \qquad r(t)V'(t) = \frac{r(t)}{n(t)} \cdot n(t) \cdot V'(t) = \frac{r(t)}{n(t)} \cdot Y'(t)$$

Thus, the taxpayer would report actual interest payments times the ratio of the real to the nominal rate of return.

For a straight capital gain without interest payments, the taxpayer would increase the purchase price by the accumulated inflation factor before subtracting it from the current value to compute the capital gain. For these assets,

$$(13.16) \qquad Y'(t) = CV - PV$$

where:

CV = current value, inclusive of inflation.

PV = original purchase value.

Adjusting $Y'(t)$ yields:

$$(13.17) \qquad Y'(t)_{\text{adjusted}} = (CV - PV) - (CV - PV)_{\text{inflation}}$$

$$(13.18) \qquad Y'(t)_{\text{adjusted}} = (CV - PV) - (PV \cdot I(t) - PV)$$

$$(13.19) \qquad Y'(t)_{\text{adjusted}} = CV - PV \cdot I(t)$$

Finally, money holdings would receive a credit equal to $i(t) \cdot V'(t)$, since there is no nominal return from which to subtract this adjustment factor. Diamond recommends ignoring this adjustment on the grounds that the bookkeeping for cash assets would be especially difficult and that the liquidity services from holding cash are untaxed anyway.[19]

These inflation adjustments are correct as given only if inflation is always fully anticipated and all income inflates at the same rate over time. In actuality, of course, neither of these is true. Nor is it clear what should be done to correct for discrepancies. As a practical matter, governments would surely have to use actual rather than expected rates of inflation for any adjustment. There is, as yet, no reliable method for translating actual inflation rates into expected rates. Indeed, economic research has not even settled upon how inflationary expectations are formed. Yet nominal interest rates and capital values almost certainly adjust to some degree for anticipated inflation. Thus, it is probably more accurate to adjust capital income by some long-run smoothed inflation

---

[19] Diamond, "Inflation and the Comprehensive Tax Base," p. 232.

index than to make no adjustment at all. Those people who anticipate incorrectly will either make windfall gains or losses relative to the theoretical ideal, but this is unavoidable.

There remains the practical question of which long-run series to use, since assets and other sources of income inflate at different rates. A broad series such as the consumer price index is probably a reasonable choice for practical purposes, although again some people will receive (suffer) windfall gains (losses) in purchasing power relative to the ideal.

The Special Treatment of Capital Gains

In contrast to the inflationary bias against capital income generally, there are a number of provisions in the tax codes which favor income taken as capital gains. Most countries confer some kind of preferential treatment on capital gains, often by not taxing them at all. The United States is somewhat less generous, but by taxing gains only as they are realized, and then only at half the personal income tax rates, the federal government offers two significant advantages to income from capital gains, at the considerable expense of both horizontal and vertical equity.

The political justification for preferential treatment has always been that it is necessary to stimulate savings for investment and growth. One can argue fairly convincingly that the steady state rate of savings in the United States is way too low,[20] but there is precious little evidence to suggest that without preferential treatment of capital gains the rate of savings would be even lower. Recently Boskin has presented some empirical evidence indicating that the interest elasticity of savings is approximately .4 in the United States,[21] but most studies of the U.S. consumption function have failed to discern any significant relationship between interest rates and consumption (hence, savings). This is hardly surprising, since economic theory tells us that an increase in the aftertax rate of return creates offsetting substitution and income effects, the former in favor of savings, the latter against savings.

Consider, for example, the simple two-period model in which a consumer has an initial endowment of income Y_0, that he will consume fully over two periods. Assume that income not consumed in period 1 can be converted to consumption in period 2 through savings at the rate $(1 + r)$.[22] Therefore, the consumer's budget line, depicted in Figure 13–1, is

(13.20)
$$Y_0 = C_t + \frac{C_{t+1}}{(1 + r)}$$

Suppose the consumer is originally in equilibrium at point A in Figure 13–1, at which the $MRS_{C_t, C_{t+1}} = (1 + r)$, the slope of the budget line. Should the

---

[20] See M. Feldstein, "Does the United States Save Too Little," *AEA Papers and Proceedings*, February 1977.
[21] M. Boskin, "On Some Recent Econometric Research in Public Finance," *AEA Papers and Proceedings*, May 1976.
[22] To simplify the analysis, assume borrowing is impossible.

FIGURE 13-1

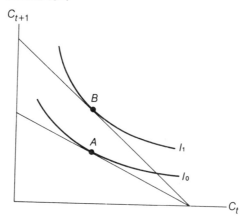

rate of return to savings rise to r^1 because of a tax break, the consumer will find a new equilibrium, say at point B. C_{t+1} will certainly rise, but the question is whether B falls to the left of A, implying lower C_t or higher savings. The substitution effect clearly favors C_{t+1}, or savings. The *equilibrium MRS* will have increased, implying a higher level of C_{t+1} and a lower level of C_t along any indifference curve. But the income effect favors both C_t and C_{t+1}. Hence, the overall effect on C_t is theoretically ambiguous. Intuitively, the higher interest rate has increased the marginal return to savings, but it has simultaneously lowered the total amount of savings required to achieve any given level of C_{t+1}. Thus, to the extent people are target savers, the actual amount of savings may well decrease.[23]

The effect on savings of preferential tax treatment may be uncertain, but its effect on vertical equity is devastating. The steeply graduated rate structure for personal income indicates that U.S. citizens desire a high degree of progression with respect to the vertical equity criterion. But according to Pechman and Okner, actual tax collections are only mildly progressive throughout the entire range of income, with a maximum effective rate of only 18 percent under their most progressive assumptions, and actually become regressive at the highest income levels.[24] The rate provisions for capital gains are not solely responsible for this, but they clearly shoulder a large portion of the blame. People in the middle to upper income levels have found it relatively easy to take

---

[23] Lawrence Summers has recently shown that analyzing the savings behavior in two-period models can be extremely misleading. Using an N period life cycle model, he was able to describe very different effects of taxation on savings behavior relative to the standard two-period treatment. In particular, he discovered a fairly high interest elasticity of savings. L. Summers, "Capital Taxation and Accumulation in a Life Cycle Growth Model," (unpublished). Paper presented at the NBER Conference on the Taxation of Capital, National Bureau of Economic Research, Inc., Cambridge, Mass., November 16 and 17, 1979.

[24] Pechman and Okner, *Who Bears the Tax Burden?*, table 4-8, p. 59.

large percentages of their incomes as capital gains, through executive stock options and similar arrangements.

President Carter recently proposed taxing capital gains at the full rates, but the proposal is unlikely to pass. George McGovern offered a similar proposal in 1972, and political observers generally agreed that it contributed significantly to his landslide defeat by President Nixon.

Accrued versus Realized Gains

To the best of our knowledge, no president or major party candidate has ever proposed taxing capital gains as they accrue rather than on a realized basis, yet this gives capital gains income another significant advantage in violation of both horizontal and vertical equity. One practical stumbling block toward adopting accrued taxation involves the evaluation of real assets. Imagine the following scenario: An elderly couple living on a modest pension owns a house free and clear, but has no other assets. The value of the house increases significantly, but the couple is forced to sell the house just to pay the tax on the accrued gain. Most people would probably object to these forced sales.[25] Another problem occurs if certain real assets are so infrequently traded (e.g., paintings) that a current market value is difficult to determine. One possible solution is to revalue all such assets at, say, 5 percent per year for purposes of capital gains taxation, adjusting for over- and underpayments, with interest, at the time of sale. People would undoubtedly balk at the arbitrary nature of such adjustments. But there is no escaping the fact that taxing capital gains on a realized basis confers real advantages relative to taxation on an accrued basis. By taxing on a realized basis, the U.S. government in effect gives annual interest-free loans to the asset holder equal in amount to the tax that would have been paid on an accrued basis. The value of these loans increases up to some point on the rate scale and then diminishes, but it is undoubtedly fairly significant in the 40–60 percent range, the rates applicable to the highest income groups.

To see how the loan arises, consider a \$1 asset growing at rate g and held for n years.[26] Ignore the problem of inflation. The asset's value at the end of n years is $(1 + g)^n$. If taxed on a *realized basis*, the capital gain is $(1 + g)^n - 1$ and the tax, at rate t, is $t[(1 + g)^n - 1]$. Hence, the asset's net of tax value at year N is:

$$(13.21) \qquad (1 + g)^n - t[(1 + g)^n - 1] = (1 - t)(1 + g)^n + t$$

If taxed on an *accrued basis*, the asset's net yearly rate of growth is $g(1 - t)$. Hence, its net of tax value at year n is:

$$(13.22) \qquad [1 + g(1 - t)]^n$$

---

[25] In fact, such forced sales actually do occur, the result of increased local property taxes which cannot be met on a fixed pension income.

[26] The following analysis of the interest-free loan is due to Diamond, "Inflation and the Comprehensive Tax Base," pp. 235–37.

Subtracting (13.22) from (13.21) yields:

(13.23) $$D = (1 - t)(1 + g)^n + t - [1 + g(1 - t)]^n$$

where:

> D = the increased net of tax value of the asset when taxed on a realized rather than an accrued basis.

To see that D is equivalent to a series of interest-free loans equal to the taxes that should have been paid on an accrued basis, note first that the series of *accrued* taxes for n periods would be:

(13.24) $gt, gt[1 + g(1 - t)], gt[1 + g(1 - t)]^2, \ldots, gt[1 + g(1 - t)]^{n-1}$

The accrued capital gains tax in the first period is obviously gt. In period 2, the value $(1 + g(1 - t))$ grows at rate $(1 + g)$. Thus, the capital gain during period 2 is $(1 + g)[1 + g(1 - t)] - [1 + g(1 - t)] = g[1 + g(1 - t)]$, on which the accrued tax is $t \cdot g[1 + g(1 - t)]$. Similar reasoning produces the series (13.24) above.

If the consumer received loans each period according to (13.24), the sum of the loans received by year n would be:

(13.25) $$L = gt[1 + (1 + g(1 - t)) + \cdots + (1 + g(1 - t))^{n-1}]$$

The principal on each loan would grow at rate $(1 + g)$, so that at the end of period n the value of the loans would be:

(13.26) $$V = gt[1 \cdot (1 + g)^{n-1} + [1 + g(1 - t)](1 + g)^{n-2} + \cdots$$
$$+ [1 + g(1 - t)]^{n-1} \cdot (1 + g)]$$

Letting $b = 1 + g(1 - t)$, and $a = (1 + g)$, (13.25) and (13.26) become:

(13.27) $$L = gt\left[\frac{1 - b^{n-1}}{1 - b}\right]$$

and

(13.28) $$V = gt\left[\frac{a^n - ab^{n-1}}{a - b}\right]$$

respectively. After repaying the principal on the loan in period n *without interest*, the consumer would have:

(13.29) $$V - L = gt\left[\frac{a^n - ab^{n-1}}{a - b} - \frac{1 - b^{n-1}}{1 - b}\right]$$

the total return on these interest-free loans. At tax rate t the net of tax return would be:

(13.30) $$(1 - t)(V - L) = (1 - t)(gt)\left[\frac{a^n - ab^{n-1}}{a - b} - \frac{1 - b^{n-1}}{1 - b}\right]$$

Recalling the definitions of a and b, (13.30) simplifies to

(13.31) $(1 - t)(V - L) = (1 - t)(1 + g)^n + t - [1 + g(1 - t)]^n$

the same as D in equation (13.23).

Finally, consider the value of the tax break with respect to the marginal tax rate, t. Differentiating D twice with respect to t shows that D attains a maximum in the range $0 < t < 100$. (At rates of either 0 or 100 percent the tax break or loan is obviously worthless.)

(13.32) $$\frac{\partial D}{\partial t} = -(1 + g)^n + n[1 + (1 - t)g]^{n-1} \cdot g + 1$$

(13.33) $$\frac{\partial^2 D}{\partial t^2} = n \cdot g(n - 1) \cdot [1 + (1 - t)g]^{n-2}(-g) < 0$$

Setting $\partial D/\partial t = 0$ gives t^*, the tax rate at which the value of the tax break is at its maximum, for given values of g and N.

(13.34) $$t^* = 1 + g - \frac{\left[\dfrac{(1 + g)^n - 1}{ng}\right]^{1/n-1}}{g}$$

As an illustration, for $g = 8$ percent and $N = 10$, $t^* = .49$, a very high-income tax bracket.

Hence, the U.S. treasury is giving the largest interest-free loans to people with the highest incomes, directly counter to society's preferences on vertical equity as represented by the graduated rate schedule.

The other major problem with a realized-basis capital gains tax is that realized gains and losses tend to occur sporadically in relatively large sums, more so than other sources of income. Bunching of gains and losses is only a problem with a graduated rate schedule since uneven increments in income tend to be taxed more heavily than smooth increments of equal amount. Presumably horizontal equity requires that two people who each earn $100,000 over a two-year period should pay the same tax, but if one earns $50,000 each year while the other earns nothing the first year and $100,000 the second year, the person with the uneven income will pay a larger tax. This bunching phenomenon can be solved by income averaging which is actually permitted by the U.S. tax codes. Capital gains (and losses) can be carried forward four years or backwards for three years to ease the tax burden.

The Taxation of Personal Income

It may seem incredible that only 40–50 percent of personal income is taxable under the federal income tax laws, but this is just testimony to the fact that the U.S. Congress uses the tax system for many purposes, not simply to help redistribute income according to accepted ability-to-pay criteria. Skeptics have termed the discrepancies between personal and taxable income tax "loopholes," arguing that they arose merely as favors to special-interest groups. There is undoubtedly some truth to this. A number of the provisions in the tax codes could hardly be explained otherwise.[27] But even a brief look at the major sources of discrepancy between personal and taxable income in the United States suggests that the "loopholes" interpretation is simply too narrow. It is not at all clear whether the tax system would be fairer if the major "loopholes" were removed.

The principal discrepancies between taxable and personal income can be classified into three broad categories: exemptions, exclusions, and deductions. An *exemption* is income that is included in the tax base but simply not taxed, the main one being the $1,000 personal exemption (as of 1979) for each dependent member of the family unit, with additional exemptions for the blind and aged. *Exclusions* are items included as personal income by the U.S. Department of Commerce in the National Accounts but not counted as taxable income by the Internal Revenue Service. The principal exclusions are federal government transfer payments, imputed income in kind (mainly rental income on owner occupied homes and farm produce consumed on the farm), and interest received on state and local bonds, commonly referred to as "municipals." *Deductions* are not sources of income at all but rather certain expenditures that can be deducted from personal income in computing taxable income. Taxpayers can elect a "standard deduction" equal to approximately 16 percent of adjusted personal income up to a maximum of $2,400 (in 1979), or they can itemize deductions. The principal itemized deductions are extraordinary medical payments or other uninsured losses; business expenses; and the so-called special deductions, the most important of which are taxes paid to state and local governments, contributions to nonprofit organizations, and interest payments on consumer debt, primarily home mortgages.

According to a strict interpretation of the Haig-Simons income criterion the only permissible item in the entire set of exemptions, exclusions, and deductions is the deduction for business expenses, because income spent to obtain income is unavailable as purchasing power. But reasonable arguments can also be made in support of most of the other items, either by appealing to other principles or to practical necessity. It is also evident that most of these "loopholes" do not relate to narrowly defined interest groups but are generally available to a broad spectrum of taxpayers. We will only offer some brief reflections on each of these items, concluding with two general principles applicable to all of them.

Exemptions.   The personal exemptions are obviously designed to prevent those with the lowest incomes from paying taxes. By themselves they are too low to prevent a family in poverty from paying taxes, since the poverty line for a family of four is now in excess of $6,000. But low-income families are also protected by various other exclusions, deductions, and tax credits, enough so that

---

[27] Philip Stern's *The Great Treasury Raid* describes the various special interest laws with a reformers zeal, his tone alternating between outrage and bemusement. P. Stern, *The Great Treasury Raid* (New York: Random House, 1964).

virtually no family below the poverty level of income pays any federal income tax.

On a more technical level, exemptions also bear a direct relationship to the progressivity of a tax. In fact, Pechman argues that the exemptions contribute to the mild progressivity of the federal income tax, especially in the low-income range.[28] There are two ways of creating a progressive tax. The obvious method is to apply a set of graduated rates to all income levels, but progression can also be achieved by using a single rate and exempting some income from taxation. (Of course, combinations of these two methods will also be progressive.) Consider a proportional tax of the form $T = tY$. If income equal to $\bar{Y}$ is exempt from taxation, the tax formula becomes:

$$(13.35) \qquad T = t(Y - \bar{Y}) = -t\bar{Y} + tY$$

Thus, with the exemption,

$$(13.36) \qquad \frac{T}{Y} = -\frac{t\bar{Y}}{Y} + t$$

and

$$(13.37) \qquad \frac{\partial(T/Y)}{\partial Y} = \frac{t\bar{Y}}{Y^2} > 0$$

as required for progression.

Exclusions. Of the three major exclusions, only the exclusion of interest income on municipals is difficult to justify. The Haig-Simons criterion notwithstanding, the U.S. Congress is understandably reluctant to tax income it has just offered to someone in the form of a transfer payment. Transfer payments, if taxed, would have to be increased to effect the same amount of net transfer, but the overall size of the federal budget has always been an important political issue in the United States. A natural reform suggested by many economists [29] would be to consolidate all the separate transfer programs into a single transfer based on income and administered by the IRS, the so-called negative income tax. President Nixon's Family Assistant Plan was a broad-based transfer program along the lines of a negative income tax. Congress rejected that plan, and no subsequent administration has submitted a similar proposal.

The problem with the negative income tax is that it does not appear possible to design one that will satisfy the following three criteria simultaneously:

1. It should bring all people above the poverty income line.
2. It should not discourage people from working rather than simply accepting a government transfer payment.
3. It should not be too costly to the taxpaying population (meaning "excessive" marginal tax rates).

---

[28] Pechman, *Federal Tax Policy*, p. 74.

[29] Milton Friedman first proposed the negative income tax in *Capitalism and Freedom* in 1962 as the most natural way of transferring income to the needy. M. Friedman, *Capitalism and Freedom* (Chicago: University of Chicago Press, 1962). James Tobin was also an early proponent. J. Tobin, "On Improving the Economic Status of the Negro," *Daedalus*, Fall 1965.

At the same time, a plan failing to meet one or more of these criteria appears unable to muster sufficient political support to pass through both Houses of Congress.

The difficulties in designing an acceptable negative income tax can be seen quite easily. Consider a negative tax or subsidy program of the form:

$$(13.38) \qquad S = s \cdot (\bar{Y} - Y_A)$$

where:

S = the negative tax or subsidy, $S \geq 0$.

s = the subsidy rate, $0 < s \leq 1$.

$\bar{Y}$ = the cutoff level of income, above which a person's income is subject to positive taxation.

Y_A = a person's actual income.

Most states determine public assistance benefit levels using a formula similar to (13.38), and transfers under Nixon's Family Assistance Plan were essentially determined the same way. Indeed, a fully general proportional income tax with negative payments below $\bar{Y}$ can be represented as:

$$(13.39) \qquad T = t \cdot (Y_A - \bar{Y})$$

where:

T = the tax payment.

t = the proportional tax rate.

Transfer programs using (13.38) have two features worth noting. First, a person with zero income receives a subsidy of $s \cdot \bar{Y}$, which defines the "income floor" or "guaranteed minimum income." Second, a person earning additional income in the range $Y_A < \bar{Y}$ is subjected to a *marginal tax* of rate s on earnings, since for every additional dollar earned the person loses s dollars of subsidy. Total gross-of-subsidy income rises throughout the subsidy range, however, to a maximum of $\bar{Y}$.

It is common to set $\bar{Y}$ at the poverty level of income so that no one above the poverty line receives a subsidy (e.g., Nixon's Family Assistance Plan).[30] The obvious problem with this, of course, is that *no one* below the poverty line escapes poverty, in dramatic contradiction of criterion 1. One possible solution is to set $\bar{Y} = 1/s \cdot$ (poverty line), in which case everyone escapes poverty, but this may well fail to satisfy criterion 3. Suppose $s = .50$. In this case $\bar{Y}$ equals twice the poverty line and the positive tax base becomes seriously eroded. Moreover, incomes immediately above this level cannot be subjected to the minimum tax rate of 14 percent, for this would create an anomaly in which

---

[30] See J. Maxwell and J. R. Aronson, *Financing State and Local Governments*, 3d ed. (Washington, D.C.: The Brookings Institution, 1977), chap. 3, for a discussion of the U.S. Public Assistance programs and President Nixon's Family Assistance Plan.

some people with lower incomes end up better off than others with higher incomes, net of tax (gross of subsidy). Presumably anomalies of this sort are unacceptable. Another possibility is to set $s = 1$. This brings everyone at least to the poverty line in the cheapest possible manner, but it clearly contradicts criterion 2. No one situated below the poverty line has any incentive to work.

The criterion of maintaining work incentives turns out to be one of the most difficult to satisfy with any subsidy program that bases the subsidy in part on earned income (that is, anything other than a lump-sum subsidy). Yet, the whole point of a negative tax scheme is to target on low-income people, so it would seem impossible to avoid relating the subsidy to income. The immediate problem is that any income based subsidy that actually increases gross-of-subsidy incomes generates an income effect in favor of leisure and against work according to the standard neoclassical labor-leisure model of labor supply. The best one can hope for in terms of work effort arises from a straight subsidy of the form

$$(13.40) \qquad\qquad S = s \cdot Y_A$$

depicted in Figure 13–2. (13.40) is exactly analogous to a (negative) income tax in the standard analysis relating taxes to work effort. Taxes lead to an income effect in favor of work and a substitution effect against work. Conversely, the subsidy (13.40) generates an income effect against work and a substitution effect in favor of work. Hence, *at best*, the overall affect on work effort is ambiguous. In terms of the diagram, B may be to the right or left, or directly above A.

(13.40) is clearly an absurb subsidy program. But more natural subsidies of the form (13.38) generate *both* income *and* substitution effects against work since the person receives more income gross of subsidy (the income effect) but is *taxed* at rate s on the margin (the substitution effect). This situation is depicted in Figure 13–3 with line segment EF representing (13.38) in the relevant range. Notice that the gross-of-subsidy wage line flattens just as it does with a positive tax, representing the negative substitution effect. The

FIGURE 13–2

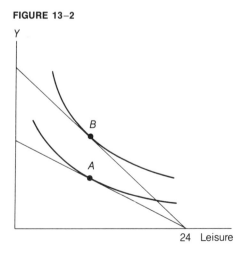

24   Leisure

FIGURE 13–3

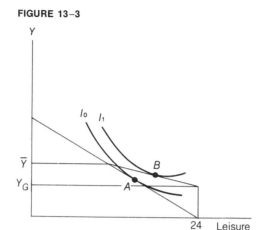

recipient is better off, but B is almost certainly to the right of A. Work effort has diminished.[31]

One final point deserves comment. If the government adopts a fully general tax with a negative portion as represented by (13.39), *all* taxpayers must receive an exemption equal to $\bar{Y}$ to avoid anomalies at the cutoff $\bar{Y}$. This can prove extremely costly if criterion 1 is even reasonably close to being satisfied. As $\bar{Y}$ rises, t must also rise to finance the program. However, a higher t implies a higher deadweight loss associated with the tax, a point that is demonstrated in Chapter 15. Indeed, Akerlof was able to show that social welfare may be higher with a "targeted," patchwork set of transfer programs, such as currently exist in the United States, than with a fully general tax of the form (13.39).[32] The essence of his analysis is that while patchwork tagging of individuals may leave some needy persons unaided, the loss in distributional power may well be offset by the efficiency gain of having lower marginal tax rates. In terms of our analysis, the losses with respect to criterion 1 may be more than offset by gains in criterion 3 (and 2). Overall, then, the case for a negative income tax is ambiguous.

The Congress is also reluctant to tackle the administrative difficulties of taxing income in kind. It is one thing for the Department of Commerce to provide aggregate estimates of in-kind income, but individual's records of their in-kind income would surely be haphazard. One can well imagine endless IRS-taxpayer disputes over individual reporting methods. Given the dollar amounts involved, it hardly seems worth the effort.

---

[31] The U.S. Department of Health, Education and Welfare financed an experimental program in New Jersey in which low-income families were offered various different kinds of subsidy formulas to test their effects on work effort. The experimental nature of the program makes it difficult to assess the results, which are summarized in H. Watts and A. Rees, eds., *The New Jersey Income Maintenance Experiment, Vol II: Labor-Supply Responses* (New York: Academic Press, Inc., 1977). 1977). Generally speaking, the supply responses were small, suggesting that neoclassical theory may overstate the problem of satisfying criterion 2. Chapter 1 by Rees contains a useful summary, pp. 5–32.

[32] G. Akerlof, "The Economics of 'Tagging,'" *American Economic Review*, March 1978.

In contrast to the other exclusions, there does not appear to be any good reason for retaining the interest exclusion on state and local bonds, other than the fact that any change in the tax laws creates a pattern of horizontal inequities (see below). The exclusion was presumably designed as a subsidy to state and local governments, the subsidy equal to the reduction in debt service made possible by the municipals' tax-free status. But this is a particularly inefficient form of subsidy from the federal government's point of view. Suppose a state government can offer an interest rate of 8 percent rather than 10 percent because of the exclusion, a savings of $20 of interest income on each $1,000 bond. The problem is that only investors who can save more than $20 in taxes will be interested in the municipal. For example, at the assumed interest rates, a person in the 25 percent tax bracket can make $80 net of tax by purchasing the tax-free bond, but only $75 net of tax if he buys the taxable bond at 10 percent. The point is that the U.S. Treasury sacrifices more than $1 in tax revenue for every $1 of interest subsidy received by a state or locality. A direct subsidy ("grant in aid") for capital expenditures will effect the same amount of subsidy on a straight dollar-for-dollar basis. The grant in aid, if designed properly (see Chapter 31), can also avoid an efficiency loss caused by having two otherwise identical debt instruments offering different rates of return.

The interest exclusion also seriously violates vertical equity as represented by the rate schedules, the more so the lower the interest rates or the wider the spread between the rates on equal-risk taxable and tax-free bonds. A number of critics find this feature particularly objectionable. For instance, if the respective interest rates were 1 percent and 2 percent, instead of 8 percent and 10 percent, only taxpayers above the 50 percent tax bracket would be interested in the municipals. In the 1940s and 1950s, when rates were roughly in this range, the vast majority of all municipal bonds were owned by taxpayers in the top 1 percent of the income scale.[33] Alternatively, high rates coupled with a wide spread would also limit the bond's appeal to the higher income investor. At a spread of 8 percent and 12 percent, for example, only investors above the 33 percent bracket would want municipals. (The actual spread will depend upon the number of potential high-income buyers relative to the supply of municipals.) For a number of reasons, then, this interest exclusion would appear to be a legitimate target of tax reform.

Deductions. All deductions (except business expenses) necessarily violate the vertical equity criterion because the value of a deduction varies directly with the marginal tax rate. Hence, deductions can only be justified on the grounds that they promote other socially desirable ends. The intent of the medical and charitable deductions in this regard is obvious. The state and local tax deduction is still another attempt to subsidize lower level governments by making it easier for them to raise taxes. The violation of vertical equity

---

[33] Ott and Meltzer review a number of studies of municipal bond holdings that were done in the 1940s and 1950s. The results of these studies vary considerably, but they suggest that anywhere from two thirds to virtually all municipal bonds outstanding at the time were held by the upper 1 percent income group. D. Ott and A. Meltzer, *Federal Tax Treatment of State and Local Securities* (Washington, D.C.: The Brookings Institution, 1963), p. 11.

inherent in that deduction is simultaneously a defect and a virtue, since every additional dollar increase in a state and local tax increases the total burden on that government's taxpayers by only $\$(1-t)$, where t is the marginal tax bracket of an individual under the federal income tax. In effect, the deduction serves as a federal revenue-sharing program.

Finally, the deduction for interest paid on mortgages (and other consumer debt) is merely one peg of a concerted effort on the part of the federal government to encourage home ownership, one that includes special below-market VA and FHA mortgage rates, the establishment of the Savings and Loans Associations in 1933 under the control of the Federal Home Loan Bank Board, and a whole host of measures designed to keep funds available to savings banks at low cost, including interest-rate ceilings on bank deposits and minimum purchase requirements for competing financial assets. In fact, there are three major inducements to home ownership within the federal income tax itself, the other two being the deduction for local property taxes and the exclusion of income in kind for owner-occupied dwellings. White and White place the direct cost of these subsidies at $10 billion in 1970.[34] Given the federal government's commitment to home ownership generally, it is understandable that Congress chooses to use the income tax to this end at some sacrifice to vertical equity.

Capitalization and Tax Reform.   It is tempting to argue for simplifying the tax system by removing all the exemptions, exclusions, and deductions and collecting taxes on the entirety of the Haig-Simons income base, with a negative tax, or subsidy, available for all families below some specified level of income. In *Federal Tax Policy*, Pechman says that this would be "difficult to implement" (p. 71), but he clearly favors a move in that direction. He concludes his discussion of the personal income tax as follows:

> Further improvement through broadening the tax base and lowering the tax rates would pay handsome dividends in still greater equity, simplification, and better economic performance (p. 122).[35]

Since Pechman is careful to present both sides of all issues, it is not entirely clear exactly how he would broaden the tax base. He does favor reducing personal deductions to the ". . . most essential items . . ." (business expenses, for one) (p. 90), and he appears to favor such reforms as removal of tax shelters (p.121), including interest income on state and local bonds (p. 113), and taxing realized capital gains at the full rate (p. 107). In any event he clearly believes the existing erosion of the tax base generates horizontal and vertical inequity and higher rates than necessary (p. 70). The rate reductions would in turn promote economic efficiency because, as we will discover in Chapter 15, the inefficiency created by any distorting tax (subsidy) is directly related to the level of its marginal tax (subsidy) rates.

Pechman's argument is certainly appealing. After all, he is proposing a simplified tax system which promises unambiguous equity and efficiency gains.

---

[34] M. J. White and L. J. White, "The Tax Subsidy to Owner-Occupied Housing—Who Benefits?," *Journal of Public Economics*, February 1977, p. 111.

[35] Pechman, *Federal Tax Policy*, pp. 70–122.

We suspect most public sector economists would accept his arguments with respect to efficiency, administrative costs, and vertical equity. But the case for horizontal equity is much less certain. If one accepts Haig-Simons income as the best tax base, and the traditional interpretation of horizontal equity that says equals should pay equal *taxes*, then there is nothing more to be said. All exemptions, exclusions, and deductions (except business expenses) violate horizontal equity and should be removed, exactly as Pechman suggests. But if one believes Haig-Simons income is at best only a proximate measure for utility, and that horizontal equity really defines equals in terms of tax burden, or utility sacrificed, in accordance with the Feldstein principle, then the situation is more complex. The problem is that the competitive market system automatically tends to react to these "loop-holes" in such a way as to remove their advantages. The market is said to *capitalize* the tax advantages into higher market prices. A complete analysis of how the market shifts the burden (gains) of taxes (subsidies) will be presented in Chapters 15 and 17. At this point we only wish to gain an intuitive feel for the adjustment process.

Consider, for example, the three concessions to home ownership that increase its attractiveness relative to renting. Once these provisions become law, or even earlier if the law is correctly anticipated, an owner-occupied house becomes a more valuable asset, and the demand for owner-occupied housing will rise relative to the demand for rental housing, bidding up its price. As a consequence, suppliers of housing will find it more profitable to build (or convert to) owner-occupied dwellings. The market's shift to home ownership will presumably continue until a new long-run equilibrium is established, at which point the marginal suppliers and demanders are once again indifferent between owning or renting. The tax advantages will then have been fully capitalized, and it would be possible to find two otherwise identical individuals, one owning and one renting, without any implication of horizontal inequity. Since they were free to choose their desired form of housing, they both must have equal utility. It also follows that the homeowner now requires all the tax breaks just to derive the same utility from owning the home as the other does from renting. Horizontal inequity will arise only if the tax "loopholes" are *removed*.[36]

---

[36] Professor Bittker tells an amusing anecdote, illustrating the principle of capitalization, about an eager young law student who searches in vain for the beneficiary of a tax-sheltered apartment building in his hometown known as Rainbow Gardens. The tax shelter had been in existence since the inception of federal income taxation, under the Revenue Act of 1913. Rainbow Gardens was for sale, but the law student quickly surmised that at the asking price he would only realize a normal return on his investment. He also learned that the current owners were selling because they, too, were only able to earn a normal return despite the existence of the tax shelter. The same had been true of the previous owner, the one before that, and so on. Alas, they all paid too much to realize a monopoly return from the tax shelter. The persistent student was able to trace the line of ownership all the way back to one R. E. Greison, who had purchased Rainbow Gardens in 1896. Mr. Greison possessed remarkable foresight. In 1896 he was clerking for a U.S. Supreme Court justice when the Court ruled that a federal income tax was unconstitutional. Greison nonetheless predicted correctly that the Court's decision would eventually be overturned by a constitutional amendment (the 16th), and further that the income tax law, when drafted, would tax shelter apartment buildings. Based on these predictions, he bought Rainbow Gardens. Sad to say, capitalization predated Greison. His epitaph read: "Sacred to the memory of R. E. Greison, who learned that before every early bird, there is an earlier bird." B. Bittker, "Tax Shelters and Tax Capitalization or Does the Early Bird Get a Free Lunch," *National Tax Journal*, December 1975.

The same analysis applies to any tax loopholes. Feldstein's analysis of the effects of capitalization can be summarized as follows:[37]

> once the market system establishes a long-run equilibrium in response to a given tax system, the tax system *per se* cannot be a source of horizontal inequity, where horizontal equity is defined in terms of burden or utility.

Corollary to this fundamental principle of *tax design* is an equally fundamental principle of *tax reform.*

> any reform of an existing tax code will create horizontal inequities through unanticipated gains and losses, and will continue to do so until a new long-run equilibrium obtains in the market place.

Continuing with the housing example, suppose the three loopholes favoring home ownership were suddenly removed in the interests of promoting horizontal equity. Assuming the long-run equilibrium had been achieved, current homeowners will be sure losers, and not necessarily because they lose a tax advantage that had been unfairly given them, as the reformers intend. Rather some of them will lose because they never received any gain in the first place, given the prices they paid for their houses. Unfortunately, these pure losses are an unavoidable consequence of any tax reform that removes the "loopholes," including Pechman's proposal. This is not necessarily a telling argument against tax reform, because the reforms do presumably improve vertical equity. But it does indicate once again the practical difficulties of achieving equitable taxation under commonly accepted ability-to-pay criteria, given that sacrifice is properly related to individual utilities and not simply to taxes paid (or subsidies received).

SUMMARY

Chapter 13 has emphasized that the problem of designing equitable general taxes is one of the most vexing in all of public sector economics. Theory offers two guidelines for tax design, the interpersonal equity conditions and the ability-to-pay doctrine. But ability to pay is subject to various interpretations, and none of them is necessarily consistent with interpersonal equity. Furthermore, even if theoretical principles can be agreed upon, it is extremely difficult to determine who has actually gained or lost from a given tax system, and who will gain or lose from particular tax reforms.

A brief review of the federal personal income tax served to highlight these problems. It pays lip service to the ability-to-pay doctrine on paper, but there are many slips in application. The chapter considered a number of reforms that would make the tax conform more closely to traditional ability-to-pay principles, but we were forced to admit these reforms would not necessarily make the tax more equitable under a broader interpretation of these same principles.

---

[37] Feldstein, "On the Theory of Tax Reform," pp. 94–97.

REFERENCES

Akerlof, G. "The Economics of 'Tagging.'" *American Economic Review*, March 1978.

Aronson, J. R., and Maxwell, J. *Financing State and Local Governments*. 3d ed. Washington, D.C.: The Brookings Institution, 1977.

Bittker, B. "Tax Shelters and Tax Capitalization or Does the Early Bird Get a Free Lunch." *National Tax Journal*, December 1975.

Boskin, M. "On Some Recent Econometric Research in Public Finance." *AEA Papers and Proceedings*, May 1976.

Diamond, P. A. "Inflation and the Comprehensive Tax Base." *Journal of Public Economics*, August 1975.

Feldstein, M. "Does the United States Save Too Little." *AEA Papers and Proceedings*, February 1977.

————. "On the Theory of Tax Reform." *Journal of Public* Economics, July–August 1976 (International Seminar in Public Economic and Tax Theory).

Friedman, M. *Capitalism and Freedom*. Chicago: University of Chicago Press, 1962.

Goode, R. *The Individual Income Tax*. Rev. ed. Washington, D.C.: The Brookings Institution, 1976.

Haig, R. M. "The Concept of Income: Economic and Legal Aspects." *The Federal Income Tax*. Edited by R. M. Haig. New York: Columbia University Press, 1921.

Kaldor, N. *An Expenditure Tax*. London: George Allen & Unwin, Ltd., 1955.

Meltzer, A., and Ott, D. *Federal Tax Treatment of State and Local Securities*. Washington, D.C.: The Brookings Institution, 1963.

Mill, J. S. *Principles of Political Economy*. Edited by W. J. Ashley. London: Longmans, Green & Co., Ltd., 1921.

Musgrave, R. A. *The Theory of Public Finance*, New York: McGraw-Hill Book Co., 1959.

Okner, B., and Pechman, J. *Who Bears the Tax Burden?* Washington, D.C.: The Brookings Institution, 1974.

Pechman, J. *Federal Tax Policy*. 3d ed. Washington, D.C.: The Brookings Institution, 1977.

Rees, A., and Watts, H., eds. *The New Jersey Income Maintenance Experiment, Vol II: Labor-Supply Responses*. New York: Academic Press, Inc., 1977.

Sadka, E. "On Progressive Taxation." *American Economic Review*, December 1976.

Simons, H. C. *Personal Income Taxation*. Chicago: University of Chicago Press, 1938.

Smith, A. *The Wealth of Nations*, vol. II. Edited by E. Cannan. New York: G. P. Putnam's Sons, 1904.

Stern, P. *The Great Treasury Raid.* New York: Random House, 1964.

Summers, L. "Capital Taxation and Accumulation in a Life Cycle Growth Model." Paper read at *NBER Conference on the Taxation of Capital*, National Bureau of Economic Research, Inc., Cambridge, Mass., November 16 and 17, 1979.

Tobin, J. "On Improving the Economic Status of the Negro." *Daedalus,* Fall 1965.

White, L. J., and White, M. J. "The Tax Subsidy to Owner-Occupied Housing—Who Benefits?" *Journal of Public Economics,* February 1977.

The theory of public expenditures and taxation:
second-best analysis

14

Introduction to second-best analysis

First-best analysis offers us a complete, tightly reasoned, internally consistent normative theory of the public sector, but despite this impressive accomplishment the theory is not entirely satisfactory. In many respects it is unrealistic and therefore unresponsive to the needs of policymakers. First-best models ignore a number of important real-world phenomena that the policymaker cannot ignore.

The strengths and weaknesses of first-best theory derive from a common source, the fact that the only restrictions on a first-best policy environment are the two sets of restrictions inherent in any economic system, the underlying production relationships and market clearance for all goods and factors. In particular, those sectors of the market economy not subject to government intervention are assumed to be perfectly competitive, and the admissible set of government policy tools includes anything necessary to achieve a social welfare maximum. For instance, the government can redistribute any good or factor lump sum; it can change the price of any good or factor to any consumer or firm; and it can commandeer inputs and supply outputs at will, subject as always to given production relationships. In short, the government has sufficient degrees of freedom to achieve the "bliss point" by designing whatever policies are necessary to restore pareto optimality and bring society to its utility-possibilities frontier, and then moving society along the frontier to the bliss point by means of lump-sum redistributions.

Second-best analysis is essentially a reaction to these heroic first-best assumptions. In an attempt to be more realistic it posits at least one additional constraint on the policy environment either in the surrounding market environment or in the set of admissible government policy tools. An immediate implication is that the search for the social welfare maximum covers a restricted set of allocations and distributions relative to first-best theory, illustrated by the shaded portion in Figure 14–1. The defining difference from first-best analysis is that the restricted set cannot include point B, the "bliss point," since adding binding restrictions must reduce the maximum attainable level of social welfare. Whether or not any points on the first-best utility-possibilities frontier are feasible depends on the nature of the additional constraints, but such points might not be policy relevant anyway. As illustrated in Figure 14–1, point A on

FIGURE 14–1

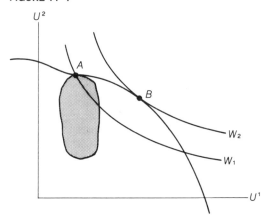

U^2-U^1 is dominated by any point within the shaded portion and above the social welfare indifference curve W_1.

The entire thrust of second-best analysis is toward increased realism. For instance, second-best theory recognizes that no government redistributes income strictly on a lump-sum basis. Taxes and transfers are almost always distorting. Similarly, all market economies contain some monopoly or monopsony elements that are unlikely to disappear in the foreseeable future. Policy analysis should incorporate these real-world phenomena, which will appear as additional constraints in a formal general equilibrium model. As noted in Chapter 3, the most common government policy restrictions employed to date in the professional literature have been the inability to make lump-sum redistributions; the necessity of raising tax revenue in a distorting manner; requiring government agencies or entire governments to operate within a legislated budget constraint; and assuming that governments will either draft some production inputs or offer some outputs free of charge, or at least at prices below opportunity costs. The most common market restriction assumes the existence of maintained monopoly power somewhere in the private sector, so that at least one private sector price does not equal marginal opportunity costs.

The set of potential policy and market restrictions is obviously limited only by the imagination of public sector theorists. Moreover, individual constraints can always be combined, each additional constraint further restricting the set of viable allocations and distributions. Thus, the possibilities for analysis are virtually endless. There can never be *a* second-best normative theory of the public sector as there is with first-best theory.

Despite the possibility for endless variation, there has been some degree of consistency in the second-best literature. Most research has followed the lead of two seminal articles, "The General Theory of Second-Best," by Archibald

Lipsey and Kelvin Lancaster, and "Optimal Taxation and Public Production," by Peter Diamond and James Mirrlees.[1]

The Lipsey-Lancaster article appeared first and clearly sparked the enormous interest in second-best theorizing over the past 15 years. In their model some specific price-cost margins are assumed to be fixed, either because of private monopoly power or distorting government taxes, neither of which the government is willing or able to change. Other than these specific restrictions, the government has as much freedom to act as it has in the first-best environment, including the ability to redistribute income lump sum. Lipsey and Lancaster were specifically interested in the following question: Given invariant distortions in some markets, are the first-best pareto-optimal rules for other markets still consistent with social welfare maximization? The answer turned out to be "no," in general. Subsequent research has expanded their analysis to consider the effects of maintained distortions on first-best public expenditure decision rules and on the welfare implications of changing the pattern of distorting taxes. One can ask, for example, whether substituting one set of distorting taxes for another, while holding tax revenue constant, increases social welfare, given the existence of still other distortions.

Another large body of literature has adopted the Diamond-Mirrlees framework of analysis. In their paper the only maintained restriction is that the government must raise some tax revenue by means of distorting taxation, but the government is otherwise free to vary all price-cost margins, exactly as in first-best analysis. One then asks the same kinds of questions as in the Lipsey-Lancaster model, with one addition. Since all tax rates are under the government's control, it is meaningful to consider the optimal pattern of distorting taxation for raising a given amount of revenue.

THE STATE OF THE ART

While most second-best research has adopted either a Lipsey-Lancaster or Diamond-Mirrlees framework, such broad classifications will undoubtedly become less useful over time as economists explore new sets of restrictions and combine them in novel ways. The future course of second-best theory can hardly be predicted, but it will almost certainly continue to challenge our ways of thinking about public sector problems. The second-best research of the past 15

---

[1] R. Lipsey and K. Lancaster, "The General Theory of Second-Best," *Review of Economic Studies*, vol. 24 (1), no. 63, 1956–57; and P. Diamond and J. Mirrlees, "Optimal Taxation and Public Production," *American Economic Review*, March, June 1971 (2 parts, Part I: Production Efficiency and Part II: Tax Rules).

There are two other seminal articles which are frequently referenced in the second-best literature: M. Boiteux, "On the Management of Public Monopolies Subject to Budgetary Constraints," *Journal of Economic Theory*, September 1971 (Boiteux's article first appeared in the January 1956 *Econometrica* in French); and J. Stiglitz and P. Dasgupta, "Differential Taxation, Public Goods, and Economic Efficiency," *Review of Economic Studies*, April 1971.

For an excellent (but difficult) summary of second-best methodology, see J. Green, "Two Models of Optimal Pricing and Taxation," *Oxford Economic Papers*, November 1975.

years may be somewhat limited in scope, but it has nonetheless had a remarkable impact on public sector economics, both tax and expenditure theory. We will conclude the chapter with some brief reflections on the current state of the art.

The allocational theory of taxation, which analyzes the welfare losses caused by distorting taxes, dates from the very beginning of public sector economics and has, by its very nature, always been part of the theory of the second-best. The recent application of formal, second-best, general equilibrium models to tax problems has mainly served to sharpen existing knowledge. But there have also been a few extensions, most notably in the context of many-person economies. We now have a more precise understanding of the trade-offs between equity and efficiency in a second-best environment. Finally, tax theory has recently become more tightly integrated with public expenditure theory.

These contributions by themselves would represent a significant achievement for second-best analysis, but they are fairly minor compared with the impact of the second-best on public expenditure theory. It has been nothing short of revolutionary.

Until 15 years ago the received doctrine on public expenditures was the first-best theory of Part II. Since then it has literally been devastated by second-best theorizing. One might have anticipated this to some extent. Adding constraints to a general equilibrium model will obviously alter its first-order conditions, and with them the resulting policy decision rules, but the alterations have hardly been trivial. Second-best public expenditure decision rules often bear little relationship to their first-best counterparts, to the point where many economists now seriously question the policy relevance of such cherished old "standards" as $\sum MRS = MRT$ for consumption externalities, or marginal cost pricing, with subsidy, for decreasing cost firms. What is worse, it is by now painfully obvious that the current state-of-the-art second-best policy rules may not have much policy relevance either. As researchers invent new ways to constrain economic systems, they will necessarily develop still different, perhaps quite different, policy guidelines for the standard problems. As noted earlier, second-best theory is inherently a theory in flux.

As if this were not disconcerting enough, three additional attributes of the second-best public expenditure results already in hand have proven especially disheartening. To begin with, second-best public expenditure rules typically lack the comfortable intuitive appeal of the first-best rules. As we discovered throughout Part II, first-best policy rules always have close competitive market analogs. The correct price for decreasing cost services is a pseudo-competitive price, and externality problems can be viewed as instances of market failure, meaning that a competitive market structure can always be described that will generate the correct pareto-optimal rules. These interpretations arise precisely because all first-best decision rules are simple combinations of marginal rates of substitution and transformation. Such is not the case for the second-best rules. The marginal terms are present, to be sure, but so are a number of terms embedded in the additional constraints that do not have natural competitive market interpretations. Hence the first-best principle that the government should do what the competitive market would have done had it been able to operate no longer applies, a discouraging note for believers in the competitive market system.

A second disappointment is that the first-order conditions of second-best general equilibrium models do not generally dichotomize into distinct sets of pareto-optimal and interpersonal equity conditions. Recall that first-best models dichotomize because the government is assumed to be able to lump sum redistribute in order to satisfy the interpersonal equity conditions of social welfare maximization. In their quest for realism, second-best models usually deny the government that option, with the result that *all* second-best optimality conditions combine elements such as marginal rates of substitution (transformation), which appear only in first-best efficiency rules, *and* social welfare terms, which first-best theory isolates into the interpersonal equity conditions. Normative prescriptions such as "place a unit tax on each person's consumption of this particular good" tend to be replaced or modified by rules such as "tax those goods that are consumed relatively more by people with low social welfare weights." But since we have no useful theory of interpersonal equity comparisons, these policy rules tend not to be terribly compelling. Economists can take some comfort in the knowledge that the second-best policy rules are useful to public officials so long as the officials are willing to provide the social welfare weights. But this is a far cry from having a complete normative theory of the public sector.

Many economists avoid the social welfare terms altogether by resorting to the fiction of the one-consumer equivalent economy, but these models can do little more than highlight the efficiency aspects of public sector problems. We will use one-consumer models for this purpose as well, but it should be understood that their policy implications are uncertain, unless it is assumed that distributional equity has been achieved. However, without lump-sum redistributions, this can occur only by chance (alternatively, does anyone seriously believe that preferences are identical and homothetic?). Moreover, given the possibility of unequal social welfare weights, it will always be possible to specify some pattern of weights such that the efficiency aspects of any given policy rule become relatively unimportant. Needless to say, this is extremely troublesome for normative public sector theory.

The final problem is that second-best restrictions tend to affect *all* markets, not just those in which public expenditures occur. By way of contrast, first-best models have the property that government intervention in any one market will not change the pareto-optimal rules for other goods and factors. They can be allocated in competitive, decentralized markets. This is no longer true in a second-best environment. The Lipsey-Lancaster theorem says that if price-cost margins are distorted in some markets, then first-best competitive efficiency rules are, in general, no longer optimal for other markets. Roughly the same result applies in the Diamond-Mirrlees framework. If the government must raise revenue by means of distorting taxation, it is generally optimal to tax all goods and factors (save one). The thrust of second-best analysis, therefore, is toward pervasive rather than limited government intervention, another discouraging result for free market advocates.

PHILOSOPHICAL AND
METHODOLOGICAL UNDERPINNINGS

Second-best theory differs from first-best theory primarily in terms of its results, the optimal policy rules. It shares the same philosophical and methodological foundations as first-best theory, by and large. For instance, consumer sovereignty remains the fundamental value judgment of second-best theory, and distributional considerations are most often represented by a Bergson-Samuelson individualistic social welfare function. Second-best analysis is also closely tied to the competitive market system. This is best illustrated by the observation that much of the second-best literature uses general equilibrium models expressed wholly or in part in terms of competitive market prices, not quantities. Analytical constructs such as indirect utility functions, expenditure functions, production functions expressed in terms of market supply (input-demand) functions, and generalized profit functions abound in second-best analysis, and they all implicitly assume competitive market behavior. Utility functions and production frontiers expressed in terms of quantities, the fundamental building block of our first-best model, are used only sparingly in second-best analysis.

There is an obvious reason why this has happened. The second-best literature has primarily been concerned with restrictions in the form of price-cost differentials. Clearly, models already specified in terms of prices can incorporate these distortions more readily than models specified in terms of quantities. In turn, the easiest way to convert a general equilibrium quantity model to a price model is by assuming competitive price-taking behavior. Thus, in nearly all second-best models, consumers are assumed to maximize utility subject to a fixed-price budget constraint. They have no monopoly or monopsony power. Producers are typically viewed as decentralized, perfectly competitive profit maximizers, often with simple production relationships exhibiting either constant costs or constant returns to scale. Even the government transacts at the competitive producer prices to the extent it buys and sells inputs and outputs. Of course, a second-best model might posit constraints implying noncompetitive behavior for a small subset of markets, but the underlying market economy is competitive. Second-best results may not have competitive interpretations, but the models used to date have been competitive through and through.

In summary, while second-best theory has severely challenged all first-best policy rules, it has taken only the smallest, most hesitant steps away from the highly stylized first-best policy environment. Second-best analysis is more realistic, but only slightly so.

PREVIEW

With these reflections in mind, we will begin our second-best analysis with the allocational theory of taxation, thereby reversing the order of presentation in Part II. This happens to coincide with the historical development of second-best theory, but that is really beside the point. There are two good analytical reasons for considering tax theory first. On the one hand, second-best tax theory is inherently simpler than second-best expenditure theory, in this sense. Public expenditure theory requires the specification of a distinct problem (e.g., an externality) and one or more distinct constraints (e.g., distorting taxation), whereas tax theory requires only the specification of a constraint. Saying that all taxes must be distorting is at once an additional constraint on the system and the source of the problem being analyzed in tax theory. Consequently, problems in tax theory can be analyzed with much simpler general equilibrium models. This is an important advantage. Second-best models are significantly different from the first-best model of Part II, enough so that it pays to begin the analysis as simply as possible. In fact, the initial chapters on tax theory have two goals. Their obvious purpose is to demonstrate some important theorems in the allocational theory of taxation, but they will also serve as a careful introduction to second-best methodology.

Second-best tax theory is also logically prior to public expenditure theory, so long as distorting taxes are one of the policy constraints. Having studied the effects of distorting taxation in isolation, its implications for externalities or decreasing cost production will be that much more apparent. Therefore, Chapters 14–17 contain a detailed analysis of the theory of distorting taxes, often without any consideration of how governments actually spend tax revenues. Chapters 18–22 will then rework selected public expenditure problems from Part II within a second-best framework—for example, aggregate externalities, nonexclusive goods, decreasing costs—using the constraints most commonly employed in the literature.

REFERENCES

Boiteux, M. "On the Management of Public Monopolies Subject to Budgetary Constraints." *Journal of Economic Theory,* September 1971 (translation from French, *Econometrica*, January 1956).

Diamond, P. A., and Mirrlees, J. "Optimal Taxation and Public Production" (2 parts, "Part I: Production Efficiency" and "Part II: Tax Rules"). *American Economic Review,* March, June 1971.

Green, J. "Two Models of Optimal Pricing and Taxation." *Oxford Economic Papers,* November 1975.

Lancaster, K., and Lipsey, R. "The General Theory of Second-Best." *Review of Economic Studies,* vol. 24 (1), no. 63, 1956–57.

Stiglitz, J., and Dasgupta, P. "Differential Taxation, Public Goods, and Economic Efficiency. *Review of Economic Studies,* April 1971.

15

The second-best theory of taxation in one-consumer economies with linear production technology

The second-best theory of taxation explores the effects of distorting taxes on social welfare. (Transfer payments are automatically included in the analysis because they can always be viewed as negative taxes.) A distorting tax is one that prevents at least one of the pareto-optimal conditions necessary for first-best allocational efficiency from holding, that is, it forces society inside its first-best utility-possibilities frontier. According to this definition, then, any tax which causes at least two economic agents in the same market to face a different set of prices will be distorting in an otherwise perfectly competitive market economy.[1] Moreover, any nondistorting tax, by definition, is a lump-sum tax. In point of fact, virtually all taxes actually employed by governments, whether they be sales, excise, income, or wealth taxes, introduce some distortion into the economy.

Because tax distortion is defined relative to pareto optimality, the bulk of the literature on second-best tax theory has treated it strictly as an allocational theory, concerned only with questions of economic efficiency. Consequently, the analysis typically occurs within the context of one-consumer economies, a simplification that makes sense if one were willing to ignore distributional issues. As Chapter 14 noted, however, recent second-best analysis has shown that allocational and distributional issues do not dichotomize in a second-best environment without lump-sum taxes and transfers, thereby questioning the policy relevance of considering the efficiency aspects of distorting taxes independently from their distributional consequences. Probably no one today would recommend a set of taxes simply on the basis of their efficiency properties. Nonetheless, it is analytically convenient to isolate the efficiency effects of taxes by using one-consumer economy models and then consider the tax rules in many-person economies as a combination of efficiency and distributional elements, with the latter represented by welfare weights derived from an individualistic social welfare function. We will take this approach in developing the theory.

There are three predominant issues in the allocational theory of taxation:

1. Relative to the first-best optimum, what is the loss in social welfare associated with any given set of distorting taxes (including a single tax)?

---

[1] Assuming continuous marginal rates of substitution and transformation.

Hotelling provided the first rigorous analysis of this issue in his 1938 article, "The General Welfare in Relation to Problems of Taxation and of Railway and Utility Rates."[2] Harberger rekindled interest in this question in two separate articles appearing in 1964, "Taxation, Resource Allocation and Welfare" and "The Measurement of Waste."[3] By now the literature is voluminous, but these three articles stand as the modern classics.

2. Relative to the first-best optimum, what pattern of distorting taxes minimizes the loss in social welfare for any given amount of tax revenue the government might wish to raise? This question has been explored under two separate assumptions: (a) that the government can tax all goods and factors and (b) that a subset of goods and factors must remain untaxed. The study of optimal taxation under the first assumption is commonly referred to as the optimal commodity tax problem, with the seminal contribution by Frank Ramsey in "A Contribution to the Theory of Taxation" (1927). Diamond and Mirrlees' "Optimal Taxation and Public Production" is a recent classic.[4]

Explorations of optimal taxation under the second assumption are a much more recent phenomenon.[5] We will defer discussion of restricted optimal taxation until Chapter 16 when we consider an important subset of that literature, the theory of optimal income taxation.

3. Holding tax revenues (or the government budget constraint) constant, what is the change in social welfare from substituting one set of distorting taxes for another. Once again, the literature on this question is voluminous, but the classic reference is Corlett and Hague, "Complementarity and the Excess Burden of Taxation."[6]

Since most of the formal analysis of these three questions employs general equilibrium models specified in terms of prices, we will switch at this point from quantity models to price models in order to familiarize the reader with the

---

[2] H. Hotelling, "The General Welfare in Relation to Problems of Taxation and of Railway and Utility Rates," *Econometrica*, July 1938.

[3] A. Harberger, "Taxation, Resource Allocation and Welfare," in National Bureau of Economic Research and the Brookings Institution, *The Role of Direct and Indirect Taxes in the Federal Revenue System*, (Princeton N.J.: Princeton University Press, 1964), and A. Harberger, "The Measurement of Waste," *American Economic Association Papers and Proceedings*, May 1964. An excellent recent reference is J. Green and E. Sheshinski, "Approximating the Efficiency Gains of Tax Reforms," *Journal of Public Economics*, April 1979.

[4] F. P. Ramsey, "A Contribution to the Theory of Taxation," *Economic Journal*, March 1927; and P. Diamond and J. Mirrlees, "Optimal Taxation and Public Production" (2 parts, "Part I: Production Efficiency" and "Part II: Tax Rules"), *American Economic Review*, March, June 1971. Two excellent surveys of the optimal tax literature are A. Sandmo, "Optimal Taxation," *Journal of Public Economics*, July–August 1976; and D. Bradford and H. Rosen, "The Optimal Taxation of Commodities and Income," *AEA Papers and Proceedings*, May 1976. Finally, P. Diamond and D. McFadden, "Some Uses of the Expenditure Function in Public Finance," *Journal of Public Economics*, vol. 3, 1974, contains an excellent analysis of some of the second-best tax issues analyzed in this chapter.

[5] Dixit presents a lucid analysis of restricted taxation using the model to be developed in this chapter. A. Dixit, "Welfare Effects of Tax and Price Changes," *Journal of Public Economics*, February 1975. Also A. Dixit and K. Munk, "Welfare Effects of Tax and Price Changes: A Correction," *Journal of Public Economics*, August 1977.

[6] W. Corlett and D. Hague, "Complementarity and the Excess Burden of Taxation," *Review of Economic Studies*, vol. 21 (1), no. 54, 1953–54.

prevalent second-best methodology. General equilibrium price models can be rather complex or extremely simple depending upon the assumptions made with respect to demand and the underlying production technology for the economy. Choices on demand range from one-consumer (equivalent) economies to H-person economies with interpersonal equity rankings determined by a Bergson-Samuelson social welfare function. The key choice with respect to production technology is whether production exhibits linear or general technology, and if the latter, whether it is constant returns to scale or something different. The choice of production technology also has direct implications for the way in which market clearance is specified.

In order to highlight the economic intuition of tax distortions we will begin with the simplest possible general equilibrium model, a one-consumer economy with linear aggregate production technology. The one-consumer assumption removes all distributional considerations so that welfare loss means inefficiency. Positing a linear technology is also enormously convenient. As discussed in Chapter 4, linear technology implies constant marginal (opportunity) costs along a linear production-possibilities frontier. But since the economy is assumed to be perfectly competitive, this means that all relevant production parameters can be described by a vector of fixed producer prices, assumed equal to the constant marginal costs (or value of marginal products for factors). Furthermore, output supply (and input demand) curves are perfectly elastic at the fixed prices within the boundaries of the aggregate production frontier. Hence, market clearance is implicit because supplies (input demands) auto- matically expand or contract to meet the consumer's demands (factor supplies). That is, output is completely demand determined. Market clearance is also irrelevant to the determination of prices.

The only problem with the linear technology assumption is that its simplicity tends to mask the role of production in determining the welfare costs of tax the distortions. Fortunately, however, a fair number of properties of distorting taxes do carry over virtually intact from linear to general technologies, especially if the latter exhibit constant returns to scale. In any case, we will relax the assumption of linear technology in Chapter 16.

THE MEASUREMENT OF LOSS
FROM DISTORTING TAXES

Let us turn first to question 1: Relative to the first-best optimum, what is the social welfare loss resulting from any given pattern of distorting taxes, within the context of a one-consumer, linear production economy? With one consumer, loss in social welfare is equivalent to the consumer's loss in utility. To be con- crete, assume the distorting taxes (transfers) take the form of unit taxes on both the consumer's purchases of goods and services and his supply of factors, paid by the consumers. In principle, then, the taxes include most forms of sales and excise taxes on the product side and income taxes on the factor side. In practice, however, only income taxes are typically paid by consumers. Sales and excise taxes are usually paid by the firm. But, as we shall discover in Chapter 17, it makes no difference to loss measurement which side of a given market actually pays a tax, so the assumption that consumers pay the tax is of no consequence. Hence, the only distorting taxes specifically ruled out at this point are taxes paid by certain firms (consumers) but not others, such as a tax on corporate income.

The Geometry of Loss Measurement:
Partial Equilibrium Analysis

The analysis of welfare loss from distorting unit taxes dates from the beginnings of public sector theory and has appeared for decades in economic texts at all levels, including introductory principles texts. Figure 15–1 depicts the standard textbook analysis of the loss from a single tax. S and D represent the zero-tax market supply and demand curves for a particular product, and D' is the demand curve given that the government levies a unit tax paid by the consumers, equal in amount to the vertical distance between D and D'. As a result of the tax, equilibrium output drops from X_0 to X_T, and the price to the consumer rises to $q = p + t$, where t is the unit tax. With constant producer prices, the price to the consumer rises by the full amount of the tax. The government collects revenue equal to $X_T \cdot t$. The so-called *deadweight* or *efficiency* loss of the tax is measured by the triangle *abc*, according to the following argument.

Because the tax causes the consumer price to rise from p to q, the consumer loses Marshallian consumer surplus in amount equal to the trapezoidal area *qpac*. Some of this loss is captured by the government as revenue $X_T \cdot t$, the rectangle $q \cdot pbc$. Presumably it will be used to finance some socially beneficial expenditures. But the loss of triangle *abc* is captured by no one. It is a pure or deadweight welfare loss, created directly by the distorting tax which forces producers and consumers to face different prices for a given product. The loss triangle is indicative of the fact that the pareto-optimal condition $MRS = MRT$ no longer holds in this market.

FIGURE 15–1

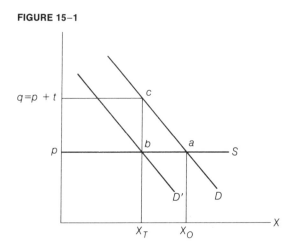

FIGURE 15–2

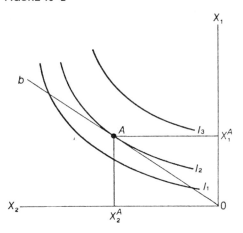

The traditional analysis is intuitively instructive, but it is obviously not a valid general equilibrium presentation of the loss question. It cannot capture the effects on loss of further price changes in other markets. Nor is Marshallian consumer's surplus a meaningful compensation measure of loss, in general.[7] In fact, as one might suspect, its use can be seriously misleading. For instance, one "theorem" commonly derived from this framework is that the government should tax products whose demand (or supply) is perfectly inelastic in order to avoid deadweight loss. If either the demand or supply curve in Figure 15–1 were vertical, output will remain constant, and there will be no deadweight loss triangle resulting from the unit tax. Unfortunately, this proposition is not accurate. Unit taxes can generate welfare loss, properly measured, even if demand or supply is perfectly inelastic.

The Geometry of Loss Measurement:
General Equilibrium Analysis[8]

The first task, then, is to develop a proper and unambiguous measure of the welfare loss resulting from distorting taxes in a full general equilibrium context. To capture the intuition behind the measure, we will continue with a graphical analysis but switch from the partial equilibrium supply-demand framework to a valid general equilibrium representation using the consumer's indifference curves and the economy's production-possibilities frontier.

Suppose the consumer buys a single good X_1 and supplies a single factor, X_2, (e.g., labor, measured negatively), with preferences $U(X_1, X_2)$, represented by the indifference curves I_1, I_2, and I_3 in Figure 15–2. In addition, assume

---

[7] Refer to Chapters 4 and 9 for a discussion of this point.
[8] The analysis in this section draws heavily on unpublished class notes provided to us by Professors Peter Diamond and Paul Samuelson of MIT. See also Diamond and McFadden, "Some Uses of the Expenditure Function in Public Finance."

FIGURE 15-3

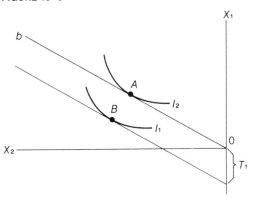

producers can transform X_2 into X_1 according to the linear technology $X_1 = a \cdot X_2$, where a is the marginal product of X_2 (labor). The pp frontier is depicted as line segment Ob in Figure 15–2. All feasible (X_1, X_2) combinations lie on or to the southwest of Ob. Given the consumer's preferences and the economy's production possibilities, point A is obviously the first-best welfare optimum for the economy. A can be achieved by a competitive equilibrium, with relative prices p_{X_2}/p_{X_1} equal to the slope of the production frontier. That is, $p_{X_1} = p_{X_2}/a = MC_{X_1}$, the standard competitive result. To see that this is a general market equilibrium, note that with $p_{X_2}/p_{X_1} = a$, the pp frontier Ob becomes a budget line for the consumer, with zero lump-sum income (payment).

(15.1)
$$\frac{p_{X_2}}{p_{X_1}} = a = \frac{X_1}{X_2}$$

(15.2)
$$p_{X_1} \cdot X_1 = p_{X_2} \cdot X_2$$

Thus, the consumer will purchase the bundle (X_1^A, X_2^A). Furthermore, with competitive pricing Ob represents the objective profit function for the firm and indicates that the firm just breaks even. There are no pure economic profits (losses) to distribute to the consumer. Thus, (15.2) applies for both the consumer and producer, and point A is the pretax competitive general equilibrium for the economy.

The first point to stress is that *any* tax on the consumer creates a loss in utility. Suppose the government places a lump-sum tax on the consumer in amount equivalent to T_1 units of X_1. Lump-sum taxes are nondistorting by definition, but the tax shifts the consumer's budget line down everywhere by T_1 and forces him to a new equilibrium, point B in Figure 15–3. Clearly the utility at B is less than the utility at A; the consumer has suffered a loss. Yet because lump-sum taxes are nondistorting, they cannot possibly create any "deadweight" loss. Hence the loss $U(A) - U(B)$ must be considered an unavoidable consequence of any tax and should not be included in the measure of loss arising from tax distortion.

FIGURE 15-4

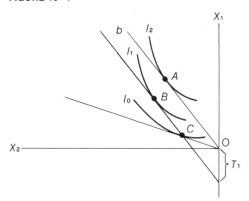

To see that a distorting tax creates loss in addition to this unavoidable loss, place a unit tax, t_1, on the consumption of X_1 such that it raises the same amount of revenue as the lump-sum tax. This tax will change the relative prices faced by the consumer from p_{X_2}/p_{X_1} to $p_{X_2}/(p_{X_1} + t_1)$, while leaving the relative producer prices at p_{X_2}/p_{X_1}. Since the consumer and producers now face different relative prices, $MRS_{X_1,X_2} \neq MRT_{X_1,X_2} (\equiv MP_{X_2}^{X_1})$, pareto optimality cannot obtain, and the tax is distorting, by definition. The consumer will arrive at a new equilibrium, depicted by point C in Figure 15-4. Notice that the lump-sum and the unit taxes raise the same amount of revenue, T_1 units of X_1,[9] but equilibrium points B and C differ. In general, C will be to the south and east of B, as drawn. The reason is that the unit tax introduces a *substitution effect* because of the relative price change that is absent from the lump-sum tax. The *income effects* of the two taxes are identical by construction, each measured by the lost tax revenue, but the added substitution effect will cause the consumer to purchase less X_1 and *less* X_2 (more negative X_2, the "good"—for example, leisure) than with the lump-sum tax. Moreover, C will generally offer a lower level of utility than B, also as drawn. This follows from revealed preference. When the consumer purchased B with the lump-sum tax, he was able to purchase C. However, when he purchased C, he was unable to purchase B. Hence, B is revealed preferred to C. Only if the indifference curves are right angled, so that there will be no substitution effect with the unit tax, will the two taxes generate the same aftertax equilibrium and thus the same loss in utility.

The additional loss in utility from B to C, then, can be considered the *avoidable loss* of the distorting unit tax, the loss equivalent to the deadweight loss triangle in the supply and demand presentation of Figure 15-1. This is the loss society will be interested in minimizing. Furthermore, the graphical analysis suggests that the amount of the avoidable loss for any distorting tax

---

[9] It is always possible to construct equal-revenue taxes by positing any given unit tax, finding the new equilibrium, and constructing a line through this equilibrium parallel to the no-tax budget line to represent the equivalent lump-sum tax.

depends upon the magnitude of the substitution effect between goods and factors, and the level of the tax rate.

Of course, we would not want to measure the avoidable loss as the difference in utility levels $U(B) - U(C)$, since this measure is not invariant to monotonic transformations of the utility index. What is required is an unambiguous income measure of the avoidable utility loss. As we have already discussed in Chapter 9 when considering the "hard case" for decreasing cost services, such income measures involve the notion of compensation. There is an infinity of acceptable choices, one of which can be obtained from the following conceptual experiment:

1. Place a unit tax on the consumer's purchases of one of the goods or factors, say, X_1.
2. Simultaneously transfer to the consumer enough income, lump sum, to keep him on the original zero-tax indifference curve.
3. Include in this income the tax revenue collected from the unit tax.
4. Ask if the tax revenue alone is sufficient compensation. If not, then measure the loss as the difference between the lump-sum income necessary to compensate the consumer less the tax revenue collected and then returned lump sum. Since utility is being held constant at the original no-tax equilibrium, this measure utilizes Hicks Compensating Variation resulting from the (relative) price change.

Consider first the lump-sum tax by this measure of loss. No matter what the size of the tax, if the consumer receives the revenue lump sum simultaneously as it is collected from him lump sum, he will obviously remain at the original no-tax equilibrium. No further lump-sum income will be necessary as compensation, and the loss measure will be zero, as it must be. With the unit tax, however, the tax revenue will not be sufficient compensation and the loss measure will be positive, providing the substitution effect is nonzero. This case is depicted in Figure 15–5.

FIGURE 15–5

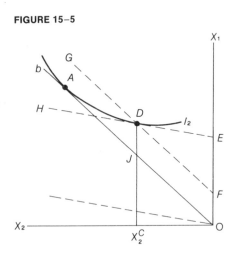

Given the compensation, the consumer remains on indifference curve I_2 as the budget line rotates in response to the tax. Suppose the consumer winds up at point D. D is a market equilibrium in which the consumer faces the with-tax price line HE and simultaneously receives compensation lump-sum equal to OE (in terms of X_1). The tax revenue collected (and returned) *at the compensated equilibrium D* equals EF units of X_1, the difference between the no-tax and with-tax price lines at D projected back to the X_1 axis. Hence, the distance OF measures the loss, the income (in units of X_1) required in excess of the tax revenue to compensate the consumer for the tax. So long as the tax produces a substitution effect, OF will be positive.

Note, finally, that society cannot produce the compensated equilibrium D since it lies outside its production-possibilities frontier Ob. This is another useful way of conceptualizing the notion of deadweight or avoidable loss, that society cannot satisfy the entire set of *compensated* goods-demands and factor-supplies from its own resources given distorting taxes. For suppose the consumer supplies the compensated amount of X_2, X_2^C. Producers can only supply J units of X_1 given this amount of X_2. Hence, the vertical distance $(D-J)$ provides an alternative measure of loss, equal to OF, the amount of X_1 which the government would have to obtain from an outside source to compensate the consumer fully for the unit tax.[10]

It should be understood that these compensation experiments are merely conceptual exercises, useful for deriving certain analytical properties of distorting taxes but not indicative of actual government policies. There is no reason to suppose a compensated equilibrium would ever actually be observed, and of course there is nothing in the normative theory of the public sector to suggest that governments ought to return the tax lump sum.

The Analytics of General Equilibrium Loss Measurement

Extending the concept of efficiency loss from distorting taxation to N goods and factors, and any given pattern of existing taxes, can be accomplished quite easily by means of the expenditure function from the theory of consumer behavior, defined as:

$$M(\vec{q}; \bar{U}) = \sum_{i=1}^{N} q_i X_i^C(\vec{q}; \bar{U})$$

where:

$\vec{q}$ = the vector of consumer prices, with element q_i.

$X_i^C(\vec{q}; \bar{U})$ = the compensated demand (supply) for good (factor) i.

$M(\vec{q}; \bar{U})$ gives the lump-sum income for any vector of consumer prices necessary to keep the consumer at utility level $\bar{U}$. But if $\bar{U}$ is set equal to the

---

[10] Alternatively, the dotted line $G-F$ represents a production-possibilities frontier in which producers receive a lump-sum transfer of OF units of X_1 from an outside source. Given this transfer, and with the ratio of *producer* prices $p_{X_2}/p_{X_1} = a$, competitive production can achieve the compensated equilibrium D.

original zero-tax utility level, that is, $\bar{U} = U^0$, then $M(\vec{q}; \bar{U}^0)$ is precisely the income measure required for the conceptual experiment described in the preceding section.[11] Furthermore, with linear technology there can be no pure profits (losses) in the economy. Hence, it is reasonable to assume that

$$M(\vec{p}; \bar{U}^0) \equiv 0$$

where:

    $\vec{p}$ = the vector of producer prices, assumed fixed and equal to marginal costs.

With this assumption, the loss for any given tax vector is simply the value of the expenditure function at the gross of tax consumer price vector less the tax revenues collected and returned (conceptually) lump sum, or

$$(15.3) \qquad L(\vec{t}) = M(\vec{q}; \bar{U}^0) - \sum_{i=1}^{N} t_i \cdot X_i^C(\vec{q}; \bar{U}^0)$$

where:

    $\vec{q} = \vec{p} + \vec{t}$, and $\vec{t}$ is the vector of unit taxes, with element t_i.

The tax revenue is the only source of income available to the consumer.

Notice that the tax revenue is the revenue that would be collected at the fully compensated equilibrium, corresponding to point D in Figure 15–5. To be consistent, the conceptual experiment must assume that compensation is actually paid, in which case the tax revenues collected from the vector of rates $\vec{t}$ is $\vec{t} \cdot X(\vec{q}; \bar{U}^0)$. Actual tax collections, equal to $\sum_{i=1}^{N} t_i X_i(\vec{q}; 0)$, where $X(\vec{q}; 0)$ represents the consumer's ordinary or Marshallian demand (supply) curves, are irrelevant to this conceptual loss experiment.

Relating equation (15.3) to Figure 15–5, then, $M(\vec{q}; U^0)$ corresponds to the distance OE, $\sum_{i=1}^{N} t_i X_i^C(\vec{q}; \bar{U}^0)$ corresponds to the distance EF, and $L(\vec{t})$ corresponds to the distance OF.

Before analyzing the expression for loss further, we want to stress that the expenditure function $M(\vec{q}; \bar{U}^0) \equiv M(\vec{p} + \vec{t}; \bar{U}^0)$ is, *by itself*, a valid general equilibrium model of a one-consumer economy with linear technology, when coupled with the standard assumption of perfectly competitive markets. On the demand side, the expenditure function incorporates all relevant aspects of the consumer's behavior. On the supply side, the price vector $\vec{p}$ specifies all relevant production parameters, since relative producer prices will equal marginal rates of transformation with perfect competition. Finally, market

---

[11] It should be noted that the choice of $\bar{U}$ is arbitrary in that any constant utility level will generate the same analytical expressions for total and marginal loss. Setting $\bar{U} = U^0$ is certainly a natural choice when measuring the loss from distorting taxation, since loss is then defined explicitly with reference to the zero-tax, nondistorted economy. As noted in the text, setting $\bar{U} = U^0$ coincides with the conceptual loss experiment described above. On the other hand, setting $\bar{U}$ equal to the utility level obtained with lump-sum taxation would also define loss with respect to a nondistorted economy, and would correspond to our introductory discussion of loss as represented in Figure 15–4, in which loss is defined in terms of $U(C)$ versus $U(B)$, two equal-tax-revenue equilibria.

clearance is implicit. It is understood that supplies (input demands) respond with perfect elasticity to the consumer's demands (factor supplies) at the specified price vector $\vec{p}$, and that the consumer automatically supplies all factors used in production and receives all the goods produced. Moreover, the resource limitations defining the outward limits to these supply responses depend entirely on the consumer's willingness to supply factors, which is already incorporated in $M(\vec{q}; \bar{U}^0)$. Also, once $\vec{t}$ is set by the government, $\vec{q}$ is determined by the relationships $\vec{q} = \vec{p} + \vec{t}$. Separate market clearance equations are not needed to determine equilibrium price vectors. Thus, given that $M(\vec{q}; \bar{U})$ is a valid general equilibrium specification of a one-consumer economy with linear technology, it follows immediately that equation (15.3), along with the relations $\vec{q} = \vec{p} + \vec{t}$, is a valid general equilibrium specification of the conceptual loss experiment described in the preceding section.

Marginal Loss

As a first step in determining the policy implications of distorting taxation, consider the marginal loss from a small change in one of the unit taxes, t_k, all other taxes held constant.

$$(15.4) \quad \frac{\partial L(\vec{t})}{\partial t_k} = \frac{\partial M(\vec{q}; \bar{U}^0)}{\partial t_k} - \frac{\partial \left[\sum_{i=1}^{N} t_i X_i^C(\vec{q}; \bar{U}^0) \right]}{\partial t_k} \quad k = 1, \ldots, N$$

$$(15.5) \quad \frac{\partial L(\vec{t})}{\partial t_k} = M_k - M_k - \sum_{i=1}^{N} t_i M_{ik} \quad k = 1, \ldots, N$$

$$(15.6) \quad \frac{\partial L(\vec{t})}{\partial t_k} = - \sum_{i=1}^{N} t_i M_{ik} \quad k = 1, \ldots, N$$

where:

$$M_k = \frac{\partial M}{\partial q_k}$$

$$M_{ik} = \frac{\partial X_i^C}{\partial q_k} \quad \text{the substitution terms in the Slutsky equation}$$

The derivatives take on these values because of the assumption of linear technology, which fixes the vector of producer $\vec{p}$. In the kth market, represented by Figure 15–6, demand shifts down by the amount of the tax, and in the new equilibrium the consumer price q_k increases by the full amount of the tax. Thus $dq_k = dt_k$, with p_k constant. The change in t_k may well affect demand (factor supply) in some other markets, say, the market for good j, as represented in Figure 15–7. Output increases from X_j^0 to X_j^1, but there will be no change in the equilibrium price q_j, since neither p_j nor t_j can change as t_k is varied. p_j is constant because technology is linear, and t_j is a control variable for the government, assumed constant.

FIGURE 15–6

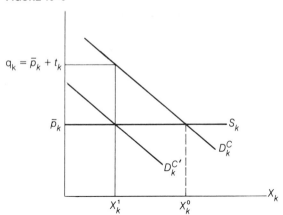

FIGURE 15–7

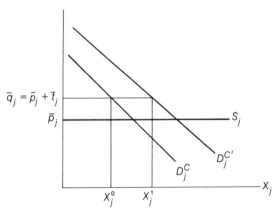

Hence the derivative $\partial M/\partial t_k = \sum_{i=1}^{N} (\partial M/\partial q_i)(\partial q_i/\partial t_k)$ contains the single term $(\partial M/\partial q_k)(\partial q_k/\partial t_k) = \partial M/\partial q_k = M_k$, and similarly for $\partial X_i^C(\bar{q}; \bar{U}^0)/\partial t_k$.

Notice that expression (15.6) for marginal loss confirms the results suggested by the one-good, one-factor graphical analysis, and that the marginal loss from changing a distorting tax depends only upon the level of taxes already in existence and the Slutsky substitution effects between all pairs of goods and factors, the M_{ik}.

Total Loss for Any Given Pattern of Taxes

Equation (15.3) gives one valid general equilibrium measure of the total loss from any given vector of distorting taxes, $\bar{t}$. An alternative expression for total loss can be derived by integrating the N expressions for marginal loss and summing over all markets. Hence:

$$(15.7) \quad L(\vec{t}) = \sum_{i=1}^{N} \int_0^{t_i} \frac{\partial L}{\partial t_i} dt_i = \sum_{i=1}^{N} \int_0^{t_i} \frac{\partial L(q_1, \ldots, q_{i-1}; s; p_{i+1}, \ldots, p_N)}{\partial s} ds$$

Substituting (15.6) into (15.7) yields:

$$(15.8) \qquad L(\vec{t}) = \sum_{i=1}^{N} \int_0^{t_i} - \sum_{j=1}^{i} t_j M_{ij} dt_i$$

The summation inside the integral sign of (15.8) indicates that the taxes are being introduced market by market. Thus $t_j = 0, j > i$. Moreover, since $M_{ij} = M_{ji}$ from the symmetry of the Slutsky substitution terms, the order of integration is irrelevant. That is, the order in which the government actually levies the given vector of taxes will not affect the measurement of total welfare loss resulting from the entire set of taxes.

As it stands, (15.8) is an exact measure ot total welfare loss for a one-consumer economy with linear technology. It can be related to the standard notion of deadweight loss triangles, properly measured using compensated demand curves, if the compensated demand derivatives, $M_{ik} = \partial X_i^C(\vec{q}; \bar{U}^0)/\partial q_k$ are assumed constant, that is, if compensated demand curves are assumed to be linear over the relevant range of prices. With this assumption, the M_{ij} can be taken outside the integrals so that (15.8) becomes:

$$(15.9) \qquad L(\vec{t}) = \sum_{i=1}^{N} \left(-\sum_{j=1}^{i-1} t_j M_{ji} \int_0^{t_i} dt_i - M_{ii} \int_0^{t_i} t_i dt_i \right)$$

Performing all N integrations yields:

$$(15.10) \qquad L(\vec{t}) = -\sum_{i=1}^{N} \left(\sum_{j=1}^{i-1} t_j t_i M_{ji} + \frac{1}{2} M_{ii} t_i^2 \right)$$

Rearranging terms:

$$(15.11) \qquad L(\vec{t}) = -\frac{1}{2} \sum_i \sum_j t_i t_j M_{ij}$$

Arnold Harberger first derived an expression of this form in his 1964 articles "Taxation, Resource Allocation and Welfare" and "The Measurement of Waste."[12]

---

[12] Harberger, "Taxation, Resource Allocation and Welfare," and Harberger, "The Measurement of Waste." Harberger refers to the Slutsky substitution terms specifically in each article, but only as special cases. Generally, his $\partial X_i/\partial q_j$ refer to the general equilibrium response of the X_i along the production-possibilities frontier, not the movement along the consumer's zero-tax indifference curve. See Chapter 26 for additional discussion. Harberger clarifies the meaning of his "demand" derivatives in A. Harberger, "Three Basic Postulates for Applied Welfare Economics," *Journal of Economic Literature*, September 1971; and A. Harberger, *Taxation and Welfare* (Boston, Mass.: Little, Brown and Co., 1974), pp. 86–90.

FIGURE 15–8

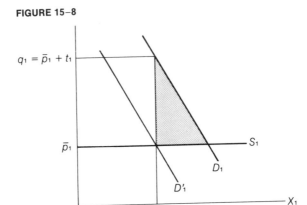

To relate this expression to deadweight loss triangles, rewrite (15.11) as:

$$(15.12) \qquad L(\vec{t}) = -\frac{1}{2} \sum_{i=1}^{N} t_i \sum_{j=1}^{N} t_j M_{ij} = -\frac{1}{2} \sum_{i=1}^{N} t_i \sum_{j=1}^{N} t_j \frac{\Delta X_i^C}{\Delta q_j}$$

$$= -\frac{1}{2} \sum_{i=1}^{N} t_i \Delta X_i^C$$

under the assumptions of constant M_{ij}, and $dq_j = dt_j$ for a linear technology economy. (15.12) suggests that the total loss from a given vector of taxes can be approximated as the sum, over all markets, of deadweight loss triangles in each market, as taxes are added seriatim. But one has to be very careful with this interpretation, since the quantity base of these triangles, the ΔX^C in (15.12), represents the total general equilibrium change in each X_i in response to the *entire set* of tax distortions $t_j, j = 1, \ldots, N$. Thus, it is not correct to sum deadweight loss triangles as they are traditionally presented in partial equilibrium analysis, even with the proper compensated demand curves.

Consider a two-good example in which the imposition of t_1 precedes the imposition of t_2.[13] As t_1 is imposed, the loss at that point is correctly approximated by the shaded triangle in Figure 15–8. D_1 and D'_1 are the pre- and post tax compensated demand curves for X_1 (at the zero-tax utility level) under the assumption that $q_2 = p_2$, the producer price of good 2. D_2 may shift in response to t_1, but with no resulting addition to (subtraction from) loss since its price equals marginal cost. Hence, loss is properly measured as

$$\frac{1}{2} t_1^2 \frac{\partial X_1^C}{\partial q_1} = \frac{1}{2} \cdot t_1 \cdot \frac{\partial X_1^C}{\partial q_1} \cdot \Delta q_1 = \frac{1}{2} \cdot t_1 \cdot \Delta X_1^C$$

FIGURE 15-9

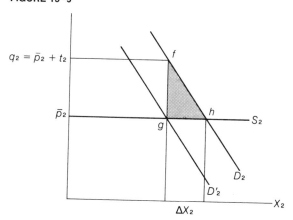

the shaded triangle. It immediately follows that the traditional representation of loss as a triangle in D-S space is accurate for a single tax, providing the compensated demand curves are employed.

When t_2 is imposed, it creates an additional loss in the market for good 2 which can be represented by the shaded triangle in Figure 15-9. The compensated pre- and post tax demand curves D_2 and D'_2 assume that $q_1 = p_1 + t_1$, the gross of tax price for good 1. The triangle equals $\frac{1}{2} \cdot t_2 \cdot M_{22} \cdot t_2 = \frac{1}{2}t_2 \cdot \Delta X_2^C$. However, if we simply add this loss triangle to the loss triangle in Figure 15-8 for good 1 and stop, we will have ignored a third term in the expression for loss given by equation (15.10), equal to $(-)t_1 \cdot t_2 \cdot M_{12}$, ot $t_1 \cdot \partial X_1^C/\partial q_2 \cdot \Delta q_2$. Given that t_1 exists, the response of X_1 to a change in the price of X_2 entails a further source of loss since price no longer equals marginal cost for good 1. This loss equals the change in tax revenue collected from good 1 as its demand shifts. If demand shifts to D''_1 as depicted in Figure 15-10, then the shaded rectangular area (*abcd*) must be added to the standard deadweight loss triangle

FIGURE 15-10

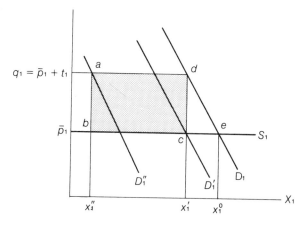

(*cde*) to compete the total loss associated with the market for good 1 resulting from the entire set of taxes t_1 *and* t_2. Note that D_1'' assumes $q_2 = p_2 + t_2$, whereas D_1' assumes $q_2 = p_2$. Thus, total loss from both markets is the trapezoidal area *abed* in Figure 15–10 plus the triangle (*fgh*) in Figure 15–9.

The analysis generalizes directly to N goods (and factors) in which rectangles of the form $t_i \cdot \Delta X_i$ in markets for which taxes already exist are added (subtracted) to the standard dead weight loss triangles $\frac{1}{2} t_k \cdot \Delta X_k$ as taxes t_k are added seriatim. The triangles correspond to the terms $-\sum_i \frac{1}{2} M_{ii} t_i^2$ in equation (15.10); the rectangles to the terms $-\sum_{i=1}^{N} \sum_{j=1}^{i-1} t_j t_i M_{ji}$.[14]

Policy Implications of the Loss Measures

Despite the simplicity of the one-consumer, linear technology model, the expressions (15.6) and (15.11) for marginal and total loss, respectively, convey a number of important policy implications on distorting taxation, all of which follow directly from the fact that both marginal and total loss depend only upon the level of existing tax rates and the Slutsky substitution effects. We will offer seven such implications as a representative sampling.[15]

a. The Zero Tax Economy versus the Existing Tax Economy. An immediate implication from the expression for marginal loss (15.6) is that if there are no tax distortions in the economy, then the imposition of a marginal tax on one of the goods or factors will not create any significant deadweight loss. Under these conditions the *level* of all tax rates is either exactly or approximately equal to zero so that marginal loss is also (approximately) zero. In other words, the first marginal distortion is free. The intuition behind this result is that all resource transfers in response to the new marginal tax occur at values (approximately) equal to their marginal costs. But if so, then returning the tax revenue will be sufficient compensation for the distortion.

---

[14] The loss measure (15.11) can be directly related to our earlier discussion of the gain or loss to the consumer for any given change in consumer prices. In Chapter 9 we showed that the gain or loss for any price change can be represented as a summation of areas behind the consumer's compensated demand (and supply) curves between the old and new prices in each market. The result followed from the fact that

$$(15.13) \qquad M(q^1; \bar{U}) - M(q^0; \bar{U}) = \sum_{i=1}^{N} \int_{q_i^0}^{q_i^1} \frac{\partial M(q_1^1, \ldots, q_{i-1}^1; s; q_{i+1}^0, \ldots, q_N^0; \bar{U})}{\partial s} ds$$

$$(15.14) \qquad = \sum_{i=1}^{N} \int_{q_i^0}^{q_i^1} X_i^C(q_1^1, \ldots, q_{i-1}^1; s; q_{i+1}^0, \ldots, q_N^0; \bar{U}) ds$$

where: $X_i^C(\bar{q}^1; s; \bar{q}^0; \bar{U})$ is the demand for X^i compensated at utility level $\bar{U}$, and evaluated at $q_j = q_j^1$, $j < i$ and $q_j = q_j^0$, $j > i$. With $\bar{U} = U^0$, these areas measure Hicks Compensating Variation. In the tax problem $t_i = \Delta q_i = q_i^1 - q_i^0$ and $M(\bar{q}_0; \bar{U}) = 0$, so the loss measure from distorting taxes corresponds directly to this earlier loss measure. The original measure gives the entire area behind each demand curve, for example, area $p_1 e d q_1$, in Figure 15–10. As such it captures only the change in the value of the expenditure function in response to the tax, that is, it ignores the disposition of the tax revenue. The tax loss measure recognizes that the revenue $p_1 b a q_1$ can be put to some socially useful purpose. Conceptually, it is simply returned lump sum to the consumer. Hence, the net or deadweight loss caused by the distortion is just the trapezoidal area *abed*.

[15] An unpublished paper by P. A. Samuelson entitled "Theory of Optimal Taxation" discusses a number of the implications presented here.

Of course, the zero-tax, zero-loss result is really just a theoretical *curiosum*. All developed countries have complex tax structures that raise substantial amounts of revenue. Thus, the policy relevant conclusion to be drawn from (15.6) is that even a marginal tax change can generate significant losses in welfare, precisely because resources are shifting from an initial position in which marginal values may be far from their marginal costs. The government cannot choose to ignore the efficiency implications of minor changes in the tax structure simply because the changes are "small."

b. Proportional Taxes Generate No Deadweight Loss. Equations (15.6) and (15.11) indicate that the deadweight loss from distorting taxes depends fundamentally on the Slutsky substitution terms, the M_{ij}. But substitution effects can only arise from changes in *relative* prices, which move the consumer along a given indifference curve. Thus, if all prices change in the same proportion, relative prices will remain unchanged, and there can be no deadweight loss from these taxes.

This can be seen directly from rewriting equation (15.11) as

$$(15.15) \qquad\qquad L(\vec{t}) = -\frac{1}{2} \sum_{i=1}^{N} t_i \sum_{j=1}^{N} t_j M_{ij}$$

Suppose $t_j = \alpha q_j^0$, all $j = 1, \ldots, N$ so that all prices change in the same proportion, $(1 + \alpha)$.[16] (15.15) becomes:

$$(15.16) \qquad L(\vec{t}) = -\frac{1}{2} \sum_{i=1}^{N} t_i \sum_{j=1}^{N} \alpha \cdot q_j^0 M_{ij} = -\frac{1}{2} \sum_{i=1}^{N} t_i \alpha \sum_{j=1}^{N} q_j^0 M_{ij}$$

But compensated demands (factor supplies), $M_i = X_i^C(\vec{q}; \bar{U}^0)$, are homogeneous of degree zero in all prices. Thus, $M_i[(1 + \alpha)\vec{q}^0; \bar{U}^0] = M_i(\vec{q}^0; \bar{U}^0)$, and from Euler's theorem on homogeneous functions $\sum_{j=1}^{N} q_j M_{ij} = 0$, all $\vec{q}$. Hence, $L(\vec{t}) = 0$.

Unfortunately, governments may not be able to use proportional taxation. With no pure profits in the system, the value of the expenditure function at the zero-tax equilibrium $M(\vec{p}; \bar{U}^0)$ could well be zero, as we have been assuming. In this case a proportional tax on all goods *and factors* raises no revenue because

$$\sum_{i=1}^{N} t_i X_i(\vec{q}; \bar{U}) = \alpha \sum_{i=1}^{N} q_i^0 X_i(\vec{q}; \bar{U}^0) = 0$$

Since variable factor supplies enter the expenditure function with a negative sign, the rule "set $t_j = \alpha q_j^0$, all $j = 1, \ldots, N$" implies taxing goods and *subsidizing* factors, the net effect of which raises no revenue for the government. If, instead, $M(\vec{q}^0; U^0) = k, k > 0$, then a proportional tax (subsidy) on all goods and factors at rate α will collect revenue equal to $\alpha \cdot k$. But since $M(\vec{q}^0; U^0)$ includes both goods and variable factor supplies, k must be a source of lump-sum income, most likely, income from a factor in *absolutely* fixed supply, meaning that both its substitution and income effects are identically zero. Thus, an alternative would be simply to tax the income from this factor at rate α, a tax which cannot

---

[16] $q_j = \bar{p}_j + t_j = \bar{p}_j + \alpha q_j^0$. But $q_j^0 = \bar{p}_j$. Hence, $q_j = \bar{p}_j + \alpha \bar{p}_j = (1 + \alpha)\bar{p}_j$.

possibly be distorting. Henry George once proposed a tax on land rents for just this reason.[17] Less obvious is the equivalent alternative of taxing all goods and subsidizing all variable factors at the same rate (assuming land rents are the only source of lump-sum income).

In conclusion, the ability to levy proportional taxes is essentially the ability to tax lump sum. For this reason proportional taxation is hardly an interesting proposition from the view-point of second-best tax theory. The allocational theory of taxation ought properly concern itself only with taxes that generate distortions by changing the vector of *relative* prices.

c. The Efficiency Properties of Income Taxes. Income taxes are held in high regard by many public sector economists. On the one hand, a number of economists view income taxes as the most equitable of all general taxes. As we discussed in Chapter 13, they believe that income broadly defined as accretion in purchasing power best satisfies the ability-to-pay principle of equitable taxation.

Income taxes are also seen as being reasonably efficient, based on a large empirical literature which indicates that the supply of labor and capital are both extremely price inelastic. Recent analysis using micro data sets has suggested that there may be some wage elasticity in the supply of labor for certain subsets of the labor market, principally women, and that the interest elasticity of household savings may be as high as $|.4|$,[18] but the weight of all the empirical evidence on these elasticities places their values very close to zero. If these elasticities actually were zero, there would be a presumption for supporting income taxation on efficiency grounds as well, since factor supplies would not respond to the imposition of a tax.

This argument must be made very carefully however. Nearly all the empirical studies measure $\partial X_i/\partial q_i$, the derivative of the ordinary market supply curves with respect to changes in supply prices, whereas the relevant derivatives for efficiency loss are the Slutsky substitution effects $M_{ii} = \partial X_i^c/\partial q_i$. These two derivatives are related, of course, through the Slutsky equation, $\partial X_i/\partial q_i = \partial X_i^c/\partial q_i - X_i(\partial X_i/\partial I)$. If one observes $\partial X_i/\partial q_i = 0$, the crucial question is whether the ordinary price derivative takes on a zero value because both the substitution and income effects are zero, or because the substitution and income effects cancel one another out. If the former is true, then indifference curves are right angled, the compensated factor supply is invariant to changes in relative prices, and taxing the factor will not produce any deadweight loss. Income from these factors is truly lump sum. However, if the derived elasticity merely reflects a canceling of income and substitution effects, the ordinary supply curve may be vertical, but taxing the factor can nonetheless generate a considerable amount of deadweight loss.

Unfortunately, the canceling story is quite possible for both the supply of labor and capital, since in each case the income and substitution effects work in

---

[17] H. George, *Progress and Poverty* (New York: Doubleday & Co., Inc., 1914), Book VII.

[18] See the excellent survey article by Michael Boskin on the savings and labor force participation effects of taxation. M. Boskin, "On Some Recent Econometric Research in Public Finance," *AEA Papers and Proceedings*, May 1976.

FIGURE 15–11

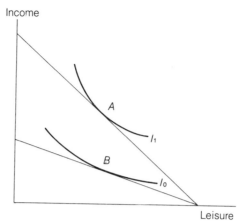

opposite directions. We argued the case for savings in Chapter 13. The same conclusion applies for the supply of labor. Consider the standard income-leisure model of neoclassical theory in which the consumer equates his *MRS* between income and leisure with the wage rate, as depicted in Figure 15–11.

The slope of the budget line equals the net-of-tax wage rate. Suppose the consumer is initially in equilibrium at point *A*, with no tax on wages. If the government imposes a wage tax, the budget line rotates downward and the consumer reaches a new equilibrium, at point *B*. The key issue is whether *B* is to the right or left of *A*, that is, whether work effort has increased or decreased. The substitution effect of the tax says that the consumer will substitute leisure for income. In turn, more leisure implies less work effort. Intuitively, marginal effort is penalized, so why work harder? The income effect says that because the price of one of the goods (income) has risen, real purchasing power has diminished, and the consumer will tend to "buy" less of both goods, income and leisure. But less leisure implies more work effort. Intuitively, the consumer has to work harder to maintain his standard of living. Thus, the overall effect of the tax on work effort is ambiguous. Therefore, unless empirical research can provide us with better estimates of the relevant substitution effects, it will not be of much help in assessing the efficiency implications of income taxes.

d. Direct versus Indirect Taxation. There is a large literature on the relative inefficiencies caused by direct versus indirect taxes, where direct taxes refer to taxes on factor supplies and indirect taxes to taxes on consumer goods and services. On balance the literature tends to favor direct taxation on efficiency grounds, but the logic of the presumption is unclear.[19] In theory, at least, equations (15.6) and (15.11) convey everything we need to know to settle the

---

[19] For example, see M. Friedman, "The Welfare Effects of an Income and an Excise Tax," *Journal of Political Economy*, February 1952; and more recently, E. K. Browning, "The Excess Burden of Excise vs. Income Taxes: A Simplified Comparison," *Public Finance*, 3, 1975. Clearly, the bias in favor of income taxes results from special assumptions in the models which, in effect, place restrictions on the values of certain M_{ij} terms.

issue of which taxes are best. Obviously there can be no general presumption in favor of direct taxes over indirect taxes, or vice versa. One can always postulate a set of M_{ij}'s and tax rates t_k that would tip the balance one way or the other.

The issue is ultimately an empirical one, but our current econometric knowledge of the relevant M_{ij}'s is very sparse indeed, and likely to remain so. There are at least three reasons for this. One problem is that the relevant M_{ij}'s are the individuals' M_{ij}'s, whereas econometric work is often forced to estimate aggregate market derivatives. In most empirical work it is never very clear what biases are created by using aggregated data. Second, even if these biases were well known, empirical demand equations for goods and services of the form $X^i = X^i(\vec{q}; I; \vec{Z})$, where $\vec{Z}$ represents a set of exogenous influences other than prices $(\vec{q})$ or income (I), are typically misspecified, in that the measure of income is seldom a true lump-sum measure. Rather it is most often a combination of income from lump-sum sources and variable factor supplies. As a consequence, if the researcher uses the estimated price and income coefficients to compute an estimated pure substitution effect via the Slutsky equation, the measure of this effect will be biased by the misspecification of the income term.[20] A third problem is that we would need to know the entire set of M_{ij}'s over time to resolve the issue, but our current knowledge of intertemporal Slutsky terms is virtually nil. As an empirical matter, then, statements in favor of either direct or indirect taxes must be largely conjectural, given current econometric knowledge. Furthermore, as the next section will demonstrate, the optimal pattern of taxes for raising any given amount of tax revenue will generally be a mix of both direct and indirect taxes, not one or the other.

e. If the Government Chooses to Collect All Revenue by Imposing a Single Distorting Tax, which Good or Factor Should It Tax?

Equation (15.11) provides the answer to this question. Consider the use of a single tax on good (factor) k versus a single tax on the good (factor) j to raise a given amount of revenue, $\bar{T}$. The loss using tax t_k is:

$$(-)\tfrac{1}{2}t_k^2 M_{kk} \qquad \text{assuming } t_i = 0, i \neq k$$

Similarly, the loss with the single tax t_j is $(-)\tfrac{1}{2}t_j^2 M_{jj}$. Which one dominates depends entirely on two factors: the relative values of M_{kk} and M_{jj} and the relative size of t_K and t_j necessary in each instance to raise the required revenue $\bar{T}$. The only real issue, then, is the standard empirical question: What confidence do we place in our estimates of M_{kk} and M_{jj}?

---

[20] In his Ph.D. thesis William Spaeth tried to isolate the lump-sum income effect in estimating the price and income responses of labor supply to a negative income tax. He used unearned income as the measure of income, and a proxy variable for the negative income tax rate based on unemployment compensation benefits. The results were mixed in that the computed Slutsky substitution effect had a perverse sign for all but prime-aged males, but at least he tried to avoid the misspecification noted in the text. On a positive note, the prime-aged males constituted the largest subset in his sample. W. Spaeth, *Labor Effort Disincentives of Negative Income Taxation*, unpublished Ph.D. dissertation, Boston College, April 17, 1974. See, also S. Rea, Jr., "Incentive Effects of Alternative Negative Income Tax Plans," *Journal of Public Economics*, vol. 3, 1974, pp. 237–49, for an attempt to isolate substitution and income effects on work effort.

f. The Issue of Tax Avoidance. People tend to favor taxes they can avoid fairly easily, meaning taxes on goods with high price elasticities for which substitutes are readily available. But these are precisely the taxes governments should avoid if they are concerned about deadweight loss, especially if the high price elasticities reflect large substitution effects as opposed to income effects. One immediate implication is that on efficiency grounds alone, taxes of goods and services ought to be levied by higher rather than lower level governments in the fiscal hierarchy, that is, the national government rather than the state governments, and by state governments rather than the local governments. If a city taxes some good such as cigarettes, substitutes are readily available in the form of cigarettes sold outside the city limits. In effect the tax artificially creates two goods, city cigarettes and non city cigarettes.[21] Obviously, a national cigarette tax is least likely to create artificial distinctions of this type.

g. Single Market Measures of Loss. Because of data limitations, empirical research is often forced to adopt partial equilibrium techniques and focus entirely on the market directly under considertaion. Unfortunately, partial equilibrium measures of tax loss can be especially misleading. They would compute the loss from a tax, t_k, as $(-)\frac{1}{2}t_k^2 M_{kk}$, ignoring all cross-product terms in equation (15.11). If t_k were the only tax this would be entirely appropriate, but since many goods and factors are taxed, it is not clear that the cross-product terms can be safely ignored.

One assumption commonly employed in empirical research to "justify" partial equilibrium analysis is that all cross-price elasticities are zero, but this assumption can only hold for ordinary demand (factor supply) derivatives. It cannot be imposed on the M_{ij}. Consumer theory offers precious few general theorems about consumer behavior, but it does tell us that $M_{kk} \leq 0$, and $\sum_{i=1}^{N} q_i M_{ik} = 0$, all $k = 1, \ldots, N$. These results, in turn, imply that at least one M_{kj} must be greater than zero, $j \neq k$. In other words, if the compensated demand (supply) for one good (factor) changes in response to a relative price change, then the compensated demand (supply) for at least one other good (factor) must change as well. As always it is the substitution terms that are relevant to second-best tax questions.[22]

Despite these lessons from consumer theory, public sector economists have been willing to employ the assumption that $M_{ij} = 0$, $i \neq j$, in order to get some rough indication of tax loss, even though there is no way of judging how accurate the resulting estimate is. To cite one recent example that is now widely referenced, Edgar Browning has estimated that the marginal cost of raising a dollar of income tax in the United States is currently in the range of $1.07 to $1.16, equal to the $1 of revenue plus $[.07–.16] of deadweight loss.[23] To obtain this

---

[21] City dwellers would also waste resources by traveling outside the city to purchase cigarettes. This waste is an addition to the standard deadweight loss.

[22] Researchers will also frequently assume away all income effects, so that $\partial X_i/\partial q_j = \partial X_i^C/\partial q_j$, all $i, j = 1, \ldots, N$, in order to justify the use of ordinary demand (factor supply) derivatives in their loss measures. Given this assumption, one cannot then assume away all ordinary cross-price derivatives.

[23] E. Browning, "The Marginal Cost of Public Funds," *Journal of Political Economy*, April 1976.

estimate Browning assumes that the loss for an individual consumer from a marginal increase in the income tax rate can be written as:

$$(15.17) \qquad d\mathscr{L}^h = (-)\alpha^h E_{LW}^h \cdot WL_h d\alpha^h$$

where:

α^h = the marginal tax rate for consumer h.

$E_{LW} = (\partial L_h / \partial W_h)(W_h / L_h)$, the compensated elasticity of labor supply with respect to the wage rate, assumed equal for all consumers.

W = the gross of tax wage (the "producer price"), assumed constant.

L_h = supply of labor for consumer h.

This is equivalent to our one-consumer measure of marginal loss for unit taxes,

$$dL = (-)t_k M_{kk} dt_k$$

with $t_k = \alpha^h W$ (α^h is an ad valorem tax on the gross of tax wage W), $M_{kk} = \partial L_h / \partial W$, $M_{ik} = 0$, $i \neq k$, and W constant (so that $dt_k = W d\alpha^h$). Making these substitutions into our measure, and multiplying and dividing by L_h, produces equation (15.17). Assuming that $E_{LW}^h = E_{L,W}$, all $h = 1, \ldots, H$, and that all consumers are in the same marginal tax bracket, α,

$$(15.18) \qquad dL^{\text{aggregate}} = (-)\alpha E_{LW}(W \cdot L)d\alpha$$

Next, Browning assumes as a first-order approximation that

$$(15.19) \qquad dT = (W \cdot L)d\alpha$$

Substituting (15.19) into (15.18) and rearranging terms yields:

$$(15.20) \qquad \frac{dL}{dT} = (-)\alpha E_{LW}$$

Browning believes the best single estimate of the marginal tax rate is .35 and cites some recent evidence that $E_{LW} \approx .2$ for the United States. Hence, he estimates $dL = .2(.35) = .07$.

Browning also provides a more complicated estimate based on the following considerations: (1) consumers with different incomes face different marginal tax rates; (2) exemptions and deductions in the federal income tax increase the marginal rates necessary to raise a dollar of revenue; and (3) a person's marginal tax rate is in part determined by other federal, state, and local taxes. With these additional considerations Browning is able to derive a range of estimates for dL/dT bounded by the values $|.07|$ and $|.16|$.

Browning's research is very carefully done, but the analysis rests on the illegitimate assumption that all compensated cross-elasticities with respect to wages are zero. As a result his single market estimates may well be unreliable.

THE OPTIMAL PATTERN OF COMMODITY TAXES

The second allocational question posed at the beginning of Chapter 15 asks the following: Suppose the government has to raise a given amount of tax revenue, $\bar{T}$, subject to the constraint that it must use distorting unit taxes paid by the consumer. If the government is free to tax or subsidize any good (or factor), what pattern of taxes raises the required revenue in such a way as to minimize deadweight loss in the economy? This is commonly referred to as the optimal "commodity" tax problem, with the understanding that "commodities" include both goods and factors.

Having defined the appropriate loss function for a one-consumer, linear technology economy, the optimal tax problem is a straightforward constrained loss minimization problem of the form[24]

$$\min_{(t_k)} L(\vec{t})$$

$$\text{s.t.} \sum_{i=1}^{N} t_i X_i^C = \bar{T}$$

Two assumptions are necessary to ensure that the first-order conditions will yield interesting results. First, we will continue to assume that the value of the consumer's expenditure function in the pretax equilibrium is zero, that is, $M(\vec{p}; \bar{U}^0) = 0$. If, to the contrary, $M(\vec{p}; \bar{U}^0) = k$, the loss-minimizing strategy obviously involves taxing the lump-sum income k at rate α such that $\bar{T} = \alpha k$. Since k is lump-sum income, there would be no deadweight loss with this tax. If $k < \bar{T}$, the loss-minimizing strategy involves taxing away all of k and then using distorting taxes to collect revenue equal to $(\bar{T} - k)$. Since the problem can always be redefined in this way, it is convenient to assume $k = 0$ at the outset so that lump-sum income taxation is impossible.

Second, with zero lump-sum income, both demand and production are homogeneous of degree zero in prices $\vec{q}$ and $\vec{p}$, respectively. Hence we are permitted two separate normalizations which, for convenience, can be taken on the same good, say, the first. Therefore set $q_1 \equiv p_1 \equiv 1$, which in turn implies $t_1 \equiv 0$, or that the government can avoid taxing the first good. These normalizations also remove the uninteresting possibility of proportional taxation, which would entail no deadweight loss, and given the assumption of zero lump-sum income and constant producer prices, raise no revenue. By leaving good one untaxed, however, any set of tax rates on the remaining $(N - 1)$ goods and factors must necessarily change the vector of *relative* prices and create distortions. Moreover, a set of rates can generally be found to meet the revenue requirements, $\bar{T}$.

Given these two assumptions, define the Lagrangian[25] for the optimal tax problem as:

$$\min_{(t_k)} L = L(\vec{t}) + \lambda \left(\sum_{i=1}^{N} t_i X_i^C - \bar{T} \right) = M(\vec{q}; \bar{U}^0) - \sum_{i=1}^{N} t_i X_i^C$$

$$+ \lambda \left(\sum_{i=1}^{N} t_i X_i^C - \bar{T} \right)$$

with $t_1 \equiv 0$.

---

[24] The optimal tax problem can also be modeled using social welfare as the objective function, in which the goal is to maximize welfare subject to a revenue constraint and distorting taxation. The resulting tax rules will be identical.

[25] Whether the tax revenue summations go from $1, \ldots, N$ or $2, \ldots, N$ is immaterial since $t_1 \equiv 0$.

The first-order conditions are:

$$(15.21) \quad \frac{\partial L}{\partial t_k} = X_k^C - X_k^C - \sum_{i=1}^{N} t_i \frac{\partial X_i^C}{\partial q_k} + \lambda \left(X_k^C + \sum_{i=1}^{N} t_i \frac{\partial X_i^C}{\partial q_k} \right) = 0$$

$$k = 2, \ldots, N$$

(recall that $\partial q_k = \partial t_k$ with linear technology)

Rearranging terms:

$$(15.22) \quad -(1-\lambda)\left(\sum_{i=1}^{N} t_i \frac{\partial X_i^C}{\partial q_k} \right) + \lambda X_k^C = 0 \qquad k = 2, \ldots, N$$

$$(15.23) \quad \frac{\sum_{i=1}^{N} t_i \frac{\partial X_i^C}{\partial q_k}}{X_k^C} = \frac{\lambda}{(1-\lambda)} \qquad k = 2, \ldots, N$$

and

$$(15.24) \quad \sum_{i=1}^{N} t_i X_i^C = \bar{T}$$

Notice that the right-hand side of (15.23) is independent of k. Furthermore, since $\partial X_i^C/\partial q_k = M_{ik} = M_{ki} = \partial X_k^C/\partial q_i$ from the symmetry of the Slutsky substitution terms, (15.23) can be rewritten as:

$$(15.25) \quad \frac{\sum_{i=1}^{N} t_i M_{ki}}{X_k^C} = C \qquad k = 2, \ldots, N$$

The numerator, $\sum_{i=1}^{N} t_i(\Delta X_k^C/\Delta q_i) = \sum_{i=1}^{N} t_i(\Delta X_k^C/\Delta t_i)$, approximates the total change in X_k in response to marginal changes in all the taxes, $t_k = 2, \ldots, N$. Hence, the left-hand side is the percentage change in X_k^C, $\Delta X_k^C/X_k$, in response to the tax package. The first-order conditions, then, require a set of taxes that produce equal changes in the compensated demands and supplies for all goods and factors.[26],[27]

---

[26] If all the taxed goods and factors, $k = 2, \ldots, N$, undergo equal percentage changes, then the first untaxed good will undergo the same percentage change as well, although the base for computing the percentage change differs.

[27] The equal percentage change interpretation applies, strictly speaking, only to marginal changes in each of the tax rates from the no-tax position, that is, to a marginal revenue package. For discrete tax changes, the rule implies that there must be an equal percentage change in quantity demanded in response to a further infinitesimal proportional change in all the tax rates from their optimum values. This interpretation is necessary because the compensated demand curves in the discrete case will all be evaluated at the gross of tax consumer prices existing at the optimum when solving for the optimal pattern of the t_k. On the other hand, if all the M_{ik} are constant in the relevant range, then the rule needs no modification for the discrete case. This follows because

$$\Delta X_k^C = \sum_{i=1}^{N} \int_0^{t_i} M_{ik} dq_i = \sum_{i=1}^{N} \int_0^{t_i} M_{ki} dq_i = \sum_{i=2}^{N} M_{ki} \int_0^{t_i} dq_i$$

$$= \sum_{i=1}^{N} t_i M_{ki} = \sum_{i=1}^{N} t_i M_{ik}$$

when the M_{ik} are constant (and $t_1 \equiv 0$).

Notice that (15.25) describes percentage changes in terms of quantities and not the tax rates themselves. Unfortunately, the pattern of tax rates cannot be described by an equivalently simple rule. However, their general pattern is clear: goods (factors) whose compensated demands (supplies) are relatively inelastic should be subjected to relatively higher rates of taxation. This is the only way the "equal percentage charge" rule can possibly be satisfied.

A rough intuitive explanation of the rule can be obtained by considering the optimal tax problem as one of minimizing the sum of the deadweight loss triangles in each market (this ignores the cross-substitution terms M_{ij}, $j \neq i$, and their corresponding loss rectangles depicted in Figure 15–10).[28]

If the compensated demand for one good is highly inelastic and the compensated demand for another highly elastic, most of the required revenue should be raised from the inelastic good. Even with a relatively high tax rate, its quantity demanded will not change much. Consequently, it will raise a relatively large amount of revenue with a relatively small deadweight loss triangle. Conversely, placing an equal tax rate on a good with a relatively elastic demand will create a larger change in quantity demanded. Hence, the revenue collected will be smaller and the deadweight loss triangle larger. Per dollar of revenue then, it pays to tax the relatively inelastic goods (factors). In the limit, if one good (factor) has a perfectly inelastic compensated demand (supply), it should be used to collect all the revenue. There can be no deadweight loss, and the percentage changes in output will be equalized among all goods at a value equal to zero.

Policy Implications of the Optimal Tax Rule

The equal percentage change rule is a deceptively simple representation of the optimal tax equilibrium. Computing the actual tax rates involves solving N first-order conditions for λ and the t_k, $k = 2, \ldots, N$, a devastatingly complex task, especially given present econometric knowledge of the crucial Slutsky substitution terms. Furthermore, all goods and factors (except the untaxed numeraire) will either be taxed or subsidized at the optimum, in general. Thus it is extremely unlikely that any government could ever even approximate the *optimal* pattern of tax rates. On the other hand, the equal percentage charge rule does yield a number of useful qualitative insights for tax policy. We will consider four of them.

a. Broad-Based Taxation. Equation (15.25) creates a strong presumption against broad-based taxes such as general sales or general income taxes, which tax a broad range of goods or factors at a single rate. Additional restrictions on preferences will clearly be required to generate the result that $t_k = t$, with k defined over a significant range of goods or factors. Atkinson and Stiglitz explored the nature of these restrictions in an article entitled, "The Structure

---

[28] See W. Baumol and D. Bradford, "Optimal Departures from Marginal Cost Pricing," *American Economic Review*, June 1970, on this point. Generally speaking, their article offers an excellent intuitive feel for the optimal tax problem and the properties of its solutions.

of Indirect Taxation and Economic Efficiency," using a model virtually identical to ours.[29] Their N goods and factors consisted of $(N - 1)$ goods and labor, a common practice when studying the relative efficiency of direct and indirect taxation. They were particularly interested in describing conditions under which equal proportional taxation of all the commodities is optimal, with labor the untaxed numeraire. This is especially compelling because of a theorem we will prove in Chapter 17, that the efficiency implications of an equal proportional tax on all commodities can be duplicated by replacing it with a proportional tax on all factors. Hence, if uniform commodity taxation is optimal, it need not be used. A single tax on labor (in the Atkinson-Stiglitz model) is also optimal.

Unfortunately the restrictions required for a uniform (or even "simplified") set of taxes are extremely stringent. Atkinson and Stiglitz prove that uniform taxation is optimal if either (a) labor is in absolutely fixed supply (see pp. 319–20) or (b) preferences are homothetic. Beyond that they were able to show that if preferences have an additive representation (i.e., $U(X_1, \ldots, X_{n-1}, L) = g_1(X_1) + \ldots + g_{n-1}(X_{n-1}) + g_n(L)$), then tax rates are inversely proportional to each commodity's income elasticity of demand. This implies uniform taxation if preferences are additive in logarithms with equal coefficients, in which case all income elasticities equal one. They also proved that if preferences have an additive representation, and the marginal disutility of labor is constant (i.e., (i.e., $\partial g_N / \partial L = k$), then tax rates are inversely proportional to each commodity's own price elasticity of demand (refer to the discussion of the inverse elasticity rule, below).[30]

b. The Exemption of "Necessities." There is also a presumption, long recognized in the profession, against the common practice of exempting necessities such as food and clothing from sales tax bases. If anything, these items can be expected to have relatively low substitution effects, as well as income elasticities less than one. Therefore, by the efficiency criterion, they should be taxed at *higher* than average rates, not exempted from taxation. But governments exempt these items anyway for equity reasons, in an attempt to make sales taxes somewhat less regressive. This particular trade-off between efficiency and equity goals with distorting taxation has long been recognized. Careful analysis within the context of a many-consumer economy, the subject of Chapter 16, can effect a reconciliation, but only in principle. Many-person tax rules are extremely difficult to apply. Nonetheless, it is clear that governments have been swayed more by equity than efficiency arguments for these taxes. This is usually the case whenever equity and efficiency goals conflct. Favoring equity considerations is not peculiar to tax policy.

---

[29] A. Atkinson and J. Stiglitz, "The Structure of Indirect Taxation and Economic Efficiency," *Journal of Public Economics*, vol. 1, 1972.

[30] Subsequent analysis with models of optimal income taxation, to be discussed in Chapter 16, showed that this last set of restrictions implies uniform commodity taxation if the government also institutes a lump-sum subsidy and adopts a utilitarian social welfare function with equal social marginal utilities, $\partial W / \partial U^h$. A. Atkinson and J. Stiglitz, "The Design of Tax Structure: Direct vs. Indirect Taxation," *Journal of Public Economics*, July/August 1976.

c. **Percentage Charge Rules for Ordinary Demand (Factor Supply) Relationships.** Some additional qualitative policy information can be obtained by rewriting (15.25) in terms of the price and income derivatives from ordinary demand curves by means of the Slutsky equation.

$$(15.26) \qquad \frac{\partial X_k}{\partial q_i} = M_{ki} - X_i \frac{\partial X_k}{\partial I}$$

or

$$(15.27) \qquad M_{ki} = \frac{\partial X_k}{\partial q_i} + X_i \frac{\partial X_k}{\partial I}$$

Substituting (15.27) into (15.25) yields:

$$(15.28) \qquad \frac{\sum_{i=1}^{N} t_i \left(\frac{\partial X_k}{\partial q_i} + X_i \frac{\partial X_k}{\partial I} \right)}{X_k} = C \qquad k = 2, \ldots, N$$

Rearranging terms:

$$(15.29) \qquad \frac{\sum_{i=1}^{N} t_i \frac{\partial X_k}{\partial q_i}}{X_k} = C - \sum_{i=1}^{N} t_i X_i \frac{\frac{\partial X_k}{\partial I}}{X_k} \qquad k = 2, \ldots, N$$

Multiplying and dividing the second term on the right-hand side of (15.29) by I yields:

$$(15.30) \qquad \frac{\sum_{i=1}^{N} t_i \frac{\partial X_k}{\partial q_i}}{X_k} = C - \frac{\sum_{i=1}^{N} t_i X_i}{I} (E_{k,I}) \qquad k = 2, \ldots, N$$

where $E_{k,I}$ is the income elasticity for good k.

Assuming the $\partial X_k / \partial q_i$ are constant in the relevant range, the left-hand side of (15.30) gives the percentage change in the *ordinary* demand (supply) of the kth good (factor). Notice that these percentage changes are not equal. Goods with higher income elasticities should change by a greater amount (in absolute value; C is presumably negative for goods). It makes intuitive sense to "exploit" income effects, since they do not contribute to deadweight loss. Of course the optimal tax rates are no more easily solved by equations (15.30) than by equations (15.25) (including the revenue constraint in each instance). If we had excellent econometric knowledge of the price and income derivatives for ordinary demand at the individual level, the Slutsky equation could then be used to find the M_{ij} to be used in equations (15.25). But the same econometric problems exist for obtaining these estimates as for obtaining the M_{ij} (refer to the discussion on page 322). At the same time, common sense will often suggest which goods tend to have relatively high income elasticities. Notice, for example, that (15.30) gives a partial efficiency justification for taxing necessities lightly.

d. The Inverse Elasticity Rule. In another effort to mine the policy implications of the optimal tax rule, a number of economists have proposed an interpretation called the inverse elasticity rule (IER), which says that tax rates should be increased in inverse proportion to a good's (factor's) price elasticity of demand.[31] The basis for this interpretation of (15.25) is as follows. Suppose, as an approximation, that all income effects are ignored as being empirically unimportant, and, further, that all cross-price derivatives are set equal to zero on the grounds that own price effects will dominate the cross-price effects. With these two assumptions, equation (15.25) reduces to:

$$(15.31) \qquad \frac{t_k M_{kk}}{X_k} = C \qquad k = 2, \ldots, N,$$

where:

M_{kk} = the own price derivative for *both* compensated and ordinary demand (supply) curves, since there are no income effects.

Multiplying and dividing the left-hand side of (15.31) by q_k yields:

$$(15.32) \qquad \left(\frac{t_k}{q_k}\right) \cdot \left(\frac{\partial X_k}{\partial q_k} \cdot \frac{q_k}{X_k}\right) = C \qquad k = 2, \ldots, N$$

Alternatively,

$$(15.33) \qquad \left(\frac{t_k}{q_k}\right) = \frac{C}{E_{kk}} \qquad k = 2, \ldots, N$$

where:

E_{kk} = the own-price elasticity of demand.

Hence, the tax rate as a percentage of the gross of tax price, q, should be inversely related to the own-price elasticity of demand (supply) for each good (factor), the inverse elasticity rule.

The IER is an intuitively appealing interpretation of the optimal tax rules, especially if one thinks in terms of minimizing deadweight loss triangles, but the assumptions supporting this interpretation are heroic, to say the least. As noted in the preceding section on marginal loss, if all income effects are zero, then ordinary price derivatives must follow the same laws as compensated price derivatives, in particular the homogeneity result that $\sum_{i=1}^{N} q_i M_{ik} = 0$, all $k = 1, \ldots, N$. But this implies $M_{ki} \neq 0$ for some i, $i \neq k$. One legitimate possibility is to assume that $M_{ki} = 0$, all $i \neq k$, for all *taxed* goods (factors). This says that all cross-price effects occur with respect to the untaxed numeraire,

---

[31] A. Kahn, *The Economics of Regulation: Principles and Institutions*, (New York: John Wiley & Sons, Inc., 1970), vol. I, pp. 144–45, contains a discussion of the inverse elasticity rule in the context of price discrimination. Kahn's analysis reflects the fact that the IER has also become popular in the industrial organization literature. As we shall discover in Chapter 21, second-best pricing rules for multiproduct decreasing cost industries with profit constraints are virtually identical to the optimal tax rule.

that is, $M_{k1} \neq 0$, all $k = 2, \ldots, N$. In particular, with $q_1 \equiv 1$ (the numeraire),

$$(15.34) \qquad M_{k1} = -q_k M_{kk} \qquad k = 2, \ldots, N$$

Unfortunately, there is no reason why (15.34) should be true. Thus, the IER may not be very useful even as a rough guideline to the policymaker. It would perhaps make more sense to select one or two M_{ki}, $i \neq k$, that are likely to be nonzero, place reasonable values on them that satisfy the homogeneity condition $\sum_{i=1}^{N} q_i M_{ik} = 0$, and apply a simplified version of the equal percentage change rule (15.25). It will still have a rough inverse elasticity interpretation. For example, suppose one assumes only M_{kk} and M_{kj} nonzero when evaluating the first-order condition for t_k. The kth relation in (15.25) becomes:

$$(15.35) \qquad \frac{t_k M_{kk} + t_j M_{kj}}{X_k} = C$$

Multiplying and dividing the two terms on the left-hand side by q_k and q_j, respectively, yields:

$$(15.36) \qquad \frac{t_k}{q_k} \cdot E_{kk} + \frac{t_j}{q_j} E_{kj} = C$$

Rearranging terms:

$$(15.37) \qquad \frac{t_k}{q_k} E_{kk} = C - \frac{t_j}{q_j} E_{kj}$$

and

$$(15.38) \qquad \left(\frac{t_k}{q_k} \right) = \frac{1}{E_{kk}} \left[C - \left(\frac{t_j}{q_j} \right) E_{kj} \right]$$

In this form, the IER says that the percentage tax on good (factor) k is inversely related to its own-price elasticity corrected by a term incorporating the relevant cross-price elasticity and the percentage tax (at the optimum) on the other good.

This simplification at least avoids having to impose patently unrealistic assumptions on the compensated cross-price elasticities. Moreover, the resulting simultaneous system of equations would not be much more difficult to solve than the standard IER applied to all goods and factors.

SUBSTITUTIONS AMONG TAXES— IMPLICATIONS FOR WELFARE LOSS

The third and final issue to be considered within the context of a simple one-consumer linear technology economy is the implication on social welfare of substituting one set of taxes for another while holding revenue constant. This tax substitution experiment is perhaps the most compelling of all second-best exercises within the pure allocational theory of taxation, if only because governments occasionally engage in just such tax substitutions.

So long as the tax changes are "small," the expressions for marginal loss and total tax revenue are all that are needed to determine the efficiency implications for any given equal-revenue substitution among taxes. Begin with the total differential of deadweight loss with respect to all the taxes:

$$(15.39) \qquad dL = - \sum_{k=1}^{N} \sum_{i=1}^{N} t_i M_{ik} dt_k$$

(there is no need to assume an untaxed good in this exercise). (15.39) is an appropriate measure of loss for any given change in the vector of tax rates, since a tax substitution can always be viewed as a multistep series of individual loss experiments, in which one tax is reduced and the revenue returned to the government lump sum, after which a second tax is imposed, with its revenue returned to the consumer lump sum, and so on, for any number of tax changes, dt. Moreover, since $M_{ik} = M_{ki}$, the order of substitution is irrelevant. All we need know, in addition, are the values of given dt_k that hold revenue constant. But this can be determined by totally differentiating the tax revenue equation.

$$(15.40) \qquad dT = \sum_{k=1}^{N} \left(M_k + \sum_{i=1}^{N} t_i M_{ik} \right) dt_k$$

Setting $dT = 0$, (15.40) determines all possible tax substitutions that keep revenue unchanged. Once the appropriate values for dt_k have been determined from (15.40), they can be substituted back into (15.39) to determine the resulting change in deadweight loss.

When only two taxes change, (15.40) describes the exact relationship between the two changes necessary to hold revenue constant. Suppose, for example, t_j and t_k are to be changed, $dt_i = 0$, $i \neq j, k$. From (15.40),

$$(15.41) \qquad dT = 0 = \left(M_k + \sum_{i=1}^{N} t_i M_{ik} \right) dt_k + \left(M_j + \sum_{i=1}^{N} t_i M_{ij} \right) dt_j$$

or

$$(15.42) \qquad \frac{dt_k}{dt_j} = - \frac{\dfrac{\partial T}{\partial t_j}}{\dfrac{\partial T}{\partial t_k}}$$

As expected, the two rates must change in direct ratio to the marginal changes in tax revenue with respect to each of the taxes. Presumably one tax is increased, the other decreased. Notice also that the relevant marginal revenue changes are the changes at the compensated equilibria, not the actual equilibria. This is consistent with the definition of loss in terms of compensated equilibria.

To complete the analysis, the marginal loss with respect to changes in t_j and t_k is:

$$(15.43) \qquad dL = - \left(\sum_{i=1}^{N} t_i M_{ik} dt_k + \sum_{i=1}^{N} t_i M_{ij} dt_j \right)$$

from (15.39). Substituting in the equal-revenue constraint (15.42) and recalling that $\partial L/\partial t_k = -\sum_{i=1}^{N} t_i M_{ik}$ yields:

$$
(15.44) \qquad dL = \left[\frac{\partial L}{\partial t_k} \left(-\frac{\dfrac{\partial T}{\partial t_j}}{\dfrac{\partial T}{\partial t_k}} \right) dt_j + \frac{\partial L}{\partial t_j} dt_j \right]
$$

Rearranging terms:

$$
(15.45) \qquad \frac{dL}{dt_j} = \left[\frac{\partial L}{\partial t_k} \left(-\frac{\dfrac{\partial T}{2t_j}}{\dfrac{\partial T}{\partial t_k}} \right) + \frac{\partial L}{\partial t_j} \right] = \left[\frac{\partial L}{\partial t_k} \left(+\frac{dt_k}{dt_j}\bigg|_{R=\bar{R}} \right) + \frac{\partial L}{\partial t_j} \right]
$$

Equation (15.45) gives an entirely plausible result. The change in loss from increasing one tax (say, t_j) and lowering another tax (say, t_k) to keep total tax revenue constant is a linear combination of the marginal losses from changing t_k and t_j individually, with the marginal loss for the compensating (in a revenue sense) tax, t_k, weighted by the amount that t_k must be changed per unit change in t_j in order to keep revenue unchanged. Put another way, the second term on the right-hand side of (15.45) measures the direct effect on loss because of a change in t_j. The first term measures the indirect effect on loss working through the required change in t_k in response to dt_j in order that $dT = 0$. In the two-tax case, then, equation (15.45) gives an exact expression for the change in loss arising from a "small" equal revenue tax substitution.

When more than two taxes change there is obviously an infinity of combinations for the dt that will satisfy (15.40). The natural way to proceed in this case is to impose values on all but one of the tax changes, use (15.40) to solve for the remaining tax change, and then substitute for the dt in (15.39).

Other than the obvious point that given approximately equal revenue effects, taxes which generate small changes in loss should replace taxes which generate large losses in order to reduce loss, equations such as (15.45) are not particularly illuminating for policy purposes. However, with additional restrictions added to the model in the form of limited possibilities for substitution and/or limitations in the number of taxed goods, equation (15.45) can yield some interesting results. One of the most famous exercises along these lines is due to Corlett and Hague, who examined the efficiency implications of moving from equal proportional taxes on two goods in the context of a three-good economy, in which leisure is the third good and is incapable of being taxed.[32] Label the two goods k and j, and let good 1 be leisure, the untaxed numeraire ($q_1 \equiv 1 \equiv p_1; t_1 \equiv 0$). Assume initially that $t_j = \alpha \bar{p}_j$ and $t_k = \alpha \bar{p}_k$, with α the equal proportional rate of tax, and consider the efficiency implications of a marginal increase in t_j

---

[32] Corlett and Hague, "Complementarity and the Excess Burden of Taxation." See also Diamond and McFadden, "Some Uses of the Expenditure Function in Public Finance."

coupled with a marginal decrease in t_k to hold revenue constant, that is, an equal revenue movement away from proportionality.

With proportional taxes α,

(15.46)
$$q_j = \bar{p}_j + \alpha \bar{p}_j = (1 + \alpha)\bar{p}_j$$

and

(15.47)
$$q_k = \bar{p}_k + \alpha \bar{p}_k = (1 + \alpha)\bar{p}_k$$

Substituting the expressions for marginal loss into (15.45) yields:

(15.48)
$$\frac{dL}{dt_j} = -\left[+ \sum_{i=k,j} t_i M_{ik}\left(\frac{dt_k}{dt_j}\bigg|_{R=\bar{R}}\right) + \sum_{i=k,j} t_i M_{ij} \right]$$

To replace the terms $\sum_{i=k,j} t_i M_{ik}$ and $\sum_{i=k,j} t_i M_{ij}$ make use of the homogeneity conditions:

(15.49)
$$\sum_{i=1}^{3} q_i M_{ik} = \sum_{i=1}^{3} q_i M_{ij} = 0$$

Rewrite $\sum_{i=1}^{3} q_i M_{ik} = 0$ as

(15.50)
$$M_{1k} = -q_j M_{jk} - q_k M_{kk} \qquad \text{(with } q_1 \equiv 1\text{)}$$

But from (15.46) and (15.47),

(15.51)
$$M_{1k} = -\left[(1 + \alpha)\bar{p}_j M_{jk} + (1 + \alpha)\bar{p}_k M_{kk}\right]$$

Furthermore,

(15.52)
$$t_j M_{jk} + t_k M_{kk} = \alpha \bar{p}_j M_{jk} + \alpha \bar{p}_k M_{kk}$$

Hence, from (15.52) and (15.51),

(15.53)
$$\sum_{i=k,j} t_i M_{ik} = -\left(\frac{\alpha}{1 + \alpha}\right) M_{1k}$$

Similarly,

(15.54)
$$\sum_{i=k,j} t_i M_{ij} = -\left(\frac{\alpha}{1 + \alpha}\right) M_{1j}$$

Therefore, (15.48) becomes:

(15.55)
$$\frac{dL}{dt_j} = +\left(\frac{\alpha}{1 + \alpha}\right)\left(M_{1k}\frac{dt_k}{dt_j}\bigg|_{R=\bar{R}} + M_{1j}\right)$$

Next, totally differentiate M_1, the demand for leisure, with respect to t_j, subject to the total revenue constraint, and $q_1 \equiv 1$.

(15.56)
$$\frac{dM_1}{dt_j} = M_{1k}\frac{dt_k}{dt_j}\bigg|_{R=\bar{R}} + M_{1j}$$

Substituting (15.56) into (15.55) yields:

(15.57)
$$\frac{dL}{dt_j} = +\left(\frac{\alpha}{1+\alpha}\right)\frac{dM_1}{dt_j}$$

Thus if leisure decreases (work increases) in response to the changes in $t_j(+)$ and $t_k(-)$, loss decreases, in which case equal proportional taxes are dominated by a system of nonproportional taxes on goods k and j.[33]

Whether or not dM_1/dt_j is negative depends on the Slutsky substitution terms M_{ij} and M_{ik}. To see this write (15.56) as:

(15.58)
$$\frac{dM_1}{dt_j} = M_{1k}\left[-\frac{\dfrac{\partial T_j}{\partial t_j}}{\dfrac{\partial T_k}{\partial t_k}}\right] + M_{1j}$$

(15.59)
$$\frac{dM_1}{dt_j} = M_{1k}\left[-\frac{M_j + \sum\limits_{i=k,j} t_i M_{ij}}{M_k + \sum\limits_{i=k,j} t_i M_{ik}}\right] + M_{1j}$$

Substitute (15.53) and (15.54) into (15.59) to obtain:

(15.60)
$$\frac{dM_1}{dt_j} = M_{1k}\left[-\frac{\left(M_j - \left(\dfrac{\alpha}{1+\alpha}\right)M_{1j}\right)}{\left(M_k - \left(\dfrac{\alpha}{1+\alpha}\right)M_{1k}\right)}\right] + M_{1j}$$

(15.60) assumes proportional taxes initially. Placing (15.60) over a common denominator and rearranging terms yields:

(15.61)
$$\frac{dM_1}{dt_j} = \frac{-M_j M_{1k} + M_k M_{1j}}{\left[M_k - \left(\dfrac{\alpha}{1+\alpha}\right)M_{1k}\right]}$$

$$= \frac{M_k M_j}{\left[M_k - \left(\dfrac{\alpha}{1+\alpha}\right)M_{1k}\right]} \cdot \left(\frac{M_{1j}}{M_j} - \frac{M_{1k}}{M_k}\right)$$

Assuming the first term on the right-hand side of (15.61) is positive, the sign of (15.61) depends upon the relative magnitudes of M_{1j}/M_j and M_{1k}/M_k. Consider the various possibilities. With $M_{11} < 0$, one possibility is for $M_{1k} > 0$, $M_{1j} < 0$. In the Slutsky sense, goods k and 1 are substitutes, goods j and 1 complements. If this is the case $dM_1/dt_j < 0$ as required for a decrease in loss. Hence the government should raise the tax on the good that is complementary

---

[33] By similar manipulations it can be demonstrated that $dL/dt_k = +(\alpha/1 + \alpha)(dM_1/dt_k)$. Hence if either dM_1/dt_k or dM_1/dt_j is negative, nonproportional taxes dominate proportional taxes.

with leisure. If $M_{1k} < 0$, $M_{1j} > 0$, t_k should be raised.[34] If both are substitutes, such that M_{1k}, $M_{1j} > 0$, then equation (15.61) implies raising the tax on the good relatively more complementary (less substitutable) with leisure, for example, raising t_j if, roughly speaking, $M_{1j} < M_{1k} > 0$, and vice versa. The only other possibility in a three-good world is for one of the goods to be a Slutsky substitute for leisure (say, $M_{1k} > 0$) while the other is neither a substitute nor a complement ($M_{1j} = 0$). In this case, the tax should be increased on the good whose cross-price derivative is zero, since it is *relatively* more complementary with leisure. Of course, both goods cannot be Slutsky complements, since $\sum_{k=1}^{3} q_k M_{1k} = 0$ from homogeneity of the compensated demand functions and $M_{11} < 0$.

Note, finally, that the Corlett-Hague analysis applies, strictly speaking, only for small changes in taxes. Using the homogeneity conditions to obtain expressions in terms of M_{1k} and M_{1j} required evaluating all demand relationships (M_k, M_{jk}, etc.) at the original proportional tax prices. The larger the tax changes, the more inaccurate this evaluation becomes. There are no longer any simple relationships between M_{1k} and $\sum_{i=j,k} t_i M_{ik}$, or between M_{1j} and $\sum_{i=j,k} t_i M_{ij}$.

REFERENCES

Atkinson, A., and Stiglitz, J. "The Design of Tax Structure: Direct vs. Indirect Taxation." *Journal of Public Economics,* July/August 1976.

————, and Stiglitz, J. "The Structure of Indirect Taxation and Economic Efficiency." *Journal of Public Economics,* vol. 1, 1972.

Baumol, W., and Bradford, D. "Optimal Departures from Marginal Cost Pricing." *American Economic Review,* June 1970.

Boskin, M. "On Some Recent Econometric Research in Public Finance." *AEA Papers and Proceedings,* May 1976.

Bradford, D., and Rosen, H. "The Optimal Taxation of Commodities and Income." *AEA Papers and Proceedings,* May 1976.

Browning, E. "The Excess Burden of Excise vs. Income Taxes: A Simplified Comparison." *Public Finance,* 3, 1975.

————. "The Marginal Cost of Public Funds." *Journal of Political Economy,* April 1976.

Corlett, W., and Hague, D. "Complementarity and the Excess Burden of Taxation." *Review of Economic Studies,* vol. 21 (1), no. 54, 1953–54.

Diamond, P. A., and McFadden, D. "Some Uses of the Expenditure Function in Public Finance." *Journal of Public Economics,* vol. 3, 1974.

---

[34] Were the analysis carried out with respect to dt_k, the equation replacing (15.61) would be:

$$(15.61\text{N}) \qquad \frac{dL}{dt_k} = \frac{M_k M_j}{\left[M_j - \left(\frac{\alpha}{1+\alpha} \right) M_{1j} \right]} \cdot \left(\frac{M_{1k}}{M_k} - \frac{M_{1j}}{M_j} \right)$$

————, and Mirrlees, J. "Optimal Taxation and Public Production" (2 parts, Part I: "Production Efficiency," Part II: "Tax Rules"). *American Economic Review,* March, June 1971.

Dixit, A. "Welfare Effects of Tax and Price Changes." *Journal of Public Economics,* February 1975.

————, and Munk, K. "Welfare Effects of Tax and Price Changes: A Correction." *Journal of Public Economics,* August 1977.

Friedman, M. "The Welfare Effects of an Income and an Excise Tax." *Journal of Political Economy,* February 1952.

George, H. *Progress and Poverty.* Book VIII. New York: Doubleday & Co. Inc., 1914.

Green, J., and Sheshinski, E. "Approximating the Efficiency Gains of Tax Reforms." *Journal of Public Economics,* April 1979.

Harberger, A. *Taxation and Welfare.* Boston, Mass.: Little, Brown and Co. 1974.

————. "Taxation, Resource Allocation and Welfare." In *The Role of Direct and Indirect Taxes in the Federal Revenue System.* The National Bureau of Economic Research and The Brookings Institution. Princeton, N.J.: Princeton University Press, 1964.

————. "The Measurement of Waste." *American Economic Association Papers and Proceedings,* May 1964.

————. Three Basic Postulates for Applied Welfare Economics," *Journal of Economic Literature.* September 1971.

Hotelling, H. "The General Welfare in Relation to Problems of Taxation and of Railway and Utility Rates." *Econometrica,* July 1938.

Kahn, A. *The Economics of Regulation: Principles and Institutions.* vol. I. New York: John Wiley & Sons, Inc., 1970.

Ramsey, F. P. "A Contribution to the Theory of Taxation." *Economic Journal,* March 1927.

Rea, Jr., S. "Incentive Effects of Alternative Negative Income Tax Plans." *Journal of Public Economics,* vol. 3, 1974.

Samuelson, P. A. "Theory of Optimal Taxation" (unpublished).

Sandmo, S. "Optimal Taxation." *Journal of Public Economics,* July–August 1976.

Spaeth, W. "Labor Effort Disincentives of Negative Income Taxation." Unpublished Ph.D. dissertation, Department of Economics, Boston College, April 17, 1974.

16

The second-best theory of taxation with general production technologies and many consumers

In order to make the second-best analysis of Chapter 15 more responsive to real-world economies it must be extended to incorporate general production technologies, with increasing cost production-possibilities frontiers, and many consumers, with different tastes and different marginal social welfare weights. Neither extension is analytically trivial by any means. With general technologies, producer prices vary as government policy variables move society along (or inside of) its production-possibilities frontier. Moreover, pure economic profits or losses are possible and have to be accounted for in a general equilibrium framework. As a consequence of these features the loss from taxation depends not only on consumption derivatives but on production derivatives as well. The many-consumer economy brings the social welfare function back into the analysis in a fundamental way, such that distinctions between equity and efficiency aspects of government policy become blurred. In addition, it is no longer possible to define a general aggregate income measure of tax loss.

The modeling implications of either extension are sufficiently complex that the chapter will consider each separately before combining them into a fully general model. Hence, the first section of Chapter 16 will rework two of the main results of Chapter 15 in the context of a one-consumer, general technology economy. The second section will consider the many-consumer economy with fixed producer prices. The third and final section will then present the full general model, emphasizing how the results of Chapter 15 must be modified to accommodate a more realistic economic environment. It will also review the the recent literature on optimal second-best income taxation.

A ONE-CONSUMER ECONOMY WITH GENERAL TECHNOLOGY

Dead Weight Loss from Taxation

Replacing the assumption of linear technology with the more realistic specification of general technology affects the analysis of tax loss in two ways. The most direct implication is that production terms enter into the loss function in a nontrivial manner. In addition, general technology reintroduces market clearance explicitly into the analysis because the full set of market clearance

FIGURE 16–1

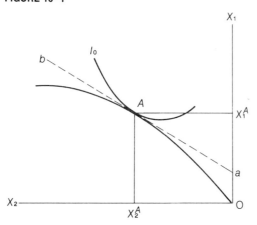

equations are necessary to determine the relationship between producer and consumer prices. Let us consider each of these points in turn.

With linear technology the loss resulting from a vector of commodity taxes is defined as the lump-sum income necessary to keep the consumer indifferent to the taxes less the tax revenue collected at the compensated equilibrium and returned lump sum to the consumer, or $L(\vec{t}) = M(\vec{q}; \bar{U}) - \sum_{i=2}^{N} t_i X_i^C(\vec{q}; \bar{U})$. There is no need to keep track of production because as society moves along a linear production frontier there can never be any pure profits in the system that could also be given to the consumer. If, as we assumed, the competitively determined producer prices for the goods and factors generate no pure profits in the initial equilibrium, then there can never be pure profits because these prices never change. With general technologies, however, the competitively determined producer prices may well generate pure profits and losses, both at the initial zero-tax equilibrium and at the final with-tax equilibrium, and the pure profits may vary from one equilibrium to another. Consider, for example, the decreasing returns to scale technology depicted in Figure 16–1.

The competitive price ratio P_{X_2}/P_{X_1} at the initial no-tax equilibrium A equals the slope of the line ab. Notice that at these prices the factor payments $P_{X_2} \cdot X_2$ do not exhaust the product $P_{X_1} \cdot X_1$. The firm earns pure profits equal to Oa (in units of X_1), which presumably accrue to the single consumer. Moreover, as society moves along the frontier in response to commodity taxes the value of the pure profits changes. As a result, loss must be reinterpreted more generally as the lump-sum income necessary to keep the consumer indifferent to the new consumer prices less *all* sources of lump-sum income available to the consumer at the new with-tax equilibrium. These include *both* the tax revenue which is returned lump sum *and* any pure profits existing at the new equilibrium. In Figure 16–2, the loss from a unit tax on X_1 that changes the slope of the consumer's budget line to that of line segment cd is ae (in units of X_1). The income necessary to compensate the consumer for the new price vector is oc. The tax revenue collected and returned is ce, equal to the difference between the

FIGURE 16-2

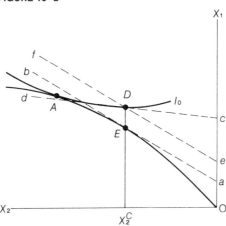

consumer prices (slope of *cd*) and the producer prices (slope of *ab* or *ef*) at the compensated equilibrium *D*, projected back to the X_1 axis. But loss is no longer the difference, *oe*, because production at the compensated equilibrium gives rise to pure profits equal to *oa* at the net-of-tax producer prices. These profits are also available to the consumer. Hence, the consumer's loss is only *ae*, equal to the difference between the consumer's required lump-sum compensation and the lump-sum income received from all sources within the general equilibrium system. Notice that *ae* also equals the difference between the amount of X_1 required to compensate the consumer at *D*, less the amount of X_1 society is able to produce at *E*, given that the compensated supply of X_2 is satisfied.

In order to retain the loss-minimizing approach in general equilibrium analysis, then, the first requirement is to develop a valid production relationship, specified in terms of producer prices, that measures the pure economic profits in the economy for any given vector of producer prices. As was shown in Chapter 4, if we assume perfectly competitive goods and factor markets, the proper analytical construct is the general equilibrium profit function. Recall that the profit function, $\pi(\vec{p}) = \sum_{i=1}^{N} p_i Y_i(\vec{p})$ is derived by first maximizing aggregate profits at fixed producer prices subject to the aggregate production-possibilities frontier $f(\vec{Y}) = 0$, and then substituting the resulting goods supply and input demand functions, $Y_i(\vec{p})$, back into the objective profit function, $\sum_{i=1}^{N} p_i Y_i$. Recall also that, analogous to the consumer's expenditure function, $\partial \pi(p)/\partial p_k = Y_k(\vec{p})$, the supply of (demand for) the kth good (factor).

Since the profit function $\pi(\vec{p})$ incorporates all relevant aspects of production for the economy, the expression

$$(16.1) \qquad L(\vec{t}) = M(\vec{q}; \bar{U}) - \sum_{i=1}^{N} t_i M_i(\vec{q}; \bar{U}) - \pi(\vec{p})$$

is a valid general equilibrium expression for the deadweight loss resulting from any given vector of taxes, $\vec{t}$, assuming competitive market structures, general

FIGURE 16–3

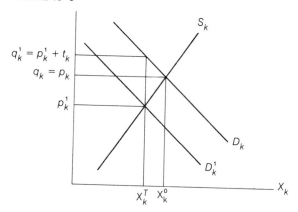

production technology, and tax revenues measured at the new with-tax compensated equilibrium. The expression $M(\vec{q}; \bar{U})$ measures the income necessary to compensate the consumer, and the final two expressions measure the (lump-sum) income actually available at the new compensated equilibrium.[1] As before, $\vec{q}$, is the vector of gross-of-tax consumer prices, $\vec{p}$ is the vector of net-of-tax producer prices, and $\vec{q} = \vec{p} + \vec{t}$.

Unlike the loss expression with a linear technology, however, equation (16.1) is not a complete general equilibrium specification of the economy. While $M(\vec{q}; \bar{U})$ captures the preferences of the consumer and $\pi(\vec{p})$ completely specifies the production technology, $L(t)$ does not incorporate market clearance. Recall that with linear technology, market clearance was implicit. There was only one consumer, and aggregate production and producer prices were fixed. Therefore, once $\vec{t}$ was specified, $\vec{q}$ was determined through the identities $\vec{q} = \vec{p} + \vec{t}$. There is still only one consumer and aggregate production with general technology, but the crucial difference is that producer prices are no longer fixed. In general, goods supply curves (input demand curves) will be upward (downward) sloping so that any given producer price p_i is now a function of the entire vector of taxes, $\vec{t}$, that is, $p_i = p_i(\vec{t})$. To see this, consider the response to a tax, t_k, in both the market for k and the market for some other good, i

In the market for good k, depicted in Figure 16–3, the tax t_k generates a new equilibrium X_k^T, with new consumer *and* producer prices q_k^1 and p_k^1. Similarly, in some other market i, if D_i shifts in response to the tax t_k (as pictured in Figure 16–4 the goods i and k are substitutes), both the consumer and the producer prices will change, from $q_i = p_i$ to $q_i' = p_i'$.[2] By contrast with linear technologies, all supply (input demand) curves were horizontal so that a tax t_k could only

---

[2] This ignores subsequent changes as D_k shifts in response to the change in q_i, which changes q_k and further shifts D_i, and so on.

FIGURE 16–4

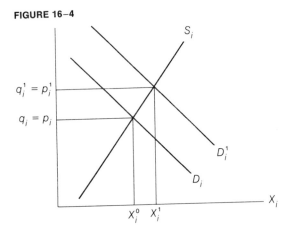

change the consumer price q_k by the full amount of the tax. p_k could not change, nor could any other producer or consumer price, even if the tax t_k caused demand shifts in these other markets. With general technology, however, market clearance relationships of the form

$$(16.2) \qquad M_i(\vec{q}; \bar{U}) = M_i[\vec{p}(\vec{t}) + \vec{t}; \bar{U}] = Y_i[\vec{p}(\vec{t})] \qquad i = 1, \ldots, N$$

become necessary to determine the vector of producer prices $\vec{p}$ for any given vector of taxes, $\vec{t}$. Once $\vec{p}$ has been determined through these relationships, $\vec{q}$ is determined by the identities $\vec{q} = \vec{p} + \vec{t}$.

The market clearance relationships (16.2) can be incorporated into the analysis in one of two ways. One possibility is to replace either M_i or Y_i in equation (16.1), the expression for loss. The other choice is to keep (16.1) exactly as it is and use the market clearance relationships to simplify derivatives of $L(t)$. We will use the second method throughout the chapter.

There is one additional complication. The loss expression (16.1) is specified in terms of *compensated* goods demands and factor supplies. To be consistent, the market clearance relationships (16.2) must also be specified in terms of the compensated demands and supplies, the $M_i(\vec{q}; \bar{U})$, as written. But market clearance cannot possibly hold in terms of *all* N compensated supplies and demands, for if society could provide the full vector of *compensated* supplies and demands the consumer would not suffer any loss as a result of the commodity taxes. As noted above, the compensated equilibrium for the consumer in Figure 16–2, point D (the $M_i(\vec{q}; \bar{U})$), is not attainable with the given production technology. Production at the compensated equilibrium (the $Y_i(\vec{p})$) is represented by point E. Thus specifying that $M_i = Y_i$, all $i = 1, \ldots, N$, requires that E and D coincide which cannot possibly occur if there is deadweight loss. This is simply an alternative way to consider the notion of loss.

The most natural resolution to this problem is to impose market clearance on all but one of the goods and factors, say, the first, and assume that compensation occurs through this good. It is also natural to let good one serve as the untaxed numeraire, with $q_1 \equiv p_1 \equiv 1$, and $t_1 \equiv 0$. From the discussion of loss in Chapter 15 we know that loss requires a change in *relative* prices, and setting $t_1 = 0$ ensures that any tax vector will change the vector of relative prices. Moreover, with $q_1 \equiv p_1 \equiv 1$, units of X_1 can be interpreted as units of purchasing power. These assumptions are consistent with Figure 16–2 in which loss is depicted as *ae* units of X_1, equal to the amount of X_1 demanded at the compensated equilibrium less the amount of X_1 actually produced given the producer prices at that equilibrium. In fact, given that $M_i = Y_i, i = 2, \ldots, N$, and $q_1 \equiv p_1 \equiv 1, t_1 \equiv 0$, the loss from taxation can be written as

$$(16.3) \qquad\qquad L(\vec{t}) = M_1(\vec{q}; \bar{U}) - Y_1(\vec{p})$$

Equations (16.3) and (16.1) are equivalent specifications of deadweight loss.

Assuming that compensation occurs in good 1 is not entirely satisfactory, however. Compensation could just as well occur with respect to any of the other $(N - 1)$ goods and factors, which could then serve as the untaxed numeraire. Unfortunately the choice of the compensating good (factor) matters, since the remaining $(N - 1)$ market clearance equations will determine a different vector $\vec{p}$ for any given $\vec{t}$ each time. Moverover, no matter what good is chosen, the vector $\vec{p}$ solved through the $(N - 1)$ market clearance equations will, in general, differ from the actual $\vec{p}$ observed in the economy in response to any given $\vec{t}$. Hence, there is an unresolveable dilemma here. If we want to define deadweight loss for a general technology economy, all components of the loss function must be defined in terms of the compensated equilibrium resulting from any given tax vector. If the actual and compensated equilibria are mixed together by, say, returning the *actual* tax revenue collected, then the loss minimization specification of a particular problem will not generate the same analytical results as a welfare maximum specification. Thus, to be an entirely consistent general equilibrium exercise, the conceptual loss experiment must assume, in effect, that the consumer is actually compensated by some outside agent, and that the compensation takes place in terms of some particular good. Were such compensation to occur, the price vector $\vec{p}$ solved for by this experiment would be the actual price vector observed in the economy. The dilemma, of course, is that such compensation will not actually occur so that the price vector $\vec{p}$ resulting from the conceptual loss experiment will not equal, or bear any necessary relationship to, the actual $\vec{p}$ resulting from any given pattern of taxes, $\vec{t}$. On the other hand, the actual $\vec{p}$ are irrelevant to a carefully designed conceptual experiment defining deadweight loss.

So long as one remains interested in defining a legitimate loss measure there appears to be no way out of this dilemma. Of course, there is always the analytical choice of modeling all second-best tax questions as welfare maximization problems using the indirect utility function, in which case everything is defined in terms of the actual post- and pretax equilibria. There is no need to define a loss function in order to analyze second-best tax (or expenditure) questions. However, the loss minimization framework is compelling since deadweight loss has been the traditional notion of tax inefficiency.

This dilemma does not arise with linear technologies because producer prices are fixed. The conceptual loss experiment still involves the compensated rather than actual tax collections and is therefore somewhat awkward, but it at least employs the observed vector of prices, both $\vec{q}$ and $\vec{p}$, for any given vector of tax rates, $\vec{t}$. The fixed vector $\vec{p}$ is the same in each equilibrium.

Marginal Loss—General Technology

With these comments in mind, we begin an examination of tax loss with general technology by computing the marginal loss with respect to the kth tax, t_k, using the loss expression (16.1), $L(\vec{t}) = M(\vec{q}; \bar{U}) - \sum_{i=1}^{N} t_i M_i(\vec{q}; \bar{U}) - \pi(\vec{p})$; the $(N - 1)$ market clearance relationships

$$(16.4) \qquad M_i(\vec{q}; \bar{U}) = Y_i(\vec{p}) \qquad i = 2, \ldots, N$$

and the pricing identities

$$(16.5) \qquad q_i = p_i + t_i \qquad i = 2, \ldots, N$$

and

$$(16.6) \qquad q_1 \equiv p_1 \equiv 1 \qquad t_1 \equiv 0$$

Recalling that $p_i = p_i(\vec{t})$, $i = 2, \ldots, N$, $\partial\pi/\partial p_i \equiv Y_i$, and noting that $p_1 \equiv 1$, a constant

$$(16.7) \qquad \frac{\partial L}{\partial t_k} = M_k + \sum_{i=2}^{N} M_i \frac{\partial p_i}{\partial t_k} - M_k - \sum_{i=2}^{N} t_i \left(M_{ik} + \sum_{j=2}^{N} M_{ij} \frac{\partial p_j}{\partial t_k} \right)$$
$$- \sum_{i=2}^{N} Y_i \frac{\partial p_i}{\partial t_k}$$

$$(16.8) \qquad \frac{\partial L}{\partial t_k} = \sum_{i=2}^{N} M_i \frac{\partial p_i}{\partial t_k} - \sum_{i=2}^{N} t_i \left(M_{ik} + \sum_{j=2}^{N} M_{ij} \frac{\partial p_j}{\partial t_k} \right) - \sum_{i=2}^{N} Y_i \frac{\partial p_i}{\partial t_k}$$

(16.8) can be simplified further by means of the market clearance equations (16.4). Multiplying (16.4) by $\partial p_i/\partial t_k$ yields:

$$(16.9) \qquad M_i \frac{\partial p_i}{\partial t_k} = Y_i \frac{\partial p_i}{\partial t_k} \qquad i = 2, \ldots, N$$

Next, sum (16.9) over all $(N - 1)$ relationships to obtain:

$$(16.10) \qquad \sum_{i=2}^{N} M_i \frac{\partial p_i}{\partial t_k} = \sum_{i=2}^{N} Y_i \frac{\partial p_i}{\partial t_k}$$

Hence, (16.8) simplifies to:

$$(16.11) \qquad \frac{\partial L}{\partial t_k} = - \sum_{i=2}^{N} t_i \left(M_{ik} + \sum_{j=2}^{N} M_{ij} \frac{\partial p_j}{\partial t_k} \right)$$

(16.11) is similar to equation (15.6), the expression for marginal loss with a linear technology, since with $q_i = p_i + t_i$, $i = 2, \ldots, N$, (16.11) can be rewritten as:

$$(16.12) \qquad \frac{\partial L}{\partial t_k} = - \sum_{i=2}^{N} t_i \frac{\partial X_i^{\text{comp}}}{\partial q_j} \frac{\partial q_j}{\partial t_k} = - \sum_{i=2}^{N} t_i \frac{\partial X_i^{\text{comp}}}{\partial t_k} \qquad k = 2, \ldots, N$$

Once again, we see that marginal loss depends upon the pattern of existing taxes and the change in compensated demands (factor supplies) in response to the tax. With a linear technology, $\partial q_k = \partial t_k$ and $\partial q_j / \partial t_k = 0, j \neq k$, so that (15.6) is just a special case of the general expression (16.11). The major qualitative difference between the two expressions is that the derivative $\partial X_i^{comp} / \partial t_k$ depends on both consumption *and* production responses, since $\partial q_j / \partial t_k$ depends upon all the consumption and production elasticities through the $(N - 1)$ market clearance equations (16.4). Of course, this is hardly a trivial difference.

In order to develop this point further, rewrite the $(N - 1)$ market clearance relationships (16.4) and the expression for loss, (16.11), in vector notation:[3]

(16.13)
$$dL = -(t)(M_{ij})\left(\frac{dq}{dt}\right)(dt)$$

(16.14)
$$M_i(q; \bar{U}) = \pi_i(q - t)$$

where:

(t) = the $1 \times (N - 1)$ row vector $(t_2, \ldots, t_N)$.

(M_{ij}) = the $(N - 1) \times (N - 1)$ matrix: $\begin{bmatrix} M_{22} & \cdots & M_{2N} \\ \vdots & & \vdots \\ M_{N2} & \cdots & M_{NN} \end{bmatrix}$

$\left(\dfrac{dq}{dt}\right)$ = the $(N - 1) \times (N - 1)$ matrix of differentials: $\begin{bmatrix} \dfrac{dq_2}{dt_2} & \cdots & \dfrac{dq_2}{dt_N} \\ \vdots & & \vdots \\ \dfrac{dq_N}{dt_2} & \cdots & \dfrac{dq_N}{dt_N} \end{bmatrix}$

(dt) = the $(N - 1) \times 1$ column vector of differentials: $\begin{bmatrix} dt_2 \\ \vdots \\ dt_N \end{bmatrix}$

M_i = the $(N - 1) \times 1$ column vector of compensated demands (factor supplies): $\begin{bmatrix} M_2 \\ \vdots \\ M_N \end{bmatrix}$

π_i = the $(N - 1) \times 1$ column vector of supplies (input demands): $\begin{bmatrix} Y_2 \\ \vdots \\ Y_N \end{bmatrix}$

q, p = vectors of prices.

Totally differentiating (16.14) yields:

(16.15)
$$M_{ij}dq = Y_{ij}(dq - dt)$$

---

[3] This technique was first demonstrated to us by Peter Diamond in a set of unpublished class notes.

FIGURE 16–5

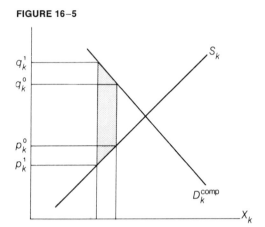

Solving for dq/dt, and substituting the notation X for M_i and Y for π_i yields:

(16.16)
$$\frac{dq}{dt} = \frac{-\left(\dfrac{\partial Y}{\partial p}\right)}{\left(\dfrac{\partial X}{\partial q} - \dfrac{\partial Y}{\partial p}\right)}$$

Substituting (16.16) into (16.13), the expression for loss becomes:

(16.17)
$$dL = -(t)(M_{ij})\left[\frac{-\dfrac{\partial Y}{\partial p}}{\dfrac{\partial X}{\partial q} - \dfrac{\partial Y}{\partial p}}\right] dt$$

Hence marginal loss depends upon both consumption and production derivatives.

As one additional comparison of marginal losses in general versus linear technology economies, consider the simple (and unlikely) case in which t_k is the only existing tax, only the kth prices, q_k and p_k, vary in response to a marginal change in the kth tax, t_k, and all cross-price derivatives are zero.[4] With these assumptions, (16.13) (or (16.17)) simplifies to:

(16.18)
$$dL = -t_k \frac{\partial X_k}{\partial q_k} \frac{dq_k}{dt_k} dt_k = -t_k \frac{\partial X_k}{\partial q_k} dq_k = -t_k \Delta X_k$$

The marginal loss occurs entirely within the market for good (factor) k, and is approximately equal to the shaded trapezoidal area depicted in Figure 16–5.

---

[4] Assuming $M_{ij} = 0$, all $i \neq j$ is actually improper, but the example is meant to be illustrative only. This analysis, along with the result (16.17) can be found in R. Boadway, "Cost-Benefit Rules and General Equilibrium," *Review of Economic Studies*, June 1975. Boadway derives (16.17) in a utility-maximizing framework.

This area can be thought of as the combined (marginal) decrease in consumer's and producer's surplus from consuming and producing good k, where the former is measured with reference to the compensated demand for good k and the latter with reference to the generalized supply function $Y_k = \partial \pi(\vec{p})/\partial p_k$. By contrast, with linear technology, loss was approximated by a set of triangles, equal in each market to the loss in consumer's surplus measured with reference to the set of compensated demand (factor supply) curves. Since a linearly technology has perfectly elastic supplies (input demands) at constant producer prices, there can never be a generalized producer's surplus.

Optimal Commodity Taxation

One of the most striking results in the allocational theory of taxation is that the equations describing the optimal pattern of commodity taxes in a one-consumer, general technology economy are *identical* with their linear technology counterparts if the technology exhibits constant returns to scale (CRS), the technology most compatible with competitive market structures. The first-order conditions for optimal taxation continue to depend *only* upon compensated demand (factor supply) derivatives despite the fact that marginal tax loss with CRS in general technology depends upon *both* consumption and production derivatives. Having already discussed the notion of loss from taxation with general technologies, this result can be derived fairly easily, as follows.

The optimal commodity tax problem in a one-consumer general technology economy can be represented as:

$$\min_{(t_k)} L(t) = M(\vec{q}; \bar{U}) - \sum_{i=2}^{N} t_i M_i - \pi(\vec{p})$$

$$\text{s.t.} \quad \sum_{i=2}^{N} t_i M_i(\vec{q}; \bar{U}) = \bar{T}$$

along with the market clearance equations (16.4) and the pricing identities (16.5) and (16.6). Notice once again that tax revenue is measured at the compensated equilibrium. The first order conditions are:

(16.19)
$$\frac{\partial L}{\partial t_k} - \lambda \frac{\partial T}{\partial t_k} = 0 \quad k = 2, \ldots, N$$

and

(16.20)
$$\sum_{i=2}^{N} t_i M_i = T$$

But

(16.21)
$$\frac{\partial L}{\partial t_k} = -\sum_{i=2}^{N} t_i \left(M_{ik} + \sum_{j=2}^{N} M_{ij} \frac{\partial p_j}{\partial t_k} \right)$$

and

(16.22)
$$\frac{\partial T}{\partial t_k} = M_k + \sum_{i=2}^{N} t_i \left(M_{ik} + \sum_{j=2}^{N} M_{ij} \frac{\partial p_j}{\partial t_k} \right)$$

Therefore, (16.19) becomes:

$$(16.23) \qquad (1 + \lambda)\frac{\partial L}{\partial t_k} - \lambda M_k = 0 \qquad k = 2, \ldots, N$$

or

$$(16.24) \qquad -(1 + \lambda)\left[\sum_{i=2}^{N} t_i \left(M_{ik} + \sum_{j=2}^{N} M_{ij} \frac{\partial p_j}{\partial t_k} \right) \right] - \lambda M_k = 0$$

$$k = 2, \ldots, N$$

Without imposing the assumption of CRS all we can do is rewrite (16.24) in a form corresponding to, but not identical with, the optimal tax rules for a linear technology. The term

$$(16.25) \qquad \left(M_{ik} + \sum_{j=2}^{N} M_{ij} \frac{\partial p_j}{\partial t_k} \right) = \sum_{j} \frac{\partial X_i^{\text{comp}}}{\partial q_j} \cdot \frac{\partial q_j}{\partial t_k}$$

$$= \frac{\partial X_i^{\text{comp}}}{\partial t_k} \qquad \text{all } i = 2, \ldots, N$$

Therefore, the FOC (16.24) are equivalent to:

$$(16.26) \qquad \frac{-\sum_{i=2}^{N} t_i \dfrac{\partial X_i^{\text{comp}}}{\partial t_k}}{M_k} = \frac{\lambda}{1 + \lambda} = C \qquad k = 2, \ldots, N$$

As was true with the expression for marginal loss, the linear technology rules (15.25) are a special case of the general equations (16.26), with $\partial q_k = \partial t_k$ and $\partial q_j/\partial t_k = 0$, $j \neq k$. But with general technology the derivatives $\partial X_i^{\text{comp}}/\partial t_k$ in (16.26) refer to the general equilibrium changes in X_i^{comp} in response to the tax, which in turn depend upon the changes in the full set of producer and consumer prices as t_k changes. And, as demonstrated above, these price changes are functions of both demand and supply price derivatives through the market clearance equations.

It is not immediately obvious why the assumption of CRS should reduce the general equations (16.26) to their linear technology counterparts. After all, even with CRS supply (input demand) curves will generally be upward (downward) sloping, which means that producer prices will vary in response to variations in government taxes. But the key is that there can be no pure profits in the economy with CRS technology and perfectly competitive market structures. $\pi(\vec{p}) \equiv 0$, so that

$$\frac{\partial \pi}{\partial t_k} = \sum_{i=1}^{N} \pi_i \frac{\partial p_i}{\partial t_k} = 0$$

With $p_1 \equiv 1$ as the numeraire, $\sum_{i=2}^{N} \pi_i(\partial p_i/\partial t_k) = 0$ as well. But this implies, from market clearance, that

$$(16.27) \qquad \sum_{i=2}^{N} M_i \frac{\partial p_i}{\partial t_k} = \sum_{i=2}^{N} \pi_i \frac{\partial p_i}{\partial t_k} \equiv \sum_{i=2}^{N} Y_i \frac{\partial p_i}{\partial t_k} = 0$$

Using this result, subtract $\lambda \sum_{i=2}^{N} M_i(\partial p_i/\partial t_k)$ $(=0)$ from equations (16.24), obtaining:

$$(16.28) \quad -(1+\lambda)\sum_{i=2}^{N} t_i\left(M_{ik} + \sum_{j=2}^{N} M_{ij}\frac{\partial p_j}{\partial t_k}\right) - \lambda\left(M_k + \sum_{j=2}^{N} M_i\frac{\partial p_i}{\partial t_k}\right) = 0$$

$$k = 2, \ldots, N$$

Writing all $(N-1)$ of these equations in matrix notation,

$$(16.29) \quad -(1+\lambda)(t)(M_{ij})\left[I + \left(\frac{\partial p}{\partial t}\right)\right] - \lambda(M_i)\left[I + \left(\frac{\partial p}{\partial t}\right)\right] = 0$$

where:

t, M_{ij}, and M_i are defined as above.

λ and $(1-\lambda)$ are scalars.

I is the $(N-1)$ identity matrix.

$\left(\dfrac{\partial p}{\partial t}\right) =$ the $(N-1) \times (N-1)$ matrix of price derivatives:

$$\begin{bmatrix} \dfrac{\partial p_2}{\partial t_2} & \cdots & \dfrac{\partial p_2}{\partial t_N} \\ \vdots & & \vdots \\ \dfrac{\partial p_N}{\partial t_2} & \cdots & \dfrac{\partial p_N}{\partial t_N} \end{bmatrix}$$

$0 =$ an $(N-1)$ column vector of zeros.

Since $[I + (\partial p/\partial t)]$ is nonsingular, conditions (16.29) imply:

$$(16.30) \quad -(1+\lambda)(t)(M_{ij}) - \lambda(M_i) = 0$$

(16.30) will hold for each of the $(N-1)$ relationships. Hence:

$$(16.31) \quad -(1+\lambda)\sum_{i=2}^{N} t_i M_{ik} - \lambda M_k = 0 \quad\quad k = 2, \ldots, N$$

Rearranging terms:

$$(16.32) \quad \frac{\displaystyle\sum_{i=2}^{N} t_i M_{ik}}{M_k} = -\frac{\lambda}{1+\lambda} = C \quad k = 2, \ldots, N$$

with C independent of k. Equations (16.32) are identical to equations (15.25) and imply that the pattern of optimal taxes depends only upon the compensated demand (factor supply) derivatives $\partial X_i^{\text{comp}}/\partial q_k$. Moreover, the equal percentage change interpretation applies to (16.32) exactly as it applies to (15.25)[5]

---

[5] The independence of the optimal tax rules to supply responses with constant returns-to-scale production was first pointed out to us by Paul Samuelson in a set of unpublished class notes. Refer to J. Stiglitz and P. Dasgupta, "Differential Taxation, Public Goods, and Economic Efficiency," *Review of Economic Studies*, April 1971, for an alternative derivation of this result.

The assumption of CRS, then, greatly simplifies the application of second-best results. Admittedly (16.32) would be difficult to apply in practice given our limited econometric knowledge of the relevant Slutsky substitution terms, but at least the general equilibrium supply responses to the tax can be ignored.

That the assumption of CRS for private production simplifies the optimal commodity tax rules is not unique to that problem. CRS tends to simplify all second-best results, both tax and expenditure theory. Therefore it is somewhat encouraging that econometric studies of stylized aggregate production functions for the U.S. economy so often support (or at least do not reject) the assumption of constant returns to scale production,[6] even granting the fairy-tale quality of these simplistic models and the fact that a significant proportion of U.S. output is produced in markets that are far from perfectly competitive.

MANY-PERSON ECONOMIES—FIXED PRODUCER PRICES

Social Welfare Maximization versus Loss Minimization

Until very recently, public sector economists chose to analyze second-best tax theory almost exclusively within the context of one-consumer economies in order to highlight the efficiency aspects of that theory. The results derived in Chapters 15 and 16 provide a representative sampling of the received theory in the professional journals as late as 1970. In the past few years, however, a number of the leading public sector theorists—Boadway, Diamond, Feldstein, Green, Hartwick, and Mirrlees to name just a few[7]—have reworked second-best tax theory within the more realistic context of many-person economies, with nothing short of a devastating impact on the received doctrine. One of the most striking implications of their work is that it might not be very useful to consider efficiency aspects of various taxes independently of their distributional effects, at least not for the purposes of practical application. Economists have long known that distributional considerations would modify the standard one-consumer results of second-best tax theory, but the recent work has made it painfully obvious just how hopelessly intertwined distributional and efficiency

---

[6] Dale Jorgenson, for instance, argued in 1972 that the empirical literature to date justifies the assumption of constant returns to scale on production functions for the purposes of empirical investment analysis. D. Jorgenson, "Investment Behavior and the Production Function," *The Bell Journal of Economics and Management Science*, Spring 1972 (see part 3 for a review of the literature). The classic reference on aggregate production function estimation is K. Arrow, H. Chenery, B. Minhas, and R. Solow, "Capital-Labor Substitution and Economic Efficiency," *The Review of Economics and Statistics*, August 1961. Their work created an early presumption against the assumption of CRS, but Jorgenson believes subsequent work has sufficiently overridden their early reservations.

[7] R. Boadway, "Integrating Equity and Efficiency in Applied Welfare Economics," *Quarterly Journal of Economics*, November 1976; P. Diamond, "A Many Person Ramsey Tax Rule," *Journal of Public Economics*, November 1975; M. Feldstein, "Distributional Equity and the Optimal Structure of Public Prices," *American Economic Review*, March 1972; J. Green, "Two Models of Optimal Pricing and Taxation," *Oxford Economic Papers*, November 1975; J. Hartwick, "Optimal Price Discrimination," *Journal of Public Economics*, February 1978; and J. Mirrlees, "Optimal Commodity Taxation in a Two-Class Economy," *Journal of Public Economics*, February 1975.

terms become in many second-best tax (and expenditure) decision rules. This is especially disturbing because arbitrary assignment of the distributional weights embodied in an underlying social welfare function can generate almost any result one wants for these decision rules.

Along these same lines, it may not be very useful to think of the effects of distorting taxes in terms of deadweight loss, even though public sector economists have characterized distortion as loss since the very beginnings of the discipline. Unambiguous notions of efficiency loss involve the use of the expenditure function, which is best suited to one-consumer economies. Loss minimization and welfare minimization generate identical results in second-best analysis if the objective function is the welfare or loss of a single individual. In a many-person economy, however, loss minimization and *social* welfare maximization are no longer equivalent except under the highly restrictive assumptions which render the many-person economy essentially equivalent to the one-person economy. Indeed the concept of loss is not generally well defined in a many-person economy. This point is worth considering before analyzing a specific second-best problem in a many-person context.[8]

Loss measures using the expenditure function model of the economy in terms of market prices. Therefore, loss can be directly compared with social welfare expressed in terms of each consumer's indirect utility function, $V^h(\vec{q}; I^h)$, obtained by plugging the consumer's demand (input supply) functions $X_{hk} = X_{hk}(\vec{q}; I^h)$ obtained from utility maximization back into the (negative of the) utility function $U^h(X_{hk})$. Let:

$$(16.33) \qquad W^*[V^h(\vec{q}; I^h)] = V(\vec{q}; I^1, \ldots, I^h, \ldots, I^H)$$

represent the Bergson-Samuelson individualistic social welfare function expressed as a function of the vector of consumer prices, $\vec{q}$, and the distribution of lump-sum incomes, $(I^1, \ldots, I^H)$.

The problem is that, in general, there exists no aggregate expenditure function of the form $M(\vec{q}; \bar{V}^1, \ldots, \bar{V}^H)$, corresponding to the social welfare function, which can be incorporated into a many-person loss measure, because there is no general method for specifying the vector of constant utilities, $\bar{V}_1, \ldots, \bar{V}_H$, to be inserted into M. Suppose, for example, that the government were to change the vector of consumer prices, $\vec{q}$, by instituting a set of distorting taxes, $\vec{t}$. A natural way of defining M would be to hold each consumer at his pretax utility level and ask how much lump-sum income in the aggregate would be required to do this given the new gross of tax consumer prices. In effect, each consumer would be fully compensated for the tax, with (16.33) evaluated at the pretax utility levels $(\bar{V}_0^1, \ldots, \bar{V}_0^H)$. Imagine that the government actually borrowed (at no cost) the required income from some third country and compensated each consumer. Clearly, this amount of income would differ from the income required to keep *social welfare* constant in response to the tax, because by returning *each* consumer to his pretax utility the government has foregone the possibility of exploiting differences in the social welfare weights $\partial W^* / \partial V^h$.

---

[8] Refer also to the discussion of this point in Chapter 4.

By judiciously offering more income to people with high marginal social utilities and less to those with low marginal social utilities, the government can restore the pretax level of *social* welfare without necessarily returning *each* consumer to his pretax utility level. The only appropriate vector of utilities $(\bar{V}_1, \ldots, \bar{V}_H)$ to plug into M, therefore, is the vector of individual utilities that would exist once social welfare has been "compensated" at its pretax level, but there is no general method of solving for this vector. Thus, there is no general many-person loss measure of the form $L(t) = M(\vec{q}; \bar{V}^1, \ldots, \bar{V}^H) - \sum_{h=1}^{H} \sum_{i=2}^{N} t_i X_{hi}$ that would correspond to a one-consumer loss measure. In particular, defining aggregate loss as the sum of individual losses,

$$L(\vec{t}) = \sum_{h=1}^{H} L^h(\vec{t}) = \sum_{h=1}^{H} \left[M^h(\vec{q}; \bar{U}^h) - \sum_{i=2}^{N} t_i X_{hi} \right]$$

bears no necessary relationship to the social welfare function $V(\vec{q}; I^1, \ldots, I^H)$.

One might think that weighting each $L^h(\vec{t})$ by the marginal social welfare terms $\partial W^*/\partial V^h$ and defining aggregate loss as

$$L(\vec{t}) = \sum_{h=1}^{H} \frac{\partial W^*}{\partial V^h} \cdot L^h(\vec{t})$$

would be equivalent to (16.33), but that is not so. It turns out that the proper weighting scheme for individual losses is problem specific. Terms from second-best constraints must be incorporated into the vector of weights to make loss minimization equivalent to social welfare maximization.

The aggregate expenditure function will be unambiguously defined for a many-consumer economy only if the economy is equivalent to a single-consumer economy in the sense that the level of social welfare is independent of any distributional considerations, including both the distribution of lump-sum income and the pattern of consumption (and factor supply) among the various consumers. Recall from the discussion in Chapter 4 that three sufficient conditions have been described that will generate one-consumer equivalence, two by Samuelson and one by Green, as follows:[9]

1. Lump-sum income is continuously and optimally redistributed in accordance with the interpersonal equity conditions of first-best social welfare maximization. That is, the social marginal utility of income is always equal for all consumers.
2. Consumers have identical and homothetic tastes so that for any given consumer price vector, $\vec{q}$, and all lump-sum income distributions $I^1, \ldots, I^H$ the aggregate Engel's (income-consumption) curves are straight parallel lines.
3. The covariance of person h's social marginal utility of income and his proportion of aggregate consumption of any one good (X_{hk}/X_k) is identical for all goods (and factors) $k = 1, \ldots, N$ (Green's condition).

---

[9] P. Samuelson, "Social Indifference Curves, "*Quarterly Journal of Economics*, February 1956; and Green, "Two Models of Optimal Pricing and Taxation." See Chapter 4, pp. 81–85.

Under any of these conditions, the function $V(\vec{q}; I^1, \ldots, I^H)$ is equivalent to $V(\vec{q}; I)$, which in turn is identical to the specification of indirect utility for a single consumer. Moreover, if social welfare can be expressed as $V(\vec{q}; I)$ then the problem

$$\max_{(q)} V(\vec{q}; I)$$

$$\text{s.t. } \vec{q} \cdot \vec{X} = I$$

where:

$\vec{X} =$ the vector of aggregate quantities.

$I =$ aggregate lump-sum income.

has the dual form:

$$\min_{(X)} \vec{q} \cdot \vec{X}$$

$$\text{s.t. } V = \bar{V}$$

The dual can be solved unambiguously for an aggregate expenditure function

$$(16.34) \qquad \sum_{i=1}^{N} q_i X_i^{\text{comp}}(\vec{q}; \bar{U}) = M(\vec{q}; \bar{U})$$

In this case, then, aggregate deadweight loss from taxation is also unambiguously defined as:

$$(16.35) \qquad L(\vec{t}) = M(\vec{q}; \bar{U}) - \sum_{k=2}^{N} t_k X_k^{\text{comp}}(\vec{q}; \bar{U})$$

exactly analogous to the one-consumer economy.

Unfortunately, none of the sufficient conditions is particularly compelling. Thus, it would seem more realistic to analyze second-best tax (and expenditure) problems within the context of social welfare maximization and *actual* general equilibria using (16.33) as the maximand, and under the assumptions of non-identical individual preferences, a fixed distribution of lump-sum incomes $(I^1, \ldots, I^H)$ and unequal social welfare weights, $\partial W^*/\partial V^h$. We will adopt this approach for the remainder of the chapter.

Optimal Commodity Taxation in a Many-Person Economy

As one illustration of the differences in second-best analysis between one-person (equivalent) and many-person economies let us reconsider the optimal commodity tax problem in a many-person context, while retaining the assumption of fixed producer prices. As in the one-consumer economies, assume good 1 is the untaxed numeraire to ensure that *relative* prices change as tax rates are varied, with resulting losses in social welfare. Note also that with fixed producer prices, $\vec{p}$, the social welfare function

$$W^*[V^h(\vec{q}; \bar{I}^h)] = V(\vec{q}; \bar{I}^1, \ldots, \bar{I}^H)$$

along with the pricing identities $\vec{q} = \vec{p} + \vec{t}$ provides a complete general equilibrium description of the economy. Production is entirely specified by the producer price vector, $\vec{p}$. Market clearance is implicit, since production is perfectly elastic at the prices $\vec{p}$, expanding or contracting as needed to meet the aggregate vector of consumer demands. Moreover, $\vec{q}$ is determined by the pricing identities given $\vec{t}$. The government's problem, then, is to:

$$\max_{(t)} W^*[V^h(\vec{q};\bar{I}^h)] = V(\vec{q};\bar{I}^1, \ldots, \bar{I}^H)$$

$$\text{s.t.} \sum_{h=1}^{H} \sum_{i=2}^{N} t_i X_{hi} = \bar{T}$$

along with the identities $\vec{q} = \vec{p} + \vec{t}; q_1 \equiv p_1 \equiv 1; t_1 \equiv 0,$

where:

$\bar{T}$ = the fixed amount of revenue to be collected with distorting taxes.

Assuming the distribution of lump-sum income is fixed, the first-order conditions are:[10]

(16.36)
$$-\sum_{h=1}^{H} \frac{\partial W^*}{\partial V^h} \lambda^h X_{hk} + \lambda \sum_{h=1}^{H} \left(X_{hk} + \sum_{i=2}^{N} t_i \frac{\partial X_{hi}}{\partial q_k} \right) = 0 \text{[11]}$$

$$k = 2, \ldots, N$$

and

(16.37)
$$\sum_{h=1}^{H} \sum_{i=2}^{N} t_i X_{hi} = \bar{T}$$

where:

λ^h = the private marginal utility of income for person h.

Letting $\beta^h = (\partial W^*/\partial V^h)\lambda^h$ represent the social marginal utility of income for person h, rewrite (16.36) as:

(16.38)
$$-\sum_{h=1}^{H} \beta^h X_{hk} + \lambda \sum_{h=1}^{H} \left(X_{hk} + \sum_{i=2}^{N} t_i \frac{\partial X_{hi}}{\partial q_k} \right) = 0$$

$$k = 2, \ldots, N$$

Conditions (16.38) cannot be manipulated into simple and intuitive equal percentage change rules as in the one-consumer case, even in terms of individual's compensated demands (factor supplies). About all that is left by way of a simple general interpretation is that, at the optimum, the marginal change in social welfare resulting from a change in any given tax rate must be proportional

---

[10] The derivation of (16.36) employs Roy's theorem on individual's indirect utility functions, $\partial V^h/\partial q_k = -\lambda^h X_{hk}, k = 1, \ldots, N$. Refer to Chapter 4.
[11] Recall that with fixed producer prices, $\partial q_k/\partial t_k = 1$, and $\partial q_i/\partial t_k = 0, i \neq k$.

to the change in tax revenues resulting from changing the tax rate or

(16.39)
$$\frac{\partial W^*}{\partial t_k} = \lambda \frac{\partial T}{\partial t_k}$$

To see how the equal percentage change rule must be modified, substitute the individual consumers' Slutsky equations:

(16.40)
$$\frac{\partial X_{hi}}{\partial q_k} = S_{ik}^h - X_{hk} \frac{\partial X_{hi}}{\partial I^h} \qquad \begin{array}{l} h = 1, \ldots, H \\ k = 1, \ldots, N \end{array}$$

into (16.38) to obtain:

(16.41)
$$-\sum_{h=1}^{H} \beta^h X_{hk} + \lambda \sum_{h=1}^{H} X_{hk} + \lambda \sum_{h=1}^{H} \sum_{i=2}^{N} t_i S_{ik}^h$$

$$-\lambda \sum_{h=1}^{H} \sum_{i=2}^{N} t_i X_{hk} \frac{\partial X_{hi}}{\partial I^h} = 0 \qquad k = 2, \ldots, N$$

Rearranging terms, dividing through by $\lambda \sum_{h=1}^{H} X_{hk} = \lambda X_k$, and noting that $S_{ik}^h = S_{ki}^h$, yields:

(16.42)
$$\frac{\displaystyle\sum_{i=1}^{H} \sum_{i=2}^{N} t_i S_{ki}^h}{X_k} = -1 + \frac{\frac{1}{\lambda} \displaystyle\sum_{h=1}^{H} \beta^h X_{hk}}{X_k} + \frac{\displaystyle\sum_{i=2}^{N} \sum_{h=1}^{H} t_i X_{hk} \frac{\partial X_{hi}}{\partial I^h}}{X_k}$$

Recalling the definition of Feldstein's distributional coefficient for good k (see Chapter 4):

$$\lambda^k = \sum_{h=1}^{H} \beta^h \frac{X_{hk}}{X_k}$$

(16.42) becomes:

(16.43)
$$\frac{\displaystyle\sum_{h=1}^{H} \sum_{i=2}^{N} t_i S_{ki}^h}{X_k} = -1 + \frac{\lambda^k}{\lambda} + \frac{\displaystyle\sum_{h=1}^{H} \sum_{i=2}^{N} t_i \frac{\partial X_{hi}}{\partial I^h} X_{hk}}{X_k} \qquad k = 2, \ldots, N$$

The left-hand side of (16.43) gives the percentage change in the aggregate compensated demand for good k (approximately), but the right-hand side is no longer independent of k. Rather, the percentage changes depend in a complicated manner on Feldstein's distributional coefficients and the change in tax revenue in response to changes in the pattern of lump-sum incomes. Moreover, the right-hand side cannot readily be divided into two distinct sets of terms, with one set containing all relevant efficiency considerations and the second containing all relevant distributional information.

One can shed some additional light on the pattern of optimal taxes by considering changes in actual demands, even though these changes cannot be described in a simple way either. From the individual Slutsky equations:

(16.44)
$$S_{ki}^h = \frac{\partial X_{hk}}{\partial q_i} + X_{hi} \frac{\partial X_{hk}}{\partial I^h}$$

Substituting for the S_{ki}^h in equation (16.43) and rearranging terms:

$$(16.45) \quad \frac{\sum_{h=1}^{H} \sum_{i=2}^{N} t_i \frac{\partial X_{hk}}{\partial q_i}}{X_k} = -1 + \frac{\lambda^k}{\lambda} + \frac{\sum_{h=1}^{H} \sum_{i=2}^{N} t_i \frac{\partial X_{hi}}{\partial I^h} X_{hk}}{X_k}$$

$$-\frac{\sum_{h=1}^{H} \left(\sum_{i=2}^{N} t_i X_{hi} \right) \frac{\partial X_{hk}}{\partial I^h}}{X_k} \qquad k = 2, \ldots, N$$

$$(16.46) \quad \frac{\sum_{h=1}^{H} \sum_{i=2}^{N} t_i \frac{\partial X_{hk}}{\partial q_i}}{X_k} = -1 + \frac{\lambda^k}{\lambda} + \frac{\sum_{h=1}^{H} \sum_{i=2}^{N} t_i \frac{\partial X_{hi}}{\partial I^h} X_{hk}}{X_k}$$

$$-\sum_{h=1}^{N} \left(\frac{\sum_{i=2}^{N} t_i X_{hi}}{I^h} \cdot \frac{\partial X_{hk}}{\partial I^h} \cdot \frac{I^h}{X_{hk}} \right)$$

$$k = 2, \ldots, N$$

(16.46) says that the actual percentage changes in demand (factor supply) resulting from the optimal pattern of commodity taxes should be greater:

1. The lower its distributional coefficient λ^k, or the more it is demanded by people with low social marginal utilities of income ($\Delta X_k / X_k$ is presumably negative for goods, λ positive). Presumably these people are the rich. If so, the rule says, other things equal, taxes should be heaviest on those goods consumed most heavily by the rich.
2. The more it is demanded by people whose total taxes change least as lump-sum income changes.
3. The more it is demanded by people for whom, other things equal, the product of the fraction of income paid as taxes and the income elasticity of demand for the good is highest.

Unfortunately, there is no clear presumption as to who the people referred to in 2 and 3 might be, so that rewriting the first-order conditions in terms of actual demand changes still fails to provide any really clear intuitive feel for the optimal pattern of taxation.

A Covariance Interpretation of Optimal Taxation

Peter Diamond has recently provided an ingenious interpretation of these rules that does give one a better intuitive appreciation of the tax rules.[12] Suppose the government, in addition to the commodity taxes, has the ability to offer a single head or poll subsidy of equal value to all consumers. While this is admittedly a lump-sum subsidy, it is not the sophisticated variable subsidy necessary to satisfy the interpersonal equity conditions of first-best theory.

---

[12] P. Diamond, "A Many Person Ramsey Tax Rule."

With the additional head subsidy, the governments problem becomes:

$$\max_{(\vec{t},I)} V(\vec{q};I^1,\ldots,I^H)$$

$$\text{s.t.} \quad \sum_{h=1}^{H} \sum_{i=2}^{N} t_i X_{hi} = \bar{T} + H \cdot I$$

where:

I = the equal per-person subsidy.

The first-order conditions with respect to the t_k are obviously unchanged by the presence of the subsidy. Reproducing (16.41):

(16.47)
$$-\sum_{h=1}^{H} \beta^h X_{hk} + \lambda \sum_{h=1}^{H} X_{hk} + \lambda \sum_{h=1}^{H} \sum_{i=2}^{N} t_i S_{ik}^h$$

$$-\lambda \sum_{h=1}^{H} \sum_{i=2}^{N} t_i X_{hk} \frac{\partial X_{hi}}{\partial I^h} = 0 \qquad k = 2, \ldots, N$$

The first-order condition with respect to the head tax, I, is:

(16.48)
$$\sum_{h=1}^{H} \beta^h + \lambda \left(\sum_{h=1}^{H} \sum_{i=2}^{N} t_i \frac{\partial X_{hi}}{\partial I} - H \right) = 0$$

with $\partial I = \partial I^h$, all $h = 1, \ldots, H$. Diamond then defines

(16.49)
$$\gamma^h = \beta^h + \lambda \sum_{i=2}^{N} t_i \frac{\partial X_{hi}}{\partial I^h}$$

as the full social marginal utility of income for person h, consisting of the conventional direct increase in social utility when I^h increases, the β^h term, *plus* the social marginal utility of the increased tax revenues when I^h increases, equal to $\lambda \sum_{i=2}^{N} t_i(\partial X_{hi}/\partial I^h)$. With γ^h defined in this manner, the first-order conditions (16.47) can be rewritten as:

(16.50)
$$\lambda \sum_{i=2}^{N} \sum_{h=1}^{H} t_i S_{ik}^h = \sum_{h=1}^{H} (\gamma^h - \lambda) \cdot X_{hk} \qquad k = 2, \ldots, N$$

Furthermore, (16.48) becomes simply:

(16.51)
$$\lambda H = \sum_{h=1}^{H} \gamma^h$$

or

(16.52)
$$\lambda = \frac{\displaystyle\sum_{h=1}^{H} \gamma^h}{H}$$

Thus, λ can be interpreted as the *average* full social marginal utility of income given that the government employs an optimal head subsidy. Moreover, once λ is expressed in this form, the first-order conditions (16.50) have a simple covariance interpretation. To see this, divide (16.50) by $X_k = \sum_h X_{hk}$ and note that $S_{ik}^h = S_{ki}^h$, to obtain:

(16.53)
$$\frac{\sum\limits_{h=1}^{H} \sum\limits_{i=2}^{N} t_i S_{ki}^h}{X_k} = \frac{\sum\limits_{h=1}^{H} (\gamma^h - \lambda) X_{hk}}{\lambda X_k} \qquad k = 2, \ldots, N$$

But, from (16.51), $\sum_{h=1}^{H} (\gamma^h - \lambda) = 0$. Hence, $\sum_h (\gamma^h - \lambda) \cdot \bar{X}_k = 0$, where

$$\bar{X}_k = \frac{\sum\limits_{h=1}^{H} X_{hk}}{H},$$

so that (16.53) can be rewritten as:

(16.54)
$$\frac{\sum\limits_{i=1}^{H} \sum\limits_{i=2}^{N} t_i S_{ki}^h}{X_k} = \frac{\sum\limits_{h=1}^{H} (\gamma^h - \lambda)(X_{hk} - \bar{X}_k)}{H\lambda\bar{X}_k} \qquad k = 2, \ldots, N$$

(16.54) says that the aggregate percentage change in the compensated demand (supply) of good (factor) k should be proportional to the covariance between the full marginal social utility of income and the consumption (supply) of good (factor) k. This is the simplest interpretation of the many-person optimal tax rule to date.

A Two-Class Tax Rule

Defining an optimal per-person income subsidy and the full social marginal utility of income yields some additional intuition into the pattern of optimal taxes. Consider again the first-order conditions (16.50) with λ interpreted as the average full social marginal utility of income given a head subsidy. Multiply each equation by t_k and sum over $k = 1, \ldots, N$ to obtain:[13]

(16.55)
$$\sum_{h=1}^{H} \left[(\gamma^h - \lambda) \sum_{k=1}^{N} t_k X_{hk} \right] = \lambda \sum_{h=1}^{H} \sum_{i=1}^{N} \sum_{k=1}^{N} t_i S_{ik}^h t_k$$

Since S_{ik}^h is negative semidefinite,

$$\sum_{i=1}^{N} \sum_{h=1}^{H} \sum_{k=1}^{N} t_i S_{ik}^h t_k \leq 0.$$

Therefore,

(16.56)
$$\sum_{h=1}^{H} \left[(\gamma^h - \lambda) \sum_{k=1}^{N} t_k X_{hk} \right] \leq 0$$

Suppose the government is willing to think of the H consumers as divided into two subsets, the rich and the poor, such that all rich people are identical and all poor people are identical (equal preferences and equal full social marginal

---

[13] With $t_1 = 0$, k or i can be summed from 1 or 2 to N.

utilities of income). Let there be R rich people each with full social marginal utility γ^R, and $(H - R)$ poor people each with full social marginal utility of income γ^P, such that $\gamma^P > \gamma^R$ and $\gamma^P > \lambda$, where λ is the average full social marginal utility of income over all H people.[14] With an optimal head subsidy (equation (16.51) satisfied):

$$(16.57) \qquad \sum_{h=1}^{H} \gamma^h = \lambda H = R \cdot \gamma^R + (H - R)\gamma^P$$

Substituting (16.57) into (16.56) yields:

$$(16.58) \qquad R(\gamma^R - \lambda) \sum_{k=1}^{N} t_k X_{Rk} + (H - R)(\gamma^P - \lambda) \sum_{k=1}^{N} t_k X_{Pk} \leq 0$$

But from (16.57),

$$(16.59) \qquad [R + (H - R)]\lambda = R\gamma^R + (H - R)\gamma^P$$

Rearranging terms:

$$(16.60) \qquad R(\gamma^R - \lambda) = -(H - R)(\gamma^P - \lambda)$$

Substituting for $R(\gamma^R - \lambda)$ in (16.58) yields:

$$(16.61) \quad -(H - R)(\gamma^P - \lambda) \sum_{k=1}^{N} t_k X_{Rk} + (H - R)(\gamma^P - \lambda) \sum_{k=1}^{N} t_k X_{Pk} \leq 0$$

Rearranging terms:

$$(16.62) \qquad (H - R)(\gamma^P - \lambda)\left(\sum_{k=1}^{N} t_k X_{Pk} - \sum_{k=1}^{N} t_k X_{Rk} \right) \leq 0$$

Hence, assuming $(\gamma^P - \lambda) > 0$ implies that $\sum_{k=1}^{N} t_k X_{Rk} \geq \sum_{k=1}^{N} t_k X_{Pk}$, or that the optimal pattern of commodity taxes should, in general, collect more taxes from the rich than the poor. This result is certainly consistent with one's intuitive sense of the effect of social welfare considerations on the optimal pattern of commodity taxes, although equation (16.56) will not necessarily yield such simple guidelines when there are more than two classes of people.

A MANY-PERSON ECONOMY WITH GENERAL TECHNOLOGY

Synthesizing the separate analyses of a one-person economy with general technology and the many-person economy with linear technology (constant producer prices) is relatively straightforward, especially under the assumption of CRS production.

Let us begin by considering the optimal commodity tax problem. We saw that assuming CRS in the context of a one-consumer economy generated the same optimal tax rules that resulted when production technology was characterized by fixed producer prices. The key to this result lay in the fact that there

---

[14] Refer to equation (16.52) and its derivation, above.

can never be pure economic profits or losses with CRS and perfectly competitive markets, so that the value of the general equilibrium profit function $\pi(\vec{p})$ is identically zero for all values of the producer price vector $\vec{p}$.

The same correspondence exists in the many-person economy. So long as we assume CRS, the original distribution of lump-sum incomes $(I^1, \ldots, I^H)$ will remain unchanged as producer prices vary in response to taxation. Hence, the many-person optimal tax rule is identical to its linear technology counterpart. In fact, Diamond used a general technology CRS model to generate the many-person optimal tax rules.

A model appropriate for analyzing second-best tax (and expenditure) problems in a many-person, general technology economy was presented in Chapter 4. To review briefly, the object of government policy is to maximize a social welfare function of the form

$$W[V^h(\vec{q}; I^h)] = V(\vec{q}; I^1, \ldots, I^H)$$

specified in terms of consumer prices, exactly as in the many-person, linear technology case. The only new wrinkle is that general technology production can no longer be specified by means of the generalized profit function, $\pi(\vec{p})$, as in the one-consumer economy, because social welfare is not measured in terms of lump-sum income. Nonetheless, production must still be specified in terms of prices and actual general equilibria to be compatible with social welfare. Moreover, it must be amenable to various kinds of technologies. Given these considerations, the natural choice is to use an implicit aggregate production frontier of the form $F(\vec{Y}) = 0$, exactly as in first-best analysis, where $\vec{Y}$ = the vector of aggregate goods (factors) supplies (demands), but with the general equilibrium market supply (input demand) functions $Y_i = Y_i(\vec{p})$, $i = 1, \ldots, N$, replacing the quantities $\vec{Y}$. The resulting function, $F[\vec{Y}(\vec{p})] = 0$, which we labeled the production-price frontier in Chapter 4, specifies all relevant production parameters assuming competitive market behavior.

Finally, general technology requires explicit market clearance equations of the form

(16.63) $$\sum_{h=1}^{H} X_{hi}(\vec{p} + \vec{t}; I^h) = Y^i(\vec{p}) \qquad i = 1, \ldots, N$$

to solve for the vector of producer prices given a vector of tax rates. The pricing identities $\vec{q} = \vec{p} + \vec{t}$ then solve for the vector of consumer prices.

Thus, a full general equilibrium model useful for analyzing any problem in the second-best theory of taxation can be represented as:

$$\max_{(\vec{q}, \vec{t}, \vec{p})} W[V^h(\vec{q}; \overline{I}^h)]$$

s.t. (1) $F[\vec{Y}(\vec{p})] = 0$

(2) $\sum_{h=1}^{H} X_{hi}(\vec{q}; I^h) = Y_i(\vec{p}) \qquad i = 1, \ldots, N$

(3) $q_i = p_i + t_i \qquad i = 2, \ldots, N$

(4) $q_1 \equiv p_1 \equiv 1 \qquad t_1 = 0$

As always, setting $t_1 = 0$ ensures that the tax vector $\vec{t}$ will change the vector of relative consumer and producer prices and thereby create distortions.

The model can be greatly simplified by incorporating market clearance directly into the production frontier and thinking of the government as solving directly for the vector of consumer prices, $\vec{q}$, rather than the vector of taxes, $\vec{t}$, as follows:

$$\max_{(\vec{q})} W[V^h(\vec{q}; I^h)]$$

$$\text{s.t.} \quad F\left[\sum_{h=1}^{H} X_{hi}(\vec{q}; I^h) \right] = 0$$

The vector of producer prices $\vec{p}$ can then be determined through the market clearance equations, after which the $(N - 1)$ optimal tax rates are given by the pricing identities, $t_i = q_i - p_i$, $i = 2, \dots, N$. The final point is that there is no need to include the government's budget constraint,

$$\sum_{h=1}^{H} \sum_{i=2}^{N} t_i X_{hi}(\vec{q}; I^h) = \bar{T},$$

explicitly in the model. Since the model describes an actual market general equilibrium, Walras' law guarantees that the budget constraint is satisfied. Recall from the discussion of Chapter 4 that Walras' law can have either of two interpretations:

1. If each economic agent is on his budget constraint (firms are profit maximizing) and all but one market is in equilibrium, the final market must also be in equilibrium.
2. If all but one economic agent is satisfying its budget constraint and *all* markets are in equilibrium, then the last economic agent must also be on its budget constraint. It is the second interpretation which allows us to exclude the government's budget constraint since the model: (a) explicitly posits market clearance in all markets, (b) implicitly assumes all consumers are on their budget constraints as a prerequisite for defining indirect utility functions, and (c) implicitly assumes all producers are maximizing profits when substituting the general equilibrium supply (input demand) functions $\vec{Y}(\vec{p})$ into the aggregate production frontier $F(\vec{Y}) = 0$.

This is the model actually used by Diamond to generate many-person optimal taxes rules identical to equations (16.50) and (16.52) above.[15] To see that the assumption of general technology makes no difference so long as the technology exhibits constant returns to scale, consider the first-order conditions of the model with respect to q_k and an equal head subsidy, I.

---

[15] The model is not identical to Diamond's model, since he included a Samuelson nonexclusive public good and assumed all consumers had identical initial endowments of lump-sum income.

$$(16.64) \qquad \sum_{h=1}^{H} \frac{\partial W}{\partial V^h} \frac{\partial V^h}{\partial q_k} = \lambda \sum_{i=1}^{N} \sum_{h=1}^{H} F_i \frac{\partial X_{hi}}{\partial q_k} \qquad k = 2, \ldots, N$$

$$(16.65) \qquad \sum_{h=1}^{H} \frac{\partial W}{\partial V^h} \frac{\partial V^h}{\partial I} = \lambda \sum_{i=1}^{N} \sum_{h=1}^{H} F_i \frac{\partial X_{hi}}{\partial I}$$

Equation (16.64) implicitly embodies the assumption of CRS production in that the initial distribution of lump-sum income, $(I^1, \ldots, I^H)$, is assumed unchanged by a marginal change in the kth consumer price.

From Roy's theorem on indirect utility functions, the definition of marginal social utility β^h and the assumption of profit maximization with $p_1 \equiv 1$ (16.64) can be rewritten as:[16]

$$(16.66) \qquad -\sum_{h=1}^{H} \beta^h X_{hk} = \lambda \sum_{h=1}^{H} \sum_{i=1}^{N} p_i \frac{\partial X_{hi}}{\partial q_k} \qquad k = 2, \ldots, N$$

But $p_i = q_i - t_i$, $i = 1, \ldots, N$. Hence

$$(16.67) \qquad -\sum_{h=1}^{H} \beta^h X_{hk} = \lambda \sum_{h=1}^{H} \sum_{i=1}^{N} \left(q_i \frac{\partial X_{hi}}{\partial q_k} - t_i \frac{\partial X_{hi}}{\partial q_k} \right) \qquad k = 2, \ldots, N$$

Further, if consumers are on their budget constraints,

$$(16.68) \qquad \sum_{i=1}^{N} q_i \frac{\partial X_{hi}}{\partial q_k} = -X_{hk} \qquad h = 1, \ldots, H$$

Therefore:

$$(16.69) \qquad -\sum_{h=1}^{H} \beta^h X_{hk} = \lambda \sum_{h=1}^{H} \left(-X_{hk} - \sum_{i=1}^{N} t_i \frac{\partial X_{hi}}{\partial q_k} \right) \qquad k = 2, \ldots, N$$

which is identical to equation (16.38).[17]

Turning to the optimal head tax, make use of profit maximization, the definition of marginal social utility, and the definitional relationships among prices and taxes, as above, to rewrite (16.65) as:

$$(16.70) \qquad \sum_{h=1}^{H} \beta^h = \lambda \sum_{h=1}^{H} \sum_{i=1}^{N} (q_i - t_i) \frac{\partial X_{hi}}{\partial I}$$

If consumers are on their budget constraints,

$$(16.71) \qquad \sum_{i=1}^{N} q_i \frac{\partial X_{hi}}{\partial I} = 1 \qquad h = 1, \ldots, H$$

---

[16] From profit maximization $F_i/F_1 = p_i/p_1$. But $p_1 \equiv 1$ and F can be scaled such that $F_1 = 1$, so that $F_i = p_i$, $i = 2, \ldots, N$.

[17] $\sum_{i=1}^{N} t_i \frac{\partial X_{hi}}{\partial q_k} = \sum_{i=2}^{N} t_i \frac{\partial X_{hi}}{\partial q_k}$ with $t_1 = 0$.

Hence,

$$(16.72) \qquad \sum_{h=1}^{H} \beta^h = \lambda H - \lambda \sum_{h=1}^{H} \sum_{i=1}^{N} t_i \frac{\partial X_{hi}}{\partial I}$$

But

$$\gamma^h = \beta^h + \lambda \sum_{i=1}^{N} t_i \frac{\partial X_{hi}}{\partial I}$$

the full social marginal utility of income. Therefore:

$$(16.73) \qquad \lambda = \sum_{h=1}^{H} \frac{\gamma^h}{H}$$

the average full social marginal utility of income, exactly as in equation (16.52). Consequently, the many-person optimal tax rules continue to have a simple covariance interpretation.

OPTIMAL INCOME TAXATION

The models of optimal taxation in this and the preceding chapter have been assuming that the government is free to tax all goods and factors. Parallel with the development of these models, research in the theory of taxation over the past ten years has also been focusing on more restricted, and realistic, cases in which the government is constrained to vary only a few taxes. Roughly speaking, this line of inquiry has proceeded along two separate paths. One group of economists has adopted the basic model for optimal commodity taxation and attempted to develop theorems on optimal charges (or levels) of taxes for a subset of the goods and factors (Dixit, Guesnerie, Hatta).[18] A second group, following the lead of Mirrlees and Fair in 1971, has concentrated specifically on optimal income taxation (e.g., Mirrlees, Fair, Sheshinski, Atkinson, Stiglitz, Sadka, Stern, and Searde).[19] Since the income tax models differ considerably

---

[18] A. Dixit, "Welfare Effects of Tax and Price Changes," *Journal of Public Economics*, February 1975. Also, A. Dixit, and K. Munk, "Welfare Effects of Tax and Price Changes: A Correction," *Journal of Public Economics*, August 1977; R. Guesnerie, "On the Direction of Tax Reform," *Journal of Public Economics*, April 1977; R. Guesnerie, "Financing Public Goods with Commodity Taxes: A Tax Reform Viewpoint," *Econometrica*, March 1979; and T. Hatta, "A Theory of Piecemeal Policy Recommendations, *Review of Economic Studies*, February 1977.

[19] J. Mirrlees, "An Exploration in the Theory of Optimum Income Taxation," *Review of Economic Studies*, April 1971 (the seminal article); J. Mirrlees, "Optimal Tax Theory: A Synthesis," *Journal of Public Economics*, November 1976; R. Fair, "The Optimal Distribution of Income," *Quarterly Journal of Economics*, November 1971; E. Sheshinski, "The Optimal Linear Income Tax," *Review of Economic Studies*, July 1972; A. Atkinson, "How Progressive Should Income Tax Be?," in M. Parkin, ed., *Essays in Modern Economics*, London: Longman Group Ltd., 1973; A. Atkinson and J. Stiglitz, "The Design of Tax Structure: Direct vs. Indirect Taxation," *Journal of Public Economics*, July/August 1976; E. Sadka, "On Income Distribution, Incentive Effects, and Optimal Income Taxation, *Review of Economic Studies*, June 1976; N. Stern, "On the Specification of Models of Optimum Income Taxation," *Journal of Public Economics*, July/August 1976; J. Searde, "On the Shape of Optimal Tax Schedules," *Journal of Public Economics*, April 1977; and D. Bradford and H. Rosen, "The Optimal Taxation of Commodities and Income," *American Economic Association Papers and Proceedings*, May 1976.

from those employed to study commodity taxation, we will discuss the optimal income tax literature in this section as an example of optimal restricted taxation.

The study of income taxation in a second-best environment is compelling for a number of reasons, foremost among them being that income taxes are such an important revenue source for most governments. Tax reform often implies reform of an existing income tax system. Beyond this practical consideration, however, income taxes have a number of analytical properties that are of special interest. For instance, it is possible to design income tax schedules with varying average rates of taxation, either by means of a general tax schedule of the form $T = T(Y)$, $T' > 0$, with varying marginal rates T', or a two-part schedule consisting of a fixed subsidy and a constant marginal rate, $T = -\alpha + \beta$. Y, the so-called linear income tax. The taxation of individual commodities, by contrast, will almost certainly have to be at one fixed rate, either ad valorem or per unit, a feature central to the optimal commodity tax models. The flexibility to vary average tax rates in turn makes income taxes an excellent instrument for pursuing society's distributional goals. Rather than attempting to tax everything in accordance with rules such as (16.38), a government might choose to levy a single income tax in order to meet its revenue requirements, hoping thereby to effect a reasonable compromise between efficiency and equity. Of course, if labor or some other factor of production is in absolutely fixed supply, taxing that source of income will not entail any efficiency loss, and the government can try to approximate the first-best interpersonal equity conditions. In general, though, one would expect some efficiency loss with an income tax. A final, and related point is that the analysis of income taxation in second-best environments is a natural outgrowth of the attempt to design taxes according to accepted ability-to-pay principles. As indicated in Chapter 13, these principles were developed entirely under first-best assumptions, in which the main thrust of the analysis was to describe a tax base and rate schedule that best satisfied purely distributional notions such as equal treatment of equals, or equal marginal social utilities of income. We also saw that income, broadly defined, is considered by many to be the best tax base for these purposes. The recent second-best analysis of income taxation has tried to determine how first-best distributional criteria are modified by considerations of efficiency loss, but it is still firmly grounded in the ability to pay or neoclassical interpersonal equity tradition.

Unfortunately, we will not be able to analyze the standard optimal tax model in any great detail since its solution requires knowledge of the calculus of variations, which is beyond the scope of this text. But the structure of the model is easy enough to understand and it is worth noting the principal results obtained to date, some of which have important implications for commodity taxation.

Stripped to its bare essentials, the optimal income tax problem can be represented as follows. Suppose each consumer has a preference function defined over the consumption of a composite commodity (c), and labor (ℓ):

(16.74) $$U = U(c, \ell)$$

All individuals have identical preferences but varying abilities or skills indexed by the parameter N.[20] N transfers one unit of labor, ℓ, into $N\ell$ efficiency units which are assumed to be perfect substitutes in the production of c. Let W be the wage rate per efficiency unit of labor. Hence an N-person's income is equal to:

$$(16.75) \qquad Y = WN\ell$$

Assume further that the index of skills N is distributed across the population in accordance with a probability density function $\int_0^\infty f(N)dN$.

The government is interested in maximizing a Bergson-Samuelson social welfare function of the form:

$$(16.76) \qquad \omega = \frac{1}{V} \int_0^\infty U^V(c, \ell) f(N) dN$$

where V defines society's aversion to inequality. For example, $V = 1$ implies utilitarianism with equal social marginal utilities for all. At the other extreme, $V = -\infty$ implies the Rawls criterion of maximizing the utility of the individual with lowest utility.

The policy instrument is an income tax schedule of the general form:

$$(16.77) \qquad T = T(Y)$$

which the government will levy to satisfy an aggregate budget constraint of the form

$$(16.78) \qquad \int_0^\infty T(WN\ell) f(N) dN = R$$

where R could reflect some public goods or the deficits from decreasing cost production. $R = 0$ implies that the government is solely interested in income redistribution.

Faced with the income tax, each individual will have income available for consumption equal to:

$$(16.79) \qquad C = y - T(Y) = WN\ell - T(WN\ell)$$

Hence, maximizing (16.74) with respect to ℓ, given (16.79), implies

$$(16.80) \qquad WN(1 - T')U_C + U_\ell = 0$$

The government's problem, then, is to maximize (16.76) with respect to the parameters of $T(Y)$, subject to (16.78) and (16.80). The constraint (16.80) highlights the second-best nature of the problem, that the marginal tax rate T' distorts each consumer's choice between consumption and labor (leisure). For suppose the government's social welfare function is utilitarian ($V = 1$). With identical consumers, the first-best interpersonal equity conditions would imply

---

[20] For our purposes it doesn't matter whether these differing abilities are innate or the result of varying educational experiences, so long as N is exogenous to each individual.

equal posttax (transfer) income for all. If the income tax were lump sum (e.g., labor in absolutely fixed supply), the optimal marginal tax rate would be 100 percent. But with variable labor supply, increases in marginal rates increase the distortion, or efficiency loss, thereby partially offsetting the gains from an improved distribution. The optimal solution, then, finds the tax parameters that just equalize the efficiency losses and distributional gains on the margin.

Two aspects of the solution are of interest, the optimal tax parameters themselves, and the conditions under which an optimal income tax is also *the* optimal second-best tax, that is, the conditions under which taxation of commodities is unnecessary. Despite the relative simplicity of the models analyzed to date, a number of interesting results have emerged.

With respect to the tax parameters themselves, their values clearly depend on the structure of the tax schedule (e.g., linear or general) and the values of the parameters of the model, including: V, the aversion to inequality; the elasticity of labor supply; the distribution of skills throughout the population; and R, the revenue requirement. Numerical analysis with a *linear* tax schedule has yielded a number of intuitively appealing results. Generally speaking, the marginal tax rate is higher:

1. The higher society's aversion to inequality (Atkinson and Stern).[21] The more to be gained from redistribution, the more inefficiency society can tolerate;
2. The greater the dispersion of skills (Mirrlees and Stern)[22]. With an individualistic social welfare function, increased dispersion increases the gains from redistribution.
3. The lower the labor supply elasticity (Stern)[23]. Generally speaking, the efficiency loss implies by a given marginal rate varies inversely with the elasticity. In the limiting case, with the elasticity identically zero, the tax rate would be 100 percent with a utilitarian social welfare function, as noted above. Stern's experiments showed that the marginal rate is extremely sensitive to the elasticity parameter.
4. The higher the revenue requirement R (Stern)[24]. Roughly, a given tax rate entails less redistribution when some of the revenues must be used for other purposes. But this tends to increase the marginal returns from still further redistribution, implying a higher marginal rate.

The most striking result with *general* tax schedules is that the marginal rates are not uniformly increasing throughout the range of income, in contrast to many actual tax schedules. In fact, as Sadka first demonstrated,[25] with a finite

[21] Atkinson, "How Progressive Should Income Tax Be?" and Stern, "On the Specification of Models of Optimum Income Taxation."
[22] Mirrlees, "An Exploration in the Theory of Optimum Income Taxation," and Stern, "On the Specification of Models of Optimum Income Taxation."
[23] Stern, "On the Specification of Models of Optimum Income Taxation.
[24] Ibid.
[25] Sadka, "On Income Distribution, Incentive Effects, and Optimal Income Taxation."

population the optimal marginal rate at the top of the income scale will be *zero* if the social welfare function is utilitarian! To see why this must be so, suppose there exists someone who earns more income than anyone else, say $Z, and that the marginal tax rate on the $(Z + 1)^{st}$ dollar is positive. Given that rate, the individual chose to stop at Z. Now set the marginal rate on the $(Z + 1)^{st}$ dollar at zero. Presumably he will now choose to work harder and take the extra dollar of income. If so, he is obviously better off. Moreover, his total tax payments remain unchanged so the government's revenue constraint remains satisfied and no one else is affected. Hence social welfare increases.

Searde demonstrated a similar result for the lowest incomes,[26] namely that so long as everyone who faces a positive wage chooses to work, the optimal marginal rate for the lowest income level is also zero. This follows because the only reason to levy positive rates at any income level, given that inefficiency will arise, is to redistribute the revenue to people below that income level. But no one is below the lowest income level. Hence there is only an efficiency loss from taxing that income. Combining the Sadka and Searde results, the optimal general tax schedule must have a segment of rising marginal rates near the bottom and a segment of falling marginal rates near the top, contrary to usual practice.

With respect to the second issue of overall optimality, Atkinson and Stiglitz[27] showed that the ability to levy either linear or general income taxes significantly reduces the restrictions on preferences sufficient to render an income tax *the* optimal second best tax. Specifically, a linear income tax of the form $T = -\alpha + \beta Y$ is optimal if preferences have an additive representation and the marginal disutility of labor is constant. Without the lump-sum subsidy, $-\alpha$, these same conditions imply that levying per-unit or ad valorem taxes on all commodities remains the optimal tax structure, with the tax rates inversely proportional to the own-price elasticity of demand. More importantly, they were able to prove that a general income tax is optimal if preferences have a representation in which labor is weakly separable, meaning that $\partial(U_{Xi}/U_{Xj})/\partial l = 0$, all $i, j = 1, \ldots, N$.[28] This is perhaps the strongest analytical result yet achieved with the optimal income tax models.

THE SOCIAL WELFARE IMPLICATIONS OF
ANY GIVEN CHANGE IN TAXES

We will conclude the chapter by considering the social welfare implications of a marginal change in a single tax, or of substituting one vector of tax rates for another, equal revenue vector of rates in the context of a many-person, general technology economy.[29] Begin by totally differentiating the social

[26] Searde, "On the Shape of Optimal Tax Schedules."

[27] Atkinson and Stiglitz, "The Design of Tax Structure: Direct vs. Indirect Taxation."

[28] Searde also derived this result. Searde, "On the Shape of Optimal Tax Schedules."

[29] The analysis in this section draws heavily from Boadway, "Integrating Equity and Efficiency in Applied Welfare Economics."

welfare function $W^* = W[V^h(\vec{q}; I^h)]$ with respect to prices and income. Using Roy's theorem and the definition of social marginal utility of income β^h:

(16.81) $$dW = -\sum_{h=1}^{H} \sum_{i=1}^{N} \frac{\partial W}{\partial V^h} \alpha^h X_{hi} dq_i + \sum_{h=1}^{H} \frac{\partial W}{\partial V^h} \alpha^h dI^h$$

(16.82) $$dW = -\sum_{h=1}^{H} \sum_{i=1}^{N} \beta^h X_{hi} dq_i + \sum_{h=1}^{H} \beta^h dI^h$$

Next, totally differentiate the production-price frontier $F(\sum_{h=1}^{H} X_{hi}) = 0$, in which the market clearance equations have been used to substitute consumers' demands and factor supplies for the production aggregates Y_i.

(16.83) $$\sum_{i=1}^{N} F_i \sum_{h=1}^{H} dX_{hi} = 0$$

Assuming perfect competition and $p_1 \equiv 1$, (16.83) becomes:

(16.84) $$\sum_{i=1}^{N} p_i \sum_{h=1}^{H} dX_{hi} = 0$$

But $q_i = p_i + t_i$, $i = 1, \dots, N$. Multiplying each price by dX_{hi}, and summing over all goods and people yields:

(16.85) $$\sum_{i=1}^{N} \sum_{h=1}^{H} q_i dX_{hi} = \sum_{i=1}^{N} \sum_{h=1}^{H} (p_i + t_i) dX_{hi}$$

which, from (16.84) becomes:

(16.86) $$\sum_{i=1}^{N} \sum_{h=1}^{H} q_i dX_{hi} = \sum_{i=1}^{H} \sum_{h=1}^{H} t_i dX_{hi}$$

Next, totally differentiate each consumer's budget constraint and sum over all consumers to obtain:

(16.87) $$\sum_{h=1}^{H} dI^h = \sum_{h=1}^{H} \sum_{i=1}^{N} q_i dX_{hi} + \sum_{h=1}^{H} \sum_{i=1}^{N} X_{hi} dq_i$$

Combining (16.87) and (16.86) yields:

(16.88) $$\sum_{h=1}^{H} dI^h - \sum_{h=1}^{H} \sum_{i=1}^{N} X_{hi} dq_i = \sum_{h=1}^{H} \sum_{i=1}^{N} t_i dX_{hi}$$

Thus, (16.82) can be rewritten as:

(16.89) $$dW = -\sum_{h=1}^{H} \sum_{i=1}^{N} \beta^h X_{hi} dq_i + \sum_{h=1}^{H} \beta^h dI^h - \sum_{h=1}^{H} dI^h$$
$$+ \sum_{h=1}^{H} \sum_{i=1}^{N} X_{hi} dq_i + \sum_{i=1}^{N} \sum_{h=1}^{H} t_i dX_{hi}$$

Finally, the dX_{hi} in the last term of (16.89) can be eliminated by noting that

(16.90)
$$X_{hi} = X_{hi}(\vec{q}; I^h) \qquad \begin{matrix} h = 1, \ldots, H \\ i = 1, \ldots, N \end{matrix}$$

Totally differentiating (16.90) yields:

(16.91)
$$dX_{hi} = \sum_{j=1}^{N} \frac{\partial X_{hi}}{\partial q_j} dq_j + \frac{\partial X_{hi}}{\partial I^h} dI^h \qquad \begin{matrix} h = 1, \ldots, H \\ i = 1, \ldots, N \end{matrix}$$

Substituting (16.91) into (16.89) and combining terms yields:

(16.92)
$$dW = \sum_{h=1}^{H} \left(\beta^h - 1 + \sum_{i=1}^{N} \sum_{h=1}^{H} t_i \frac{\partial X_{hi}}{\partial I^h} \right) dI^h$$
$$+ \sum_{h=1}^{H} (1 - \beta^h) \sum_{i=1}^{N} X_{hi} dq_i + \sum_{h=1}^{H} \sum_{i=1}^{N} t_i \sum_{j=1}^{N} \frac{\partial X_{hi}}{\partial q_j} dq_j$$

(16.92) highlights the importance of constant returns to scale in second-best analysis. With general technology, pure profits or losses can occur in production, thereby changing the pattern of lump-sum incomes $(I^1, \ldots, I^H)$ received by the consumers. As indicated by the first term in (16.92), the government would then have to keep track of these changes, and their subsequent effects on social welfare. With the constant returns assumption, on the other hand, the first term can be ignored since pure profits and losses will be zero and the vector of lump-sum income can remain unchanged.

Even with CRS, however, it is clear that production derivatives will affect second-best decision rules, in general, even if they do not do so in the optimal tax problem. The change in the vector of consumer prices, $\vec{q}$, in (16.92) will be determined by the combined interaction of general equilibrium demand and supply schedules. To see this explicitly, ignore changes in lump-sum income and use market clearance to express the change in welfare in terms of changes in taxes rather than prices, exactly as we did for the one-consumer, general technology case. Totally differentiating the market clearance equations

$$\sum_{h=1}^{H} X_{hi}(\vec{q}; \overline{I^h}) = Y_i(\vec{p}) = Y_i(\vec{q} - \vec{t}) \qquad i = 1, \ldots, N$$

yields:

(16.93)
$$\sum_{h=1}^{H} \sum_{j=1}^{N} \frac{\partial X_{hi}}{\partial q_j} dq_j = \sum_{j=1}^{N} \frac{\partial Y_i}{\partial p_j} (dq_j - dt_j) \qquad i = 1, \ldots, N$$

Solving for $d\vec{q}$ and expressing the N equations (16.93) in vector notation yields:

(16.94)
$$dq = E^{-1} \left(-\frac{\partial Y}{\partial p} \right) dt$$

where:
$$E = \left(\frac{\partial X}{\partial q} - \frac{\partial Y}{\partial p} \right) \text{ in vector notation.}$$

Finally, substitute (16.94) into (16.92), with $dI^h \equiv 0$, to obtain, in vector notation,

$$(16.95) \qquad dW = \left[-((1 - \beta)'X)' - t' \frac{\partial X}{\partial q} \right] E^{-1} \frac{\partial Y}{\partial p} \, dt$$

where:

$$\beta = \begin{bmatrix} \beta^1 \\ \vdots \\ \beta^H \end{bmatrix}, \text{ a } (H \times 1) \text{ column vector of marginal social utilities of income.}$$

$X = [X_{hi}]$, an $(H \times N)$ matrix of individual consumer demands and factor supplies.

$1 =$ a $(H \times 1)$ unit column vector.

(16.95) is the fundamental equation for evaluating tax changes in a many-consumer economy with CRS general production technology. By inspection, the supply responses $(\partial Y / \partial p)$ clearly affect the change in social welfare.

Equation (16.95) can also be compared directly with the results from a one-consumer equivalent economy. Equation (16.17), reproduced here as (16.96), calculated the change in loss as

$$(16.96) \qquad dL = (t)(M_{ij})E^{-1} \frac{\partial Y}{\partial p} \, dt$$

The second term in (16.95) is very close to (16.96) but not identical. A trivial difference is the minus sign, resulting from the fact that $dW = -dL$. More importantly, the demand derivatives $(\partial X / \partial q)$ in (16.96) are the compensated Slutsky terms, not the actual demand derivatives, reflecting the fact that (16.96) derives from a conceptual compensation experiment that is not particularly meaningful in a many-person environment. In practical applications, however, it may prove useful to think of the change in social welfare resulting from any change in tax rates as a linear combination of social welfare considerations and deadweight efficiency loss, with the former embodied in the first term of (16.95) and the latter in the second term. This interpretation maintains the dichotomy between equity and efficiency that exists in all first-best analysis, but it can only be viewed here as a rough "interpretative" approximation. Whether it is useful or not will depend on the particular problem under consideration. We saw, for example, that equity and efficiency terms were fairly tightly intertwined in the many-person optimal commodity tax rules. But it could be more compelling for simple tax change problems, such as in the Corlett and Hague analysis. The welfare effects of such changes can be evaluated directly by (16.95),[30] once the equal-revenue pattern of tax changes, $d\vec{t}$, has been determined.

---

[30] Alternatively, (16.92) with nonconstant returns to scale production. In this case, the vector of income changes dI^h would have to be specified and incorporated into the total differential of the market clearance equations (16.93).

REFERENCES

Arrow, K. Chenery, H; Minhas, B.; and Solow, R. "Capital-Labor Substitution and Economic Efficiency." *The Review of Economics and Statistics,* August 1961.

Atkinson, A. "How Progressive Should Income Tax Be?" In *Essays in Modern Economics,* edited by M. Parkin. London: Longman Group, Ltd., 1973.

————, and Stiglitz, J. "The Design of Tax Structure: Direct vs. Indirect Taxation." *Journal of Public Economics,* July/August 1976.

Boadway, R. "Cost-Benefit Rules and General Equilibrium." *Review of Economic Studies,* June 1975.

————. "Integrating Equity and Efficiency in Applied Welfare Economics." *Quarterly Journal of Economics,* November 1976.

Bradford, D., and Rosen, H. "The Optimal Taxation of Commodities and Income." *American Economic Association Papers and Proceedings,* May 1976.

Diamond, P. A. "A Many Person Ramsey Tax Rule." *Journal of Public Economics,* November 1975.

Dixit, A. "Welfare Effects of Tax and Price Changes." *Journal of Public Economics,* February 1975.

————, and Munk, K. "Welfare Effects of Tax and Price Changes: A Correction." *Journal of Public Economics,* August 1977.

Fair, R. "The Optimal Distribution of Income." *Quarterly Journal of Economics,* November 1971.

Feldstein, M. "Distributional Equity and the Optimal Structure of Public Prices." *American Economic Review,* March 1972.

Green, J. "Two Models of Optimal Pricing and Taxation." *Oxford Economic Papers,* November 1975.

Guesnerie, R. "Financing Public Goods with Commodity Taxes: A Tax Reform Viewpoint." *Econometrica,* March 1979.

————. "On the Direction of Tax Reform." *Journal of Public Economics,* April 1977.

Hartwick, J. "Optimal Price Discrimination." *Journal of Public Economics,* February 1978.

Hatta, T. "A Theory of Piecemeal Policy Recommendations." Review *of Economic Studies,* February 1977.

Jorgenson, D. "Investment Behavior and the Production Function." *The Bell Journal of Economics and Management Science,* Spring 1972.

Mirrlees, J. "An Exploration in the Theory of Optimum Income Taxation." *Review of Economic Studies,* April 1971.

————. "Optimal Commodity Taxation in a Two-Class Economy." *Journal of Public Economics,* February 1975.

————. "Optimal Tax Theory: A Synthesis." *Journal of Public Economics,* November 1976.

Sadka, E. "On Income Distribution, Incentive Effects and Optimal Income Taxation." *Review of Economic Studies,* June 1976.

Samuelson, P. A. "Social Indifference Curves." *Quarterly Journal of Economics,* February 1956.

Searde, J. "On the Shape of Optimal Tax Schedules." *Journal of Public Economics,* April 1977.

Sheshinski, E. "The Optimal Linear Income Tax." *Review of Economic Studies,* July 1972.

Stern, N. "On the Specification of Models of Optimum Income Taxation." *Journal of Public Economics,* July/August 1976.

Stiglitz, J., and Dasgupta, P. "Differential Taxation, Public Goods and Economic Efficiency." *Review of Economic Studies,* April 1971.

17

The theory and measurement of tax incidence

When an economic agent sends a tax payment to a government it is said to bear the *impact* of a tax. But public sector economists have long recognized that the actual tax payment may not be a very good measure of the true economic burden arising as a consequence of the tax. The problem, of course, is that the tax payment will initiate an entire chain of general equilibrium market effects that will change the vectors of equilibrium consumer and producer prices. These price changes, in turn, will generate welfare losses and gains throughout the economy affecting, potentially, every economic agent, not just the person(s) who paid the tax.

The *incidence* of a tax, then, is a measure of the full changes in welfare arising from the tax, incorporating both the initial *impact* of the tax and the gains and losses associated with the general equilibrium market responses to the tax. As such, incidence measures the true economic burden of the tax and is, therefore, the central concept for either a normative or positive distributional theory of taxation.

TAX INCIDENCE—A PARTIAL EQUILIBRIUM ANALYSIS

All students of economics are introduced to the distinction between the impact and incidence of a tax at the principles level, at least in a partial equilibrium context. Recall the standard discussion of a unit sales tax paid by all producers in a competitive market, depicted in Figure 17–1. The suppliers of X will try to pass the tax on to the consumers of X. S shifts to S' by the full amount of the unit tax. Whether or not they are successful depends upon the elasticities of both supply and demand. As drawn in Figure 17–1, the price to the consumer rises, but only from q_0 to q_T, less than the full amount of the tax. The producer price falls to p_T (equal to $q_T - t$), the new equilibrium output is X_T, and the tax revenue is $X_T \cdot t = X_T(q_T - p_T)$. The *impact* of the tax falls on the producers and is equal to the total tax payment, but the *incidence*, or true burden, of the tax is shared by the producers and consumers in the example. Because the consumer price (the "gross-of-tax" price) rises from q_0 to q_T, the consumers suffer a loss of consumer surplus (ignoring income effects) equal to $q_T \cdot B \cdot C \cdot q_0$. Because the producer price (the "net-of-tax" price) falls from p_0 to p_T the producers suffer a decrease in returns to capital of $p_0 \cdot C \cdot D \cdot p_T$. Using the *impact*, or tax revenue, as a measure of the true burdens, then, would

FIGURE 17–1

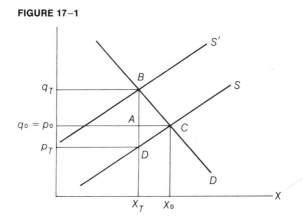

overstate the producers' true economic losses by $[q_T B A p_0 - CAD]$ and understate the consumers' true economic losses by $q_T \cdot B \cdot C \cdot p_0$.[1] Even though this example is only a partial equilibrium analysis of tax incidence, it illustrates a fundamental point: that market responses to a tax are a crucial determinant of its ultimate pattern of burdens.

FIRST-BEST THEORY, SECOND-BEST THEORY, AND TAX INCIDENCE

We have delayed discussing the general theory of tax incidence until this part of the text because the most interesting questions in tax incidence are inherently of a second-best nature, precisely because they depend on the market's response to distorting taxation. In first-best theory, all questions of distributional equity are incorporated into the interpersonal equity conditions,

$$(17.1) \qquad \frac{\partial W}{\partial U^h} \frac{\partial U^h}{\partial I^h} = \frac{\partial W}{\partial U^j} \frac{\partial U^j}{\partial I^j} \qquad \text{all } h, j = 1, \dots, H,$$

which the government satisfies through a set of lump-sum taxes and transfers among the consumers. As a general rule these lump-sum redistributions will affect equilibrium market prices, contrary to the common assumption that they do not, and these price changes will in turn affect peoples' utilities. The incidence, or burden, on each consumer could presumably be measured as the difference in his utility level before and after government redistribution, but computing this change in utility for each person is not especially interesting. Consider the various possibilities.

On the one hand, the equilibrium market prices may *not* change if, for example, aggregate production technology is linear with constant marginal

---

[1] This example is meant only as an illustration of the distinction between tax impact and tax incidence. As we have noted in other contexts, its measures of "true" consumer and producer losses are not generally valid.

opportunity costs. If producer prices remain unchanged, so too will the vector of consumer prices with lump-sum redistributions. In this case the tax and transfer payments are a perfect income proxy for the change in utility in this sense—if any one person received (paid) the tax (transfer) back from (to) the government, his original utility level would be restored. Therefore, the impact and incidence of the redistribution is identical, so that the incidence question is trivial. In point of fact, tax theorists have usually been willing to define the burden of a tax (transfer) solely in terms of the distribution of tax (transfer) payments if they believe the tax (transfer) is (approximately) lump sum. It is common practice, for example, to allocate the distributional burdens of personal income taxes solely on the basis of the tax payments by income class.

Suppose, on the other hand, general equilibrium prices do change in response to a lump-sum redistribution. Now if the government restores the original income level for any *one* person that person will not be able to achieve his original utility level. That is to say, the tax (transfer) payment (receipt) is no longer necessarily an accurate proxy for the change in utility. Even so, the pattern of incidence is still not an especially compelling question, for two reasons. In the first place, the relevant alternative to a given program of lump-sum taxes and transfers can always be viewed as the complete unraveling of the redistribution, in which the government restores *everyone's* original income level *simultaneously*. If this were done, the original *utility levels* would also be restored. Under this assumption, then, the payments (receipts) by any one person are still a perfect proxy for the pattern of burdens, so that impact and incidence are again identical. Suppose, however, one insisted on viewing the problem strictly at the individual level, asking what the consequences would be to an individual of restoring his original income level while leaving the remaining patterns of taxes and transfers intact. Because prices have changed, the income payment would not accurately proxy the utility change, but the utility effects of the price changes are still not terribly interesting in a first-best environment. Presumably the government's distribution branch has taken account of the price-induced utility changes in reaching the final equilibrium, at which point the marginal social utilities of income are equalized. The fact that actual taxes and transfers may not be good proxies for individual's utility gains and losses is really beside the point, because whatever changes in utility have actually occurred, they are the optimal changes required for a first-best social welfare maximum. Thus, there is ultimately no *need* to measure the incidence of the redistributions, because if the interpersonal equity conditions have been satisfied, no other pattern of redistributions could possibly dominate the given redistributions in the sense of being more equitable.

The same cannot be said for second-best taxes. In a second-best environment, taxes are raised in a distorting manner to meet certain revenue requirements. Particular taxes may be chosen simply on the basis of convenience, or by some efficiency criterion such as minimizing deadweight loss, in which case it may well be possible to design more (or less) equitable taxes. If so, then measuring the incidence of the tax is crucial. Only if the taxes are optimally designed to maximize social welfare in accordance with equation (16.38) would the question of tax incidence be more or less irrelevant, as it is in a first-best environment. But since equation (16.38) is unlikely to hold in practice, the motivation for developing accurate measures of incidence in a second-best environment is especially compelling.

The theory of tax incidence has been a central focus of public sector economics since the very beginning of the discipline, with the result that there exists a voluminous literature on the subject. The incidence of every major tax has been studied in detail, both theoretically and empirically, whether it be federal, state, or local income taxes, the payroll tax for social security, various wealth taxes including local property taxes, various selective excise and factor taxes, general sales taxes, inheritance taxes, and so forth. Rather than address each tax separately, Chapter 17 will stress the fundamental methodological issues involved in both the theory and empirical measurement of tax incidence in a second-best environment, issues applicable to all taxes.

METHODOLOGICAL DIFFERENCES IN THE MEASUREMENT OF TAX INCIDENCE

The tax incidence literature is bound to be confusing to the beginning student of public sector economics. Empirical studies of individual taxes are fraught with controversy, in part because empirical analysis of tax incidence is inherently so difficult, but also because there exist serious methodological differences among experts in the field on the appropriate theoretical approaches to the measurement of incidence. Our goal is simply to provide a general perspective on the existing theoretical differences in the literature.

By way of illustration, consider the following bewildering examples which the beginning student must confront. A large number of researchers have tried to determine, empirically, the incidence of the U.S. corporate income tax. Their results could not possibly be more divergent, ranging all the way from Richard Musgrave's finding that the tax is borne *at least* 100 percent by the consumers of corporate output to Arnold Harberger's estimate that under the most plausible assumptions, corporate stockholders almost certainly bear virtually the entire burden of the tax. To confuse matters further, Friedlaender and Vandendorpe have shown that the analytical framework Harberger used to determine corporate tax incidence should have generated the result that no one bears a burden from the tax.[2]

The corporate income tax may be the most dramatic instance of empirical uncertainty with regard to tax incidence, but the incidence of most other important taxes has hardly been settled either. To give just one further example, a few years ago most public sector economists agreed that local property taxes were at least mildly regressive, but even this is no longer certain. Recent work

---

[2] Marion Krzyzaniak and Richard Musgrave, *The Shifting of the Corporation Income Tax* (Baltimore, Md.: Johns Hopkins Press, 1963); Arnold C. Harberger, "The Incidence of the Corporation Income Tax," *Journal of Political Economy*, June 1962, pp. 215–40; and A. L. Vandendorpe and A. F. Friedlaender, "Differential Incidence in the Presence of Initial Distorting Taxes," *Journal of Public Economics*, October 1976, pp. 205–29.

on tax incidence within the context of one-sector growth models strongly suggests that local property taxes may well be progressive.[3]

Perhaps it is not surprising that empirical estimates of the incidence of any tax should vary considerably, given the nature of the problem. Empirical researchers must select what they think are the most important market responses to the tax from a staggering set of possibilities, and methods of selection are bound to differ. Unfortunately, empirical tax incidence analysis appears not to be especially robust to assumptions made about sectors of the economy not explicitly under examination. But, as indicated above, matters are made even more confusing by the fact that researchers often employ different *theoretical* measures of incidence as a basis for their empirical work, and it is this problem we wish to focus on here.

THEORETICAL MEASURES OF TAX INCIDENCE

Three distinct theoretical approaches to incidence measurement currently exist in the literature: (1) Some research merely reports the pattern of tax payments by income class and judges the equity of the tax on this basis alone, thereby equating the impact and incidence of the tax. As noted above, nearly all research on income taxation employs this measure, on the assumption that income taxes are essentially lump sum. For example, Joseph Pechman and Bernard Okner allocate personal income tax burdens in this manner in their recent Brookings study, *Who Bears the Tax Burden?*[4] (2) At the other end of the spectrum, a large group of incidence studies bases their measures of incidence on changes in certain market prices in response to a tax. The change in the wage-rental ratio is the usual choice. Actual tax payments *influence* this incidence measure in that their impact and size affect both the pattern of general equilibrium price changes and the degree to which they change, but the tax payments themselves are usually not a direct part of the final incidence measure. Arnold Harberger pioneered this approach in his 1962 classic, *The Incidence of the Corporation Income Tax*,[5] and numerous other tax theorists have followed his lead, including those (e.g., Martin Feldstein) who have studied tax incidence within the context of one-sector growth models.[6] Harberger's paper has certainly been one of the most influential works on the incidence question.

(3) Finally, a third set of studies relate tax incidence to changes in welfare, measured either directly as changes in individual's utility levels, or indirectly as compensated income changes using the expenditure (and profit) function.

---

[3] Martin Feldstein, "Incidence of a Capital Income Tax in a Growing Economy with Variable Savings Rates," *Review of Economic Studies*, October 1974, pp. 505–13. Refer also to the *American Economic Review, Papers and Proceedings*, May 1974, articles by Henry Aaron, "A New View of Property Tax Incidence", Richard Musgrave, "Is a Property Tax on Housing Regressive?" and comments. Also, Henry Aaron, *Who Pays The Property Tax?* (Washington, D.C.: The Brookings Institution, 1975).

[4] Joseph A. Pechman and Bernard A. Okner, *Who Bears the Tax Burden?* (Washington, D.C.: The Brookings Institution, 1974.)

[5] Harberger, "The Incidence of the Corporation Income Tax."

[6] Feldstein, "Incidence of a Capital Income Tax."

Shoven and Whalley's analyses of tax incidence by means of Scarf's algorithm use this approach, as do Friedlaender and Vandendorpe.[7] These studies typically report changes in general equilibrium price ratios as an intermediate step, following in the spirit of Harberger's analysis.

Faced with such diverse incidence measures the natural question is whether or not they can be reconciled. In our opinion they cannot be, at least not fully, since they each view the problem of measuring the burden of taxation from different perspectives, and in some respects these perspectives are irreconcilable. Moreover, there appears to be no clear-cut presumption in favor of any one of them, or some other candidate not currently in vogue. They each have their advantages and disadvantages, and choosing among them will depend ultimately on the researcher's personal preferences.

GENERAL PRINCIPLES OF TAX INCIDENCE

Despite differences in the way they measure tax incidence, nearly all tax theorists agree on two general principles. The first is that people, as consumers, ultimately bear the burden of taxation so that any notion of burden must relate either directly or indirectly to the welfare of the individuals in the society. This is merely a specific application of the first principle in all of normative public sector economics, that the government's task is to promote the interests of its constituents. Thus, while the government may levy a corporate tax on General Motors, the interesting question in tax incidence is not the harm done to General Motors as a legal entity but rather which *people* bear the burden of this tax: GM stockholders, the workers at GM, consumers of GM products, other consumers, other stockholders, other workers, and so forth, and how much harm do each of them suffer. This principle also implies that any measure of burden should incorporate, at least in part, each individual's own perception of the burden he or she suffers as a result of the tax. As always in public sector theory, individual preference is a fundamental datum for public sector decision making.

The second generally accepted principle of tax incidence is that measurement must occur within the context of a general equilibrium framework. The preponderance of tax incidence models assumes a fully employed economy with competitive markets, although there has been some work done on tax incidence in the presence of noncompetitive markets and/or unemployed resources.[8] In keeping with the rest of the text, we will adopt the full-employment, competitive markets assumptions.

---

[7] J. Shoven, "The Incidence and Efficiency Effects of Taxes on Income from Capital," *Journal of Political Economy*, December 1976. Also, J. Shoven and J. Whalley, "A General Equilibrium Calculation of the Effects of Differential Taxation of Income from Capital in the U.S.," *Journal of Public Economics*, November 1972; and Vandendorpe and Friedlaender, "Differential Incidence in the Presence of Initial Distorting Taxes."

[8] Refer to A. Asimakopulos and J. Burbidge, "The Short-Period Incidence of Taxation," *Economic Journal*, June 1974; and M. Kalecki, "A Theory of Commodity, Income and Capital Taxation," *Economic Journal*, September 1937.

That tax theorists insist on general equilibrium modeling is altogether appropriate, given that the final burden of a tax depends directly on the pattern of general equilibrium market responses to the tax, but this principle has simultaneously created some sticky conceptual problems for tax incidence measurement. In the first place, general equilibrium analysis challenges the very notion that it is possible to consider unambiguously the incidence of a single tax. The heart of the matter is that in a proper general equilibrium framework the disposition of the tax revenue must be accounted for explicitly. Tax revenue collected by the government cannot simply disappear without continued repercussions throughout the economy. Most likely, the government will spend the revenues in some manner, but it could simply save them. In any case, the disposition of the revenues will generate its own pattern of welfare gains and losses. In what sense, then, can "the incidence of *a* tax" have meaning as an isolated phenomenon within a general equilibrium, interdependent market economy? This point deserves some careful thought.

In an attempt to isolate the incidence of a particular tax, suppose one assumes that the government simply saves the tax revenues. This would appear to be the spirit of the income tax studies, which assume the taxes are lump sum and thereby equate the impact of the tax with its incidence, without reference to the disposition of the revenues. As noted above, however, if the vector of general equilibrium prices changes in response to the tax, then impact and incidence are not generally equivalent for any one individual. Moreover, if one also assumes continued full employment, as is common with incidence analysis, then at least one price must change. Suppose, for purposes of illustration, one chooses the simple standard *IS–LM* model of macroeconomics with competitive factor markets, depicted in Figure 17–2, to analyze the consequences of taxation with savings of the tax revenues. According to this model, the real rate of interest changes from the pretax to the posttax equilibrium. The tax shifts the *IS* curve to *IS'*, resulting in excess supply in the goods market. As a consequence, the absolute price level declines, increasing real money balances, and shifting the

FIGURE 17–2

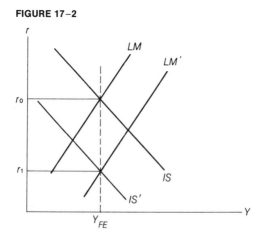

LM curve to *LM'*. The full employment level of real income is restored, but *r* has dropped from r_0 to r_1. Thus, in this model, the final burden of the tax will depend not only on the pattern of tax payments but also on the welfare consequences of the decline in the real rate of interest. The impact and incidence of the tax will not be identical, and the tax payments may be a poor proxy for the true pattern of welfare changes even with destruction of the tax revenue.

Suppose, more realistically, that the tax revenue is used to finance government expenditures. The combined distributional effect of the tax-cum-expenditure policy is commonly referred to as *balanced-budget incidence*, and will obviously depend upon the particular expenditures being financed. In order to highlight the role of the expenditures in the analysis, assume that the taxes are lump sum and consider the following possibilities by way of illustration. If the expenditures are simply lump-sum transfer payments, then the tax and transfer program is first best, a case we have already considered. Note, however, that if the taxes are not lump sum, then the analysis is second best, even though the transfers are lump sum. We will return to this point below.

If the expenditures take any other form, including nonlump-sum transfers or exhaustive expenditures, then the measure of balanced budget incidence obviously requires specific measures of the incidence of the expenditure programs as well as that of the taxes, a difficult problem which we will consider in Chapter 18. Furthermore, any of these expenditure programs will change the vector of equilibrium prices in general, so that the lump-sum tax payment is no longer necessarily an accurate measure of the *tax* burden suffered by any individual consumer. In conclusion, then, tax studies that use income tax payments as the measure of incidence ought to be assuming that the taxes are lump sum, *and* that they are being used to finance lump-sum transfer payments in a balanced budget manner (no shift in the *IS* curve). To be absolutely unambiguous, these studies should also assume a linear technology with unchanged producer prices. Then, as was also discussed above, if any *one* consumer received his tax payment back, that payment would restore the consumer's original utility level. Otherwise, incidence and impact are identical only in the aggregate sense described above.

PURE TAX INCIDENCE THEORY— DIFFERENTIAL INCIDENCE

Is there any way of focusing on the incidence of taxes per se in a general equilibrium framework without complicating the analysis with difficult questions of expenditure incidence? Theoretically the answer is yes, but one should keep in mind that since taxes are usually changed in response to particular expenditure initiatives, the empirical relevance of pure tax incidence measures may be limited.

One very popular method of analysis, initiated by Harberger, is to assume that the revenues collected are returned lump sum.[9] In a one-consumer or

---

[9] Harberger, and others, actually assume that the government spends the revenue exactly as the consumer(s) would have had they received it, but this is equivalent to redistributing the revenue lump sum and letting the consumer(s) spend it.

one-consumer-equivalent economy, there is no ambiguity over the pattern of lump-sum returns, but in a many-person economy the pattern of returns is crucial, whether one considers the incidence affects from the aggregate viewpoint of social welfare, or from each individual's perspective of the loss he suffers as a result of the tax with redistribution. The natural assumption for analytical purposes is that each person receives a lump-sum transfer exactly equal to his tax payment, so that the *impact* of the tax-cum-transfer program on each individual is zero. While this assumption is surely a disservice to reality, it is a useful analytical device for considering the *incidence of a single tax* within the context of a general equilibrium framework. Assuming lump-sum returns of the revenues at least neutralizes the expenditure side of the budget as much as possible.

The other more realistic possibility is to consider the incidence of substituting one tax for another, while holding constant either total tax revenues or the entire government budget surplus (taxes − expenditures). This method of analysis is known as *differential incidence*, and since governments might actually do this, many researchers find it especially appealing. The method of returning tax collections lump sum to analyze the incidence of a single tax can be considered a specific instance of differential incidence, in which the taxes being substituted for are head taxes levied on each individual consumer.

It is important to note that whether one chooses to hold tax revenues or the entire government budget surplus constant in a differential incidence analysis is a matter of some consequence. In order to focus strictly on differential *tax* incidence the tax-revenue-constant assumption might appear to be the preferred alternative, but it may well violate the dictates of a full general equilibrium analysis. Suppose, for example, the government buys and sells goods and factors in the competitive market system either at the producer or consumer prices. With general technology production, both producer and consumer prices will change in response to a tax substitution, thus changing both the level of government expenditures and the amount of revenue from the new tax necessary to balance the overall government budget. If tax collections are held constant in the process of substituting one tax for another, then the overall budget surplus will change and this will have to be considered as part of the incidence analysis. Adding an assumption that government expenditures are also held constant simply creates different problems, for then government inputs and outputs will have to change, with corresponding changes in consumers' welfare. If, on the other hand, the overall budget is held constant, then the incidence analysis can properly focus on the differential effects of the taxes. Government *expenditures* may change, but so long as the government does not vary the vector of government inputs and outputs there will be no change in consumer(s) welfare arising from the expenditure side of the budget. Thus, the government-budget-constant assumption is preferred, even though total tax collections will vary as one set of taxes is substituted for another. Only if one assumes that linear production technologies exist in both the private and public sectors, *and* that government purchases (sales) are at *producer* prices, will the tax-revenue-constant and government-budget-surplus-constant assumptions be equivalent. Since producer prices cannot change in response to taxation, neither will the level of government expenditures. These considerations highlight the care that must be taken in order to specify a well-defined problem within a general equilibrium framework.[10]

Welfare Measures of Tax Incidence—One-Consumer Economy

Having determined that taxation with selective lump-sum return and, more generally, differential incidence are the only appropriate methods for considering tax incidence independently from expenditure incidence in a general equilibrium framework, there remains the difficult theoretical problem of actually measuring the resulting incidence effects. Recall that three measures have been commonly employed: the impact of a tax, the change in (some) general equilibrium prices, and changes in utility or equivalent income compensation measures.

While a many-person economy would appear to be the relevant context of an incidence study, the theoretical issues of measurement are sufficiently complex to warrant a preliminary discussion within the context of a one-consumer or one-consumer-equivalent economy.

The first principle of tax incidence is that it should measure the burden on the consumer for any given pattern of taxation. But if so, then the natural interpretation of burden in the one-consumer-equivalent economy is the deadweight loss measure developed in Chapter 15. For instance, if it is assumed that any tax revenue collected is simply returned to the consumer lump sum, and that there are no government expenditures, the incidence of any given (set of) tax(es) would be appropriately measured as:

$$(17.2) \qquad L(\vec{t}) = M(\vec{q}; \bar{U}^0) - \sum_{i=1}^{N} t_i X_i^{comp} \qquad \text{(linear technology)}$$

$$(17.3) \qquad L(\vec{t}) = M(\vec{q}; \bar{U}^0) - \sum_{i=1}^{N} t_i X_i^{comp} - \pi(\vec{p}) \qquad \text{(general technology)}$$

identical to the measure of deadweight loss from taxation. Recall that $M(\vec{q}; \bar{U}^0)$ measures the lump-sum income necessary to compensate the consumer for a given vector of taxes, $\vec{t}$, with $\bar{U}^0$ equal to the zero-tax level of utility. Strictly speaking, this assumes a linear technology with constant producer prices. With general technology there may be pure profits or losses from production as producer prices, $\vec{p}$, vary in response to the tax rates. In this case, the appropriate income measure of welfare loss is $M(\vec{q}; \bar{U}^0) - \pi(\vec{p})$, where $\pi(\vec{p})$ is the general equilibrium profit function. With the tax revenues returned lump sum, (17.2) and (17.3) measure the consumer's loss.

Tax incidence and tax inefficiency are equivalent because with the taxes returned lump sum, the *only* source of welfare loss is the change in the vector of consumer (and producer) prices resulting from the taxes. The tax payments,

---

[10] For an excellent general discussion of alternative equivalent taxes, see J. Shoven and J. Whalley, "Equal Yield Tax Alternatives: General Equilibrium Computational Techniques," *Journal of Public Economics*, October 1977.

or impact of the tax, affect this measure only in that the level of the tax rates, $\vec{t}$, will in part determine the degree to which the consumer (and producer) price vectors change, exactly as in loss measurement.

The loss measure is also relevant to the measure of differential incidence, since if tax revenue is always returned lump sum, the substitution of one tax for another with revenue held constant can be thought of as follows: impose one set of taxes and return the revenues lump sum. Then impose a different set of taxes with its revenues returned lump sum. In short, differential incidence is equivalent to differential efficiency in a one-consumer economy and follows exactly the Corlett-Hague analysis presented in Chapter 15. Recall that for marginal changes in tax rates, the relevant equations, in vector notation, are:

$$(17.4) \qquad dL = \frac{\partial L}{\partial t} dt$$

and

$$(17.5) \qquad dT = 0 = \frac{\partial (tX)}{\partial t} dt$$

Equation (17.5) determines the changes in tax rates necessary to maintain tax revenues constant, and equation (17.4) computes the resulting change in the consumer's welfare in terms of the lump-sum income required to hold utility constant.

In the case of general technologies, the market clearance equation relevant to the compensated equilibrium

$$(17.6) \qquad X_i(\vec{q}; \bar{U}^0) = X_i(\vec{p} + \vec{t}; \bar{U}^0) = \pi_i(\vec{p}) \qquad i = 2, \ldots, N$$

would also be necessary to relate market price changes to the tax changes in computing (17.4). (Recall that compensation is assumed to occur in terms of the numeraire good, the first good as written, which is also assumed to be untaxed.) These assumptions have already been discussed in the development of the deadweight loss from taxation. For linear technologies, $dq = dt$, and $dp = 0$, so that market clearance is unnecessary. Note, finally, that according to these measures the incidence or loss from lump-sum taxes is zero, precisely because they entail zero deadweight loss. Clearly, in a one-consumer or one-consumer-equivalent economy, collecting lump-sum taxes and returning the revenues lump sum cannot create an economic burden.

The equivalence between incidence and deadweight loss from taxation carries over intact in the presence of government expenditures. Suppose the government's budget constraint is:

$$(17.7) \qquad \sum_{i=1}^{N} t_i X_i + \sum_{i=1}^{N} p_i Z_i = S$$

where:

$S = $ the fixed government surplus (possibly equal to zero).

$Z_i = $ the government purchase (supply) of input (good) i, and all government transactions at competitive producer prices.

So long as any government surplus, S, is returned to the consumer lump sum, an appropriate assumption for general equilibrium analysis, then the dead-weight-loss measures for any given pattern of government decision variables $(\vec{t}; \vec{Z})$ are:

$$(17.8) \quad L(\vec{t}; \vec{Z}) = M(\vec{q}; \bar{U}^0) - \sum_{i=1}^{N} t_i X_i - \sum_{i=1}^{N} p_i Z_i \quad \text{(linear technology)}$$

$$(17.9) \quad L(\vec{t}; \vec{Z}) = M(\vec{q}; \bar{U}^0) - \sum_{i=1}^{N} t_i X_i - \sum_{i=1}^{N} p_i Z_i - \pi(\vec{p})$$

$$\text{(general technology)}$$

as discussed in Chapter 16. For Z constant, these are also the appropriate measures for the incidence of any given vector of taxes $\vec{t}$ providing the government surplus is returned lump sum. Moreover, the equations (in vector notation):

$$(17.10) \quad dL = \frac{\partial L}{\partial t} dt$$

and

$$(17.11) \quad dS = 0 = \frac{\partial(\sum t_i X_i - \sum p_i Z_i) \cdot dt}{\partial t}$$

(along with the market clearance equations (17.6)) determine the differential incidence of any tax substitutions which leave the overall government budget surplus unchanged.[11] If the surplus is held constant, one can think of differential incidence as replacing one set of taxes with the surplus returned lump sum with another set of taxes also with the (same) surplus returned lump sum.

The Relative Price Measure of Differential Tax Incidence—One-Consumer Economy

While the notion of income compensation provides a nice theoretical bridge between tax inefficiency as represented by deadweight loss and tax incidence, these loss measures may well have limited applicability to the practical requirement of deriving empirical measures of tax incidence. The problem, which was also addressed in Chapter 15, is that these loss measures require knowledge of compensated equilibria and they quite obviously will not be observed in practice. This is not so serious with linear production technologies, since any pattern of tax rates will generate the same set of producer and consumer prices at both the compensated and actual with-tax equilibrium, although the amount of taxes collected for any given set of rates will differ between the two equilibria. The incidence of a given set of taxes can be thought of as the incidence of establishing a given set of tax *rates* and then returning the resulting revenues

---

[11] Market clearance is also required for linear technology with government production.

lump sum. Thus, the loss measure will be unambiguously defined for the given tax rates, but not for a given amount of revenue. Differential incidence would be measured analogously. Presumably one would determine a set of tax rates as an alternative to a given set of tax rates that held *actual* tax collections (or the overall budget surplus) constant and then use those changes to compute (17.4) ((17.10)). Since $dq = dt$, and $dp = 0$ in both the actual and compensated equilibria, (17.4) can be evaluated unambiguously for the given pattern of dt. Of course the vector dt which keeps actual tax collections constant will not, in general, hold compensated tax revenues constant, but it is still possible to mix compensated and actual equilibria in the manner suggested.

With general technologies, however, it is not clear how to use the loss measure. Consider the problem of measuring the incidence of a given set of tax rates when the tax revenue has been returned lump sum to the consumer. Presumably one wants to measure the loss implied by the given set of tax rates, $\vec{t}$, and the market prices, $\vec{q}_A$ and $\vec{p}_A$, observed in the actual with-tax equilibrium. With general technologies, however, any given vector $\vec{t}$ will generate one set of market prices $(\vec{q}_A, \vec{p}_A)$ in the actual equilibrium and different set of prices $(\vec{q}_C, \vec{p}_C)$ in the compensated equilibrium. This follows because the market clearance equations for the actual and compensated equilibria,

(17.12)
$$X_i^{\text{actual}}(\vec{p} + \vec{t}) = \pi_i(\vec{p}) \qquad i = 1, \ldots, N$$

and

(17.13)
$$X_i^{\text{comp}}(\vec{p} + \vec{t}; \vec{U}^0) = \pi_i(\vec{p}) \qquad i = 2, \ldots, N$$

respectively, will produce a different vector of producer prices $\vec{p}$ for any given $\vec{t}$. Moreover, the compensated $\vec{p}$ will depend as well on the good picked for compensation (good 1 in all of our examples). Notice, too, that the level of pure profits will also differ in the two equilibria, equal to $\pi(\vec{p}_A)$ in the actual equilibrium and $\pi(\vec{p}_C)$ at the compensated equilibrium. (So will the tax revenues collected, but this is true even for the linear technology case.) For the loss measure to be well defined, then, compensation in some stated good must actually be paid by some agent outside the economy so that the compensated price vectors will actually be observed. Without actual compensation it is not clear how to evaluate loss. In particular, evaluating loss using (17.3) ((17.9)) at actual tax and price vectors $(\vec{t}, \vec{p}_A, \vec{q}_A)$, the only vectors observed in practice, is not a well-defined theoretical measure.

Price Change Measure of Incidence

Because of this ambiguity many researchers have been content to compute actual changes in consumer prices as *the* measure of incidence, stopping short of relating the price changes directly to changes in welfare in any formal manner. This is obviously a pragmatic compromise. The resulting measures have no firm theoretical justification, but at least they can be computed fairly easily from the actual data. Using the profit function to represent production, the procedure for computing price changes for differential incidence can be represented as a three-step process, already outlined above:

First, totally differentiate the actual government budget constraint with respect to the tax rates being changed (usually two of them) to determine the exact changes required to hold the budget surplus constant, for example:

$$(17.14) \qquad dS = 0 = \frac{\partial(tx^A + pZ)dt}{\partial t} \qquad \text{(in vector notation)}$$

Second, totally differentiate the actual market clearance relationships

$$(17.15) \qquad X_i^{\text{actual}}(\vec{p}_A + \vec{t}; I) = \pi_i(\vec{p}_A) + Z_i \qquad i = 1, \ldots, N$$

with respect to the tax rates to solve for the producer price changes given the changes in taxes determined from differentiating the government budget constraint. (The demand curve should have an income term to allow for the possibility of deadweight loss which reduces real income, even if there is zero pure profit or loss from production. If pure profits exist it is natural to assume they are received by the consumer as income.) Finally, use the relationships

$$(17.16) \qquad dq_i = dp_i + dt_i \qquad i = 1, \ldots, N$$

to determine the resulting changes in consumer prices.

The price changes could be directly related to welfare losses by positing an indirect utility function of the form $V(\vec{q})$ and totally differentiating it to obtain (in vector notation):

$$(17.17) \qquad dV = -\lambda X dq \qquad \text{with } \lambda = \text{ the marginal utility}$$
$$\text{of income}$$

Since $dq = dp + dt$, dV can easily be calculated as a fourth and final step, with dV/λ representing a money index of utility. But it will not be uniquely valued, in general (path dependent). Consequently, incidence analysis using the change-in-actual price measure typically concludes the formal analysis with the price changes. The link to consumer's welfare is then simply presented in heuristic terms.

In summary, then, the theory of tax incidence remains somewhat in a quandary even for simple one-consumer-equivalent economies. Despite the obvious motivation for developing empirically testable measures of tax incidence there appear to be no obvious candidates for the task unless production technology is linear. With general technologies, unambiguous measures of welfare loss involve compensated equilibria which cannot be observed in practice, and observed tax and price vectors offer at best only intuitive guidance to welfare losses. As a practical matter economists may have to be content with measures of price changes in response to different sets of tax that leave the government budget surplus unchanged, especially given that production technologies are certainly general and not linear. The only firm conclusion one can draw is that if the incidence of a given set of taxes per se is to have any meaning in a general equilibrium context, tax incidence must be defined in such a way as to render the impact of a tax only indirectly relevant to the incidence measure. Tax revenues (or the resulting budget surplus) from distorting taxes must be returned lump sum to the consumer to have a well-defined problem focusing on a single tax. The actual tax payment will, therefore, affect incidence only through its influence on market price changes. Regardless of whether one chooses the income compensation or change-in-actual-price approach, the final incidence measure will be fully determined by the resulting changes in the general equilibrium price vectors.

THE EQUIVALENCE OF GENERAL TAXES

Although the income compensation and change-in-actual-price measures of incidence approach the problem from different perspectives, they each imply the following important result:

In a perfectly competitive, profitless economy, in which tax revenues (or budget surplus) are always returned lump sum, any two (sets of) taxes will have identical incidence if they create the same distortions in relative prices.

Consider, first, the relative price measure of incidence. If production is profitless and tax revenues are returned to the consumers, actual consumer demands (factor suppliers) will be functions only of relative prices. Moreover, producers' supply (input demand) relationships are also functions only of relative prices. Therefore, two taxes that generate the same vector of relative prices will generate the same with-tax general equilibrium solution. Consequently, they must have the same incidence by the relative price criterion.

That two taxes creating the same vector of relative prices will have the same incidence using the income compensation measure can be most easily demonstrated as follows. Suppose compensation is paid in good 1 so that the market for good 1 remains uncleared in the compensated equilibrium. With compensation defined in terms of good 1, loss can be represented as:

$$(17.18) \qquad\qquad L(t) = M_1(\vec{q}; \bar{U}) - \pi_1(\vec{p})$$

Equation (17.18) measures the difference between the amount of good 1 required for compensation less the amount of good 1 available to the consumer from production, given that all other compensated demands (factor supplies) have been satisfied $(M_i(\vec{q}; \bar{U}) = \pi_i(\vec{p}), i = 2, \ldots, N)$. But both M_1 and π_1 are homogenous of degree 0 in prices. Therefore, any two taxes creating the same vector of relative prices must generate the same deadweight loss or incidence.

These considerations lead to the following well-known theorem applicable to a competitive, profitless economy:

Theorem: The Equivalence of General Taxes

Define a general tax as one with the following properties: (1) if levied on a single consumer good (factor supply), all consumers pay the same tax rate; (2) if levied on more than one good (and/or factor), property (1) holds for each taxed good (factor), and all the taxed goods (factors) are taxed at the same rate. Let $(X_1, \ldots, X_N)$ be the vector of goods and factors for a competitive, profitless economy with producer prices $(p_1, \ldots, p_N)$. Levy a general ad valorem tax at rate t, paid by consumers, on any subset of the goods and factors, say, $X_1, \ldots, X_K$, so that $q_i = p_i(1 + t)$, $i = 1, \ldots, K$; $q_j = p_j$, $j = k + 1, \ldots, N$, where $(q_1, \ldots, q_N)$ define the consumer prices. It is always possible to define another general ad valorem tax t^* on the remaining goods and factors $(X_{K+1}, \ldots, X_N)$ such that the two taxes have equivalent incidence.

Notice that if $(X_1, \ldots, X_K)$ is the subset of goods and $(X_{K+1}, \ldots, X_N)$ the subset of factors, the theorem establishes the equivalence between a general sales tax and a general income tax (or general value added tax), but dividing the goods and factors in this way is not necessary. It also establishes the equivalence between a tax on one good (or factor) and a tax on all the remaining goods and factors, a specific example of which was discussed in Chapter 15.

Proof: With the ad valorem tax t on the subset $(X_1, \ldots, X_K)$ the following relationships will hold in equilibrium:

$$(17.19a) \qquad MRS_{ij} = \frac{p_i}{p_j} = MRT_{ij} \qquad i, j \text{ both in } (K + 1, \ldots, N)$$

$$(17.19b) \quad MRS_{ij} = \frac{p_i(1 + t)}{p_j(1 + t)} = \frac{p_i}{p_j} = MRT_{ij} \qquad i, j \text{ both in } (1, \ldots, K)$$

$$(17.19c) \quad MRS_{ij} = \frac{p_i(1 + t)}{p_j} = (1 + t)MRT_{ij} \qquad \begin{matrix} i \text{ in } (1, \ldots, K) \\ j \text{ in } (K + 1, \ldots, N) \end{matrix}$$

With the ad valorem tax t^* on the subset $(X_{K+1}, \ldots X_N)$, the following relationships will hold:

$$(17.19a') \qquad MRS_{ij} = \frac{p_i}{p_j} = MRT_{ij} \qquad i, j \text{ both in } (1, \ldots, K)$$

$$(17.19b') \quad MRS_{ij} = \frac{p_i(1 + t^*)}{p_j(1 + t^*)} = \frac{p_i}{p_j} = MRT_{ij} \qquad i, j \text{ both in } (K + 1, \ldots, N)$$

$$(17.19c') \quad MRS_{ij} = \frac{p_i}{p_j(1 + t^*)} = \frac{1}{1 + t^*}MRT_{ij} \qquad \begin{matrix} i \text{ in } (1, \ldots, K) \\ j \text{ in } (K + 1, \ldots, N) \end{matrix}$$

In a profitless economy, only relative prices matter in determining the general equilibrium. For the taxes to be equivalent, then, (17.19c) must equal (17.19c'). But they will be equal if t^* is set such that

$$(17.20) \qquad \frac{p_i(1 + t)}{p_j} = \frac{p_i}{p_j(1 + t^*)}$$

or

$$(17.21) \qquad (1 + t)(1 + t^*) = 1$$

Implications:

1. If $t > 0$, then $t^* < 0$. For example, if $t = 100$ percent, t^* must be set equal to -50 percent. Thus, a general sales tax of 100 percent on all goods is

FIGURE 17–3

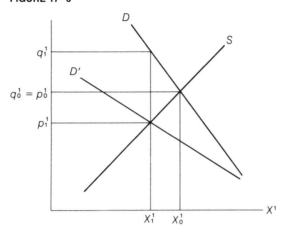

equivalent to a 50 percent tax on all factors (factors are measured negatively, so that a negative t^* applied to a factor supply is a tax). If the subsets $X = 1, \ldots, K$ and $i = K + 1, \ldots, N$ each include some goods and factors, then some elements of *each* subset will be taxed, others subsidized, depending on whether they are goods or factors.

2. The numerical example illustrates second point, that one of the ad valorem rates, in the case t^*, is applied to the gross-of-tax price and the other, in this case t, to the net-of-tax price. This merely reflects the fact that the producer price for factors is a gross-of-tax price, while the producer price for goods is a net-of-tax price. To see this, consider Figures 17–3 and 17–4 and assume the economy consists of a single factor and a single good.

An ad valorem tax paid by the consumer shifts the demand curve down in the goods market and the supply curve up in the factor market. For q_1/q_2 to

FIGURE 17–4

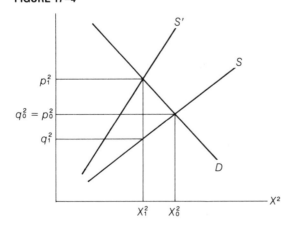

be the same for either tax, the tax rate applied to p_1 must exceed the tax rate applied to p_2. In the graphical example, t raises q_1 100 percent above p_1, the net-of-tax price, and t^* lowers q_2 50 percent below p_2, the gross-of-tax price. At these rates

$$(17.22) \qquad \frac{q_1}{q_2} = \frac{p_1(1+1)}{p_2} = \frac{p_1}{\left(1-\frac{1}{2}\right)p_2} = \frac{2 \cdot p_1}{p_2}$$

3. In these examples the consumers actually pay the tax. The same theorem applies if the producers paid the tax, the only difference being that

$$(17.23) \qquad p_i = (1+t) \cdot q_i \qquad i = 1, \ldots, K$$

$$(17.24) \qquad p_i = (1+t^*) \cdot q_i \qquad i = K+1, \ldots, N$$

$(1+t)(1+t^*) = 1$ is still required for equivalence. In Figures 17–3 and 17–4, the opposite curves would shift, the only difference being that t would now apply to the gross-of-tax price in the goods market, and t^* to the net-of-tax price in the factor market. Whether the impact of a general tax falls on the buyer or supplier in any market can never affect the ultimate incidence of the tax in this or any other context.

4. The two taxes will not generate the same tax revenue in either the actual or compensated general equilibrium. Consider, first, the actual equilibrium.

$$(17.25) \qquad T_t^A = \sum_{i=1}^{K} t \cdot p_i^A X_i^A = t \cdot \sum_{i=1}^{K} p_i^A X_i^A$$

$$(17.26) \qquad T_{t^*}^A = \sum_{i=K+1}^{N} t^* p_i^A X_i^A = t^* \cdot \sum_{i=K+1}^{N} p_i^A X_i^A$$

In a profitless economy, $\sum_{i=1}^{N} p_i Y_i = 0$, where Y_i is the supply of (demand for) good (factor) i. Therefore, from market clearance, $\sum_{i=1}^{N} p_i X_i = 0$, or $\sum_{i=1}^{K} p_i X_i = -\sum_{i=K+1}^{N} p_i X_i$. Thus $T_t = T_{t^*}$ only if $t = -t^*$, which in general will not be true. The theorem, therefore, is a variant of differential incidence as defined above. In this case one tax is substituted for another so as to generate equal incidence, not to hold either tax revenues or the government budget surplus constant.

Tax revenues will not be equal in the compensated equilibrium, either. By design, deadweight loss is equal with each tax. Thus,

$$(17.27) \qquad L(t) = M(\vec{q}^t; \bar{U}^0) - \sum_{i=1}^{K} tp_i X_i^{\text{comp}}$$

$$(17.28) \qquad L(t^*) = M(\vec{q}^{t^*}; \bar{U}^0) - \sum_{i=K+1}^{N} t^* p_i X_i^{\text{comp}}$$

Since $\vec{q}^t$ and $\vec{q}^{t^*}$ are identical vectors of relative prices by the design of t and t^*, $X_i^{\text{comp}}(\vec{q}^t) = X_i^{\text{comp}}(\vec{q}^{t^*})$, all i. But $M(\vec{q}; \bar{U}^0)$ is homogeneous of degree 1 in the vector of absolute prices and $\vec{q}^t = (1+t)\vec{q}^{t^*}$. Therefore $M(\vec{q}^t; \bar{U}^0) \neq M(\vec{q}^{t^*}; \bar{U}^0)$, in general. Since $L(t) = L(t^*)$, it follows immediately that

$$(17.29) \qquad \sum_{i=1}^{K} t \cdot p_i X_i^{\text{comp}} \neq \sum_{i=K+1}^{N} t^* p_i X_i^{\text{comp}}$$

5. The theorem applies only to a one-period profitless economy. If there were pure profits or losses in production, they would have to be accounted for to define incidence equivalence. And designing equivalent taxes in a multi-period model is much more difficult, since all contemporaneous and inter-temporal price ratios have to be equal with the two sets of taxes, but it is at least possible to describe such taxes. Despite these qualifications, the theorem on the equivalence of any two general taxes which span the entire set of goods and factors is one of the most powerful results in all of tax incidence theory, especially since it applies for either measure of tax incidence.

MEASURING TAX INCIDENCE— A MANY-CONSUMER ECONOMY

Tax incidence theory is ultimately concerned with the relative burdens from taxation suffered by various consumers or groups of consumers within the economy. As such it requires analysis within the context of a many-person consumer economy. Unfortunately, it is not entirely clear how to conceptualize a valid incidence analysis for the many-person economy. There is, at the outset, a fundamental and ambiguous issue centered around the question of one's point of view: What matters to incidence theory in a many-person economy, the losses suffered by each of the (H) consumers in the economy as *individually* perceived, or the *aggregate* loss from a social welfare perspective? Presumably the aggregate perspective would incorporate the individuals' self-perceived losses, but weight them according to the rankings of a social welfare function. Optimal second-best policy analysis certainly requires the aggregate viewpoint, as was demonstrated for the many-person optimal tax problem in Chapter 16, but one could reasonably argue that incidence analysis merely tries to describe the pattern of burdens as perceived by each individual (group of) consumer(s). This view, in effect, says that tax incidence is meant to fall within the domain of the positive theory of the public sector, not the normative theory.

The individual perspective on tax incidence is certainly appealing, but it is not at all clear how to maintain an individual perspective in a many-person economy. The same issue arose in Chapter 16 when we discussed deadweight loss in the context of a many-person economy, as it must, since incidence and loss are equivalent under the theoretically appropriate measure of incidence in the one-consumer case. Consider, for example, the problem of measuring the incidence of a single tax from the viewpoint of each individual's loss. Determining the incidence of a single tax requires, at the outset, a specific assumption about how the revenue is given back to the consumers. The natural assumption for incidence analysis is that each consumer receives exactly the revenue he or she pays. Any other distribution of the revenues blurs the focus on the incidence of the tax, per se.

There are three possible ways to view each individual's loss with this assumption, two of them virtually identical with the one-consumer case. The first method would compute the loss function for each individual as:

$$(17.30) \qquad L^h(\vec{t}) = M^h(\vec{q}; \bar{U}^0) - \sum_{i=1}^{N} t_i X_{hi}^{comp} - \pi^h(\vec{p})$$

where $\pi^h(\vec{p}) = $ person h's share of pure profits (losses) from private production, and compare individual losses.

While this would give unambiguous individual measures of loss that could be compared across consumers, it suffers the same defects as its one-consumer counterpart, with one additional problem. As already noted in the discussion of one-person measures, it implies a conceptual experiment in which not only are all the tax revenues returned to each individual exactly as collected but one in which each person simultaneously receives additional lump-sum income (from an agent outside the economy) to fully compensate him for the given pattern of tax rates. Moreover, the compensated equilibrium would not exhibit the same vector of market prices $(\vec{q}, \vec{p})$ as the actual general equilibrium if production employs general technology. In a many-person context it suffers the further handicap that the government would generally not be interested in compensating individuals in that way even if it could, since compensating each individual fully for his self-perceived loss is generally not optimal.

The second option is simply to compute the actual change in market prices $(\vec{q}_A, \vec{p}_A)$ and infer the pattern of burdens from these changes, although how such inferences are to be made is difficult to see. As noted in the one-consumer case, the government could use each individual's indirect utility function to compute individual money indexes of utility loss, although their value is questionable.[12]

A third option, not open in the one-consumer case, is to focus on the welfare loss of a single person (or one "small" group of consumers) and ask how much income this person (group) would require as compensation for the actual change in market prices resulting from the tax. That is, compute for some person, *but only for that person,*

$$(17.31) \qquad L^h(\vec{t}) = M^h(\vec{q}_A; \bar{U}^0) - \sum_{i=1}^{N} t_i X_{hi}^{comp}(\vec{q}_A; \bar{U}^0) - \pi^h(\vec{p}_A)$$

where the loss function is evaluated at the *actual* gross of tax market prices. Since only one person (or one "small" group) is conceptually being compensated, this compensation will presumably not affect the actual structure of market prices, so that this conceptual experiment is well defined. Thus we can consider the loss suffered by one person (group) as he (it) perceives the loss, although we cannot do this for all people (groups) and compare results. Conpensating *everyone* simultaneously at the *actual* market prices is *not* a well-defined conceptual experiment with general technologies. This could only be done un-

---

[12] Peter Diamond takes this approach in P. Diamond, "Tax Incidence in a Two-Good Model," *Journal of Public Economics*, June 1978.

ambiguously if technology were linear, in which case the observed vector of consumer prices will obtain no matter how a conceptual compensation experiment is defined.

The same considerations apply to differential incidence, in which one tax is substituted for another. Presumably one would be interested in computing the tax changes necessary for a constant government budget surplus at the actual equilibrium. Given these tax changes, the question remains whether compensation tests could be mixed with actual market results, a question which has been fully discussed in the context of a one-consumer (equivalent) economy.

If the aggregate social welfare point of view is adopted, there is no ambiguity. One would simply compute changes in actual market equilibria and their resulting effects on the social welfare function. The aggregate differential incidence problem has already been presented at the end of Chapter 16 for a profitless, competitive economy with no government production. Recall that the two key relationships are the government budget constraint

$$(17.32) \qquad \sum_h \sum_i t_i X_{hi} = \bar{T}$$

which can be totally differentiated to determine the change in tax rates necessary to hold tax revenues constant,[13] and equation (16.95) (in vector notation)

$$(17.33) \qquad dW = \left\| \left[-(1 - \beta)'X \right]' - t' \frac{\partial X}{\partial q} \right| E^{-1} \frac{\partial y}{\partial p} \, dt$$

which relates changes in social welfare to changes in tax rates.

$\beta = \begin{bmatrix} \beta^1 \\ \beta^h \\ \beta^H \end{bmatrix}$ is the vector of social marginal utilities of income.

The aggregate perspective thus reduces the differential incidence question to one of determining which of two sets of taxes creates the highest level of social welfare. This is certainly a well-defined general equilibrium problem but it would appear to violate the spirit of most existing incidence studies, which have typically adopted the individual perspective.

THE HARBERGER ANALYSIS

Arnold Harberger's 1962 analysis of the incidence of the corporate income tax stands as a landmark without rival in the literature on tax incidence theory. Its contributions were twofold. In the first place, his study firmly established the fundamental principle that incidence analysis, properly conceived, requires a full general equilibrium model of the underlying economic system. Second, Harberger developed the methodology of measuring incidence in terms of changes in actual general equilibrium consumer and producer prices, focusing

---

[13] With government production, the overall surplus should be held constant.

primarily on changes in factor prices. While, as noted above, this measure cannot possibly be the definitive measure of tax incidence, no other single measure is infallible either. Furthermore, most tax theorists have chosen Harberger's method of analysis in their own studies, regardless of the tax being analyzed. For all these reasons, Harberger's study of the corporate income tax deserves careful attention. It also happens to be, somewhat ironically, an excellent vehicle for demonstrating the limitations of the change-in-actual-prices measure of incidence as a measure of true economic burdens. Thus it serves as an excellent conclusion to the chapter.

For his analytical framework, Harberger chose a one-consumer (equivalent), profitless, perfectly competitive market economy with general, constant returns to scale (CRS) production technology. His basic methodology can be stated very simply in terms already outlined in the preceding sections of this chapter. First, he chose to analyze the incidence of a single "small" tax in which the revenues were returned to the consumer lump sum. Specifically, Harberger posited a single tax on the use of capital services by all firms in one of two sectors within the economy, the "corporate" sector,[14] the proceeds of which are spent by the government exactly as the consumer would have spent them. This assumption is equivalent to returning the taxes lump sum, and it automatically maintains budgetary balance (at level zero) and consumers' lump-sum income.[15] Once the tax rate is specified, all that is required to determine the resulting price changes is differentiating the market clearance equations of the form

(17.34) $$D^i[p(t) + t] = \pi_i[p(t)] \qquad i = 1, \ldots, N$$

where:

$D^i(\ )$ = demand (supply) of good (factor) i by the consumer.

π_i = the supply (demand) of good (factor) i, the first derivative of the competitive profit function for the economy.

These equations will determine the producer price changes, after which the consumer price changes follow directly from the price relationships, $q_i = p_i + t_i$, all $i = 1, \ldots, N$.

As a general rule, with N goods and factors it is impossible to determine a priori how these prices will change, but in much simpler economies these price changes will often follow predictable patterns. Harberger chose the standard two-good–two-factor model used in most geometric presentations of general equilibrium analysis and was able to describe precisely how the various demand and production parameters of this model would affect changes in the wage-rental ratio resulting from the corporate tax. He concluded that under most reasonable values of these parameters capitalists would bear all or nearly all of the burden of the tax.

---

[14] Notice that this is a "specific" or "selective" tax as opposed to a "general" tax, since only a subset of all the demanders of capital are taxed.

[15] For a more careful discussion of the effect of this tax and transfer on the consumer's income, see page 407.

Harberger's analytics are actually much more complicated than the three-step process described above because he works directly with the underlying production functions for the economy, rather than the profit functions, in order to highlight the manner in which production parameters influence the pattern of tax incidence. Most other researchers have followed his lead in this regard. Consequently, Harberger's general equilibrium model contains five basic sets of assumptions, as follows:

1.   There are two goods, X and Y, each produced by two factors of production, capital (K) and labor (L). Consumers supply the factors in absolutely fixed amounts, a standard assumption that permits one to draw a pareto-optimal production frontier in capital-labor space, since the boundaries of the Edgeworth box are thereby fixed.

2.   Production is CRS for each good, according to the production relationships:

$$(17.35) \qquad\qquad X = X(K_X, L_X)$$

$$(17.36) \qquad\qquad Y = Y(K_Y, L_Y)$$

Furthermore, the two industries are unequally factor intensive, meaning that $K_X/L_X > K_Y/L_Y$ (X relatively capital intense) or $K_X/L_X < K_Y/L_Y$ (Y relatively capital intense) at *any* given feasible factor price ratio, P_K/P_L. This assumption, along with CRS, creates a production-possibility frontier that is uniformly concave to the origin, so that general equilibrium price ratios vary systematically as the economy moves along the frontier. The CRS assumption rules out the possibility of pure profits or losses at any competitive allocation.

3.   Despite the fact that capital is one of the factors of production, there is no savings in the economy. All economic decisions occur within a single time period. Moreover, all markets are competitive,[16] which has two very important implications:

a.   There is always full employment in equilibrium so that $K_X + K_Y = \bar{K}$ and $L_X + L_Y = \bar{L}$, where $\bar{K}, \bar{L}$ are the fixed factor supplies.

b.   In equilibrium, all consumers pay the same prices for X and Y no matter where purchased, and receive the same returns for their factors of production no matter where supplied, whether to industry X or industry Y. Moreover, the equilibrium factor prices equal the value of their marginal products in each industry.

4.   The government levies a "small" tax on the use of capital services in industry X, identified as the corporate sector. There are no other taxes in the economy. To dispose of the revenue, the government spends the proceeds exactly as the consumers would have had they kept the revenue but were confronted with the new general equilibrium vector of prices. As mentioned, this is equivalent to simply returning the tax revenues lump sum. It also preserves the total level of national income within the economy.

---

[16] Harberger relaxes this assumption in the last part of his article by permitting monopoly power in the market for X, the taxed corporate sector.

5. Since Harberger does not introduce a social welfare function, he implicitly assumes a one-consumer equivalent economy.

With these five sets of conditions, Harberger is able to describe the change in the factor price ratio P_K/P_L in response to the tax. The changes in factor incomes accruing to capital and labor as a result of the changes in the P_K/P_L ratio measure, for Harberger, the true economic burdens of the tax borne by capital and labor. Before turning to his analytical equations, which are fairly complex, let us first develop a feel for Harberger's results by undertaking a geometric-intuitive analysis of the general equilibrium response to the tax in a simple two-good–two-factor economy.

A tax on the use of capital in industry X will have the immediate effect of driving a wedge between the returns to capital in the two sectors. Investors in industry X receive the net-of-tax return $(P_K^0 - T_{KX})$, where T_{KX} is the unit tax on capital in industry X. Investors in industry Y continue to receive the gross of tax return P_K^0. Presumably firms in industry X will shift up their supply curves by an amount sufficient to restore the original rate of return P_K^0. Whether or not this will succeed depends upon the demand elasticity for good X. In a two-good economy, one would expect the demand for X to have some price elasticity and that X and Y would be substitutes. Therefore, the demand for Y could increase in response to a rise in the price of X. If this is true, then p_X will not rise sufficiently to cover the tax in the short run, creating losses in industry X. Profits will develop in industry Y, and firms will have an incentive to shift resources from X to Y in order to equalize returns to capital in both industries. What happens then depends on relative factor intensities. Suppose X is relatively capital intensive. If so, then at the initial factor price ratio P_K^0/P_L^0, industry X will be releasing capital and labor in different proportions from those desired by industry Y, creating excess supply in the capital market and excess demand in the labor market. The factor price ratio P_K/P_L will begin to fall, and *both* industries will respond by becoming more capital intensive as factor markets continue to equate factor prices with values of marginal products. Equilibrium will be achieved only when full employment is restored in *both* factor markets. The amount of factor price change required to bring this about will depend not only on the relative factor intensities but also on elasticities of substitution between capital and labor in both industries.

To give one extreme example indicating how elasticities of substitution matter, if the elasticity of substitution between capital and labor is infinite (straight-line isoquants) in the untaxed sector, then there can be only one equilibrium price ratio for industry Y, the original P_K^0/P_L^0. For a given P_L, the demand schedule for capital in industry Y is perfectly elastic at the original P_K. Hence capital will shift until $(P_K - T_{KX})$ in industry X just equals P_K^0 in industry Y, and the return to capital will not fall as a result of a tax on capital in industry X. This case is depicted in Figure 17–5.

Finally, returning to the goods markets, the shift in resources to industry Y will tend to lower the goods price ratio P_X/P_Y. This follows because the price of capital has fallen relative to the price of labor, and industry X uses capital

FIGURE 17-5

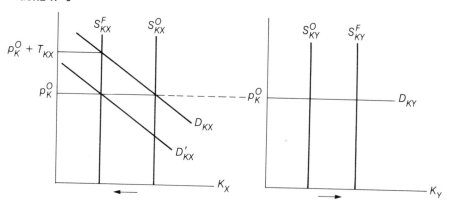

relatively more intensively than industry Y, whereas industry Y is relatively labor intensive. Consequently, production (marginal) costs should fall in industry X and rise in Y. What this says, in effect, is that the long-run supply curves for both goods are expected to be upward sloping with CRS and unequal factor intensities. Overall, the final change in the goods price ratio is indeterminant, a priori. Figure 17–6 gives one possible outcome in which there is no change in P_X/P_Y.

In this example, the shift in the demand curve for Y in response to the original increase in the price of X is just enough to restore (the posited) equality of P_Y and P_X, so that the *ratio* of these prices will remain unchanged. The tax tends to increase P_X relative to P_Y, but the demand response moves the prices in the other direction. In fact, because Harberger focuses entirely on the changes in the factor price ratio P_K/P_L for his measure of incidence, he is implicitly assuming that there is no change in the equilibrium goods price ratios, exactly as depicted in Figure 17–6, or at least that the final change is relatively small and can be ignored.

The descriptive analysis indicates that the incidence of the corporate tax (a tax on use of capital in sector X) will depend on three sets of parameters: the

FIGURE 17-6

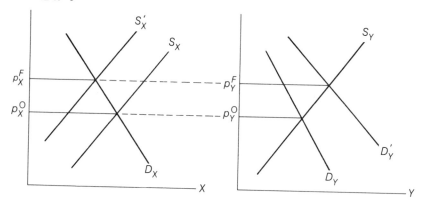

relative factor intensities of the two sectors, the elasticity of substitution between capital and labor in each sector, and the price elasticities of demand for goods X and Y. The analytics will determine a fourth factor as well, the shares of both capital and labor income originating in each sector. Finally, the descriptive analysis emphasizes another important fact about tax incidence, that it is impossible to isolate the burden of a tax to one sector of an economy even though the tax is placed selectively within that one sector. Since competitive factor markets will equalize returns to capital everywhere in the economy, if investors in the taxed sector suffer a decrease in the return to capital, investors elsewhere will suffer the same burden as well. Moreover, since markets are interdependent, the tax burdens could spread to other untaxed factors, and to consumers through changes in goods prices. In general, then, a selective tax is selective in impact only, not in its incidence.

THE HARBERGER ANALYTICS

Harberger describes the demand, supply, and market clearance equations for his economy with ten equations designed to highlight changes in the equilibrium values of factor prices and factor supplies in response to the tax on the use of capital in sector X. Since he selects the price of labor as the numeraire, the change in the factor price ratio equals the change in the price of capital, dP_K. The only unusual feature of his analysis is that all goods and factors are defined in units such that the value of all goods and factor prices in the original pretax equilibrium is one. This is done strictly as a matter of convenience. It implies no loss of generality.

The Demand Equations

Harberger describes the demand side of the general equilibrium model with a single demand equation for X of the form

(17.37)
$$X = X\left(\frac{P_X}{P_Y}\right)$$

With fixed factor supplies, once the change in X is determined in response to the tax, the change in Y follows immediately, since all income is spent on either X or Y. Thus a separate demand equation for Y would be redundant. Moreover, there is no need to write the demand for X as a function of P_L and P_K. Production is CRS so that factor income exhausts the product—there can be no pure profits or losses. Furthermore, the government essentially returns all tax revenue to the consumers. Thus there is no change in the consumers' disposable income even if P_L and P_K change.[17] Finally, given Harberger's one-consumer equivalent assumption, there is only a single aggregate demand relationship for X.

---

[17] There may be an income effect in the form of deadweight loss, but Harberger ignores this. We will return to this point below.

Totally differentiating the demand for X,

(17.38)
$$dX = \frac{\partial X}{\partial \left(\dfrac{P_X}{P_Y}\right)} \frac{P_Y dP_X - P_X dP_Y}{P_Y^2}$$

Dividing by X to express the change in percentage form

(17.39)
$$\frac{dX}{X} = \frac{\partial X}{\partial \left(\dfrac{P_X}{P_Y}\right)} \frac{1}{X} \left[\frac{dP_X}{P_Y} - \frac{P_X}{P_Y^2} dP_Y\right]$$

Finally, with units defined such that $P_X = P_Y = 1$, (17.39) can be rewritten as:

(17.40)
$$\frac{dX}{X} = E[dP_X - dP_Y]$$

where:

(17.41)
$$E = \frac{\partial X}{\partial \left(\dfrac{P_X}{P_Y}\right)} \frac{\dfrac{P_X}{P_Y}}{X} = \text{the demand elasticity for } X \text{ in terms of the relative prices } P_X/P_Y.$$

The Goods-Supply and Input-Demand Equations

From market clearance, the percentage change in demand for X must equal the percentage change in supply of X. To determine the percentage change in the supply of X, totally differentiate the production function $X = f(K_X, L_X)$, obtaining:

(17.42)
$$dX = \frac{\partial f}{\partial K_X} dK_X + \frac{\partial f}{\partial L_X} dL_X$$

Therefore:

(17.43)
$$\left.\frac{dX}{X}\right|_{\text{supply}} = \frac{\dfrac{\partial f}{\partial K_X}}{f} dK_X + \frac{\dfrac{\partial f}{\partial L_X}}{f} dL_X$$

(17.44)
$$\left.\frac{dX}{X}\right|_{\text{supply}} = \frac{\dfrac{\partial f}{\partial K_X} K_X}{f} \frac{dK_X}{K_X} + \frac{\dfrac{\partial f}{\partial L_X} L_X}{f} \frac{dL_X}{L_X}$$

(17.45)
$$\left.\frac{dX}{X}\right|_{\text{supply}} = \theta_{KX} \frac{dK_X}{K_X} + \theta_{LX} \frac{dL_X}{L_X}$$

where:

$\theta_{KX} =$ the share of capital's income in the value added for industry X.
$\theta_{LX} =$ the share of labor's income in the value added for industry Y.

(17.45) follows from (17.44) because: (1) with CRS, factor payments exhaust the product; and (2) factors are paid the value of their marginal products in competitive factor markets. Hence:

$$\frac{\partial f}{\partial K_X} \frac{K_X}{f} = \frac{P_k}{P_X} \frac{K_X}{X} = \begin{array}{l}\text{capital's share of income} \\ \text{in industry } X\end{array}$$

and similiarly for labor's share.

By Walras' law, both the demand and supply equations for Y are redundant.

Turning next to the industries' demands for factors, changes in factor demands can be specified in terms of their direct elasticities of substitution. Define:

(17.46)
$$S_Y = \frac{d \log\left(\dfrac{K_Y}{L_Y}\right)}{d \log\left(\dfrac{f_{L_Y}}{f_{K_Y}}\right)}$$

(17.47)
$$S_X = \frac{d \log\left(\dfrac{K_X}{L_X}\right)}{d \log\left(\dfrac{f_{L_X}}{f_{K_X}}\right)}$$

where:

S_Y = the direct elasticity of substitution between capital and labor in industry Y.

S_X = the direct elasticity of substitution between capital and labor in industry X.

But with competitive markets and CRS production,

(17.48)
$$d \log\left(\frac{f_{L_X}}{f_{K_X}}\right) = d \log\left(\frac{f_{L_Y}}{f_{K_Y}}\right) = d \log\left(\frac{P_K}{P_L}\right)$$

Therefore:

(17.49)
$$d \log\left(\frac{K_Y}{L_Y}\right) = S_Y d \log\left(\frac{P_K}{P_L}\right)$$

and

(17.50)
$$d \log\left(\frac{K_X}{L_X}\right) = S_X d \log\left(\frac{P_K}{P_L}\right)$$

Consider equation (17.49):

(17.51)
$$d \log\left(\frac{K_Y}{L_Y}\right) = \frac{1}{\dfrac{K_Y}{L_Y}} d\left(\frac{K_Y}{L_Y}\right) = \frac{1}{\dfrac{K_Y}{L_Y}} \left[\frac{L_Y dK_Y - K_Y dL_Y}{L_Y^2}\right]$$

$$= \frac{dK_Y}{K_Y} - \frac{dL_Y}{L_Y}$$

Similarly,

$$(17.52) \quad d \log\left(\frac{P_K}{P_L}\right) = \frac{dP_K}{P_K} - \frac{dP_L}{P_L} = dP_K - dP_L \qquad \text{with } P_K = P_L = 1$$

Substituting (17.51) and (17.52) into (17.49) yields:

$$(17.53) \qquad \frac{dK_Y}{K_Y} - \frac{dL_Y}{L_Y} = S_Y(dP_K - dP_L)$$

Similarly,[18]

$$(17.54) \qquad \frac{dK_X}{K_X} - \frac{dL_X}{L_X} = S_X(dP_K + T_{KX} - dP_L)$$

Market Clearance

Since capital and labor are in fixed supply, capital and labor must move between sectors in equal amounts to maintain full employment. Therefore:

$$(17.55) \qquad\qquad\qquad dK_Y = -dK_X$$

$$(17.56) \qquad\qquad\qquad dL_Y = -dL_X$$

Also, the market for X must remain in balance so that

$$(17.57) \qquad\qquad\qquad \left.\frac{dX}{X}\right|_{\text{demand}} = \left.\frac{dX}{X}\right|_{\text{supply}}$$

As indicated above, a market clearance equation for Y is redundant given the formulation of the model.

Additional Price Relationships

Because Harberger is ultimately interested only in changes in relative factor prices as the measure of tax incidence, he presents two additional equations relating changes in the goods prices to changes in the factor prices. Consider, first, the market equilibrium for industry X.

$$(17.58) \quad P_X X = P_L L_X + (P_K + T_{KX}) K_X \qquad \text{from product exhaustion with CRS}$$

Totally differentiating:

$$(17.59) \qquad P_X dX + X dP_X = P_L dL_X + L_X dP_L + (P_K + T_{KX}) dK_X$$
$$+ (dP_K + T_{KX}) K_X$$

But with competitive pricing,

$$(17.60) \qquad \frac{\partial f}{\partial L_X} = \frac{P_L}{P_X} \quad \text{and} \quad \frac{\partial f}{\partial K_X} = \frac{P_K + T_{KX}}{P_X}$$

---

[18] Recall that Harberger begins with zero taxes, so that $T_{KX} = dT_{KX}$ and $T_{KX} \approx 0$. Equations (17.45), (17.48), and (17.50) implicitly include T_{KX} in P_K for industry X.

Moreover, from differentiating the production function:

$$(17.61) \qquad dX = \frac{\partial f}{\partial K_X} dK_X + \frac{\partial f}{\partial L_X} dL_X$$

Therefore:

$$(17.62) \qquad P_X dX = P_L dL_X + (P_K + T_{KX}) dK_X$$

and

$$(17.63) \qquad X dP_X = L_X dP_L + K_X (dP_K + T_{KX})$$

Thus

$$(17.64) \qquad dP_X = \frac{L_X}{X} dP_L + \frac{K_X}{X} (dP_K + T_{KX})$$

With all prices equal to 1, and the level of taxes equal to 0 to a first order of approximation,

$$(17.65) \qquad \frac{P_L}{P_X} = \frac{P_K + T_{KX}}{P_X} = 1$$

so that (17.64) can be rewritten as:

$$(17.66) \qquad dP_X = \theta_{LX} dP_L + \theta_{KX} (dP_K + T_{KX})$$

By similar analysis,

$$(17.67) \qquad dP_Y = \theta_{LY} dP_L + \theta_{KY} dP_K$$

Finally, labor is chosen as the numeraire. Thus $P_L \equiv 1$, and

$$(17.68) \qquad dP_L = 0$$

Summary

Equations (17.40, 17.45, 17.53–17.57, 17.66–17.68) describe the comparative static changes in the general equilibrium quantities and prices. Plugging equations (17.66) and (17.67) into (17.40) and employing equations (17.45, 17.55–17.57, and 17.68), the ten equation system can be collapsed into the following three-equation system, with dP_K, dL_X/L_X, and dK_X/K_X as the dependent variables.

$$(17.69) \qquad E(\theta_{KY} - \theta_{KX}) dP_K + \theta_{LX} \frac{dL_X}{L_X} + \theta_{KX} \frac{dK_X}{K_X} = E \theta_{KX} T_{KX}$$

$$(17.70) \qquad S_Y dP_K - \frac{L_X}{L_Y} \frac{dL_X}{L_X} + \frac{K_X}{K_Y} \frac{dK_X}{K_X} = 0$$

$$(17.71) \qquad - S_X dP_K - \frac{dL_X}{L_X} + \frac{dK_X}{K_X} = S_X T_{KX}$$

For purposes of tax incidence, the variable of interest is dP_K $(=d(P_K/P_L)$, with $P_K = P_L = 1$, and $dP_L = 0$). Using Cramer's rule and combining terms:

$$(17.72) \quad dP_K = \frac{E\theta_{KX}\left(\dfrac{K_X}{K_Y} - \dfrac{L_X}{L_Y}\right) + S_X\left(\dfrac{\theta_{LX}K_X}{K_Y} + \dfrac{\theta_{KX}L_X}{L_Y}\right)T_{KX}}{E(\theta_{KY} - \theta_{KX})\left(\dfrac{K_X}{K_Y} - \dfrac{L_X}{L_Y}\right) - S_Y - S_X\left(\dfrac{\theta_{LX}K_X}{K_Y} + \dfrac{\theta_{KX}L_X}{L_Y}\right)}$$

All the relevant information necessary to determine the incidence of the corporate tax is contained in equation (17.72).

Comments on the Solution

1. As indicated in the preliminary intuitive analysis, the change in relative factor prices will depend upon the demand elasticity for X, the elasticities of substitution between capital and labor in each industry, the relative capital (labor) intensities in the two sectors, and the share of capital and labor income in each sector.

Once the change in the price of capital is obtained, it can then be used to compute changes in capital's income relative to changes in national income as a summary measure of incidence, with all changes measured in units of labor, the numeraire. Because the overall supply of capital is fixed, the change in capital's income is simply dP_K. With $P_K = 1$, dP_K also equals the percentage change in income to capital. National income equals the sum of all factor payments, or

$$(17.73) \qquad I = (P_K + T_{KX})K_X + P_K K_Y + P_L L_X + P_L L_Y$$

Totally differentiating and recalling that $T_{KX} = dT_{KX}$,

$$(17.74) \qquad \begin{aligned} dI &= (dP_K + T_{KX})K_X + dP_K K_Y + dP_L L_X + dP_L L_Y \\ &\quad + (P_K + T_{KX})dK_X + P_K dK_Y + P_L dL_X + P_L dL_Y \end{aligned}$$

But $P_X = P_Y = P_L = P_K = 1$, $dP_L = 0$, $dL_X = -dL_Y$, and $dK_X = -dK_Y$. Hence:

$$(17.75) \qquad dI = T_{KX}K_X + (K_X + K_Y)dP_K$$

and

$$(17.76) \qquad \frac{dI}{I} = \frac{T_{KX}K_X + (K_X + K_Y)dP_K}{K_X + K_Y + L_X + L_Y}$$

Three cases are of special interest.

Suppose, first, that $dP_K = -T_{KX}K_X/(K_X + K_Y)$. This would leave national income unchanged measured in units of labor, whereas capital's share would fall by the entire amount of the tax revenue. In this case, then, capital can be said to bear the entire burden of the tax. Suppose, secondly, that $dP_K = 0$. Since $dP_L \equiv 0$, both capital's and labor's income would fall in proportion to their initial share in national income. This would imply equal sharing of the tax burden. Finally, suppose the percentage change in the price of capital net of tax (dP_K) just equals the percentage change in national income. This would imply that labor bears the entire burden of the tax, which will occur if

$$dP_K = \frac{dI}{I} = \frac{[T_{KX}K_X + (K_X + K_Y)dP_K]}{L_X + L_Y + K_X + K_Y}$$

$$dP_K = \frac{T_{KX}K_X}{L_X + L_Y}$$

2. How the burden will actually be shared between capital and labor will of course depend upon the exact solution to (17.72), which will in turn depend upon the four demand and production parameters imbedded in the right-hand side of the equation. Moreover, the specific cases mentioned above do not place limits on the possible results. Capital could bear a burden greater than its share of the tax revenue $(dP_K < -T_{KX}K_X/(K_X + K_Y)$; similarly capitalists could actually gain at the expense of labor despite being taxed $(dP_K > T_{KX}K_X/(L_X + L_Y))$. Harberger presents ten theorems derived from equation (17.72), each highlighting how the four supply and demand parameters will determine the final incidence of the tax. We will present just three of them, indicating how the three special cases mentioned above might occur. The first two theorems were also suggested by the introductory discriptive analysis of the corporate tax.

a. Labor can bear most of the burden of the tax only if the taxed sector is relatively labor intensive.

Proof: For labor to bear most of the burden of the tax dP_K must be positive. But examination of (17.72) reveals that this can only occur if industry X is relatively labor intensive. To see this, consider the denominator. The last two terms can be expected to be positive, by inspection. The first term will generally be positive also. E can be expected to be negative. $(\theta_{KY} - \theta_{KX})$ and $|K_X/K_Y - L_X/L_Y|$ must necessarily have opposite signs, since if capital's share of income is greater in industry Y, $((\theta_{KY} - \theta_{KX}) > 0)$, then industry Y must be relatively capital intensive, or $(K_X/K_Y - L_X/L_Y) < 0$. Thus, the denominator is positive. Turning to the numerator, its second term can be expected to be negative. Hence, for dP_K to be positive, the first term must be positive and greater in absolute value than the second term. Since $E < 0$, and $f_K > 0$, this can only occur if $(K_X/K_Y - L_X/L_Y) < 0$, or if the taxed sector, X, is relatively labor intensive.

The exact conditions for which labor bears precisely the full burden of the tax are not easily stated and will not be derived.

b. If the elasticity of substitution between capital and labor in the untaxed industry is infinite, then capital and labor will share equally the burden of taxation.

Proof: Equal sharing of the tax burden requires that $dP_K = 0$. But if S_Y, the elasticity of substitution between capital and labor in the untaxed sector, is infinitely large, dP_K must $= 0$.

c. If both industries are initially equally factor intensive, and each has the same elasticity of substitution between capital and labor, then capital will bear the full burden of the tax.

Proof: Capital will bear the full burden of the tax if $dP_K = -T_{KX}K_X/(K_X + K_Y)$. If both industries are equally capital intensive, then $K_X/K_Y = L_X/L_Y$ and (17.72) reduces to:

$$(17.77) \quad dP_K = \frac{S_X\left(\theta_{LX}\dfrac{K_X}{K_Y} + \theta_{KX}\dfrac{L_X}{L_Y}\right)T_{KX}}{-S_Y - S_X\left(\theta_{LX}\dfrac{K_X}{K_Y} + \theta_{KX}\dfrac{L_X}{L_Y}\right)} = -\frac{S_X\dfrac{K_X}{K_Y}(\theta_{LX} + \theta_{KX})T_{KX}}{S_Y + S_X\dfrac{K_X}{K_Y}(\theta_{LX} + \theta_{KX})}$$

But $\theta_{LX} + \theta_{KX} = 1$. Therefore,

$$(17.78) \quad dP_K = -\frac{S_X\dfrac{K_X}{K_Y}T_{KX}}{S_Y + S_X\dfrac{K_X}{K_Y}} \quad \text{or} \quad dP_K = \frac{-S_XK_XT_{KX}}{S_YK_Y + S_XK_X}$$

If, in addition, $S_X = S_Y$, then

$$(17.79) \quad dP_K = \frac{-T_{KX}K_X}{K_Y + K_X}$$

3. Harberger presents a large number of conditions for which capital bears the full burden of the tax. Given that much econometric analysis of the U.S. economy has found that elasticities of substitution between capital and labor are -1, and further that empirical research often assumes that elasticities of substitution in demand are also -1, one of the most compelling theorems is the following: Capital will bear the full burden of the tax if the elasticities of substitution between capital and labor are equal in both industries, and equal as well to the elasticity of substitution in demand between the two goods. The proof of this theorem requires extensive manipulation of equation (17.72) so we have chosen not to present it, but this is one of the most striking of the ten Harberger theorems.

In the final section of his paper, Harberger performs a sensitivity analysis on the U.S. economy, computing $dP_K^{U.S.}$ for what he believes to be a plausible range of estimates for the various elements on the right hand side of equation (17.72). His analysis leads him to the following conclusion:

> It is hard to avoid the conclusion that plausible alternative sets of assumptions about the relevant elasticities all yield results in which capital bears very close to 100 percent of the tax burden. The most plausible assumptions imply that capital bears more than the full burden of the tax.[19]

Harberger also reworks the analysis to include the special taxation of capital gains and the existence of monopoly elements in the corporate sector. Neither

---

[19] Harberger, "The Incidence of the Corporation Income Tax," pp. 235–36.

of these considerations affect his basic result, that in all likelihood the incidence of the corporate tax in the United States falls substantially upon capital.

4. Harberger's analysis brings into sharp focus the possible differences between tax incidence measured as changes in actual general equilibrium prices and tax incidence measured as changes in welfare or, equivalently, the lump-sum income required to compensate consumers for a given pattern of taxation. A suitable welfare measure would indicate that the tax described by Harberger *creates no burden at all*, precisely because his tax is an infinitesimally small change from a zero-tax general equilibrium. With the tax revenues (effectively) returned lump-sum to the consumer(s), deadweight loss is an appropriate welfare measure, and we saw in Chapter 15 that deadweight loss is zero for a single, infinitesimally small tax. Actually the analysis in Chapter 15 is not strictly appropriate since it applies only to general taxes paid by consumers. Harberger, on the other hand, considers a selective tax paid by some, but not all, of the firms for the use of a specific factor. Nonetheless, it can be easily shown that the deadweight loss is still zero.

It is important to note that Harberger had to posit a selective tax in order to have an interesting problem. Had he chosen a general tax on the use .of capital in both sectors the tax could not possibly have created a burden even using the change-in-actual price measure of incidence. Clearly a tax on the *supply* of a factor in absolutely fixed supply in a one-consumer-equivalent economy could not create a burden if the revenues are returned. Any tax on a fixed factor is equivalent to a lump-sum tax, and returning all the revenues would return the economy to its original equilibrium. But a tax has the same incidence effects if applied to either side of a market. Hence a tax cum transfer on the total demand for capital would also keep the economy at its original equilibrium. Figure 17–7 depicts the case of a tax on all capital. The price of capital remains at P_K^0 whether the suppliers are taxed and S remains unshifted, or all firms are taxed and demand shifts to D_K' with the shift equal to the full amount of the tax. Assuming the tax revenue is returned in each case, the consumers suffer no loss in income either.

FIGURE 17–7

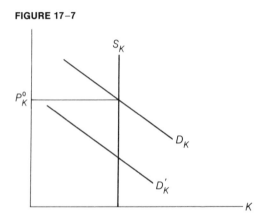

5.   Harberger's assumption that the corporate tax represents an infinitesimal movement away from a world of zero taxes may be an analytical convenience for illustrating his approach to the measurement of tax incidence, but it is certainly an extreme departure from reality. Moreover, as noted in the preceding comment, if one chooses the deadweight loss measure of tax incidence, the existence of initial taxes is required for a tax burden to exist. While the Harberger measure does not require initial taxes to generate a pattern of tax burdens, the change in relative factor prices in response to a marginal change in any given tax will obviously be affected by the presence of initial taxes. Ballentine and Eris have recently reworked the original Harberger analysis to include an existing corporate tax, while retaining the assumption of zero taxes elsewhere in the economy.[20] The assumption of an existing tax changes rather significantly such calculations as the share of income going to capital in the taxed industry and the change in tax revenues in response to a marginal change in the tax rate, but the major analytical distinction occurs in the equation determining the percentage change in the demand for X (equation (17.40), above). Because there is now a marginal deadweight loss from the tax change, the consumers' real income declines, and the change in the demand for X will include this income effect as well as Harberger's relative price effect. When Ballentine and Eris reworked Harberger's empirical sensitivity analysis for the U.S. economy to include this income effect, they found that the burden on capital fell somewhat for plausible values of the income elasticity of demand, although not enough to alter the conclusion that capital bears the major portion of the tax burden.

6.   Harberger's equations are easily modified to analyze per unit commodity taxes on X or Y, or other selective factor taxes such as a tax on the use of capital or labor in Y, or a tax on the use of labor in X. For instance, a per-unit commodity tax on X involves adding T_X $(=dT_X)$ to the right-hand side of (17.66), with all other equations unchanged (and, of course, removing all T_{KX} terms). A tax on the use of labor in Y requires replacing dP_L by $(dP_L + T_{LY})$ in equations (17.53) and (17.67), all other equations unchanged, and similarly for the other taxes.[21] More than one tax change can also be considered, with the addition of a government budget constraint whose derivatives determine the relationship among equal yield tax alternatives.

7.   Finally, Harberger's analysis assumes that the U.S. corporate tax actually does change the opportunity cost of capital and hence the investment margin within the corporate sector, thereby distorting investors' preferences away from the corporate sector in favor of the unincorporated sector. No attention is given to the characteristics of the tax itself, yet it happens to be a fairly complex tax. For instance, firms are allowed to deduct interest payments on debt and an estimate of depreciation from total returns in computing taxable

---

[20] J. Ballentine and I. Eris, "On the General Equilibrium Analysis of Tax Incidence," *Journal of Political Economy*, June 1975, pp. 633–44.

[21] Refer to P. Mieszkowski, "On the Theory of Tax Incidence," *Journal of Political Economy*, June 1967, for an analysis of the various possibilities.

returns. Moreover net-of-tax returns are taxed again under the federal (and state) personal income tax(es), but differentially depending on the exact form of the returns. Dividends and interest income from bonds are taxed as ordinary income, but retained earnings which ultimately generate capital gains are taxed at preferential rates, and only when realized. There are also reasonably complex provisions relating to the offset of losses against income. Many other provisions affect the net-of-tax returns as well, too numerous to cite here. The point, however, is that the distortionary effects of this or any other tax depend crucially on its particular design characteristics.

Suppose the corporate tax turned out to be a tax on pure economic profits. In that case the tax would be lump sum *and* nondistortionary. Corporate investors would simply pay the tax without any adjustment in their investment plans. There would be no incentive to shift investment to the unincorporated sector, and no change in relative prices. This point has long been understood; yet it was thought that the corporate tax was not simply a tax on pure economic profits. Recently, however, Stiglitz argued that the tax may well approximate a pure profits tax especially in a world of certainty, which the Harberger analysis assumes. Given that both interest payments on debt and depreciation are deductible, corporate investment decisions may be independent of the tax.[22]

To see this, consider a firm's decision to borrow \$1 in time $(t - 1)$ to finance an additional unit of capital in time t, all other investment plans unchanged (and optimal). Let:

r = the one period rate of interest on borrowing.

δ = the true rate of economic depreciation.

t_c = the corporate profits tax rate.

$\dfrac{\partial \pi}{\partial K_t}$ = the increased profits arising from a marginal increase in the capital stock, the gross-of-tax returns to capital.

The decision to invest an additional dollar in time $(t - 1)$ leads to $\partial \pi / \partial K_t$ of gross returns in time t, less r dollars of interest costs and δ dollars of depreciation. If both interest payments and the true economic rate of depreciation are tax deductible, the net-of-tax returns from the investment are $(\partial \pi / \partial K_t - r - \delta)(1 - t_c)$. Hence the firm should borrow to invest to long as $(\partial \pi / \partial K_t - \delta) \geq r$. Similar analysis for a unit decrease in investment shows that the appropriate disinvestment margin is $(\partial \pi / \partial K_t - \delta) \leq r$. Hence, the optimal investment plan occurs when $(\partial \pi / \partial K_t - \delta) = r$. The opportunity cost of capital is just r, equal to gross-of-tax returns net of depreciation. It is entirely *independent* of t_c. Therefore, if actual depreciation allowances are reasonably close approximations of true

---

[22] The seminal paper is J. Stiglitz, "Taxation, Corporate Financial Policy, and the Cost of Capital," *Journal of Public Economics*, vol. 2, 1973, but the following papers are far simpler and more accessible: J. Stiglitz, "The Corporation Tax," *Journal of Public Economics*, April–May 1976; M. King, "Taxation, Corporate Financial Policy, and the Cost of Capital: A Comment," *Journal of Public Economics*, August 1975; and J. Flemming, "A Reappraisal of the Corporate Income Tax," *Journal of Public Economics*, July–August 1976. The analysis in the text borrows heavily from Stiglitz (1976) and King.

economic depreciation, the interest deductibility feature of the corporate tax renders it nondistortionary.[23]

Harberger's analysis turns out to be most compatible with a corporate tax without interest deductibility, in which the net-of-tax returns equal $(1 - t_c)(\partial\pi/\partial K_t - \delta) - r$, or $(\partial\pi/\partial K_t - \delta) = r/(1 - t_c)$ on the margin. The cost of capital is directly proportional to increases in t_c, as Harberger intended.

Determining whether or not the tax is actually distortionary would require a full analysis of all its design characteristics, as well as the underlying market environment. For instance, some firms may be subject to borrowing constraints which would change their investment margins. Also, estimated depreciation allowances may not reflect true economic depreciation as assumed above. All things considered, the tax is undoubtedly distortionary to some extent. But in light of Stiglitz' analysis, assuming the U.S. corporate tax is nondistortionary may be a good approximation of reality.

REFERENCES

Aaron, H. J. "A New View of Property Tax Incidence." *AEA Papers and Proceedings,* May 1974.

————. *Who Pays the Property Tax?* Washington D.C.: The Brookings Institution, 1975.

Asimakopulos, A., and Burbidge, J. "The Short-Period Incidence of Taxation." *Economic Journal,* June 1974.

Ballentine, J. G., and Eris, I. "On the General Equilibrium Analysis of Tax Incidence." *Journal of Political Economy,* June 1975.

Diamond, P. A. "Tax Incidence in a Two-Good Model." *Journal of Public Economics,* June 1978.

Feldstein, M. "Incidence of a Capital Income Tax in a Growing Economy with Variable Savings Rates." *Review of Economic Studies,* October 1974.

Fleming, J. "A Reappraisal of the Corporation Income Tax." *Journal of Public Economics,* July–August 1976.

Friedlaender, A. F., and Vandendorpe, A. "Differential Incidence in the Presence of Initial Distorting Taxes." *Journal of Public Economics,* October 1976.

Harberger, A. "The Incidence of the Corporation Income Tax." *Journal of Political Economy,* June 1962.

Kalecki, M. "A Theory of Commodity, Income and Capital Taxation." *Economic Journal,* September 1937.

---

[23] The same result obtains without interest deductibility, but with immediate depreciation of full investment costs. In this case, the firm only needs to borrow $(1 - t_c)$ dollars to finance a dollar of additional investment. The remainder can be financed out of tax savings. Hence the firm's net returns in period t are $(1 - t_c)(\partial\pi/\partial K_t - \delta) - r(1 - t_c)$, with the investment margin again defined by $(\partial\pi/\partial K_t - \delta) = r$, independent of t_c.

King, M. "Taxation, Corporate Financial Policy, and the Cost of Capital: A Comment." *Journal of Public Economics,* August 1975.

Krzyzaniak, M., and Musgrave, R. A. *The Shifting of the Corporation Income Tax.* Baltimore, Md.: Johns Hopkins University Press, 1963.

Mieszkowski, P. "On the Theory of Tax Incidence." *Journal of Political Economy,* June 1967.

Musgrave, R. A. "Is a Property Tax on Housing Regressive?" *AEA Papers and Proceedings,* May 1974.

Okner, B., and Pechman, J. *Who Bears the Tax Burden?* Washington, D.C.: The Brookings Institution, 1974.

Shoven, J. "The Incidence and Efficiency Effects of Taxes on Income from Capital." *Journal of Political Economy,* December 1976.

————, and Whalley, J. "A General Equilibrium Calculation of the Effects of Differential Taxation of Income from Capital in the U.S." *Journal of Public Economics,* November 1972.

————, and Whalley, J. "Equal Yield Tax Alternatives: General Equilibrium Computational Techniques." *Journal of Public Economics,* October 1977.

Stiglitz, J. "Taxation, Corporate Financial Policy, and the Cost of Capital," *Journal of Public Economics,* vol. 2, 1973.

————. "The Corporation Tax." *Journal of Public Economics,* April–May 1976.

18

Expenditure incidence

Although governments will occasionally increase one set of taxes to replace another set of taxes, most often taxes are raised to finance particular government expenditure programs. Once this obvious point is conceded, it is no longer as compelling to speak only of the incidence of the tax revenues. The policy relevant decision with regard to the income distribution is clearly the entire tax-cum-expenditure package. One might still argue that tax incidence per se remains relevant in that alternative sets of taxes could have financed the given expenditure program, but ignoring the expenditure side is always dangerous since the very existence of a new expenditure program will affect the evaluation of both incidence measures discussed in Chapter 17.

Government inputs and outputs enter into the market clearance and government budget equations, thereby influencing the price responses to any change in tax rates. Moreover, there is every reason to assume that the distributional consequences of expenditure programs will be every bit as significant as the distributional consequences of the tax revenues raised to finance them. Thus, to the extent incidence analysis is an aid to governmental distributional policies, there may be no useful alternative to considering the incidence of an entire tax-cum-expenditure package.

This is bound to be a difficult assignment, even in theory, since tax-cum-expenditure incidence theory is fraught with the same difficulties as the pure theory of tax incidence, *plus* some other problems as well. At very least, an analysis of various tax-cum-expenditure alternatives must confront these issues at the outset:

a. What measure of incidence will be employed? The three most likely candidates are income compensation or welfare loss measures at the individual level, aggregate changes in a many-person social welfare function, or the Harberger change-in-actual-relative-prices measure, the same as for the pure theory of tax incidence.

b. For any given set of taxes, exactly what expenditure programs are being financed? The obvious candidates are transfer payments, Samuelsonian nonexclusive public goods, and government operated decreasing cost services, but the government might be buying goods and services that could have been provided by a perfectly competitive private sector. The theoretical problem is not merely that the choice of a particular type of expenditure will have particular distributional consequences, but rather that the way in which the researcher models an incidence study will be determined by that choice as well.

c. Will the analysis consider marginal, balanced budget changes in taxes and expenditures, or must it focus on a total package of finite taxes and expenditures? Marginal analysis makes sense for transfer payments, but not for decreasing cost services.

d. For any given expenditure program, how are the taxes being raised? The point that the choice of expenditures will affect the measurement of tax incidence is reversible—the way in which expenditures are financed will dictate the approach to the measurement of expenditure incidence. It matters greatly, for example, whether expenditures are financed with lump-sum taxes or by a set of distorting taxes. To give one example by way of illustration, if the deficits arising from exhaustive government expenditure programs are assumed to be financed with lump-sum taxes, then the incidence analysis could take place within a first-best context, so long as other appropriate assumptions are made, such as perfectly competitive private production and marginal cost pricing of government services. This would also permit an incidence analysis at the individual level, since optimal lump-sum income redistributions would effectively turn the many-person economy into a one-consumer-equivalent economy. Lump-sum financing would also provide an unambiguous method for considering the incidence of a single (set of) government programs(s), or a pure theory of expenditure incidence, analogous to the incidence of a single tax program when the revenues are returned lump sum. This is an important consideration, since first-best expenditure incidence is more compelling than first-best tax incidence. Exhaustive expenditures will be undertaken solely for effeciency reasons in a first-best enviornment, but they will also have distributional consequences, and knowing these will aid the distribution branch in its search for the optimal pattern of lump-sum redistributions.

If, on the other hand, governments use distorting taxes to finance the deficits from government projects, the analysis is inherently second best, and unless the expenditures happen to be self-financing, it is not possible to separate tax and expenditure incidence. Moreover, as we saw in the discussion of tax incidence in a many-consumer world, one may have no choice but to adopt the aggregate-social-welfare perspective on incidence in a second-best environment in order to have a well-defined problem.

Chapter 18 will not attempt an exhaustive analysis of all possible tax-cum-expenditure combinations with all possible incidence measures. Rather, we will only highlight some of the problems involved with introducing specific expenditure programs into an analysis of incidence. Thus, in order to keep the discussion somewhat manageable, the numerous possibilities will be limited in three ways:

1. Tax-cum-expenditure packages will be evaluated by the income compensation or loss measure of incidence.[1] Hence, we will assume a one-consumer-equivalent economy, with an optimal income distribution.

---

[1] The many-person social welfare measure of incidence will be discussed in Chapter 22. For an analysis of expenditure incidence in the Harberger tradition, see C. McClure and W. Thirsk, "A Simplified Exposition of the Harberger Model, II: Expenditure Incidence," *National Tax Journal*, June 1975.

2. Only three expenditure programs will be considered: transfer payments, decreasing costs services, and nonexclusive Samuelsonian public goods.
3. We will assume that lump-sum tax revenues finance the two *exhaustive* expenditure programs, Samuelsonian public goods and decreasing cost services, and analyze their incidence in a first-best environment. Since the theory of exhaustive public expenditures in a second-best environment will not be considered until the next chapter, a discussion of second-best expenditure incidence at this point in the text would be premature.

Note that these last comments apply only to exhaustive expenditures. As will be seen immediately below, all the tools necessary for a comprehensive analysis of the incidence of transfer payments in a second-best environment have already been developed.

THE INCIDENCE OF GOVERNMENT TRANSFER PAYMENTS

Transfer payments, or subsidies, are formally identical to negative taxes. Consequently, the theory of tax incidence is fully applicable to government transfer payments, with the sole exception that all signs are reversed. All we need do, then, is review the major results of the previous chapter as they apply to subsidies.

a. If lump-sum taxes finance lump-sum transfers, there will be no burden or incidence in a one-consumer-equivalent economy. In a many-person economy, the tax paid or transfer received by any one person will be an appropriate income proxy for the welfare gain or loss by that person under either one of two assumptions: (1) technology is linear so that the taxes and transfers cannot change the equilibrium vector of consumer and producer prices; or (2) the policy relevant alternative to a given transfer-tax program is for the government to completely undo the program, recalling all transfers and returning all taxes, thereby restoring the original pretax and transfer equilibrium. Otherwise the tax-transfer program will change relative prices, and an individual's gain or loss would be measured by the value of his expenditure function evaluated at the new prices and original utility level, less the tax paid or transfer received.

b. A set of distorting subsidies offered to consumers and financed by lump-sum taxes is formally equivalent to the single-tax incidence problem of instituting a set of distorting taxes and returning the revenues lump sum. The distorting subsidy-cum-lump-sum tax will create a deadweight loss measured, in the case of linear technology, by

$$(18.1) \qquad L(\vec{s}) = M(\vec{q}; \bar{U}^0) + \sum_{i=1}^{N} s_i X_i^{\text{comp}}$$

where:

$\vec{s}$ = the vector of unit subsidies with element s_i.

$\vec{q}$ = the vector of consumer prices net of subsidy.

414

FIGURE 18–1

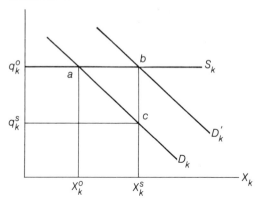

The appropriate measure in the case of general technology is:

(18.2)
$$L(\vec{s}) = M(\vec{q}; \bar{U}^0) + \sum_{i=1}^{N} s_i X_i^{comp} - \pi(\vec{p})$$

(18.1) or (18.2) measures the required lump-sum income *payment* less the *payment* consumers are willing to make as a consequence of the subsidies.[2]

Figure 18–1 illustrates the measure of loss created by a unit subsidy s_k on the consumption of X_k, with linear technology.

The subsidy shifts D_k upward by s_k, reduces the price of X_k to the consumer from q_k^0 to q_k^s, and increases consumption from X_k^0 to X_k^s. The gain to the consumer is the area $acq_k^s q_k^0$, the area behind the original compensated demand curve (compensated at utility level $\bar{U}^0$) between the old and new prices, the Hicks Compensating Variation. The subsidy at the new compensated equilibrium is $s_k \cdot X_k^s$, the area $bcq_k^s q_k^0$, which the consumer must pay for with lump-sum taxes. The net loss, therefore, is the triangle abc. Under the income compensation measure of incidence, this deadweight loss is the incidence of the subsidy.

Similarly, the incidence of marginal changes in an entire set of distorting subsidies is measured by summing the changes in deadweight loss each time, equal (for linear technologies) to:

(18.3)
$$dL = \sum_k \sum_i s_i M_{ik} ds_k$$

where:

M_{ik} = the Slutsky substitution terms.

---

[2] Since, from the consumer's point of view, goods prices are falling and factor prices are rising, $M(\vec{q}; \bar{U}^0)$ measures the income consumers are willing to pay for the subsidies and is a negative number. Hence, loss is the addition of $M(\vec{q}; \bar{U}^0)$ and $\sum_{i=1}^{N} s_i X_i^{comp}$, where $s_i > 0$ for goods, <0 for factors. Similarly, good prices are rising, factor prices falling from the firm's point of view, both of which tend to increase profits. Hence, $\pi(\vec{p})$ must be subtracted from the subsidy payment in equation (18.2).

c. One set of distorting subsidies may be substituted for another while holding the total subsidy constant, a case of differential expenditure analysis. This is exactly analagous to the pure case of differential tax incidence, in which the substitution is viewed as removing one set of subsidies, returning the tax savings lump sum, and instituting a second set of subsidies, paid for by lump-sum taxes. As in the tax case, the first step involves totally differentiating the government's budget constraint

$$(18.4) \qquad \sum_{i=1}^{N} s_i X_i^{comp} = \overline{S}$$

with $dS = 0$, to determine the changes in the s_i necessary to maintain a balanced budget. The resulting changes are then substituted into equation (18.3) to evaluate the change in loss (for linear technologies). Finally, the practical difficulties of applying these compensated measures, especially for general technologies, which were discussed in previous chapter on tax incidence, apply to transfer incidence as well.

TAX-CUM-EXPENDITURE INCIDENCE WITH DECREASING COST SERVICES

So long as decreasing cost services are being analyzed within the context of first-best theory, it is natural to assume that the government is charging a price equal to the marginal cost of providing the service and financing the deficits arising because $MC < AC$ with lump-sum taxes. The appropriate comparison is a total all-or-none test in which having the service with these characteristics is compared to not having the service at all. Marginal incidence analysis is not relevant for decreasing cost services.

The income compensation measure of incidence has already been developed in Chapter 9. Assuming linear or constant returns-to-scale (CRS) general production technology elsewhere in the economy, the net benefit of providing the decreasing cost service with lump-sum financing of its deficit is:[3]

$$(18.5) \qquad B = -M(\vec{q}; \overline{U}^0) - T$$

where:

$\vec{q}$ = vector of consumer prices with the service.

$\overline{U}^0$ = the utility level without the service.

T = the lump-sum payment required to finance the deficit.

$-M(\vec{q}; \overline{U}^0)$ = the amount consumers are willing to pay for the new prices, $\vec{q}$.

---

[3] Alternatively,

$$(18.5N) \qquad B = [M(\vec{q}^o; \overline{U}^0) - M(\vec{q}; \overline{U}^0)] - T, \text{ with } M(\vec{q}^o; \overline{U}^0) = 0$$

The term in brackets is the Hicks Compensating Variation measure of the willingness to pay for the price change, where $\vec{q}^o$ = the vector of consumer prices without the service.

SAMUELSONIAN NONEXCLUSIVE GOODS

Chapter 6 developed the standard pareto-optimal decision rule for a nonexclusive good in a first-best environment, $\sum_{h=1}^{H} MRS = MRT$, but did not consider the incidence of providing the good, that is, the resulting gain in welfare to each consumer from being able to consume the good at its optimal level, less the loss in welfare from having to finance the good. As a first step in deriving an incidence measure, recall that all government decisions with respect to financing and providing the good are lump-sum events from any one consumer's point of view. Since the market system completely breaks down because of the revelation problem, the government has no choice but to select a given quantity of the good that will be available in equal amounts to all consumers, hope that it has satisfied the $\sum MRS = MRT$ rule, and then finance its purchases with lump-sum taxes in order to preserve efficiency in all other markets.

For the purposes of this discussion, assume that the government has selected the correct quantity, so that $\sum_{h=1}^{H} MRS = MRT$. Assume further that production of the nonexclusive good, and all other goods and services, exhibits CRS or linear technology.

Consumers will react in two ways to the existence of a nonexclusive good. On the one hand, the good will enter each consumer's utility function directly as one of the arguments, although the sign of the argument is uncertain. Some consumers may view it as a "good," others as a "bad," especially at the margin.

On the other hand, consumers may well adjust their own goods demands and factor supplies in response to the nonexclusive good. That is, the nonexclusive good may be a substitute for or complement to other goods and factors.

Thus, it makes sense to represent a consumer's indirect utility function as:

$$(18.6) \qquad V(\vec{q}; \bar{I}; e) = U[X_i(\vec{q}; \bar{I}; e); e]$$

with

$$(18.7) \qquad \frac{\partial V}{\partial e} = \sum_{i=1}^{N} \frac{\partial U}{\partial X_i} \frac{\partial X_i}{\partial e} + \frac{\partial U}{\partial e}$$

where:

$\vec{q}$ = the vector of consumer prices.

X_i = good (factor) i demanded (supplied) by the consumer.

$\bar{I}$ = A source of lump-sum income other than profits from production, assumed constant unless taxed by the government.

e = the quantity of the nonexclusive good selected by the government.

Two results useful for the measure of incidence follow directly from the first-order conditions of utility maximization. First, differentiate the budget constraint with respect to e to obtain:

$$(18.8) \qquad \sum_{i=1}^{N} q_i \frac{\partial X_i}{\partial e} = 0$$

Furthermore, from the primal of the consumer problem,

(18.9)
$$\frac{\partial U}{\partial X_i} = \lambda q_i \qquad i = 1, \ldots, N$$

Substituting (18.9) into (18.8) yields:

(18.10)
$$\frac{1}{\lambda} \sum_{i=1}^{N} U_i \frac{\partial X_i}{\partial e} = 0$$

Thus equation (18.7) simplifies to:

(18.11)
$$\frac{\partial V}{\partial e} = \frac{\partial U}{\partial e}$$

Hence, the change in utility from a marginal change in the nonexclusive good equals its direct marginal effect on utility. While the consumer may change his other purchases and factor supplies in response to the change in e, these changes will have no further effect on utility.

Second, equation (18.11) implies that the marginal rate of substitution between e and ith good or factor, MRS_{e,X_i}, is defined exactly as it would be for any exclusive good.

(18.12)
$$MRS_{e,X_i} = -\frac{\dfrac{\partial U}{\partial e}}{\dfrac{\partial U}{\partial X_i}}$$

If good i is the numeraire,

(18.13)
$$MRS_{e,X_i} = -\frac{1}{\lambda} \frac{\partial U}{\partial e}$$

Thus the marginal rate of substitution establishes the value of a marginal increase in the public good to the consumer, as it does for any good.

The value of a finite amount of the public good can be derived from the consumer's expenditure function. In the presence of a nonexclusive good, the dual to the standard consumer problem is:

$$\min_{(X_i)} \sum_{i=1}^{N} q_i X_i$$

$$\text{s.t.} \quad U = \bar{U}(\vec{X}; e)$$

whose first-order conditions yield compensated demand (supply) functions of the form:

(18.14)
$$X_i^{\text{comp}} = X_i[\vec{q}; \bar{U}(\vec{X}; e)] \qquad i = 1, \ldots, N$$

and the expenditure function:

(18.15)
$$M[\vec{q}; \bar{U}(\vec{X}; e)] = \sum_{i=1}^{N} q_i X_i^{\text{comp}}[\vec{q}; \bar{U}(\vec{X}; e)]$$

418

Thus, even though the consumer does not purchase e, the expenditure function has e as an argument because e appears in the utility function, which is being held constant. All we need establish, then, is that $\partial M/\partial e \neq 0$, so that as e varies, the income required to keep the consumer at the same utility level will also change.

(18.16)
$$\frac{\partial M}{\partial e} = \sum_{i=1}^{N} q_i \frac{\partial X_i^{\text{comp}}[\vec{q}; \bar{U}(\vec{X};e)]}{\partial e}$$

Substituting (18.9) into (18.16) yields:

(18.17)
$$\frac{\partial M}{\partial e} = \frac{1}{\lambda} \sum_{i=1}^{N} \frac{\partial U_i}{\partial X_i} \frac{\partial X_i^{\text{comp}}[\vec{q}; \bar{U}(\vec{X};e)]}{\partial e}$$

But $U = \bar{U}(\vec{X};e)$. Thus,

(18.18)
$$\sum_{i=1}^{N} \frac{\partial U_i}{\partial X_i} \frac{\partial X_i^{\text{comp}}}{\partial e} + \frac{\partial U}{\partial e} = 0$$

if utility is held constant, or

(18.19)
$$\sum_{i=1}^{N} \frac{\partial U_i}{\partial X_i} \frac{\partial X_i^{\text{comp}}[\vec{q}; \bar{U}(\vec{X};e)]}{\partial e} = -\frac{\partial U}{\partial e}$$

Hence:

(18.20)
$$\frac{\partial M}{\partial e} = -\frac{1}{\lambda} \frac{\partial U}{\partial e} = -\frac{\dfrac{\partial U}{\partial e}}{\dfrac{\partial U}{\partial I}} = -\frac{\partial I}{\partial e}\bigg|_{u=\bar{u}}$$

As expected, the derivative of the expenditure function with respect to the nonexclusive good yields the change in lump-sum income that would make the consumer indifferent to a change in the nonexclusive good. From (18.18), this will be nonzero, in general. Moreover, from (18.13), $\partial M/\partial e$ is also the marginal rate of substitution between e and the numeraire good.

Therefore, an appropriate income measure of the gain from having a finite amount of a nonexclusive good is:[4]

(18.21)
$$B = \bar{I} - M[\vec{q}; \bar{U}^0(\vec{X};e)]$$

where:

$\vec{q}$ = the vector of consumer prices in the presence of the nonexclusive good.

$\bar{U}^0$ = the consumer's utility when $e = 0$.

$\bar{I}$ = the consumer's lump-sum income, assumed constant.

---

[4] Alternatively, $B = (I_e - I_o) + [M(\vec{q}^0; \bar{U}^0(e=0)) - M(\vec{q}; \bar{U}^0(e))]$. The gain equals $(I_e - I_o)$, the actual change in lump-sum income as e moves from o to e, plus the amount the consumer is willing to pay to have e increased from o to e. Recall that $\bar{I}_o = M[\vec{q}^0; \bar{U}^0(e=0)]$.

If consumers are asked to make a lump-sum tax payment to finance e or changes in e, then the incidence of the entire tax-income-expenditure package is straightforward. Since the expenditure function expresses welfare changes in terms of lump-sum income, the lump-sum tax is just subtracted from (18.21) to obtain the incidence of the entire package. Thus,

$$(18.22) \qquad B^N = -M[\vec{q}; \bar{U}^0(\vec{X}; e)] + (\bar{I} - T)$$

For marginal charges:

$$(18.23) \qquad \frac{\partial B^N}{\partial e} = -\frac{\partial M}{\partial e} - \frac{\partial T}{\partial e} = MRS_{e, \text{ numeraire}} - \partial T/\partial e$$

where:

$$\frac{\partial T}{\partial e} = \text{the change in lump-sum taxes per unit change in } e.$$

(18.23) establishes the following result. Suppose the government is able to establish a per-unit tax on each person equal to his MRS, in accordance with the competitive interpretation of the benefits-received principle of taxation as discussed in Chapter 6. If $\sum MRS = MRT$ and all production exhibits CRS, these taxes will be sufficient to cover the full costs of the public good. This tax scheme will also guarantee positive net benefits to all consumers so long as the MRS declines as e increases, or that compensated demand for e is downward sloping. Even consumers who think e is a "bad" will gain net benefits with decreasing MRS under the competitive benefits-received "tax." Since their $MRS < 0$, they would actually receive subsidies, and these unit subsidies would be greater than required on the inframarginal units of e. On the other hand, marginal changes in e, accompanied by taxes equal to each consumer's MRS, will generate no net benefits or losses. This, of course, is true for any good whose price equals its MRS (defined in terms of the numeraire good).

THE INCIDENCE OF NONEXCLUSIVE GOODS— EMPIRICAL EVIDENCE

While it is fairly easy to derive theoretical formulas for the total or marginal incidence of nonexclusive goods, regardless of how they are financed, the formulas will always be very difficult to apply in practice. The problem is the familiar one that consumers have no incentive to reveal their true demands for nonexclusive goods. In particular, we saw that the marginal benefit to the consumer, $\partial M/\partial e = -\partial I/\partial e|_{U=\bar{U}}$, is the marginal rate of substitution between the nonexclusive good and an exclusive numeraire good, but there is no natural market or political mechanism through which the government can accurately measure each consumer's MRS, and incentive revealing schemes such as "Clarke taxes" have never been used. Thus, empirical analysis must resort to indirect methods in order to determine the incidence of these goods.

The best-known empirical study of public goods incidence is that of Aaron and McGuire in their 1970 paper "Public Goods and Income Distribution," in which in they divide the benefits from U.S. defense expenditures among various income classes on the basis of estimates of the MRS for each income class.[5] Their analysis rests on five key assumptions:

1. The government has achieved the proper quantity of defense, so that $\sum MRS = MRT$.
2. All consumers have identical preferences which can be represented by an additive utility index of the form:

(18.24) $$U^h(Y_h, P) = f^h(Y_h) + g^h(P)$$

where:

Y_h = income for person h.
P = units of defense.

3. All consumers within a given income class have identical incomes, equal to the mean income for that class.
4. The total value of P units of defense to consumers in income class i is $MRS^i_{y_i,P} \cdot P$, which they define as the pseudo competitive market value of the good to the consumer.
5. Defense technology exhibits CRS, and defense suppliers receive prices equal to marginal costs.

Given these five assumptions it is possible to allocate the benefits of defense among the various income classes. The first step is the define the MRS for each income class as:

(18.25) $$MRS^i_{y_i,P} = \frac{g^i_p}{f^i_{Y_i}}$$

where:

$$g^i_P = \frac{\partial g^i(P)}{\partial P}$$

$$f^i_{Y_i} = \frac{\partial f^i(Y_i)}{\partial Y_i}$$

Next compute the ratio of MRS's between any two income classes, i and j, as:

(18.26) $$\frac{MRS^i_{Y_i,P}}{MRS^j_{Y_j,P}} = \frac{\dfrac{g^i_p}{f^i_{Y_i}}}{\dfrac{g^j_p}{f^j_{Y_j}}} \qquad \text{all } i, j$$

[5] H. Aaron and M. McGuire, "Public Goods and Income Distribution," *Econometrica*, November 1970. Also, S. Maital, "Apportionment of Public Goods Benefits to Individuals," *Public Finance*, 3, 1975. The original classic is W. Gillespie, "Effect of Public Expenditures on the Distribution of Income," ed, R. Musgrave, *Essays in Fiscal Federalism* (Washington, D.C.: The Brookings Institution, 1965). Gillespie uses simple allocation formulas that do not derive from public goods theory.

But with identical tastes for all consumers:

(18.27) $$g_P^i = g_P^j \qquad \text{any } i, j$$

Hence:

(18.28) $$\frac{MRS_{Y_i,P}^i}{MRS_{Y_j,P}^j} = \frac{f_{Y_j}^j}{f_{Y_i}^i}$$

or

(18.29) $$MRS_{Y_i,P}^i \cdot f_{Y_i}^i = MRS_{Y_i,P}^j \cdot f_{Y_j}^j = \cdots = k \qquad \text{all } i, j$$

Next, employ the assumption that the government has properly allocated defense, so that

(18.30) $$\sum_{i=1}^{I} MRS_{Y_i,P}^i = MRT_{y_i,P} = \frac{MC_P}{MC_Y}$$

Letting $MC_Y = 1$ (private income is the numeraire) yields:

(18.31) $$\sum_{i=1}^{I} MRS_{Y_i,P}^i = MC_P$$

Furthermore, if the price of defense equals its marginal costs and defense technology exhibits CRS,

(18.32) $$\sum_{i=1}^{I} MRS_{Y_i,P}^i \cdot P = MC_P \cdot P = E$$

where:

$E =$ the total defense budget.

From assumption 4 the total value of P units of defense to consumers in income class i, designated as Y_P^i, is $MRS_{Y_i,P}^i \cdot P$. Hence, from (18.31) and (18.32)

(18.33) $$Y_P^i = MRS_{Y_i,P}^i \cdot P = MRS_{Y_i,P}^i \left(\frac{MC_P}{\sum\limits_{i=1}^{I} MRS_{Y_i,P}^i} \right) \cdot P$$

(18.34) $$Y_P^i = \frac{MRS_{Y_i,P}^i}{\sum\limits_{i=1}^{I} MRS_{Y_i,P}^i} E$$

But from (18.29)

$$MRS_{Y_i,P}^i = \frac{k}{f_{Y_i}^i}.$$

Therefore,

(18.35) $$\sum_{i=1}^{I} MRS_{Y_i,P}^i = k \sum_{i=1}^{I} \left(\frac{1}{f_{Y_i}^i} \right)$$

and,

$$(18.36) \qquad Y^i_P = \frac{1}{f^i_{Y_i}} \frac{E}{\sum_{i=1}^{I} \left(\frac{1}{f^i_{Y_i}} \right)}$$

Finally, since only the ratios Y^i_P/Y^j_P are of interest, utility can be normalized by scaling the $f^i_{Y_i} = f^{i*}_{Y_i}$ such that $\sum_{i=1}^{I} (1/f^{i*}_{Y_i}) = 1$. With this normalization (18.36) becomes:

$$(18.37) \qquad Y^i_P = \frac{1}{f^{i*}_{Y_i}} E$$

To derive a plausible range of empirical estimates for the benefits, Aaron and McGuire posit a number of different utility functions, normalize each one such that $\sum_{i=1}^{I} (1/f^{i*}_{Y_i}) = 1$, and divide total defense expenditures among income classes using equation (18.37). Unfortunately, their results are quite sensitive to the specification of the underlying utility function.

Despite the obvious care Aaron and McGuire have taken to measure the distributional consequences of the defense budget in accordance with accepted neoclassical principles, it is difficult to have much confidence in their results. While their third assumption is commonly employed in empirical analysis, the first two assumptions are clearly heroic. Moreover, while it is reasonable to define $MRS^i_{Y_i, P} \cdot P$ as the pseudo competitive market value of the public good, it is not reasonable to suppose that this is an accurate measure of the gross benefit to the consumer. In general, $Y^i_P \neq B$ from equation (18.21), unless marginal rates of substitution are constant for all levels of defense, an unlikely occurrence. In terms of our analysis, $(-)M[\bar{q}; \bar{U}^0(P)]$ is almost certainly greater than $MRS \cdot P = (-)\partial M/\partial P \cdot P$. Finally, the sensitivity of their results to the choice of a utility function is troublesome, although certainly to be expected.

CONCLUSION

It is all too easy to criticize. The Aaron and McGuire study is merely one specific example of the difficulties of obtaining reliable empirical estimates of incidence, whether it be expenditure or tax incidence. Governments would dearly love to know the distributional consequences of their policies, but they face a discouraging dilemma. Theoretically appropriate welfare measures of incidence require data that are not readily observable, if at all, while measures using observable data typically have no firm theoretical underpinning. Given the current state of the art, the best any empirical research can hope for is some rough estimates of incidence under fairly restrictive assumptions, which is exactly the spirit of the Aaron and McGuire analyis.

REFERENCES

Aaron, H., and McGuire, M. "Public Goods and Income Distribution." *Econometrica.* 1970.

Gillespie, W. "Effect of Public Expenditures on the Distribution of Income." In *Essays in Fiscal Federalism*, edited by R. A. Musgrave, Washington, D.C.: The Brookings Institution, 1965.

Maital, S. "Apportionment of Public Goods Benefits to Individuals." *Public Finance*, 3, 1975.

McLure, C., and Thirsk, W. "A Simplified Exposition of the Harberger Model, II: Expenditure Incidence." *National Tax Journal*, June 1975.

19

The second-best theory of public expenditures—overview

For the past 20 years public expenditure theory has been at the forefront of theoretical developments in public sector economics. By extending the methodology of second-best tax theory to expenditure theory, public sector theorists have shattered the received doctrine of first-best expenditure theory in a barrage of challenges that must now number well into the hundreds. No longer is it possible to accept, even as approximations, such time-honored decisions rules as $\sum MRS = MRT$ for externalities, and marginal cost pricing for decreasing cost services, rules which bear such a remarkably close intuitive relationship to the competitive market system. As it now stands, public expenditure theory is more than a little chaotic, each new journal article pushing in new directions, and offering new insights, with as yet little in the way of synthesis to provide some perspective on where second-best expenditure theory will eventually lead. Perhaps this is as it must be. The essence of second-best analysis involves adding constraints to the basic first-best general equilibrium analysis beyond the fundamental constraints of production technology, market clearance, and resource limitations. The promise of second-best theory is that these additional constraints are much more representative of real-world conditions, such as the existence of monopoly elements in the private sector and distorting taxes in the public sector. The discouraging aspect, however, is that the decision rules derived from a second-best analysis will vary depending upon both the form of a particular constraint and the number of constraints added to the system. Unlike first-best analysis, then, the set of policy prescriptions is virtually unlimited. Moreover, no second-best theory can possibly incorporate all the additional constraints that would be necessary to approximate reality. As was noted in Chapter 14, current second-best models accurately portray only a very few specific distortions operating in the economy. They model the remaining parts of the economic system along standard first-best lines. Hence the state of the art is but a hesitant first step toward reality. Even so, virtually none of the old first-best decision rules have remained standing. Needless to say, the goal of developing a widely accepted normative economic theory of the public sector appears increasingly less plausible.

A few chapters in a broad text such as this one cannot hope to review adequately all the various ways in which public sector theorists have chosen to rework public expenditure theory in a second-best context, much less provide a comprehensive synthesis of this large and varied literature. In lieu of that, the next few chapters will undertake a far more modest task. We merely want to highlight a few of the major second-best public expenditure results to date, and demonstrate the most common methodological tools used to analyze public expenditure theory in a second-best context.

With respect to the first goal, the main pedagogical problem is simply lending some coherence to the presentation. We hope to achieve this by limiting the analysis by and large to the specific public expenditure problems discussed in Part II under first-best theory. Furthermore we will always assume, unless otherwise noted, that the policy environment is second best because the government must use distorting unit "commodity" taxes (subsidies) on consumer goods and factors in order to raise revenue (grant subsidies) for financing its expenditures. We will also usually assume that the government's budget must balance. The market environment, by contrast, will always be assumed perfectly competitive, and therefore first best. These are the assumptions most commonly employed in the second-best literature. They will also allow us to draw directly upon the models developed in Chapters 15–17 for analyzing the second-best theory of taxation. More often than not, these tax models require only slight modifications to incorporate public expenditure questions. This is why it made sense to reverse the development of Part II and consider second-best tax theory prior to second-best expenditure theory. It is natural to introduce distorting taxes as the additional constraint necessitating a second-best approach to public expenditure questions. The tax models also prove convenient as an analytical framework for developing two of the most striking results in all of second-best theory: first, that the optimal commodity tax rules are unaltered by the presence of government expenditures and, second, that second-best public expenditure decision rules tend to have their most appealing and simplest interpretations when distorting taxes are set optimally to maximize social welfare or minimize loss. Given the current state of the art, these rather tentative statements about the interrelationships between tax and expenditure rules are about as far as one would dare venture toward a generalization of second-best results.

With respect to methodology, some of the expenditure problems will be analyzed from the perspective of social welfare maximization, others from the perspective of loss minimization. The latter is especially useful when distributional considerations are not central to the point being developed. Switching the analytical framework in this manner should not be confusing since both approaches have already been fully explored in the preceding chapters on second-best tax theory. In any case, the risk of some initial confusion is worth taking in order to demonstrate a variety of models suitable for analyzing second-best expenditure questions.

With these goals in mind, a selection of second-best public expenditure results will be presented in three relatively brief and self-contained chapters. Chapter 20 will rework the first-best theory of externalities contained in Chapters 6–8. In a first-best environment, whether one considers a nonexclusive

Samuelsonian public good or exclusive activities generating either "individualized" or "aggregate" externalities, we saw that the government should achieve an allocation in which $\sum_{h=1}^{H} MRS^h = MRT$.[1] For nonexclusive goods, the government must simply try to select the proper allocation. With exclusive goods the government can, in principle, tax (subsidize) the externality-generating activity to achieve the desired result.

Unfortunately, the summation rule fails to hold for any of these cases in a second-best environment. Chapter 20 will demonstrate this for two of them. The first example, following an analysis by Leuthold,[2] will derive the second-best tax rules for an aggregate externality when society cannot redistribute lump sum to satisfy the first-best interpersonal equity conditions. As a spin-off from this analysis, we will also indicate how failure to satisfy interpersonal equity in a many-person economy destroys the optimal properties of competitive markets even for purely private goods that are not generating any external effects. The government must tax (subsidize) these goods as well. The second example will reconsider the proper allocation of a Samuelsonian nonexclusive good when the revenues to pay for this good must be raised with distorting "commodity" taxes. This problem was first considered by Pigou in 1947, but formalized more precisely in the 1970s, first by Atkinson and Stern, and then Diamond.[3]

Chapter 21 will turn to a well-known second-best result for decreasing cost industries. We saw in Chapter 9 that these services should be provided at marginal cost prices in a first-best policy environment, with lump-sum taxes covering the resulting losses to the firm. However, Chapter 10 noted that these services are typically priced at average cost in the United States, and considered a number of equity issues arising from this practice. It also explored an important efficiency implication of "average cost" pricing for the single product firm, the so-called Averch-Johnson effect. Chapter 21 will expand the efficiency implications by analyzing the average cost pricing philosophy applied to the multiproduct firm. Marcel Boiteux wrote the classic article here in 1956, five years before Averch and Johnson described the overcapitalization effect for public utilities. He considered the pricing and investment implications of requiring that a multiservice decreasing cost industry cover its full costs out of total revenues. Price does not have to equal average cost for each service,[4] but the prices on all the services combined must raise enough revenue in the aggregate

---

[1] This applies, of course, only to consumption externalities. The standard production-externality rule is that $MRS = \sum_{j=1}^{J} MRT^j$, J firms

[2] J. Leuthold, "The Optimal Congestion Charge When Equity Matters," *Economica*, February 1976. Also, J. Hartwick, "Optimal Price Discrimination," *Journal of Public Economics*, February 1978.

[3] A. C. Pigou, *A Study in Public Finance*, 3d ed. (London: MacMillan & Co., Ltd., 1947); A. Atkinson and N. Stern, "Pigou, Taxation, and Public Goods," *Review of Economic Studies*, January 1974; and P. Diamond, "A Many Person Ramsey Tax Rule," *Journal of Public Economics*, November 1975.

[4] If two or more services commonly use one or more resources, it is not always possible to define average costs for each of them, even in the long run. M. Boiteux, "On the Management of Public Monopolies Subject to Budgetary Constraints," *Journal of Economic Theory*, September 1971 (translated from the original version in French, *Econometrica*, January 1956).

to cover all costs. The Boiteux problem is especially intriguing for public sector economics because it closely parallels the optimal commodity tax problem of Chapters 15 and 16, in which the government has to set taxes (consumer prices) to collect a given amount of revenue. As we shall see, the optimal pricing rules for the multiproduct decreasing cost firm have virtually the same interpretation as the optimal tax rules. Moreover, they also apply to any government agency which operates under a legislated budget constraint, whether or not the agency's output exhibits decreasing cost production.

Chapter 22 will extend second-best public expenditure theory by considering the general problem of government production in a second-best environment. There will be no specific constraints on government production possibilities. They can exhibit decreasing, increasing, or constant returns to scale. Furthermore, the government is permitted to produce anything that the private sector produces. We will place only two restrictions on government activity, generally. If government producers buy and sell inputs and outputs, they must do so at the (competitive) prices faced by the private sector producers. Second, if government production incurs a deficit (surplus) at these prices, the government must use distorting commodity taxes (subsidies) to cover the deficit (return the surplus).

This type of general expenditure model has been explored in depth by a number of economists in the 1970s, most notably Diamond and Mirrlees, and Boadway.[5] In their classic entitled "Optimal Taxation and Public Production," Diamond and Mirrlees asked the following questions: (a) does the existence of government production alter the optimal commodity tax rules derived in the context of raising revenue simply for the sake of raising revenue? and (b) what production rules should the government follow in the presence of optimal commodity taxation to cover production deficits (return surpluses)? They found that government production does not change the optimal tax rules. Even more striking, however, was their answer to the second question. They were able to show that if the distorting taxes are optimal, the government should follow standard *first-best* production rules.

Boadway generalized their analysis to consider the welfare effects of raising additional taxes (subsidies) and/or marginally increasing government production from *any* initial values of distorting taxes and government production, not necessarily the optimal values. As might be imagined, the resulting tax and expenditure rules are extremely complex. One nice result, however, is that the addition of government production does not affect the nonoptimal marginal tax loss rules developed in Chapters 15 and 16.

Chapter 22 will highlight each of these results and set the stage for Part IV, *The Theory and Practice of Cost-Benefit Analysis*. Cost-benefit analysis asks

---

[5] P. Diamond and J. Mirrlees, "Optimal Taxation and Public Production," *American Economic Review*, March, June 1971 (2 parts, Part I: Production Efficiency, Part II: Tax Rules); R. Boadway, "Cost-Benefit Rules and General Equilibrium," *Review of Economic Studies*, June 1975; and R. Boadway, "Integrating Equity and Efficiency in Applied Welfare Economics," *Quarterly Journal of Economics*, November 1976.

how one can use normative public sector theory to analyze real-world government investment projects. In applying the theory, the predominant issue is the underlying policy environment one is willing to assume. Is it "approximately" first best, or second best; and if second best, exactly what constraints make it so? The answers given to these questions will always be a compromise of sorts, since the real world is many times more complex than any of our theoretical models. But the answers are crucial, nonetheless, for any subsequent cost- benefit study and its policy recommendations. With the conclusion of Chapter 22, all the major first- and second-best results of public expenditure theory will be in hand, ready for application to real-world problems.

REFERENCES

Atkinson, A., and Stern, N. "Pigou, Taxation, and Public Goods." *Review of Economic Studies,* January 1974.

Boadway, R. "Cost-Benefit Rules and General Equilibrium." *Review of Economic Studies,* June 1975.

―――――. "Integrating Equity and Efficiency in Applied Welfare Economics." *Quarterly Journal of Economics,* November 1976.

Boiteux, M. "On the Management of Public Monopolies Subject to Budgetary Constraints." *Journal of Economic Theory,* September 1971 (translated from French in *Econometrica,* January 1956).

Diamond, P. A. "A Many Person Ramsey Tax Rule." *Journal of Public Economics,* November 1975.

―――――, and Mirrlees, J. "Optimal Taxation and Public Production" (2 parts, "Part I: Production Efficiency," "Part II: Tax Rules"). *American Economic Review,* March, June 1971.

Hartwick, J. "Optimal Price Discrimination." *Journal of Public Economics,* February 1978.

Leuthold, J. "The Optimal Congestion Charge When Equity Matters." *Economica,* February 1976.

Pigou, A. C. *A Study in Public Finance.* 3d ed. London: MacMillan Co., Ltd., 1947.

20

Externalities in a second-best environment

First-best models of externalities dichotomize in two important respects for policy purposes. On the one hand, the government can pursue appropriate tax or expenditure policies to restore pareto optimality in the presence of externalities without regard to distributional considerations. All distributional issues are embodied in the interpersonal equity conditions, which can be satisfied by an appropriate set of lump-sum taxes and transfers. First-best models further dichotomize in that externalities arising in a subset of all goods and factor markets can be corrected independently of behavior in the other markets, in the sense that the perfectly competitive allocations in these markets remain pareto optimal. These two properties greatly facilitate policy design when correcting for externalities.

Unfortunately, neither of these dichotomies obtains in a second-best environment. Consequently even the simplest externalities require highly complex forms of government intervention, so complex in fact that it is entirely implausible to expect governments to achieve them. To understand this fundamental point, we will consider the simple example of a single aggregate consumption externality in a many-person economy made second best because the government does not have the ability to tax and transfer lump sum to achieve the first-best interpersonal equity conditions. As a result, marginal social utilities of income are initially unequal, and remain so at the optimum.

AN AGGREGATE EXTERNALITY[1]

Recall the definition of an aggregate externality: an exclusive activity k generates an aggregate externality if the aggregate amount of k consumed, $X_k = \sum_{h=1}^{H} X_{hk}$, enters into each person's utility function. If all other goods are

---

[1] A number of authors have discussed optimal pricing rules when the distribution of income is nonoptimal and lump-sum redistributions are infeasible, although not necessarily in the context of an aggregate externality. See P. Diamond, "A Many Person Ramsey Tax Rule," *Journal of Public Economics*, November 1975; J. Hartwick, "Optimal Price Discrimination," *Journal of Public Economics*, February 1978; J. LeGrand, "Public Price Discrimination and Aid to Low Income Groups," *Economica*, February 1975; and J. Leuthold, "The Optimal Congestion Charge When Equity Matters," *Economica*, February 1976 (Leuthold does analyze an aggregate externality in her model).

purely private goods, the utility of person h can be written as:

(20.1) $\qquad U^h(X_{h1}, \ldots, X_{hk}, \ldots, X_{hN}; X_k) \qquad h = 1, \ldots, H$

(20.2) $$X_k = \sum_{h=1}^{H} X_{hk}$$

Society's problem is to maximize social welfare subject to aggregate production possibilities and market clearance. Formally,

$$\max_{(X_{hi})} W[U^h(X_{hi}; X_k)] \qquad \begin{array}{l} h = 1, \ldots, H \\ i = 1, \ldots, N \end{array}$$

$$\text{s.t.} \quad F\left(\sum_{h=1}^{H} X_{hi}\right) = 0$$

where:

$$X_k = \sum_{h=1}^{H} X_{hk}$$

Chapter 6 showed that if the policy environment is first best and each consumer ignores his own contribution to the aggregate externality, the government should:

a. Let all (competitive) markets $i = 1, \ldots, k - 1, k + 1, \ldots, N$ determine the allocation of resources by the laws of supply and demand, without government intervention of any kind.

b. Use lump-sum redistributions to satisfy the interpersonal equity conditions for any one purely private good, say, the first, such that

(20.3) $$\frac{\partial W}{\partial U^h}\frac{\partial U^h}{\partial X_{h1}} = \frac{\partial W}{\partial U^j}\frac{\partial U^j}{\partial X_{j1}} \qquad \text{all } h, j = 1, \ldots, H$$

c. Place a single unit tax on the consumption of X_k, such that (with $p_1 \equiv 1$, the numeraire)

(20.4) $$t_k = - \sum_{h=1}^{H} MRS^h_{X_k, X_{h1}}$$

the aggregate *marginal* external effect of any person's additional consumption of good k, equal for all people (and defined as the sum of each individual's MRS between his own consumption of good 1 and the aggregate consumption of good k).[2] (20.4) is the well-known Pigovian tax (subsidy, for an external economy).

Suppose, however, that the government is unable to satisfy (20.3) because it cannot redistribute lump sum. In this case, neither conditions (a) nor (20.4)((c)) will maximize social welfare in general.

The model used to analyze the many-person optimal tax rule with general technology in Chapter 16 turns out to be a convenient model for analyzing an aggregate externality when lump-sum redistributions are not possible. Recall that this model assumes competitive markets everywhere, individual utility maximization and profit maximization, and represents social welfare maxi-

---

[2] X_k and/or X_1 can be factor supplies.

mization in terms of each individual's indirect utility function, as follows:

$$\max_{(q_i)} W[V^h(X_{hi}(\vec{q};\bar{I}^h))] = V(\vec{q};\bar{I}^1,\ldots,\bar{I}^H)$$

$$\text{s.t.}\quad F\left(\sum_{h=1}^{H} X_{hi}(\vec{q};\bar{I}^h)\right) = 0$$

where:

$\vec{q}$ = the $(N \times 1)$ vector of consumer prices, with element q_i.

$\bar{I}^h$ = the fixed amount of lump-sum income for person h, which the government cannot change through lump-sum redistributions.

The production constraint embodies market clearance in the usual manner.

The first problem, then, is to introduce into this model an aggregate consumption externality arising from the consumption of good k. This turns out to be relatively straightforward. So long as we continue to assume that consumers ignore the effect of own consumption on the aggregate, each individual consumer will consider $X_k = \sum_{h=1}^{H} X_{hk}$ as a parameter when maximizing utility and solve the following problem:

$$\max_{(X_{hi})} U^h(X_{h1},\ldots,X_{hN};X_k)$$

$$\text{s.t.}\quad \sum_{i=1}^{N} q_i X_{hi} = \bar{I}^h$$

where:

$$X_k = \sum_{h=1}^{H} X_{hk}$$

The first-order conditions generate demand (factor supplies) functions of the form:

(20.5) $$X_{hi} = X_{hi}(\vec{q};\bar{I}^h;\bar{X}_k) \qquad i = 1,\ldots,N$$

and an indirect utility function:

(20.6) $$U^h[X_{hi}(\vec{q};\bar{I}^h;\bar{X}_k)] = V^h(\vec{q};\bar{I}^h;\bar{X}_k)$$

Thus, society's problem in the presence of this aggregate externality becomes:

$$\max_{(q_i)} W[V^h(\vec{q};\bar{I}^h;X_k)] = W[U^h(X_{hi}(\vec{q};\bar{I}^h;X_k))]$$

$$\text{s.t.}\quad F\left[\sum_{h=1}^{H} X_{hi}(\vec{q};\bar{I}^h;X_k)\right] = 0$$

with corresponding Lagrangian:[3]

$$\max_{(q_i)} L = W[V^h(\vec{q};\bar{I}^h;X_k)] - \lambda F\left[\sum_{h=1}^{H} X_{hi}(\vec{q};\bar{I}^h;X_k)\right]$$

---

[3] The distribution of lump-sum income I^h is assumed fixed. Also, the market clearance equations $\sum_{h=1}^{H} X_{hi}(\vec{q};\bar{I}^h;X_k) = Y_i(\vec{p})$ have been incorporated directly into $F(\ )$ to substitute out the producer prices, $\vec{p}$. They still serve to solve for $\vec{p}$, given $\vec{q}_{\text{opt}}$, however.

Notice that from society's viewpoint X_k is not a parameter. Its optimal value must be derived, along with the optimal values of all other X_i, $i \neq k$. Moreover, production possibilities are unaffected by the existence of the consumption externality, the standard assumption with consumption externalities.

With $q_1 \equiv 1$, the untaxed numeraire, the $N - 1$ first-order conditions for this problem are (along with the production constraint):

$$(20.7) \qquad \sum_{h=1}^{H} \frac{\partial W}{\partial V^h} \frac{\partial V^h}{\partial q_k} + \sum_{h=1}^{H} \frac{\partial W}{\partial V^h} \frac{\partial V^h}{\partial X_k} \frac{\partial X_k}{\partial q_k} = \lambda \sum_{i=1}^{N} F_i \frac{\partial X_i}{\partial q_k}$$

$$(20.8) \qquad \sum_{h=1}^{H} \frac{\partial W}{\partial V^h} \frac{\partial V^h}{\partial q_j} + \sum_{h=1}^{H} \frac{\partial W}{\partial V^h} \frac{\partial V^h}{\partial X_k} \frac{\partial X_k}{\partial q_j} = \lambda \sum_{i=1}^{N} F_i \frac{\partial X_i}{\partial q_j}$$

$$j = 2, \ldots, k - 1, k + 1, \ldots, N, \text{ the}$$
set of pure private goods

where:

$$F_i = \frac{\partial F}{\partial X_i} = \frac{\partial F}{\partial X_{hi}} \qquad \text{all } h = 1, \ldots, H$$

Recalling Roy's theorem, that $\partial V^h / \partial q_i = -\alpha^h X_{hi}$, $i = 1, \ldots, N$, where $\alpha^h =$ the marginal utility of income for person h, and letting $\beta^h = (\partial W / \partial V^h) \alpha^h =$ the social marginal utility of income for person h, equations (20.7) and (20.8) can be rewritten as:

$$(20.9) \qquad -\sum_{h=1}^{H} \beta^h X_{hk} + \sum_{h=1}^{H} \frac{\partial W}{\partial V^h} \frac{\partial V^h}{\partial X_k} \frac{\partial X_k}{\partial q_k} = \lambda \sum_{i} F_i \frac{\partial X_i}{\partial q_k}$$

$$(20.10) \qquad -\sum_{h=1}^{H} \beta^h X_{hj} + \sum_{h=1}^{H} \frac{\partial W}{\partial V^h} \frac{\partial V^h}{\partial X_k} \frac{\partial X_k}{\partial q_j} = \lambda \sum_{i} F_i \frac{\partial X_i}{\partial q_j}$$

$$j = 2, \ldots, k - 1, k + 1, \ldots, N$$

It is immediately obvious from (20.9) and (20.10) that *all* first-order conditions are affected by *both* the social welfare weights and the aggregate externality, including those for the purely private goods $j = 2, \ldots, k - 1, k + 1, \ldots, N$. Clearly, the social optimum cannot be achieved by the standard competitive market forces for the pure private goods. In general, government intervention will be required in every market.

To understand exactly what these first-order conditions imply for public policy, consider separately the social welfare effects from the externality effect. Suppose for the moment that all goods (factors) are purely private goods (factors), including k, but retain the assumption that the government cannot redistribute lump-sum to equalize the β^h. The social welfare maximization problem now becomes:

$$\max_{(q_i)} W[V^h(X_{hi}(\vec{q}; \bar{I}^h))] = V(\vec{q}; \bar{I}^1, \ldots, \bar{I}^H)$$

$$\text{s.t.} \quad F\left[\sum_{h=1}^{H} X_{hi}(\vec{q}; \bar{I}^h)\right] = 0$$

This is *identical* to the many-person optimal tax problem considered in Chapter 16, in which the government finds a set of commodity taxes $(t_2, \ldots, t_N)$ that will maximize social welfare subject to raising a given amount of revenue. Recall that the government's budget constraint is automatically contained within the structure of the model because of Walras' law, which states that if each consumer is on his budget constraint, each firm is maximizing profits, and all markets are cleared, then the government must be satisfying its budget constraint.

Hence the inability to redistribute lump-sum forces the government to re-adjust all consumer prices in accordance with the optimal tax rule even if it has no need to collect any tax revenue. The implied government budget constraint is

$$\sum_{h=1}^{H} \sum_{i=1}^{N} t_i X_{hi} = \bar{T} = 0.$$

Indeed, conditions (20.9) and (20.10) are identical to conditions (16.64) except for the addition of the externality terms:

$$\sum_{h=1}^{H} \frac{\partial W}{\partial V^h} \frac{\partial V^h}{\partial X_k} \frac{\partial X_k}{\partial q_i} \quad i = 2, \ldots, N$$

(The production derivatives $F_i(\partial X_i / \partial q_k)$ are also more complicated because the $X_{hi}(\ )$ are functions of X_k, which varies with $\bar{q}$.)

To gain some additional insight into the consequences of nonoptimal income distribution, totally differentiate social welfare for the case of all purely private goods, obtaining:[4]

(20.11)
$$dW = -\sum_{k=1}^{N} \sum_{h=1}^{H} \beta^h X_{hk} dq_k$$

Suppose first that the distribution is optimal, so that $\beta^h = \beta$, all $h = 1, \ldots, H$. (20.11) becomes:

(20.12)
$$dW = -\beta \sum_{k=1}^{N} X_k dq_k$$

With lump-sum income constant, and each consumer on his budget constraint,

(20.13)
$$\sum_{k=1}^{N} X_{hk} dq_k = -\sum_{k=1}^{N} q_k dX_{hk} \quad \text{all } h = 1, \ldots, H,$$

(20.14)
$$\sum_{k=1}^{N} X_k dq_k = -\sum_{k=1}^{N} q_k dX_k$$

by totally differentiating each budget constraint and adding across all consumers. But from totally differentiating the aggregate production constraint,

(20.15)
$$\sum_{k=1}^{N} F_k dX_k = 0$$

---

[4] Recall that I^h is constant, all $h = 1, \ldots, H$.

With $p_1 \equiv 1$, the numeraire, and scaling $F(\ )$ such that $F_1 = 1$, (20.15) can be rewritten as:

$$(20.16) \qquad \sum_{k=1}^{N} p_k dX_k = 0$$

Finally, if all markets are competitive and there is no government intervention, $q_i = p_i$, all $i = 1, \ldots, N$. Therefore:

$$(20.17) \qquad \sum_{k=1}^{N} q_k dX_k = 0 = -\sum_{k=1}^{N} X_k dq_k$$

from which it follows that

$$(20.18) \qquad dW = 0$$

Hence, with optimal income distribution and all purely private goods and factors, competitive allocations generate a social welfare maximum.

Suppose, instead, that $\beta^h \neq \beta$, all $h = 1, \ldots, H$, or that the distribution of income is nonoptimal. In this case competitive markets will not generate a welfare optimum. For even though $\sum_{k=1}^{N} X_k dq_k = 0$ with $q_i = p_i$, all $i = 1, \ldots, N$,

$$(20.19) \qquad dW = -\sum_{h=1}^{H} \sum_{k=1}^{N} \beta^h X_{hk} dq_k \neq 0$$

in general. The government can improve social welfare by finding a vector of consumer prices that differs from the vector of producer prices by means of unit taxes. As we have seen, the optimal pattern of the $\bar{q}$ is obtained by setting taxes in accordance with the optimal commodity tax problem.

Returning once again to the aggregate externality arising from good k, the first-order conditions tell the government to adjust the optimal commodity taxes by the terms

$$\sum_{h=1}^{H} \frac{\partial W}{\partial V^h} \frac{\partial V^h}{\partial X_k} \frac{\partial X_k}{\partial q_i}, \qquad i = 2, \ldots, N,$$

which reflect the marginal social cost of the externality as prices are changed. The last two terms in the expression give the marginal external effect on each individual as X_k changes in response to changes in the ith consumer price. The terms $\partial W / \partial V^h$ multiply these individual effects by the appropriate social welfare weight.

In Chapter 16 the first-order conditions for optimal commodity taxes were manipulated to form the percentage change rule (16.42) (reproduced here as (20.20)):

$$(20.20) \qquad \frac{\sum_{i=1}^{N} \sum_{h=1}^{H} t_i S_{ki}^h}{\sum_{h=1}^{H} X_{hk}} = -1 + \frac{\frac{1}{\lambda} \sum_{h=1}^{H} \beta^h X_{hk}}{\sum_{h=1}^{H} X_{hk}} + \frac{\sum_{h=1}^{H} \sum_{i=1}^{N} t_i X_{hk} \frac{\partial X_{hi}}{\partial I^h}}{\sum_{h=1}^{H} X_{hk}}$$

where the left-hand side of (20.20) gives the aggregate percentage change in the compensated demand (supply) for good (factor) j. Conditions (20.9) and (20.10) will obviously generate the same percentage change rule with the addition of the externality term.

$$(20.21) \qquad (-) \frac{\dfrac{1}{\lambda} \sum_{h=1}^{H} \dfrac{\partial W}{\partial V^h} \dfrac{\partial V^h}{\partial X_k} \dfrac{\partial X_k}{\partial q_j}}{\sum_{h=1}^{H} X_{hk}} \qquad j = 2, \ldots, N \text{ (including } k)$$

in all equations for which $\partial X_k / \partial q_j \neq 0$, $j = 2, \ldots, N$. This gives the sensible interpretation that percentage changes in the jth good should be decreased (roughly speaking, q or t lower) the more that a marginal increase in the jth consumer price induces consumption of a good generating an external diseconomy ($\partial V^h / \partial X_k < 0$), and vice versa. Unfortunately, such interpretations do not necessarily ease the task of finding the social optimum. Even if $\partial X_k / \partial q_j = 0$, all $j \neq k$, so that only equation (20.9) need be adjusted, the adjustment occurs with respect to the optimal vector of commodity taxes (prices), not with respect to competitive market prices. Clearly, any time policy must adjust all markets simultaneously there is obviously little or no hope for success. Of course, one could argue that nonoptimal income distribution is the real culprit since it necessitates finding an optimal vector of prices in the first place. The externality adds a rather modest increment to the problem, especially if nearly all $\partial X_k / \partial q_j = 0$. But unless society feels it has generated the correct vector of consumer prices independently of any external effects, an unlikely occurrence to say the least, it can never be entirely confident that social welfare will be improved by incremental adjustments to account for an externality or two, even though the first-order conditions imply intuitively appealing adjustments for externalities. The externalities become hopelessly intertwined with society's interpersonal equity problems.

SAMUELSONIAN NONEXCLUSIVE GOODS

Providing nonexclusive goods in a second-best environment is somewhat easier than the aggregate externality case in the narrow sense that decision rules for these goods can be described independently of second-best optimal tax rules because the government, not the individual consumers, selects the quantity for common consumption. But, as we saw in Chapter 6, finding the optimum allocation of these goods is an extraordinarily complex practical problem even in a first-best policy environment because of the "free-rider" problem. The optimal decision rule, $\sum_{h=1}^{H} MRS^h = MRT$, is easy to describe but difficult to achieve. The first-best assumptions do help somewhat, however, in that if the government happens to select the proper quantity, it can finance the good with any lump-sum payment scheme. Moreover, undistorted competitive markets can be used to allocate all the pure private goods.

These policy prescriptions will generally not apply in a second-best environment, although as is always true with second-best analysis, the ways in which the first-best optimal decision rules change will depend upon the nature of the additional constraints placed on the system. One natural way to pose a second-best problem is to let the government freely choose the quantity of the non-exclusive good, but constrain it to finance the good with distorting unit commodity taxes. This would also implicitly preclude lump-sum redistributions to equalize marginal social utilities of income, because if lump-sum taxes could be used for distributional purposes they should also be available to finance the public good. Otherwise, assume that the economy is perfectly competitive with all other goods (factors) being purely private.

Given this particular second-best environment, there are two compelling policy questions to be asked: (a) how does the required distorting taxation affect the provision of the public good, and (b) how does the presence of the public good affect the optimal tax rules when revenue is raised for its own sake?

The general equilibrium framework used above to analyze an aggregate externality is also well suited to the nonexclusive good for this problem since the "public good" enters the analysis in much the same way as the aggregate externality. Let e stand for the nonexclusive good, defined in units such that its price equals 1. Since the government is selecting the quantity of e, consumers will of necessity treat e as a parameter, even though e enters their utility functions. Hence, as we saw in Chapter 18, each individual will solve the following utility maximization problem:

$$\max_{(X_{hi})} U^h(X_{hi}; \overline{e})$$

$$\text{s.t.} \sum_{h=1}^{N} q_i X_{hi} = \overline{I}^h$$

All other terms are defined as in the aggregate externality case. This leads to demand (factor supply) functions of the form:

$$(20.22) \qquad X_{hi} = X_{hi}(\vec{q}; \overline{I}^h; \overline{e}) \qquad \begin{matrix} i = 1, \ldots, N \\ h = 1, \ldots, H \end{matrix}$$

and indirect utility functions:

$$(20.23) \qquad U^h[X_{hi}(\vec{q}; \overline{I}^h; \overline{e})] = V^h(\vec{q}; \overline{I}^h; \overline{e}) \qquad h = 1, \ldots, H$$

Social welfare, then, is:

$$(20.24) \qquad W^*[U^h(X_{hi}(\vec{q}; \overline{I}^h; e))] = W[V^h(\vec{q}; \overline{I}^h; e)] = V(\vec{q}; \overline{I}; e)$$

Notice that (20.22) and (20.23) are virtually identical to (20.5) and (20.6).

Finally, e must also enter the aggregate production constraint since it uses real resources, or

$$(20.25) \qquad F(X_i; e) = 0 \qquad i = 1, \ldots, N$$

Society's problem, then, is:[5]

$$\max_{(q_i;e)} W[V^h(\vec{q};\bar{I}^h;e)]$$

$$\text{s.t. } F\left[\sum_{h=1}^{H} X_{hi}(\vec{q};\bar{I}^h;e);e\right] = 0$$

with corresponding Lagrangian:

$$\max_{(q_i;e)} L = W[V^h(\vec{q};\bar{I}^h;e)] - \lambda \cdot F\left[\sum_{h=1}^{H} X_{hi}(\vec{q};\bar{I}^h;e);e\right]$$

As above, the government's budget constraint

$$\sum_{h=1}^{H} \sum_{i=2}^{N} t_i X_{hi} = e$$

is implied by utility maximization, profit maximization, market clearance in all markets, and Walras' law.

Consider the first-order conditions with respect to the consumer prices, q_i:

(20.26) $$\sum_{h=1}^{H} \frac{\partial W}{\partial V^h} \frac{\partial V^h}{\partial q_k} = \lambda \sum_{i=1}^{N} F_i \frac{\partial X_i}{\partial q_k} \qquad k = 2, \ldots, N$$

Conditions (20.26) are identical to conditions (16.64). Therefore, the existence of a nonexclusive good does not affect the form of the many-person optimal tax rule relative to the case in which the government simply raises revenue for its own sake. Of course the choice of e will determine the amount of revenue required, which will in part determine the level of the tax rates, but otherwise the optimal tax rules will have all the same interpretations as developed in Chapter 16.

Consider, next, the first-order conditions with respect to e.

(20.27) $$\sum_{h=1}^{H} \frac{\partial W}{\partial V^h} \frac{\partial V^h}{\partial e} = \lambda \sum_{h=1}^{H} \sum_{i=1}^{N} F_i \frac{\partial X_{hi}}{\partial e} + \lambda F_e$$

Defining F such that $\partial F/\partial X_1 = 1$, assuming perfectly competitive profit maximization, and given that $p_1 \equiv q_1 \equiv 1$, the untaxed numeraire, (20.27) can be rewritten as:

(20.28) $$\sum_{h=1}^{H} \frac{\partial W}{\partial V^h} \frac{\partial V^h}{\partial e} = \lambda \sum_{h=1}^{H} \sum_{i=1}^{N} p_i \frac{\partial X_{hi}}{\partial e} + \lambda F_e$$

But $p_i = q_i - t_i, i = 1, \ldots, N$. Therefore,

(20.29) $$\sum_{h=1}^{H} \frac{\partial W}{\partial V^h} \frac{\partial V^h}{\partial e} = \lambda \sum_{h=1}^{H} \sum_{i=1}^{N} (q_i - t_i) \frac{\partial X_{hi}}{\partial e} + \lambda F_e$$

---

[5] Recall that maximizing W with respect to $\vec{q}$ is equivalent to maximizing W with respect to $\vec{t}$, with $\vec{q} = \vec{t} + \vec{p}$, and the market clearance equations establishing the relationships among $\vec{q}$, $\vec{t}$, and $\vec{p}$ in equilibrium. This is the model used by Peter Diamond in Diamond, "A Many Person Ramsey Tax Rule."

Next, differentiate each consumer's budget constraint, $\sum_{i=1}^{N} q_i X_{hi}(\bar{q}; \bar{I}^h; e) = \bar{I}^h$ with respect to e.

$$(20.30) \qquad \sum_{i=1}^{N} q_i \frac{\partial X_{hi}}{\partial e} = 0 \qquad h = 1, \ldots, H$$

Hence, substituting (20.30) into (20.28) yields:

$$(20.31) \qquad \sum_{h=1}^{H} \frac{\partial W}{\partial V^h} \frac{\partial V^h}{\partial e} = -\lambda \sum_{i=1}^{N} t_i \frac{\partial X_i}{\partial e} + \lambda F_e$$

Peter Diamond has recently proposed the following $\sum_{h=1}^{H} MRS = MRT$ interpretation of conditions (20.31).[6] Rewrite (20.31) as:

$$(20.32) \qquad \sum_{h=1}^{H} \frac{\partial W}{\partial V^h} \frac{\partial V^h}{\partial e} + \lambda \sum_{i=1}^{N} t_i \frac{\partial X_i}{\partial e} = \lambda F_e$$

The right-hand side of (20.32) measures the marginal social cost, through production, of increasing the public good. The left-hand side is the social marginal value of increasing the public good, the first terms representing the social marginal value of having each person consume an additional unit of e, and the second term representing the social value of the increased tax revenues resulting from a marginal increase in e. Thus, (20.32) has the natural interpretation that e should be increased until its marginal social value just equals its marginal social cost. To change this to a $\sum_{h=1}^{H} MRS = MRT$ form, define:

$$(20.33) \qquad \delta^h = \frac{\partial W}{\partial V^h} \frac{\partial V^h}{\partial e} + \lambda \sum_{i=1}^{N} t_i \frac{\partial X_{hi}}{\partial e}$$

But $\beta^h = (\partial W / \partial V^h) \alpha^h = (\partial W / \partial V^h)(\partial V^h / \partial I^h)$. Therefore, δ^h can be expressed as:

$$(20.34) \qquad \delta^h = \beta^h \left(\frac{\dfrac{\partial V^h}{\partial e}}{\dfrac{\partial V^h}{\partial I^h}} \right) + \lambda \sum_{i=1}^{N} t_i \frac{\partial X_{hi}}{\partial e} = \beta^h MRS_{e, X_{h1}}^h + \lambda \sum_{i=1}^{N} t_i \frac{\partial X_{hi}}{\partial e}{}^{[7]}$$

the marginal social value of letting person h consume an additional unit of e. Substituting (20.33) into (20.32) yields:

$$(20.35) \qquad \sum_{h=1}^{H} \delta^h = \lambda F_e$$

---

[6] Ibid., p. 341.

[7] $MRS_{e, X_{h1}}^h \equiv \dfrac{\dfrac{\partial V^h}{\partial e}}{\dfrac{\partial U^h}{\partial X_{h1}}} = \dfrac{\dfrac{\partial V^h}{\partial e}}{\alpha^h q_1} = \dfrac{\dfrac{\partial V^h}{\partial e}}{\dfrac{\partial V^h}{\partial I^h}}$, from utility maximization and $q_1 \equiv 1$.

or

$$(20.36) \qquad \sum_{h=1}^{H} \frac{\delta^h}{\lambda} = F_e$$

With F defined such that $F_1 = 1$, and $p_1 \equiv q_1 \equiv 1$, the right-hand side is the marginal rate of transformation between the public good and the numeraire good. To interpret the left-hand side of (20.36), recall from Chapter 16 that if the government offers an optimal equal-value head subsidy to all individuals, λ can be interpreted as the average social marginal utility of income, equal to $\sum_{h=1}^{H} \gamma^h / H$, where $\gamma^h = \beta^h + \lambda \sum_{i=1}^{N} t_i (\partial X_{hi}/\partial I)$, the social marginal utility of giving additional income to person h. Given this interpretation of λ, the left-hand side of (20.36) can be interpreted as a $\sum_{h=1}^{H} MRS^h$, the sum of the *social* marginal rate of substitution between consumption of e by each individual and income (or, equivalently, the numeraire good) averaged over the population.

NONEXCLUSIVE GOODS—RELATIONSHIPS
BETWEEN FIRST- AND SECOND-BEST ALLOCATIONS

Diamond's interpretation of the social marginal rate of substitution is obviously far removed from the usual notion of a social marginal rate of substitution for nonexclusive goods from first-best analysis. The Diamond concept weights the standard individual marginal rates of substitution by social welfare weights (the β^h) and includes a tax term, so that there is no obvious quantitative relationship between the first-best and second-best decision rules for the allocation of e. Clearly, the true social MRS (the Diamond measure) could be arbitrarily larger or smaller than the first-best social MRS depending upon the choice of the β^h, the social marginal utilities of income. It has long been recognized, at least intuitively, that a nonoptimal income distribution requires dividing the benefits (and costs) of public projects into socially relevant components and weighting each component by the appropriate social marginal utilities of income. But notice that even if the income distribution is optimal, such that $\beta^h = \beta$, all $h = 1, \ldots, H$, the straight summation of individual MRS^h will still misrepresent the true social marginal rate of substitution if distorting taxes are used to finance these public projects, since the tax term, $\lambda \sum_i t_i (\partial X_i/\partial e)$ remains as part of the true social marginal rate of substitution. This point has only recently been subjected to formal analysis by Atkinson and Stern, although Pigou presented an intuitive analysis as early as 1947.[8]

To isolate the effect of the tax term on the social valuation of nonexclusive goods, assume all consumers have identical tastes and endowments, $\bar{I} = \bar{I}^1, \ldots, \bar{I}^h, \ldots, \bar{I}^H$. Further, let $\partial W/\partial V^h = 1$, all $h = 1, \ldots, H$, so that the distribution is optimal from society's point of view. Hence, $\beta^h = \beta = \alpha = \partial V^h/\partial I^h$, all $h = 1, \ldots, H$, the common private marginal utility of income.

---

[8] A. Atkinson and N. Stern, "Pigou, Taxation, and Public Goods," *Review of Economic Studies*, January 1974; and A. C. Pigou, *A Study in Public Finance*, 3d ed. (London: MacMillan & Co., Ltd., 1947).

Under these assumptions, (20.36) becomes (using (20.34)):

$$(20.37) \qquad \frac{\alpha}{\lambda}(H \cdot MRS^h_{e,X_{h1}}) + \sum_{i=1}^{N} t_i \frac{\partial X_i}{\partial e} = F_e = MRT_{e,X_1}$$

where:

$(H \cdot MRS^h_{e,1}) = $ the standard first-best interpretation of the social marginal rate of substitution for a nonexclusive good.

Thus, according to (20.37), the true second-best social MRS (the entire left-hand side of (20.37)) will tend to exceed the first-best social MRS the more increasing the public good increases tax revenues through its effect on the demands (supplies) of all other goods (factors), and vice versa. Assuming the revenues increase, this provides an additional source of marginal social value which the first-best measure misses.

Suppose, however, that all purely private demands (and factor suppliers) are independent of e ($\partial X_i/\partial e = 0$, all $i = 1, \ldots, N$), so that the revenue effect vanishes. The true social MRS still differs from the first-best measure by the factor α/λ in a world with distorting taxes. The question remains, then, whether the first-best measure over or understates the true measure, that is, whether $\alpha/\lambda \lessgtr 1$.

α/λ can be evaluated if we assume the government is raising tax revenue optimally. With identical consumers and $\beta^h = \beta = \alpha$, the first-order conditions for optimal taxation, equations (20.26), become:

$$(20.38) \quad -H\alpha X_{hk} = \lambda \sum_{h=1}^{H} \sum_{i=1}^{N} F_i \frac{\partial X_{hi}}{\partial q_k} = \lambda H \cdot \sum_{i=1}^{N} F_i \frac{\partial X_{hi}}{\partial q_k} \qquad k = 2, \ldots, N$$

Reproducing the derivation of the optimal rule in Chapter 16:

$$(20.39) \qquad -\alpha X_{hk} = \lambda \sum_{i=1}^{N} F_i \frac{\partial X_{hi}}{\partial q_k}$$

$$(20.40) \qquad -\alpha X_{hk} = \lambda \sum_{i=1}^{N} p_i \frac{\partial X_{hi}}{\partial q_k}$$

$$(20.41) \qquad -\alpha X_{hk} = \lambda \sum_{i=1}^{N} (q_i - t_i) \frac{\partial X_{hi}}{\partial q_k}$$

$$(20.42) \qquad -\alpha X_{hk} = \lambda \left(-X_{hk} - \sum_{i=1}^{N} t_i \frac{\partial X_{hi}}{\partial q_k} \right)$$

$$(20.43) \qquad -\alpha X_{hk} = \lambda \left(-X_{hk} - \sum_{i=1}^{N} t_i S^h_{ik} + X_{hk} \sum_{i=1}^{N} t_i \frac{\partial X_{hi}}{\partial I} \right)$$

where:

$$S^h_{ik} = \frac{\partial X_{hi}}{\partial q_k}\bigg|_{compensated}, \text{ the Slutsky substitution term.}$$

Rearranging terms:

$$(20.44) \qquad \left(\frac{\alpha}{\lambda} - 1 + \sum_{i=1}^{N} t_i \frac{\partial X_{hi}}{\partial I} \right) = \frac{\displaystyle\sum_{i=1}^{N} t_i S_{ik}^h}{X_{hk}} \qquad k = 2, \ldots, N$$

Next, multiply the numerator and denominator of the right-hand side of (20.44) by t_k and sum over $k = 1, \ldots, N$, to obtain:

$$(20.45) \qquad N \cdot \left(\frac{\alpha}{\lambda} - 1 + \sum_{i=1}^{N} t_i \frac{\partial X_{hi}}{\partial I} \right) = \frac{\displaystyle\sum_{i=1}^{N} \sum_{k=1}^{N} t_i S_{ik}^h t_k}{\displaystyle\sum_{k=1}^{N} t_k X_{hk}}$$

So long as total tax revenue ($\sum_{k=1}^{N} t_k X_{hk}$) is positive,[9] the right-hand side of (20.45) will be negative because the Slutsky matrix is negative definite. Other things equal, this tends to lower the value of α/λ and thereby reduce the value of the true social MRS. Pigou identified this as the "indirect damage" of having to raise additional revenues with distorting taxes to finance increases in the public good.[10] The second effect involves the term $\sum_{i=1}^{N} t_i(\partial X_{hi}/\partial I)$, which Atkinson and Stern call the "revenue effect" of distorting taxes.[11] If this term is positive, that is, if tax collections rise with increases in lump-sum income, then α/λ is surely less than one and the first-best social MRS overstates the true social MRS. However, this term could well be negative to the extent factor supplies are taxed (recall that factors enter the analysis with a negative sign). If so, then α/λ may be greater than, less than, or equal to 1 despite the (negative) distortionary effect of second-best taxes. Hence, there is no way of knowing, a priori, whether the true social MRS is less than, greater than, or equal to the first-best social MRS in the presence of distorting taxes, even if (a) the distribution of income is optimal; (b) there are no direct revenue effects of increasing the nonexclusive good; and (c) the distorting taxes used to raise revenue are optimally set.

CONCLUSION

The public good example reemphasizes an important yet discouraging fact that was uncovered in the aggregate externality example: even small departures from a first-best environment create staggering problems for public sector decision making. And when one considers that the number of real-world distortions is likely to be far greater than represented in our second-best model, the implications for normative analysis are discouraging indeed.

---

[9] It may not be, given that factors are subsidized.

[10] Pigou, *A Study in Public Finance*, p. 34.

[11] Atkinson and Stern, "Pigou, Taxation, and Public Goods," p. 123. The analysis of α/λ closely follows their derivation.

REFERENCES

Atkinson, A., and Stern, N. "Pigou, Taxation, and Public Goods." *Review of Economic Studies,* January 1974.

Diamond, P. A. "A Many Person Ramsey Tax Rule." *Journal of Public Economics,* November 1975.

Hartwick, J. "Optimal Price Discrimination." *Journal of Public Economics,* February 1978.

LeGrand, J. "Public Price Discrimination and Aid to Low Income Groups." *Economica,* February 1975.

Leuthold, J. "The Optimal Congestion Charge When Equity Matters." *Economica,* February 1976.

Pigou, A. C. *A Study in Public Finance.* 3d ed. London: MacMillan & Co., Ltd., 1947.

21

Decreasing costs and the theory of the second best— the Boiteux problem

Chapter 9 explored the theory of decreasing costs in a first-best environment with a bare-bones general equilibrium model consisting of a one-consumer-equivalent economy and production of a single good (X), with a single factor, labor (L), under increasing returns to scale or decreasing unit costs. The three first-best decision rules mimicked standard competitive pricing principles in that:

a. The price of X should equal its marginal production costs. Achieving this result would require government interference since we also showed that the industry for X should consist of a single firm, and an unregulated profit-maximizing monopolist would presumably set marginal revenues equal to marginal costs.

b. Since marginal cost pricing implies operating losses with decreasing unit costs, the government should subsidize the firm's losses with a lump-sum transfer. This transfer simply becomes part of the first-best interpersonal equity conditions for optimal income distribution. That is, in satisfying interpersonal equity, the "Distributional Branch" must collect sufficient taxes from one subset of consumers to subsidize all decreasing cost producers as well as the remaining subset of consumers.

c. Finally, the government should allow competitive allocations in all other nondecreasing cost markets.[1]

Chapter 10 then departed from the first-best paradigm by discussing some of the equity and efficiency implications of actual U.S. policy for decreasing cost services, which tends to follow an average cost pricing philosophy whenever prices (or taxes or tolls) are charged for these services. But that discussion ignored the fact that many of the decreasing cost firms offer a variety of services to different customers (e.g., the Post Office and most public utilities). In Chapter 21 we extend the efficiency implications of the average cost pricing philosophy

---

[1] The simple model of Chapter 9 would have had to add one other good to show this formally, but it is clear that marginal cost pricing of all other goods achieves pareto optimality.

to the multiservice firm following the analysis of this problem by Marcel Boiteux.[2]

Specifically, Boiteux considered the optimal pricing and investment rules for multiservice decreasing cost monopolies that are required to raise a given amount of revenue. Thinking in terms of the public utilities one can consider the revenue as just sufficient to generate break-even production given the firm's allowable returns to capital, although Boiteux did not explicitly attempt to model the U.S. regulatory process for public utilities. Boiteux analyzed this problem in the context of a many-person, N goods and factors, general equilibrium model in which all other markets are perfectly competitive and the government has the ability to redistribute endowment income lump sum to satisfy interpersonal equity. In order to highlight the efficiency aspects of the problem, we will simply posit a one-consumer equivalent economy. By way of introduction, it should also be noted that the Boiteux problem has general interest for public sector economics far beyond the theory of decreasing costs. It stands as the intellectual precursor to a fair portion of all second-best tax and expenditure theory developed over the past 15 years. For instance, it turns out to be quite similar to the optimal commodity tax problem of Chapters 15 and 16. Furthermore, it may also be used as a basis for developing production decision rules for any public agency subject to a legislated budget constraint, whether or not the agency supplies decreasing cost services. Since most governments do restrict agencies in this way, the Boiteux analysis obviously has far reaching practical significance for government policy.

THE ANALYTICS OF THE BOITEUX PROBLEM

The essence of the Boiteux problem can be described as follows. Let one production sector ("industry") of the economy be under the control of the government because it exhibits increasing returns to scale production.[3] Moreover, assume this particular government activity employs many inputs and produces many goods and services according to the implicit government production-possibilities relationship

$$(21.1) \qquad G(Z_1, \ldots, Z_i, \ldots, Z_N) = G(\vec{Z}) = 0$$

$\vec{Z}$ = an $(N \times 1)$ vector of government inputs and supplies, with element Z_i.

---

[2] M. Boiteux, "On the Management of Public Monopolies Subject to Budgetary Constraints," *Journal of Economic Theory*, September 1971 (translated from the original in French, *Econometrica*, January 1956). Dreze presents a useful interpretation of Boiteux's results in J. Dreze, "Some Postwar Contributions of French Economists to Theory and Public Policy," *American Economic Review*, June 1964 (Supplement), pp. 27–34. Our analysis closely follows these two papers. We would also recommend W. Baumol and D. Bradford, "Optimal Departures from Marginal Cost Pricing," *American Economic Review*, June 1970, for an excellent intuitive discussion of the Boiteux problem, including its relationship to the optimal tax literature. The article also presents a brief historical account of the optimal second-best price and tax literature.

[3] As will become evident, the increasing returns to scale assumption merely provides a convenient motivation for government control. It is not a necessary condition for any of the theorems derived in this chapter.

(The government need not literally employ all inputs and produce all goods and services in the economy, although it is analytically convenient to use the most general formulation possible. Some (perhaps most) of the Z_i will be identically equal to zero for any given application). Assume further that government production is twice constrained, in that:

a.   The government must buy all inputs and sell all outputs at the vector of producer prices, $\vec{p} = (p_1, \ldots, p_i, \ldots, p_N)$, as viewed by the economy's perfectly competitive private sector firms. These prices reflect private sector marginal costs (or values of marginal products). Since there will be no taxation in this model, $\vec{p}$ also serves as the vector of consumer prices.

b.   Government purchases and sales must satisfy an overall budget constraint of the general form

$$(21.2) \qquad \sum_{i=1}^{N} p_i Z_i = B$$

where B is set by some legislative body. For the decreasing cost interpretation of this problem, it is natural to set $B = 0$ and require that revenues from the sale of all government goods and services at actual market prices just equal total costs of production. This can be thought of as the average or full cost pricing philosophy applied to a multiservice firm.

The problem, then, is to derive optimal production decision rules for the government control variables, the $\vec{Z}$, given the government's production possibilities and its self-imposed budget constraint.

This problem can be analyzed quite easily by the loss minimization technique. Assume a one-consumer (equivalent) economy in which all relevant information on the consumer can be summarized by the expenditure function

$$(21.3) \qquad M(\vec{p}; \bar{U}) = \sum_{i=1}^{N} p_i X_i^{\text{comp}}(\vec{p}; \bar{U})$$

Assume, further, that private production exhibits general technology with constant returns to scale (CRS) and can be summarized by means of the profit function

$$(21.4) \qquad \pi(\vec{p}) = \sum_{i=1}^{N} p_i Y_i(\vec{p})$$

Since production comes from two sources, market clearance must also be specified as:

$$(21.5) \qquad M_i(\vec{p}; \bar{U}) = \pi_i(\vec{p}) + Z_i \quad i = 2, \ldots, N$$

Recall that all markets cannot clear in terms of compensated demand (supply) functions. Therefore, let the first market remain uncleared, with compensation occurring in terms of good 1. The first good will also serve as the numeraire ($p_1 \equiv 1$). Finally, as a matter of convenience, define the government's production possibilities such that $\partial G / \partial Z_1 = G_1 = 1$, or $Z_1 = -g(Z_2, \ldots, Z_N)$, with inputs measured negatively. ($\partial g/\partial Z_k \equiv g_{Z_k}$ measures the marginal product of Z_k as a positive number.[4])

Loss is defined as the lump-sum income required to keep the consumer at utility level $\bar{U}$ less all sources of lump-sum income for any given values of the Z_i. In general,[5]

(21.6)
$$L(\vec{Z}) = M(\vec{p};\bar{U}) - \pi(\vec{p}) - \sum_{i=1}^{N} p_i Z_i - B$$

Loss must be minimized with respect to the Z_i, subject to the constraints that $\sum_{i=1}^{N} p_i Z_i = B$ and government production. Formally[6]:

$$\min_{(Z_i)} M(\vec{p};\bar{U}) - \pi(\vec{p}) - \sum_{i=1}^{N} p_i Z_i - B$$

$$\text{s.t.} \quad \sum_{i=1}^{N} p_i Z_i = B$$

$$Z_1 = -g(Z_2, \ldots, Z_N)$$

Alternatively, directly incorporating the government budget constraint,

$$\min_{(Z_i)} M(\vec{p};\bar{U}) - \pi(\vec{p}) + p_1 g(\vec{Z}) - \sum_{i=2}^{N} p_i Z_i - B$$

$$\text{s.t.} \quad -p_1 g(\vec{Z}) + \sum_{i=2}^{N} p_i Z_i = B$$

The corresponding Lagrangian is:

$$\min_{(Z_i)} L = M(\vec{p};\bar{U}) - \pi(\vec{p}) + p_1 g(\vec{Z}) - \sum_{i=2}^{N} p_i Z_i - B$$

$$+ \lambda \left[-p_1 g(\vec{Z}) + \sum_{i=2}^{N} p_i Z_i - B \right]$$

With general technology, the producer prices, p_i, are functions of the Z_i. Therefore the first-order conditions with respect to the Z_k are (with $p_1 \equiv 1$):

(21.7)
$$\sum_{i=2}^{N} M_i \frac{\partial p_i}{\partial Z_k} - \sum_{i=2}^{N} \pi_i \frac{\partial p_i}{\partial Z_k} + p_1 g_{Z_k} - \sum_{i=2}^{N} Z_i \frac{\partial p_i}{\partial Z_k} - p_k$$

$$+ \lambda \left[-p_1 g_{Z_k} + \sum_{i=2}^{N} Z_i \frac{\partial p_i}{\partial Z_k} + p_k \right] = 0^{[7]} \qquad k = 2, \ldots, N$$

---

[4] Since Z_1 and Z_k can either be goods or factors, g_{Z_k} can also be interpreted as a technical rate of substitution or a marginal rate of transformation.

[5] With CRS production ($\pi(\vec{p}) = 0$) and the requirement that $\sum_{i=1}^{N} p_i Z_i = B$, the loss function can be simplified to $L(\vec{Z}) = M(\vec{p};\bar{U})$, but for generality the expanded version of loss will be maintained.

[6] Following the practice in Chapter 16, the market clearance equations will be kept outside the loss minimization framework. In this example they solve for the prices $\vec{p}$ once the loss-minimizing $\vec{Z}$ has been determined.

[7] Recall that $M_i = X_i^{\text{comp}}(\vec{p};\bar{U})$ and $\pi_i = Y_i(\vec{p})$.

From market clearance,

(21.8) $$M_i = \pi_i + Z_i \qquad i = 2, \ldots, N$$

Multiply (21.8) by $\partial p_i/\partial Z_k$ and sum over all $(N-1)$ equations to obtain:

(21.9) $$\sum_{i=2}^{N} M_i \frac{\partial p_i}{\partial Z_k} = \sum_{i=2}^{N} \pi_i \frac{\partial p_i}{\partial Z_k} + \sum_{i=2}^{N} Z_i \frac{\partial p_i}{\partial Z_k}$$

Thus, equations (21.7) simplify to:

(21.10) $$p_1 g_{Z_k} - p_k + \lambda \left(-p_1 g_{Z_k} + \sum_{i=2}^{N} Z_i \frac{\partial p_i}{\partial Z_k} + p_k \right) = 0$$

$$k = 2, \ldots, N$$

or

(21.11) $$(\lambda - 1)(-p_1 g_{Z_k} + p_k) + \lambda \sum_{i=2}^{N} Z_i \frac{\partial p_i}{\partial Z_k} = 0 \qquad k = 2, \ldots, N$$

In order to interpret conditions (21.11), use the market clearance equations to substitute out the price derivatives, $\partial p_i/\partial Z_k$. Differentiate each of the market clearance equations (21.8) with respect to Z_k to obtain:

(21.12) $$\sum_{j=2}^{N} (M_{ij} - \pi_{ij}) \frac{\partial p_j}{\partial Z_k} = \alpha_{ik} = \begin{cases} 0, & i \neq k \\ 1, & i = k \end{cases}$$

Differentiating the market clearance relationships with respect to all other Z_i, $i = 2, \ldots, k-1, k+1, \ldots, N$, and writing the results in matrix notation yields:

(21.13) $$(M_{ij} - \pi_{ij}) \left(\frac{\partial p}{\partial Z} \right) = I$$

where:

M_{ij} = an $(N-1) \times (N-1)$ matrix of derivatives $\partial M_i/\partial p_j$.
π_{ij} = an $(N-1) \times (N-1)$ matrix of derivatives $\partial \pi_i/\partial p_j$.
$\partial p/\partial Z$ = an $(N-1) \times (N-1)$ matrix of derivatives $\partial p_i/\partial Z_j$.
I = the $(N-1) \times (N-1)$ identity matrix.

Thus,

(21.14) $$\frac{\partial p}{\partial Z} = (M_{ij} - \pi_{ij})^{-1}$$

Using (21.14), the entire set of first-order conditions (21.11) can be expressed in matrix notation as:

(21.15) $$(\lambda - 1)(-p_1 g_Z + p) + \lambda(M_i - \pi_i)(M_{ij} - \pi_{ij})^{-1} = 0$$

where:

M_i = the $1 \times (N-1)$ vector $(M_2, \ldots, M_N)$.
π_i = the $1 \times (N-1)$ vector $(\pi_2, \ldots, \pi_N)$ and

$$(M_i - \pi_i) = Z_i$$

g_Z = the $1 \times (N-1)$ vector $(g_{Z_2}, \ldots, g_{Z_N})$.

Multiplying (21.15) by $(M_{ij} - \pi_{ij})$ yields:

(21.16) $(\lambda - 1)(-p_1 g_z + p)(M_{ij} - \pi_{ij}) + \lambda(M_i - \pi_i) = 0$

Select the kth relationship from (21.16):

(21.17) $(\lambda - 1) \sum_{i=2}^{N} (-p_1 g_{z_i} + p_i)(M_{ik} - \pi_{ik}) + \lambda(M_k - \pi_k) = 0$

Rearranging terms:

(21.18) $$\frac{\sum_{i=2}^{N} (-p_1 g_{z_i} + p_i)(M_{ik} - \pi_{ik})}{M_k - \pi_k} = \frac{-\lambda}{\lambda - 1} \qquad k = 2, \ldots, N$$

where the right-hand side is a constant independent of k. Written in this form, the first-order conditions can be given an interpretation remarkably similar to the optimal commodity tax rules of Chapters 15 and 16.

As originally defined, the problem asks us to interpret the first-order conditions (21.11) as decision rules for the government production variables, the Z_i, that is, as government "investment" rules. Using (21.18), they can also be given a pricing interpretation if one thinks of the government as making "competitive" production decisions in the usual manner. Given a production function $Z_1 = -g(Z_2, \ldots, Z_N) = 0$, and a vector of fixed *shadow* prices for the inputs and outputs $\vec{\gamma} = (\gamma_2, \ldots, \gamma_i, \ldots, \gamma_N)$ a profit-maximizing firm will equate $g_i/g_j = \gamma_i/\gamma_j$, all $i, j = 2, \ldots, N$. Furthermore, if the shadow prices reflect true social opportunity costs for the inputs and outputs, the firm's decision rule will be pareto optimal. Conditions (21.18) describe, in effect, how to define the optimal shadow prices for the government sector. To see this, let $\vec{p} = \vec{\gamma} + \vec{t}$, with elements p_i, γ_i, and t_i, respectively, where $\vec{p}$ is the vector of actual market prices, $\vec{\gamma}$ the vector of optimal shadow prices, and $\vec{t}$ a vector of *implicit* taxes driving a wedge between the two sets of prices. Given our normalization, $p_1 \equiv \gamma_1$, $t_1 = 0$. Substituting for the p_i in equation (21.18),

(21.19) $$\frac{\sum_{i=2}^{N} (\gamma_i + t_i - p_1 g_{z_i})(M_{ik} - \pi_{ik})}{M_k - \pi_k} = \frac{-\lambda}{\lambda - 1} = C \qquad k = 2, \ldots, N$$

But if the government sector is using the γ_i as shadow prices,

(21.20) $$\gamma_i = p_1 g_{z_i} \qquad i = 2, \ldots, N$$

(21.20) says that the government producer will hire an input until the value of its marginal product just equals its shadow price. Substituting (21.20) into (21.19) yields:

(21.21) $$\frac{\sum_{i=2}^{N} t_i(M_{ik} - \pi_{ik})}{M_k - \pi_k} = C \qquad k = 2, \ldots, N$$

which is virtually identical to the optimal commodity tax rule of Chapters 15 and 16. Equations (21.21) say that the government should define a new set of shadow prices for use in production decisions by establishing a set of implicit taxes having the following properties (in the words of Boiteux): "... [The taxes] are proportionate to the infinitesimal variations in price, that, when accompanied by compensating variations in incomes, entail the same proportional change in the demands (supplies) of the goods produced (consumed) by the nationalized sector...."[8] Boiteux's interpretation follows directly from the fact that $M_{ik} = M_{ki}$ and $\pi_{ik} = \pi_{ki}$, so that (21.21) can be rewritten as:

$$(21.22) \qquad \frac{\sum_{i=2}^{N} t_i(M_{ki} - \pi_{ki})}{M_k - \pi_k} = C \qquad k = 2, \ldots, N$$

M_{ki} gives the change in the compensated demand (supply) for good (factor) k in response to a change in the ith consumer price. Similarly, π_{ki} gives the change in supply (demand) of good (factor) k in private production in response to a change in the ith price. Consequently, $(M_{ki} - \pi_{ki})$ gives the change in government supply (demand) of good (factor) k required to maintain compensated market clearance in response to a change in the ith price. The denominator $(M_k - \pi_k) = Z_k$, from market clearance. Thus, conditions (21.22) gave the familiar equal percentage rule, except that they apply only to percentage changes entirely within the government sector.

The crux of the matter, then, can be viewed as defining a correct set of shadow prices on which to base standard "competitive" government production decisions. This suggests that the original problem could have been formulated as a tax-price problem rather than as a quantity problem. Viewed in this way, the problem is indistinguishable from the problem of designing a set of optimal commodity taxes on part of production, to be paid by the producer. The partial tax problem was first described for a single tax in the discussion of corporate tax incidence in Chapter 17. It can be easily generalized for $(N - 1)$ goods and factors by dividing the profit function into two sectors, one taxed, the other untaxed, and using the loss minimization technique. Consumer and producer prices would differ only in the taxed sector. In the Boiteux problem the taxes $\bar{t}$ are implicit and the $\bar{y}$ are shadow prices. They are not actually observed in the market. In contrast, the taxes in the partial tax problem would be real, so that the $\bar{y}$ define observed gross (for factor) or net (for goods) of tax prices to the firm.

Whether or not these implicit valuations in the Boiteux formulation affect actual market prices depends upon the relationship of the government producer to the entire market. There are a number of possibilities. Suppose, for example, that the government is merely one of thousands of firms hiring a particular factor of production. It would then be reasonable to assume that its implicit

---

[8] Boiteux, "On the Management of Public Monopolies," p. 230 (in translation). (21.21) also points out that our formulation of $G(\ )$ implies that the government retains control over all prices in the economy, an assumption we have been using all along. If the government is constrained from changing some distorted price-cost margins in the private sector, these additional constraints would change the optimal decision rules, both here and elsewhere in the text. Formally, the new constraints could be represented as $q_i = k_i \cdot p_i$, some i, with k_i constant for good i, and would have Lagrangian multipliers associated with them in the loss minimization problem.

FIGURE 21–1

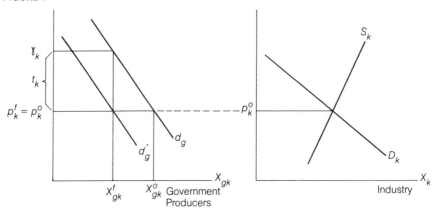

tax had no effect on actual market prices, a situation depicted in Figure 21–1. The government sets an implicit tax of t_k on the purchase of X_k, which drives the factor's shadow price to γ_k and causes a reduction in its purchase of X_k from X_{gk}^o to X_{gk}^f. However, because it is small relative to the total market of X_k, the price of X_k remains at p_k^o for all other firms and all consumers.

In fact, Figure 21–1 is misleading in that the government need not design implicit taxes in markets for which the tax does not affect market prices. Consider the kth equation of (21.11). If Z_k is "small" relative to the entire market for good (factor) k such that $\partial p_i / \partial Z_k = 0$, all $i = 2, \ldots, N$, (21.11) becomes:

$$(21.23) \qquad (\lambda - 1)(-p_1 g_{Z_k} + p_k) = 0$$

which will be satisfied if $t_k = 0$. In other words, the government should use the actual market price of p_k in deciding how much Z_k to employ (supply).

Suppose, however, that the government is the only supplier of a particular output X_j. In this case, the implicit tax is virtually identical to a real tax. Refer to Figure 21–2. The shadow price γ_j equals the firm's actual marginal costs at X_j^F, but because of the implicit tax the firm charges the consumer p_j, equal to measured marginal costs plus the implicit tax t_j. Thus, the consumer is indifferent between the implicit tax or a real partial tax with lump-sum return of the revenues. (Notice that although the firm receives p_j for each unit, it pretends it is receiving only γ_j for the purposes of implicit profit maximization.)

These results indicate that the first-order conditions for optimal implicit taxes, equations (21.22), may be much easier to approximate than appears at first pass, certainly much easier than the optimal tax rules for the economy as a whole. In most cases the government producer will be supplying a few services that are unique to it, and buying generalized factors whose prices are set in large national markets. Thus, it only need determine implicit taxes on these few services. In effect, then, conditions (21.22) tell the government how to raise prices above measured marginal costs on each of its services in order to satisfy an overall budget constraint. Viewed in this way, conditions (21.22)

FIGURE 21–2

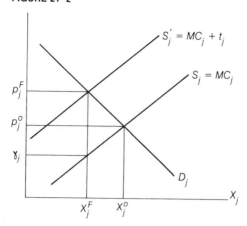

provide an efficient second-best algorithm for applying full or "average" cost pricing to the multiproduct firm.

The full-cost interpretation of the Boiteux tax rules has actually found its way into public policy discussions. In the 1975 Postal rate hearings, economists representing the Post Office used conditions similar to (21.22) to argue for relatively large percentage increases in first-class rates as the appropriate second-best method for balancing the Postal budget.[9] Given that the government has a virtual monopoly in first-class service, and that these demand elasticities are quite low, the Boiteux rule quite naturally suggested rather large implicit taxes for first-class mail, or consumer prices well in excess of marginal production costs. (Think of the inverse elasticity rule as an approximate interpretation of (21.22).) As it turned out, their argument did not carry the day, but it is at least noteworthy that second-best tax rules have been referenced in public policy debates.

CONSTRAINED GOVERNMENT AGENCIES

While Boiteux's analysis was motivated by an attempt to develop optimal second-best rules for public monopolies, the resulting decision rules (21.11) or (21.22) are directly applicable to any government agency subject to a legislated budget constraint. That this is so is obvious from our original formulation of the Boiteux problem, in which the government is constrained to meet a given target B from the purchase and sales of inputs and outputs at actual market prices $(p_1, \ldots, p_i, \ldots, p_N)$, or $\sum_{i=1}^{N} p_i Z_i = B$. The government has a production function $Z_1 = -g(Z_2, \ldots, Z_N)$ but there are no formal restrictions on $g(\vec{Z})$

---

[9] Postal Rate and Fee Increases, *Docket No: R75-1.* The IER was first proposed by William Vickrey in the 1974 hearings as a means of determining postal rates on the various classes of mail. Docket No: R74-1.

(other than that it be continuous and twice differentiable). It does not even have to be a homogeneous function. Clearly, then, the original formulation is a fairly general statement covering any constrained public agency engaged in the production of goods and services. Conditions (21.22) suggest that constrained agencies should follow standard competitive production decision rules, based on shadow prices determined by the solution of (21.22). Once again, the number of shadow prices to be determined depends upon the importance of the agency relative to the national markets for its outputs and inputs. Finally, Boiteux was able to prove as an extension of his results that if there is more than one such constrained sector (agency), each sector will have its own set of rules similar to (21.22).[10] This is obviously of some importance, since most government agencies operate under imposed budget constraints, but we will not exhibit that result here.

REFERENCES

Baumol, W., and Bradford, D. "Optimal Departures from Marginal Cost Pricing." *American Economic Review,* June 1970.

Boiteux, M. "On the Management of Public Monopolies Subject to Budgetary Constraints." *Journal of Economic Theory,* September 1971 (translated from French in *Econometrica,* January 1956).

Dreze, J. "Some Post-War Contributions of French Economists to Theory and Public Policy." *American Economic Review,* June 1964 (Supplement).

"Postal Rate and Fee Increases." *Docket No: R75-1; Docket No: R74-1.*

---

[10] Boiteux, "On the Management of Public Monopolies," p. 231.

22

General production rules in a second-best environment

Chapter 22 will conclude the survey of second-best public expenditure theory by exploring some fairly general propositions about government production in an environment made second best because of distorting taxation. A major goal of the chapter is to integrate our previous results on second-best tax theory with second-best public expenditure theory. Therefore, all the analysis in Chapter 22 will employ basically the same set of assumptions regarding government activity and the underlying structure of the private sector that we have been using all along. With respect to the former, the government is making a set of production decisions under two constraints: (a) it must buy inputs and sell outputs at the established private sector producer prices and (b) it must cover any resulting deficit (surplus) with distorting commodity taxes levied on the consumer. Otherwise, government production is fully general in that it may buy or sell any inputs or outputs, including those traded in the private sector, and that there are no restrictions on the form of the aggregate government production function other than the exclusion of externalities. Following Chapter 21, we will represent the government's production possibilities by $G(Z) = 0$, or $Z_1 = -g(Z_2, \ldots, Z_N)$, where $\check{Z}$ spans (potentially) the entire set of the economy's inputs and outputs. The only difference between the specification of the government sector in this chapter and the specification employed in the Boiteux analysis is that the government taxes (subsidizes) all consumer transactions to cover its deficits (surpluses), not just those between the consumers and the government.

With respect to the private sector, it is assumed that all markets are perfectly competitive and that private production exhibits general technology with constant returns to scale (CRS). Thus, the only distortions in the economy that render the analysis second best are the distorting commodity taxes used to cover government production deficits. Second, since private production is CRS, there can be no pure profits or losses from private production. We will also assume that the consumers have no other sources of lump-sum income either, so that all income derives from the sale of variable factors. These assumptions about the private sector are not necessary, but they greatly facilitate the analysis.

Given this analytical framework, the first problem to be considered is the so-called Diamond-Mirrlees problem, which Peter Diamond and James Mirrlees set out in their two-part article in the 1971 *American Economic Review* entitled "Optimal Taxation and Public Production."[1] By 1968, when their paper was first drafted, the optimal tax rule for a one-consumer (equivalent) economy was well known, but only under the assumption that the government simply raised revenue to be returned lump sum to the consumer. Diamond and Mirrlees added government production to the standard second-best general equilibrium tax model and asked, first: How does the existence of government production affect the optimal tax rule? In particular, if the revenue were raised to cover a government production deficit under the conditions set forth above, what form will the tax rules take? They found that the optimal tax rule was unchanged. This result could have been anticipated since it was well known by then that the tax rules as originally derived did not contain any production terms even when *private* production exhibited general technology. Turning the question around, they then asked what effect distorting taxation had on government production rules. Their answer to this question was startling. They proved that so long as the taxes were set optimally, the government should follow the standard *first-best* production rules, using the private sector producer prices and equating these price ratios to marginal rates of transformation. Distorting taxation forces society underneath its utility-possibilities frontier, but it should remain on the production-possibilities frontier. This result will surely stand as a classic in the annals of public sector theory.

Having established the Diamond and Mirrlees production result, their analysis will then be generalized to consider government production rules under conditions of nonoptimal distorting taxation. As one might suspect, production efficiency no longer holds. In fact, the production rules become fairly complicated. This is especially unfortunate since real-world taxes are likely to be far from optimal.

Any analysis incorporating both second-best tax and expenditure theory is bound to be complex, although the assumptions on the private sector help somewhat in simplifying the analysis. To simplify even further, and highlight the efficiency aspects of taxation and government production, we will analyze them first in the context of a one-consumer (equivalent) economy using the technique of loss minimization. We will then conclude the chapter by reworking one of the production exercises in a many-person economy to suggest how equity considerations modify the one-consumer rules.[2]

THE DIAMOND-MIRRLEES PROBLEM— ONE-CONSUMER ECONOMY

Let us establish the general equilibrium framework for the Diamond-Mirrlees problem with some care since we will be using this same analytical structure

[1] P. Diamond and J. Mirrlees, "Optimal Taxation and Public Production" (2 parts, Part I: Production Efficiency, Part II: Tax Rules), *American Economic Review*, March, June 1971.

[2] These analyses draw heavily from two papers by R. Boadway: R. Boadway, "Cost-Benefit Rules and General Equilibrium," *Review of Economic Studies*, July 1975; and R. Boadway, "Integrating Equity and Efficiency in Applied Welfare Economics," *Quarterly Journal of Economics*, November 1976. We also benefitted from a set of unpublished class notes provided by Peter Diamond.

throughout most of the chapter. The private sector consists of a single consumer and a set of perfectly competitive producers with general technologies and CRS production. Loss minimization requires that the consumer's decisions be represented by the expenditure function

$$(22.1) \qquad M(\vec{q}; \bar{U}) = \sum_{i=1}^{N} q_i X_i^{\text{comp}}(\vec{q}; \bar{U})$$

where:

$\vec{q}$ is the $(N \times 1)$ vector of consumer prices (gross of tax for outputs; net of tax for inputs) with element q_i.

$\vec{X}^{\text{comp}} = \vec{M}_i =$ the $(N \times 1)$ vector of demand and factor supplies, with element X_i^{comp} (or M_i).

Let private production be represented by an aggregate profit function

$$(22.2) \qquad \pi(\vec{p}) = \sum_{i=1}^{N} p_i Y_i(\vec{p})$$

where:

$\vec{p} =$ the $(N \times 1)$ vector of producer prices (gross of tax for inputs, net of tax for outputs) with element p_i.

$\vec{Y} = \vec{\pi}_i =$ the $(N \times 1)$ vector of private supplies and factor demands, with element Y_i (or π_i).

With CRS, $\pi(\vec{p}) \equiv 0$.

The government has an $(N \times 1)$ vector of production decision variables $\vec{Z}$, with element Z_i, related by the aggregate government production function

$$(22.3) \qquad G(\vec{Z}) = 0 \quad \text{or} \quad Z_1 = -g(Z_2, \ldots, Z_N)$$

Since it buys and sells at the private producer prices, the resulting deficit (surplus) from government production is:

$$(22.4) \qquad D = \sum_{i=1}^{N} p_i Z_i$$

with inputs measured negatively following the usual convention. The government will cover the deficit (surplus) by using an $(N \times 1)$ vector of unit "commodity" taxes $\vec{t}$, with element t_i, placed on the consumer, such that $\vec{q} = \vec{p} + \vec{t}$. The revenue raised at the compensated equilibrium[3] is $\sum_{i=1}^{N} t_i M_i$, so that the government's budget constraint has the generalized form

$$(22.5) \qquad \sum_{i=1}^{N} t_i M_i + \sum_{i=1}^{N} p_i Z_i = B$$

---

[3] Recall from the discussion of the optimal tax problem that loss minimization requires measurement at the compensated equilibrium.

If B is not equal to zero, the resulting surplus or deficit is returned lump sum to the consumer.

With two sources of production and general production technology, market clearance must be introduced explicitly into the analysis. We know, however, that all markets cannot clear at the compensated with-tax equilibrium.[4] Therefore, specify

$$(22.6) \qquad M_i(\vec{q};\bar{U}) = \pi_i(\vec{p}) + Z_i \qquad i = 2, \ldots, N$$

and assume that compensation occurs in terms of good 1.

Furthermore, let good 1 serve as the untaxed numeraire so that $q_1 \equiv p_1 \equiv 1$, $t_1 = 0$. This completes all the relevant elements of the general equilibrium framework. The government has $2N - 1$ control variables at its disposal, $(Z_1, \ldots, Z_N)$ and $(t_2, \ldots, t_N)$.

The loss function the government will minimize with respect to these control variables has the general form:

$$(22.7) \qquad L(\vec{t};\vec{Z}) = M(\vec{q};\bar{U}^0) - \sum_{i=2}^{N} t_i M_i - \sum_{i=1}^{N} p_i Z_i - \pi(\vec{p})$$

where, with general technology,

$$(22.8) \qquad \vec{q} = q(\vec{t};\vec{Z}) \qquad \text{and} \qquad \vec{p} = p(\vec{t};\vec{Z})$$

Loss equals the lump-sum income required to keep the consumer indifferent to the gross of tax prices less all sources of lump-sum income resulting from decisions on the government control variables. In this model lump-sum income derives from two sources, pure economic profits (losses) from private production and the remaining government surplus after taxes have been collected. With CRS the profit term need not be included. Similarly, if tax revenues just cover government production deficits, the second and third terms could be dropped as well, with loss defined simply as $M(\vec{q};\bar{U}^0)$. In the interests of presenting a more general methodology, however, all these terms will be retained in the subsequent analysis.

Loss must be minimized subject to government production technology and the government budget constraint. Formally, the problem is:

$$\min_{(\vec{t},\vec{z})} M(\vec{q};\bar{U}^0) - \sum_{i=2}^{N} t_i M_i - \sum_{i=1}^{N} p_i Z_i - \pi(\vec{p})$$

$$\text{s.t.} \quad \sum_{i=2}^{N} t_i M_i + \sum_{i=1}^{N} p_i Z_i = B$$

$$Z_1 = -g(Z_2, \ldots, Z_N)$$

Incorporating the government production constraint directly into the analysis,

---

[4] Refer to Chapter 16 for a discussion of the compensated market clearance relationships.

and noting that $\vec{q} = \vec{p} + \vec{t}$, the problem can be restated as:

$$\min_{(\vec{t},\vec{Z})} M(\vec{p} + \vec{t}; \vec{U}^0) - \sum_{i=2}^{N} t_i M_i + p_1 g(Z_2, \ldots, Z_N) - \sum_{i=2}^{N} p_i Z_i - \pi(\vec{p})$$

$$\text{s.t.} \sum_{i=2}^{N} t_i M_i - p_1 g(Z_2, \ldots, Z_N) + \sum_{i=2}^{N} p_i Z_i = B$$

Also, $q_1 \equiv p_1 \equiv 1, t_1 = 0$, so that there are $2N - 2$ control variables, $(t_2, \ldots, t_N)$ and $(Z_2, \ldots, Z_N)$.

Finally, the market clearance equations will be used to simplify the first-order conditions. Formally, they solve for $\vec{p}$ given the solution for $\vec{t}$ and $\vec{Z}$. The Lagrangian for this problem is:

$$\min_{(\vec{t},\vec{z})} \mathscr{L} = M(\vec{p} + \vec{t}; \vec{U}^0) - \sum_{i=2}^{N} t_i M_i + p_1 g(Z_2, \ldots, Z_N)$$

$$- \sum_{i=2}^{N} p_i Z_i - \pi(\vec{p}) + \lambda \left[\sum_{i=2}^{N} t_i M_i - p_1 g(Z_2, \ldots, Z_N) \right.$$

$$\left. + \sum_{i=2}^{N} p_i Z_i - B \right]$$

To derive the Diamond-Mirrlees results, begin by considering the first-order conditions with respect to t_k, computing $\partial L / \partial t_k$ as an intermediate step.

(22.9)
$$\frac{\partial L}{\partial t_k} = M_k + \sum_{i=2}^{N} M_i \frac{\partial p_i}{\partial t_k} - M_k - \sum_{i=2}^{N} t_i \left(M_{ik} + \sum_{j=2}^{N} M_{ij} \frac{\partial p_j}{\partial t_k} \right)$$

$$- \sum_{i=2}^{N} Z_i \frac{\partial p_i}{\partial t_k} - \sum_{i=2}^{N} \pi_i \frac{\partial p_i}{\partial t_k} \qquad k = 2, \ldots, N$$

Multiply each market clearance equation (22.6) by $\partial p_i / \partial t_k$ and sum over all $(N-1)$ relationships to obtain:

(22.10)
$$\sum_{i=2}^{N} M_i \frac{\partial p_i}{\partial t_k} = \sum_{i=2}^{N} \pi_i \frac{\partial p_i}{\partial t_k} + \sum_{i=2}^{N} Z_i \frac{\partial p_i}{\partial t_k}$$

Therefore (22.9) simplifies to:

(22.11)
$$\frac{\partial L}{\partial t_k} = - \sum_{i=2}^{N} t_i \left(M_{ik} + \sum_{j=2}^{N} M_{ij} \frac{\partial p_j}{\partial t_k} \right) \qquad k = 2, \ldots, N$$

Next, differentiate the budget constraint with respect to t_k.

(22.12)
$$\frac{\partial B}{\partial t_k} = M_k + \sum_{i=2}^{N} t_i \left(M_{ik} + \sum_{j=2}^{N} M_{ij} \frac{\partial p_j}{\partial t_k} \right) + \sum_{i=2}^{N} Z_i \frac{\partial p_i}{\partial t_k}$$

$$k = 2, \ldots, N$$

From (22.11):

(22.13)
$$\frac{\partial B}{\partial t_k} = - \frac{\partial L}{\partial t_k} + \left(M_k + \sum_{i=2}^{N} Z_i \frac{\partial p_i}{\partial t_k} \right)$$

With CRS in private production, $\sum_{i=1}^{N} \pi_i(\partial p_i/\partial t_k) = 0$. Furthermore, since $\partial p_1/\partial t_k = 0$, $\sum_{i=2}^{N} \pi_i(\partial p_i/\partial t_k) = 0$. Hence, from (22.10):

$$(22.14) \qquad \sum_{i=2}^{N} Z_i \frac{\partial p_i}{\partial t_k} = \sum_{i=2}^{N} M_i \frac{\partial p_i}{\partial t_k}$$

Given (22.14), (22.13) can be rewritten as:

$$(22.15) \qquad \frac{\partial B}{\partial t_k} = -\frac{\partial L}{\partial t_k} + \left(M_k + \sum_{i=2}^{N} M_i \frac{\partial p_i}{\partial t_k} \right)$$

Combining (22.11) and (22.15), and incorporating λ, the first-order conditions with respect to t_k are:

$$(22.16) \qquad (1 - \lambda) \frac{\partial L}{\partial t_k} + \lambda \left(M_k + \sum_{i=2}^{N} M_i \frac{\partial p_i}{\partial t_k} \right) = 0$$

or

$$(22.17) \qquad (\lambda - 1) \left[\sum_{i=2}^{N} t_i \left(M_{ik} + \sum_{j=2}^{N} M_{ij} \frac{\partial p_j}{\partial t_k} \right) \right] + \lambda \left(M_k + \sum_{i=2}^{N} M_i \frac{\partial p_i}{\partial t_k} \right) = 0$$

$$k = 2, \ldots, N$$

But equation (22.17) is identical to equation (16.28), the first-order conditions when revenue was simply raised for its own sake. Following the manipulations of Chapter 16, these conditions imply the standard optimal commodity tax rule (15.25), or

$$(22.18) \qquad \frac{\sum_{i=2}^{N} t_i M_{ik}}{M_k} = -\frac{\lambda}{\lambda - 1} = C \qquad k = 2, \ldots, N$$

Thus, introducing government production into the analysis does not alter the optimal tax rules, the first of the two main Diamond-Mirrlees results. As was noted in Chapter 16, this result depends crucially on the assumption of CRS in private production.

To derive their second, more interesting result, differentiate the first-order conditions with respect to the Z_k. As before, begin with a preliminary consideration of $\partial L/\partial Z_k$.

$$(22.19) \qquad \frac{\partial L}{\partial Z_k} = \sum_{i=2}^{N} M_i \frac{\partial p_i}{\partial Z_k} - \sum_{i=2}^{N} \sum_{j=2}^{N} t_i M_{ij} \frac{\partial p_j}{\partial Z_k} + p_1 g_{Z_k} - p_k$$

$$- \sum_{i=2}^{N} Z_i \frac{\partial p_i}{\partial Z_k} - \sum_{i=2}^{N} \pi_i \frac{\partial p_i}{\partial Z_k} \qquad k = 2, \ldots, N$$

Multiplying each market clearance equation (22.6) by $\partial p_i/\partial Z_k$, and summing over all $(N - 1)$ relationships yields:

$$(22.20) \qquad \sum_{i=2}^{N} M_i \frac{\partial p_i}{\partial Z_k} = \sum_{i=2}^{N} \pi_i \frac{\partial p_i}{\partial Z_k} + \sum_{i=2}^{N} Z_i \frac{\partial p_i}{\partial Z_k}$$

Hence, (22.19) simplifies to:

$$(22.21) \qquad \frac{\partial L}{\partial Z_k} = - \sum_{i=2}^{N} \sum_{j=2}^{N} t_i M_{ij} \frac{\partial p_j}{\partial Z_k} + p_1 g_{z_k} - p_k \qquad k = 2, \ldots, N$$

Next, consider $\partial B / \partial Z_k$:

$$(22.22) \qquad \frac{\partial B}{\partial Z_k} = \sum_{i=2}^{N} \sum_{j=2}^{N} t_i M_{ij} \frac{\partial p_j}{\partial Z_k} - p_1 g_{z_k} + p_k + \sum_{i=2}^{N} Z_i \frac{\partial p_i}{\partial Z_k}$$

$$k = 2, \ldots, N$$

From market clearance and CRS in private production, (22.22) can be restated as:

$$(22.23) \qquad \frac{\partial B}{\partial Z_k} = \sum_{i=2}^{N} \sum_{j=2}^{N} t_i M_{ij} \frac{\partial p_j}{\partial Z_k} - p_1 g_{z_k} + p_k + \sum_{i=2}^{N} M_i \frac{\partial p_i}{\partial Z_k}$$

Thus,

$$(22.24) \qquad \frac{\partial B}{\partial Z_k} = - \frac{\partial L}{\partial Z_k} + \sum_{i=2}^{N} M_i \frac{\partial p_i}{\partial Z_k} \qquad k = 2, \ldots, N$$

Combining (22.21) and (22.24), and incorporating λ, the first-order conditions with respect to the Z_k are:

$$(22.25) \qquad (1 - \lambda) \frac{\partial L}{\partial Z_k} + \lambda \sum_{i=2}^{N} M_i \frac{\partial p_i}{\partial Z_k} = 0 \qquad k = 2, \ldots, N$$

Substituting the expression for $\partial L / \partial Z_k$, and changing the summation index on the $M_i (\partial p_i / \partial Z_k)$ terms, (22.25) becomes:

$$(22.26) \qquad (\lambda - 1) \left[\sum_{i=2}^{N} \sum_{j=2}^{N} t_i M_{ij} \frac{\partial p_j}{\partial Z_k} + p_k - p_1 g_{z_k} \right] + \lambda \sum_{j=2}^{N} M_j \frac{\partial p_j}{\partial Z_k} = 0$$

$$k = 2, \ldots, N$$

To consider the effect that optimal taxation has on these rules, rewrite (22.26) as:

$$(22.27) \qquad \sum_{j=2}^{N} \left[(\lambda - 1) \sum_{i=2}^{N} t_i M_{ij} + \lambda M_j \right] \frac{\partial p_j}{\partial Z_k} + (\lambda - 1)(p_k - p_1 g_{z_k}) = 0$$

$$k = 2, \ldots, N$$

But if commodity taxes are set optimally in accordance with (22.18):

$$(22.28) \qquad (\lambda - 1) \sum_{i=2}^{N} t_i M_{ij} + \lambda M_j = 0 \qquad j = 2, \ldots, N$$

Thus, the government production rule is simply:

$$(22.29) \qquad p_k - p_1 g_{z_k} = 0 \qquad k = 2, \ldots, N$$

or

$$(22.30) \qquad p_k = p_1 g_{z_k} \qquad k = 2, \ldots, N$$

(22.30) is the standard first-best rule for production efficiency in competitive markets. Alternatively,

$$(22.31) \qquad \frac{p_k}{p_j} = \frac{g_{z_k}}{g_{z_j}} = MRT_{z_k, z_j} \qquad k, j = 2, \ldots, N$$

with the government using the competitively determined producer prices as shadow prices in its production decisions.

This may well be the most striking result in all of second-best public expenditure theory, one of the precious few examples of a simple second-best decision rule. It implies overall production efficiency for the economy,[5] or that the economy should remain on its aggregate production-possibilities frontier. Of course, with distorting taxation the economy cannot also be on its first-best utility-possibilities frontier. A final implication is that in an intertemporal context, government investment decisions should use the private sector's gross-of-tax returns to capital as the rate of discount in present value calculations (recall that P_k is a gross-of-tax price for an imput such as capital).[6] Since the U.S. corporate tax rate is 48 percent, this implies a fairly high government rate of discount, the rate of return the government must beat to justify public investment at the expense of private investment. We will return to this point in Part IV when discussing the rate of discount in cost-benefit analysis.

PRODUCTION DECISIONS WITH NONOPTIMAL TAXES

The Diamond-Mirrlees problem provides a clear example of just how far removed second-best theory is from the complexities of the real world, even though it contains elements that are more realistic than the traditional first-best assumptions. Taxes are distorting in this model, but assuming that current tax rates are (even approximately) at their optimal values is every bit as heroic as assuming taxes are (approximately) lump sum, which first-best theory requires. We can move somewhat closer to reality by assuming explicitly that the current rates are nonoptimal and asking how this affects the government's production decision rules. Formally, this assumption is equivalent to adding further constraints to the original Diamond-Mirrlees problem of the form that a subset of the tax rates are predetermined at nonoptimal levels. Given these predetermined rates, the first-order conditions of the new problem will indicate how the government can adjust its production decisions to minimize loss. Unfortunately, the resulting production rules are extremely complex. They have a plausible interpretation, but it is doubtful whether any government would have sufficient information to implement them. Moreover, even this problem is far removed from reality, for it retains the assumption of a perfectly competitive private

---

[5] Recall that the private sector is assumed to be perfectly competitive, and therefore first-best pareto efficient.

[6] Intertemporally, all budget constraints in the general equilibrium framework must balance in terms of present value, not year by year, and there must be perfect capital markets for borrowing and lending.

sector.[7] Were we to introduce monopoly elements in private production, the optimal production rules would change once again. Consequently, the normative policy content of this model is not especially compelling either, but it will be instructive to explore the production decision rules when taxes are nonoptimal if only to give a flavor for this kind of analysis.

In order to keep the notation as simple as possible, rewrite the loss function entirely in vector notation as:

$$(22.32) \qquad L(t;Z) = M(q;\bar{U}^0) - t'M_i + p_1 g(Z) - (q - t)'Z - \pi(q - t)$$

Written in this form the loss function incorporates every relevant constraint except for the market clearance equations (22.6), expressed in vector notation as:

$$(22.33) \qquad\qquad M_i(q;\bar{U}^0) = \pi_i(q - t) + Z$$

The nonoptimal tax and production rules are derived by totally differentiating the loss function with respect to t and Z, and using (22.33) to simplify the resulting expression.

$$(22.34) \quad dL(t;Z) = M_i' \frac{\partial q}{\partial t} dt + M_i' \frac{\partial q}{\partial Z} dZ - M_i' dt - t' M_{ij} \frac{\partial q}{\partial t} dt$$

$$- t'M_{ij} \frac{\partial q}{\partial Z} dZ + p_1 g_z dZ - Z' \frac{\partial q}{\partial t} dt + Z' dt - Z' \frac{\partial q}{\partial Z} dZ$$

$$- (q - t)' dZ - \pi_i' \frac{\partial q}{\partial t} dt - \pi_i' \frac{\partial q}{\partial Z} dZ + \pi_i' dt$$

From market clearance:

$$(22.35) \qquad\qquad M_i' dt = \pi_i' dt + Z' dt$$

$$(22.36) \qquad\qquad M_i' \frac{\partial q}{\partial t} dt = \pi_i' \frac{\partial q}{\partial t} dt + Z' \frac{\partial q}{\partial t} dt$$

$$(22.37) \qquad\qquad M_i' \frac{\partial q}{\partial Z} dZ = \pi_i' \frac{\partial q}{\partial Z} dZ + Z' \frac{\partial q}{\partial Z} dZ$$

Also,

$$(22.38) \qquad\qquad q - t = p$$

Using (22.35)–(22.38), (22.34) simplifies to:

$$(22.39) \qquad dL(t;Z) = -t'M_{ij} \frac{\partial q}{\partial t} dt - t'M_{ij} \frac{\partial q}{\partial Z} dZ + p_1 g_z dZ - p' dZ$$

Next, totally differentiate (22.8), obtaining:

$$(22.40) \qquad\qquad dq = \frac{\partial q}{\partial t} dt + \frac{\partial q}{\partial Z} dZ$$

---

[7] The assumption of private sector CRS production is also retained.

Substituting (22.40) into (22.39) yields:

(22.41) $$dL(t; Z) = -t'M_{ij}dq + p_1g_zdZ - p'dZ$$

The first point to notice is that the Diamond-Mirrlees production rules follow directly from (22.41). Suppose taxes are set optimally. Since setting taxes is equivalent to setting consumer prices, this means that the vector dq is also optimal. But at the optimum, $dL = 0$. Hence, optimal taxation implies a dq such that the first term in equation (22.41) is zero ($dL = -t'M_{ij}dq = -t'dX = 0$ at the optimum, t^*). But the vector dZ must also be compatible with $dL = 0$. Hence,

(22.42) $$p_1g_zdZ - p'dZ = 0$$

or

(22.43) $$p_1g_z = p'$$

If taxes are not optimal, however, the decision rules for government production are more complex, since changes in Z will change q, and thereby indirectly affect dL through the (nonzero) tax term in (22.41). The separate effects of taxes and government production on loss in the general case can be obtained by totally differentiating the market clearance equations, solving for dq in terms of dt and dZ and substituting the resulting expression for dq into the first term of equation (22.41), as follows:

(22.44) $$M_{ij}dq = \pi_{ij}dq - \pi_{ij}dt + dZ$$

(22.45) $$dq = (-\pi_{ij}dt + dZ)E^{-1}$$

where:

$E = [M_{ij} - \pi_{ij}]$, the matrix of compensated demand and private production price derivatives (as defined in Chapter 16).

Substituting (22.45) into (22.41), and rearranging terms:

(22.46) $$dL = t'(M_{ij})E^{-1}\pi_{ij}dt - (-p_1g_z + p' + t'M_{ij}E^{-1})dZ$$

Equation (22.46) can be used to compute the change in loss, or welfare, resulting from any combination of changes in the t's and Z's, the remaining t's and Z's held constant. One immediate and important implication of (22.46) is that the addition of government production does not affect any of the theorems in Chapter 16 on the deadweight loss from changes in tax rates. In this sense, the welfare effects of government production are separable from the welfare effects of distorting taxes. The term $[t'M_{ij}E^{-1}\pi_{ij}]dt$ is identical to equation (16.17) in Chapter 16, with

$$M_{ij} = \frac{\partial X^{comp}}{\partial q} \quad \text{and} \quad \pi_{ij} = \frac{\partial Y}{\partial p}$$

As indicated in that chapter, the marginal loss from a small increase in a distorting tax can be interpreted as a change in consumer and producer surpluses, where consumer surplus is defined in terms of compensated demand curves. This result continues to hold in the presence of government production because with $dZ = 0$, the market clearance derivatives imply $dq = -\pi_{ij}E^{-1}dt$, or

$$(22.47) \qquad dL(t;\bar{Z}) = t'M_{ij}dq = t'\frac{\partial X}{\partial q}\,dq = t'dX = (q-p)'dX$$

exactly as in Chapter 16.

The government's production rules can be stated in a number of different ways depending upon the manner in which the control variables are manipulated. The most straightforward example to consider is the welfare implication of marginally increasing one of the inputs, say, Z_k, in order to increase output of Z_1 through the marginal product relationship g_{Z_k}, all other Z and the tax rates constant. According to equation (22.46) the change in loss from this move would be:

$$(22.48) \qquad dL(\bar{t};Z) = -(-p_1 g_{Z_k} + p_k + t'M_{ik}E^{-1})dZ_k$$

The *optimal* adjustment of Z_k is one for which $dL = 0$, or

$$(22.49) \qquad -(-p_1 g_{Z_k} + p_k + t'M_{ik}E^{-1})dZ_k = 0$$

In a first-best environment, the government would hire Z_k until its price equaled the value of its marginal product, or $p_1 g_Z = p_k$ (recall that Z_k enters negatively in $g(z)$). With distorting and nonoptimal taxes, however, equation (22.49) implies that the true social costs of hiring Z_k are $(p_k + t'M_{ik}E^{-1})$. Hence, the government should use these true costs as the shadow price for decision making and equate them to the value of marginal product, or set (generally)

$$(22.50) \qquad p_1 g_Z = (p' + t'M_{ij}E^{-1})$$

The term $t'M_{ij}E^{-1}$ turns out to have an intuitively appealing interpretation. With taxes held constant, $dt = 0$, $dq = dp$, and the market clearance derivatives (22.44) become:

$$(22.51) \qquad M_{ij}dq = \pi_{ij}dp + dZ$$

Substituting $dq = dp$ and solving for dZ yields:

$$(22.52) \qquad dZ = (M_{ij} - \pi_{ij})dq = Edq$$

Substituting (22.52) into the last term of (22.46), and letting only Z_k change:

$$(22.53) \qquad -(-p_1 g_{Z_k}dZ_k + p_k dZ_k + t'M_{ik}dq) = 0$$

Rearranging terms:

$$(22.54) \qquad p_1 g_{Z_k} = \left(p_k + t'M_{ik}\frac{dq}{dZ_k}\right)$$

But

$$(22.55) \qquad t'M_{ik}\frac{\partial q}{dZ_k} = t'\frac{\partial X}{\partial q}\frac{dq}{dZ_k} = t'dX$$

FIGURE 22-1

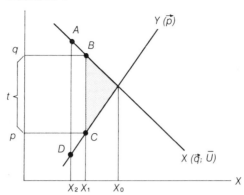

the change in tax revenues caused by a change in Z_k at constant tax rates. This revenue change represents an additional deadweight burden to the consumer because with nonzero taxes, changes in market equilibria will change the sum of producers' and consumer's surpluses lost as a result of the tax distortions, as indicated in Figure 22–1.

X_0 is the original no-tax equilibrium, and X_1 is the equilibrium with taxes (and government production), with loss equal to the shaded triangle. If a marginal increase in Z_k shifts X again, generating a new equilibrium X_2, then the loss area in the market for X increases by the trapezoidal area $ABCD$, which can be approximated for small changes by $t'dX$. The full social opportunity costs of using Z_k, then, are the standard market opportunity costs as represented by p_k plus the additional excess burden implied by the tax revenue response to changes in Z_k. Finally, since this result holds for all k, the production rule can be expressed in the traditional format as $MRT_{i,j} = \theta_i/\theta_j, i,j = 2, \ldots, N$, where $\theta_i = p_i + t'M_{ij}(dq/dZ_i)$, the optimal shadow price for good (factor) i.

The government production shadow prices $\theta_k = (p_k + t'M_{ik}E^{-1})$ also have a very appealing weighted-average interpretation if one assumes, as an approximation, that all cross-price derivatives in demand and private production are zero.[8] With this assumption, the shadow price simplifies to:

$$(22.56) \qquad \theta_k = p_k + t_k \frac{\partial X_k}{\partial q_k}\left[\frac{\partial X_k}{\partial q_k} - \frac{\partial Y_k}{\partial p_k}\right]^{-1}$$

$$(22.57) \qquad \theta_k = p_k + (q_k - p_k)\frac{\partial X_k}{\partial q_k}\left[\frac{\partial X_k}{\partial q_k} - \frac{\partial Y_k}{\partial p_k}\right]^{-1}$$

---

[8] This assumption is tenable for production derivatives but not for the demand derivatives which are expressed in terms of compensated demand curves. At least one $M_{ij}, i \neq j$, must be positive. Thus, the assumption can only be approximately true. See Boadway, "Cost-Benefit Rules and General Equilibrium," pp. 365, 366, and 370.

Rearranging the second term on the right-hand side of (22.57) yields:

$$\text{(22.58)} \qquad \theta_k = p_k + (q_k - p_k)\left[\cfrac{1}{1 - \cfrac{\dfrac{\partial Y_k}{\partial p_k}}{\dfrac{\partial X_k}{\partial q_k}}}\right]$$

Let

$$\alpha = \cfrac{\dfrac{\partial Y_k}{\partial p_k}}{\dfrac{\partial X_k}{\partial q_k}}.$$

Therefore:

$$\text{(22.59)} \qquad \theta_k = p_k + (q_k - p_k)\left[\frac{1}{1 - \alpha}\right].$$

Rearranging terms:

$$\text{(22.60)} \qquad \theta_k = q_k\left(\frac{1}{1 - \alpha}\right) + p_k\left(\frac{-\alpha}{1 - \alpha}\right)$$

(22.60) says that the optimal shadow price for the input Z_k is a weighted average of the consumer and producer prices, with the weights equal to the proportions in which the increased Z_k comes at the expense of either decreased demand for the input by the private sector or increased supply of the input from consumers. Given market clearance, these are the only possibilities. If the entire increase in Z_k comes from an increase in consumer supply, $\partial Y_k/\partial p_k = 0$, $\alpha = 0$, and $\theta_k = q_k$. The only opportunity cost of increasing Z_k is the private opportunity cost to the consumer of supplying the additional Z_k. If, on the other hand, the entire increase in Z_k comes from a decrease in private demand, $\partial X_k/\partial q_k = 0$, $\alpha \to \infty$, and $\theta_k = p_k$, the market opportunity cost for Z_k. This is effectively what happens with optimal taxation—all changes in government production come entirely at the expense of private production.

The case of $\partial X_k/\partial q_k = 0$ generalizes to linear technologies with fixed producer prices. With private production input demands and output supplies perfectly elastic at the fixed producer prices, all changes in government production must come entirely at the expense of private production. Thus, we would expect the optimal shadow prices to equal the producer prices, $\vec{p}$, even if cross-price derivatives are nonzero. That this is so can be seen directly from equation (22.41). With $\vec{p}$ constant, $dq = dt$ and (22.41) becomes:

$$\text{(22.61)} \qquad dL = -t'M_{ij}dt + (p_1 g_Z - p')dZ$$

Even with nonoptimal distorting taxes, then, the government should use the competitive private sector producer prices as shadow prices to avoid any additional increases in deadweight loss.

Thus far government production variables have been allowed to change without any reference to the government's budget constraint. Any changes in the budget surplus (deficit) are simply returned to the consumer lump sum. If, in fact, the government is required to maintain budgetary balance, then increasing Z_k may require a simultaneous change in at least one of the tax rates. One can imagine the following policy: Suppose the government increases Z_k (and, implicitly, Z_1) and simultaneously changes the jth tax, t_j, in order to maintain a balanced budget. Under these circumstances, what is the appropriate shadow price for Z_k? Given equation (22.46) the solution is straightforward. Totally differentiate the government's budget $t'M_i - p_1 g(Z) + p'Z = B$ with respect to t_j and Z_k to determine the required change in t_j for any given (small) change in Z_k, and substitute the resulting solution $dt_j = f' \cdot dZ_k$ into equation (22.46) to obtain an expression for the change in loss solely as a function of dZ_k. The optimal shadow price can then be computed by setting $dL = 0$. Without actually carrying out the calculations, the effect of the budget constraint on the optimal shadow prices can be seen by writing:

$$(22.62) \qquad \frac{dL}{dZ_k} = t'M_{ij}E^{-1}\pi_{ij}\frac{dt_j^*}{dZ_k} - (-p_1 g_{Z_k} + p_k + t'M_{ik}E^{-1}) = 0$$

where:

$\dfrac{dt_j^*}{dZ_k}$ is the required change in t_j for maintaining budgetary balance.

The new shadow price to be equated to the value of marginal product $p_1 g_{Z_k}$ is:

$$(22.63) \qquad \theta_k = p_k + t'M_{ik}E^{-1} - t'M_{ij}E^{-1}\pi_{ij}\frac{dt_j^*}{dZ_k} = p_1 g_{Z_k}$$

There are now two necessary adjustments to p_k, the private opportunity costs, to obtain the full social opportunity costs of Z_k. The first is the additional deadweight loss as tax revenues adjust directly to the change in Z_k, measured at constant tax rates, the same effect as above. The second is the additional deadweight loss due to the required increase in t_j in order to maintain budgetary balance. Since marginal changes in different Z's will affect the budget equation differently, this second source of additional burden is, in general, unique to each Z. Quite obviously, governments are going to have a most difficult time computing these optimal shadow taxes, unless the distorting taxes are optimal, or technology is linear. As we have seen, in either of these cases the optimal shadow prices are just the p_k. Moreover, using p_k implies that the government's budget constraint will necessarily hold, since if $p_1 g_{Z_k} = p_k$,

$$(22.64) \qquad -p_1 g_{Z_k} dZ_k + p_k dZ_k = 0 \qquad k = 2, \dots, N$$

$$(22.65) \qquad -p_1 dZ_1 + p_k dZ_k = 0 \qquad k = 2, \dots, N$$

SECOND-BEST PRODUCTION RULES WHEN
EQUITY MATTERS

Assuming a one-consumer-equivalent economy in second-best analysis is always somewhat contradictory. Unless consumers' tastes are severely restricted, one-consumer equivalence implies that the government is optimally redistributing income lump sum in accordance with the first-best interpersonal equity conditions, thereby equilibrating social marginal utilities of income. But if the government can do this, why would it ever have to use distorting taxes? It is far more natural in a second-best framework to deny the existence of optimal income redistribution and assume explicitly that social marginal utilities of income are unequal. This means, however, that the optimal shadow prices for government production decisions will depend upon both efficiency and equity considerations, just as the many-person optimal tax and nonexclusive goods decision rules were seen to incorporate both efficiency and equity terms. And, as we noted when discussing those problems, this is doubly discouraging for policy purposes. Not only are optimal shadow prices further complicated by the addition of equity terms but society may well not agree on the proper equity weights for each individual. Thus, the analysis runs the risk of becoming totally subjective, since different sets of ethical weights will imply different optimal shadow prices. Nonetheless, if society can agree on a ranking of social marginal utilities of income, a big if, then the proper shadow prices for government production can be determined. Moreover, the shadow prices can be expressed as a simple combination of distinct equity and efficiency effects, at least for the particular government production decisions and second-best distortions being considered in this chapter.

Recall that analyzing a many-person economy with a nonoptimal income distribution requires a social welfare orientation, because there is no unambiguously defined aggregate loss function. As in the previous many-person problems, a natural choice for the objective function is the individualistic Bergson-Samuelson social welfare function whose arguments are the individuals' indirect utility functions defined over all consumer prices and lump-sum income. Once this objective function is chosen, the analysis occurs with respect to actual and not compensated equilibria. However, in order to relate the many-person results as closely as possible to the one-person rules, we will assume away all sources of lump-sum income by requiring that private production exhibits *CRS*, the government budget exactly balances, and all factor supplies are variable. These assumptions also greatly simplify the analysis, while capturing the flavor of many-person second-best analysis.[9]

The government's objective function, then, is:

$$(22.66) \qquad W = W[V^h(\vec{q})] = V(\vec{q})$$

---

[9] With only minor changes, the analysis of this section is taken directly from Boadway, "Integrating Equity and Efficiency in Applied Welfare Economics."

Differentiating totally

$$(22.67) \qquad dW = \sum_{h=1}^{H} \sum_{i=1}^{N} \frac{\partial W}{\partial V^h} \frac{\partial V^h}{\partial q_i} dq_i = - \sum_{h=1}^{H} \sum_{i=1}^{N} \beta^h X_{hi} dq_i$$

from Roy's theorem and the definition of an individual's social marginal utility of income $\beta^h = (\partial W/\partial V^h)\alpha^h$, where α^h = the private marginal utility of income for person h. It will be convenient to express the change in social welfare in terms of Feldstein's distributional coefficient of X:

$$(22.68) \qquad R_i = \sum_{h=1}^{H} \beta^h \frac{X_{hi}}{X_i} \qquad i = 1, \ldots, N$$

in order to work with aggregate consumption.[10] Substituting (22.68) into (22.67) yields:

$$(22.69) \qquad dW = - \sum_{i=1}^{N} R_i X_i dq_i$$

The problem is to define dW in terms of the government control variables $\vec{t} = (t_2, \ldots, t_N)$ and $\vec{Z} = (Z_1, \ldots, Z_N)$, given the following constraints:

a. Private production possibilities, $F(Y_1, \ldots, Y_N) = 0$, assumed to exhibit CRS.
b. The government production function, $G(Z_1, \ldots, Z_N) = 0$, or $Z_1 = -g(Z_2, \ldots, Z_N)$, with inputs measured negatively.
c. The government budget constraint, $\sum_{i=2}^{N} t_i X_i + \sum_{i=1}^{N} p_i Z_i = 0$.
d. N market clearance relationships, $X_i(\vec{q}) = Y_i(\vec{p}) + Z_i$, $i = 1, \ldots, N$. In the actual general equilibrium, *all* markets clear.
e. $\vec{q} = \vec{p} + \vec{t}$, with $q_1 \equiv p_1 \equiv 1, t_1 \equiv 0$.

As always, the first good serves as the untaxed numeraire.

The analysis proceeds much as in the one-consumer case. Begin by totally differentiating the market clearance equations:

$$(22.70) \qquad dX_i = dY_i + dZ_i \qquad i = 1, \ldots, N$$

Multiply each equation by $q_i = (p_i + t_i)$ and sum over all N equations to obtain:

$$(22.71) \qquad \sum_{i=1}^{N} q_i dX_i = \sum_{i=1}^{N} (p_i + t_i) dY_i + \sum_{i=1}^{N} (p_i + t_i) dZ_i$$

Equation (22.71) can be simplified as follows. Totally differentiate the individual consumers' budget constraints $\sum_{i=1}^{N} q_i X_{hi} = 0$, all $h = 1, \ldots, H$, and sum over all individuals to obtain:

$$(22.72) \qquad \sum_{i=1}^{N} q_i dX_i = - \sum_{i=1}^{N} X_i dq_i$$

---

[10] M. Feldstein, "Distributional Equity and the Optimal Structure of Public Prices," *American Economic Review*, March 1972. Also, see our discussion of Feldstein's distributional coefficient in Chapter 4.

Next, differentiate the aggregate private production possibilities $F(\vec{Y}) = 0$,

$$(22.73) \qquad \sum_{i=1}^{N} F_i dY_i = 0$$

But if markets are perfectly competitive,

$$(22.74) \qquad \frac{F_i}{F_1} = \frac{p_i}{p_1} = p_i \qquad \text{with } p_1 \equiv 1, i = 2, \dots, N$$

Therefore:

$$(22.75) \qquad \sum_{i=1}^{N} F_i dY_i = 0 = F_1 \sum_{i=1}^{N} p_i dY_i$$

or

$$(22.76) \qquad \sum_{i=1}^{N} p_i dY_i = 0$$

Substituting (22.72) and (22.76) into (22.71) yields:

$$(22.77) \qquad - \sum_{i=1}^{N} X_i dq_i = \sum_{i=1}^{N} t_i dY_i + \sum_{i=1}^{N} t_i dZ_i + \sum_{i=1}^{N} p_i dZ_i$$

Using (22.70), (22.77) can be expressed as:

$$(22.78) \qquad - \sum_{i=1}^{N} X_i dq_i = \sum_{i=1}^{N} t_i dX_i + \sum_{i=1}^{\tilde{N}} p_i dZ_i$$

Substituting (22.78) into (22.69) yields:

$$(22.79) \qquad dW = - \sum_{i=1}^{N} R_i X_i dq_i + \sum_{i=1}^{N} X_i dq_i + \sum_{i=1}^{N} t_i dX_i + \sum_{i=1}^{N} p_i dZ_i$$

or

$$(22.80) \qquad dW = \sum_{i=1}^{N} (1 - R_i) X_i dq_i + \sum_{i=1}^{N} t_i dX_i + \sum_{i=1}^{N} p_i dZ_i$$

Next, incorporate the government production function, $Z_1 = -g(Z_2, \dots, Z_N)$, and note that $t_1 \equiv 0$, $dq_1 = 0$, to rewrite (22.80) as:

$$(22.81) \qquad dW = \sum_{i=2}^{N} (1 - R_i) X_i dq_i + \sum_{i=2}^{N} t_i dX_i + \sum_{i=2}^{N} (-p_1 g_{Z_i} + p_i) dZ_i$$

In order to eliminate the dX_i, totally differentiate the individual demand (factor supply) functions $X_{hi} = X_{hi}(\vec{q})$, $h = 1, \dots, H$, and sum over all individuals to obtain:

$$(22.82) \qquad dX_i = \sum_{j=2}^{N} \frac{\partial X_i}{\partial q_j} dq_j \qquad i = 1, \dots, N$$

Substituting (22.82) into (22.81), and rearranging terms yields:

$$(22.83) \quad dW = \sum_{i=2}^{N} \sum_{j=2}^{N} \left[(1 - R_i)X_i + t_j \frac{\partial X_j}{\partial q_i} \right] dq_i + \sum_{i=2}^{N} (-p_1 g_{Z_i} + p_i) dZ_i$$

Finally, utilize the market clearance equations:

$$(22.84) \qquad X_i(\vec{q}) = Y_i(\vec{q} - \vec{t}) + Z_i \qquad i = 1, \ldots, N$$

to express dq_i in terms of the control variables dt_i and dZ_i, as follows. From Walras' law only $(N - 1)$ of these relationships are independent. Since good 1 is the numeraire, eliminate the first equation and totally differentiate equations $2, \ldots, N$ to obtain:

$$(22.85) \qquad \sum_{j=2}^{N} \frac{\partial X_i}{\partial q_j} dq_j = \sum_{j=2}^{N} \frac{\partial Y_i}{\partial p_j} dq_j - \sum_{j=2}^{N} \frac{\partial Y_i}{\partial p_j} dt_j + dZ_i$$

$$i = 2, \ldots, N$$

Writing all $(N - 1)$ equations in matrix notation:

$$(22.86) \qquad \left(\frac{\partial X}{\partial q} \right) dq = \left(\frac{\partial Y}{\partial p} \right) dq - \left(\frac{\partial Y}{\partial p} \right) dt + dZ$$

(All matrices have dimension $(N - 1) \times (N - 1)$; all vectors have dimension $((N - 1) \times 1)$.) Solving (22.86) for dq yields:

$$(22.87) \qquad dq = E^{-1} \left[-dt' \left(\frac{\partial Y}{\partial p} \right) + dZ \right]$$

where:

$$E = \left[\left(\frac{\partial X}{\partial q} \right) - \left(\frac{\partial Y}{\partial p} \right) \right]$$

Substituting (22.87) into (22.83), rearranging terms, and writing the resulting equation in matrix notation yields:

$$(22.88) \quad dW = -\left[[(1 - R)' \cdot X]' + t' \frac{\partial X}{\partial q} \right] E^{-1} \left(\frac{\partial Y}{\partial p} \right) dt$$

$$+ \left[[(1 - R)' \cdot X]' E^{-1} + t' \frac{\partial X}{\partial q} E^{-1} - p_1 g_Z + p' \right] dZ$$

Equation (22.88) gives the change in social welfare for any given (marginal) changes in the government control variables, evaluated at the existing levels of the t's and Z's. Notice that if the distribution of income were optimal so that $\beta^h = \beta$, all $h = 1, \ldots, H$, then $R_i = \sum_{h=1}^{N} \beta_h X_{hi}/X_i = \beta$, all $i = 1, \ldots, N$, the common social marginal utility of income. Since W can be defined such that

$\beta = 1$, by setting $\partial W/\partial V^h = 1/\alpha^h$, all $h = 1, \ldots, H$, dW simplifies to:

$$(22.89) \quad dW|_{\beta^h = \beta = 1} = -\left(t'\frac{\partial X}{\partial q}\right)E^{-1}\left(\frac{\partial Y}{\partial p}\right)dt + \left[t'\left(\frac{\partial X}{\partial q}\right)E^{-1} - p_1 g_Z + p'\right]dZ$$

But equation (22.89) is identical to equation (22.46), with $dW|_{\beta^h = \beta = 1} = -dL$, $(\partial X/\partial q) = M_{ij}$, and $(\partial Y/\partial p) = \pi_{ij}$. Since equation (22.46) captures all the efficiency implications of distorting taxation, equation (22.88) can be viewed as a simple linear combination of the efficiency and equity effects of tax distortion, where the latter are embodied in the coefficients $[(1 - R)' \cdot X]'E^{-1}(\partial Y/\partial p)$ for changes in tax rates, and $[(1 - R)' \cdot X]'E^{-1}$ for changes in the government production variables. Thus, if the government were able to approximate the efficiency effects of the tax distortions, and if it could provide an acceptable set of social marginal utilities of income, adjusting tax and production decision rules for equity considerations would be a straightforward exercise. Of course, while it is nice to be able to separate the equity and efficiency effects of government policies in principle, there is still no reason to suppose that the government will be able to find an acceptable set of distributional coefficients R_i, much less compute the efficiency distortions with any confidence.

What is worse, the full social costs (benefits) for public sector inputs and outputs in a many-person environment will generally consist of the coefficients on (some of) the dt terms as well as the coefficients on the appropriate dZ terms. For, suppose the government increases its purchase of input Z_k, thereby increasing production of Z_1 through g_{Z_k}. It is tempting to conclude that the social cost for Z_k is p_k plus the appropriate terms in $[[(1 - R) \cdot X]'E^{-1} + t'(\partial X/\partial q)E^{-1}]$, to be equated to $p_1 g_{Z_k}$, the value of marginal product for Z_k. But this ignores the fact that the government's budget must remain in balance. When computing the dq as functions of dt and dZ in equation (22.86), we invoked Walras' law to eliminate the market clearance equation for good 1. But the N market clearance equations are dependent only if all consumers are on their budget constraints, all firms are maximizing profits, *and* the government budget always remains in balance. Thus, although the government budget constraint was never explicitly mentioned in deriving the expression for dW, the solution for dq in equation (22.86) and dX_i in equation (22.82) implicitly assumed that it holds, since lump-sum income was held constant. Therefore, any policy experiments evaluated with equation (22.88) must be consistent with the government's budget constraint. However, if the government follows the optimal shadow price for Z_k derived above, the budget will surely not remain in balance, since this would require $p_1 g_{Z_k} = p_k$, or $p_1 dZ_1 = p_k dZ_k$. In general, then, the government will also have to vary at least one of the tax rates to maintain budgetary balance, in which case the full social costs price of Z_k will contain terms of the form

$$\left[[(1 - R)' \cdot X]' + t'\frac{\partial X}{\partial q}\right]E^{-1}\left(\frac{\partial Y}{\partial p}\right)\frac{dt^*}{dZ_k}$$

where dt^*/dZ_k are the tax changes necessary to keep

$$\sum_{i=2}^{N} t_i X_i + \sum_{i=1}^{N} p_i Z_i = 0^{11}$$

The only simple case for optimal shadow prices occurs when the producer prices, $\bar{p}$, are fixed, such as with linear technologies or for a small country facing perfectly elastic supplies (input demand) at world prices. With $dq = dt$, equation (22.83) becomes:

$$(22.90) \qquad dW|_{p=\bar{p}} = \sum_{i=2}^{N} \sum_{j=2}^{N} \left[(1 - R_i)X_i + t_j \frac{\partial X_j}{\partial q_i} \right] dt_i$$

$$+ \sum_{i=2}^{N} (-p_1 g_{Z_i} + p_k) dZ_i$$

The optimal shadow prices are just the private sector or producer prices p_k, exactly as in the one-consumer (equivalent) economy. With perfectly elastic supplies (input demands), changes in government production variables will not change consumer prices. Therefore, they will have no equity effects, and no efficiency implications other than the requirement that government producers do just as well as the private opportunity costs reflected in the p_k. Furthermore, as noted in the preceding sections, with $p_1 g_{Z_k} = p_k$, or $p_1 dZ_1 = p_k dZ_k$, all $k = 2, \ldots, N$, marginal changes in government production are always self-financing so that the government's budget constraint will automatically be satisfied.

CONCLUSION

Equation (22.88) provides a fairly comprehensive guideline for government decision making. The many-person problem considered above imposes no restrictions on the form of the government production function and allows the government to tax all goods and factors. Furthermore, the analysis of Chapter 17 showed that it makes no difference whether distorting taxes are levied on producers or consumers. Finally, equation (22.88) holds at the existing values of all government tax and production control variables.

It is important to realize, however, that the analysis is not fully general. There are, for example, no externalities arising from the government's activity, private production is assumed to be perfectly competitive and exhibit CRS, and the government is free to vary all price-cost margins. Changes in any or all of these assumptions can be expected to alter the implied optimal shadow prices for public production. Nonetheless, we will refer to equation (22.88) in the discussion of cost-benefit analysis in Part IV as representative of a large portion of existing second-best public expenditure theory.

---

[11] If many Z's change it is possible for the budget to remain in balance without changing taxes, but unlikely.

REFERENCES

Boadway, R.   "Cost-Benefit Rules and General Equilibrium." *Review of Economic Studies,* July 1975.

————.   "Integrating Equity and Efficiency in Applied Welfare Economics." *Quarterly Journal of Economics,* November 1976.

Diamond, P. A., and Mirrlees, J.   "Optimal Taxation and Public Production" (2 parts, "Part I: Production Efficiency," "Part II: Tax Rules"). *American Economic Review,* March, June 1971.

Feldstein, M.   "Distributional Equity and the Optimal Structure of Public Prices." *American Economic Review,* March 1972.

IV

Cost- benefit analysis

23

Introduction—the issues of cost-benefit analysis

Cost-benefit analysis is the practitioner's art, the application of normative public sector theory to an imperfect world which does not conform to the underlying assumptions of any one theoretical model. Strictly speaking, it refers to the systematic evaluation of government *investment* projects, as distinguished from transfer programs or consumption-oriented allocational expenditures such as judicial services.

What criteria should the government employ to determine whether or not a particular investment project is worthwhile? If funds are limited for some reason, which of a number of worthwhile projects should be chosen? How can the government compare investments meant to serve very different functions, for example, building a new highway versus subsidizing private manpower development training programs? Practical questions such as these are the substance of cost-benefit analysis. They often tend not to have clear-cut answers, but at very least attempts to answer them should recognize three fundamental principles.

THREE PRINCIPLES OF COST-BENEFIT ANALYSIS

The first principle merely reaffirms the notion that cost-benefit analysis is as much an art as a science, for which the rule of reason is every bit as important as strict analytical rigor. Our theoretical knowledge on project costs and benefits comes from two sources, first-best models in which all markets are perfectly competitive and government policy responses to particular problems are totally unrestricted, and second-best models which, to date at least, have taken only the smallest steps toward the myriad of real-world imperfections and complexities. Second-best theory has also shown us just how sensitive normative policy prescriptions are to both the number and substance of restrictions added to the basic first-best general equilibrium framework. Consequently, analytical rigor cannot be the sole arbiter in practical policy deliberations. At best these theoretical models provide a consistent analytical framework for thinking about practical problems, with their results serving as guidelines to the policymaker.

The essence of any cost-benefit study derives from the assumptions it chooses. To this end, the most important prior consideration is whether or not first-best assumptions are reasonable for analyzing a given investment project, and, if not, what specific second-best assumptions are appropriate to the analysis. As might be expected, using the first-best assumptions tends to simplify the analysis in most instances, but there is no sense using them if they are clearly unreasonable. To give but one example, can the policymaker reasonably assume that the distribution of income is (approximately) optimal? The answer to this one question is central to the analysis of a whole host of practical issues.

One of the main goals of Part IV will be to indicate how the choice between first- and second-best assumptions dictates the approach to each of the practical problems being considered. For the most part we will simply be recalling theoretical results from Parts II and III and reflecting upon their application to specific problems. In our view it makes little sense to push forward with new second-best models unless absolutely necessary, especially since no new second-best theoretical model will capture all elements of reality in any event. Of course, no such problem arises if the first-best assumptions are deemed appropriate because first-best theory offers a single, well-defined set of policy guidelines for any given problem. There is only one possible set of first-best assumptions.

The second principle is that a cost-benefit analysis of government investments proceeds exactly as the analysis of private investments undertaken by individual firms. In either case the basic analytical tool is the present value formula, which is necessary to render all benefits and costs commensurate over time. Let the present value of a government project be defined as:

$$(23.1) \qquad PV = -I_0 + \sum_{n=1}^{N} \frac{R_n}{(1 + r)^n}$$

where:

PV = the present value of the investment,
I_0 = initial investments costs,
R_n = a measure of net benefits (benefits − costs) in period n,
r = the appropriate rate of discount (assumed constant over time),
N = the endpoint of the planning horizon,

exactly as for private sector investments. The same decision rules apply for the government as well:

a. The government should accept all investments, and only those investments, that have a positive present value. This is the meaning of a "worthwhile" project.[1]

b. If funds are limited for some reason, the goal is to select the subset of projects that maximizes aggregate present value subject to the budget constraint. The solution to this problem requires programming techniques and may leave some of the funds unexpended, depending on the size of each individual project.

---

[1] If a subset of these investments contains mutually exclusive projects, the project with the highest present value within the subset should be chosen.

Ideally, the government should subject all potential investments to these present value tests regardless of function or purpose.

The present value formula (23.1) represents an addition to the theoretical tools developed in Parts II and III, which ignored the investment aspect of government expenditures entirely by adopting a one-period, static general equilibrium framework. But it is only a trivial addition in and of itself. Our previous models can easily be modified to incorporate government investments by appropriately time subscripting all variables and writing all budget constraints (profit functions) in present value form.

The underlying analytical framework for cost-benefit analysis, then, is perfectly straightforward. Its interest lies in developing reasonable guidelines for quantifying each element in the present value formula. The same can also be said of private investment analysis.

The final principle is that cost-benefit analysis assumes a fully employed economy, unless specifically stated otherwise. Thus, it is meant as an exercise in microeconomic analysis, designed to help governments select among alternative uses of scarce resources. One immediate implication of the full-employment assumption is that government investment projects not only compete directly among themselves for scarce resources. Each one must also dominate all alternative private sector uses of the same scarce resources to be deemed worthwhile.

The formal structures of public sector cost-benefit and private sector investment analysis may be identical, but the former is ultimately more difficult and, in many ways, more subjective than the latter. Broadly speaking, the differences between them in application center around the point that market prices do not always reflect marginal *social* values, a fact that the private sector typically ignores but the government cannot. Indeed, the very name "cost-benefit" analysis suggests that government project evaluation goes well beyond the straight calculation of profits at current and expected future market prices and interest rates that one normally associates with private sector investment analysis. Profitability is generally not the proper criterion for selecting among alternative public sector projects.

In trying to evaluate the present value formula, government policymakers face the same class of problems that beset private investment analysts, plus another whole range of difficult issues unique to the public sector. The common issues are the choice of an appropriate rate of discount and the general problem of uncertainty. Even so, the solutions to these problems are often markedly different. Let us consider each of them briefly.

ISSUES COMMON TO COST-BENEFIT AND PRIVATE INVESTMENT ANALYSIS

The Discount Rate

By inspection of (23.1) it is obvious that choosing the proper rate of discount is crucial to any investment analysis. Using a rate that is too low (high) introduces two types of errors. On the one hand, too many (few) projects will pass the present value test. On the other hand, the present value formula will bias selection toward projects whose net returns occur later (earlier) rather than earlier (later), given equal undiscounted streams of returns. Moreover, project selection tends to be very sensitive to even small absolute errors as a general rule. Choosing a discount rate of 5 percent when the "true" rate is 10 percent or 15 percent may cause the government to choose far too many projects, especially those whose returns occur far into the future.[2]

It is well-accepted that the rate of discount for private investments should reflect the returns generally available to the owners of the firm on alternative investments of equal risk. That is to say, r defines the opportunity cost of capital for the firm.

The role of the discount rate in cost-benefit analysis is less clear-cut, however, and the subject of considerable disagreement among public sector economists. Two well-defined positions have emerged in the literature, although some economists hold neither view. One group (Harberger, Sjaastad and Wisecarver, for example)[3] argue that the rate of discount remains an opportunity cost, in this case reflecting the returns generally available in the private sector. Even so, they do not necessarily agree on a numerical value for r.

There are really two problems here. The first is a conceptual issue relating to the precise meaning of "the returns available in the private sector." Different interpretations can imply vastly different social rates of discount. Second, even when economists agree on the interpretation, they often disagree on the numerical value for r that best reflects the private sector returns.

A second group of economists (Marglin, Arrow, Feldstein, for example)[4] maintains that the discount rate in cost-benefit analysis has nothing whatsoever to do with opportunity cost. Rather it reflects the interest rate which the government deems appropriate for discounting any stream of consumption over time, commonly referred to as the social rate of time preference. According to this view, the net benefits resulting from any given project should simply be considered an addition to the stream of consumption available to society. The fact that public investment causes society to forego private consumption and investment opportunities is relevant, but is properly accounted for by applying an appropriate shadow price to the initial investment costs, I_0 (and any subsequent *cash* deficits (surpluses) that may arise throughout the life of the project).

---

[2] These generalizations ignore the problem that any one project may have multiple internal yields, defined as a rate of discount that just sets $PV = 0$. With multiple yields, a project may pass the present value test over numerous regions of r, so that applying higher (lower) rates of discount may not generate a bias against (in favor of) the project.

[3] A. C. Harberger, *Project Evaluation: Collected Papers* (Chicago: Markham Publishing Co., 1974). See also, "The Opportunity Costs of Public Investment Financed by Borrowing," in R. Layard, ed., *Cost-Benefit Analysis* (Harmondsworth, Middlesex, England: Penguin Education, Penguin Books, Ltd., 1972); and L. Sjaastad and D. Wisecarver, "The Social Cost of Public Finance," *Journal of Political Economy*, June 1977.

[4] K. J. Arrow, "Discounting and Public Investment Criteria," in A. Kneese and S. Smith, eds., *Water Resources Research* (Baltimore: 1966); M. Feldstein, "The Inadequacy of Weighted Discount Rates," in Layard, ed., *Cost-Benefit Analysis*; and S. Marglin, "The Opportunity Costs of Public Investment," *Quarterly Journal of Economics*, May 1963.

To date a full reconciliation of these conflicting positions has not been achieved. This is a matter of some importance, since the social rate of time preference is likely to be well below any rate reflecting the opportunity cost of funds in the private sector and, as noted above, present value calculations are extremely sensitive to the rate of discount chosen. These issues will be discussed at length in Chapter 24.

Uncertainty

Uncertainty is obviously a fundamental problem for any investment analysis. No one can know for sure what the stream of net benefits will be for any project, nor the appropriate rate of discount in each future time period. All such numbers will have probability distributions associated with them.

We have no intention of undertaking a detailed analysis of decision making under uncertainty in this section of the text. Parts II and III assumed perfect certainty when developing the normative theories of public expenditure and taxation, and the chapters on cost-benefit analysis will generally continue in this vein. However, Chapter 25 will present a remarkable theorem due to Arrow and Lind which shows that under fairly plausible conditions, government investment analysis can actually *ignore* uncertainty.[5] Their proof uses nothing more sophisticated than the definition of a derivative, and their results hold not only in a first-best environment but for a broad range of second-best environments as well. The Arrow-Lind theorem also provides a striking exception to the general rule that public sector investment analysis is more difficult than private sector investment analysis, for it can also be used to demonstrate that private firms will typically not be able to ignore uncertainty. For all these reasons we decided to present the Arrow-Lind theorem of public investment under uncertainty, along with a more recent note by Foldes and Rees,[6] which shows that the Arrow-Lind theorem does not hold for all possible second-best environments. Indeed, it may fail to hold in the presence of general income taxation.

PROBLEMS UNIQUE TO COST-BENEFIT ANALYSIS

Chapters 26 and 27 consider two exceedingly complex issues in cost-benefit analysis that are not likely to be of much consequence for private investment analysis. Chapter 26 analyzes a broad set of measurement problems relating to both costs and benefits that arise whenever market prices do not reflect marginal social values. Chapter 27 then considers a number of issues relating to the distribution of project costs and benefits.

---

[5] K. J. Arrow and R. C. Lind, "Uncertainty and the Evaluation of Public Investment Decisions," *American Economic Review*, June 1970.

[6] L. P. Foldes and R. Rees, "A Note on the Arrow-Lind Theorem," *American Economic Review*, March 1977.

Measurement Problems

The most common measurement problems associated with government projects can be grouped into four broad categories: intangibles, lumpiness, resources or services that are either drafted or given away, and the computation of shadow prices for government inputs and outputs. As a practical matter, resolving any one of them will necessarily involve large doses of judgment and common sense, with theoretical analysis offering only broad guidelines to the policymaker.

Intangibles are costs or benefits that are impossible to evaluate in dollar terms, such as the "national security" derived from a particular weapons system. Private industry may occasionally consider intangibles such as "goodwill" in its investment analysis, but such items are bound to be peripheral. By and large, projects will be accepted or rejected on more objective, and measurable, grounds, such as the investment's expected profitability or its projected effect on the firm's market share. In contrast, both proponents and opponents of public projects often view the presence of intangibles as the decisive factor in accepting or rejecting the project. This, of course, is devastating to objective cost-benefit analysis, since the present value formula is useful only to the extent its various elements can be quantified. By the same token, however, certain legitimate benefits and costs of public projects may well be intangible. This does not render them any less relevant to the overall evaluation of the project.

Lumpiness refers to the fact that a government project may be large enough to have a significant impact on the economy, meaning that the project will change the general equilibrium vector of consumer and producer prices. For example, a hydroelectric project might significantly lower the price of electricity for an entire region of the country. Conversely, private investment analysis can usually assume that any one project is small so that it will not affect prices. The two situations are compared in Figure 23–1.

In the case of the private sector firm, its additional capacity is so small relative to the overall market that the firm's demand curve essentially remains horizontal at P_0. Thus, the benefits are simply the additional revenues at

FIGURE 23–1

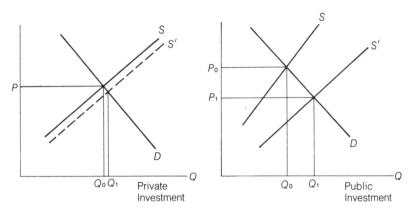

existing (and expected future) market price(s), equal to $P_0(Q_1 - Q_0)$. In the case of the public sector project, however, the supply curve shifts significantly, changing the equilibrium prices from P_0 to P_1. Normative theory may suggest that P_1 is the correct price to charge for the project's output, but if this project is being compared with other projects, there remains the problem of placing a dollar value on the benefits derived from the lower price and increased output. As it turns out, neither $P_0(Q_1 - Q_0)$ nor $P_1(Q_1 - Q_0)$, two obvious *revenue* measures, are reasonable approximations of the benefits in this market. Furthermore, if this price has changed, prices in other markets will likely change as well. As we have discovered throughout the text, public sector theory offers specific guidelines for measuring benefits and costs when prices change, but computing the appropriate measures with real-world data is almost never an easy task.

Whenever the government *commandeers resources* (e.g., military conscription) or offers *the benefits of certain projects free of charge* (e.g., flood control benefits from a hydroelectric project), two issues arise. The first concerns the propriety of setting a zero price—is it justified or not? The second concerns the method of computing costs or benefits when price is zero. Obviously the zero price by itself offers no useful information on costs or benefits. While only the second issue appears to be directly relevant to a cost-benefit study, the answer to the first question will in part determine how the benefits and costs should be evaluated. For example, suppose the price of some service is zero because the short-run marginal costs or providing the service are zero. In this case, the zero price is consistent with first-best pricing principles and the analyst could choose to evaluate the benefits using first-best assumptions. If marginal costs differ from zero, however, the analytical framework must necessarily be second best. In formal terms, setting the price equal to zero acts as a binding constraint on the range of possible government policy responses, and this (additional) constraint must be incorporated into the analysis.

The final measurement problem, establishing appropriate *shadow* prices for government inputs and outputs, is a catchall residual category applying generally to any analysis using second-best assumptions. The theoretical analysis in Chapters 21 and 22 showed that if there are market imperfections throughout the economy or if government policy responses are constrained in any way, such as by the use of distorting taxes to finance government projects, then the evaluation of costs and benefits generally requires the computation of shadow prices which differ from observed market prices. Once again, the nature of the second-best restrictions will determine exactly how the shadow prices are to be computed, so that a cost-benefit study employing second-best assumptions must carefully specify the assumed policy environment. Unfortunately, for most real-world situations the information required to compute these shadow prices is difficult, if not impossible, to obtain. This helps explain the enormous appeal of first-best assumptions in cost-benefit analysis, despite the fact that they are often not terribly realistic. In a first-best environment, observed market prices are the basic data for all benefit and opportunity cost measures.

The Distribution of Income

The distribution question is certainly unique to the evaluation of government projects. Private investment analysis quite properly ignores the fact that profits from its investments will accrue to the firm's owners in proportion to the distribution of ownership rights. Its only concern is determining the aggregate present value for each project.

Governments, on the other hand, are concerned with the equity implications of their policy actions. Consequently, the present value of the aggregate benefits and costs, which can be taken as an indicator of the efficiency of a project, may well be an incomplete measure of the project's contribution to social welfare. The government would presumably be justified in selecting a project with lower present value over another project with higher present value on the basis of a superior distribution of the discounted benefits and costs. Given that all distributional evaluations are inherently subjective, this is an extremely uncomfortable possibility. The whole purpose of cost-benefit analysis is to provide the policymaker with objective measures of project costs and benefits, which can then be applied consistently to all government investments. But if the distribution of costs and benefits matters, complete objectivity is virtually impossible to maintain. Consequently, many cost-benefit studies ignore distributional considerations entirely. Of course, ignoring the distributional problem does not solve it. It merely consigns to cost-benefit analysis the more modest task of determining the relative efficiency of government projects, rather than ranking projects according to their contributions to social welfare. Perhaps this is all cost-benefit analysis can hope to achieve.

Chapter 27 explores two fundamental questions relating to the distribution of costs and benefits. First, under what conditions can the distribution question safely be ignored in cost-benefit analysis? Second, if these conditions do not exist, how should distributional considerations enter into the analysis? With respect to the second question, we will consider two different methods of incorporating distributional parameters that have been suggested in the literature. Unfortunately, neither avoids the problem of subjectivity. Using either method, one can always design a set of subjective distributional weights that will overwhelm whatever objective efficiency information a cost-benefit study might contain.

PITFALLS IN COST-BENEFIT ANALYSIS

Chapter 28 will conclude Part IV by discussing a number of common pitfalls in cost-benefit analysis. It may seem odd to spend time on false claims, but the sad truth is that public debate on government projects all too often focuses on irrelevancies and misconceptions. Furthermore, people tend to repeat the same mistakes over and over again. Ronald McKean has labeled these errors "secondary benefits" (costs), implying that people find new sources of benefits (costs) to add to the true benefits (costs) in order to make the project seem all the more attractive (unattractive).[7] What is worse, these secondary or bogus benefits (costs) can be many times greater than the project's true benefits (costs). We will consider five of the most common pitfalls:

a. *The chain-reaction game*—in which profits (losses) generated throughout the economy are indiscriminately attached to the benefits (costs) of the project.
b. *The regional multiplier game*—in which Keynesian-type multipliers are used to enhance the benefits (costs) of the project.
c. *The labor game*—a variation of (a) and (b) in which the employment effects of the project are viewed as one of its major benefits, perhaps even the principal benefit.
d. *Double counting*—in which the same benefits (costs) appear twice in the analysis.
e. *The public sector bias charge*—which says that public investments have an unfair advantage over private investments because they do not have to make a profit. Hence, it is intended as an additional implicit cost for all government projects.

Many of these items contain the proverbial germ of truth, but they are misused to the point of being totally misleading. Hence, it seemed fitting to conclude Part IV with a fair warning of these practices. They may arise because the public simply misunderstands the nature of true costs and benefits, but it is easy to be skeptical. Partisans always stand ready to exploit them for their own ends.

CONCLUSION

Chapters 24–28 do not pretend to be an exhaustive treatise on cost-benefit analysis. Many excellent books, filled with detailed and illustrative examples, have already been written on the subject.[8] Rather, these chapters are meant to highlight the major problems that the policy analyst is likely to encounter when evaluating a project, and indicate the extent to which public sector theory can help resolve them. In our view, if a cost-benefit analysis pays close attention to the issues raised in Chapters 24–27 and the theory underlying them, and avoids the pitfalls discussed in Chapter 28, it will serve to enlighten public policy discussions. The inverse is equally true.

---

[7] R. N. McKean, *Efficiency of Government through Systems Analysis* (New York: John Wiley & Sons, Inc., 1958), chaps, 8 and 9.

[8] We would especially recommend any of the following:

Layard, *Cost-Benefit Analysis*. A thoroughly excellent choice of readings on all aspects of cost-benefit analysis.

McKean, *Efficiency of Government*.

E. J. Mishan, *Cost Benefit Analysis*, new and expanded edition (New York: Praeger Publishers, 1976). Comprehensive, but at times unconventional. Excellent references throughout.

E. Stokey and R. Zeckhauser, *A Primer for Policy Analysis* (New York: W. W. Norton & Co. Inc., 1978). Not strictly a treatise on cost-benefit analysis but an excellent methods-tools text.

J. N. Wolfe, ed., *Cost-Benefit and Cost-Effectiveness: Studies and Analysis* (London: George Allen & Unwin, Ltd., 1973).

REFERENCES

Arrow, K. J. "Discounting and Public Investment Criteria." In *Water Resources Research,* edited by A. Kneese and S. Smith, Baltimore, 1966.

————, and Lind, R. C. "Uncertainty and the Evaluation of Public Investment Decisions." *American Economic Review,* June 1970.

Feldstein, M. "The Inadequacy of Weighted Discount Rates." In *Cost-Benefit Analysis,* edited by R. Layard, Harmondsworth, Middlesex, England: Penguin Education, Penguin Books, Ltd., 1972.

Foldes, L. P., and Rees, R. "A Note on the Arrow-Lind Theorem." *American Economic Review,* March 1977.

Harberger, A. C. *Project Evaluation: Collected Papers.* Chicago: Markham Publishing Co., 1974.

————. "The Opportunity Costs of Public Investment Financed by Borrowing." In *Cost-Benefit Analysis,* edited by R. Layard. Harmondsworth, Middlesex, England: Penguin Education, Penguin Books Ltd., 1972.

Layard, R., ed. *Cost-Benefit Analysis.* Harmondsworth, Middlesex, England: Penguin Education, Penguin Books, Ltd., 1972.

Marglin, S. "The Opportunity Costs of Public Investment." *Quarterly Journal of Economics,* May 1963.

McKean, R. *Efficiency of Government through Systems Analysis.* New York: John Wiley & Sons, Inc., 1958.

Mishan, E. J. *Cost-Benefit Analysis.* New and expanded edition. New York: Praeger Publishers, 1976.

Stokey, E., and Zeckhauser, R. *A Primer for Policy Analysis.* New York: W. W. Norton & Co., Inc., 1978.

Sjaastad, L., and Wisecarver, D. "The Social Cost of Public Finance." *Journal of Political Economy,* June 1977.

Wolfe, J. N., ed. *Cost-Benefit and Cost-Effectiveness: Studies and Analysis.* London: George Allen & Unwin, Ltd., 1973.

24

The rate of discount for public investments

What rate of discount should the government use for computing the present values of various investment alternatives? As indicated in Chapter 23, this question has stirred considerable debate among public sector economists, one which goes far beyond attaching a particular numerical value to the rate of discount. There is a fundamental conceptual disagreement over exactly what the discount rate is meant to represent.

Roughly speaking, the division within the profession is threefold. One group, following Harberger,[1] believes that the rate of discount for public projects ought to reflect the opportunity cost of public funds, much as the discount rate for private investments measures the opportunity cost of capital to the firm. A second group, following Marglin and Feldstein,[2] argues that the discount rate, per se, has nothing whatsoever to do with opportunity cost. It simply reflects society's rate of time preference, the social marginal rate of substitution between the present and future. The opportunity cost of public funds is relevant, but is properly accounted for by means of a separate shadow price applied directly to these funds. It is not relevant for discounting a future stream of net benefits. A final group remains eclectic (e.g., Diamond, McKean),[3] arguing that it is pointless to associate the rate of discount with any one concept such as opportunity cost or time preference. Rather, the rate of discount is simply another shadow price among many in a second-best environment that will depend, as do all shadow prices, on the structure of that environment. Under some assumptions the appropriate discount rate will appear to represent the opportunity cost of public funds, under different assumptions, society's rate of time preference. Yet it is always possible to describe reasonable assumptions under which there is no obvious relationship between the discount rate and either concept. On strictly theoretical grounds the eclectic view is unassailable,

---

[1] A. C. Harberger, *Project Evaluation: Collected Papers* (Chicago: Markham Publishing Co., 1974). Also, "The Opportunity Costs of Public Investment Financed by Borrowing," in R. Layard, ed., *Cost-Benefit Analysis* (Harmondsworth, Middlesex, England: Penguin Education, Penguin Books, Ltd., 1972).

[2] M. Feldstein, "The Inadequacy of Weighted Discount Rates," in Layard, ed., *Cost-Benefit Analysis*; and S. Marglin, "The Opportunity Costs of Public Investment," *Quarterly Journal of Economics*, May 1963.

[3] P. Diamond, "The Opportunity Costs of Public Investment: Comment," *Quarterly Journal of Economics*, November 1968; and R. N. McKean, "Tax Wedges and Cost-Benefit Analysis," *Journal of Public Economics*, February 1974.

but it bears reemphasizing that most issues in cost-benefit analysis cannot be decided by appealing strictly to theoretical notions. Ultimately governments must choose some rate of discount to apply consistently to all projects. Proponents in each of the first two groups would undoubtedly concede the theoretical point that the appropriate rate of discount is model sensitive. Nonetheless, they argue that their principles offer reasonable guidelines for real-world policy evaluation.

Despite their differences of opinion, virtually all public sector economists agree that the present value of government projects depends crucially upon three factors: (a) the opportunity cost of public funds, (b) the degree to which the net benefits of government projects are reinvested or consumed, and (c) society's rate of time preference. This disagreement arises over the emphasis placed on each of these factors, and their precise role in the present value formula.

In order to bring some structure to the description of the controversy, we will begin with an intuitive discussion of these common factors. We will then consider what the theoretical models of public expenditure and tax theory developed in Parts II and III can tell us about the rate of discount. It turns out that they do not settle the debate, by any stretch of the imagination. Therefore, we will conclude the chapter with an alternative model developed by Bradford that is specifically designed to highlight the three factors listed above, and use it as a vehicle for comparing some of the conflicting views on the appropriate rate of discount.

THREE FACTORS RELEVANT TO PRESENT VALUE CALCULATIONS

The Opportunity Cost of Public Funds

Given the full employment assumption, there is no question that bringing resources into the public sector for investment projects entails an opportunity cost, equal to the value of those resources if left in the private sector. What public sector economists cannot agree upon is how the present value formula should account for these opportunity costs. In particular, should they affect the rate of discount, or simply be reflected in the initial investment costs, I_0 in equation (23.1) (and any subsequent cash deficits that may arise). Regardless of one's view on this issue, there remains the important question of how to evaluate these opportunity costs. At this point in the chapter we will only consider the latter question.

The major conceptual problem in evaluating the opportunity cost of public funds is that there are two natural claimants of scarce resources in the private sector, private consumption and private investment. This can be seen directly by returning to the first principles of national income accounting and writing:

$$(24.1) \qquad Y = C + I + G \qquad \text{(ignoring the foreign sector)}$$

Assuming full employment, and differentiating:

(24.2) $$dY_{FE} = 0 = dC + dI + dG$$

or

(24.3) $$1 = -\frac{dC}{dG} - \frac{dI}{dG}$$

Clearly, an extra dollar of government spending, in this case government investment, implies either a dollar decrease in consumption spending, or a dollar decrease in private investment spending, or some combination of the two adding to one dollar. Consequently, the opportunity cost of public funds must be a combination of at least three factors: (a) a rate of return that reflects the opportunity costs of consumption, (b) a rate of return that reflects the opportunity costs of private investment, and (c) the proportion in which an extra dollar of government investment comes at the expense of consumption and private investment.

The Marginal Rate of Substitution

To the extent government investment comes at the expense of private consumption, the government is, in effect, forcing consumers to save now in exchange for a specific stream of future consumption in the form of the net benefits from the government investment. Conceptually, then, we seek a rate of return sufficient to induce consumers to save now for future consumption. For any one consumer this is simply the (private) marginal rate of substitution between present and future consumption, which we will assume is constant over time. For purposes of illustration, suppose a consumer has an initial endowment Y which he will convert to a stream of consumption over his lifetime.[4] A utility-maximizing consumer will solve the following problem:

$$\max_{(C_t)} U(C_1, \ldots, C_t, \ldots, C_N)$$

$$\text{s.t.} \quad \sum_{t=1}^{N} \frac{C_t}{(1 + r_C)^t} = Y$$

where:

C_t = consumption at time t.

Y = initial endowment income.

r_C = the one-period rate of return on savings, assumed constant over time.

N = the last year of life.

---

[4] The example assumes no final bequest, although this is easily accounted for by adding one more time period, the year after death. We are also assuming no borrowing, and that the undiscounted price of the consumer good equals unity.

For any two consecutive periods, the first-order conditions imply:

(24.4)
$$\frac{U_{C_t}}{U_{C_{t+1}}} \equiv MRS_{C_t, C_{t+1}} = 1 + r_c$$

Graphically, the consumer would be at point A in Figure 24–1, with the slope of the budget line equal to $(1 + r_c)$. The relevant point for public investment analysis is that if the government is going to force a (marginal) reduction in C_t to finance a government project, say, by means of taxation, the project should guarantee the consumer at least $(1 + r_c)$ units of consumption next period to compensate for each unit of C_t.

The analysis is straightforward enough, but selecting a single number from observable data to represent the marginal rate of substitution between present and future consumption is extremely difficult. There are hundreds of different savings instruments, each with a specific array of characteristics, such as function, liquidity, return, risk, term to maturity, and so forth. There are millions of consumers, each with his own set of preferences. Actually, the large number of consumers would not matter so much except that various capital market imperfections force different groups of consumers into vastly different savings opportunity sets. Generally speaking, large-income savers tend to have more options than small-income savers because of minimum purchase requirements in many financial markets, and greater access to borrowed funds. Moreover, consumers face varying marginal income tax rates so that different consumers receive different effective returns on any given asset. Finally, some consumers, especially the poor, do not save at all. In order to protect their interests, the government must presumably finance only projects which exceed the net-of-tax returns available to these people if it is going to ask them to forego current consumption for future benefits. Ideally, one would want some weighted average of returns available to various subgroups of consumers.

Despite these difficulties, there does appear to be a consensus among public sector economists that relatively small rates of return, in the 3–6 percent range, accurately reflect consumers' marginal rate of substitution between present and

FIGURE 24–1

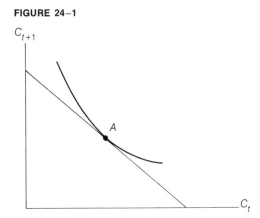

FIGURE 24–2

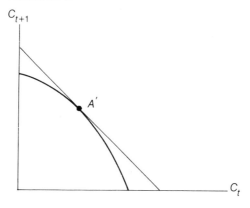

future consumption in the United States.[5] These are meant to be real rates of return, net of the expected rate of inflation. If there is an expected rate of inflation, e, the discount factor would simply be multiplied by $(1 + e)$. However, the stream of returns would presumably be adjusted by the expected rate of inflation as well, so for purposes of this discussion it does not really matter if we consider present value in nominal or real terms. The 3–6 percent rates are also meant to reflect *net-of-tax returns* on assets, since the aftertax return is the relevant parameter for consumers' savings decisions.

The Marginal Rate of Transformation

To the extent government investment comes at the expense of private investment, society is foregoing the productivity of the private investment alternatives. In line with the consumer example, think of competitive private sector producers transforming current consumption into future consumption by means of an aggregate production function

(24.5) $$F(C_1, \ldots, C_t, \ldots, C_N) = 0$$

in order to maximize the present value of profits, $\sum_{t=1}^{N} P_t/(1 + r_P)^t \cdot C_t$, where r_P = the opportunity cost of capital to the firm. For any two consecutive periods the first-order conditions imply:

(24.6) $$\frac{F_{C_t}}{F_{C_{t+1}}} \equiv MRT_{C_t, C_{t+1}} = \frac{P_t}{P_{t+1}} = 1 + r_P$$

The equilibrium condition (24.6) is depicted as point A' in Figure 24–2. Hence, r_P equals the one-period rate of return, or productivity, of private investment on the margin.

Selecting a single number to represent the marginal productivity of private sector investment is every bit as difficult as selecting a representative marginal rate of substitution, given that there are thousands of business firms in the United States, each one with its own distinct set of investment alternatives,

---

[5] We have never seen an estimate outside this range.

subject to varying degrees of risk and earning quite different rates of return. One can only be confident of two points. First, the measure of a firm's productivity is its *gross-of-tax return* on investment. By taxing these returns the government is merely sharing in the distribution of the benefits. Second, returns to capital are fairly heavily taxed in the United States. Corporate returns are taxed twice, first by the federal (and some state) corporate income taxes and again by federal (and some state and local) personal income taxes as they are distributed.[6] Moreover, the tax rates are substantial. The federal corporate rate is 48 percent for most corporations, and personal income tax rates can reach 60 percent (30 percent for capital gains). Inflation introduces a further bias against income from capital (see Chapter 13 for a discussion of this point). Hence if rates of 3–6 percent are taken as reasonable estimates of the marginal rate of substitution between present and future consumption, then the private marginal rate of transformation is likely to be many times higher, in the 10–25 percent range. Estimates of private sector productivity vary considerably among public sector economists, but the majority are certainly within this range.[7]

The Consumption-Investment Mix

The wide divergence between the MRS and MRT for the United States presents a serious problem because the third factor relevant to the opportunity cost of public funds is the proportion in which increases in government investment come at the expense of consumption and private investment. Unfortunately, it is virtually impossible to determine what the mix is likely to be for any one project. For suppose one were willing to assume that each dollar of some government investment requires an additional dollar of taxes. The problem remains that there are many different kinds of taxes, each presumably implying a different consumption-investment sacrifice. Moreover, it is generally impossible to relate specific taxes to specific projects in any event. All this would hardly matter if the marginal rates of substitution and transformation were approximately equal, but with the former in the 3–6 percent range and the latter between 10 and 25 percent, the consumption-investment mix is obviously crucial.

The point takes on even more force to the extent one agrees with Harberger, et al., that the opportunity cost of funds ought to be incorporated directly into the rate of discount.[8] Lacking precise information on the consumption-investment mix, the government could make different assumptions and hope that the same projects pass and fail each time. But this is unlikely to happen.

---

[6] While unincorporated businesses escape the corporate tax, the more successful ones will be subjected to fairly high personal income tax rates.

[7] The most recent estimates we have seen place the MRS^{US} at 5 percent and the MRT^{US} at 12 percent. M. Feldstein, "Does the United States Save Too Little?" *AEA Papers and Proceedings.* February 1977, pp. 116–17.

[8] At this point, think of the rate of discount as a simple weighted average of the MRS and MRT, with the weights equal to the proportion in which government investment comes at the expense of consumption and private investment according to (24.3). This rate is the rate of discount proposed by Harberger and is the theoretically appropriate rate under certain assumptions. We will discuss these points at length further along in the chapter.

Discounting at rates varying from 3 percent to 25 percent will generally produce very different results. As discussed in Chapter 23, the lower rates will tend to favor far more investments, and those whose net benefits occur farther in the future.

Reinvestment of Project Benefits

The goal of normative public sector theory is the maximization of an individualistic social welfare function, which depends ultimately upon the consumption possibilities available to consumers over time. Viewed in these terms, the essence of public sector investment is that it changes the stream of aggregate consumption, presumably to the benefit of society. Similarly, the opportunity cost of taking scarce resources from the private sector can be thought of as the stream of aggregate consumption that would have arisen had those resources been left in the private sector. To the extent private investment is foregone, the entire stream of consumption will be altered simply by extracting resources for the initial public investment. But even so, the repercusions of public projects clearly extend beyond the original source of the funds, because the future stream of net benefits from the government investment will affect the future paths of private consumption and investment if government benefits are either substitutes for or complements to either component of private sector demand. Moreover, these future effects may well differ from the future impacts of the benefits from private investment, and these differences must also be accounted for in determining the present value of public investment.

Unfortunately, determining the private consumption and investment repercussions of project benefits is every bit as difficult as determining the consumption-investment mix of the source of funds. There are a number of problems. For example, suppose one could safely assume that the benefits from a certain project, say, a park, were in the nature of a consumption good. Even so, it remains uncertain whether such public consumption is a substitute or complement to private consumption. There is precious little econometric evidence on this score. A related problem is that the benefits from private investment are typically not so specific. They generally accrue in the form of income, out of which consumers decide either to save or consume. That is to say, the time stream of future consumption resulting from private investments will depend largely upon consumers' marginal propensity to consume (save). Yet the mpc (mps) is unlikely to be relevant for highly specific public benefits. This merely underscores the point that differential consumption effects from public and displaced private investment will almost certainly arise. Finally, we expect private firms to save in order to replace depreciated assets. Can we also expect governments to save some of the benefits from its projects in the form of capital consumption allowances, or will the public insist on consuming all the net benefits as they arise? That is clearly a difficult question, but it is reasonable to suppose that private and public sector depreciation practices differ, creating still another factor that will generate differential future consumption effects from the returns of public and private investments.

The Social Rate of Time Preference

The final issue concerns a possible divergence between consumers' private marginal rates of substitution over time and the appropriate social marginal rate of substitution over time, the so-called social rate of time preference. There is a consensus within the profession that the stream of additional *consumption* available to society as the result of a worthwhile government project ought to be discounted at the marginal rate of substitution. For instance, any formal intertemporal model of social welfare maximization would be cast in present value terms, with the maximand and all relevant constraints discounted at the marginal rate of substitution. The only source of controversy is whether this marginal rate of substitution should simply reflect the consumers' private marginal rates of substitution, or be adjusted to reflect additional social considerations. Harberger has argued the former position but he would appear to be in the minority.[9] Most economists writing in this area favor an adjusted MRS that is below the private market rate. Two arguments have been advanced in favor of the adjusted rate.

The first is a distributional point, that private individuals will tend to ignore the desires of unborn generations, whereas the government should not do so. Specifically, by ignoring future generations, the current population will tend to consume too much, leaving too little capital for the future. Hence, the argument is that the government should counteract this tendency by using a lower MRS, thereby increasing the stock of capital.

The second point in favor of a socially adjusted MRS is due to Sen and Marglin,[10] who argue that savings has a Samuelsonian public good aspect to it which the government should take into consideration, just as it would any intratemporal externality. The situation is somewhat akin to the issue of pareto-optimal redistributions discussed in Chapter 12, in that the benefits received by any one individual saving for future generations are twofold: (a) a direct benefit arising from the increased income of one's own heirs, plus (b) an external benefit arising because savings are taxed and distributed throughout the population, thereby increasing the income of others' heirs. To the extent people receive utility from the indirect effect, Sen and Marglin show a social contract in which all are forced to save for the future is generally pareto superior to the situation of privately determined savings, from the current generation's point of view. Without presenting the details, the essence of the proof is identical to that for any external economy, that subsidizing any activity generating external economies will yield net benefits otherwise unexploited by private decision making. In this instance, the subsidy consists of setting the $MRS^{soc} < MRS^{priv}$ for purposes of project evaluation.

---

[9] Harberger, *Project Evaluation: Collected Papers.*

[10] S. Marglin, "The Social Rate of Discount and the Optimal Rate of Investment," *Quarterly Journal of Economics*, February, 1963; A. Sen, "The Social Time Preference Rate in Relation to the Market Rate of Interest," Layard, ed., *Cost-Benefit Analysis*; and A. Sen, "Isolation, Assurance, and the Social Rate of Discount," *Quarterly Journal of Economics*, February, 1967.

494

FIGURE 24–3

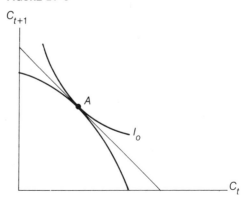

THEORETICAL CONSIDERATIONS FROM NORMATIVE PUBLIC EXPENDITURE AND TAX THEORY

Before proceeding to a model specifically designed to incorporate these three features, let us briefly consider the implications of the theoretical models of public expenditures and taxation developed in Parts II and III. It turns out they describe a number of special cases for which computing the rate of discount would be relatively straightforward, but the assumptions each time are so stringent that these results may not have much practical value. One "easy" case occurs if the economic and policy environment can reasonably be assumed to be first best. This would greatly simplify computations of the discount rate because the MRS and MRT between the present and future would be equal for investments of equal risk. Hence, the consumption-investment mix would be irrelevant. Optimal income distribution would render the economy equivalent to a one-consumer economy and, with perfect markets everywhere, the economy would reach an equilibrium such as point A in Figure 24–3, at which the common MRS just equals the common MRT. Hence, the MRS^{soc} *is* the opportunity cost of public funds, so the two major views on the rate of discount coincide.[11]

As usual, the first-best assumptions make life easy, but they are clearly inappropriate for computing the public sector rate of discount, at least in the United States and probably for all other developed market economies as well. As indicated above, the MRS and MRT are almost certainly driven far apart by the U.S. tax system. Thus, determining the proper discount rate must fall within the domain of the second best. Unfortunately, however, the second-best results developed in Part III suggest a wide range of possibilities.

---

[11] I_o in Figure 24–3 is meant to be a social indifference curve under the first-best assumption of optimal income distribution. If $MRS^{soc} < MRS^{priv}$ because of a Sen-Marglin intergenerational savings externality, the private market MRT is the proper rate of discount, not the private market MRS. At a first-best optimum, $MRS^{priv} > MRS^{soc} = MRT$.

To interpret our previous models intertemporally think of the economy as consisting of a single good produced and consumed over N time periods rather than N goods and factors in a single time period, and let the good in period N serve as the untaxed numeraire. The good can be consumed directly or used to produce additional units of the good in future periods. The maximand is the present value of social welfare, discounted at the MRS^{soc}. The consumer prices, q_j, represent the MRS^{priv} ($U_j/U_{j+1} = q_j/q_{j+1} = 1 + r_c$). Similarly, the producer prices p_j define the MRT for the competitive private sector ($f_j/f_{j+1} = p_j/p_{j+1} = 1 + r_p$). In addition, the government's production function $Z_N = -g(Z_1, \ldots, Z_{N-1})$ defines the public sector's rate of transformation over time, with $g_{z_j}/g_{z_{j+1}}$ equal to the one-period rate of discount for public projects. Finally, all budget constraints (profit functions) are satisfied in terms of present value over the entire N periods, not period by period, discounted at the MRS^{soc}. Hence, $\sum_{i=1}^{N} p_i Z_i$ refers to the present value of the government deficit, and $\sum_{i=1}^{N} t_i M_i$ the present value of (compensated) tax collections. Requiring period-by-period balance, or $t_j M_j = p_j Z_j, j = 1, \ldots, N$, would add N constraints to the models, implying entirely different tax and expenditure rules.

Given this interpretation, let us simply recall the main results from Chapter 22.

1. Surely the most striking result is the Diamond-Mirrlees theorem, which says that even if the government uses distorting taxes to finance government expenditures, the appropriate rate of discount is the private sector's MRT between present and future outputs, or the gross-of-tax producer prices for inputs. But the Diamond-Mirrlees theorem depends crucially upon two conditions: (a) private production exhibits CRS; and (b) the distorting taxes are set optimally. While the first condition may be reasonable, the second is unlikely to hold in practice, even approximately.

2. Given the same model, but assuming nonoptimal distorting taxation, equation (22.46) applies,[12] reproduced here as equation (24.7) with the numeraire changed from the first to the Nth good.

$$(24.7) \qquad dL = \left[t' \frac{\partial X}{\partial p} E^{-1} \frac{\partial Y}{\partial p} \right] dt - \left[-p_N g_Z + p' + t' \frac{\partial X}{\partial q} E^{-1} \right] dZ$$

(24.7) illustrates the important point that the government's rate of discount is simply another shadow price defined in a temporal context.[13] Thus, all the difficulties of determining optimal shadow prices discussed in Chapter 22 apply directly to the computation of the proper social rate of discount. As we discovered, there were only three relative easy cases. The first applies to the existence of optimal taxation already mentioned above. Second, if private sector production technology is linear, then the constant producer prices are the

---

[12] In order to focus on the rate of discount assume an optimal distribution of income among all living persons.

[13] See McKean, "Tax Wedges and Cost-Benefit Analysis," for further discussion of this point.

optimal shadow prices for public production. This implies discounting government investments at the private marginal rate of transformation.[14] Finally, if all cross-price derivatives over time are zero, then the rate of discount in any given period (with respect to period N) is a straight weighted average of the MRS and MRT specific to that period. Reinterpret equation (22.60) as:

$$(24.8) \qquad r_{\text{pub}}^{j} = \left(\frac{-\alpha}{1-\alpha}\right) MRT_j + \left(\frac{1}{1-\alpha}\right) MRS_j$$

where:

$$\alpha = \frac{\dfrac{\partial Y_j}{\partial p_j}}{\dfrac{\partial X_j}{\partial q_j}}$$

Y_j = private sector production (use) of the good (factor) in period j.

p_j = the producer price in period $j \equiv MRT_j \equiv f_j/f_N$.

X_j = consumption (supply) of the good (factor) in period j.

q_j = the consumer price in period $j \equiv MRS_j \equiv U_j/U_N$.

Hence, if $\partial X_j/\partial q_j = 0$, or the government's investment comes entirely at the expense of private production (investment), $r_{\text{pub}} = MRT$, as expected, and vice versa if $\partial Y_j/\partial p_j = 0$.

(24.8) is the formula recommended by Harberger. It obviously corresponds to the notion that r_{pub} should reflect the opportunity cost of extracting scarce resources from the private sector.[15]

THE BRADFORD MODEL OF THE PUBLIC SECTOR RATE OF DISCOUNT

The simplest cases from our second-best models appear to imply that the appropriate rate of discount is biased toward the private MRT, but that would be a hasty conclusion. David Bradford has recently developed a second-best model which highlights the relationship between the three factors discussed above—the opportunity cost of public funds, reinvestment of project benefits, and the social rate of time preference—and the discount rate, and which leads

---

[14] Diamond and Mirrlees later generalized this result, proving that in all private sectors exhibiting CRS production, the shadow prices must be such that profits in these sectors equal zero calculated at the shadow prices. This holds true for any vector of distorting "commodity" taxes. Their theorem implies, for example, that if there are $N - 1$ CRS industries each using one input, then the shadow prices are the market prices (the social rate of discount is the MRT in a temporal context). P. A. Diamond and J. Mirrlees, "Private Constant Returns and Public Shadow Prices," *Review of Economic Studies*, February 1976.

[15] Harberger, "The Opportunity Costs of Public Investment Financed by Borrowing." He also presents an alternative formula which aggregates across consumers and firms who face different MRS's and MRT's, respectively. Finally, it should be noted that Harberger equates MRS^{soc} with MRS^{priv}. He does not believe there is a significant divergence between the two.

him to conclude that the consumers' MRS is probably closer to the true rate.[16] Bradford's model is more general than the ones we have been using in that it permits any underlying market structure. Furthermore, his model does not necessarily require the existence of distorting taxation, nor even that the government's budget constraint must balance, assumptions which we used repeatedly in the theoretical chapters on second-best expenditure theory. Rather, his analysis is second-best simply because the government has certain investment opportunities that are not open to the private sector. In terms of our previous models, if the government produces some output Z_i, there cannot be a corresponding private sector output Y_i. Of course, our previous models were general enough to consider this possibility, but they placed a considerable number of restrictions on the underlying policy environment. Bradford avoids these restrictions by defining the relationship between private investment and the future stream of consumption broadly enough to encompass any specific set of market or policy assumptions one might choose to make.

Following Bradford, let V_t = the present value of the stream of consumption, discounted at the social MRS, that is created by \$1 of private investment at time t. The stream of consumption benefits begins in time $t + 1$. Presumably V_t could be calculated for any specific model, such as those in Parts II and III of this text. The calculations may be extremely complex, but V_t would nonetheless be well defined for any given intertemporal general equilibrium model.

Bradford completes his model by assuming that:

a. The one-period rate of return on private investment, the MRT, is constant over time at rate r. That is, \$1 of private investment at time t yields \$$(1 + r)$ of income in time $t + 1$.
b. The government's objective function is the discounted stream of aggregate consumption over time, where the discount rate is the social MRS, equal to i. We will assume that the government's social MRS equals the consumer's private MRS.

Notice that this objective function is more restrictive than the one we were implicitly assuming above when we considered the intertemporal specification of the one-consumer equivalent models in Chapter 22, in that it assumes the consumer's utility has an additive representation with constant undiscounted marginal utilities. That is,

$$(24.9) \qquad U(C_1, \ldots, C_N) = \sum_{j=1}^{N} (1 + i)^{-j} \phi^j(C_j)$$

with

$$\frac{\partial \phi^j}{\partial C_j} = k \qquad j = 1, \ldots, N$$

---

[16] D. F. Bradford, "Constraints on Government Investment Opportunities and the Choice of the Discount Rate," *American Economic Review*, December 1975. Bradford's principal contribution is that his model includes the reinvestment of project benefits. In other respects, his approach is well represented in the literature (e.g., Marglin, "The Opportunity Costs of Public Investment"; and Feldstein, "The Inadequacy of Weighted Discount Rates").

Maximizing (24.9) is equivalent to maximizing the stream of consumption discounted at i. These restrictions may seem particularly severe, but they are commonly employed in intertemporal economic analysis.

Given the concept V_t, and his assumptions with respect to private investment (a), the government's objective function (b), and the government's investment opportunities, Bradford is able to derive specific expressions for the social rate of discount. To capture the flavor of his analysis, consider first the simple example of a government project which costs \$1 in period t, yields \$$(1 + p)$ of income in period $(t + 1)$, and nothing thereafter. Think of p as a variable, equal to the internal yield on the government investment, and ask: How large must p be to justify the project? The answer, p^*, defines the appropriate rate of discount for the project.

From our earlier discussion of the opportunity cost of public funds, we know that i (the MRS), r (the MRT), and the percentage decreases in C_t and I_t resulting from the financing of each dollar of government investment are all relevant to the calculation of p^*. Given Bradford's framework, we can also easily incorporate the future repercussions on both consumption and private investment, $(C_{t+1}, \ldots, C_{t+N})$ and $(I_{t+1}, \ldots, I_{t+N})$, resulting from the \$$(1 + p)$ of benefits generated by the government project in period $(t + 1)$, the reinvestment factor.

Let a_t = the fraction of each dollar of government investment that comes at the expense of private investment in time t. Hence $(1 - a_t)$ represents the decrease in C_t. Similarly, let α_{t+1} = the fraction of each dollar of the net benefits from the government project that is saved (invested) in time $(t + 1)$. Hence, $(1 - \alpha_{t+1})$ is the increase in C_{t+1} per dollar of net benefits.

Since the government's objective function is just the stream of discounted consumption over time, its investment decision rule is straightforward. p must be such that the increase in the discounted stream of consumption arising from the net benefits of the government project is at least as large as the discounted stream of consumption sacrificed by having to finance the project. The point of equality, or indifference, defines p^*, the rate of discount. Using the concept V_t, the loss in discounted consumption per dollar of government investment can be represented as:

$$(24.10) \qquad L_C = (1 - a_t) + a_t V_t$$

The first term equals the direct loss in C_t. The second term represents the indirect consumption loss caused by the decrease in I_t. a_t dollars of I_t translate, through V_t, into a discounted loss of consumption equal to $a_t \cdot V_t$.

Similarly, the gain in discounted consumption per dollar of government investment is:

$$(24.11) \qquad G_C = \frac{1}{(1 + i)} \left[(1 - \alpha_{t+1})(1 + p) + (1 + p)(\alpha_{t+1} V_{t+1}) \right]$$

The first term in brackets is the direct gain in C_{t+1} arising from \$$(1 + p)$ of benefits. The second term is the indirect gain in discounted consumption arising from an increase of $(\alpha_{t+1})(1 + p)$ dollars of I_{t+1}. Since these benefits accrue in $(t + 1)$, they must be discounted by $(1 + i)$ to make them commensurate with L_C. Hence, the investment criterion is simply $G_C \geq L_C$, or

(24.12) $$\frac{(1 + p)}{(1 + i)} [(1 - \alpha_{t+1}) + \alpha_{t+1} V_{t+1}] \geq [(1 - a_t) + a_t V_t]$$

Rearranging terms:

(24.13) $$\frac{(1 + p)}{(1 + i)} \geq \frac{(1 - a_t) + a_t V_t}{(1 - \alpha_{t+1}) + \alpha_{t+1} V_{t+1}}$$

n-Period Government Investments

The generalization of (24.13) to government projects whose costs and benefits occur over all n periods is straightforward.

Let:

$e_t = (1 - a_t) + a_t V_t$ be the present value, *at time t*, of the decrease in consumption occasioned by \$1 of costs incurred by a government project at time t.

$\beta_t = (1 - \alpha_t) + \alpha_t V_t$ be the present value, *at time t*, of the increase in consumption arising from \$1 of benefits associated with a government project at time t.

$\delta_t = \dfrac{1}{(1 + i)^t}$, the discount factor for time t.

$b_t = $ the total dollar value of the project's benefits at time t.

$E_t = $ the total dollar value of the project's costs at time t.

Given these definitions, the present value rule for government investments is simply:

(24.14) $$PV = \sum_{t=0}^{N} \delta_t (b_t \beta_t - E_t e_t) > 0$$

Suppose $\beta_t = B$, all t and $e_t = e$, all t. Then,

(24.15) $$PV = \sum_{t=0}^{N} \delta_t \left(b_t - E_t \frac{e}{B}\right) > 0^{17}$$

---

[17] In the two-period government project analyzed in the preceding section, $E_t = \$1$, $E_{t+1} = 0$, $b_t = 0$, $b_{t+1} = (1 + p)$, so that

(24.15N) $$PV = -[(1 - a_t) + a_t V_t] + \frac{1 + p}{1 + i}(1 - \alpha_{t+1} + \alpha_{t+1} V_{t+1}) > 0$$

which is equivalent to (24.13).

(24.15) implies that the government should discount all projects by the *MRS*, but scale the costs by the factor

(24.16)
$$\frac{e}{B} = \frac{1 - a + aV}{1 - \alpha + \alpha V}$$

The evaluation of V is the key to understanding why Bradford favors discounting at δ. He proceeds as follows. Suppose there is a constant savings rate, s. \$1 of I_t yields \$$(1 + r)$ of income in time $(t + 1)$. Of this, $(1 - s)$ is consumed in $(t + 1)$ and s is saved and invested. The amount saved and invested yields $(1 + r)$ dollars of additional income in time $(t + 2)$, of which $(1 - s)$ is consumed and s is saved and invested, and so on. Hence,

(24.17)
$$V_t = \frac{(1 + r)(1 - s)}{1 + i} + \frac{s(1 + r)^2(1 - s)}{(1 + i)^2} + \frac{s^2(1 + r)^3(1 - s)}{(1 + i)^3} + \cdots$$

Factoring out $(1 + r)/(1 + i) \cdot (1 - s)$ yields:

(24.18)
$$V_t = \frac{(1 + r)}{(1 + i)}(1 - s)\left[1 + \frac{s(1 + r)}{(1 + i)} + \frac{s^2(1 + r)^2}{(1 + i)^2} + \cdots + \frac{s^N(1 + r)^N}{(1 + i)^N}\right]$$

Letting $\gamma = (1 + r/1 + i) > 1$, and taking the limit as $N \to \infty$:

(24.19)
$$V_t = \gamma(1 - s)\left[\frac{1}{1 - s\gamma}\right] > \gamma$$

(24.19) permits a simple calculation of V_t. For example, setting $i = .05$, $r = .15$, and $s = .10$, as reasonable values for the *MRS*, *MRT*, and the rate of savings, respectively, in the United States, $V_t = 1.11$. Bradford, in fact, believes $V_t = 1.05$ is even more plausible for the United States. Given that V is close to unity, Bradford reasonably concludes that discounting by the *MRS* is a safe rule of thumb on the grounds that the "... *extreme* range for [the scale] factor $[e/\beta]$ is $1/V \geq e/\beta \geq V$, with $e/\beta = 1/V$ for $a_t = 0$, $\alpha_t = 1$, and $e/\beta = V$ for $a_t = 1$, $\alpha_t = 0$."[18] With $V = 1.11$ (Bradford; 1.05), the errors from assuming $e/\beta = 1$ are within a range of ± 11 percent (Bradford: 5 percent), which are probably within the range of cost estimation errors, as Bradford contends.

ALTERNATIVE VIEWS OF THE APPROPRIATE RATE OF DISCOUNT

Bradford's conclusion is hardly the last word on the appropriate rate of discount. Indeed, we have already presented a number of theoretical cases in which the appropriate discount factor is the *MRT*, or a weighted average of the *MRS* and *MRT*. Moreover, Bradford's V_t calculation assumes a simple model in which there is essentially only one good and a constant savings rate out of private sector income. Preferences are also severely restricted in other ways. More importantly, in calculating V he assumes that private investment

---

[18] Bradford, "Constraints on Government Investment Opportunities," p. 897.

yields returns r for one period only, and nothing thereafter. Hence, the maximum value of V, which occurs if all returns are consumed ($s = 0$), is $(1 + r)/(1 + i)$, a number still reasonably close to one. All other economists' using his basic framework (e.g., Marglin, Feldstein, Sjaastad, and Wisecarver[19]) assume private investment is a perpetuity yielding r forever, which implies a $V = r/i$ with zero savings. This V is almost certainly much greater than 1, perhaps in the [2.5–4.0] range. Hence, under the perpetuity assumption one would certainly not be willing to ignore the scaling factor e/β. The "best" assumption for private investment undoubtedly lies somewhere between the extremes of one-period and perpetual yields, but, in any event, results such as the Diamond-Mirrlees theorem suggests that the limits implied for the scaling factor in Bradford's model may be wide of the mark for many second-best environments, especially those with variable savings rates. This merely reemphasizes the general proposition demonstrated throughout the text that second-best results can be extremely sensitive to underlying assumptions.

Despite these reservations, Bradford's model is comprehensive enough to serve as a convenient vehicle for summarizing some of the conflicting views in the literature. For instance, the Marglin-Feldstein view that the appropriate present value calculation consists of discounting project benefits at the social rate of time preference and adjusting project costs by a shadow price reflecting second-best distortions follows directly from (24.15). To see this, suppose all investment costs occur immediately and yield a stream of benefits forever. Under these assumptions, $e_t = 0$, $t \geq 1$ and (24.15) becomes:

(24.20)
$$PV = \sum_{t=1}^{N} \delta^t b_t - \frac{e}{\beta} E_0 > 0$$

This is essentially the original Marglin result,[20] with the shadow price of project costs equal to Bradford's scale factor, e/β. The only difference is that Marglin is not so willing to ignore the shadow price, given his assumption that private investment is a perpetuity. For instance, ignoring reinvestment ($\alpha = 0$), and assuming all private benefits are consumed,

(24.21)
$$\frac{e}{\beta} = e = (1 - a) + aV = (1 - a) + a\frac{r}{i}$$

which may differ substantially from 1.

Feldstein extended Marglin's analysis to include cash deficits whenever they occur.[21] His recommended procedure also follows immediately from (24.15), although care must be taken to distinguish between true project costs and out-of-pocket costs. Suppose that some project benefits are sold and some costs paid for by the government each period.

---

[19] Marglin, "The Opportunity Costs of Public Investment"; Feldstein, "The Inadequacy of Weighted Discount Rates"; and L. Sjaastad and D. Wisecarver, "The Social Cost of Public Finance," *Journal of Political Economy*, June 1977.

[20] Marglin, "The Opportunity Costs of Public Investment." Marglin uses a continuous time model.

[21] Feldstein, "The Inadequacy of Weighted Discount Rates."

Let:

b_t = true project benefits in time t.

E_t = true project costs in time t.

R_t = project revenues in time t.

C_t = project cash payments in time t.

Net consumption benefits are $(b_t - R_t)$, and net transfers to consumers are $(C_t - E_t)$. The cash deficit is $(C_t - R_t)$, to which the shadow price of funds must be applied. Assuming no reinvestment of net project benefits ($\alpha = 0$), Feldstein's version of Bradford's formula is:

$$(24.22) \quad PV = \sum_{t=0}^{\infty} \delta^t [(b_t - R_t) + (C_t - E_t) - ((1 - a) + aV_t)(C_t - R_t)] > 0$$

Rearranging terms:

$$(24.23) \qquad PV = \sum_{t=0}^{\infty} \delta^t [(b_t - E_t) - (V - 1)a(C_t - R_t)] > 0$$

One immediate implication of (24.23) is that the net benefits of self-financing projects should be discounted at the social rate of time preference, with no further corrections applied. (24.23) is also obviously consistent with (24.20) and (24.15), assuming $\alpha = 0$, $R_t = 0$ and $C_t = E_t$.

Harberger's "opportunity cost" point of view that the rate of discount should be a weighted average of r and i, with weights equal to a and $(1 - a)$, respectively, can also be derived from (24.15) under special assumptions. For instance, it has long been known that the two-period model so often used in public sector analysis will generate this result.[22] The two-period version of (24.15) can be represented by (24.13) under the assumption that all project costs are incurred immediately, and all project benefits occur in period 1, equal to $1 + p$. However, since life ends in period 1, all benefits from public *and* private investments will be entirely consumed in period 1. Hence $\alpha = 0$, $V_0 = (1 + r)/(1 + i)$, with $s = 0$. Therefore, (24.13) becomes:

$$(24.24) \qquad \frac{1 + p}{1 + i} - (1 - a) - a\frac{(1 + r)}{(1 + i)} > 0$$

Rearranging terms:

$$(24.25) \qquad (1 + p) > (1 - a)(1 + i) + a(1 + r)$$

or

$$(24.26) \qquad p > (1 - a)i + ar$$

the Harberger formula.

---

[22] See, for example, Diamond, "The Opportunity Costs of Public Investment: Comment."

Sjaastad and Wisecarver have recently argued that using (24.26) is always appropriate no matter how long the investment horizon.[23] Consider, first, the extreme case in which both public and private investments are perpetuities, yielding p and r respectively. Under this assumption it is reasonable to assume that all benefits are consumed as they arise, since capital never depreciates. Thus, \$1 of public investment in time 0 will cause a loss in consumption equal to:

$$(24.27) \qquad L_C = (1 - a) + a\frac{r}{i}$$

and a gain equal to:

$$(24.28) \qquad G_C = \frac{p}{i}$$

in present value terms. $G_C > L_C$ implies:

$$(24.29) \qquad \frac{p}{i} > (1 - a) + a\frac{r}{i}$$

or

$$(24.30) \qquad p > (1 - a)i + ar$$

Notice that (24.29) is simply the Marglin-Feldstein algorithm, so that the two rules are equivalent for perpetuities.

In a world of finite investments the "opportunity cost" and "social rate of time preference with shadow price" approaches will differ, but Sjaastad and Wisecarver believe the former is still the appropriate technique. To compare the two, return to the special case of the Bradford model given by (24.13) in which all costs of public investment are incurred immediately, all the returns from the public project occur in period 1, but life continues beyond period 1, so reinvestment is possible. (24.13) does not necessarily imply (24.26), the Harverger "opportunity cost" rule, but Sjaastad and Wisecarver believe that appropriate assumptions on the functioning of capital markets and the treatment of public sector capital depreciation will generate the opportunity cost rule. In effect, they argue that the reinvestment parameter, α, in (24.13) must be such as to generate (24.26). It is not free to assume an arbitrary value.

The argument is as follows. $(1 + p)$ measures the gross returns to public investment, of which \$1 is depreciation. The key question is whether or not society will choose to consume the depreciation, or save it in an attempt to maintain the stock of public capital. They believe it is natural to assume that society will try to save the \$1 and view the true benefits of the project as p, the net benefits. However, the attempt to inject an additional dollar of savings into the capital market will lower interest rates, and discourage some savings such that only $a \cdot \$1$ of savings and reinvestment will actually result. $(1 - a) \cdot \$1$ will be consumed. Notice that the actual amount of savings is precisely the amount required to restore the total (and private) capital stock, since private

---

[23] Sjaastad and Wisecarver, "The Social Cost of Public Finance."

investment declined by $a \cdot \$1$ in the initial period, and the $1 of public investment fully depreciated by $1. Furthermore, with the private capital stock remaining constant, the future investment effects on consumption beyond period 1 cancel, so all one need do is compare the direct consumption effects over the two periods. The immediate loss is:

$$(24.31) \qquad\qquad L_C = (1 - a)$$

The consumption gain in the first period is[24]

$$(24.32) \qquad\qquad G_C = \frac{p - ar + (1 - a)}{1 + i}$$

$G_C > L_C$ implies:

$$(24.33) \qquad\qquad \frac{p - ar + (1 - a)}{1 + i} > (1 - a)$$

$$(24.34) \qquad\qquad p > (1 - a)i + ar$$

the Harberger formula once again.

Sjaastad Wisecarver are able to show that this example is not a special case. So long as interest rate effects change $1 of intended savings into a of actual savings, and society saves the depreciation on public capital, the weighted-average formula will apply (with one insignificant adjustment) to all public projects yielding returns over any finite number of periods.[25] Of course, it is problematical whether capital markets function as the authors posit, or whether society adjusts its savings for public capital depreciation, assumptions crucial to their result. On the other hand, ignoring savings for public depreciation and interest rate effects on intended savings, a common feature of other models, is certainly suspect.[26]

It is difficult to know what to make of the debate over the appropriate rate of discount for public projects. More than anything else, it reemphasizes the frustrating point that no single "rule of thumb" derived from a particular second-best model is likely to be very robust to changes in the underlying policy and market environment. We have seen many different rules in just these few pages covering a wide range of discount rates,[27] and yet the entire discussion ignores one final caveat, the *intragenerational* distribution of income.[28] It may

---

[24] The displacement of $a \cdot \$1$ of private investment at time 0 will cause a loss of consumption equal to ar in period 1. This loss will not recur in subsequent periods once the capital stock is restored to its original level in period 1.

[25] Sjaastad and Wisecarver, "The Social Cost of Public Finance"; see pp. 524–528 for the development of their adjusted formula.

[26] P. Diamond has shown that models positing a constant marginal propensity to save, a constant stream of returns from private investment, and utility of consumption diminishing at a constant geometric rate over time, such as Marglin's, will generate the MRS^{soc} discounting rule. Diamond, "The Opportunity Costs of Public Investment: Comment."

[27] The situation is actually worse than represented. Bradford demonstrates special cases for which the discount rate lies outside the range of rates bounded by the MRS^{soc} and the MRT. Bradford, "Constrants on Government Investment Opportunities," pp. 891–892.

[28] The *intergenerational* distribution is embodied in the social rate of time preference, however.

be natural to ignore distributional considerations when modeling the rate of discount, but if the underlying distribution is nonoptimal, an equation such as (22.88) applies to the rate of discount, as it does to all government shadow prices. Hence, it is always possible that intratemporal social welfare rankings will overwhelm the pure efficiency aspects of the discount rule, which are all these models consider.

EMPIRICAL EVIDENCE ON THE RATE OF DISCOUNT

In our view, it would be difficult to mount a decisive case for or against any rate of discount governments might choose over a range of 3 percent to 20 percent or even 25 percent. All one can say for certain is that whatever rate the government selects, it should be applied equally to all potential investments (standardizing for risk—see Chapter 25). In fact, consistent project evaluation seldom occurs. Most state and local governments do not use present value analysis at all in their investment decisions. The situation is more hopeful at the federal level in that the Office of the Management of the Budget is charged with overseeing all agency investment proposals, but its power is largerly illusory. Many agencies enjoy considerable political influence among House and Senate members, enough so that they can effectively circumvent the OMB. Consequently, fully standardized review procedures have never been achieved. The data in Table 24–1 on discount rates used by various U.S. government agencies in 1969 are indicative of the variations that persist to this day.

These 1969 data are especially revealing in two respects. First, 1969 was a year characterized by relatively full employment and expectations of low rates

TABLE 24–1

Agency	Rate of Discount (percentage)
Defense	10–12 (but only on shipyard projects and air and other stations)
Agency for International Development	8–12 (but this applies to investments in less-developed countries and may be far too low)
Department of the Interior	6–12 (energy programs) 3–6 (all other projects)
Department of Health, Education, and Welfare	0–10
Tennessee Valley Authority Department of Agriculture Office of Economic Opportunity Department of Transportation	≤ 5
All other agencies	No discounting

Source: Elmer B. Staats, "Survey of Use by Federal Agencies of the Discounting Technique in Evaluating Future Programs," in H. Hinrichs and G. Taylor, eds., *Program Budgeting and Benefit Cost Analysis* (Pacific Palisades, Calif.: Goodyear Publishing Co., Inc., 1969), appendix I, pp. 222–24.

of inflation, surely less than 3 percent. Hence, the rates in Table 24–1 give a fairly good reading of what each agency felt to be the appropriate real rate of discount. The fact that most chose rates of 5 percent or less, with only a few as high as 10 percent, perhaps suggests that most government officials believe the appropriate rate of discount is closer to the *MRS* than the *MRT*. Secondly, investment criteria vary considerably not only across agencies but *within* agencies. For example, the Department of Interior's energy projects must yield far greater returns that its other projects to be acceptable. Similarly, HEW obviously applies quite different standards across programs. It is difficult to justify such wide discrepancies without resorting to perceived differences in the distributional implications of various types of projects, or noneconomic considerations such as intra-agency political biases.[29] One might reasonably expect to find more standardized evaluation procedures within each agency.

REFERENCES

Bradford, D. F.   "Constraints on Government Investment Opportunities and the Choice of the Discount Rate." *American Economic Review,* December 1975.

Diamond, P. A.   "The Opportunity Costs of Public Investment: Comment." *Quarterly Journal of Economics,* November 1968.

————, and Mirrlees, J.   "Private Constant Returns and Public Shadow Prices." *Review of Economic Studies,* February 1976.

Feldstein, M.   "Does the United States Save Too Little?" *AEA Papers and Proceedings,* February 1977.

————.   "The Inadequacy of Weighted Discount Rates." In *Cost-Benefit Analysis,* edited by R. Layard. Harmondsworth, Middlesex, England: Penguin Education, Penguin Books Ltd., 1972.

Harberger, A. C.   *Project Evaluation: Collected Papers.* Chicago: Markham Publishing Co., 1974.

————.   "The Opportunity Costs of Public Investment Financed by Borrowing." In *Cost-Benefit Analysis,* edited by R. Layard. Harmondsworth, Middlesex, England: Penguin Education, Penguin Books Ltd., 1972.

Haveman, R.   "Policy Analysis and the Congress: An Economist's View." In *Public Expenditure and Policy Analysis,* edited by R. Haveman and J. Margolis. 2d ed. Chicago: Rand McNally College Publishing Co., 1977.

---

[29] It is not at all clear that matters have improved since 1969. For an analysis of recent trends in project evaluation, see A. Schick, "A Death in the Bureaucracy: The Demise of the Federal PPB"; and R. Haveman, "Policy Analysis and the Congress: An Economist's View," in R. Haveman and J. Margolis, eds., *Public Expenditure and Policy Analysis,* 2d ed. (Chicago: Rand McNally College Publishing Co., 1977).

Layard, R., ed. *Cost-Benefit Analysis.* Harmondsworth, Middlesex, England: Penguin Education, Penguin Books Ltd., 1972.

Marglin, S. "The Social Rate of Discount and the Optimal Rate of Investment." *Quarterly Journal of Economics,* February 1963.

————. "The Opportunity Costs of Public Investment." *Quarterly Journal of Economics,* May 1963.

McKean, R. N. "Tax Wedges and Cost-Benefit Analysis." *Journal of Public Economics,* February 1974.

Schick, A. "A Death in the Bureaucracy: The Demise of the Federal PPB." In *Public Expenditure and Policy Analysis,* edited by R. Haveman and J. Margolis. 2d ed. Chicago: Rand McNally College Publishing Co., 1977.

Sen, A. "Isolation, Assurance, and the Social Rate of Discount." *Quarterly Journal of Economics,* February 1967.

————. "The Social Time Preference Rate in Relation to the Market Rate of Interest." In *Cost-Benefit Analysis,* edited by R. Layard, Harmondsworth, Middlesex, England: Penguin Education, Penguin Books Ltd., 1972.

Sjaastad, L., and Wisecarver, D. "The Social Cost of Public Finance." *Journal of Political Economy,* June 1977.

Staats, E. B. "Survey of Use by Federal Agencies of the Discounting Technique in Evaluating Future Programs." In *Program Budgeting and Benefit Cost Analysis,* edited by H. Hinricks and G. Taylor. Pacific Palisades, Calif.: Goodyear Publishing Co., Inc., 1969.

25

Uncertainty—the Arrow-Lind theorem

When speaking of the rate of return or internal yield on an investment in the preceding chapter we were obviously referring only to a project's expected return. Given the fact of uncertainty about the future, the actual returns have an entire probability distribution associated with them dependent upon the possible states of nature that can occur. Uncertainty presents a problem for investment analysis, public or private, because people are generally not neutral with respect to risk. Most are risk averse, meaning that they would be willing to pay a premium to change an asset's uncertain stream of returns into a certain return. In other words, an asset's expected return exceeds its true value to a risk-averse individual. Therefore, if society consists mainly of risk-averse consumers, and the government acts on the basis of individuals' preferences, then one would naturally expect cost-benefit analysis of government projects to reflect society's risk aversion in order to maximize social welfare. For example, suppose the government determines that the appropriate rate of discount on riskless projects is 10 percent. Should it not add a few percentage points to the 10 percent rate as a risk premium when evaluating its own risky projects? In general the answer is yes, but Arrow and Lind[1] have shown that under certain fairly broad conditions the government can actually *ignore* risk. In particular, they prove that if—

a. The returns on a government project are distributed independently of national income, and
b. The benefits and costs of the project are each spread over a sufficiently large population,

then the value of a project is accurately measured by its expected value. For under these two conditions, the risk premium that society *in the aggregate* would be willing to pay to convert a stream of uncertain returns into a certain return goes to zero in the limit.

The Arrow-Lind theorem is especially powerful because it makes no assumptions about the underlying market environment. For instance, it need not be perfectly competitive. Moreover, there are no restrictions on government policy

---

[1] K. Arrow and R. Lind, "Uncertainty and the Evaluation of Public Investment Decisions," *American Economic Review*, June 1970.

other than those directly associated with the project. Hence, their result is applicable to a wide range of second-best (and the first-best) policy environments. The only potentially unrealistic aspect of their model concerns the distribution of project costs and benefits. Arrow and Lind guarantee that condition (a) holds by assuming that the government pays all the costs of the investment, receives all the benefits, and then distributes the net benefits lump sum to each individual. They assume further that the project's net benefits are free of tax. Thus, there can be no further fiscal repercussions of the project that could lead to an indirect correlation between its net benefits and each consumer's disposable income. These assumptions are clearly not meant to be realistic. Arrow and Lind use them merely as an analytically convenient way of satisfying condition (a). However, they turn out not to be innocuous. Foldes and Rees contend that it may not be possible to satisfy the independence condition for very many projects in the context of an actual fiscal system.[2] We will consider their analysis at the end of the chapter.

PROOF OF THE ARROW-LIND THEOREM

A discussion of the Arrow-Lind theorem hardly constitutes a comprehensive analysis of public decision making under uncertainty, but a general analysis of uncertainty is well beyond the scope of this text. Rather, we chose to highlight their theorem because of its remarkable implications for policy analysis, and the fact that its proof requires nothing more sophisticated than the definition of a derivative and some rudimentary properties of the expected value operator.

Begin by assuming that society consists of N identical consumers, each of whom has initial income equal to A, where A is a random variable. In line with accepted practice in uncertainty analysis, assume further that each consumer maximizes expected utility. (The assumption that the consumers are identical is not necessary to the proof but it greatly simplifies the derivation.) Let $B =$ the total net returns from some government project. Assume B is also a random variable, equal to its expected value, $\bar{B}$, and a random component X, or

$$(25.1) \qquad\qquad B = \bar{B} + X$$

with:

$$E[X] = 0$$

Finally assume that B and A are independently distributed (condition (a)) and that each of the N identical individuals receives an equal share of the returns B. Hence, each person's share is $s = 1/N$.

Under these assumptions an individual's income without the project is A. With the project the individual receives $A + sB = A + s\bar{B} + sX$. The corresponding expected utilities with and without the project are $E[U(A + s\bar{B} + sX)]$ and $E[U(A)]$.

---

[2] L. Foldes and R. Rees, "A Note on the Arrow-Lind Theorem," *American Economic Review*, March 1977.

Define each person's expected utility with the project as a function of s, or

$$(25.2) \qquad W(s) = E[U(A + s\bar{B} + sX)]$$

Differentiate $W(s)$ with respect to s and evaluate the derivative at $s = 0$.

$$(25.3) \qquad W'(s) = E[U'(A + s\bar{B} + sX)(\bar{B} + X)]$$

Hence:

$$(25.4) \qquad W'(0) = E[U'(A)(\bar{B} + X)] = \bar{B}E[U'(A)] + E[U'(A) \cdot X]$$

But if A and X are independently distributed

$$(25.5) \qquad E[U'(A) \cdot X] = E[U'(A)] \cdot E[X] = 0$$

with:

$$E[X] = 0$$

Therefore:

$$(25.6) \qquad W'(0) = \bar{B}E[U'(A)]$$

By the definition of a derivative, (25.6) implies that

$$(25.7) \qquad \lim_{s \to 0} \frac{E[U(A + s\bar{B} + sX) - U(A)]}{s} = \bar{B}E[U'(A)]$$

Substituting $s = 1/N$ into (25.7) yields:

$$(25.8) \qquad \lim_{N \to \infty} N \cdot E\left[U\left(A + \frac{\bar{B}}{N} + \frac{X}{N}\right) - U(A)\right] = \bar{B}E[U'(A)]$$

Next incorporate the notion of a risk premium. Assuming each individual is risk averse, there will exist a number $k(N)$ such that the individual is indifferent between accepting the risky stream of returns $\bar{B}/N + X/N$ and paying $k(N)$ for $\bar{B}/N$, certain. Hence, define $k(N)$ such that

$$(25.9) \qquad E\left[U\left(A + \frac{\bar{B}}{N} + \frac{X}{N}\right)\right] = E\left[U\left(A + \frac{\bar{B}}{N} - k(N)\right)\right]$$

Substituting the certainty equivalent (25.9) into (25.8) yields:

$$(25.10) \qquad \lim_{N \to \infty} N \cdot E\left[U\left(A + \frac{\bar{B}}{N} - k(N)\right) - U(A)\right] = \bar{B}E[U'(A)]$$

But

$$(25.11) \qquad \lim_{N \to \infty} \frac{\bar{B}}{N} - k(N) = 0$$

Clearly, as N becomes large without limit *each individual's* share of the return and the risk approach zero. The fact that exposure to risk approaches zero in turn implies that the risk premium any individual would be willing to pay to convert the returns into a certain stream also approaches zero. But if,

$\lim_{N \to \infty} \bar{B}/N - k(N) = 0,$

(25.12)
$$\lim_{N \to \infty} \frac{E\left[U\left(A + \dfrac{\bar{B}}{N} - k(N)\right) - U(A)\right]}{\dfrac{\bar{B}}{N} - k(N)} = E[U'(A)]$$

Dividing (25.10) by (25.12) yields:

(25.13)
$$\lim_{N \to \infty} N \cdot \left[\frac{\bar{B}}{N} - k(N)\right] = \bar{B}$$

or

(25.14)
$$\lim_{N \to \infty} N \cdot k(N) = 0$$

(25.14) says that the risk premium society *in the aggregate* would be willing to pay goes to zero, or that the value to society of the risky stream of returns B is simply its expected value, $\bar{B}$.

Professor James has offered an important caveat to this result, however, that the Arrow-Lind theorem applies to a single investment project.[3] Suppose it happened that each of M projects would be accepted if analyzed individually, in part because the Arrow-Lind "risk-spreading" effect virtually removes the aggregate risk associated with each project. Society still could be in a position of wishing to reject the entire set of projects, if analyzed collectively. In other words, the piecemeal or marginal decision process might not generate a global optimum.

To see how this anomaly can arise, assume that the returns and risks associated with each project are identical and that their returns are perfectly correlated. In this case the returns accruing to any one consumer from the entire set of projects is $M \cdot \bar{B}/N$, and the consumer's exposure to risk is $M \cdot X/N$. For purposes of illustration, assume $M = N$ (the population is finite and the set of projects is extremely large). In this case, the individual consumer receives returns $\bar{B}$, with risk X, exactly as if he received the entire returns and bore the entire risk associated with any one of the M projects. If the consumer's risk premium k exceeds $\bar{B}$ under these conditions, society should reject all M projects even though it would accept each of them if analyzed individually. In short, a sufficiently large number of projects with perfectly correlated returns can negate the Arrow-Lind risk-spreading effect.

The anomaly can be avoided if the returns on the M projects are independently distributed, in which case the aggregate risk premium is reduced by a second effect, the "risk pooling," or dispersion effect. This says that the risk premium associated with a portfolio of assets whose returns are independently distributed goes to zero as the number of assets becomes large without limit.

---

[3] E. James, "A Note on Uncertainty and the Evaluation of Public Investment Decisions," *American Economic Review*, March 1975.

Hence, even if society consisted of a single individual so that risk spreading is impossible, the individual might be willing to accept all M projects collectively if M were large enough and the returns on each project were independently distributed. Clearly, then, risk pooling supports risk spreading and reduces the chances of anomaly with independent projects. In general, the likelihood of an anomaly occurring depends upon the values of M and N, and the extent to which the returns on individual projects are correlated.

Assuming the anomaly does not arise, the Arrow-Lind theorem has two important policy implications. First, there is no need to adjust the riskless rate of discount because of uncertainty. Second, the government can simply compare alternative investments on the basis of their expected returns *no matter how risky each of them may be*. Furthermore, the risk-spreading phenomenon is likely to apply uniquely to public sector projects, for even if the returns on some private investment were distributed independently of national income, they would generally not be spread over a sufficiently "large" population to render the theorem applicable. On the other hand, private investors can benefit from risk pooling through portfolio diversification, although it is doubtful that private sector diversification is sufficient to reduce private sector risk premia to zero. Hence the response to uncertainty may be the only instance whereby government investment analysis is conceptually easier than private investment analysis.

FURTHER REFLECTIONS ON THE ARROW-LIND THEOREM

The remaining issue is whether or not the conditions of the theorem are likely to apply for a very many government projects. It is easy to be skeptical on this score.

One can advance the following arguments in support of the theorem. First, projects at the national or (large) state level ought to satisfy condition (b) that the population be sufficiently large. The only clear exception would arise in cases for which either the costs or benefits were very narrowly conceived. Second, if the typical cost-benefit assumption of full-employment is retained, it might be argued that the level of (real) national income is not a random variable but a single number determined independently of any one project, whose value is assured either by the corrective actions of monetary and fiscal policy or by the workings of a perfectly competitive market system. Hence, condition (a) is also likely to hold.

There are problems with either of these positions, however. The population condition is not simply that the population be sufficiently large. Embedded in the proof of the theorem is the additional condition that the individuals expected net benefits, $\bar{B}/N$, approach zero as $N \to \infty$. Arrow and Lind guarantee this result by assuming that the expected benefits are bounded, but this might not be true if externalities are present. For example, if the government is financing a Samuelsonian nonexclusive public good, each person consumes the same "benefit" stream. If these benefits are positive for all individuals (as they would be for identical individuals assuming the project is worthwhile), they will not be bounded as $N \to \infty$. Hence, $\lim_{N \to \infty} \bar{B}/N - k(n) \neq 0$ and equation (25.11) would not hold. Given that externalities are a major justification for government intervention, this point is troublesome. The theorem may only be broadly applicable to investments in decreasing cost services.[4]

Second, the assumption of independence between project benefits and national income may not be justified. It is natural to assume that national income is a random variable in an uncertain world, even under the standard assumption of full employment. Corrective monetary and fiscal policy, or perfectly competitive markets, can only guarantee that the *expected value* of income is the full employment level. But if national income is a random variable, one can easily identify many government projects whose returns might well be correlated with national income in violation of condition (a), projects such as irrigation, recreational facilities, transportation infrastructures, education, research and development, job training programs, and so forth. Furthermore, even if the returns on these projects have a particular form that turns out not to be correlated with national income (defense, possibly), the fiscal system itself can create a statistical dependence between income and the returns on *any* project. Arrow and Lind preclude this possibility by their assumption that the government pays all the costs and distributes the benefits lump sum, with no further taxation of the benefits. But, realistically, the net benefits of many projects will undoubtedly be subject to income taxation, simply because they increase each person's income. Moreover, if the government simultaneously adjusts the tax rate on other income to maintain budgetary balance given that net benefits are taxed, the independence between disposable income without the project and the project's returns may be destroyed, even though gross incomes and project returns are independent. Recall that the relevant arguments of each individual's utility function are the share of the project's net benefits and each person's *disposable income* without the project.

Consider two distinct cases. First, with identical individuals, or a one-consumer-equivalent economy, changes in the income tax rate to offset taxation of project net benefits cannot matter with a balanced government budget. If gross incomes and total project returns are independent, so too must be each person's disposable income and share of net benefits, because the income tax reductions will just equal the revenues from taxing the benefits. With non-identical individuals, however, this no longer holds. An individual's disposable income and share of the benefits may be correlated if the government varies income taxes to meet an aggregate budget constraint. Thus, the "convenience" of lump-sum distributions of untaxed net benefits and identical individuals may disguise the relevant point that for most realistic fiscal structures the assumed independence between project benefits and disposable income is extremely unlikely.

---

[4] Anthony Fisher first made this point in A. Fisher, "A Paradox in the Theory of Public Investment," *Journal of Public Economics*, vol. 2, 1973. See, also, the discussion in Foldes and Rees, "A Note on the Arrow-Lind Theorem."

THE FOLDES-REES ANALYSIS

To see this, consider the following fiscal system, a simplified version of a model suggested by Foldes and Rees.[5] Imagine an initial situation in which the government provides a pure public good G^0 which it finances with an income tax, at rate t_0, on total income A. $A = \sum_{i=1}^{N} A_i$, where $A_i =$ the gross income of person i before the project, assumed to be a random variable. The government's budget constraint without the project is:

$$(25.15) \qquad G^0 = t^0 A$$

and each consumer's disposable income is initially

$$(25.16) \qquad D_i = (1 - t^0)A_i + G^0$$

Suppose the government then undertakes a project with net benefits B which are distributed independently of the A_i and subject to taxation at rate, λ. If G^0 is unchanged, and the government's budget constraint continues to hold, the government will have to adjust t^0 to offset the increased tax revenues on the project's benefits. The new government budget constraint is now

$$(25.17) \qquad G^0 = t^1 A + \lambda B$$

Let person i's share of the net benefits be B_i, where $B = \sum_{i=1}^{N} B_i$. Each consumer's disposable income with the project is therefore:

$$(25.18) \qquad r_i + D_i = (1 - t^1)A_i + G^0 + (1 - \lambda)B_i \qquad i = 1, \ldots, N$$

where r_i is the net benefit from the project. Combining (25.15) and (25.16), and defining $a_i = A_i/A$, disposable income without the project can be expressed as:

$$(25.19) \qquad D_i = a_i(A - G^0) + G^0 = \frac{(Na_i)(A - G^0)}{N} + \frac{G^0}{N} \cdot N$$

Substituting (25.16) into (25.18) to solve for r_i yields:

$$(25.20) \qquad r_i = (t^0 - t^1)A_i + (1 - \lambda)B_i$$

Next, combine (25.15) and (25.17) to solve for $(t^0 - t^1)$:

$$(25.21) \qquad t^0 A = t^1 A + \lambda B$$

or

$$(25.22) \qquad (t^0 - t^1) = \frac{\lambda B}{A}$$

Substituting for $(t^0 - t^1)$ in (25.20) yields:

$$(25.23) \qquad r_i = \frac{\lambda B A_i}{A} + (1 - \lambda)B_i$$

or

$$(25.24) \qquad r_i = a_i \lambda B + (1 - \lambda)B_i$$

---

[5] Foldes and Rees, "A Note on the Arrow-Lind Theorem."

Finally, multiply (25.24) by N to obtain:

$$(25.25) \qquad\qquad Nr_i = (Na_i)\lambda B + N(1 - \lambda)B_i$$

For nonidentical individuals, the Arrow-Lind theorem requires that D_i and Nr_i converge to finite limits as $N \to \infty$, and that D_i and Nr_i be independently distributed.[6] Assume all the elements of D_i and Nr_i do converge, as required. By inspection of equations (25.19) and (25.25), however, D_i and Nr_i will generally be statistical *dependent* because each contains the term Na_i. Independence can be preserved in only one of two ways:

1. (Na_i) is constant across all possible states of nature. This condition would be satisfied if $a_i = 1/N$, that is, if all consumers had identical initial incomes, as Arrow-Lind assume. With nonidentical individuals, however, (Na_i) will almost certainly vary with the state of nature. This result highlights the point that the Arrow-Lind assumption of identical individuals is no longer innocuous once a more realistic fiscal structure is assumed.

2. The limit of the *coefficients* on (Na_i) approach zero as $N \to \infty$, either in equation (25.19) or (25.25), or both. But this condition is not plausible for equation (25.19). It would imply either that $(A - G_0) \to 0$, which in turn implies a 100 percent tax rate t^0, or that $A/N \to 0$. For any realistic economy, however, A/N is obviously quite different from zero. Thus, the only remaining possibility is that $\lim_{N \to \infty} \lambda B = 0$, from equation (25.25). Since B is certainly finite, this implies that $\lim_{N \to \infty} \lambda = 0$, or that the benefits from the project are untaxed. While this is possible, it is unlikely to apply for very many government projects in an economy with income taxation, in which case the Arrow-Lind theorem would not be applicable.

These results provide yet another clear example of the general principle on second-best modeling emphasized repeatedly throughout Part III of the text, that there can never be an ultimate second-best model. One can always place additional effective constraints on any second-best model in the name of realism, after which the policy implications of the model are bound to change. In this particular instance Foldes and Rees imposed a more realistic fiscal structure on the basic Arrow-Lind model, which was already second best, and were able to generate quite different results. The Foldes-Rees attack on Arrow-Lind would appear to be fairly devastating for many government projects, but there is always the possibility that some clever person will define a net set of realistic constraints that, when attached to the Foldes-Rees model, recapture the Arrow-Lind theorem. Any second-best model is potentially vulnerable in this way.

CONCLUSION

By way of concluding these brief remarks on cost-benefit analysis under uncertainty, let us assume that the Arrow-Lind theorem applies at least to a subset of government projects, and that the James global anomaly does not occur. Two additional implications of the theorem deserve comment. First, the

---

[6] See Foldes and Rees, "A Note on the Arrow-Lind Theorem," p. 190, for a proof.

point that the government can take the expected value of government projects as the measure of their true value to society regardless of their riskiness facilitates comparisons among various government investment alternatives, but it does not eliminate the problem of uncertainty when comparing all government projects to private sector alternatives.[7] Uncertainty within the private sector will still tend to obscure the proper value for the public sector's rate of discount. To facilitate discussion of this point, assume a Diamond-Mirrlees optimal-taxation environment, in which the proper rate of discount is the productivity of private sector investments, the MRT between present and future consumption. As noted in Chapter 24, the MRT can be reasonably approximated by observed gross-of-tax returns on private investments. The problem is that *observed* private rates of return undoubtedly have risk premia built into them. But this implies that the government's true social rate of discount is *not* the observed MRT but the observed MRT less the private risk premium, or

$$(25.26) \qquad MRT_{\substack{\text{government} \\ \text{opportunity} \\ \text{cost}}} = MRT_{\text{observed}} - \text{risk premium}$$

The fact that the government can spread risk in a manner unavailable to the private sector is a real cost advantage which the public sector ought to exploit by using a lower rate of discount on its projects. The problem, however, is that there is no commonly accepted method for unscrambling risk premia from observed market rates of return. Thus, even if—

1. The Arrow-Lind theorem applies to a given set of government projects,
2. The real world is reasonably approximated by the assumptions underlying the Diamond-Mirrlees theorem, and
3. Cost-benefit analysts could agree that some particular rate measures the MRT_{private}

the proper rate of discount for these projects would still remain unknown.[8]

A second important implication of the Arrow-Lind analysis is that if the benefits (costs) of a project accrue to a small subset of the population, an additional risk premium should be applied to them in the form of a higher rate of discount. This provides some solace for those who dislike projects that are narrowly conceived to benefit (harm) particular interest groups, since they must pass a more stringent test to be judged worthwhile. It should be stressed,

---

[7] We are assuming that the possibilities for risk pooling in the private sector are limited.

[8] We have been stating throughout the chapter that risk premia, if relevant, ought to be incorporated by adjusting the rate of discount in the present value formula. This implicitly assumes that the government's discount rate will depend, in part, on the gross-of-tax and net-of-tax returns available in the private sector. To the extent these returns incorporate risk premia, some adjustment in them will be required when computing the public sector rate. If, on the other hand, one agrees with Marglin and Bradford that the discount rate ought to equal the social rate of time preference, risk premia would only be reflected in the shadow price of project deficits. Perhaps both kinds of adjustments make sense, although the proper adjustment undoubtedly depends upon the underlying general equilibrium model being assumed. Theory is unlikely to reveal a single correct method. See R. Boadway, *Public Sector Economics* (Cambridge, Mass.: Winthrop Publishers, Inc., 1979), pp. 202–5, for an analysis of various approaches and their justifications.

however, that this adjustment has nothing whatsoever to do with the distribution question, per se. It is strictly a consequence of uncertainty, applicable to any subset of a risk-averse population, whether its members happen to have high or low social marginal utilities of income.

REFERENCES

Arrow, K. J., and Lind, R. C. "Uncertainty and the Evaluation of Public Investment Decisions." *American Economic Review,* June 1970.

Boadway, R. *Public Sector Economics.* Cambridge, Mass.: Winthrop Publishers, Inc., 1979.

Fisher, A. "A Paradox in the Theory of Public Investment." *Journal of Public Economics,* vol. 2, 1973.

Foldes, L. P., and Rees, R. "A Note on the Arrow-Lind Theorem." *American Economic Review,* March 1977.

James, E. "A Note on Uncertainty and the Evaluation of Public Investment Decisions." *American Economic Review,* March 1975.

26

Measurement problems in cost-benefit analysis

Determining the proper rate of discount and adjusting for uncertainty are problems shared by both private and public sector investment analysis. Chapter 26 will explore a set of problems associated with the measurement of public sector costs and benefits that are unlikely to arise in the private sector. They derive either from the nature of the government projects themselves or the policy environment in which project selection occurs.

Generally speaking, private investment analysis attempts to measure expected profitability as the difference between revenues and costs evaluated at current and expected future market prices. In public sector analysis, however, profitability is usually not the proper criterion for project selection. Market prices always convey useful information, but they often must be combined with other evaluative concepts in rather complex ways to determine government project costs and benefits.

Chapter 23 identified four common types of measurement problems in cost-benefit analysis:

a. The presence of intangibles.
b. The fact that government projects are often lumpy, not marginal additions to an existing market environment.
c. The fact that some project benefits are often given away free of charge, or at least priced below marginal costs; similarly, some project resources may simply be commandeered, or bought at prices below marginal opportunity costs.
d. The presence of a second-best market or policy environment which requires the computation of shadow prices different from existing market prices.

With the exception of intangibles, all necessary tools for analyzing these problems have been developed in Parts I–III of the text, so for the most part Chapter 26 will simply be recalling past results. There will be a considerable shift in perspective, however, because there is a clear distinction between optimal normative policy prescriptions and policy evaluation. The former, which was stressed in the theoretical analysis, tells the government what it ought to do given the underlying policy and economic environment. Policy evaluation, on the other hand, is concerned with the measurement of costs and benefits given the underlying environment and the policies *actually* undertaken by the government regardless of whether or not they are optimal. If optimal normative policy prescriptions have not been followed, they are simply not relevant to cost and benefit measurement. Hence there must be a shift in emphasis away from theorems derived in tightly controlled policy environments toward the development of reasonable guidelines in the face of staggering real-world complexities. Nontheless, the theoretical *tools* necessary for developing "reasonable" guidelines are the same as those used in developing the normative theory, concepts such as the expenditure function, the general equilibrium profit function, and the individualistic social welfare function. Furthermore, the underlying policy environment is as important to cost-benefit evaluation as it is to notions of optimality. It matters whether first-best or second-best assumptions apply, and if the latter, exactly how the environment is second best. Perhaps the outstanding example in this regard concerns the distribution of income. If the underlying distribution is optimal, either by accident or through application of optimal first-best lump-sum taxes and transfers, the measurement of costs and benefits is a relatively straightforward exercise, at least in principle. Otherwise policy evaluation becomes extremely complex, enough so that it will pay to discuss the measurement problems listed above under the assumption of an optimal distribution of income. This is the only fruitful way of analyzing the implications of these problems, per se. The distribution issue will then be considered in Chapter 27.

INTANGIBLES

Intangibles are the most intractible of the measurement problems. An intangible is a benefit or cost for which there is no known method of assigning a dollar value. Examples are easy to come by: national security in defense; loss of life from environmental damage; the boost to national prestige of developing the first commercial supersonic airplane; the nation's inherent love affair with passenger rail travel; and so forth. By their very nature there is little that economic analysis can offer by way of guidance on intangibles. Indeed, if they are thought to be the major benefit (cost) of a particular project, as they undoubtedly are in many defense applications, there is no sense even attempting a full cost-benefit study. Cost-benefit analysis is only useful for evaluation purposes if costs and benefits can be reasonably quantified.

It is not surprising, therefore, that cost-benefit analysis is not used to evaluate alternative advanced weapons systems. Rather, the Department of Defense determines certain military objectives, requests proposals for weapons designed to meet these objectives, and then awards contracts on the basis of three broadly defined criteria—ability to meet the objectives, time to completion of the project, and cost.[1] The military objectives are the benefits, but they are simply assumed at the outset and not subjected to much further analysis in the awarding

---

[1] Peck and Scherer's book, *The Weapons Acquisition Process: An Economic Analysis*, remains the classic source on the evaluation procedures for military hardware. M. Peck and F. Scherer, *The Weapons Acquisition Process: An Economic Analysis* (Boston, Mass.: Division of Research, Graduate School of Business Administration, Harvard University, 1962).

of contracts. There is an obvious loss of accountability which cost-benefit analysis is meant to promote, because the military itself largely determines the relevant objectives, but there is probably no other practical way to proceed.

The increased (decreased) probability of death (or illness or serious injury) associated with many nondefense projects (e.g., nuclear power plants, public innoculation programs, interstate highways) is another obvious example of an external diseconomy (economy) that may well be intangible. Public sector economists universally agree that this type of externality ought to be included as a true project cost (benefit), but there is widespread disagreement over whether or not the value of a person's life is measurable, and if so, how to do it. The following three examples should suffice as an illustration of the broad range of opinions on this issue. One popular method, generally attributed to Kneese,[2] equates the value of life to the economic value of life, equal to the present discounted value of an individual's gross earnings over his lifetime, with each year's earnings weighted by the probability that the person will live through that year. Should the individual die unexpectedly as a result of a government project, the discounted earnings stream defines the cost of that death. Mishan[3] rejects this approach in favor of computing each individual's subjective evaluation of the Hicks Compensating Variation required to offset his *involuntary exposure* to the increased risk of death (or disability) resulting from the project. According to Mishan, these subjective *HCV*'s will consist of three components:

a. The compensatory payment required to offset the (subjectively determined) increased risk of death per se, either directly (e.g., directly exposure to radiation) or indirectly (e.g., the spread of an infectious disease originally contacted by someone else).
b. The psychic costs of bereavement over the increased risk of death to others.
c. The financial gain or loss to the individual associated with the increased risk of death of others.

These individual *HCV*'s are then simply aggregated to determine the total costs (benefits) of the probable loss (savings) of life across the entire population. Mishan also distinguishes between involuntary and voluntary exposure to the increased risk of death, arguing that the latter is already built into ordinary demand curves. For instance, an individual's demand for a particular mode of transportation already includes an assessment of the subjective probability of incurring death (or injury) while traveling. Hence, including the voluntary exposure to these risks in addition to the *HCV* computed directly from that demand curve would entail double counting.

To cite one last opinion, Broome[4] argues that it is virtually impossible to place a value on life so long as one believes that individuals view death, with

---

[2] A. Kneese, "Research Goals and Progress toward Them," in H. Jarrett, ed., *Environmental Quality in a Growing Economy* (Washington, D.C.: Johns Hopkins Press, 1966).

[3] E. Mishan, "Evaluation of Life and Limb: A Theoretical Approach," *Journal of Political Economy*, March/April 1971.

[4] J. Broome, "Trying to Value a Life," *Journal of Public Economics*, February 1978.

certainty, as infinitely costly. Speaking directly to Mishan's position, Broome contends that each individual's subjective assessment of the increased probability of dying is irrelevant from a social perspective once one concedes that some people are virtually certain to die as a result of a project. The problem is really one of misinformation. Suppose the government announces that 10 people out of a population of 1,000 will die as a consequence of building a nuclear power plant. Each of the thousand people might reasonably assume everyone's chances of death have increased by 1 percent, and proceed to compute "Mishan" *HCV*'s based on this assessment. Suppose, on the other hand, the government could name the ten individuals who will die. The aggregate "Mishan" *HCV*'s would surely be much different in this case, perhaps infinitely large. In all likelihood the former situation will apply, but even so, Broome argues that the latter calculation is the appropriate one if the government adopts an *HCV* approach to the valuation of life. From the government's point of view, the relevant points are that ten people *will* die, each person views death as infinitely costly, and each individual *HCV* receives equal weight.

Of course, this leads one immediately to the position that any project involving any expected loss of life should not be undertaken, a position Broome views as equally nonsensical. His final judgment is that loss of life is a true intangible that cannot be subjected to the usual willingness-to-pay calculation. Public officials must simply make decisions given the existence of the intangible.

It should be noted, however, that Broome's position has not exactly carried the day. He was sharply criticized in a number of negative "Comments," some supporting Mishan and others suggesting still different approaches to the evaluation of a person's life.[5] However, even if one believes that the value of life is measurable in principle, there remains the difficult task of evaluating such concepts as Mishan's individual *HCV*'s or Kneese's economic value of life. In that sense Broome's pessimism is easily shared.

The real danger with true intangibles is that they can easily undermine objective cost-benefit analysis in nondefense areas when they are realistically only a fraction of overall benefits or costs, thereby turning the analysis into a blatantly political exercise. By placing a sufficiently large implicit dollar value on some intangible element of a project, the project's present value can arbitrarily be made positive or negative. Partisans will undoubtedly always be able to discover "significant" intangible benefits or costs in any government project, but this should not preclude undertaking a careful cost-benefit analysis. To the contrary, the only possible way of obtaining any proximate valuation of the intangibles is by means of a cost-benefit analysis of tangible project costs and benefits. The tangible data can then be used to place an implicit lower bound on the value of the intangible elements. For example, suppose the government must choose between two mutually exclusive alternatives, *A* and *B*, with the

---

[5] J. M. Buchanan and R. L. Faith, "Trying Again to Value a Life"; M. W. Jones-Lee, "Trying to Value a Life: Why Broome Does Not Sweep Clean"; A. Williams, "A Note on 'Trying to Value a Life'"; and J. Broome, "Trying to Value a Life: A Reply," *Journal of Public Economics*, October 1979.

FIGURE 26–1

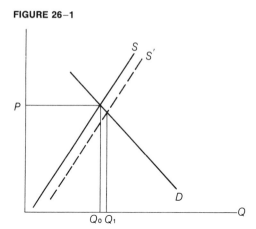

following properties: the quantifiable present value of A is greater than the quantifiable present value of B, but B is perceived to contain some intangible benefits. For B to be chosen, the implicit dollar value of its intangible benefits must be at least $(PV_A - PV_B)$. One can then ask whether society would conceivably be willing to pay that much for the alleged intangible benefits. Without a cost-benefit study, even a lower bound on the value of intangible benefits (costs) is unobtainable.

LUMPINESS

If a private firm invests in a new machine that will increase its annual production capacity by, say, 1,000 units, it will typically measure the benefits of the machine as the increase in expected revenues from the 1,000 units, equal to 1,000 × the existing and expected future market price of the item each year for the projected life of the machine. The revenue measure $P \times \Delta Q$ is usually considered to be a reasonable approximation of the social benefits of the machine so long as the 1,000 units represents a "small" increment to overall market capacity. As depicted in Figure 26–1, $(Q - Q_0) = 1,000$, is such a small addition to the overall market that it has virtually no effect on the market price.[6]

Government investments, on the other hand, often represent substantial additions to existing market capacity, enough so that they do significantly affect prices. This situation is depicted in Figure 26–2. Obvious examples would include hydroelectric projects which can significantly reduce the price of electricity to an entire region, or large additions to a public transportation network in an urban area. In these cases $P \cdot \Delta Q$ revenue calculations are no longer good approximations of the benefits. Unfortunately the proper benefit measures are a good deal more complex. However, they have all been developed

---

[6] Further discussion of this point follows.

FIGURE 26-2

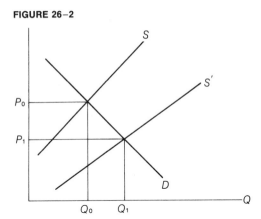

in various contexts scattered throughout the theoretical analysis in Parts I–III. Our purpose here will be to collect and summarize these results within the single context of benefit measurement when prices change significantly (with chapter references included).

First-Best Benefit Measures—A Single Price Change

As always in public sector analysis it matters whether the underlying policy environment is considered first best or second best, although perhaps less so here than in other areas. To keep matters straight, however, we will assume to begin with that the environment is first best, that only a single price changes, and that there are no additional relevant supply effects from changes in production (e.g., linear or constant returns to scale (CRS) general technology). Under these conditions, we saw that the appropriate benefit measures can be approximated by areas behind various demand curves. Our previous analysis developed three such area measures, each depicted in Figure 26–3. (For purposes of discussion, assume price drops from P_0 to P_1.)

FIGURE 26-3

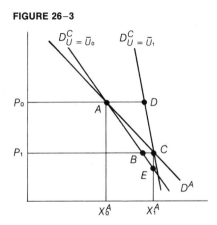

1.   *Marshallian consumer surplus*, equal to the area behind the actual market demand curve, D^A, between the initial and final equilibrium prices P_0 and P_1, area $P_0 P_1 C A$ (Chapters 4, 9, and 15).

2.   *The Hicks Compensating Variation* (*HCV*), equal to the area behind the demand curve compensated at the original utility level, U^0, $D^c_{U = \bar{U}^0}$, between the prices P_0 and P_1, area $P_0 P_1 B A$. This measures the lump-sum income the consumer would be willing to sacrifice in order to purchase X at the new lower price P_1. Notice that the demand compensated at the original utility level exceeds actual demand at prices greater than P_0, equals X^A_0 at P_0, and is less than actual demand at prices lower than P_0. At P_0 the required lump-sum income is the actual income. At prices above P_0 the consumer would receive compensation so that his income is greater than actual income, and vice versa for prices less than P_0 (Chapters 4, 9, and 15).

3.   *The Hicks Equivalent Variation* (*HEV*), equal to the area behind the demand curve compensated at the new utility level U^1, $D^c_{U = \bar{U}^1}$, between the prices P_0 and P_1, area $P_0 P_1 C D$. This area represents the payment the consumer requires to return to the original price P_0. Notice that demand compensated at the new utility level exceeds actual demand at prices greater than P_1, equals actual demand at P_1, and is less than actual demand at prices less than P_1, by similarly reasoning applied to the position of the demand curve compensated at U^0 (Chapters 4, 9, and 15).

4.   A fourth measure commonly employed in the literature, which we have not developed formally, is *the compensating surplus*, which is equal to the area *under* the demand curve compensated at the original utility level U^0, $D^C_{U = \bar{U}_0}$, between the initial and final equilibrium outputs, X^A_0 and X^A_1, area $A E X^A_1 X^A_0$. The measure represents the amount of the numeraire good the consumer would be willing to sacrifice to be able to consume (supply) the actual quantities of all other goods (factors) existing at the new equilibrium. In sacrificing the numeraire good, the consumer returns to the initial utility level.[7]

The differences in these areas clearly turn on income effects, since the consumer is paying or receiving different amounts of lump-sum income in each case. Therefore, to avoid having to choose among them, and also because of data limitations, empirical researchers often assume away all income effects, so that all the compensated curves will coincide with the actual market demand curve. This assumption is inconsistent with measurement of benefits in a single market, however, because changes in compensated demand in response to a price change in one market imply a change in demand in at least one other market. This point is often ignored in empirical research. It is also empirically unrealistic to assume away income effects.

Recognizing income effects, the researcher is faced with choosing among these alternative measures. Since they place different values on the benefits, he will want to choose one of them and apply it consistently across all projects.

---

[7] P. Diamond and D. McFadden, "Some Uses of the Expenditure Function in Public Finance," *Journal of Public Economics*, February 1974, and W. Moss, "Some Uses of the Expenditure Function in Public Finance: A Comment," *Journal of Public Economics*, April–May 1976.

In theory, measures (2)–(4) dominate (1) because the last three all have valid willingness-to-pay interpretations whereas Marshallian consumer surplus does not. For example, the HCV is the difference between the consumer's expenditure function evaluated at the original utility level,

$$(26.1) \qquad HCV = M(q_1^0; \bar{q}_2, \ldots, \bar{q}_N; \bar{U}^0) - M(q_1^1; \bar{q}_2, \ldots, \bar{q}_N; \bar{U}^0)$$

$$= \int_{q_1^1}^{q_1^0} \frac{\partial M(q_1; \bar{q}_2, \ldots, \bar{q}_N; \bar{U}^0) dq_1}{\partial q_1}$$

$$\int_{q_1^1}^{q_1^0} X_1(q_1; \bar{q}_2, \ldots, \bar{q}_N; \bar{U}^0) dq_1$$

and similarly for the HEV and the compensating surplus. Marshallian consumer surplus, on the other hand, is simply a money index of utility change that depends on the path taken by prices and income between the initial and final equilibrium. Of course, if the researcher maintains the assumption of a single price change, with income and all other prices constant, the path dependency problem does not arise.

In practice, the prior choice will undoubtedly come down to Marshallian consumer surplus along an estimated market demand curve versus any one of the compensated measures, since if there are sufficient data to compute any one of the compensating measures they can all be computed.

Ron Willig has recently shown that the Marshallian measure will be a reasonable choice for empirical work (Chapter 9)[8] under the assumptions of a single price change and linear technologies. Empirical research has long used the Marshallian measure anyway, accepting more or less on faith what Willig was finally able to prove. It should be stressed, however, that Willig's theorem applies strictly to an individual's demand curve, not the more commonly observed market demand curve. The aggregation problem is sticky, one which researchers typically avoid by assuming identical individuals (or a few subsets of identical individuals), with homothetic preferences. Lacking data at the individual level, this assumption is probably unavoidable.

Whatever measure is chosen it is also important to understand that these area measures of benefits do not create a bias for or against public sector projects relative to the standard private sector revenue measure. $q \cdot \Delta X$ is also a willingness-to-pay measure under the assumption that ΔX is sufficiently small so that it has no effect on price. This can be seen directly by comparing $q \cdot \Delta X$ with the compensating surplus measure (4). Relative to the numeraire, $q_x = MRS_{X,\text{numeraire}}$, or the amount of the numeraire good the consumer would be willing to sacrifice in exchange for an additional unit of X. Hence, $q_x \cdot \Delta X$ gives the total amount of the numeraire the consumer would be willing to sacrifice for all additional units of X, under the assumption that q_x has not changed. But this is exactly what the compensating surplus measures.

---

[8] R. Willig, "Consumer's Surplus without Apology," *American Economic Review*, September 1976.

FIGURE 26-4

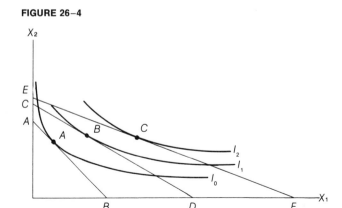

As a final note, some economists have expressed a preference for the Hicks Equivalent Variation if more than one project is being evaluated and the government for some reason can only finance a limited subset of all those with positive present value.[9] All the measures will indicate whether accepting any given project and moving to a new equilibrium is preferred to the original situation, but with limited funds the Hicks Compensating Variation and the compensating surplus can be misleading. Consider the situation depicted in Figure 26-4, in which the economy is at point A, and the government is considering two projects, one (B) which will bring the economy to point B, and another (C) which will bring the economy to point C. Suppose the government can finance only one of them. Clearly the government should choose project C.

The Hicks Equivalent Variation will indicate C is the preferred alternative since the same price line AB is first moved tangent to I_1 to evaluate B and then tangent to I_2 to evaluate C. At this common parallel, I_2 must be the farthest from the axis. The Hicks Compensating Variation, on the other hand, first measures the distance from I_1 to I_0 at the parallel CD, and then the distance from I_2 to I_0 at the parallel EF. Despite the fact that CPB, the first distance measure could easily be greater than the second, indicating a preference for B. A similar demonstration applies to the compensating surplus. The anomaly can occur because the distances are taken in different ways from one curve to the next. Hence the preference for the Hicks Equivalent Variation, which standardizes the distance measures by selecting the same parallel each time.

First-Best Analysis—Multiple Price Changes

The compensating measures easily generalize to situations in which more than one price changes. If producer prices are assumed unchanged, the Hicks

---

[9] See, for example, J. F. Oiesen, "A Theoretical Justification of Cost-Benefit Analysis," *Staff Study: Report No. 55-213-U9-5* (Cambridge, Mass.: U.S. Department of Transportation, Transportation Systems Center, Kendall Square), pp. 29–30 (draft).

Compensating Variation is:

(26.2) $$HCV = M(\vec{q}^0;\bar{U}^0) - M(\vec{q}^1;\bar{U}^0)$$

where:

$\vec{q}^0 =$ the vector of consumer prices at the original equilibrium.

$\vec{q}^1 =$ the vector of consumer prices at the final equilibrium.

and similarly for the other two measures. The multiple price change measures can also be interpreted as summations of areas under compensated demand (factor supply) curves in each market, as was shown in Chapter 15 when discussing deadweight loss from taxation. Prices are assumed to change one at a time with each demand curve evaluated at a vector of prices containing the new prices for those markets for which areas have been computed, and the initial prices in the remaining markets. Because these are compensated demand curves, the final value of the measure obtained in this manner will be invariant to the order of summation because $\partial X_i^C/\partial q_j = \partial X_j^C/\partial q_i$, all i, j, and income is assumed constant. This again is the notion of path independence, that any assumed path of price changes from the initial to the final general equilibrium will generate the same value for any of these measures. Path independence does not hold for Marshallian consumer surplus with multiple price changes, but if the researcher is willing to assume away income effects there is no problem, since all benefit measures are then identical.[10]

First-Best Analysis—General Technology

Up to this point we have been considering the lump-sum income the consumer would be willing to pay for the price changes resulting from a lumpy government investment. This is only the demand side of the problem. The

---

[10] The following set of references provide an excellent overview of consumer surplus and, more generally, the welfare implications of price changes:

P. Samuelson, "Social Indifference Curves," *Quarterly Journal of Economics*, February 1956.

P. Samuelson, *Foundations of Economic Analysis* (New York: Atheneum, 1965).

P. Samuelson, "Constancy of the Marginal Utility of Income," in O. Lange, et al., eds., *Studies in Mathematical Economics and Econometrics: In Memory of Henry Schultz* (Plainview, N.Y.: Brooks for Libraries Press, 1968).

D. Patinkin, "Demand Curves and Consumer's Surplus," in C. Christ, et al., eds., *Measurement in Economics* (Stanford, Calif.: Stanford University Press, 1963).

A. Harberger, "Three Basic Postulates for Applied Welfare Economics," *Journal of Economic Literature*, September 1971.

D. Richter, "Games Pythagoreans Play," *Public Finance Quarterly*, October 1977.

A. Dixit, "Welfare Effects of Tax and Price Changes," *Journal of Public Economics*, February 1975. Also, A. Dixit and K. Munk, "Welfare Effects of Tax and Price Changes: A Correction," *Journal of Public Economics*, August 1977.

R. Willig, "Consumer's Surplus without Apology," *American Economic Review*, September 1976.

J. Searde, "Consumer's Surplus and Linearity of Engel's Curves," *Economic Journal*, September 1978.

G. McKenzie, "Measuring Gains and Losses," *Journal of Political Economy*, June 1976.

G. McKenzie and I. Pearce, "Exact Measures of Welfare and the Cost of Living," *Review of Economic Studies*, October 1976.

benefit measure must also include supply side effects, in particular, any changes in actual *pure economic profits from private production* in response to the government investment. Notice the emphasis on pure economic profits, a source of lump-sum income. Changes in factor incomes, including opportunity returns to capital, are already incorporated in the consumer's expenditure function in so far as the factor supplies are variable (income changes accruing to factors in absolutely fixed supply can be considered part of the pure profits from private production).

Analytically, equation (26.2) is simply extended to incorporate the change in the value of the general equilibrium profit function at the final and initial producer prices. Hence, the general technology Hicks Compensation Variation measure of benefits is

$$(26.3) \qquad HCV = [M(\vec{q}_0; \bar{U}^0) - M(\vec{q}_1; \bar{U}^0)] + [\pi(\vec{p}_1) - \pi(\vec{p}_0)]$$

(26.3) can be given one of two interpretations. As written it compares the lump-sum income the consumer is willing to sacrifice for the change in prices plus the change in pure profits from production. However, $M(\vec{q}_0; \bar{U}^0) = \pi(\vec{p}_0)$. Therefore,

$$(26.4) \qquad\qquad HCV = \pi(\vec{p}_1) - M(\vec{q}_1; \bar{U}^0)$$

interpreted as the pure lump-sum income the consumer receives from production at the new equilibrium less the lump-sum income the consumer requires at the new equilibrium to attain the original utility level. Similar modifications apply to the HEV and the compensating surplus.

BENEFIT MEASURES—
SECOND-BEST CONSIDERATIONS

Equations (26.3) and (26.4) remain appropriate general equilibrium measures of the benefits of government projects in a second-best environment for one consumer equivalent economies. However, they may be incomplete in a second-best environment if some additional constraint implies a further source of lump-sum income change, for example, a constraint that the government's budget deficit must be simultaneously decreased by a certain amount or be maintained at some non-zero level. We saw this when analyzing the dead-weight loss from taxation, in which the budget deficit was part of the loss measure. However, most second-best applications with budget constraints assume that the budget will remain balanced at level zero, in which case these equations are complete specifications of the net benefits from lumpy government investments. They incorporate all relevant general equilibrium reactions to an investment expressed in the form of lump-sum income changes. In principle the measures are straightforward, but they may be difficult even to approximate in actual practice. For instance, will any researcher ever be able to estimate the full pattern of pure economic profits and losses in the private sector resulting from any given project? Beyond questions such as this, there is an additional serious conceptual problem with applying these measures. If compensation actually occurs, and production exhibits general technology, the compensated general equilibrium price vector will differ from the actual observed general equilibrium price vector, so it is unclear how to evaluate equations such as (26.3). (Refer to the discussion of this point in Chapters 16 and 17.)

This particular ambiguity has led Harberger to suggest an alternative method of evaluating price changes with distorted equilibria. Recall equation (15.11),

$$(26.5) \qquad L(\vec{t}) = -\frac{1}{2} \sum_{i=2}^{N} \sum_{j=2}^{N} t_i t_j \frac{\partial X_i^c}{\partial q_j}$$

which approximates the total loss from a vector of distorting unit taxes $\vec{t} = (t_2, \ldots, t_N)$ with constant producer prices by assuming that the compensated demand derivatives $\partial X_i^c / \partial q_j$ are constant over the relevant range of prices. In general, (26.5) can be represented as

$$(26.6) \qquad L(Z^*) = \int_{Z^0}^{Z^*} \sum_{i=1}^{N} D^i(\vec{Z}) \frac{\partial X_i}{\partial Z} d\vec{Z}$$

where:

$\vec{Z}$ = a vector of policy variables (not necessarily unit taxes).

$D^i(\vec{Z})$ = the difference between the consumer and producer prices, $\vec{q}$ and $\vec{p}$ respectively, expressed as a function of $\vec{Z}$ ($= t_i$, when unit taxes are the policy variables and the only source of distortion).

Harberger recommends applying (26.5) or (26.6) for both linear *and* general technologies, in which the derivatives $\partial X_i / \partial Z$ represent changes in the general equilibrium values of the quantities X_i given that the government acts in such a way as to keep all resources fully employed.[11] The practical advantage of this technique is that the loci of general equilibrium values of the X_i and their derivatives are observable, but notice that his approach lacks strict theoretical justification. Compensation is occuring, but only to maintain production on the production possibilities frontier, not necessarily to keep the consumer at a particular utility level. The difference is depicted in Figure (26–5), with X_2 serving as the numeraire. Suppose the economy is originally at the undistorted equilibrium A, with P_{X_1} equal to (minus) the slope of the line segment ab. The government then levies a unit tax on X_1, raising P_{X_1} to (minus) the slope of line segment cd. Assume the government spends the revenues (and engages in

---

[11] He argues his case most forcefully in A. Harberger, "Three Basic Postulates for Applied Welfare Economics," although his methodology is also spelled out in A. Harberger, "Taxation, Resource Allocation, and Welfare," in *The Role of Direct and Indirect Taxes in the Federal Revenue System*, National Bureau of Economic Research and The Brookings Institution (Princeton, N.J.: Princeton University Press, 1964), and A. Harberger, "The Measurement of Waste," *American Economic Association Papers and Proceedings*, May 1964. See also, A. Harberger, *Taxation and Welfare* (Boston, Mass.: Little, Brown and Company, 1974), pp. 86–90. Harberger is also willing to ignore distributional considerations, the third of his three basic postulates for applied work.

FIGURE 26-5

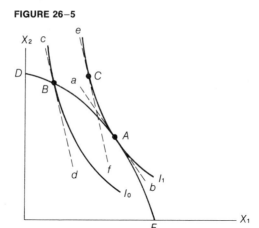

further lump-sum distribution) in such a way as to keep society on its production-possibilities frontier DE, thereby establishing a new general equilibrium at B. The change from A to B is represented by $\sum_j (\partial X_i/\partial t_j) t_j$ in (26.5) ($\int_{Z^0}^{Z^*} (\partial X_i/\partial Z)dZ$ in (26.6)) where the $\partial X_i/\partial t_j (\partial X_i/\partial Z)$ represent the (constant) marginal general equilibrium changes in X_i in response to the tax. Because of the nature of the X_i, (26.6) is a path dependent money index of utility change.

On the other hand, C represents the fully compensated equilibrium, with the change from A to C given by $\sum_j (\partial X_i^c/\partial t_j) t_j$ ($\int_{Z^0}^{Z^*} (\partial X_i^c/\partial Z)d\check{Z}$), where the $\partial X_i^c/\partial t_j (\partial X_i^c/\partial Z)$ represent the (constant) Slutsky substitution terms evaluated at the utility level associated with I_1. The fully compensated loss measure would also incorporate the change in the value of pure economic profits as society moves from A to C. The two measures of loss will clearly differ, in general, begging the question of whether Harberger's approach is a reasonable practical compromise. Harberger obviously thinks that it is, but others may well disagree.[12]

NONMARKETED BENEFITS OR COSTS

When evaluating government services offered free of charge (e.g., toll-free bridges and highways, free access to over-the-air commercial television, free recreational facilities, and so forth), the first important consideration is whether the analysis can assume a first-best or second-best environment.[13] First-best assumptions are only appropriate if the service *ought* to have a zero price at the optimum, in that short-run marginal costs are zero and there are no

---

[12] Don Richter provides a lucid critique of the Harberger loss measure in Richter, "Games Pythagoreans Play."

[13] To keep the analysis as simple as possible, the discussion in this section will be limited to benefits offered free of charge. The analysis is easily generalized to benefits that are in some meaningful sense "underpriced," or to conscripted resources.

capacity constraints. Otherwise the zero price cannot possibly be first best. These supply characteristics are, of course, in addition to all the other conditions necessary for first-best analysis, such as an optimal income distribution, perfectly competitive markets everywhere, and so forth.

Some public services may actually approximate these supply conditions. The marginal costs of having another viewer turn on his television set are virtually zero no matter how many people watch a particular program, nor are there any effective capacity constraints on over-the-air telecasts. A rural road between two cities, or rural bridges, do not typically suffer congestion either, and maintenance costs may be as much a function of weathering as travel. Clearly the marginal costs of a few additional vehicles is near zero for any given average traffic flow. Thus, the fact that public television is free at the point of viewing, and rural roads and bridges generally do not charge per-use tolls can reasonably be viewed as examples of first-best pricing. In these cases the benefit measure is straightforward, equal to the area under an appropriate compensated demand curve over its full length less the full costs of providing the service (assuming that costs are covered through lump-sum taxation). If providing the services changes prices in other markets, then these price changes (and profit effects) would enter into the measure as well. In other words, these services are just another example of lumpy public projects, and equations such as (26.3) or (26.4) can be applied directly in measuring their net benefits.

These formulas may not be too useful, however, because if price has never been different from zero, the relevant demand curves cannot possibly be estimated. All one can project is the zero-price point on the demand curve. It may be possible to estimate how many people will actually use the service at zero price. But since the slope through this point on the demand curve is unknown, even the standard restrictions placed on demand curves in empirical analysis—linearity, zero income effects, and so forth—are not much use. Faced with this problem, researchers have to resort to indirect benefit measures, trying, in effect, to determine the underlying sources of value giving rise to the unknown demand curve. For instance, suppose the government builds a straight, four-lane superhighway between two small cities which had previously been connected by a twisting, two-lane highway, an example relevant to many segments of the U.S. Interstate Highway System. In lieu of estimating an unknowable demand curve, the analyst could obtain estimates of projected travel demand at zero price and multiply this estimate by the per trip value to the average user of having this new road. The sources of value to the average passenger (or commercial user) clearly derive from factors such as increased safety, improved gasoline economy, reduced wear and tear on the vehicle, and time saved per trip. Having identified these sources, one then tries to obtain reasonable dollar estimates of their value to users. For example, accident records and medical expenses might be used to evaluate the safety factor (with some arbitrary evaluation for each life saved), and depreciation data on trucks and automobiles to evaluate the "wear and tear" factor. In transportation analysis, economists typically choose the average wage rate, or some multiple thereof, to evaluate time saved, which turns out to be a major component of total value in most studies. This practice stems from the neoclassical view of the labor-leisure choice, in which the $MRS_{labor,\,leisure}$ is the wage. If the time savings are considerable, a multiple of the wage is sometimes used to reflect the value of inframarginal hours.[14]

Indirect evaluations are also common in cost-benefit studies of public recreational facilities, noise pollution reduction and other similar areas in which the government has been unwilling or unable to set price equal to benefits received in pseudo-market fashion. These indirect valuations are often ingenious, but they always serve to emphasize the judgmental nature of cost-benefit analysis. If the demand curves could be estimated, each study would proceed in the same way, trying to obtain the best possible estimates of the relevant price and income elasticities. But with indirect evaluations it is always possible that different researchers will identify somewhat different sources of value from one study to the next, and evaluate commonly perceived sources in different ways. Consequently choosing a "best" estimate will almost certainly be a matter of subjective judgment and taste.

So far we have been considering nonmarketed benefits under the first-best assumption that a zero-price is pareto-optimal because marginal costs are (approximately) zero. If, on the other hand, services are given away for which marginal costs exceed zero, the analysis of benefits is inherently second best. This further complicates the valuation of the benefits, because as in all second-best analysis, valuation depends upon the complete specification of the second-best environment, and there are endless possible variations. For instance, the cost-benefit study must specify the supply conditions for this market. Is the good being rationed because of a capacity constraint and, if so, how: first-come, first-served? rationing coupons? are resales possible? and so forth. Presumably researchers could agree on the answers to these questions, but still further questions pose more difficult problems. For example, what are the underlying cost conditions? Is the capital stock optimal for the quantity demanded at zero price so that short-run and long-run marginal costs are equal, or are short and long-run marginal costs substantially different. Second, how is the good being financed? Since first-best assumptions have been discarded in this market, is the analyst willing to add more realistic assumptions elsewhere, such as financing with distorting taxation? Evaluation of the benefits and costs will depend upon the answers to all such questions, and there is obviously broad scope for disagreement.

To get some feel for the sensitivity of cost-benefit evaluation to these kinds of questions, let us consider two quite different conditions under which goods are given away free. Mumy and Hanke have recently analyzed the case of a

---

[14] For further analysis of the valuation of time savings, see E. Mishan, *Cost-Benefit Analysis*, new and expanded edition (New York: Praeger Publishers, 1976), chap. 41. Mishan analyzes various benefit and cost valuation problems throughout Part V. For further analysis of time-savings valuation, see D. Tipping, "Time Savings in Transport Studies," *Economic Journal*, December 1968. Another useful source is R. Layard, ed., *Cost-Benefit Analysis* (Harmondsworth, Middlesex, England: Penguin Education, Penguin Books, Ltd., 1972).

FIGURE 26-6

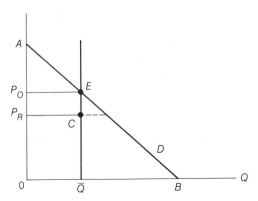

good given away on a rationed basis in which, except for rationing in this one market, the underlying environment is first best.[15] In particular, they assume that the distribution of income is optimal, project costs are paid by lump-sum taxation, all other markets are perfectly competitive, and other prices are unaffected by the project. With these assumptions they can concentrate solely on the rationed market in evaluating the benefits.

They then make two further simplifying assumptions in the rationed market. First, they assume away income effects, so that the ordinary demand curve (assumed to be known) can be used in their benefit measure. Second, they assume all costs associated with the project result from additions to capacity, which is infinitely divisible. Thus, they avoid distinctions between short-run and long-run marginal costs, and possible resulting "lumpiness" problems.

With all these assumptions, the analysis turns on the single question of how the good is rationed. Consider a variation of the Mumy-Hanke model depicted in Figure 26-6 in which the government supplies a single quantity of some good, $\bar{Q}$, at fixed costs $\bar{C}$. The demand for the good, D, is linear in price, and independent of income (assuming a fixed quantity $\bar{Q}$ does not restrict the analysis in any way since the focus is on the rationing mechanism). The pareto-optimum price is P_0, which allocates $\bar{Q}$ exactly to those users willing to pay the highest price for the service. The net benefits using P_0 can be represented by the compensating surplus measure

(26.7) $$CS(\bar{Q}) = \int_0^{\bar{Q}} P(Q)dQ - \bar{C}$$

where:

$P(Q)$ = the inverse of D.

$\bar{C}$ = the fixed costs of $\bar{Q}$ expressed in terms of the numeraire good.

---

[15] G. Mumy and S. Hanke, "Public Investment Criteria for Underpriced Public Projects," *American Economic Review*, September 1975.

If the government gives the service away, consumers would want to consume $0B$ units of the good. Since only $\bar{Q}$ units are available, the good must be rationed. This could be done in any number of ways, but suppose rationing occurs randomly so that all consumers have an equal probability of consuming the good.[16] Under this assumption the expected value of a unit of consumption equals the average price along the demand curve, or

$$(26.8) \qquad P_R = \frac{1}{B} \int_0^B P(Q) dQ$$

If the demand curve is linear, as pictured,

$$(26.9) \qquad P_R = \frac{1}{2} 0A$$

With consumption rationed at $\bar{Q}$ units, therefore, the *total* expected net benefits of the rationed service are:

$$(26.10) \qquad CS_R(\bar{Q}) = \frac{\bar{Q}}{B} \int_0^B P(Q) \cdot dQ - \bar{C} = P_R \cdot \bar{Q} - \bar{C}$$

using the compensating surplus measure of net benefits. As expected, rationing lowers the net compensating surplus relative to the first-best price of P_0, by an amount equal to the area $AP_R CE$. This is the penalty incurred by foregoing the pricing mechanism, which naturally "rations" use to those willing to pay the highest prices.

Analyzing rationing schemes in a first-best environment is somewhat inconsistent because given the ability to generate an optimal distribution of income the government would have no real interest in rationing and incurring the welfare loss. Why allow the service to be consumed by other than those who most want it? In real life the primary motivation for pricing below the natural market-clearing price, and rationing, is surely distributional. In recognition of the fact that it has been unable to correct distributional imbalances through general tax and transfer mechanisms, the government tries to offset the social ills of a nonoptimal distribution by foregoing the pricing mechanism and offering the poor a chance to consume certain goods. Distributional considerations in cost-benefit analysis are the subject of the following chapter, but it is intuitively clear that if consumers along the demand curve from P_0 to A have sufficiently low social marginal utilities, and consumers along the demand curve from 0 to P_0 have sufficiently high social marginal utilities, social welfare could conceivably be improved by the zero price, rationing mechanism.

The preceding analysis indicates that measuring net benefits when the government gives away services on a rationed basis involves fairly straightforward adaptations of standard net benefit measures, so long as the analysis

---

[16] Mumy and Hanke analyze other rationing schemes as well. We chose this one because it is realistic and provides a simple illustration of net benefit measurement with rationing.

is able to retain all other first-best assumptions. It is also fairly easy to introduce nonmarketed benefits into a second-best model. To illustrate this point, let us return to the second-best model of Chapter 22 in which the government produces goods and services that may also be produced in the private sector, and covers the resulting deficit with unit "commodity" taxes on the (one) consumer's goods demanded and factors supplied. It was also assumed that the government bought and sold all inputs and outputs at the producer prices $\vec{p} = (p_1, \ldots, p_N)$. Recall that the measure of loss which the government sought to minimize was given by:

(26.11) $L(\vec{t}; \vec{Z}) = M(\vec{q}; \overline{U}) -$ Government surplus $- \pi(\vec{p})$

where:

$\vec{t} = (t_2, \ldots, t_N)$, the vector of commodity taxes.

$\vec{Z} = (Z_1, \ldots, Z_N)$, the vector of government inputs and outputs.

$\vec{q} = \vec{p} + \vec{t} = $ the vector of consumer prices, with $q_1 \equiv p_1 \equiv 1, t_1 = 0$.

$\overline{U} = $ the utility level when $\vec{Z} = \vec{t} = \vec{0}$.

$\pi(\vec{p}) = $ the general equilibrium profit function.

and

$$\text{Government surplus} = \sum_{i=2}^{N} t_i M_i + \sum_{i=2}^{N} p_i Z_i - p_1 g(Z_2, \ldots, Z_N)$$

where:

$M_i = $ the compensated demand (supply) for good (factor) i.

$Z_1 = -g(Z_2, \ldots, Z_N)$, the government's production function.

Since Loss $= -$Benefits, the benefits from taxation and government production are simply:

(26.12) $B(t; Z) = \pi(\vec{p}) - M(\vec{q}; \overline{U}) + $ Government surplus

If the government's budget constraint balances at level zero, then:

(26.13) $$B(t; Z) = \pi(\vec{p}) - M(\vec{q}; \overline{U})$$

which is just the Hicks Compensating Variation version of benefits with general private production technology, equation (26.4) above.

The basic structure of this model can be maintained when some government outputs are given away (or resources drafted) under the following assumptions.[17] Suppose only a subset $i = k + 1, \ldots, N$ of the Z_i are either given away or drafted. The remaining $i = 1, \ldots, K$, are bought and sold at the producer prices $(p_1, \ldots, p_K)$. To keep the analysis as general as possible, assume further that the goods (factors) given away (drafted) are routinely produced (purchased) in the private sector so that producer and consumer prices have been established

---

[17] The adaptation presented here appears in a set of unpublished class notes distributed by Peter Diamond.

for these goods (factors), and that the tax base to which the $\vec{t}$ apply is consumption (supply) less goods (factors) received free of charge (drafted) by the government. Write $\check{Z} = [Z_1, \ldots, Z_K; \check{0}]$ to represent the goods and factors bought and sold by the government, and $\check{X} = [\check{0}; X_{k+1}, \ldots, X_N]$ to represent the subset of goods (factors) given away (drafted) by the government. With this notation, and the preceding assumptions, the government's budget surplus at the compensated equilibrium becomes:

$$(26.14) \qquad S = \sum_{i=2}^{N} t_i(M_i - X_i) + \sum_{i=2}^{K} p_i Z_i - p_1 g(\check{Z}; \check{X})$$

where:

$Z_1 = -g(\check{Z}; \check{X})$, the government's production function incorporating both sold outputs (purchased inputs) and outputs (inputs) given away (drafted).

Notice that the tax revenue has to be sufficient to cover the deficit on government goods and factors bought and sold and still produce the desired surplus. Goods (factors) given away (drafted) do not directly reduce (increase) the government's surplus (deficit) from production.

The total benefits, considering taxation, government production of bought and sold inputs and outputs, and goods (factors) given away (drafted) by the government are therefore:

$$(26.15) \qquad B(\vec{t}; \check{Z}; \check{X}) = \pi(\vec{p}) - \left[M(\vec{q}; \bar{U}) - \sum_{i=k+1}^{N} q_i X_i^{\text{comp}} \right] + S$$

There are two differences, then, in the benefits measure when goods are given away. First, the form of the government surplus equation changes. Second, the lump-sum income required to keep the consumer indifferent to the initial pre-government situation is less than the value of the expenditure function by the value of the goods (factors) received from ("donated" to) the government free of charge, valued at the consumer prices, $\vec{q}$, established in the private production and sale of these goods at the compensated equilibrium. Because the consumer simply receives (offers) these goods (factors) from (to) government in amounts dictated by the government, the vector $\check{X}$ is a lump-sum event from the consumer's point of view. Thus it is appropriate to subtract its value in B, all the elements of which are in the form of lump-sum income.

It should be emphasized that the relatively minor adjustments in the benefits measure from the original model of government production with commodity taxation depend upon being able to retain the basic structure of that model. The modified model with free goods (factors) is fairly general and allows for second-best taxation, but it does contain some fairly restrictive assumptions that might not be applicable in real life applications. For example, it differs fundamentally from the Mumy-Hanke model in one crucial respect—there is no rationing of any goods that are given away. Furthermore it implicitly assumes optimal private and government production decisions so there is no distinction between long-run and short-run costs. Thus, the model is inherently long run. It also requires private purchase (sale) of all goods (factors) which the government provides (drafts) free of charge in order to evaluate these goods. Removing any one of these assumptions would require significant modifications in the government production-tax model of Chapter 22. Nonetheless, the model as it stands remains of a fairly general description of government policy in a second-best environment. It would appear to be applicable to government hydroelectric projects in which some of the benefits are sold (electricity) while others (recreational facilities) are given away even though they are routinely marketed in other contexts. We leave it to the reader to derive and interpret the first-order conditions for this model. The normative policy rules yield a number of interesting conclusions, including the fact that the existence of goods (factors) given away (drafted) does not change either the optimal tax rules or the result that with optimal taxation (and CRS in private production) the government should discount all *marketed* inputs and outputs at the marginal rate of transformation. On the other hand, a different discount rate applies to all *free* goods and *drafted* factors.

THE USE OF SHADOW PRICES FOR GOVERNMENT PROJECTS

The preceding sections discussed three problems commonly associated with government projects—intangibles, lumpiness, and nonmarketed benefits (costs)—that are unlikely to arise in private sector analysis. These problems need not always occur, however. In many instances government projects will be virtually identical to their private sector counterparts in that they represent marginal additions to capacity and all inputs and outputs are bought and sold at competitive private sector prices.[18] Even when this occurs, however, there will still be substantial differences between the *evaluation* of private and public sector costs and benefits, as a general rule.

As noted above, competitive producer prices are the proper values to attach to *each* unit of private inputs or outputs under these conditions, from society's point of view. $p \cdot \Delta Q$ is an appropriate gross benefit measure for a private project in either a first or second-best environment.

By contrast, equation (22.46), reproduced here as equation (26.16) (with a negative sign, since $B = -dL$):

$$(26.16) \qquad dB = -t'(M_{ij})E^{-1}\pi_{ij}dt + (-p_1 g_Z + p' + t'M_{ij}E^{-1})dZ$$

gives the proper shadow prices for government inputs and outputs in the one-consumer equivalent second-best economy of Chapter 22, under the twin assumptions of government purchase and sale at competitive private sector producer prices, and that changes in government production are infinitesimal,

---

[18] One may wonder why the government is involved in the production of these services, but that is beside the point for cost-benefit analysis.

meaning that they have virtually no effect on established market prices. Hence, even if the projects are "small," the government should not use the competitive producer prices for project evaluation, as a general rule, despite the fact these prices are appropriate for evaluating "small" changes in private sector inputs and outputs. Rather, the government should use the coefficients on $\vec{Z}$ which will differ, in general, from $\vec{p}$.[19]

These differences in public and private sector evaluation of similar kinds of production processes stem from the underlying assumptions of the model in Chapter 22. Recall that the derivation of (22.46) (26.16) *assumed* that private sector production is first-best efficient, using competitive producer prices for its decisions, and satisfying pareto-optimal rules of the form

$$(26.17) \qquad -\frac{dY_j}{dY_k} = \frac{f_k}{f_j} = \frac{p_k}{p_j} \qquad \text{all } j, k = 1, \ldots, N,$$

where:

$\vec{Y} = (Y_1, \ldots, Y_N) =$ the vector of private sector inputs and outputs.

$f(\vec{Y}) = 0 =$ the aggregate production possibilities for the private sector.

$\vec{p} = (p_1, \ldots, p_N) =$ the vector of competitively determined producer prices.

Given this assumed private sector behavior, if the government introduces distortions by means of per-unit taxes, it should also evaluate its own production decisions in accordance with (26.16). The cost coefficients on the $\vec{Z}$ will equal $\vec{p}$ only for special cases, such as if the underlying environment is first best, or the tax rates are optimal, or private sector production technology is linear. While it is true that (26.16) applies to a specific second-best model and that other models will generate different vectors of shadow prices, the same general principle will continue to apply: if the private sector is first-best efficient, changes in government production must be evaluated at shadow prices different from competitive producer prices, given government induced second-best distortions.

If the private sector is itself second best, then it would generally follow that the private sector would not use the competitive prices, $\vec{p}$, to evaluate the benefits and costs of its own projects. One would then expect the government shadow prices to differ from those in (26.16) under these circumstances. These conclusions once again underscore the point that when cost-benefit analysis employs second-best assumptions, it must carefully specify all aspects of the underlying policy environment assumed to be second best. Neither normative decision rules nor cost-benefit evaluations generalize across all second-best environments.

---

[19] Notice that, as an approximation, (26.16) is to be evaluated at the existing *levels* of $\vec{t}$, $\vec{Z}$, $\vec{p}$, and $\vec{q}$, which are assumed to be unchanged (approximately) when the elements of $\vec{t}$, or $\vec{Z}$ are subject to infinitesimal changes.

REFERENCES

Broome, J. "Trying to Value a Life." *Journal of Public Economics,* February 1978.

―――. "Trying to Value a Life: A Reply." *Journal of Public Economics,* October 1979.

Buchanan, J., and Faith, R. "Trying Again to Value a Life." *Journal of Public Economics,* October 1979.

Diamond, P., and McFadden, D. "Some Uses of the Expenditure Function in Public Finance." *Journal of Public Economics,* February 1974.

Dixit, A. "Welfare Effects of Tax and Price Changes." *Journal of Public Economics,* February 1975.

―――, and Munk, K. "Welfare Effects of Tax and Price Changes: A Correction." *Journal of Public Economics,* August 1977.

Hanke, S., and Mumy, G. "Public Investment Criteria for Underpriced Public Projects." *American Economic Review,* September 1975.

Harberger, A. "Three Basic Postulates for Applied Welfare Economics." *Journal of Economic Literature,* September 1971.

―――. *Taxation and Welfare.* Boston, Mass.: Little, Brown and Co., 1974.

―――. "Taxation, Resource Allocation, and Welfare." In *The Role of Direct and Indirect Taxes in the Federal Revenue System.* Princeton, N.J.: National Bureau of Economic Research and The Brookings Institution, Princeton University Press, 1964.

―――. "The Measurement of Waste." *American Economic Association Papers and Proceedings,* May 1964.

Jones-Lee, M. "Trying to Value a Life: Why Broome Does Not Sweep Clean." *Journal of Public Economics,* October 1979.

Kneese, A. "Research Goals and Progress toward Them." In *Environmental Quality in a Growing Economy,* edited by H. Jarret. Washington D.C.: Johns Hopkins Press, 1966.

Layard, R., ed. *Cost-Benefit Analysis.* Harmondsworth, Middlesex, England: Penguin Education, Penguin Books Ltd., 1972.

McKensie, G. "Measuring Gains and Losses." *Journal of Political Economy,* June 1976.

―――, and Pearce, I. "Exact Measures of Welfare and the Cost of Living." *Review of Economic Studies,* October 1976.

Mishan, E. J. *Cost-Benefit Analysis.* New and expanded edition. New York: Praeger Publishers, 1976.

―――. "Evaluation of Life and Limb: A Theoretical Approach." *Journal of Political Economy,* March/April 1971.

Moss, W. "Some Uses of the Expenditure Function in Public Finance: A Comment." *Journal of Public Economics,* April–May 1976.

Oiesen, J. F. "A Theoretical Justification of Cost-Benefit Analysis." *Staff Study: Report No. 55-213-U9-5.* Cambridge, Mass.: U.S. Department of Transportation, Transportation Systems Center, Kendall Square (draft).

Patinkin, D. "Demand Curves and Consumer's Surplus." In *Measurement in Economics,* edited by C. Christ et al. Stanford, Calif.: Stanford University Press, 1963.

Peck, M., and Scherer, F. *The Weapons Acquisition Process: An Economic Analysis.* Boston, Mass.: Division of Research, Graduate School of Business Administration, Harvard University, 1962.

Richter, D. "Games Pythagoreans Play." *Public Finance Quarterly,* October 1977.

Samuelson, P. A. "Constancy of the Marginal Utility of Income." In *Studies in Mathematical Economics and Econometrics: In Honor of Henry Schultz,* edited by O. Lange et al. Plainview, N.Y.: Books for Libraries Press, 1968.

———. *Foundations of Economic Analysis.* New York: Atheneum, 1965.

———. "Social Indifference Curves." *Quarterly Journal of Economics,* February 1956.

Searde, J. "Consumer's Surplus and Linearity of Engel's Curves." *Economic Journal,* September 1978.

Tipping, D. "Time Savings in Transport Studies." *Economic Journal,* December 1968.

Williams, A. "A Note on 'Trying to Value a Life.'" *Journal of Public Economics,* October 1979.

Willig, R. "Consumer's Surplus without Apology." *American Economic Review,* September 1976.

27

Cost-benefit analysis and the distribution of income

In our opinion the distribution question is the single most important issue in all of cost-benefit analysis. Should cost-benefit analysis rank government projects strictly on the basis of their aggregate present value, or should the analysis consider the distribution of the project's benefits and costs as well? Normative theory argues strongly for the latter interpretation if the income distribution is nonoptimal. Ideally, cost-benefit analysis should rank projects according to their contributions to social welfare. But if the distribution is nonoptimal, it can only do this if it includes the distributional consequences of the various projects. Ignoring distributional considerations is vastly simpler, but it limits cost-benefit analysis to an exercise in efficiency. While it may be useful to know project rankings by standard pareto-efficiency criteria, society might not be willing to choose projects on this basis alone. If not, then cost-benefit analysis becomes only an intermediate step in the overall process of project selection.

There is a clear dilemma here. To say that cost-benefit analysis should incorporate distributional considerations is one thing, but to suggest how this might be done in a clear and consistent manner is quite another. The normative analysis in Part III indicated time and again the devastating effect of distributional considerations on normative policy prescriptions. Whatever the context—"commodity" tax rules, optimal government responses to externalities, government production decision rules, and so forth—distributional considerations immensely complicated the optimal rules for social welfare maximization relative to the one-consumer equivalent case. Moreover, the policy rules became somewhat arbitrary and subjective, since the social welfare weights representing the distributional component were simply assumed to reflect the distributional preferences of society. Normative theory does not tell us how such preferences are actually determined or what they should be. Not surprisingly, cost-benefit analysis as an evaluative tool suffers an identical fate. Once distributional parameters are introduced into the evaluation, the present value calculations threaten to become so complex, and so highly subjective, that the analysis may well lose its ability to discriminate objectively among various investment alternatives. Yet ignoring the distribution of project benefits and costs may emasculate the analysis as an evaluation tool. It necessarily

FIGURE 27–1

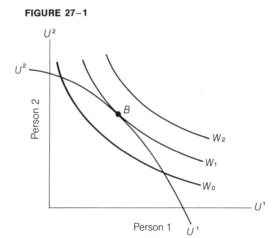

employs only part of the relevant information, and there is no way of determining the relative importance of included efficiency parameters and the excluded distributional parameters. This is the source of the dilemma and, as with all true dilemmas, there is no satisfactory resolution. All the analyst can do is decide in advance whether or not to include distributional considerations, and attempt to justify his decision. Reasonable arguments can be offered in support of either choice.

Suppose one decides that incorporating distribution judgments into the analysis is so subjective that no useful information can possibly result.[1] This argument alone would be sufficient grounds for ignoring distributional considerations, but there remains the question of whether aggregate present value calculations derived independently of distributional considerations are appropriate criteria for project selection. In other words, are cost-benefit analyses still worth doing?

There would appear to be three reasonable arguments for basing project selection solely on aggregate present value calculations. One could simply adopt the idealistic stance that the government should always be striving to reach the first-best bliss point regardless of society's current position. Recall that the bliss point is represented by point B in Figure 27–1, in which $U^2 - U^1$ is the first-best utility-possibilities frontier for persons 1 and 2, constrained only by the economy's underlying production technology and market clearance, and W_0, W_1, . . . , are a set of social indifference curves embodying society's distributional preferences. According to the social welfare rankings, B is distributionally the best of all efficient points on the utility-possibilities frontier.

---

[1] Harberger argues for ignoring distributional considerations as one of his postulates for applied research in A. Harberger, "Three Postulates for Applied Welfare Economics," *Journal of Economic Literature*, September 1971.

Attaining point B requires three conditions:

1. All markets are perfectly competitive.
2. Government policies may take any form required to satisfy first-best pareto-optimal conditions.
3. The government can tax and transfer lump sum to satisfy interpersonal welfare conditions of the form $(\partial W/\partial U^h)(\partial U^h/\partial X_{hi}) = $, all $h = 1, \ldots, H$, where the social welfare function takes the form $W = W[U^1(\ ), \ldots, U^H(\ )]$, and X_i is any one of the goods or factors. In order to continue the quest for the bliss point, the government must select all projects and only those projects with positive aggregate present value. This is just efficiency condition (2) applied to government investments. Accepting projects with aggregate present value less than zero because of their distributional consequences necessarily places society below the utility-possibilities frontier, thereby precluding attainment of the bliss point. As part of the quest, then, one must have faith that the government will tax and transfer to correct for unwanted distributional consequences arising from any given project. According to this view, cost-benefit analysis has a specific role, to ensure that the income (product) to be distributed is as large as possible. Cost-benefit analysis must *not* be concerned with distributional implications.

A second possible justification is the argument that, for all practical purposes, the economy is equivalent to a one-consumer economy. As discussed in Chapter 4 this requires one of three conditions, either that:

a. All consumers have identical and homothetic preferences; or
b. The government is continuously redistributing income lump sum to satisfy the first-best interpersonal equity conditions so that social marginal utilities of income are identical for all people; or
c. Green's condition on the covariance between social marginal utilities of income and individuals' consumption.

Of these three conditions, (b) would appear to be the most reasonable if only because it relies partially on value judgments. Econometric evidence suggests that condition (a) is violated in practice and condition (c) is simply implausible whatever value judgments one might hold with respect to social marginal utilities of income.

One is certainly free to argue that the underlying distribution of income is "about right" and that government redistributional policies tend to correct distributional imbalances if they happen to occur. Given this belief the distributional implications of any one project are obviously irrelevant, and aggregate present value is the appropriate criterion. In effect, this position argues that failure to attain the first-best bliss point is solely a matter of existing inefficiencies, which the aggregate present value criterion can help to overcome.

A final possible justification for the aggregate present value criterion is an appeal to pragmatism. Even if one believed that the underlying distribution of income were nonoptimal and that there was virtually no hope of reaching the first-best bliss point, one could still argue that the distributional implications of any one government project are likely to be small relative to the distributional impact of the government's general tax and transfer policies. For example, indexing social security benefits to the cost of living, or removing the major "loopholes" from the federal personal income tax, will have distributional impacts far beyond those of any ten government projects. Consequently, government projects *should* be chosen solely on the basis of relative efficiency by the aggregate present value criterion. It would be especially foolish to cloud the objective efficiency information that cost-benefit analysis can provide with subjective distributional judgments, given that the distributional implications of any one project are inconsequential for all intents and purposes.

Each of the preceding arguments is fairly easy to counter. The first two are simply matters of personal taste and interpretation, on which there is bound to be disagreement. With respect to the second argument, for instance, many people believe the distribution of income is far from optimal. Moreover, the personal distribution of income in the United States has not changed significantly in this century despite a marked increase in government taxes and transfers. The first argument is also suspect given that a significant portion of all U.S. GNP is marketed under conditions far from the perfectly competitive ideal. Thus, it is equally reasonable to argue that the quest for the first-best bliss point is hopelessly idealistic and should not guide economic policy decisions. According to this view, policymaking is always a second-best undertaking.

Once it is conceded that the policy environment is second best, the third argument on the "smallness" of any one project's distributional implications becomes something of a red herring from a strictly theoretical point of view. After all, the efficiency gains from any one project are "small," too. According to second-best public expenditure theory, society should take gains in social welfare where it can, and these gains include both efficiency and equity considerations. Hence, the proper decision rule for cost-benefit analysis involves ranking projects by their contribution to social welfare, not just by efficiency. Consider the situation depicted in Figure 27–2.

FIGURE 27–2

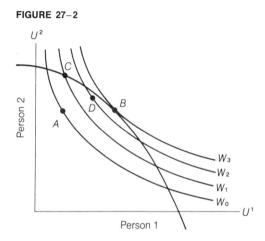

Suppose B, the first-best bliss point, is unattainable. Suppose further that society is currently at point A and that the government can invest in only one of two projects, C or D, because of a (second-best) legislated budget constraint. C is presumably the more efficient project, the one with highest *aggregate* present value, because it brings society to its pareto-optimal utility-possibilities frontier. But according to the social welfare rankings, $W_0, \ldots, W_3$, which incorporate both efficiency and equity criteria, the government should choose project D. In effect, the superior equity implications of D are sufficient to override the fact that D has lower aggregate present value. C would be preferred only if the government could simultaneously tax and transfer lump sum to move society along the frontier to a point northeast of D. If such distributions are impossible, however, D is the preferred alternative.

From a strictly theoretical point of view, then, if the policy environment is second best in part because the distribution of income is nonoptimal, and will remain so, then distributional considerations ought to enter cost-benefit analyses of alternative government projects in a consistent manner. Unfortunately, normative theory offers precious few useful guidelines for consistent distributional evaluation.

INCORPORATING DISTRIBUTIONAL PARAMETERS

The theoretical literature on cost-benefit analysis suggests two quite different ways of incorporating distributional considerations into cost-benefit calculations. The first in terms of historical development, which we shall call the "standard" neoclassical position, says that individually perceived gains and losses should be weighted by each consumer's marginal social utility of income as given by society's social welfare function. This approach is most closely associated with Burton Weisbrod.[2] Robin Boadway[3] has recently suggested a second approach which we shall call the "new" neoclassical position, in which the government computes shadow prices for public sector inputs and outputs that incorporate the distributional preferences contained in society's social welfare function. In our view only Boadway's approach is theoretically appropriate. This may be somewhat beside the point, however, since neither is likely to be of much use to the practitioner.

THE WEISBROD ANALYSIS

The "standard" neoclassical approach views the problem as follows. For simplicity, think of society as having an individualistic social welfare function

[2] B. A. Weisbrod, "Income Redistribution Effects and Benefit-Cost Analysis," in S. B. Chase, Jr., ed., *Problems in Public Expenditure Analysis* (Washington, D.C.: The Brookings Institution, 1968).

[3] R. Boadway, "Integrating Equity and Efficiency in Applied Welfare Economics, *Quarterly Journal of Economics*, November 1976.

of the form

(27.1)
$$W = W[U^1(Y_1), \ldots, U^h(Y_h), \ldots, U^H(Y_H)]$$

where:

$Y_h =$ the lump-sum income of person h, $h = 1, \ldots, H$.

Totally differentiating $W(\ )$ yields:

(27.2)
$$dW = \sum_{h=1}^{H} \frac{\partial W}{\partial U^h} \frac{\partial U^h}{\partial Y_h} dY_h$$

where:

$\dfrac{\partial W}{\partial U^h} \dfrac{\partial U^h}{\partial Y_h} =$ the social marginal utility of person h.

$dY_h =$ the change in lump-sum income incurred by person h as the result of some government project.

Thus, according to the "standard" view, the change in social welfare from a government project is a linear combination of individual gains and losses expressed as changes in lump-sum income, where the weights are the social marginal utilities of income based on the social welfare ranking W. The dY_h can be thought of as changes in one of the acceptable lump-sum income measures of individual gain or loss, such as Hicks Equivalent or Compensating Variations. Projects should be ranked according to dW in the usual manner: all projects having $dW > 0$ are acceptable since they increase social welfare. If there is a binding government budget constraint, the government should choose the affordable combination of projects yielding the highest dW. This will guarantee the greatest increase in social welfare from any given set of projects. Note, finally, that if the distribution were optimal, the first-best interpersonal equity conditions, $(\partial W/\partial U^h)/(\partial U^h/\partial Y_h) =$, all $h = 1, \ldots, H$, would be satisfied. Assuming $(\partial W/\partial U^h)/(\partial U^h/\partial Y_h) > 0$, $dW > 0$ iff $\sum_{h=1}^{H} dY_h > 0$, which is just the aggregate present value, or efficiency criterion.

Decision rule (27.2) offers a straightforward and intuitively appealing method for combining efficiency and equity criteria in project selection, but its simplicity is deceiving. It poses three immense difficulties as a practical policy rule:

1. The most severe problem is its inherent subjectivity. Applying the rule requires a two-step procedure, both parts of which are highly subjective. First, the aggregate present value must be subdivided into the relevant distributional groupings, such that

(27.3)
$$PV_{\text{agg}} = \sum_{i=1}^{I} PV_i$$

where:

$PV_i =$ the gain (loss) to subgroup i.

Second, the appropriate social marginal utilities must be applied to each subgroup, or

(27.4) $$PV^* = \sum_{i=1}^{I} \beta^i PV_i$$

where:

$$\beta^i = \frac{\partial W}{\partial U^i} \frac{\partial U^i}{\partial Y_i}$$

PV^* is equivalent to dW in equation (27.2). For consistent project evaluation, the present value of each project should be subdivided the same way, with the same social welfare weights applied to each subgroup in all projects. The problem, of course, is that normative theory does not indicate how to perform either of these operations. What, for example, is the relevant subgrouping? The government clearly will not compute gains and losses for every individual. Therefore, how should it aggregate to form subgroups? Is income the only relevant consideration, so that the relevant subdivision is rich–poor or rich–middle income–poor, or is race (sex?) also important? If so, this would suggest increasing the subdivisions to include rich–white, rich–nonwhite, poor–white, and so forth. Perhaps the personal distribution of income is not the best way to subdivide. A Marxist might prefer a functional distribution division such as wage income-capitalist income, and then maybe further subdivisions by race or sex. Whatever subdivision society chooses, there remains the issue of an appropriate weighting scheme. Should the social marginal utilities of poor–nonwhite be 10 times larger, 100 times larger, one fifth as large as the social marginal utilities of rich–whites? Should any group have a negative social marginal utility of income, contrary to the notion of an individualistic social welfare function satisfying the pareto criterion? Normative theory merely assumes that all these decisions have been made, adding only that the same subdivisions and weighting schemes be applied consistently to all projects. Government agencies are not supposed to make separate determinations of these distributional factors. There is obviously an enormous range of indeterminancy here, since by suitable choice of the relevant subdivisions and social welfare weights, a set of N projects can receive virtually any ranking regardless of their relative aggregate present values. Therefore, unless society has agreed upon these distributional parameters, there is little point in computing PV^*'s. They would simply represent the distributional biases of the cost-benefit analyst. On the other hand, ranking projects according to PV_{agg} returns us to the other horn of the dilemma: Is a project ranking devoid of distributional considerations useful as a selection criterion?

Some economists have recommended the PV_{agg} ranking on the grounds that if $PV_{agg} > 0$, the gainers could compensate the losers and still experience a net increase in utility. This is the so-called Hicks-Kaldor criterion, which bases selection on a *potential* gain in social welfare. Combined with an individualistic social welfare function, the fact that some consumers could be made better off without others being made worse off would guarantee an increase in social welfare, *if the compensation actually took place.* This is crucial qualification, however, because modern second-best analysis has developed a clear distinction between actual and potential gains in social welfare. Unfortunately, only actual gains and losses are relevant, not the potential for net social gain. In short, there can be no escaping the dilemma posed above.

2. The discussion of subjectivity assumes away an important technical problem: it may not be possible to determine gains and losses by relevant subgroups given aggregate market data, independently of the problems inherent in calculating appropriate individual welfare measures from observable market data. Suppose one were content to use Willig's approximation theorem and substitute Marshallian consumers surplus for, say, Hicks Compensating Variation. Even this would not be of much help, because Willig's theorem applies only to individual demands. Therefore, unless demand data exist for each relevant subgroup, there is, in general, no way of computing group-relevant consumer surplus measures. Of course, such individualized data seldom do exist. The only alternative is to choose an even more distant approximation to welfare change, such as the change in total factor income accruing to each relevant subgroup, and admit that these surrogate measures could be extremely wide of the mark.

These measurement problems are reversible in one very important sense. Suppose it were conceded that the distribution was nonoptimal but that for pragmatic reasons the government decided to choose projects on the basis of aggregate present value, equal to the unweighted sum of each individual's gain or loss. The problem is that the analogue to Marshallian consumer surplus equal to the area behind the *market* demand curve will give a biased estimate of the sum of individual gains and losses, and the magnitude (and possibly even the sign) of the bias will generally not be known. The bias can be demonstrated fairly simply, as follows.

A differentiable function can be approximated by the Taylor series expansion,

$$(27.5) \qquad F(q^1) = F(q^0) + \frac{\partial F}{\partial q}(q^1 - q^0) + \frac{1}{2}(q^1 - q^0)\frac{\partial^2 F}{\partial q^2}(q^1 - q^0)$$

$$+ \text{ remainder}$$

where:

$q = $ a vector argument.

Let $F(q) = M^h(q; \bar{U}^0)$, the expenditure function for person h, and assume only a single price change. Recalling that $\partial M/\partial q_1 = X_1^{\text{comp}}$

$$(27.6) \qquad M^h(q; \bar{U}^0) = M^h(q^0; \bar{U}^0)$$

$$+ X_{h1}^{\text{comp}} \cdot \Delta q + \frac{1}{2}\frac{\partial X_{h1}^{\text{comp}}}{\partial q_1} \cdot (\Delta q)^2$$

Hence (ignoring changes in the value of the general equilibrium profit function):

$$(27.7) \qquad \Delta^h M(q; \bar{U}^0) \equiv HCV^h = X_{h1}^{\text{comp}} \cdot \Delta q + \frac{1}{2}\frac{\partial X_{h1}^{\text{comp}}}{\partial q_1}(\Delta q)^2$$

FIGURE 27-3

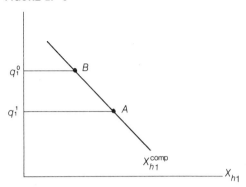

the area $q_1^1 ABq_1^0$ in Figure 27–3. The aggregate present value of a project which changes the price of X_1 from q_1^1 to q_1^0 is, therefore,

$$(27.8) \qquad PV = \sum_{h=1}^{H} \Delta M^h(q; \bar{U}^{0h}) \equiv \sum_{h=1}^{H} HCV^h = \sum_{h=1}^{H} X_{h1}\Delta q_1$$

$$+ \frac{1}{2} \sum_{h=1}^{H} \frac{\partial X_{h1}^{comp}}{\partial q_1} \cdot \Delta q_1^2 = X_1\Delta q_1 + \frac{1}{2} \sum_{h=1}^{H} \frac{\partial X_{h1}^{comp}}{\partial q_1} \Delta q_1^2$$

Suppose we estimate $\sum_{h=1}^{H} \Delta M^h(q; \bar{U}^{0h})$ by a similar area behind the aggregate demand curve, area $q_1^1 CDq_1^0$ in Figure 27–4, the analogue to individual Marshallian consumer surplus.

$$(27.9) \qquad \left[\sum_{h=1}^{H} \Delta M^h(q; \bar{U}^{0h}) \right]_{est} = X_1\Delta q_1 + \frac{1}{2} \sum_{h=1}^{H} \frac{\partial X_{h1}^{ord}}{\partial q_1} \Delta q_1^2$$

From the Slutsky equation:

$$(27.10) \qquad \frac{\partial X_{h1}^{ord}}{\partial q_1} = \frac{\partial X_{h1}^{comp}}{\partial q_1} - X_{h1} \frac{\partial X_{h1}}{\partial I^h} \qquad h = 1, \ldots, H$$

FIGURE 27-4

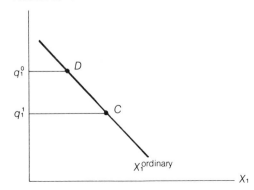

Hence:

$$(27.11) \qquad \left[\sum_{h=1}^{H} \Delta M^h(q; \bar{U}^{0h}) \right]_{\text{est}} = X_1 \Delta q_1 + \frac{1}{2} \sum_{h=1}^{H} \frac{\partial X_{h1}^c}{\partial q_1} \Delta q_1^2$$

$$- \frac{1}{2} \sum_{h=1}^{H} X_{h1} \frac{\partial X_{h1}}{\partial I^h} \Delta q_1^2$$

The first two terms on the right-hand side of (27.11) are the true approximation of the aggregate gain, equal to the summation of each individual's gain (loss). The third term is the bias term. If X_1 is a normal good, the Marshallian consumer surplus analogue clearly understates the true quadratic approximation of the aggregate gain, but the magnitude of the bias will not generally be known.

The problems intensify when more than one price changes. In this case the quadratic approximation of individual loss becomes:

$$(27.12) \qquad \Delta M^h(q; \bar{U}^0) = \sum_{i=1}^{N} X_{hi} \Delta q_i + \frac{1}{2} \sum_{i=1}^{N} \sum_{k=1}^{N} \frac{\partial X_{hi}^{\text{comp}}}{\partial q_k} \Delta q_i \Delta q_k$$

The estimated gain from aggregate demand data is:

$$(27.13) \qquad \left[\sum_{h=1}^{H} \Delta M^h(q; \bar{U}^{0h}) \right]_{\text{est}} = \sum_{h=1}^{H} \sum_{i=1}^{N} X_{hi} \Delta q_i$$

$$+ \frac{1}{2} \sum_{h=1}^{H} \sum_{i=1}^{N} \sum_{k=1}^{N} \frac{\partial X_{hi}^{\text{ord}}}{\partial q_k} \Delta q_i \Delta q_k$$

Substituting the Slutsky equation for each individual into (27.13) yields:

$$(27.14) \qquad \left[\sum_{h=1}^{H} \Delta M^h(q; \bar{U}^{0h}) \right]_{\text{est}} = \sum_{i=1}^{N} X_i \Delta q_i$$

$$+ \frac{1}{2} \sum_{i=1}^{N} \sum_{k=1}^{N} \left(\sum_{h=1}^{H} \frac{\partial X_{hi}^{\text{comp}}}{\partial q_k} \right) \Delta q_i \Delta q_k$$

$$- \frac{1}{2} \sum_{i=1}^{N} \sum_{k=1}^{N} \left(\sum_{h=1}^{H} X_{hk} \frac{\partial X_{hi}^{\text{ord}}}{\partial I^h} \right) \Delta q_i \Delta q_k$$

The bias term is now

$$- \frac{1}{2} \sum_{i=1}^{N} \sum_{k=1}^{N} \left(\sum_{h=1}^{H} X_{hk} \frac{\partial X_{hi}^{\text{ord}}}{\partial I^h} \right) \Delta q_i \Delta q_k$$

In unpublished work, Wiilig was not able to develop useful approximation theorems based on (27.14) unless individual preferences and/or the income distribution were severely restricted.[4] This is a fairly depressing conclusion. It says that even if the researcher were content to ignore distributional considerations and compare projects solely in terms of efficiency, it might not be possible to do this if the distribution is nonoptimal. The appropriate efficiency measure, the sum of each individual's gain (or loss), may not be recoverable

---

[4] See R. D. Willig, "Consumer's Surplus: A Rigorous Cookbook," *Technical Report No. 98*, Economic Series, Institute for Mathematical Studies in the Social Sciences, Stanford University, 1973. Also, R. D. Willig, "Welfare Analysis of Policies Affecting Prices and Products," *Memo No. 153*, Center for Research in Economic Growth, Stanford University, 1973.

from aggregate demand data with nonoptimal distribution. Hence, the researcher must do more than ignore distributional considerations. He must also assume that the distribution is optimal so that the economy is equivalent to a one-consumer economy. With this additional assumption Willig's approximation theorem can be applied to aggregated demand curves.

A somewhat different problem relating to multiple price changes arises because the income variable in econometric demand analysis is often an amalgam of ordinary factor income and lump-sum income. Think of a situation in which the price of good 1 changes, along with some factor prices, all of whose components are lumped into an estimated income term. When this occurs, an estimated price derivative for good 1 should really be interpreted as:

$$
(27.15) \qquad \left(\frac{\partial X_1^{\text{ord}}}{\partial q_1}\right)_{\text{est}} = \frac{\partial X_{h1}^{\text{comp}}}{\partial q_1} - X_{h1}\frac{\partial X_{h1}}{\partial I^h} + \frac{\partial X_{h1}}{\partial I^h}\frac{\partial I^h}{\partial q_1}
$$

Since $\partial I^h/\partial q_1$ can vary in sign across individuals, the aggregate bias in (27.11) can no longer be signed even if X_1 is a normal good.[5]

3. The final problem is purely theoretical in nature. Assuming away all problems mentioned in the preceding two comments, equation (27.4) recommends weighting each person's individually perceived gain or loss by a social marginal utility, β^h, where $\beta^h = (\partial W/\partial U^h)(\partial U^h/\partial Y_h)$, $h = 1, \ldots, H$. But this would not be the correct weighting scheme, in general, for second-best applications. This point was discussed in Chapter 16 when we were considering the problem of determining the optimal pattern of distorting "commodity" taxes for collecting a given level of tax revenues in a many person economy. We noted in that context that maximizing a social welfare function of the form

$$
W[V^h(\vec{q}; I^h)]
$$

where:

$V^h(\ ) =$ the indirect utility function for person h.

to determine the optimal taxes was not equivalent to minimizing an aggregate loss function of the form

$$
\sum_{h=1}^{H} \beta^h L^h(\vec{q}; \bar{U}^h)
$$

where:

$L^h(\ ) =$ the loss suffered by person h.

The equivalent loss-minimizing objective function turns out to be:

$$
\sum_{h=1}^{H} \gamma_h L^h(\vec{q}; \bar{U}^h)
$$

where:

$$
\gamma_h = \beta^h + \lambda \sum_{i=1}^{N} t_i \frac{\partial X_{hi}}{\partial I^h}.
$$

$\lambda =$ the Lagrangian multiplier associated with the government's budget constraint.

---

[5] This was first pointed out to us by our colleague James E. Anderson.

γ_h measures the full social marginal utility of income for this particular problem, equal to the direct gain arising from giving person h an additional unit of lump-sum income plus an indirect gain equal to the marginal social utility of the tax revenues collected when person h receives an additional unit of income. Since gain is simply the negative of loss for any one person, these comments would apply equally to government investment analysis.

Of course, the full social marginal utility of income will vary depending on the exact nature of the second-best environment, but in any case, the point remains that ranking projects according to equation (27.4) is not necessarily the same as ranking projects according to their contributions to social welfare in a second-best environment, even *if* the measure of each individual's gain (loss) could be agreed upon and evaluated.

Weisbrod's Empirical Analysis

Despite the problems associated with (27.4), Burton Weisbrod tried to determine the prevailing social marginal utilities of income, β^h, in the United States on the assumption that U.S. agencies actually used (27.4) for project selection.[6] Weisbrod asked the following question: Assuming that the government employs (27.4) as its decision rule, what social marginal utilities of income are consistent with projects actually selected? To answer this, he studied a set of projects

$$(P_1, \ldots, P_N)$$

with the following characteristics:

a. P_1 was rejected; $(P_2, \ldots, P_N)$ were accepted.

b. P_1 had the highest aggregate present value, equal to PV_1, of all rejected projects.

c. $PV_1 > PV_2, \ldots, PV_N$. The aggregate present value of the rejected projected exceeded the aggregate present value of any one of the accepted projects. That is to say, if efficiency were the only criterion, P_1 would have been accepted before all other projects actually accepted.

d. The (net) benefits received by each distributionally relevant subgroup within the population could be determined for each project $(P_1, \ldots, P_N)$. Weisbrod assumed the four relevant subgroups were: rich–white (1), rich–nonwhite (2), poor–white (3), and poor–nonwhite (4). Thus,

$$(27.16) \qquad PV_1 = PV_{11} + PV_{12} + PV_{13} + PV_{14}$$
$$PV_2 = PV_{21} + PV_{22} + PV_{23} + PV_{24}$$
$$PV_3 = PV_{31} + PV_{32} + PV_{33} + PV_{34}$$
$$PV_4 = PV_{41} + PV_{42} + PV_{43} + PV_{44}$$
$$\text{etc.}$$

where:

PV_{ij} = the net present value for project i accruing to population subgroup j, $i = 1, \ldots, N; j = 1, \ldots, 4$.

---

[6] Weisbrod, "Income Redistribution Effects and Benefit-Cost Analysis."

Weisbrod also approximated the PV_{ij} by the increase in factor incomes received as a result of the project.

Given a set of projects with these characteristics, Weisbrod then considered the weighting scheme (a_1, a_2, a_3, a_4) that would cause the government to reject P_1 and accept $P_2, \ldots, P_N$. The weights are a solution to the system of equations:

(27.17)
$$a_1 PV_{11} + a_2 PV_{12} + a_3 PV_{13} + a_4 PV_{14} = PV_1 = PV_1^*$$
$$a_1 PV_{21} + a_2 PV_{22} + a_3 PV_{23} + a_4 PV_{24} = PV_2^* > PV_1$$
$$a_1 PV_{31} + a_2 PV_{32} + a_3 PV_{33} + a_4 PV_{34} = PV_3^* > PV_1$$
$$a_1 PV_{41} + a_2 PV_{42} + a_3 PV_{43} + a_4 PV_{44} = PV_4^* > PV_1$$

So long as there exists one rejected project and at least three accepted projects with characteristics (a)–(d) above, the system of equations (27.17) may have a unique solution $(a_1^*, a_2^*, a_3^*, a_4^*)$ which, given Weisbrod's assumptions, can be interpreted as the social marginal utilities actually employed by the U.S. national government. Based on a selection of four water resource projects considered by the U.S. Corps of Engineers in 1950, Weisbrod determined that the Corps employed the following social marginal utilities of income:[7]

RW (1)	RNW (2)	PW (3)	PNW (4)
2.2	−2.0	−1.3	9.3

One interesting feature of this methodology is that while Weisbrod assumed the a_i reflected the social welfare weights β^h directly associated with the social welfare function, they can be thought of as representing the true marginal social utilities of income, the γ_h referred to above. The a_i presumably represent the correct marginal social utilities of income. Thus, they can be viewed as an implicit statement of the direct social welfare rankings and the prevailing second-best policy environment assumed by the government, despite Weisbrod's attempt to give them a narrower interpretation.

Perhaps the weights Weisbrod estimated are plausible, but there is really no reason to believe that the a_i are actually measuring social marginal utilities of income. They could easily be picking up other factors such as intangible costs and benefits, or blatant political partisanship. Unfortunately, Weisbrod's interpretation of the a_i is only as good as his heroic assumptions that government project selection embodies only efficiency and equity criteria, and that it combines them in accordance with the dictates of neoclassical theory. It would hardly be surprising if a similar analysis of another set of projects revealed a completely different set of a_i's, even within the same agency. In the end, one has to wonder whether estimating social welfare rankings from a selection of agency projects is the most fruitful line of attack. It may be far more plausible to assume that a government's distributional preferences are best revealed by the structure of its general taxes and its various transfer programs.

---

[7] Ibid., pp. 199–200.

NONOPTIMAL INCOME DISTRIBUTION AND
SHADOW PRICES—THE BOADWAY ANALYSIS[8]

The "new" neoclassical approach to nonoptimal income distribution accepts the notion that the goal of cost-benefit analysis is social welfare maximization, but rather than adjust individually perceived gains (losses) for distributional considerations, it adjusts the second-best optimal shadow prices on government inputs and outputs. Hence, the required adjustment depends directly upon the nature of the underlying second-best policy environment. In Chapter 22 we derived the one-person and many-person shadow prices for a general model of government production with distorting taxation, government purchases and sales at private sector producer prices, and a government budget constraint. The relevant equations, (22.46) and (22.88), respectively, are reproduced here as (27.18) and (27.19) (with $dB = -dL$):

(27.18) $$dB = -t'(M_{ij})E^{-1}\pi_{ij}dt + (-p_1 g_z + p' + t'M_{ij}E^{-1})\,dZ$$

(27.19) $$dB = -[[(1-R)' \cdot X]' + t'M_{ij}]E^{-1}\pi_{ij}dt$$
$$+[[(1-R)' \cdot X]'E^{-1}$$
$$+t'M_{ij}E^{-1} - p_1 g_z + p']\,dZ$$

Recall that the optimal shadow prices are the coefficients on the dZ, the vector of public sector inputs and outputs, with $p_1 \equiv 1$, the numeraire. Inspection of (27.18) and (27.19) reveals that the many-person rules can be thought as a linear combination of the efficiency considerations, embodied in the coefficients on the dZ in (27.18) and an equity term $[(1-R)' \cdot X]'E^{-1}$. Note also that if $\beta^h = \beta$, all $h = 1, \ldots, H$, (i,e., the distribution is optimal) then the many person shadow prices are identical to the shadow prices for a one-consumer economy, as expected.

Equation (27.19) applied as a rule for project selection views the investment process as a straight production decision. Once the shadow prices are known the government should simply try to maximize "pseudo" profits using these prices and subject to the government's production function. This yields the usual production rules: inputs and outputs should be varied until $\theta_j dZ_j = \theta_i dZ_i$, all $i, j = 1, \ldots, N$, where θ_j and θ_i are the coefficients of the dZ terms in (27.19), the optimal shadow prices (excluding $p_1 g_z$).

Note, finally, that applying (27.19) in practice is subject to most of the same pitfalls as equation (27.4). Society must somehow determine the distributionally relevant subdivision of the population and the appropriate direct marginal social utilities of income for each relevant subgroup. While the government need no longer compute each subgroup's gain or loss, it still has to determine consumption and factor supply responses for each of them. Thus, the amount of data required is forbidding, and equally unlikely to be known with any degree of certainty.

---

[8] Boadway, "Integrating Equity and Efficiency in Applied Welfare Economics."

CONCLUSION

No matter how one views the issue, a nonoptimal distribution of income poses grave difficulties for objective cost-benefit analysis. As indicated in the very first chapter of the text, normative theory has never been able to resolve the distribution question beyond the point of saying to the decision maker: "Tell us your distributional preferences and we will tell you what to do." To the extent society is unable to evolve a consistent set of distributional preferences, cost-benefit analysis is firmly trapped in a dilemma. There is no clear-cut way of incorporating distributional preferences into the analysis. At the same time, there is no way of judging the value of an analysis which chooses to ignore distributional considerations. Indeed, if the distribution is nonoptimal, it may not even be possible to compute the *efficiency* implications for any given project because of various aggregation biases. Finally, even if society's distributional preferences were well established, the data required to incorporate them consistently across all projects are formidable, to say the least.

REFERENCES

Boadway, R. "Integrating Equity and Efficiency in Applied Welfare Economics." *Quarterly Journal of Economics,* November 1976.

Harberger, A. "Three Postulates for Applied Welfare Economics." *Journal of Economic Literature,* September 1971.

Weisbrod, B. "Income Redistribution Effects and Benefit-Cost Analysis." In *Problems in Public Expenditure Analysis,* edited by S. B. Chase, Jr. Washington, D.C.: The Brookings Institution, 1968.

Willig, R. "Consumer's Surplus: A Rigorous Cookbook." *Technical Report No. 98.* Economic Series, Institute for Mathematical Studies in the Social Sciences, Stanford University, 1973.

————. "Welfare Analysis of Policies Affecting Prices and Products." *Memo No. 153.* Center for Research in Economic Growth, Stanford University, 1973.

28

Common pitfalls in cost-benefit analysis

Chapters 23–27 discussed the fundamental issues in cost-benefit analysis. Cost-benefit analysis may be as much art as science, but any study that presents a careful discussion of the social rate of discount, uncertainty, the various measurement problems outlined in Chapter 26, and the distribution of project costs and benefits, in accordance with the principles developed in those chapters, with all assumptions explicitly stated, cannot help but illuminate the decision-making process. Many cost-benefit studies stray from these issues, however, emphasizing other factors that are essentially irrelevant to the fundamental question that cost-benefit analysis attempts to answer: Does a particular government investment constitute the best possible use of society's scarce resources? Once these peripheral issues gain prominence, cost-benefit analysis loses its ability to discriminate among alternatives.

It is hardly surprising that public forums such as congressional hearings and the media tend not to emphasize these rather technical economic issues, with the possible exception of the distribution question. But since they happen to be the relevant issues, public discussions of the economic implications of proposed government projects are often badly misplaced, serving mainly to reinforce commonly held misconceptions.

Roland McKean's 1958 book, *Efficiency of Government Through Systems Analysis*, still remains one of the most comprehensive accounts of the various pitfalls in cost-benefit analysis, filled with numerous entertaining examples.[1] We will highlight five of the most common misconceptions in this chapter, all of which share two distinctive characteristics. First, as with most popular misconceptions, each contains a kernel of truth, but the kernel is blown up beyond all reasonable proportion to the point where the analysis becomes completely misleading. Whether this is done intentionally to support a particular cause or simply results from innocent misunderstanding is sometimes difficult to determine. But it clearly pays to exploit the public's biases in these matters, because their second characteristic is that the errors they entail tend to be enormous. The dollar value of the costs and/or benefits attributed to these bogus issues, which McKean facetiously labels "secondary" benefits and costs, typically swamp any reasonable estimates of the true or "primary" costs and

---

[1] R. N. McKean, *Efficiency of Government through Systems Analysis* (New York: John Wiley & Sons, Inc., 1958), especially chaps. 8 and 9.

benefits. Consequently, emphasizing the "secondary" benefits and costs can be a most effective partisan gambit, if one can get away with it.

THE CHAIN REACTION GAME

In the Chain Reaction Game, people discover numerous sources of secondary profits (or losses) arising from the particular government project under study. Suppose the government builds a hydroelectric project whose true benefits might include lowering the price of electricity to a large group of people, recreational benefits formed by damming a river, flood control, irrigation, and so forth. Presumably the lowered price of electricity is the primary objective of the project, but these other benefits are legitimate technological external economies created by the dam, and a careful analysis should try to evaluate them as part of the benefits. Proponents often go far beyond this, however, claiming as legitimate benefits profits arising in other industries as a consequence of the dam. For example, profits in the region's construction industry are almost certain to rise, as well as profits in those industries supplying the construction materials. At the retail end of the spectrum, profits in the electric appliance industry are also likely to rise. So, too, will profits in all industries whose products are complements to electricity, and so on. With all these "secondary" profits added to the other benefits of the project listed above, the hydroelectric project is virtually assured of having a positive present value. Indeed, the value of the "secondary" profits might well exceed the dollar value of the true benefits.

The kernel of truth in the Chain Reaction Game is that changes in the value of the general equilibrium profit function are a legitimate part of the true benefits measure. For example, recall that the Hicks Compensating Variation measure of benefits in a one-consumer-equivalent economy with general technology is:

(28.1) $$HCV = [M(\vec{q}_0; \bar{U}^0) - M(\vec{q}_1; \bar{U}^0)] + [\pi(\vec{p}_1) - (\vec{p}_0)]$$

where:

$(\vec{q}_0, \vec{p}_0)$ are the general equilibrium vectors of consumer and producer prices, respectively, at the initial equilibrium.

$(\vec{q}_1, \vec{p}_1)$ are the general equilibrium vectors of consumer and producer prices at the new equilibrium, which includes the project.

$M(\vec{q}; \bar{U}^0) =$ the consumer's expenditure function evaluated at the initial utility level.

$\pi(\vec{p}) =$ the general equilibrium profit function for the private sector.

Presumably the inclusion of secondary profits arising from the project is meant to capture the change in the profit function. But there are two serious problems here. The most obvious flaw is that these profits represent only a partial accounting of all secondary profit effects. The profit function measures *aggregate* profits and losses from *all* economic activity. If proponents of the project can develop a list of industries experiencing increased profits, then the project's opponents can just as easily provide a listing of "secondary" losses arising from the project. Roughly speaking, any activity that is in any way complementary to the construction of the hydroelectric project or to the benefits derived from it can be expected to show increased profits. Conversely, all activities that bear a substitute relationship to the project and its benefits can be expected to show losses. Gains in the electric appliance industry will be partially or wholly offset by decreased sales of gas and oil appliances. Bidding resources into the project may raise factor costs in other industries. The list of potential pure economic losses is equally impressive.

The second flaw is that the profit function measures pure economic profits in a long-run equilibrium, whereas the gains and losses mentioned above are likely to be short-run effects. In the long run the existence of pure profits or losses for the economy as a whole is basically a function of production characteristics industry by industry, and not changes in factor prices. Decreasing returns to scale production will exhibit pure profits in the long run; increasing returns to scale production, pure losses. The short-run effects are not irrelevant, but it may be difficult to know how long they will continue in any given industry. In any case, one would not want to represent the short-run changes as recurring annually for the life of the project.

Once these two factors are admitted, it is easy to see that the "secondary" profit game is easily overdone. We believe the safest strategy is simply to ignore profits and losses in other industries despite the fact that changes in the general equilibrium profit function are a legitimate part of benefits. Can any researcher really hope to trace through all the pure profits and losses arising from a given project, both in the short run and long run? The question, in effect, answers itself. The cost-benefit analyst would be well advised to accept the econometric evidence suggesting that aggregate production exhibits (approximately) constant returns to scale (CRS) and assume:

1. No lasting pure profit effects in other industries; and
2. That short-run gains are completely offset by short-run losses as resources move throughout the economy.

On the other hand, any profit effects directly associated with the project ought to be included. The fact that a decreasing cost service has to be financed in part out of general tax revenues if price is set equal to marginal costs is certainly a relevant project cost. Indeed, the government often invests in a particular industry precisely because it exhibits decreasing costs. Hence, it would be foolish to assume that government production necessarily exhibits CRS.

THE REGIONAL MULTIPLIER GAME

The Regional Multiplier Game attaches Keynesian multiplier analysis to the basic cost-benefit framework. Continuing with the example of the hydroelectric project, suppose the damsite were formerly a wilderness area. Presumably the construction and continued operation of the dam will support all sorts of ancillary services. The people associated with the project have to be clothed, housed, and fed. Indeed, a small town might spring up around the damsite, generating a continual flow of income in a region formerly devoid of economic activity. By the very nature of the Keynesian multiplier, these "secondary" income effects will be a multiple of the project's direct costs and/or benefits. Therefore, if they are included as project benefits, the project would necessarily have a positive present value.

Something must be wrong here, for it appears to suggest that any project placed in an underdeveloped region of a country will be worthwhile. The crux of the problem is that Keynesian multiplier analysis is simply irrelevant to the fundamental goal of cost-benefit analysis, determining the best use of society's scarce resources. Cost-benefit analysis begins with a presumption of full employment so that, strictly speaking, it is concerned with the maximum expansion of society's production-possibilities frontier. Keynesian multiplier analysis, on the other hand, is concerned with moving an unemployed economy to its production-possibilities frontier. Hence, if the full-employment assumption is retained, the multiplied increases in income associated with any one project will be exactly offset by multiplied decreases in income in other regions of the economy which lose resources to the hydroelectric project.

The kernel of truth here is that market economies are seldom fully employed and that cost-benefit analysis should be adjusted to account for unemployment. If a project creates a net gain in employment for the economy as a whole, this is a short-run benefit that can legitimately be included. But is it prudent to include these gains? A dam located in the wilderness of Colorado has obvious income effects. But a project of equal dollar amount located in the middle of New York City may well have an equal secondary income effect. Is there any reason to suppose that one type of government project will have a different multiplier from another type of project, especially given that the relevant measure is the aggregate economy-wide increase in income? Unless one can argue convincingly that some particular project will have unusually strong multiplier effects, there seems to be little point in attaching a multiplier analysis to a cost-benefit study. Of course, the reasons these effects are so often emphasized is that the residents of Colorado and New York care very much indeed whether the federal government subsidies a hydroelectric project in Colorado or an office building in New York City. But why should the federal government care? Is regional development per se a legitimate intangible? Do the people of Colorado deserve some special consideration so that the issue becomes one of income distribution viewed in a peculiarly geographic fashion? Answers to questions such as these are largely a matter of taste. We do not happen to find them compelling.

THE LABOR GAME

The Labor Game is a popular variant of the Regional Multiplier Game which focuses exclusively on the employment effects of particular projects. "The federal government should subsidize the production of supersonic commercial aircraft because if it does not, 10,000 workers in Seattle will join the ranks of the unemployed." Arguments such as this implicitly value the entire wages of these workers as a project benefit. On the surface, at least, this is an incredible proposition, since wages are normally considered part of a project's *costs*, not its benefits. Clearly, if a significant portion of some project's costs can be moved to the benefits side of the ledger, the project will almost certainly have a positive present value.

Once again, the kernel of truth resides in the possibility of an unemployed economy. Counting wages as benefits implicitly assumes that these workers are unemployable in any other alternative occupation for the duration of the project. This is unlikely, to say the least. A more careful accounting of labor's gains and losses would view the wage paid a worker on a project as having three components:

1. The opportunity wage, equal to the wage received in the worker's next best alternative employment.
2. A component equal to the nuisance cost of changing jobs to work on the project. Labor can typically be bid away from alternative employment only by an offer of increased wages, but to the extent the increase equals the nuisance cost of moving, this is a true cost of the project.
3. A pure wage rent.

Only the third component represents a true benefit. If labor receives a pure rent it is, in effect, directly capturing some of the legitimate benefits of the project.

It is true enough that a project undertaken in a high unemployment area may have a higher pure rent component than a project paying the same wages in a low unemployment area and that this gives a legitimate advantage to the former project. But even projects in high unemployment areas will draw upon some currently employed resources, and not all unemployed workers hired would have been unemployed for long periods of time. The point is that computing pure wage rents is a far more subtle exercise than merely noting that X number of workers will be hired at a certain wage. Carried to its extreme, the labor game can lead to the following absurd conclusions:

a. Pick larger projects over smaller projects because they hire more workers. If wages are viewed as benefits, large projects will tend to dominate.
b. Subsidize industries no matter how unprofitable because failure to do so will lead to unemployment.

This denies the entire dynamic behind economic growth, whereby resources are continually reallocated to better alternatives at the expense of some short-run unemployment.

The emotional appeal of employment arguments is undeniable, but they are seldom as relevant to project selection as they are made out to be. We would venture to guess that, as a first approximation, counting all wages as part of project costs is far more reasonable than counting all wages as pure wage rents for most projects, at least in the United States.

PURE DOUBLE COUNTING

Double counting project costs or benefits is undoubtedly less common than the preceding three pitfalls, but McKean points out that it was once the official policy of the Bureau of Reclamation within the U.S. Department of the Interior.[2] The Bureau's *Manual* on cost-benefit procedures required that the benefits of irrigated land be counted as the sum of—

1. The increase in the value of the land.
2. The present value of the stream of net income obtained from farming the land.

McKean recounts a humorous exchange between a congressman and one of the Bureau's administrators in which the congressman wondered how the benefits of irrigation land could be so phenomenally large if no farmer were willing to pay that much for the land. The congressman was right, of course.

The quarrel here is not with counting irrigated land as a project benefit. Since irrigation changes the land's production function, the value of these changes is a legitimate technological externality. But a landowner has only one of two choices, not both. He can farm the land himself and take the gains as a stream of net income over time, or he can sell the land and let someone else farm it. With competition, the sales price will just equal the discounted stream of net income from farming the land. A farmer clearly cannot sell the land, then farm it himself, *and* capture the resulting stream of income. Hence, the *Manual's* recommended evaluation procedure represented a double counting of the benefits, pure and simple.

THE PUBLIC SECTOR BIAS CHARGE

Public sector investments are frequently accused of enjoying an advantage over private sector investments because they are not subjected to the discipline of the profit motive. They do not have to earn a return to capital. But if cost-benefit analysis has been properly applied to all potential government investments, no such public sector bias will exist. The whole purpose of cost-benefit analysis is to ensure that government projects are selected if and only if they dominate private sector alternatives.

There are two possible sources of confusion here. On the one hand, government projects may be evaluated at a far lower rate of discount than private sector investments. Managers of private sector enterprises will be discounting projects at the marginal rate of transformation (MRT) between the present and future, the gross-of-tax rate of return. As we discovered in Chapter 24, however, government projects need not necessarily be so productive. Under certain conditions its rate of discount may be far less than the MRT, possibly even less than consumers' marginal rate of substitution, or the net-of-tax

---

[2] McKean, *Efficiency of Government through Systems Analysis*, pp. 153–54.

return. Hence, the charge arises that government projects are subjected to less stringent criteria.

But it is the public sector's rate of discount that properly discounts returns to public projects over time, not necessarily the MRT. The source of confusion here lies in viewing private investments as the only alternative to public investments when, in fact, private consumption is another possible alternative. Moreover, the net benefits of public and private investments may generate different patterns of future private consumption and investment, which also must be taken into consideration. Intertemporal externalities may also affect the public sector's rate of discount. Finally, Chapter 25 discussed how the government's ability to spread risk is a real cost advantage not necessarily shared by the private sector. All these factors suggest that private and public investments may not have to earn equivalent internal rates of return to be judged as acceptable. Furthermore, the "bias" is not necessarily one way. Chapter 24 presented a set of conditions under which the government's rate of discount exceeded the private MRT.

Computing the proper rate of discount for government projects is a devilishly complex task, but the principle is clear: Discounting government projects at that rate of discount is the proper way to protect the interests of the private sector. Using any other rate of discount creates bias, one way or the other.

The second possible source of confusion involves decreasing cost projects. With marginal cost pricing these services make losses, but this is appropriate so long as total benefits exceed total costs, where total benefits can be approximated by areas behind compensated demand curves. As was noted in Chapter 26, these area measures result from the inherent lumpiness of decreasing cost services. They are altogether equivalent to the usual revenue calculations of private sector benefits given that private investments typically represent only marginal additions of output to an already established market. This is just another instance of a principle that is not widely appreciated: profitability is not always the appropriate investment criterion for the public sector. To the contrary, forcing private sector profitability tests on public sector projects will almost certainly create an undue bias *against* the public sector.

CONCLUSION

Put the remarks in this chapter to the test. Review numerous cost-benefit studies prepared by (or for) public agencies, or read the congressional hearings or media accounts of proposed government projects (or subsidies for private investments), and see if the "issues" discussed here predominate. Our experience is that they nearly always do. Careful cost-benefit analyses, highlighting the issues presented in Chapters 24–27, are the rare exception.

REFERENCE

McKean, R. *Efficiency of Government through Systems Analysis.* New York: John Wiley & Sons, Inc., 1958.

V

Fiscal federalism

29

Optimal federalism and the allocation function

Fiscal federalism refers to a hierarchical structure of autonomous governments in which each person is, simultaneously, a citizen of more than one government. The United States is an obvious example, with its national government, 50 state governments, and over 89,000 local governmental units, including cities, townships, villages, counties, and the like. Each U.S. citizen, therefore, falls within the jurisdiction of at least three, and often four or more, distinct governmental entities.

Because it implies multiple jurisdictions, the existence of a federalist structure adds considerable depth and complexity to normative public sector theory. This is not to say that the fundamental principles of public expenditure and tax theory developed in Parts II and III of the text fail to apply. They do. In particular, government intervention still depends upon the breakdown of the technical assumptions underlying a well-functioning competitive market system, principally the existence of externalities and significant decreasing cost production. Moreover, the goal of government intervention remains social welfare maximization which, broadly speaking, translates into allocational efficiency and distributional equity (as always, stabilization problems will be ignored). As we have discovered, achieving a social welfare maximum is an incredibly difficult task for even a single government. Optimal public sector decision rules are easy enough to describe, but their application to real-world situations is problematic, at best. Unfortunately, a federalist structure of governments significantly complicates both the theory and application of public sector decision rules.

The basic problem lies at the heart of a federalist system, that more than one government has jurisdiction over any one person. Even if we assume a nonmobile population, it is all too easy to envision potential inconsistencies arising if each government simply tries to follow the single-government decision rules of public sector theory. For example, one government may try to transfer income from person 1 to person 2, whereas a second government attempts just the opposite. Or one government may encourage expansion of some decreasing cost utility which is generating ever increasing pollution externalities on the citizens of a neighboring government. Finally, a high-level government in the fiscal hierarchy may try to discourage, through taxation, the consumption of some good which from the perspective of its citizens confers a negative externality, whereas no externality is seen to exist from the narrower perspective of a lower level government in the fiscal hierarchy.

A mobile population multiplies the complications, as people move in response to desirable or undesirable governmental policies. Income redistribution is a commonly used example of a potential problem in this regard. If wealthy residents of town A are asked to provide social services to the poor, they may well move to some other town, B, which has no such policy of income redistribution. This is often referred to as the "competition" problem, in that the policies of any one government naturally compete with those of other governments in terms of attracting and maintaining a constituency. Of course, optimal decision rules must be adjusted as people move in response to them.

In essence, then, federalism requires an addition to public sector theory which tells us how to sort out the various legitimate allocational and distributional functions of government in order to avoid both inconsistencies and the special problems associated with intergovernmental competition, while at the same time pursuing the normative goal of social welfare maximization. Indeed, the very meaning of social welfare maximization requires careful attention in a federalist system since, presumably, each autonomous government has formulated its own distinct social welfare function. One would not want to characterize a federalist system as "optimal" unless each governmental unit can freely maximize its own version of social welfare. This is the obvious extension of the standard single-government policy norm to a multigovernment environment. It is, just as obviously, a most difficult norm to approach, much less achieve, in application.

ATTRIBUTES OF MODELS OF OPTIMAL FEDERALISM

Curiously enough, even the rather extensive *theoretical* literature addressing the optimal design of a federalist system has shied away from tieing the concept of optimality to social welfare maximization within each governmental unit. This is undoubtedly related to a second curiosity, that the theory of the second best, by now well entrenched in public sector theory, has had virtually no impact on the theory of optimal fiscal federalism. Rather, the major theoretical models of federalism all employ first-best policy and market assumptions, and they all exploit the dichotomization of allocational and distributional issues inherent in first-best (but only first-best) models. Moreover, the dichotomization takes a particular form, namely that only the highest level (national) government in the fiscal hierarchy concerns itself with the distributional question. The highest level government may also consider allocational issues, but the key point is that all lower level governments (state, local, county, and so forth) concern themselves *only* with allocational questions. In effect, only the highest level government is assumed to have a social welfare function. Yet public sector theory teaches us that the social welfare function is the only datum that any government qua government brings to the decision-making process.[1]

---

[1] We will wait to pursue this point in detail until Chapter 30, which analyzes distributional issues in the design of an optimal federalist system. For the moment, let us follow the standard lines of inquiry as they appear in the literature and assume a first-best policy environment in which only the highest level government has a social welfare function.

THE FUNDAMENTAL ALLOCATIONAL ISSUE IN
FISCAL FEDERALISM

Given these assumptions, the fundamental economic issue in fiscal federalism is this: why have a federalist structure in the first place? Alternatively, what possible economic advantages occur by having any lower level governments at all?

The issue can best be seen as follows. Suppose the national government pursues the norm of social welfare maximization using the traditional first-best analytical framework developed in Chapter 2:

$$\max_{(X_{hi})} W[U^h(X_{hi})]$$

$$\text{s.t.} \quad F\left(\sum_{h=1}^{H} X_{hi}\right) = 0$$

where $h = 1, \ldots, H$ includes everyone in the society. If the national government can effect a set of policies consistent with the first-order conditions of this model, given the existence of such problems as externalities, decreasing cost production, and an inappropriate distribution of income, what can additional, lower level governments possibly do to enhance the economic well-being of society? Why should the national government not do everything?

Public sector economists have provided a variety of answers to this question. None of them is entirely satisfactory, but we will consider each of them in turn. In doing so, it is important to remember that each "answer" attempts to justify a role for lower level governments only with respect to the standard allocational or efficiency questions. They all concede the distributional question to the national government. Social welfare issues are notably absent in lower level, or local, government decision making.

STIGLER'S MENU FOR OPTIMAL FEDERALISM

George Stigler, in his short masterpiece, "Tenable Range of Functions of Local Government," adopts what amounts to an axiomatic resolution of this question.[2] His justification for "local" (lower level) governments rests on two principles: first, that representative government works best the closer the government is to its constituency (presumably because local governments perceive the utilities or demands of their constituents better than a national government could, although this is unclear from his article); and second, that subsets of people within a country have the right to vote for themselves different kinds and amounts of public services. This second principle is consistent with the doctrine of "states rights" expoused so eloquently by various U.S. southern politicians in pre–Civil War days, albeit without the racial overtones normally associated with that doctrine. Similarly, the first principle is consistent with the notion of the town meeting as an optimal form of government—a notion which has held considerable sway throughout the history of the United States.

---

[2] George Stigler, "Tenable Range of Functions of Local Government," in *Federal Expenditure Policy for Economic Growth and Stability* (Washington, D.C.: Joint Economic Committee, Sub-committee on Fiscal Policy, 1957), pp. 213–19.

The growth in both the size and influence of the national government in the U.S. has diminished somewhat the commitment to these principles, but it is fair to say that they remain persuasive even today.

According to Stigler, these two principles imply that *decision making should occur at the lowest level of government consistent with the goals of allocational efficiency and distributional equity*. Notice that his conclusion provides, simultaneously, the justification for a federalist system of government and the policy norm for designing an optimal federalist system, one by which the various legitimate functions of government are best distributed among the governments within the fiscal hierarchy. In effect, Stigler has turned our original question on its head by asking when it is appropriate to have anything but small, local governments. His answer is that higher level governments may be necessary to achieve either allocational efficiency or distributional equity. In particular, he argues that the national government is the proper government for resolving the distributional question in order to avoid inconsistencies and competition among governments. As already noted above, other theorists have followed him on this point. In contrast, the responsibility for allocational functions throughout the fiscal hierarchy turns naturally on the geographic scope of both externalities and decreasing costs, the traditional allocational issues in public sector theory. A governmental body must be sufficiently large to capture all decreasing costs from a particular decreasing cost service, or to include all citizens affected by a particular externality generating activity, but it need not be any larger. Thus, the optimal-sized jurisdictional unit varies with each specific instance of a decreasing cost service or an externality.

Perfect Correspondence

Wallace Oates, in *Fiscal Federalism*, solidified Stigler's principle by suggesting the notion of a *perfect correspondence:*

> $\cdots$ the optimal form of federal government to provide the set of n public goods would be one in which there exists a level of government for each subset of the population over which the consumption of a public good is defined. This would be sufficient to internalize the benefits from the provision of each good. Such a structure of government, in which the jurisdiction that determines the level of provision of each public good includes precisely the set of individuals who consume the good, I shall call a case of *perfect correspondence* in the provision of public goods. In the ideal model, each level of government, possessing complete knowledge of the tastes of its constituents and seeking to maximize their welfare, would provide the Pareto-efficient level of output $\cdots$ and would finance this through benefit pricing.
>
> That the allocation of resources resulting from our ideal case of a perfect correspondence is Pareto-efficient is, I think, clear [assuming no private sector inefficiencies].[3]

---

[3] Excerpted from *Fiscal Federalism* by Wallace E. Oates, © 1972 by Harcourt Brace Jovanovich, Inc., pp. 34–35. Reprinted by permission of the publisher. Oates book is perhaps the best single comprehensive survey of the theory of federalism. Two points are worth noting with respect to Oates' definition of perfect correspondence. First, while he talks only of public goods, the principle clearly applies as well to any form of externality, or any decreasing cost industry. Second, Oates claims no originality for the notion of perfect correspondence, only for the terminology. Many other authors besides Stigler viewed the ideal federalist structure in a similar vein, including Albert Breton, Mancur Olson, and Vincent Ostron, et al. See pp. 34, n4, and 35.

Given the existence of a federalist system, the notion of a perfect correspondence sets a natural limit on the size of each local government. It is clearly a stringent requirement, leading one to question whether a perfect correspondence for even one public good or decreasing cost service actually exists, since political boundaries are seldom, if ever, determined solely by the extent of externalities or decreasing costs. But a more fundamental theoretical issue turns on the usefulness of perfect correspondence as a policy norm for the public sector. Is it even worth pursuing by restructuring existing jurisdictional boundaries? Oates is certainly correct when he suggests that a perfect correspondence will produce a first-best social welfare optimum, assuming that local governments follow the first-best allocational decision rules. But we must return to the original theoretical question posed above. Given a first-best policy environment in which only the national government has a social welfare function, why is local decision making necessary, the existence of a perfect correspondence notwithstanding? Why cannot the national government note the extent of each externality or decreasing cost service and make the appropriate policy response? There is something of an asymmetry here. A nonperfect correspondence can preclude local autonomy on strictly formal grounds, but a perfect correspondence does not necessarily imply local autonomy in order to achieve a social welfare maximum. If we are to make a compelling theoretical argument for a federalist structure, something besides perfect correspondence is required.

OATES' DECENTRALIZATION THEOREM

Oates provides one possible justification by adding a new constraint to the basic first-best general equilibrium model.[4] Following Oates, assume that there are two natural subgroupings, A and B, within the total population, such that all individuals within a subgroup have identical preferences, but that tastes vary across A and B. Suppose, in addition, that society produces two purely private goods, X and Y, that are both consumed by all members of the society. However, despite the fact that Y is a purely private good, it happens to be provided by a government, either national or local. Assume, finally, that the distribution of income is optimal, so that each subgroup can be viewed as containing a single individual. Under these assumptions social welfare maximization can be presented as follows:

$$\max_{(X^A, Y^A, X^B, Y^B)} U^A(X^A, Y^A)$$

$$\text{s.t.} \quad U^B(X^B, Y^B) = \bar{U}$$

$$F(X^A + X^B; Y^A + Y^B) = 0$$

We know that the first-order conditions for this problem are:

(29.1) $$MRS^A_{X^A, Y^A} = MRS^B_{X^B, Y^B} = MRT_{X,Y}$$

---

[4] Adopted from *Fiscal Federalism* by Wallace E. Oates, © 1972 by Harcourt Brace Jovanovich, Inc., p. 55. Reprinted by permission of the publisher.

Moreover, with different tastes, $X^A \neq X^B$ and $Y^A \neq Y^B$ in general, at the optimum.

Given the model as it stands, it obviously makes no difference whether a single national government provides Y^A and Y^B according to (29.1), or whether each subgroup forms its own government and individually satisfies:

(29.2) $$MRS^A_{X^A,Y^A} = MRT_{X,Y}$$

and

(29.3) $$MRS^B_{X^B,Y^B} = MRT_{X,Y}$$

Suppose, however, the national government were constrained to offer equal amounts of Y to each subgroup so that $Y^A = Y^B$ with national provision of Y. Since, in general, $Y^A \neq Y^B$ at the social welfare optimum, this would represent an additional binding constraint on the formal general equilibrium model, implying a lower level of social welfare at the optimum. It is easy to show that the new first-order conditions become:

(29.4) $$MRS^A_{X^A,Y^A} = MRS^B_{X^B,Y^B} = MRT_{X,Y} + \frac{\lambda_3}{\lambda_2 F_X}$$

where:

λ_2 = the Lagrangian multiplier associated with society's production possibilities, $F(\ ) = 0$.

λ_3 = the Lagrangian multiplier associated with the new constraint, $Y^A = Y^B$.

Local autonomy is obviously the preferred structure under these conditions because it avoids subjecting society to an unnecessary constraint upon government decision making. Oates labels this result *the decentralization theorem:*

> For a public good—the consumption of which is defined over geographical subsets of the total population, and for which the costs of providing each level of output of the good in each jurisdiction are the same for the central or the respective local government—it will always be more efficient (or at least as efficient) for local governments to provide the Pareto-efficient levels of output for their respective jurisdictions than for the central government to provide *any* specified and uniform level of output across all jurisdictions.[5]

The decentralization theorem does not actually solve the problem of justifying local level governments in a first-best policy environment. It is really an exercise in the theory of the second best, precisely because the national government is forced to offer equal service levels to all subsets of the population. Nonetheless, this is a compelling restriction. U.S. citizens have long, and successfully, argued for local autonomy over public elementary and secondary education on the grounds that a federal takeover, despite some financial

---

[5] Excerpted from *Fiscal Federalism* by Wallace E. Oates, © 1972 by Harcourt Brace Jovanovich, Inc. p. 35. Reprinted by permission of the publisher.

advantages, would imply standardized education for all children. Similarly, the FCC has promoted local television production to offset the standardized packages offered by the national networks. Chapter 8 discussed the major drawback to the federally legislated pollution control devices for all automobiles, in that the level of pollution reduction obtained is almost certainly nonoptimal for all but a few localities. In that particular case, however, effective local initiatives against automobile pollution were hard to imagine. Along these same lines, the national government is prohibited by the Constitution of the United States from varying certain taxes on a geographical basis. The point is that the particular second-best model Oates chose as an alternative to first-best local autonomy is highly relevant for the United States, and not just some arbitrary formal model that happens to be biased against national decision making.

THE THEORY OF CLUBS

There have been numerous attempts to justify local autonomy within the confines of first-best modeling. Most of these studies posit a world in which local jurisdictions have yet to form, and ask two questions simultaneously: (a) are there incentives for the formation of local jurisdictions to provide traditional public services such as Samuelsonian public goods? and (b) will the resulting local public services be provided in accordance with standard first-best decision rules, such as $\sum MRS = MRT$? The models used to analyze these questions draw heavily on Buchanan's theory of clubs.[6] Briefly, Buchanan argued that determining the optimal membership of any club has an externality element to it. On the one hand, accepting new members reduces the direct out-of-pocket costs to the current members by spreading all fixed costs over more people. On the other hand, the new members create additional external diseconomies in the form of more crowded facilities. Thus, the optimum-sized membership occurs when the marginal costs of the external diseconomies just equal the marginal savings from spreading total operating costs.

The theory of optimal club size can be adapted quite readily to explain the optimal formation of local jurisdictions. We will consider a simple model that Martin McGuire used to analyze this problem.[7]

Suppose a country consists of H identical people whose preferences are defined over two goods, X, and Y^h, where:

X = a Samuelsonian public good provided by a government.

Y^h = the income of person h (alternatively, a composite commodity with $P_y \equiv 1$).

Preferences are given by:

(29.5) $\qquad U^h(X, Y^h) \qquad$ all $h = 1, \dots, H$

---

[6] J. Buchanan, "An Economic Theory of Clubs," *Economica*, February, 1965.

[7] M. McGuire, "Group Segregation and Optimal Jurisdictions," *Journal of Political Economy*, January/February, 1974.

Rather than defining a production function relating X and the Y^h, assume first-best production efficiency and posit a cost function for X:

$$(29.6) \qquad\qquad C = C(X; \text{other arguments})$$

where C is measured in dollars, the same as the Y^h. If we assume that

a. Income is optimally distributed,
b. $C = C(X)$, and no other arguments, and
c. The costs of X are shared equally by all people,

then this representation of the Samuelsonian public good is equivalent to the formulation in Chapter 6. (Assuming equal cost sharing is convenient, but unnecessary). To see this, note that the utility of each person h is:

$$(29.7) \qquad\qquad U^h\left[X, Y^h - \frac{C(X)}{H} \right] \qquad h = 1, \ldots, H$$

Since all people are identical, and the distribution of income is optimal, all the government need do is maximize (29.7) with respect to X. The first-order conditions are:

$$(29.8) \qquad\qquad \frac{\partial U^h}{\partial X} - \frac{\partial U^h}{\partial y^h} \cdot \frac{\partial C}{\partial X} \cdot \frac{1}{H} = 0$$

where:

$$y^h = \left[Y^h - \frac{C(X)}{H} \right] \equiv \text{disposable income}$$

Rearranging terms:

$$(29.9) \qquad\qquad H \cdot \frac{\dfrac{\partial U^h}{\partial X}}{\dfrac{\partial U^h}{\partial y^h}} = \frac{\partial C}{\partial X}$$

or

$$H \cdot MRS_{X,y^h} = MC_X = MRT_{X,y^h} \qquad \text{with } P_y \equiv 1$$

(29.9) is the familiar first-best decision rule for public goods, implying national provision of X to all people within the country.

For local provision of the public good to be optimal, X must have two special properties. First, if some locality provides an amount of X to its constituents, it can effectively exclude all other people from consuming its X. In terms of the theory of clubs, the services of the club are exclusive to its own members. But that assumption alone would not be sufficient for optimal provision of X at the local level. It must be assumed further that as X is provided to more and more people, each person receiving X bears increased costs. This can be modeled in one of two ways. It may be that each person's enjoyment of X diminishes as more people consume it, along the lines of a straight consumer externality, in which utility is a function of X, Y^h, *and* N, where N is the number of people consuming X. Alternatively, the direct costs of providing X could vary directly with N, so that $C = C(X, N)$, with $\partial C / \partial N = C_N > 0$.

FIGURE 29–1

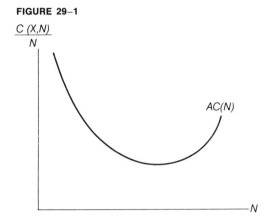

With each person bearing some of the direct cost of providing X, it hardly matters, in a formal sense, which method is chosen. One can think of the cost function as including the external diseconomies of crowding, so that the two "stories" are virtually identical. All that matters is that social welfare maximization depends directly upon N, the number of people consuming the public good. Examples might include police protection and education, in which the quantity of X co-mingles with certain quality attributes which will vary with N. Police services can be replicated as more people move into a district, but the sheer increase in numbers may make it more difficult to control criminal activity.

In fact, McGuire chooses the direct cost approach, writing:

$$(29.10) \qquad C = C(X, N) \qquad C_X, C_N > 0$$

With equal sharing of the costs, the utility of person h becomes $U^h[X, Y^h - C(X, N)/N]$. That is, each person pays the average costs of X where the average is defined relative to N, not X. McGuire further assumes that the average costs of X defined over N are U shaped. The "spreading effects" of having N in the denominator dominate up to some point, after which the marginal costs (C_N) dominate, causing the average to increase. Refer to Figure 29–1. With these cost assumptions, society's problem becomes:

$$\max_{(X,N)} U^h \left[X, Y^h - \frac{C(X, N)}{N} \right]$$

The first-order conditions are:

$$(29.11) \qquad \frac{\partial U^h}{\partial X} - \frac{\partial U^h}{\partial y^h} C_X \frac{1}{N} = 0$$

$$(29.12) \qquad \frac{\partial U}{\partial y^h} \left(\frac{-NC_N + C}{N^2} \right) = 0$$

Rearranging terms:

(29.13)
$$N \cdot \left(\frac{\frac{\partial U}{\partial X}}{\frac{\partial U}{\partial y^h}} \right) = C_X$$

(29.14)
$$\frac{C}{N} = C_N$$

Notice that both (29.13) and (29.14) are functions of X and N, so that the optimal number of jurisdictions and the provision of X within each jurisdiction are determined simultaneously. Nonetheless, each equation separately has a standard interpretation. Equation (29.13) says that, given N, each jurisdiction should follow the usual public good decision rule in providing X. Equation (29.14) says that, given X, people should form groups such that the average cost of X just equals the marginal costs of one additional person. This is the minimum AC, technically efficient, zero profit result from competitive market behavior. So long as jurisdictions can be replicated, people can always regroup until the minimum AC obtains each jurisdiction. There is no reason for anyone to bear average costs higher than the minimum. Moreover, with identical people, (29.13) and (29.14) imply equal-sized jurisdictions, H/N in number. National provision of a single X to all H people is no longer optimal, so long as AC_{min} occurs at $N^* < H$.[8]

McGuire also considers the case of a heterogeneous population consisting of homogeneous subgroupings. Without reproducing that model, it should be obvious that each jurisdiction consists of people with like tastes, and that conditions (29.13) and (29.14) hold within each jurisdiction. X has to be provided to people of like tastes in order to maximize each person's net benefit of consuming and paying for X. The only substantive difference is that the level of X will vary across jurisdictions, depending on tastes.

Curiously enough, while the McGuire model talks about the simultaneous problems of providing public goods and forming local jurisdictions, it does not actually imply local autonomy. The national government could still be the sole supplier of X. It would simply note that the costs of X vary with access to X, so that it would not be optimal to provide a national level of X with access to all, but rather exclusive subsets of X in accordance with conditions (29.13) and (29.14). With homogeneous populations, the amount of X provided to each subgroup would be equal, but these amounts would differ from the single amount

---

[8] The AC_{min} solution can be thought of as an instance of perfect correspondence even though Oates defined perfect correspondence with respect to an externality that affected a distinct subset of people (firms), whereas here the additional costs associated with N vary continuously with N. Nonetheless one can consider X as having two attributes, an externality associated with the public good quality of X and a decreasing cost aspect associated with the relationship of costs to N. For this good, perfect correspondence occurs when the decreasing costs are exhausted. Since the pure externality part of X can be made exclusive to each jurisdiction, by assumption, that aspect of X will automatically satisfy the perfect correspondence criterion once the jurisdictions have been set.

of X provided if access did not affect direct costs or create external diseconomies. All McGuire has really done is complicate the nature of the production of X (or the externality associated with X). Theoretically, the national government could anticipate this complication, even though it is difficult to imagine national provision of services such as police. Furthermore, local autonomy per se cannot guarantee that the optimal conditions will obtain because people may not actually form subgroups in an optimal manner, although failure to do so can be attributed to faulty policy tools, thereby rendering the policy environment second best. We will return to the dynamics of jurisdiction formation below. For the moment, let us continue with the attempt to justify local governments in a first-best policy environment.

MISPERCEIVED PREFERENCES

To this point we have argued that the standard attempts in the literature to justify federalism as the optimal form of government for tackling allocational problems have failed to do so if one stays strictly within the bounds of a first-best policy environment. This must be the case, for if the national government is the only government allowed to make social welfare rankings, and it has perfect knowledge and access to whatever policy tools are necessary to generate first-best allocational decision rules, there can indeed be no compelling reason for local autonomy. Having said this, there remains the nagging suspicion that local autonomy really is more appropriate for public services that are limited in scope, all the more so when Oates' perfect correspondence happens to obtain within jurisdictions that already exist. Stigler's twin axioms of "minimum sized jurisdictions consistent with allocational efficiency" and "states rights," the right to variable levels of services across localities locally determined, remain compelling despite the formal implications of first-best theory. Is it possible, therefore, to resurrect fiscal federalism as an optimal governmental structure without introducing specific second-best assumptions such as Oates did for his decentralization theorem? In our view the answer is yes, but it involves two lines of argument that have not received much, if any, attention in the theoretical literature on federalism.

In the framework of a first-best environment with perfect certainty, federalism can be justified on distributional grounds. Stigler, and others following him, have assumed that the national government resolves all distributional questions, presumably by lump-sum tax and transfers in accordance with the interpersonal equity conditions of its social welfare function. It seems obvious, though, that local jurisdictions will create their own social welfare functions, each one distinct from the national social welfare function. If this is so, then it can be shown that federalism is required for social welfare maximization even in a first-best environment. Indeed, the very notion of a "social welfare maximum" requires careful analysis in this case. These distributional issues will be considered in Chapter 30 rather than here, because Stigler's axioms clearly have nothing to do with the distribution question. He argued for local autonomy only in allocational decision making.

If one insists on placing the distribution function with the national government, then the argument for federalism would appear to require the existence of a particular kind of uncertainty. Suppose, for the sake of expositional clarity, that the only allocational problem facing society is the existence of a Samuelsonian public good, X_g, the consumption of which happens to affect only a subset of the population. Let $h = 1, \ldots, k$, be the affected subset and $h = k + 1, \ldots, H$ be the unaffected subset. All other goods are pure private goods, and there is no other (e.g., decreasing costs) problem requiring government intervention for allocational reasons. The distribution of income is optimal, and determined by the national government.

In a first-best world of perfect certainty, either the national government or a local jurisdiction comprising individuals $h = 1, \ldots, k$ could provide the proper level of X_g in accordance with the standard first-order condition:

$$(29.15) \qquad \sum_{h=1}^{k} MRS_{g,1}^{h} = MRT_{g,1}$$

where good 1 is one of the purely private goods. Suppose, however, that the local jurisdiction knows its citizens well in the sense that it can determine any individual $MRS_{g,1}^{h}$ with perfect certainty, whereas the national government knows each of these people less well in the sense that it observes each individual's $MRS_{g,1}^{h}, h = 1, \ldots, k$, as a random variable:

$$(29.16) \qquad M\hat{R}S_{g,1}^{h} = MRS_{g,1} + \alpha$$

where:

$\quad MRS_{g,1}^{h} = $ the true MRS as observed by the local jurisdiction.

$\quad \alpha = $ a random variable, with $E(\alpha) = \bar{\alpha}$, possibly 0.

Under these conditions, social welfare will be maximized, in general, by having the local jurisdiction form and decide the appropriate level of X_g, rather than letting the national government determine X_g according to the first-order condition:

$$(29.17) \qquad \sum_{h=1}^{k} M\hat{R}S_{g,1}^{h} = MRT_{g,1}$$

If $\bar{\alpha} \neq 0$, the national governments decision rule is clearly biased, implying either over- or underprovision of X_g. Even if $\bar{\alpha} = 0$, however, so that $M\hat{R}S_{g,1}^{h}$ is an unbiased estimate of $MRS_{g,1}^{h}$, a risk-averse society will prefer local provision of X_g, so long as the subset $h = 1, \ldots, k$ is small enough to violate the population condition of the Arrow-Lind theorem (Chapter 25). Expressed in terms of indirect utility functions:

$$(29.18) \qquad V^{h}(\bar{q}; I^{h}; X_g^{*}) > E[V^{h}(\bar{q}; I^{h}; \bar{X}_g)] \qquad h = 1, \ldots, k$$

where:

$\quad X_g^{*} = $ the optimal level of X_g, obtained with local provision.

$\quad \bar{X}_g = X_g^{*} + \beta$, with $E(\beta) = 0$, obtained with national provision.

Assuming risk aversion, persons $h = 1, \ldots, k$, would be willing to pay a risk premium for local rather than national provision of X_g.

Proponents of federalism obviously have this type of uncertainty in mind when they argue that local governments best know the interests of their own citizens. The sheer geographic distance from the central government to most of the people within a given society is bound to affect adversely the transmission of information. The only remaining theoretical question is whether or not this particular form of uncertainty violates the perfect knowledge assumption of first-best theory. Uncertainty, per se, is consistent with the first-best framework, but one could argue that postulating uncertainty as a function of geographic distance violates the perfect knowledge requirement, thus rendering the analysis second best. If so, then there would indeed appear to be no way to justify fiscal federalism strictly for allocational reasons in a first-best environment. One has to turn to the distributional argument of the next chapter. At very least though, it can be said that uncertainty of this type surely exists, *and* requires local autonomy for a social welfare maximum. By way of contrast, the cost phenomenon postulated by McGuire may well be equally prevalent, but it does not necessitate local autonomy. In this narrow sense, then, uncertainty is a more compelling argument for fiscal federalism, even though it may be merely another variation of a second-best decentralization theorem.

THE DYNAMICS OF JURISDICTION FORMATION

As we have seen above, it is a reasonably simple exercise to define various examples of externalities and decreasing costs over a subset of the entire population and then describe an optimal set of local jurisdictions that can act individually to correct for these problems in an optimal manner. But there remains the important question whether or not people will naturally group into subsets congruent with the set of local jurisdictions required for a social welfare optimum. The early literature on optimal federalism, following the lead of Charles Tiebout,[9] rather loosely theorized that jurisdictions would form as required. In fact, Tiebout argued that one of the great advantages of fiscal federalism was that it permitted an individual to "vote with his feet," seeking the precise combination of local services and taxes that would maximize utility. Tiebout believed that if all people were free to search in this fashion, and packages of services and taxes were infinitely replicable, then social welfare would be maximized. People of like tastes would congregate together,[10] and services

---

[9] C. M. Tiebout, "A Pure Theory of Local Expenditures," *Journal of Political Economy*, October 1956. Tiebout's article is the seminal work, the first to consider the gains from local jurisdictions in a neoclassical framework. His conclusion that voting with one's feet would generate a social welfare optimum was based on a loose formal argument that did not stand the test of more careful analysis except under special conditions, but his work fostered an entire literature on jurisdiction formation.

[10] As Stigler put it, people would choose among high service–high tax, medium service–medium tax, and low service–low tax communities. See Stigler, "Tenable Range of Functions of Local Government."

would be provided at minimum cost. No cost differences could persist across localities offering identical services because people would naturally gravitate from high-cost to low-cost towns. In effect, the "market" for local services would be perfectly competitive.

The Tiebout proposition sounds plausible enough, especially in a first-best policy environment, but more recent work has shown that the problem of actually forming optimal jurisdictions is more subtle than Tiebout originally imagined. As we have seen, each particular problem necessitating public sector intervention requires a particular set of jurisdictions. In addition, it is now known that only certain forms of taxation can create the proper incentives to form an optimal set of jurisdictions. Of course the proper form of taxation for public services would presumably be found if the policy environment were truly first best, but the important point is that these taxes are usually highly complex and/or unrealistic and, therefore, unlikely to be approximated in reality. Failing them, a federalist system might not even have a stable equilibrium.

The McGuire Model

Let us consider the McGuire model as an example since it was analyzed in some detail above. Recall that optimality entailed supplying the public good X in each community such that (29.13) and (29.14) hold simultaneously. Furthermore, these conditions imply jurisdictions of equal size if everyone has identical tastes, and (equal-sized) homogeneous subgroupings of identical people if tastes are heterogeneous across the entire population. To ensure that these conditions will actually obtain, McGuire is forced to describe the following rather complex scenario.

Imagine, at first, a single individual searching among local jurisdictions that have already been established, but only on a temporary basis. Consider an individual currently belonging to "temporary" community j. In deciding whether to move from community j to some other community, k, the individual will compare the benefits of the move with its costs. The benefits arise from the difference in the public goods provided in each community, X^k versus X^j. The costs depend upon the payment or tax scheme used by each town. According to McGuire, it is natural to assume that each town will ask a new member to pay the marginal costs of entry, so that no existing town member loses by having a new entrant. Thus, the cost comparison is $C_N^k(X^k, N^k)$ versus $C_N^j(X^j, N^j)$, where C_N is the marginal cost of X in terms of N.

Consider a move to a marginally different community. The *change* in costs can be represented as the total derivative of C_N:

$$(29.19) \qquad\qquad dC_N = C_{NX}dX + C_{NN}dN$$

Recall that N and X are simultaneously determined so that a change in N will create a change in the optimal level of X. Dividing (29.19) by dX defines the marginal cost/benefit ratio available to the individual if he moves,

$$(29.20) \qquad \frac{dC_N}{dX} = C_{NX} + C_{NN} \frac{dN}{dX}\bigg|_{\text{supply}}$$

Turning next to his preferences for such a move, an individual's

$$MRS^h_{X,Y^h} = \frac{dY^h}{dX} = -\frac{dC_N}{dX}$$

indicates his willingness to trade off increased X for increased costs (an increase in costs subtracts, dollar for dollar, from private income Y^h). Hence, the individual will search until

$$(29.21) \qquad MRS^h_{X,Y^h} = C_{NX} + C_{NN} \frac{dN}{dX}\bigg|_{\text{supply}}$$

If many people are searching under these conditions, homogenous groupings will naturally form, since localities offering a given marginal cost/benefit ratio will ultimately attract only those people whose MRS_{X,Y^h} equals that ratio. Hence:

$$(29.22) \qquad N \cdot MRS_{X,Y^i} = NC_N + NC_{NN} \frac{dN}{dX}\bigg|_{\text{supply}}$$

will hold in the final equilibrium, where N represents the number of people in a particular homogeneous subgroup i.

McGuire argues next that optimality conditions (29.14) ($C/N = C_N$) will hold in the final equilibrium. This makes sense so long as localities can be replicated, because with each person paying the marginal costs of entry, C_N, the only way in which total tax payments will equal the total costs of providing X is if MC equals AC, or $C_N = C/N$. If C_N were temporarily in excess of C/N in some towns, and below C/N in others, all of which offer equal levels of X, the people in the high-cost towns will presumably move to the lower cost communities until all profits or rents to existing members disappear. In this sense, the search acts as a competitive market mechanism.

The McGuire search procedure, then, establishes two equilibrium conditions:

$$(29.23) \qquad \frac{C}{N} = C_N$$

and

$$(29.24) \qquad N \cdot MRS_{X,Y^i} = NC_{NX} + NC_{NN} \frac{dN}{dX}\bigg|_{\text{supply}}$$

Equation (29.23) is one of the two conditions for a welfare optimum. It remains to show that equations (29.23) and (29.24) together imply the second optimality condition, the standard public goods decision rule (29.13).

To see that they do imply (29.13), totally differentiate (29.23) to obtain:

$$(29.25) \qquad C_X dX + C_N dN = NC_{NX} dX + NC_{NN} dN + C_N dN$$

Rearranging terms:

(29.26) $$(C_X - NC_{NX})dX = NC_{NN}dN$$

(29.27) $$\frac{(C_X - NC_{NX})}{NC_{NN}} = \frac{dN}{dX}\bigg|_{\text{supply}}$$

Substituting (29.27) into (29.24) and simplifying yields:

(29.28) $$N \cdot MRS_{X,Y^i} = C_X$$

as required.

The Wheaton Model

The fact that McGuire can describe a search algorithm consistent with the optimality conditions of his particular model does not really offer much confidence that anything approaching optimal jurisdiction formation will actually occur in practice. As McGuire himself notes, free-rider problems and the inability to sufficiently replicate jurisdictions are highly likely to occur in practice, in which case his search procedure will fail to achieve the welfare optimum. It is also unlikely that tax payments will ever be closely related to the marginal costs of entry. This last point is of some importance, because Wheaton has demonstrated that only certain tax payment mechanisms are consistent with an *equilibrium* of local jurisdictions, much less optimal jurisdiction formation.[11] He is also able to show that payment schema consistent with pareto optimality for nationally provided public goods will not generate pareto optimality for locally provided public goods given consumer mobility.

The model Wheaton uses to analyze the relationship between various tax mechanisms and optimality is similar to McGuire's with the exception that no particular tax is specified initially. Adopting Wheaton's notation,

Let:

X = the quantity of a Samuelsonian public good provided by some local jurisdiction.

P_0 = the price of X, assumed equal to the marginal costs of producing X.

X_i = a composite private commodity purchased by person i belonging to the jurisdiction, $i = 1, \ldots, N$.

P = the price of the composite commodity, also assumed equal to the marginal costs of producing X_i.

Y_i = the income of person i, assumed given.

T_i = taxes paid by person i.

Assume that all people have identical tastes.

---

[11] W. Wheaton, "Consumer Mobility and Community Tax Bases," *Journal of Public Economics*, November 1975.

The model consists of three sets of relationships:

$$(29.29) \qquad Y_i = T_i + PX_i \qquad i = 1, \ldots, N$$

$$(29.30) \qquad \sum_{i=1}^{N} T_i = P_0 X$$

$$(20.31) \qquad \sum_{i=1}^{N} \left(\frac{\frac{\partial U}{\partial X}}{\frac{\partial U}{\partial X_i}} \right) = \frac{P_0}{P}$$

(29.29) says that any person's income is exhausted by tax payments and expenditures on the private composite commodity. (29.30) indicates that the local officials will collect tax revenues sufficient to cover exactly the costs of the public good, in other words, pursue a balanced budget. (29.31) is the familiar public goods decision rule. Since prices equal marginal costs, the price ratio, P_0/P, is the MRT between X and X_i. Wheaton assumes that the local officials are able to select the proper level of X for any given N.

The analysis proceeds by specifying a particular kind of tax, substituting for T_i in equations (29.29) and (29.30), totally differentiating the three equations, and solving for $\partial U_i/\partial Y_1$, the effect on the utility of person i of a marginal increase in the income of person 1. This is equivalent to the effect on person i of moving into a marginally richer community, by which is meant a community all of whose people have the same income as the people in the original town except for one person, whose income is marginally higher than the income of the corresponding person in the original town. Equilibrium will only obtain if $\partial U_i/\partial Y_1$ can take on the value 0. For if it is always positive (or negative), people will always want to move, contrary to the notion of achieving an equilibrium set of local jurisdictions.

Consider, for example, the simple case of an equal head tax on all people, the tax posited by McGuire in his model. In this case,

$$(29.32) \qquad T_i = \bar{T} = \frac{P_0 X}{N}$$

The full model becomes:

$$(29.33) \qquad Y_i = \frac{P_0 X}{N} + PX_i \qquad i = 1, \ldots, N$$

$$(29.34) \qquad \sum_{i=1}^{N} \left(\frac{\frac{\partial U}{\partial X}}{\frac{\partial U}{\partial X_i}} \right) = \frac{P_0}{P}$$

(Notice that the tax itself implies equation (29.30).) Totally differentiating (29.33) and (29.34) with respect to Y_1 yields:

$$(29.35) \qquad 1 = \frac{P_0}{N} \frac{dX}{dY_1} + P \frac{dX_1}{dY_1} \qquad i = 1$$

$$(29.36) \qquad 0 = \frac{P_0}{PN} \frac{dX}{dY_1} + \frac{dX_i}{dY_1} \qquad i = 2, \ldots, N$$

$$(29.37) \qquad \sum_{i=1}^{N} \left(\frac{\partial MRS^i}{\partial X} \right) \cdot \frac{dX}{dY_1} + \sum_{i=1}^{N} \left(\frac{\partial MRS^i}{\partial X_i} \right) \frac{dX_i}{dY_1} = 0$$

Making appropriate substitutions and rearranging terms yields:

$$(29.38) \qquad \frac{dX}{dY_1} = \frac{-\left(\dfrac{\partial MRS_1}{\partial X_1} \right)}{P\left[\displaystyle\sum_{i=1}^{N} \left(\dfrac{\partial MRS_i}{\partial X} \right) - \dfrac{P_0}{PN} \displaystyle\sum_{i=1}^{N} \left(\dfrac{\partial MRS_i}{\partial X_i} \right) \right]}$$

$$(29.39) \qquad \frac{dX_i}{dY_1} = \frac{-P_0}{PN} \left(\frac{dX}{dY_1} \right) \qquad i = 2, \ldots, N$$

$$(29.40) \qquad \frac{dX_1}{dY_1} = \frac{1}{P} - \frac{P_0}{PN} \left(\frac{dX}{dY_1} \right)$$

Next, totally differentiate the utility of person i with respect to Y_1:

$$(29.41) \qquad \frac{dU_i}{dY_1} = \frac{\partial U_i}{\partial X} \left(\frac{dX}{dY_1} \right) + \frac{\partial U_i}{\partial X_i} \left(\frac{dX_i}{dY_1} \right) \qquad i = 2, \ldots, N$$

Substituting equation (29.39) into (29.41), and rearranging terms yields:

$$(29.42) \qquad \frac{dU_i}{dY_1} = \frac{dX}{dY_1} \left[\frac{\partial U_i}{\partial X} - \frac{\partial U_i}{\partial X_i} \frac{P_0}{P \cdot N} \right]$$

dU_i/dY_1 will equal zero in equilibrium because the bracketed term equals zero once the locality establishes the equilibrium level of X in accordance with the public goods decision rule (29.34). Furthermore, consumer mobility should generate this equilibrium. Presumably, X is not an inferior good, so that $dX/dY_1 > 0$. In addition, if society is out of equilibrium, one would expect $MRS_{X,Y_i} > P_0/PN$ for the rich and $MRS_{X,Y_i} < P_0/PN$ for the poor. Hence, $dU_i/dY_1 > 0$ for the rich, and < 0 for the poor. In other words, the rich will want to move to wealthier communities, the poor to poorer communities, until $dU_i/dY_1 = 0$ obtains for all people. Wheaton, therefore, reaches the same conclusions as McGuire, that with a head tax the population will divide into homogeneous subsets and form a set of jurisdictions compatible with pareto optimality. However, Wheaton's analysis can also easily establish that other tax mechanisms will not generate any equilibrium, much less an optimal equilibrium.

Consider as a final example the differential tax system whereby each person pays a tax equal to his MRS_{X,Y_i}, the so-called Lindahl price. We argued in Chapter 6 that Lindahl pricing is an especially appealing way to finance a *national* public good, since it is consistent with the competitive market interpretation of the benefits-received principle of taxation and it also preserves the pareto-optimal allocation of resources. If used to finance local public goods, however, it may not even be capable of generating an equilibrium set of jurisdictions!

To see this, rework the Wheaton analysis with Lindahl pricing instead of the head taxes. Person i will pay a per unit tax:

$$(29.43) \qquad P_0^i = P \cdot MRS^i \qquad i = 1, \ldots, N$$

Hence

$$(29.44) \qquad T_i = P_0^i \cdot X = P \cdot MRS^i \cdot X$$

Assuming CRS in the production of X, with marginal costs equal to average costs,

$$(29.45) \qquad \sum_{i=1}^{N} T_i = \sum_{i=1}^{N} P_0^i X = \sum_{i=1}^{N} MRS^i \cdot PX = P^0 X$$

so that equation (29.30) is automatically satisfied. Thus, the two remaining relevant sets of equilibrium conditions are:

$$(29.46) \qquad Y_i = PX \cdot MRS^i + PX_i \qquad i = 1, \ldots, N$$

$$(29.47) \qquad \sum_{i=1}^{N} MRS^i = \frac{P^0}{P}$$

Totally differentiating (29.46) and (29.47) with respect to Y_1 yields:

$$(29.48) \qquad 1 = PMRS^1 \frac{dX}{dY_1} + PX \frac{\partial MRS^1}{\partial X} \frac{dX}{dY_1}$$

$$+ PX \frac{\partial MRS^1}{\partial X_1} \frac{dX_1}{dY_1} + P \frac{dX_1}{dY_1} \qquad i = 1$$

$$(29.49) \qquad 0 = PMRS^i \frac{dX}{dY_1} + PX \frac{\partial MRS^i}{\partial X} \frac{dX}{dY_1}$$

$$+ PX \frac{\partial MRS^i}{\partial X_i} \frac{dX_i}{dY_1} + P \frac{dX_i}{dY_1} \qquad i = 2, \ldots, N$$

$$(29.50) \qquad 0 = \sum_{i=1}^{N} \left(\frac{\partial MRS^i}{\partial X} \right) \frac{dX}{dY_1} + \sum_{i=1}^{N} \left(\frac{\partial MRS^i}{\partial X_i} \right) \frac{dX_i}{dY_1}$$

Noting that $MRS^i = (Y_i - PX_i)/PX$, multiplying the first and last terms in (29.48) and (29.49) by X/X, and rearranging terms yields:

$$(29.51) \qquad \frac{dX_1}{dY_1} = \frac{\dfrac{1}{PX} - \dfrac{dX}{dY_1} \left[\left(\dfrac{Y_1 - PX_1}{PX^2} \right) + \dfrac{\partial MRS^1}{\partial X} \right]}{\dfrac{1}{X} + \dfrac{\partial MRS^1}{\partial X_1}}$$

and

$$(29.52) \qquad \frac{dX_i}{dY_1} = \frac{-\dfrac{dX}{dY_1} \left[\left(\dfrac{Y_i - PX_i}{PX^2} \right) + \dfrac{\partial MRS^i}{\partial X} \right]}{\dfrac{1}{X} + \dfrac{\partial MRS^i}{\partial X_i}} \qquad i = 2, \ldots, N$$

Substituting for dX_1/dY_1 and dX_i/dY_1 in (29.50) and rearranging terms to solve for dX/dY_1 yields:

(29.53)
$$\frac{dX}{dY_1} = -\frac{\left[\dfrac{\left(\dfrac{\partial MRS^1}{\partial X_1}\right)\cdot\dfrac{1}{PX}}{\left(\dfrac{1}{X}+\dfrac{\partial MRS^1}{\partial X_1}\right)}\right]}{Z}$$

where:

$$Z = \sum_{i=1}^{N}\frac{\partial MRS^i}{\partial X} - \frac{\displaystyle\sum_{i=1}^{N}\left(\dfrac{\partial MRS^i}{\partial X_i}\right)\left[\left(\dfrac{Y-PX_i}{PX^2}\right)+\dfrac{\partial MRS^i}{\partial X}\right]}{\dfrac{1}{X}+\dfrac{\partial MRS^i}{\partial X_i}}$$

It can be shown from consumer maximization that $\partial MRS^i/\partial X_i > 0$ and $\partial MRS^i/\partial X < 0$ if X is a normal good.[12] Thus, the numerator of (29.53) is negative, but Z can be $>, <, = 0$ depending on the relative magnitude of $\underset{(+)}{(Y - PX_i)/PX^2}$ and $\underset{(-)}{\partial MRS^i/\partial X}$. Assuming that neither Z nor the numerator of (29.53) equals zero, dX/dY_1 is either positive or negative.[13] Substituting for dX_i/dY_1 from (29.52), recalling that $(Y_i - PX_i)/PX = MRS^i$, noting that $(\partial U_i/\partial X_i)/(\partial U_i/\partial X) = 1/MRS^i$, and rearranging terms, (29.41) can be rewritten as

(29.54)
$$\frac{dU_i}{dY_1} = \frac{dX}{dY_1}\left(\frac{\partial U_i}{\partial X}\right)\left[1 - \frac{\dfrac{1}{X}+\dfrac{\partial MRS^i}{\partial X}}{\dfrac{1}{X}+\dfrac{\partial MRS^i}{\partial X_i}}\right]$$

With $\partial MRS^i/\partial X_i > 0$ and $\partial MRS^i/\partial X < 0$, the term in brackets must be positive. Thus, $dU_i/dY_1 > 0$ if $dX/dY_1 > 0$ and vice versa, leading to the interpretation that everyone will want to move to richer ($dU_i/dY_1 > 0$) or poorer ($dU_i/dY_1 < 0$) communities for any given existing pattern of jurisdictions. A final equilibrium will never obtain, and Lindahl pricing is simply unworkable.

The Replicability of Jurisdictions and Housing Prices

Wheaton's analysis, while instructive, cannot possibly be a complete description of jurisdiction formation with a mobile population because it ignores the response of property or housing prices as people change locations. Since Wheaton's composite commodity includes property and housing services, the price of these services is necessarily fixed. The same point applies to the McGuire model. But if some town offers a particularly attractive bundle of public services cum taxes, demand for that bundle might well cause property values there to

---

[12] Ibid., p. 379, n2.
[13] Wheaton errs in interpreting the sign of the bracketed term in the equation for Z, leading him to conclude that dX/dY_1 is always positive. Ibid., p. 383.

rise, until the annual excess value of the bundle relative to available alternatives is fully capitalized into the value of that town's property. These changes in property values will in turn affect the adjustment toward a final equilibrium. By ignoring this effect, Wheaton and McGuire are implicitly assuming that jurisdictions are sufficiently replicable so that preferences for public service bundles can be satisfied without any increase in the rental value of property. If some subset of the population desires the exact public service bundle provided by an existing town it does not necessarily have to bid for property in that town in order to acquire the bundle. If their bids begin to increase rental values above their values in some alternative, undeveloped, location, they can simply form a new town, provide the same bundle of public services and pay the same rents. This is the thrust of the second optimality condition in McGuire's model that $AC_N = MC_N$. If people pay MC_N, and $MC_N > AC_N$, the resulting "profits" will be capitalized into rental values. But if supply of public service bundles is perfectly elastic at AC_{min}, no such capitalization is possible, or desirable.

It is entirely plausible to suppose, however, that jurisdictions are not sufficiently replicable to effect a perfect match between public service bundles and preferences for those bundles at constant rental values, where rental values are understood to be standardized by property size, location, and an array of housing services. Without perfect matching, rental values will change in response to excess demands for and supplies of existing public services bundles offered by particular towns.

A model developed by Pauly is instructive for exploring the various possibilities without replicability.[14]

Let:

X = a composite commodity whose price equals 1.

G = a bundle of public services, exclusive of taxes.

g = the unit price or tax of a public service, assumed constant across all jurisdictions.

R = the rental value of a standardized vector of property and housing services.

Y = lump-sum consumer income, assumed fixed for each individual.

Assume initially that R is constant across all jurisdictions. If consumer utility is defined over X and G, each consumer will solve the following problem:

$$\max_{(X_h, G_h)} U^h(X_h, G_h)$$

$$\text{s.t.} \quad Y^h = X_h + gG_h + R \qquad h = 1, \ldots, H$$

Suppose the maximization generates a G_h^*. Person h, and all other consumers identical to h in terms of preferences and income, will form a jurisdiction providing exactly G_h^* of public services, replicating if necessary to avoid any

[14] M. Pauly, "A Model of Local Government Expenditure and Tax Capitalization," *Journal of Public Economics*, October 1976.

increases in R. In this case, preferences for public service bundles are met exactly by homogeneous subgroupings of the population, and there is no capitalization. This is the situation envisioned by McGuire and Wheaton. Furthermore, g is essentially a head tax so that the subgroups would generate a pareto-optimal equilibrium.

Suppose, however, that there are a fixed number of localities, $\ell = 1, \ldots, L$ with the following characteristics: (a) each locality offers a particular level of public services represented by the vector $\vec{G} = (G_1, \ldots, G_\ell, \ldots, G_L)$; (b) there are a fixed number of properties in each town represented by the vector $\vec{H} = (H_1, \ldots, H_\ell, \ldots, H_L)$, such that $\sum_{\ell=1}^{L} H_\ell = H$, the entire population of individuals seeking a location; and (c) rental values are specific to each location, represented by the vector $\vec{R} = (R_1, \ldots, R_\ell, \ldots, R_L)$

In this case it is possible that no one individual will find a G_h^*, given the vectors of rental values and available public service bundles. All one can say is that individual h will locate in town ℓ_1 if

(29.55) $U^h(G_{\ell_1}, R_{\ell_1}) > U^h(G_\ell, R_\ell)$ all $\ell \neq \ell_1$

Let $\eta(G_\ell) = $ the number of people that will choose to locate in locality ℓ, $\ell = 1, \ldots, L$. Equilibrium requires that

(29.56) $\eta(G_\ell) = H_\ell$ $\ell = 1, \ldots, L$

There will be no capitalization of public service bundles in equilibrium only if $R_\ell = \bar{R}$, $\ell = 1, \ldots, N$ holds as well. That is, imagine an initial situation in which rental values are equal across all localities. Rental values will remain equalized only if the search criterion (29.55) over all $h = 1, \ldots, H$, produces an exact matching of desired locations with the vector of locations available across all communities. Needless to say, a perfect matching without capitalization is unlikely, and if it does not obtain, the vector of rental values will change. For example, suppose there existed a perfect matching which was upset by a sudden decline in G_1, the public services offered in the first locality. Some consumers in town 1, those who were closest to indifference between town 1 and town 2 (assume the vector $G = (G_1, \ldots, G_\ell, \ldots, G_L)$ is indexed in order of increasing G) will now prefer town 2 at the existing rental values. This will drive up rental values in town 2. But as rental values in town 2 begin to rise, some people in town 2, those closest to indifference between town 2 and town 3 at the initial equal rental values, will now prefer town 3. Rental values in town 3 will begin to rise, and so on. The rental values in all towns may change. Equilibrium will be restored when condition (29.56) is reestablished for all ℓ, but it will be an equilibrium with capitalization of public service bundles. In this case, then, capitalization becomes a crucial part of the adjustment process.

On the other hand, equilibrium may never be restored. Pauly offers the following scenario as an intuitive counterexample relating to educational services. Suppose there are two classes of otherwise identical families: "small" families with two or fewer children, and "large" families with more than two children. Small families will naturally want to live in towns with other small families, because otherwise the small families will be subsidizing the education of the large families for any given level of educational expenditures. Thus if a given community consists of, say, an equal mix of large and small families, the small families will search for communities with a higher percentage of small families. But large families will also prefer communities with a higher proportion of small families because of the resulting educational subsidies. Hence, large families will follow the small families in their search. As rental values adjust, small families will move once again, only to be followed by the large families, and so on.

The system may reach an equilibrium if rental values in mixed communities exactly capitalize the pattern of subsidies, which are absent in the homogeneous communities. That is, rental values of small homes in mixed communities would have to be less than the rental values of small homes in a homogeneous community of small families (given equal education expenditures), to offset the subsidy paid by small families in the mixed communities. The opposite would apply to rental values of large homes in mixed communities relative to their rental values in homogeneous communities of large families.[15] But even if such capitalization occurred, there is no guarantee that (29.56) will be satisfied as required for a general equilibrium.

Empirical Analysis on Capitalization

A number of researchers, beginning with Oates in 1969,[16] have tried to determine whether or not capitalization of local public service bundles has actually occurred within the United States. The results have been mixed. Using a sample drawn from communities in southern New Jersey, Oates regressed property values on a vector of public expenditures, taxes, and various land and housing services. He found that increased public services increased property values, and increased taxes decreased property values, other things equal, consistent with the hypothesis that public service and tax bundles will be capitalized into property values. Meadows, using a more sophisticated model which allowed for simultaneous determination of expenditures and taxes, also discovered that capitalization was positively correlated with public services and negatively correlated with taxes.[17] However, the absolute values of his coefficients on both public sector variables were considerably lower than the Oates'

---

[15] Hamilton provides a similar example for high-income and low-income people. In his model, which uses a property tax, the low-income properties in mixed communities command a premium relative to their value in homogeneous communities, since their share of taxes declines in the mixed community for a given level of public services. The opposite holds for higher income properties in mixed communities. His model generates an equilibrium because properties can be expanded or contracted in each town, but it is not an efficient equilibrium. Because land values rise for low-income properties in the mixed communities, suppliers have an incentive to oversupply low-income housing in these communities. Consequently, low-income housing prices in mixed communities will no longer reflect the true value of the subsidies provided by the property taxes collected on the high-income properties. See B. W. Hamilton, "Capitalization of Intrajurisdictional Differences in Local Tax Prices," *American Economic Review*, December 1976.

[16] Oates, *Fiscal Federalism*, pp. 162–79.

[17] G. Meadows, "Taxes, Spending, and Property Values: A Comment and Further Results," *Journal of Political Economy*, August 1976.

coefficients. Edel and Sclar reproduced the Oates regression equation on a series of five cross sections of greater Boston area communities, the cross sections taken in 1930 and each subsequent decade thereafter.[18] The coefficients on the public sector variables declined (in absolute value) systematically over time. They interpreted this result as supporting the hypothesis that replication of communities would eventually reduce the possibilities for capitalization of public sector variables. Finally, Pollakowski was able to produce results quite different from the Oates-Meadows-Edel, Sclar equations.[19] Drawing from a sample of greater San Francisco area communities, he was unable to reproduce the Oates estimates. His results indicated that changes in the property tax rate were enormously overcapitalized (180 percent), an implausible estimate, and that changes in public expenditures had virtually no effect on property values.

The only reasonably safe conclusion one can draw from studies such as these is that they verify the theoretical conclusion that bundles of public sector services and taxes may be capitalized into property values. Beyond that, there is no a priori reason to expect any given pattern of coefficients on the public sector variables, whether taxes or expenditures are included in the set of regressors. They could be positive, negative, or zero, depending on people's preferences for public sector bundles relative to the bundles actually provided. If, for example, most communities in a given area are providing low service bundles, whereas most people prefer high service bundles, one would expect to find a positive correlation between property values and public services, as Oates and others actually found. But if the situation were reversed, the regression coefficient would be negative. Worse yet, suppose most towns are offering either high or low levels of public services, whereas most people prefer a medium level of service. If the distribution of public services were symmetric across communities, a regression of property values on public services would yield a zero coefficient. Yet theory would suggest that rental values in the medium service communities would capitalize the excess demand for these services. Thus, even if capitalization is occurring, regression analysis may fail to discover it.[20]

There is, then, no way to predict, a priori, the pattern of capitalization if the system is out of equilibrium. Capitalization will depend upon the pattern of excess demands and supplies for the public service bundles actually offerred, and anything is possible. Furthermore, there is no way of knowing if the system will come to an equilibrium, and, if so, what characteristics that equilibrium will possess. Local jurisdictions, each with their own public service bundles, cannot necessarily be replicated sufficiently to match exactly the preferences of (subgroups of) individuals, as the McGuire and Wheaton models require. Even

[18] M. Edel and E. Sclar, "Taxes, Spending, and Property Values: Supply Adjustment in a Tiebout-Oates Model," *Journal of Political Economy*, September/October 1974.

[19] H. Pollakowski, "The Effects of Property Taxes and Local Public Spending on Property Values: A Comment and Further Results," *Journal of Political Economy*, July/August 1973.

[20] This particular example is due to Pauly, although Hamilton has made essentially the same point. M. V. Pauly, "A Model of Local Government Expenditure and Tax Capitalization." B. W. Hamilton, The Effects of Property Taxes and Local Public Spending on Property Values: A Theoretical Comment," *Journal of Political Economy*, June 1976.

if they could be replicated, there is no guarantee that an equilibrium will exist. As we have seen, that will depend, in part, on the form of taxation actually chosen. But it is equally true that jurisdictions are not as rigidly determined as the Pauly model assumes. The truth obviously lies somewhere in between, and it remains an open question whether the U.S. federalist system of governments has enhanced social welfare by permitting localized decision making on allocational issues, rather than simply letting the national government do everything.

CONCLUSION

If the world were truly first best, a federalist system of governments could certainly do as well as a single national government in allocating resources, and perhaps even better (recall the discussion relating to uncertainty). Jurisdictions could be replicated to produce perfect correspondences, or perfect matching of individual preferences with public service bundles. If head taxes were required for efficiency they could be used. Conversely, if other taxes (e.g., Lindahl prices for public goods) were inappropriate, they could be avoided. But the real world obviously contains many second-best features, such as imperfect correspondence, nonlump-sum taxation, and the like. Given these realities, federalism creates a vast number of intriguing possibilities which public sector economists have only just begun to understand.

REFERENCES

Buchanan, J. "An Economic Theory of Clubs." *Economica*, February 1965.

Edel, M., and Sclar, E. "Taxes, Spending, and Property Values: Supply Adjustment in a Tiebout-Oates Model." *Journal of Political Economy*, September/October 1974.

Hamilton, B. "Capitalization of Intrajurisdictional Differences in Local Tax Prices." *American Economic Review*, December 1976.

———. "The Effects of Property Taxes and Local Public Spending on Property Values: A Theoretical Comment." *Journal of Political Economy*, June 1976.

McGuire, M. "Group Segregation and Optimal Jurisdictions." *Journal of Political Economy*, January/February 1974.

Meadows, G. "Taxes, Spending, and Property Values: A Comment and Further Results." *Journal of Political Economy*, August 1976.

Oates, W. *Fiscal Federalism.* New York: Harcourt Brace Jovanovich, Inc., 1972.

Pauly, M. "A Model of Local Government Expenditure and Tax Capitalization." *Journal of Public Economics*, October 1976.

Pollakowski, H. "The Effects of Property Taxes and Local Public Spending on Property Values: A Comment and Further Results." *Journal of Political Economy*, July/August 1973.

Stigler, G. "Tenable Range of Functions of Local Government." *Federal Expenditure Policy for Economic Growth and Stability.* Washington, D.C.: Joint Economic Committee, Subcommittee on Fiscal Policy, 1957.

Tiebout, C. "A Pure Theory of Local Expenditures." *Journal of Political Economy,* October 1956.

Wheaton, W. "Consumer Mobility and Community Tax Bases." *Journal of Public Economics,* November 1975.

30

Optimal federalism and the distribution function

Despite the principle that government decision making should occur at the lowest level possible in the fiscal hierarchy consistent with social welfare optimization, the literature on the optimal structure of a federalist system of governments is virtually unanimous in assigning decisions on income distribution to the national government.[1] According to the conventional wisdom, allowing redistribution by lower level ("local") governments in the fiscal hierarchy is formally inconsistent with social welfare optimization, whether one assumes that people are immobile or fully mobile across local jurisdictions.

We happen to disagree with the conventional analysis on this point. In our view, a federalist system is not only formally consistent with social welfare maximization when it contains lower government redistributions, it actually requires local redistributions to have a real meaning as an optimal fiscal system. In order to develop this argument, let us begin with a review and criticism of the conventional position.

REDISTRIBUTION—THE CONVENTIONAL ANALYSIS

Assume first that people *are* mobile, and consider a situation in which one local government tries to redistribute from its rich to its poor citizens, but that neighboring governments do not attempt any redistribution. One would expect the wealthier citizens of the redistributing locality to move to the neighboring localities. This is the so called "competition" problem, and it is clearly in evidence in many metropolitan areas in the United States.

Such migration has two obvious negative implications. First, the government that tries to redistribute is totally frustrated. Not only are its poor not made significantly better off, the total tax base of the community has declined, and it becomes more difficult to maintain per capita levels of public services. Second, if people will move in response to taxation, this tends to increase the dead-weight loss arising from taxation (assuming for the moment that lump-sum

---

[1] A notable exception is M. Pauly, "Income Redistribution as a Local Public Good," *Journal of Public Economics*, vol. 2, 1973. Pauly develops a model based on the Hochman and Rodgers notion of pareto-optimal redistributions (Chapter 12), in which, under certain conditions, local government redistributions are optimal. In this chapter we argue that local redistribution makes sense for a federalist system even if redistributions are based solely on interpersonal equity considerations.

redistributions are not viable). Thus, redistributions at the local level are seen to be inconsistent with the goal of maximizing social welfare in a federal system with mobile resources.

Even in a world without mobility, there is the possibility of incompatibilities arising throughout the system if more than one government redistributes income. Suppose local government L wants to effect a redistribution from citizens in group A to citizens in group B, but the national government prefers a net redistribution from group B to group A. One can imagine an endless chain of redistributions as each government tries to have its way. Of course this sort of game must be ruled out, and the most obvious way is to deny one government the right to redistribute.

For reasons of competition and potential incompatibility, therefore, conventional analysis assigns redistribution policy solely to the national government. In an optimal federalist system, all lower level governments in the fiscal hierarchy perform only allocational functions, in accordance with the principles outlined in the preceeding chapter. Moreover, to avoid any unintended redistributions from their allocational decisions, the prevailing model of optimal federalism also stipulates that all local allocational expenditures be financed totally according to the benefits-received theory of taxation, such as financing local public goods by taxing each person at a per-unit rate equal to his *MRS* between the public good and the numeraire good. Only the national government is allowed to tax on some basis other than benefits received, such as ability to pay, and then only to effect the goal of a just distribution. If a local government uses some tax principle other than the benefits-received principle, then it is in effect redistributing, and problems of mobility to escape taxes, excess burden, and incompatibility among governments will once again exist. Oates is very clear on the point:[2]

> The most attractive solution to this whole [distribution] problem (at a formal level at least) is that suggested in Chapter One: let the central government resolve the distribution problem and allow decentralized levels of government to provide public services that they finance with benefit taxes. The use of ability-to-pay taxation by local government, instead of a national negative income tax, may well involve a very high cost both in terms of excess burden and the failure to realize distributional objectives.

According to Oates, in an ideal world of perfect correspondence, this scheme will produce a "welfare optimum."

Two implications of the prevailing model deserve mention. Stigler and Tiebout[3] have suggested that a major incentive for citizen mobility would be to find a locality providing the right level and mix of public services. Roughly

---

[2] Excerpted from *Fiscal Federalism* by Wallace E. Oates, © 1972 by Harcourt Brace Jovanovich, Inc., p. 150. Reprinted by permission of the publisher.

[3] George Stigler, "Tenable Range of Functions of Local Government," in *Federal Expenditure Policy for Economic Growth and Stability* (Washington, D.C.: Joint Economic Committee, Subcommittee on Fiscal Policy, 1957), pp. 213–19; and Charles Tiebout, "A Pure Theory of Local ⁷xpenditures," *Journal of Political Economy*, October 1956, pp. 416–24.

speaking, people could choose among high service–high tax, medium service–medium tax, and low service–low tax localities on a more or less continuous spectrum. Distributional patterns would not enter their locational decision process because they are dictated solely by the national government. Another implication of the model in the ideal world of perfect correspondence is that there is no need for grants-in-aid among governments. Redistributions occur only among people, and at the instigation of the national government. According to Oates,[4]

> To achieve a just distribution of income among the individuals in a nation, a national program that redistributes income among individuals, not among jurisdictions, is the preferred alternative.

CRITICISM OF THE PREVAILING MODEL

To fix ideas on the meaning of a social welfare optimum in a federalist system, we will assume a first-best economic and policy environment for the remainder of the chapter. This is the only fair way to assess the conventional position, since it was developed within a first-best context.

In our view, the conventional first-best analysis of optimal federalism is deficient in three respects. In the first place, the notion that taxation according to the benefits-received principle necessarily avoids redistributions is not correct, at least with respect to decreasing cost services. To preserve efficiency with decreasing cost services, which an optimal federalist system must surely do, correct benefit taxation or pricing implies that price be set equal to marginal costs. Any other price will not result in a social welfare optimum. The problem is that setting price equal to marginal costs is not sufficient to cover full average costs if average costs are declining, so that the local government has to make up the deficit out of lump-sum taxes and transfers.[5] The question is simply this: How is the local government supposed to finance the deficit if, as in the prevailing model, it is constrained from making redistributions? Formally, this implies it is not allowed to have a social welfare function.

As we saw in Chapter 9, the decision to provide decreasing cost services in an economy with a single government is inextricably tied to the lump-sum redistributions that satisfy the interpersonal equity conditions of social welfare maximization. The only modification is that the sum of all lump-sum taxes collected from consumers will exceed the sum of all lump-sum transfers, the difference being equal to the sum of all deficits incurred by decreasing cost industries. In this case, then, allocational and redistributional considerations are also inextricably bound together. A local government cannot, by itself,

---

[4] Excerpted from *Fiscal Federalism* by Wallace E. Oates, © 1972 by Harcourt Brace Jovanovich, Inc., p. 81. Reprinted by permission of the publisher.

[5] Whether or not the service is privately or publicly owned is of little consequence. Decreasing cost industries, if correctly priced, will always involve a governmental decision because it is the government that must decide whether the benefit of having the service justifies the cost of financing the deficit.

make what is essentially an allocational decision without simultaneously having some way of ranking individuals, such as by means of a social welfare function, to decide the financing of the deficit. The alternative of reinterpreting the benefits principle of taxation to allow for average cost pricing is clearly illegitimate, because then the system of optimal federalism will not produce a welfare optimum. It cannot satisfy the pareto optimality conditions of first-best theory.

Pareto optimality would be preserved with a two-part pricing system, in which consumers paid a price equal to marginal costs to use the service, plus a one-time lump-sum fee (which potential users would have to pay as well) sufficient to cover the resulting deficit. But the one-time fee is not distributionally neutral. Nor, if the local government cannot make distributional judgments, does it have any special theoretical appeal. Why not simply charge one person for the entire deficit, with the confidence that the national government's redistribution policies will correct any undue harm suffered by that person?

Formally a model of optimal federalism can sidestep these issues by not allowing local governments to make decisions involving decreasing cost services. These must also be the sole prerogative of the national government. One might counter that the local governments could decide on the level of service to be provided with the national government merely guaranteeing to cover whatever deficit ensues. But whether or not the service is worthwhile depends both upon the demands of the individuals using the service (assume no externalities) and upon the social welfare rankings of these people as determined by the national social welfare function. Since redistributions are the sole prerogative of the national government in the conventional model, the final decision rests in part with that government. Thus, the local governments cannot make a truly autonomous decision in this area if all the tenets of the prevailing model are to be preserved. This is not a devastating blow to that model, merely uncomfortable. Since it excludes decreasing cost services from complete local autonomy, it probably excludes at least a number of transportation and recreational services. One thinks immediately of mass transit systems, highways, and parks (assuming no congestion). At this point it appears that local governments have only a single decision to make on their own, that of providing services with significant externalities among the local constituents.

A second, and more fundamental problem with the conventional solution to the distribution function is this: Within the traditional normative theory of the public sector, in what meaningful sense has an autonomous government been created if that government does not have the ability to determine a set of distributional rankings among its constituents, such as by means of a social welfare function? According to the normative theory, distributional rankings are the one datum which the government qua government brings to the analysis. Otherwise it merely accepts consumers' preferences as paramount and acts, in effect, as their agent. Without the distribution function, an autonomous government can hardly be said to exist. The conventional analysis suggests that lower level governments have essentially a single set of decisions to make on their own, those relating to markets with significant externalities among the local constituents. In doing so they merely accept the distribution of income within their jurisdictions as determined by the combination of competitive market forces and national redistribution policies. They are agents pure and simple, sounding out the preferences of their constituents to effect conditions such as $\sum MRS = MRT$.

One begins to wonder why local governments should even bother with externalities. If the national government is effecting lump-sum redistributions to achieve a just distribution of income in a first-best environment, then it is satisfying a set of first-order interpersonal equity conditions of the form:

$$\frac{\partial W}{\partial U^h}\frac{\partial U^h}{\partial X_{h1}} = \qquad \text{all } h = 1, \ldots, H$$

where:

$W = W(U^1, \ldots, U^H) =$ the social welfare function.

$U^1, \ldots, U^H$ are the utility functions of the H individuals in the society.

X_{h1} represents the consumption of good 1 by person h (one can think of good 1 as lump-sum income arising from a fixed factor of production).

But if the national government knows enough to do this, it certainly knows enough to satisfy the pareto-optimal conditions within each jurisdiction to correct for local externalities. Put differently, if the national government is establishing the distributional preferences of society, it might as well do everything else. The local governments are clearly not necessary.

We have reached an impasse here. Without social welfare functions, local governments have no input into a formal model of the public sector. On the other hand, redistributions at lower levels of government create formal problems of competition or incompatibilities among government. One might be tempted to resolve these differences by permitting all governments to have social welfare functions, but allowing only the national government to redistribute lump sum, to pursue distributional goals. The problem with this solution is that the notion of a first-best social welfare optimum loses its meaning as a general rule. Consider the situation depicted in Figure 30–1.

Suppose locality L has two people. The curve U^1–U^2 depicts the utility-possibilities frontier for the two people. L_1, L_2, and L_3 are the local government's social welfare indifference curves. Let ray OC represent an optimal distribution of utility between the two people as determined by the national social welfare function. If forced to be on the ray OC, the locality will choose point C, but this will not be a first-best optimum from its own citizens' point of view. It will be forced into a second-best optimum (formally, it will follow decision rules such as (22.88). If it can redistribute it will move to D, but then the social welfare function of the national government is not maximized. In either case it is not clear we have achieved a welfare optimum, since the citizens belong simultaneously to both governments. And a compromise solution between C and D on the utility-possibilities frontier obviously satisfies neither government.

FIGURE 30–1

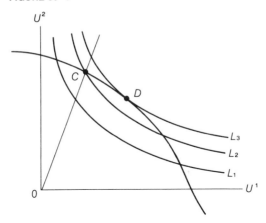

Our final criticism of the conventional analysis is simply an empirical point in support of the second criticism. It is clear that local governments in the United States (or any other country) do have distributional preferences. There are any number of examples. State and local governments in the United States often provide social services to the poor. Questions of choice among different tax programs at all levels of government turn often on their perceived incidence. States and localities clearly worry about citizen mobility in response to their policies. One can find many examples of tax policies tailored to the business interests—the threat they will leave is perceived as a very real one. These concerns all imply that states and localities make social welfare rankings.

It is also true that social welfare rankings differ among localities, states, and the national government. In general, the citizens in any given lower level government will not simply accept the national social welfare ranking as necessarily just, an assumption crucial to the prevailing model. Furthermore, these differences in distributional preferences can be given a broader interpretation. People choose different jurisdictions not only because they demand different kinds of public allocational type services but also because they choose to live with people whom they deem compatible in terms of such factors as education, cultural background, and so forth. To deny the latter point is to deny an important justification for a federal system of governments. In essence, federalism supports fraternalism, the principle of "states rights" applied to the distribution question in its broadest sense. We are not necessarily suggesting that people should pay heed to these factors. The ability to isolate oneself from "undesirables" which federalism allows may itself be undesirable. If one thought so, this would be a strong argument against creating autonomous local governments. Federalism, per se, is not sacred, and certainly not necessarily an optimal form of government.

In conclusion, we would argue that an optimal structure of fiscal federalism within the traditional theory of the public sector requires a schema whereby each government, subject to resource and generalized production constraints and market clearance, can simultaneously maximize its own social welfare function. This is so for two reasons:

1. A truly autonomous government does not exist within the traditional normative theory of the public sector unless it has a social welfare function or some such means of deciding the relative worth of its constituents.
2. In a federal system of governments social welfare maximization by each government as defined above can be the only acceptable meaning of an overall first-best social welfare optimum.

Expanding on the second point, recall that the central theoretical problem in designing an optimal federalism is to divide the functions of the public sector among the governments so as to retain the maximum degree of local autonomy without creating conflicting decisions among the governments. However, one must live with the fact that people pay allegiance simultaneously to more than one government and that inconsistencies are almost certain to arise. One manifestation of this point already referred to is that governments generally will have different social welfare rankings. Given this problem the suggested definition of a first-best social welfare optimum is the only apparent possibility.

OPTIMAL REDISTRIBUTION IN A FEDERALIST
SYSTEM OF GOVERNMENTS:
AN ALTERNATIVE SCHEMA

The basic ingredients of our search for an optimal schema were presented in the preceding section. We seek a model of federalism in which:

1. Each government simultaneously maximizes an individualistic social welfare function subject to resource and generalized production constraints and market clearance. This will serve as the definition of a first-best social welfare optimum.
2. Autonomy in the decision making process is preserved at the lowest possible level of government. Without this assumption the motivation for developing a federalist system effectively collapses. One can always design a model in which the national government does everything.

Assume perfect correspondence so that externalities (and scale economies) are entirely contained (exhausted) within each jurisdiction.

Before presenting the schema a comment is in order. It has been noted that inherent incompatibility is a central feature of a federalist system because citizens are simultaneously members of more than one government. If condition (1) is satisfied these inherent incompatibilities will simply have been dealt with in one particular way, they will not have disappeared. To the contrary, the theoretical problem of determining an optimal federalist system can be restated in the following way: What minimum restrictions must be placed on a federalist system of governments to ensure (1) and (2)? Clearly some restrictions must be placed on at least some governments. For example, not all governments can have social welfare functions whose arguments are the utility functions of their individual constituents. The prevailing model places the restriction, unacceptable in our view, that no government but the national government can have a social welfare function. Our alternative model can be thought of as one with more acceptable restrictions.

The schema that best meets these criteria in our view is the following:

> Each government has an individualistic social welfare function whose arguments are the social welfare functions of the governments *immediately* below it in the hierarchy of governments. The lowest level governments have individualistic social welfare functions whose arguments are the utility functions of their constituents.

In terms of the United States, the national government's social welfare function would contain as arguments the social welfare functions of the 50 states; each state's social welfare function would have as arguments the social welfare functions of the localities within the state; and each locality would have a social welfare function with the utility functions of its constituents as arguments.

To simplify notation, let there be a two-tiered federalist system with a national government and L local governments.

Let:

$U^{hl}(X_k^{hl})$ be the utility function of person h living in locality l.

$$h = 1, \ldots, H$$
$$l = 1, \ldots, L$$

Note: there are only H people. Each person is double subscripted according to who he is and where he lives.

> $L^l[U^{hl}(X_k^{hl})]$ be the social welfare function of locality l, whose arguments contain the utility functions of all persons (or potential persons) living in locality l.
>
> $F[L^l(U^{hl}(X_k^{hl}))]$ be the national social welfare function with L arguments, $L^1, \ldots, L^L$.
>
> X_k^{hl} be the kth good consumed by person hl, $k = 1, \ldots, N$.

The restrictions on this model consist of the arguments that are allowed to appear in each government's social welfare function.

In this model, allocational decisions are determined exactly as in the prevailing model. The local governments make all decisions on services exhibiting economies of scale and/or externalities so long as the extent of the externalities or scale economies is contained within the local jurisdiction. The national government would provide those services with spillovers across localities, or design grants-in-aid to ensure efficient solutions at the local level. Each government would maximize its own social welfare function subject to resource and generalized production constraints and market clearance. The usual first-best pareto-optimal conditions would emerge in each case because any social welfare terms would drop out from this set of first-order conditions. The difference with respect to the prevailing model is that each government would also be engaged in lump-sum redistributions to satisfy the interpersonal conditions. Let good 1 be the good transferred lump-sum. The lth local government must satisfy the following relationships:

$$\frac{\partial L^l}{\partial U^{hl}} \frac{\partial U^{hl}}{\partial X_1^{hl}} = \quad \begin{array}{l} \text{all } h \text{ in } l, \\ \text{every } l = 1, \ldots, L \end{array}$$

The national government satisfies the following interpersonal equity conditions:

$$\frac{\partial F}{\partial L^l} \frac{\partial L^l}{\partial U^{hl}} \frac{\partial U^{hl}}{\partial X_1^{hl}} = \quad \text{all } h = 1, \ldots, H$$

Notice, however, that the redistributions of the local governments will ensure that the last two terms of the expression are equal for all people within a given locality, l. Therefore, all the national government need do is tax and transfer income lump-sum among localities until the entire term is equal for all people. At that point its social welfare will also be maximized.

As an example consider two localities, 1 and 2. By their actions

$$\frac{\partial L^1}{\partial U^{h1}} \frac{\partial U^{h1}}{\partial X_1^{h1}} = \quad \text{all } h \text{ in } 1$$

and

$$\frac{\partial L^2}{\partial U^{h2}} \frac{\partial U^{h2}}{\partial X_1^{h2}} = \quad \text{all } h \text{ in } 2$$

If $\partial F/\partial L^1(\ ) > \partial F/\partial L^2(\ )$, the national government would transfer income from 2 and 1 (and the localities would redistribute to maintain social equality on the margin within each jurisdiction). Presumably, the marginal social utility of income of the citizens of 1 would drop, and that of 2 would rise (all from the national viewpoint). Redistribution continues until

(30.1)
$$\frac{\partial F}{\partial L^1}(\ ) = \frac{\partial F}{\partial L^2}(\ )$$

The same schema holds for an n-tiered hierarchy of governments.

CONCLUSIONS

The advantages of this schema over the prevailing model of optimal federalism are twofold. First, each government has an identity as traditionally defined in the theory of the public sector, that is, each government is allowed a social welfare function. Consequently, all governments provide important inputs into policy decisions and each retains the ability for truly autonomous decision making over the standard microeconomic functions assigned to the public sector. Second, the definition of a first-best social welfare optimum in a federalist system has been clarified and is consistent with the traditional definition of a first-best social welfare optimum with a single government. Both pareto optimality and the interpersonal equity conditions *in terms of individuals* are satisfied at all levels of government.

The major *operational* difference between the two models is that grants-in-aid among governments now play a central role, even if there exists a "perfect correspondence" for allocational functions. It is no longer true that redistributions among people at the national level are the "preferred alternative." In the alternative model presented here, only the lowest level governments redistribute among people. The higher governments use grants-in-aid to other governments exclusively in their redistributions.

It is interesting that the United States recognizes both models in its redistribution policies. On the one hand, there are a number of national transfer programs, such as social security, that transfer income directly to people. On the other hand, major portions of the U.S. welfare system remain essentially state (and locally) determined, for instance Medicaid and Aid for Dependent Children, with national supplementation dependent in part upon the relative fiscal capacities of the various state governments. These programs, then, are more in the spirit of our alternative model. The concept of General Revenue Sharing is also consistent with our alternative model. It is also noteworthy that recent administrations have continued to vacillate between the two models. The Nixon, Ford, and Carter administrations have all supported General Revenue Sharing, while simultaneously proposing further nationalization of the U.S. welfare system.

Finally, notice that our alternative model avoids the two problems which proponents of the conventional model perceive as potentially devastating to the federalist system if lower level governments are allowed to redistribute income. The alternative model obviously avoids the incompatibility problem with nonmobile populations, given the permissible arguments of each government's social welfare function. It also, at least formally, avoids the competition problem with mobile populations. Mobility of the kind that plagues U.S. cities today is a problem partly because the rich who leave do not adequately compensate those remaining behind for the resource drain involved when they move out. The U.S. commitment to federalism, that is, to autonomous local governments, creates the vehicle for this phenomenon, one which certainly contributes to inequality of opportunity in this country. Indeed, a number of state supreme courts have questioned the legitimacy of local autonomy in ruling that financing education primarily through local property taxes is inherently discriminatory.

The prevailing model suggests that the answer lies in stronger national redistributive policies. This may well work, but it represents a movement away from the federalist system. The model presented here suggests an alternative approach that would strengthen the federalist system. If the wealthy residents of city A move to suburb B because city A decides to redistribute income to its poor, presumably the state will insist upon a redistribution from B to A in order to maximize its own social welfare function. Upon knowing that such compensation is required, the incentive to move would diminish. Should the state fail to redistribute in this way, city A is a clear loser, but this is a matter of the state's preferences, not a formal inadequacy of the alternative model.

If, as a practical matter, lower level governments within the federal hierarchy are seen to be acting perversely, then one would not want a federalist system in which lower level governments make truly autonomous decisions. There is certainly nothing sacred about a federalist system of governments. We have only suggested that our alternative model is consistent with the notion of a first-best social welfare optimum given the existence of a federalist system.

REFERENCES

Oates, W. *Fiscal Federalism.* New York: Harcourt Brace Jovanovich, Inc., 1972.

Pauly, M. "Income Redistribution as a Local Public Good." *Journal of Public Economics,* vol. 2, 1973.

Stigler, G. "Tenable Range of Functions of Local Governments." *Federal Expenditure Policy for Economic Growth and Stability.* Washington, D.C.: Joint Economic Committee, Subcommittee on Fiscal Policy, 1957.

Tiebout, C. "A Pure Theory of Local Expenditures." *Journal of Political Economy,* October 1956.

31

The role of grants-in-aid in a federalist system of governments

Taxes and transfers among individuals play a central role in the public sector theory of a single government for resolving both distributional and allocational problems. A federalist system of governments creates the possibility of resource transfers directly among governments, commonly referred to as *grants-in-aid*.[1] Chapter 31 will begin with a theoretical discussion of the role of grants-in-aid in a federalist system, asking whether grants-in-aid among governments have functions analogous to those of taxes and transfers among individuals by a single government. Generally speaking, the answer is that they do, but their precise role depends upon two factors: (a) one's conception of the proper assignment of the public sector's basic allocative and redistributional functions across governments within the federalist system; and (b) whether or not the underlying policy environment is first-best or second-best. Chapters 29 and 30 explored the design of an optimal federalist system of governments within a first-best policy environment and, in doing so, delineated the role for grants-in-aid in that context. We will briefly review those results, and then extend the normative analysis to allow for some plausible second-best considerations.

The remainder of the chapter will explore two issues in the positive theory of grants-in-aid. There have been two rather striking features of grants-in-aid in the United States over the past few decades. First, and foremost, is simply the rapid growth of this fiscal device, especially in grants from the national government to state and local governments. In fiscal year 1950, grants to state and local governments totaled $2.25 billion, accounting for only 10.4 percent of total state and local revenues. By fiscal year 1980, national grants-in-aid totaled $82.9 billion and financed 23.6 percent of all state and local expenditures. Moreover, the growth in national grants proceeded fairly steadily throughout this period, as Table 31–1 indicates (the average annual growth rate from 1958–78 was 14.6 percent).[2] Apparently both Democrats and Republicans believe the national government should bear ever increasing financial respon-

---

[1] A grant-in-aid is usually considered to be a transfer payment, but a tax on a jurisdiction can be thought of as a negative grant.

[2] *Special Analyses: Budget of the United States Government, Fiscal Year* 1980, (Washington, D.C.: U.S. Government Printing Office, 1979), p. 212.

TABLE 31–1

Federal Grants-in-Aid to State and Local Governments

Year	Outlay ($ billions)	Percentage of State, Local Expenditures
1950	2.25	10.4
1955	3.21	10.1
1960	7.02	14.7
1965	10.90	15.3
1970	24.02	19.4
1975	49.83	22.9
1980 (estimated)	82.9	23.6

Source: *Special Analyses:* Budget of the United States Government, Fiscal Year 1980 (Washington, D.C.: U.S. Government Printing Office 1979), Table H–7, "Historical Trend of Federal Grants-in-Aid," p. 225. (Grants as a percentage of state and local expenditures peaked at 26.7 percent in 1978. *Ibid.*)

sibility for decisions that have traditionally been reserved for the state and local governments.

Not only have national grants-in-aid grown rapidly in the postwar period, they have taken on many new forms. Over the past decade, the national government has been willing to experiment with new kinds of grant-in-aid distribution formulas, especially ones which unquestionably separate the decision-making responsibilities of the state and local governments from the financial responsibilities of the national government.

Economists define grants-in-aid, or grant-in-aid formulas, along three dimensions. They may be either conditional or unconditional, matching or non-matching, open or closed ended. *Conditional grants* list specific public services on which the receiving government can spend the grant funds. Other conditions may be included as well. An *unconditional grant*, by contrast, places no restrictions on the disposition of the grant funds. In fact, a fully unconditional grant would even permit state and local tax reductions, if the receiving government chose not to increase total expenditures by the full amount of the grant.

A *matching grant* is, in effect, an ad valorem subsidy in which the grantor agrees to reimburse the receiving government for expenditures undertaken at some predetermined rate. The spending initiative remains with the receiving government. For example, a 90 percent matching grant pays the receiving government $0.90 on every dollar spent on public services covered by the grant. A *nonmatching grant* simply transfers a lump sum of money to the receiving government. This can be thought of as a two-tiered matching grant, with the matching rate equal to 100 percent up to the limit of the funds transferred, and 0 percent for any additional expenditures the receiving government might choose to make.

Finally, a *closed-ended grant* limits the total funds that the granter will transfer, whereas an *open-ended grant* places no such limit on the size of the transfer.

The vast majority of U.S. grant-in-aid programs are conditional and closed ended, using either matching or nonmatching formulas for distributing aid. In the 1950s all major national grant programs were of this form. For example, the Federal Highway Act, which provided grants to states for highway maintenance and for construction of the Interstate System, and the Public Assistance Programs (Old Age Assistance, Aid to the Blind, Aid to the Disabled, and Aid for Dependent Children), were both conditional, closed ended, matching grants. These two grants alone accounted for over 70 percent of all federal grants-in-aid as late as 1962.[3] In the 1960s the national government began experimenting with new forms of grants, to the point where each possible combination of the three grant attributes is embodied in at least one important grant-in-aid program, with the obvious exception of nonmatching, open-ended grants, which would allow recipients to ignore the opportunity costs of the grant funds.

Grant reform began in earnest in 1965, when the national government consolidated all medical vendor payments to public assistance recipients under two programs, Medicaid (for the nonaged) and Medicare (for the aged). The Medicaid program was open ended in the sense that the national government agreed to reimburse the states for a percentage of all medical payments to nonaged public assistance recipients without limit, the percentage reimbursement varying inversely with state income from 50 percent to 83 percent. The number of eligible recipients in any one state is obviously finite, but the grant placed no dollar limits on the aid any one state could receive. Even though Medicaid payments grew spectacularly throughout the late 1960s and early 1970s, the national government left this program open ended.

Reform continued in the 1970s, spurred on by the initiatives of the Nixon administration. President Nixon was an ardent federalist, strongly committed to the principle of local autonomy wherever possible, so he sought to remove the narrowly restrictive conditions that had characterized all the major national grants-in-aid. He proposed two new programs: (1) *Specific Revenue Sharing*, in which 130 existing grants-in-aid (with the notable exception of public assistance) would be consolidated into six broad categories, Education, Law Enforcement, Manpower Training, Transportation, and Urban and Rural Community Development.[4] States and localities would then be free to spend the funds within each general area as they chose. Broad-based grants of this type are referred to as *bloc grants*. (2) *General Revenue Sharing*, a new $5 billion program that would distribute funds unconditionally to states and localities by a predetermined distribution formula.

General Revenue Sharing passed through Congress and became law in 1972, on a five-year trial basis. It was renewed in 1977 during the Carter administration. This program was truly a landmark, because the U.S. Congress had never

[3] Advisory Commission on Intergovernmental Relations, *The Role of Equalization in Federal Grants*, A-19 (Washington, D.C.: U.S. Government Printing Office, January 1964), p. 97.

[4] Advisory Commission on Intergovernmental Relations, *Special Revenue Sharing: An Analysis of the Administration's Grant Consolidation Proposals*, Information Report M-70 (Washington, D.C., December 1971), p. 1.

before permitted a significant transfer of U.S. tax dollars to other governments on an unconditional basis.[5] Prior to 1972, Congress had insisted on controlling the distribution of its grant funds by means of conditional grants-in-aid, although as the analysis below will show, controlling the spending decisions of the receiving governments in some desired manner can be difficult to achieve. General Revenue Sharing clearly represented a renewed commitment to local autonomy, and with it, fiscal federalism.

Congress failed to pass Specific Revenue Sharing, but limited consolidation came anyway within four years in three important areas. In 1972 three of the Public Assistance Programs—Old Age Assistance, Aid to the Blind, and Aid to the Disabled—were combined into one program, Supplemental Security Income (effective 1974). Second, consolidation of the major categorical HUD grants into one Community Development grant occurred under the Ford administration in 1974 (effective FY 1975). Finally, the Highway Trust Fund was broken in 1974 to permit states and localities to spend these funds for rail and bus transit as well as highway maintenance and construction (effective FY 1976).[6] These bloc grants may not go so far as General Revenue Sharing in promoting local autonomy on paper, but they certainly suggest an increasing commitment to the spirit of fiscal federalism. Moreover, as our subsequent analysis will indicate, conditional bloc grants can be expected to promote local autonomy equally as well as unconditional grants, since they tend not to place any effective restrictions on the receiving government's use of the funds.

The rapid growth in national grants-in-aid, coupled with increasing flexibility in distributing the funds, raises two questions. Why, first of all, has the U.S. national government assumed ever increasing financial responsibility for state and local programs? Baumol and Oates have provided a compelling answer to this question, arguing that state and local governments are caught in a double bind.[7] On the one hand, these governments offer services that are likely to become relatively more expensive over time. On the other hand, they are stuck with taxes whose revenues will be unable to match the growth in service costs. Hence, the only way to maintain service levels is through increased national grants-in-aid. We will present the Baumol-Oates analysis in some detail.

The second question concerns the expected reactions of receiving governments to differing grant-in-aid formulas. As indicated above, grants can vary in two ways along each of three dimensions, and the national government has adopted most of the possible combinations, but does the receiving government

---

[5] Actually, GRS was not entirely unconditional. State and local governments were not permitted to spend these funds on public assistance, nor were they allowed to pass the funds back to the private sector as tax reductions. But, as the analysis below will indicate, it is exceedingly difficult to enforce these restrictions. Thus, it is hardly misleading to call GRS an unconditional program.

[6] For a description of these three changes, and an excellent survey of the history of federal grants to states generally, see J. Maxwell and J. R. Aronson, *Financing State and Local Governments*, 3d ed. (Washington, D.C.: The Brookings Institution, 1977).

[7] W. J. Baumol and W. Oates, *The Theory of Environmental Policy* (Englewood Cliffs, N.J.: Prentice-Hall, Inc., 1975), chaps. 15–17.

really care how it receives its aid? Does it matter whether grants are conditional or unconditional, matching or nonmatching, closed or open ended? Will the receiving government's spending decisions be the same, gross-of-aid, no matter what form the grant may take? We will conclude the chapter with a consumer theoretic analysis of these questions and survey the vast empirical literature on state and local governments' responses to grants-in-aid.[8]

OPTIMAL FEDERALISM AND GRANTS-IN-AID: NORMATIVE ANALYSIS

The First-Best Policy Environment

Whether or not grants-in-aid have any role in an optimal, first-best federalist system of governments depends upon the underlying model used to establish the notion of a social welfare optimum. Recall that in the traditional model of optimal federalism redistributional policy is the sole responsibility of the national government, whereas allocational functions reside in the lowest level governments consistent with pareto optimality. Consequently, only the national government is concerned with social welfare optimization as traditionally defined. The lower level governments care only about efficiency.

Grants-in-aid are totally unnecessary in this model, so long as the policy environment is truly first best and a perfect correspondence of jurisdictions exists for all allocational problems. The national government satisfies its interpersonal equity conditions with lump-sum taxes and transfers among individuals (and firms, with decreasing cost production), exactly as in the single-government model of the public sector. Similarly, all governments, whether national or "local," interact only with the individual consumers and firms within their jurisdictions when correcting for resource misallocations. Thus, they simply follow the normative decision rules derived under the assumption of a single government. There is no need for the grant-in-aid, because no government need be directly concerned with any other jurisdictions. In our view, this is yet another reason for rejecting the traditional model of optimal federalism. It seems implausible that intergovernmental relations would be of no consequence in a federalist system of governments.

Our alternative model of federalism, presented in Chapter 30, defined the social welfare optimum as an equilibrium in which each government maximized its own social welfare function, subject to the restriction that the arguments of each government's social welfare function are the social welfare functions of those governments immediately below it in the fiscal hierarchy. Grants-in-aid are required in this model to resolve the distribution question, since all but the lowest level governments must tax and transfer resources lump sum among the governments immediately below them in the fiscal hierarchy. In the parlance of grants-in-aid, these lump-sum grants would be unconditional, nonmatching,

---

[8] For a detailed taxonomic analysis of expected reactions to the various grant-in-aid formulas, consult A. D. Scott, "The Evaluation of Federal Grants," *Economica*, November 1952.

and closed ended: unconditional, because one government cannot dictate to any other government how to dispose of the funds, the "states-rights" criterion; nonmatching and closed ended, because the interpersonal equity conditions require straight resource transfers of some finite amount. Notice, too, that the "grants" will be negative for those governments which must surrender resources. Of all the major grants actually in use in the United States, General Revenue Sharing comes closest to meeting these conditions. The program appears to aid all lower level governments, but some states and localities actually do surrender resources under General Revenue Sharing, albeit indirectly through national income and excise taxes on their constituents. If General Revenue Sharing really does effect resource transfers to some states, then the citizens of some other states and localities must be contributing, in the aggregate, more in national tax revenues to finance General Revenue Sharing than their government receives as a grant-in-aid. In our model the "losing" governments would be taxed directly to pay the "gainers," whereupon the losers would have to tax their own governments or citizens to raise the required revenues. In practice, however, the resulting patterns of redistributions might not be much different.

Our alternative model shares with the traditional model the attribute that grants-in-aid are not required for allocational purposes in a first-best policy environment. Simultaneously with satisfying all possible interpersonal equity conditions, satisfying all necessary pareto-optimal conditions proceeds government by government in the usual manner. To develop a further role for grants-in-aid, then, requires introducing some second-best distortion into the policy environment.

Second-Best Policy Environment

Imperfect Correspondence. The second-best restriction most frequently analyzed in the literature is a maintained imperfect correspondence for an externality-generating activity, which causes each local government to follow the wrong decision rule. Imagine the following situation.[9] Community A, consisting of H_A individuals, provides a Samuelsonian nonexclusive public good in amount $\bar{X}_G$, the services of which are consumed only by its own citizens. In determining the amount $\bar{X}_G$, the government of A follows the standard first-best decision rule

$$(31.1) \qquad \sum_{h_A = 1}^{H_A} MRS_{X_G, X_{h_A 1}}^{h_A} = MRT_{X_G, X_1}$$

where X_1 is a private good.

Suppose that the H_B citizens of contiguous community B benefit by the existence of X_G in community A even though they cannot directly consume the services of X_G. For example, X_G may be police protection which has the spill-

---

[9] A similar example appears in Wallace Oates, *Fiscal Federalism* (New York: Harcourt Brace Jovanovich, Inc., 1972), pp. 95–104. Oates's chap. 3 and appendices provide an excellent analysis of the uses of grants-in-aid within the conventional model of fiscal federalism.

over effect of reducing criminal activity in community B. In effect, then, X_G in community A becomes an aggregate external economy for the citizens of community B, entering into each person's utility function. The aggregate gain to community B's citizens on the margin can be represented as:

$$\sum_{h_B=1}^{H_B} MRS^{h_B}_{X_G,X_{h_B1}} \qquad \text{with each } MRS^{h_B} \text{ measured positively}$$

The true first-best pareto optimal conditions are, therefore:

$$(31.2) \qquad \sum_{h_A=1}^{H_A} MRS^{h_A}_{X_G,X_{h_A1}} + \sum_{h_B=1}^{H_B} MRS^{h_B}_{X_G,X_{h_B1}} = MRT_{X_G,X_1}$$

Without any intervention from a higher level government in the fiscal hierarchy, X_G will be misallocated (presumably undersupplied), since community A ignores the second set of terms on the left-hand side of (31.2). The situation exemplifies the notion of an imperfect correspondence, since the jurisdictional boundaries of community A, which makes the allocational decision on X_G, do not encompass all citizens affected by the production and consumption of X_G.

There is no need for a grant-in-aid in this case. The next highest government in the fiscal hierarchy, one that includes the citizens of both A and B, could simply provide X_G to the citizens of A in accordance with equation (31.2). However, it has the option of allowing community A to decide on the level of X_G as before, while influencing its decision with an appropriate grant-in-aid. Hence, its choice is fully analogous to that which exists for aggregate externalities in single government models in which the government can dictate the consumption of the good, or use a Pigovian subsidy and maintain decentralization. Presumably a society committed to federalism would choose the grant-in-aid since it promotes local autonomy, much as a single government committed to free markets would choose individual subsidies for normal aggregate externalities. As discussed in Chapter 6, the appropriate subsidy is a unit subsidy, equal to the aggregate gain to the citizens of B on the margin, or

$$s = \sum_{h_B=1}^{H_B} MRS^{h_B}_{X_G,X_{h_B1}}$$

in this case a grant-in-aid from the higher level government to community A. The grant, depicted in Figure 31–1, would be conditional, matching, and open ended: conditional on expenditures for X_G; the matching rate equal to the ratio s/P_G at the optimum, where P_G is the producer price of X_G (see Figure 31–1); open ended because it is nonoptimal to limit the size of the grant to any value other than $s \cdot X_G^*$, where X_G^* is determined by the receiving government.

These simple grant-in-aid examples can be quite misleading, however. Localities tend to provide the same kinds of public services. Therefore, the actual pattern of externalities is likely to be far more complex than depicted in our simple story. If community A's police expenditures create external economies for community B (and, possibly, other neighboring communities), then community B's police expenditures can be expected to generate external

608

FIGURE 31–1

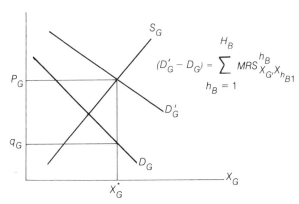

economies for all its neighbors, including A. But if so, then the spillover component of the externality is likely to be individualized by community, in which case the required pattern of grants-in-aid becomes extremely complex.

Let $X_G = X_{G_A} + X_{G_B} + \cdots + X_{Gc}$ be the aggregate output of X_G across all communities, with $(X_{G_A}, X_{G_B}, \ldots, X_{Gc})$ the vector of individual community outputs, C in number. If the aggregate X_G enters each person's utility function, then a single matching grant is appropriate, with $s = \sum_{\text{all } h} MRS^h_{X_G, X_{h1}}$. Continuing with the example on police expenditures, the spillover effects on criminal activity within a region depend upon aggregate police expenditures across all communities within the region. While this may be true, it is equally plausible to suppose that each community is most affected by police expenditures in contiguous communities, gaining increasingly less from police expenditures in ever more distant towns. If so, then the spillover externality remains individualized and pareto optimality requires a complex set of subsidies, one for each town. Moreover, the subsidies are interdependent, with each matching rate dependent upon police expenditures in every community. Thus, the situation is exactly analogous to the externalities arising from individual, private sector activities. Aggregate externalities admit to relatively simple solutions, and individualized externalities do not. The existence of federalism, with imperfect correspondences, adds nothing to the complexity of the problem. Even if the next highest government in the fiscal hierarchy chose to provide X_G, it would still follow the same decision rules, providing, of course, that the services of the individual X_{G_i}'s are consumed exclusively by members of the corresponding community, as posited in our example. If there is not even a perfect correspondence for the direct consumption of these services, then a set of grants-in-aid is unlikely to be appropriate. In that case the next highest government should decide upon the level of the aggregate $\bar{X}_G$ and its individual subcomponents. For instance, police services may be exclusive by town because the laws of each town forbid police to cross jurisdictions. But if there is really an imperfect correspondence here, then these exclusions are arbitrary and nonoptimal. Fewer, larger police departments with a regional orientation would be the optimal solution, but these would have to be provided by the next highest government in the fiscal hierarchy. Note finally that the analysis carries through in both the traditional model of federalism, in which only the national government has a social welfare function, or in our alternative model, with each government possessing a social welfare function. So long as income is optimally distributed according to the interpersonal equity conditions of each model, allocational issues will dichotomize from distributional concerns.

These same points apply to externalities generated by private sector activity. Unless the direct component of the activity can be localized within a single community, say, a production externality arising at a particular site, grants-in-aid are not likely to be pareto optimal. And even if pareto optimality could be achieved by the grants-in-aid, it may not be the most direct fiscal tool. Not surprisingly, grants-in-aid are most appropriate for publicly provided services. Consider the example of the production site, located in community A. Suppose its external diseconomies affect both citizens in A and those in other neighboring towns. If town A taxes the producer, it will undoubtedly base the tax on the marginal damages only to its own citizens. The next highest government could design a negative conditional matching grant (e.g., a tax) levied on town A that would optimally adjust for the broadened scope of the external diseconomy, but an additional direct tax on the producer would seem less cumbersome. Other more complex situations, such as the individualized pollution example of Chapter 7 in which production at multiple sites along a river generates external diseconomies for all the firms, can best be solved by producer taxes established by a higher level government and not a set of grants-in-aid to a number of localities. There seems to be no good reason to involve lower level governments as intermediaries for private sector externalities.

Nonoptimal Distribution of Income

Imperfect correspondences are merely one type of imperfection that provide a role for grants-in-aid in solving society's allocational problems. Grants can also be useful in the presence of other second best constraints as well, perhaps most importantly for the realistic case of a nonoptimal income distribution. We will let this stand as the final illustration of how grants-in-aid can be used to generate social welfare optima in a second-best policy environment.

Public expenditure analysis with a nonoptimal income distribution is sufficiently complex that it will pay to draw upon our earlier analysis of an aggregate externality developed in Chapter 20. To review briefly, we considered a model with perfectly competitive markets and general technology in which a single good, X_k, generates an aggregate consumption externality affecting all individuals. All other goods and factors are purely private. There was a single government which was constrained from redistributing resources lump sum to satisfy the first-best interpersonal equity conditions, so that the distribution of income was assumed to be nonoptimal. Finally, the standard competitive market assumptions were employed to define social welfare maximization in terms of consumer prices.

The government's problem was as follows:

$$\max_{(q_i)} W[V^h(\vec{q};\bar{I}^h;X_k)] = W[U^h(X_{hi}(\vec{q};\bar{I}^h;X_k))]$$

$$\text{s.t. } F(X_i) = 0$$

where:

$$X_i = \sum_{h=1}^{H} X_{hi}(\vec{q};\bar{I}^h;X_k) \qquad i = 1,\dots,N$$

W = the government's social welfare function.
$V^h(\ )$ = the indirect utility function of person h.
$\vec{q}$ = the vector of consumer prices.
$\bar{I}^h$ = the fixed lump-sum income of person h.
$F(\ )$ = the general technology production-possibilities frontier.

With good 1 the untaxed numeraire, the first-order conditions for this problem are:

$$(31.3) \qquad -\sum_{h=1}^{H} \beta^h X_{hk} + \sum_{h=1}^{H} \frac{\partial W}{\partial V^h}\frac{\partial V^h}{\partial X_k}\frac{\partial X_k}{\partial q_k} = -\lambda \sum_i F_i \frac{\partial X_i}{\partial q_k}$$

$$(31.4) \qquad -\sum_{h=1}^{H} \beta^h X_{hj} + \sum_{h=1}^{H} \frac{\partial W}{\partial V^h}\frac{\partial V^h}{\partial X_k}\frac{\partial X_k}{\partial q_j} = -\lambda \sum_i F_i \frac{\partial X_i}{\partial q_j}$$

$$j = 2,\dots,k-1,k+1,\dots,N$$

where:

$$\beta^h = \frac{\partial W}{\partial V^h}\frac{\partial V^h}{\partial I^h} \qquad h = 1,\dots,H$$

Conditions (31.3) and (31.4) imply that all goods and factors require taxation, not just the externality generating activity k, and that the tax rates depend upon the social welfare parameters β^h as well as the externality itself. With the single exception of the externality terms of the left-hand side of (31.3) and (31.4), these rules are identical to the many-person optimal tax rules.

To place this problem in the context of fiscal federalism, let us assume the existence of one national government and two local governments, L_1 and L_2. Assume further that there is a perfect correspondence with respect to the externality associated with X_k: purchase of X_k by citizens of L_1, $X_k^{L_1}$, affects only the citizens of L_1; and similarly, $X_k^{L_2}$ affects only the citizens of L_2.[10]

If one follows the traditional model of optimal federalism in which only the national government has a social welfare function, the modification of the single government first-order conditions is perfectly straightforward. Since purchase of good k in L_1 only affects citizens in L_1, and similarly for L_2, there

---

[10] Despite our preceding argument that grants-in-aid are not appropriate for correcting private sector externalities, we have purposely chosen an example here in which private sector activity generates an externality rather than positing local public goods. The private sector externality model of Chapter 20 is easier to modify than the public goods model and will serve the purposes of the present discussion. There is, for example, no need to worry about local budget constraints in the private sector externality model.

are two distinct externalities associated with X_k. The model can now be represented as follows:

$$\max_{(\vec{q})} W[V^{hL_1}(\vec{q};\overline{T}^{hL_1};X_k^{L_1}); V^{hL_2}(\vec{q};\overline{T}^{hL_2};X_k^{L_2})]$$

$$\text{s.t. } F\left[\sum_{h \text{ in } L_1} X_{hi}(\vec{q};\overline{T}^{hL_1};X_k^{L_1}); \sum_{h \text{ in } L_2} X_{hi}(\vec{q};\overline{T}^{hL_2};X_k^{L_2})\right] = 0$$

Given that the purchase of X_k generates two distinct externalities, social welfare can be increased by establishing separate prices, $q_k^{L_1}$ and $q_k^{L_2}$, for X_k, rather than a single price q_k.[11] Thus $\vec{q} = (q_1, \ldots, q_{k-1}; q_k^{L_1}; q_k^{L_2}; q_{k+1}, \ldots, q_N)$. The first-order conditions are:

$$(31.5) \quad -\sum_{h \text{ in } L_1} \beta^h X_{hk} + \sum_{h \text{ in } L_1} \frac{\partial W}{\partial V^{hL_1}} \frac{\partial V^{hL_1}}{\partial X_k^{L_1}} \frac{\partial X_k^{L_1}}{\partial q_k^{L_1}} = -\lambda \sum_{i=1}^{N} F_i \frac{\partial X_i}{\partial q_k^{L_1}}$$

$$(31.6) \quad -\sum_{h \text{ in } L_2} \beta^h X_{hk} + \sum_{h \text{ in } L_2} \frac{\partial W}{\partial V^{hL_2}} \frac{\partial V^{hL_2}}{\partial X_k^{L_2}} \frac{\partial X_k^{L_2}}{\partial q_k^{L_2}} = -\lambda \sum_{i=1}^{N} F_i \frac{\partial X_i}{\partial q_k^{L_2}}$$

$$(31.7) \quad -\sum_{h=1} \beta^h X_{hj} + \sum_{h \text{ in } L_1} \frac{\partial W}{\partial V^{hL_1}} \frac{\partial V^{hL_1}}{\partial X_k^{L_1}} \frac{\partial X_k^{L_1}}{\partial q_j} + \sum_{h \text{ in } L_2} \frac{\partial W}{\partial V^{hL_2}} \frac{\partial V^{hL_2}}{\partial X_k^{L_2}} \frac{\partial X_k^{L_2}}{\partial q_j}$$

$$= -\lambda \sum_{i} F_i \frac{\partial X_i}{\partial q_j} \qquad j = 2, \ldots, k-1, k+1, \ldots, N$$

In the context of the example, $q_k^{L_1}$ and $q_k^{L_2}$ can be achieved by means of conditional, matching, open-ended grants-in-aid to L_1 and L_2 sufficient to change the consumer price of X_k by $(p_k - q_k^{L_1})$ in L_1 and $(p_k - q_k^{L_2})$ in L_2, each price calculated at the social welfare optimum. This is obviously an enormous task, but the source of the problem is more the fact of nonoptimal income distribution than the existence of two distinct externalities associated with X_k. Calculating the optimal price vector using equations (31.5)–(31.7) is only trivially more difficult than using equations (31.3) and (31.4). However, the implications for maintaining a federalist system of governments are staggering. The national government has to resolve the externality problem because only it can determine the role of the social welfare terms. Even if each locality adjusted for its own externality by taxing according to the usual first-best decision rule, the national government would have to adjust these taxes to establish the optimal q_k^* from equations (31.5)–(31.7). Since this applies to any externality, or decreasing cost service, there is literally nothing left for the local governments to do!

Local governments remain important in our alternative model of federalism even with a nonoptimal income distribution, but the notion of optimality becomes ambiguous. To see this, represent the local communities' social welfare functions by:

$$L^1 = L^1[V^{hL_1}(\vec{q};\overline{T}^{hL_1};X_k^{L_1})] \quad \text{and} \quad L^2 = L^2[V^{hL_2}(\vec{q};\overline{T}^{hL_2};X_k^{L_2})]$$

---

[11] Social welfare could be further increased by having separate prices for all the goods, but we will assume this is beyond the power of the national government.

respectively, and the national social welfare function by:

$$W = W[L^1[V^{hL_1}(\vec{q}; \bar{T}^{hL_1}; X_k^{L_2})], L^2[V^{hL_2}(\vec{q}; \bar{T}^{hL_2}; X_k^{L_2})]]$$

If the income distribution is nonoptimal from *each* government's point of view because they are all constrained from using lump-sum taxes and transfers, they will each try to satisfy first-order conditions similar to those of (31.3) and (31.4). In particular, the proper first-order conditions from the point of view of L^1 are:[12]

$$(31.8) \quad \sum_{h \text{ in } L_1} \beta^{hL_1} X_{hL_1 k} + \sum_{h \text{ in } L_1} \frac{\partial L^1}{\partial V^{hL_1}} \frac{\partial V^{hL_1}}{\partial X_k^{L_1}} \frac{\partial X_k^{L_1}}{\partial q_k} = -\lambda \sum_i F_i \frac{\partial X_i}{\partial q_k}$$

$$(31.9) \quad \sum_{h \text{ in } L_1} \beta^{hL_1} X_{hL_1 j} + \sum_{h \text{ in } L_1} \frac{\partial L^1}{\partial V^{hL_1}} \frac{\partial V^{hL_1}}{\partial X_k^{L_1}} \frac{\partial X_k^{L_1}}{\partial q_j} = -\lambda \sum_i F_i \frac{\partial X_i}{\partial q_j}$$

$$j = 2, \ldots, k-1, k+1, \ldots, N$$

where:

$$\beta^{hL_1} = \frac{\partial L^1}{\partial V^{hL_1}} \alpha^{hL_1}, \text{ and } \alpha^{hL_1} = \text{ the marginal utility of income for person } h \text{ in } L_1$$

Community L_2 will solve an identical set of first-order conditions, with L_2 replacing L_1 everywhere. In general, these will generate different relative consumer prices for all goods, at the optima, in each community.

Viewing the problem from the perspective of the national government, two features stand out. First, the national government's social welfare expressions differ from each local expression by a single term, $\partial W/\partial L^1$ and $\partial W/\partial L^2$, respectively. For instance,

$$(31.10) \quad \beta^{hN} = \frac{\partial W}{\partial L^1} \beta^{hL_1} \quad \text{all } h \text{ in } L_1$$

$$(31.11) \quad \beta^{hN} = \frac{\partial W}{\partial L^2} \beta^{hL_2} \quad \text{all } h \text{ in } L_2$$

Second, the national government should not be constrained to adopt a single price vector q_i, $i \neq k$, as was assumed above for the traditional model of federalism. Consistent with the notion of states rights, it will accept the possibility that citizens in L_1 and L_2, by the separate actions of their governments, may face different prices. Thus, national social welfare is maximized with respect to $2(N-1) + 1$ prices, $(q_1; q_2^{L_1}; q_2^{L_2}; \ldots; q_N^{L_1}; q_N^{L_2})$, generating four sets of first-order conditions:

$$(31.12) \quad \frac{\partial W}{\partial L^1} \left(\sum_{h \text{ in } L_1} \beta^{hL_1} X_{hL_1 k} + \sum_{h \text{ in } L_1} \frac{\partial L^1}{\partial V^{hL_1}} \frac{\partial V^{hL_1}}{\partial X_k^{L_1}} \frac{\partial X_k^{L_1}}{\partial q_k^{L_1}} \right) = -\lambda \sum_i F_i \frac{\partial X_i}{\partial q_k^{L_1}}$$

---

[12] The following discussion assumes no differences in production technologies across local jurisdictions, or nationally.

(31.13) $\dfrac{\partial W}{\partial L^2}\left(\sum_{h \text{ in } L_2} \beta^{hL_2} X_{hL_2 k} + \sum_{h \text{ in } L_2} \dfrac{\partial L^2}{\partial V^{hL_2}} \dfrac{\partial V^{hL_2}}{\partial X_k^{L_2}} \dfrac{\partial X_k^{L_2}}{\partial q_k^{L_2}}\right) = -\lambda \sum_i F_i \dfrac{\partial X_i}{\partial q_k^{L_2}}$

(31.14) $\dfrac{\partial W}{\partial L^1}\left(\sum_{h \text{ in } L_1} \beta^{hL_1} X_{hL_1 j} + \sum_{h \text{ in } L_1} \dfrac{\partial L^1}{\partial V^{hL_1}} \dfrac{\partial V^{hL_1}}{\partial X_k^{L_1}} \dfrac{\partial X_k^{L_1}}{\partial q_j^{L_1}}\right)$

$= -\lambda \sum_i F_i \dfrac{\partial X_i}{\partial q_j^{L_1}} \quad j = 2, \ldots, k-1, k+1, \ldots, N$

(31.15) $\dfrac{\partial W}{\partial L^2}\left(\sum_{h \text{ in } L_2} \beta^{hL_2} X_{hL_2 j} + \sum_{h \text{ in } L_2} \dfrac{\partial L^2}{\partial V^{hL_2}} \dfrac{\partial V^{hL_2}}{\partial X_k^{L_2}} \dfrac{\partial X_k^{L_2}}{\partial q_j^{L_2}}\right)$

$= -\lambda \sum_i F_i \dfrac{\partial X_i}{\partial q_j^{L_2}} \quad j = 2, \ldots, k-1, k+1, \ldots, N$

These $2(N-1)$ conditions, together with the production constraint and the fact that $q_1 = 1$, will solve for the $2(N-1)+1$ prices, and λ. Inspection of conditions (31.12)–(31.15) reveals that the locally determined price structures will be maintained only if $\partial W/\partial L^1 = \partial W/\partial L^2$. With community marginal utilities equalized from the perspective of the national government, appropriate division of equations (31.12)–(31.15) will eliminate the national social welfare terms as well as λ. The remaining $2(N-1)-1$ conditions, together with the production frontier and $q_1 = 1$, will solve for the same vector of prices as were determined by each locality's social welfare maximization. There is no need for national grants-in-aid, or any other national response. If, on the other hand, $\partial W/\partial L^1 \neq \partial W/\partial L^2$, division of conditions (31.12)–(31.15) equation by equation can eliminate the national social welfare terms in only $2(N-2)$ equations. At least one equation in the required set of $2(N-1)-1$ equations will contain the term $\partial W/\partial L^1 / \partial W/\partial L^2 \neq 1$. Hence, the nationally determined optimal price vector

$$\overset{N}{\vec{q}} = \left(q_1; \overset{N_{L_1}}{q_2}; \overset{N_{L_2}}{q_2}; \ldots; \overset{N_{L_1}}{q_N}; \overset{N_{L_2}}{q_N}\right)$$

will differ from the locally determined price vectors, in general. This creates an inherent incompatibility. Suppose the national government readjusts $\vec{q}_{L_1}$ and $\vec{q}_{L_2}$ through a series of taxes and subsidies to generate $\overset{N}{\vec{q}}$. Since neither local government is a price taker, there is no reason for L_1 or L_2 to accept $\overset{N}{\vec{q}}$. From their own perspectives, the optimal policy is to reestablish $\vec{q}_{L_1}$ and $\vec{q}_{L_2}$, respectively. But if they do this, the national government will try to reestablish $\overset{N}{\vec{q}}$, and so on. There is obviously no equilibrium price vector, in general, nor is it clear what a social welfare optimum means. This is precisely the situation that the traditional model seeks to avoid. The alternative model had been able to avoid incompatibilities in all previous analysis because income was always optimally distributed. First-best analysis naturally generates optimal redistributions, and our previous second-best example simply assumed an optimal income distribution at the outset. That nonoptimal distributions should generate incompatibilities in our alternative model of federalism is understandable, given that jurisdictions' preferences regarding the distribution of income will differ from one another and from the nation's preferences, that people are citizens of more than one jurisdiction, and that each jurisdiction has the ability to adjust prices. Moreover, there is no obvious way to resolve the incompatibilities. In this example, the spirit of federalism might best be served by allowing the locally determined price vectors to prevail. But suppose this particular externality coexists with another externality that cuts across L_1, L_2, creating an imperfect correspondence. Since these second-best models with nonoptimal distributions suggest that *all* prices should change, it makes little sense to have the localities adjust for the first externality and the national government for the second. The optimal prices for the purely private goods will differ in each case.

Whether this analysis implies that our alternative model of fiscal federalism should be abandoned is a matter of personal preference. On the one hand, our model produces incompatibilities and ambiguous notions of social welfare optima. On the other hand, the traditional model strips local governments of all economic functions, thereby denying the very fiscal structure that it is supposed to model. For this reason we prefer to maintain the alternative view that all governments possess social welfare functions despite its problems. The real issue would appear to be nonoptimal income distributions which, even for single governments, create enormously complex normative decision rules that have little hope of practical application. The fact that a federalist system suffers incompatibilities when the distribution is nonoptimal may not really matter all that much. Society will be unable to achieve a social welfare optimum in any case, no matter how that optimum is defined, but at very least it must decide which government's distributional preferences will predominate.

THE GROWTH OF NATIONAL GRANTS-IN-AID IN THE UNITED STATES

As noted in the introductory remarks to this chapter, the national government in the United States has vastly increased the number and magnitude of grants-in-aid to states and localities over the past 30 years, to the point whereby grants now finance 23.6 percent of all state and local expenditures (FY 1980 (est)).[13] The explanation for this phenomenon appears to be three pronged. First, demand for the kinds of services traditionally offered by state and local governments—primary and secondary education, transportation, public assistance, public safety and so forth—appears to have been exceptionally buoyant. State and local expenditures increased 14.2 times from 1950 to 1978, whereas personal incomes increased by a factor of 7.6.[14] Second, state and local taxes are not especially well suited for keeping pace with rapidly increasing expenditures. Localities rely overwhelmingly on the property tax. States have more varied revenue sources, including sales taxes, property taxes, and various kinds

---

[13] See Table 31–1.

[14] Computations based on data contained in the *Economic Report of the President, January 1979* (Washington, D.C.: U.S. Government Printing Office, 1979), Table B–1, p. 183, and Table B–18, p. 203. Personal income increased from $226.1 billion in 1950 to $1707.3 billion in 1978 (preliminary).

of income taxes, with sales taxes by far the most important of those. Public sector economists generally concede that these taxes are not especially income elastic, certainly relative to national personal and corporate income taxes. Nonetheless, states and localities have chosen them over graduated income taxes for various reasons, including the avoidance of *in situs* problems, ease of collection, fear of the competition problem if any one state or locality choses less "progressive" taxes, constitutional restrictions against graduated taxes, and more stable revenue growth relative to graduated taxes. Revenue stability is desirable since it increases the accuracy of revenue forecasts and thereby reduces the probability of sizable revenue shortfalls in times of recession which, given that most states and localities cannot readily issue debt, might necessitate periodic cutbacks in expenditures.

State and local governments have countered the relatively low income elasticities of their taxes to some extent by expanding tax bases and raising rates, but there are obvious political pressures against these kinds of changes. Consequently, in order to satisfy the growing demands for state and local public services, national grants-in-aid have had to fill an increasing expenditure-revenue gap. In effect, the grant-in-aid allows these services to be financed by the relatively income elastic national taxes.

The third, and final, point centers on the behavior of prices for state and local public services over time. We noted above that state and local expenditures have grown more rapidly than personal incomes over the past 30 years, suggesting that demand for local public sector output has been growing relative to private sector output. Such inferences are risky, however, all the more so when talking about public services, since economists have never been able to devise any reliable method for separating public service expenditure data into its price and output components. What exactly are the appropriate output measures for the products of public schools, police departments, libraries, the judicial system, and so forth? This question has always clouded public sector analysis, most of which is based on expenditure data. The relevant point here is that higher public expenditures may not be indicative of increasing demand for public service output. Higher expenditures may simply reflect ever increasing (real) prices for the same output. In fact, Baumol and Oates[15] argue convincingly that even though they are difficult to observe, prices of local public services can be expected to rise geometrically over time relative to prices of private sector goods and services. They believe local public services such as education, public safety, the judiciary, general government, and so forth do not experience much productivity growth over time, at least not relative to the private sector. Consequently, the relative costs of public services will rise geometrically over time, at a rate equal to the difference between private and public sector productivity growth. Since prices presumably reflect costs in each sector, the same applies to relative

---

[15] This section of the text draws heavily on the analysis contained in William J. Baumol, Wallace E. Oates, *The Theory of Environmental Policy: Externalities, Public Outlays, and the Quality of Life,* © 1975, pp. 243–44, 248, 258–63, 265–66. Reprinted by permission of Prentice-Hall, Inc., Englewood Cliffs, N.J.

prices. This "cost disease" makes it ever more difficult to satisfy demands for these services, especially given state and local tax structures.

Baumol and Oates may not be correct. Without knowing how to measure local public sector output it is impossible to measure productivity growth. But their speculation is certainly plausible and, if accurate, would go a long way toward explaining the rapid growth in state and local expenditures and the consequent pressures for increased national grants-in-aid.

THE BAUMOL-OATES MODEL OF COST DISEASE

To see the effect of productivity differentials on relative prices and its implication for public services, consider a simple, perfectly competitive economy which produces two goods (Y_1 and Y_2) using only labor (L), by means of the following production relationships:

(31.16) $$Y_{1t} = aL_{1t}$$

(31.17) $$Y_{2t} = bL_{2t} \cdot e^{rt}$$

where:

The subscript t refers to time, and r is the rate of growth of labor productivity in the production of Y_2. Y_1 experiences no productivity growth.

Assume, further, that the supply of labor is perfectly inelastic and equal to L_0, constant over time. Hence:

(31.18) $$L_0 = L_{1t} + L_{2t} \qquad \text{all } t$$

With competitive markets labor must receive the same wage in each time period, W_t, and there can be no pure profits in the production of either good. Under these conditions, and given that labor is the only factor of production, the average and marginal costs of producing Y_{1t} and Y_{2t} are:[16]

(31.19) $$C_{1t} = \frac{W_t L_{1t}}{Y_{1t}} = \frac{W_t L_{1t}}{aL_{1t}} = \frac{W_t}{a} = AC_{Y_{1t}} = MC_{Y_{1t}}$$

(31.20) $$C_{2t} = \frac{W_t L_{2t}}{Y_{2t}} = \frac{W_t L_{2t}}{be^{rt} L_{2t}} = \frac{W_t}{be^{rt}} = AC_{Y_{2t}} = MC_{Y_{2t}}$$

Hence:

(31.21) $$\frac{C_{1t}}{C_{2t}} = \left(\frac{b}{a}\right) e^{rt}$$

According to (31.21), the average and marginal costs of producing Y_1 rise over time relative to the costs of producing Y_2 at a rate r, the difference in productivity growth in the two sectors. Since $P_{1t} = C_{1t}$ and $P_{2t} = C_{2t}$ with competitive markets, the *relative* price of Y_1 also increases at rate r. Letting Y_1 represent

---

[16] Note that a is the average and marginal product of labor in Y_1 and be^{rt} is the average and marginal product of labor in Y_2.

FIGURE 31-2

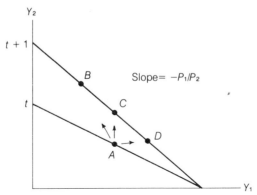

public sector output, and Y_2 private sector output, (31.21) demonstrates the "cost disease" suffered by the public sector.

What actually happens to the *demand* for Y_1 depends upon the relative strengths of two conflicting forces. On the one hand, the increasing relative price of Y_1 lowers the quantity demanded for Y_1, a movement along its demand curve. On the other hand, society is generating more real income over time because of the productivity growth in Y_2. The production-possibilities frontier is moving outward over time, as represented in Figure 31-2. Increases in real income will shift the demand curves for both Y_1 and Y_2 outward over time. The net effect on Y_1 depends, then, on the relative strengths of the negative relative price (or opportunity cost) effect and the positive real income effect. Anything is possible depending on tastes.[17] Society could move from A to points such as B, C, or D in Figure 31-2 implying less, equal, or more Y_1, respectively. Let us consider two such possibilities, a movement to either C or D (we will assume that the demand for public service outputs has not decreased over time).

Suppose, at first, that the demand for Y_1 remains constant over time. This result could be generated by a Cobb-Douglas utility function, which implies

---

[17] In a more realistic setting, with many factors of production and a convex production-possibilities frontier, relative prices or opportunity costs could decrease over time, but we will consider this an anomaly. As shown in the accompanying figure, the movement from A to B lowers the price ratio P_1/P_2.

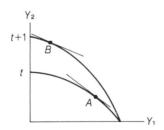

price elasticities of -1, and income elasticities of $+1$ for all goods, or constant expenditure shares. Let:

(31.22)
$$\frac{P_{1t}Y_{1t}}{P_{2t}Y_{2t}} = k$$

With total revenues equal to total costs in each sector

(31.23)
$$\frac{C_{1t}Y_{1t}}{C_{2t}Y_{2t}} = k = \frac{W_tL_{1t}}{W_tL_{2t}} = \frac{L_{1t}}{L_{2t}}$$

In this case, society would allocate a constant proportion of its total labor supply to both goods. Y_{1t} remains constant as required, and Y_{2t} grows at rate r over time. The conflicting relative price and income effects for Y_1 just balance one another, and society takes all its real income gains in increased consumption of Y_2.

Suppose, on the other hand, that society wants to take its real income gains in the form of increased consumption of both Y_1 and Y_2 over time. The implications of *any* steady growth in Y_1 over time are rather remarkable. Consider as one possible example the simple case in which society demands a constant proportion of Y_1 and Y_2 over time, such that

(31.24)
$$\frac{Y_{1t}}{Y_{2t}} = C$$

Substituting the production functions for Y_{1t} and Y_{2t} yields:

(31.25)
$$\frac{aL_{1t}}{bL_{2t}e^{rt}} = C$$

Rearranging terms:

(31.26)
$$\frac{L_{1t}}{L_{2t}} = C \cdot \frac{b}{a} \cdot e^{rt} = k \cdot e^{rt}$$

or

(31.27)
$$L_{1t} = ke^{rt}L_{2t}$$

But

(31.28)
$$L_{2t} = L_0 - L_{1t}$$

Substituting (31.27) into (31.28) yields:

(31.29)
$$L_{2t} = L_0 - ke^{rt}L_{2t}$$

Solving for L_{2t}:

(31.30)
$$L_{2t} = \frac{L_0}{1 + ke^{rt}}$$

But

(31.31)
$$\lim_{t \to \infty} L_{2t} = \frac{L_0}{1 + ke^{rt}} \to 0$$

Thus, in order to maintain Y_{1t}/Y_{2t} constant, society has to increase the proportion of its labor supplied to Y_1 to the point where virtually all labor is employed in the production of Y_1. Since Y_1 experiences no productivity growth, constantly increasing its labor supply is the only way to maintain constant growth. Furthermore, since W_t is equal in both sectors,

$$(31.32) \qquad \frac{W_t L_{1t}}{W_t L_{2t}} = ke^{rt}$$

Following the same reasoning as above:

$$(31.33) \qquad W_t L_{2t} \to 0$$

$$(31.34) \qquad W_t L_{1t} \to W_t L_0 \text{ as } t \to \infty$$

Society has to allot an ever increasing proportion of its total expenditures (total income) to Y_1 until, in the limit, all of its income is used to purchase Y_1. Even so, Y_2 continues to grow over time, at the same rate as Y_1. This is possible since Y_2 is becoming cheaper over time relative to Y_1 (the obverse of Y_1's cost disease). For example, suppose W_t is actually constant over time. Then P_{1t} will also be constant over time, since $P_{1t} = W_t/a$. But P_{2t} will decline at rate r, since $P_{2t} = W_t/be^{rt}$. Of course, this is just one of an infinite variety of possible solutions for P_{1t}, P_{2t}, and W_t, but it clearly illustrates how Y_2 can increase over time as ever more of society's expenditures become allocated to Y_1.

That *any* steady growth in Y_1 over time will generate these results can be seen by assuming that Y_1 grows at some rate s, with $s < r$. Suppose:

$$(31.35) \qquad Y_{1t} = Y_1^0 e^{st} = aL_{1t}^0 e^{st}$$

Since there is no productivity growth in Y_1, L_{1t} must be growing at rate s, or $L_{1t} = L_{1t}^0 e^{st}$. This further implies that L_{2t} must be declining at rate s. Therefore, in the limit, all labor will be used in the production of Y_1 as above. However, Y_2 will still continue to grow, at rate $(r - s)$, since with L_{2t} declining at rate s, but its productivity growing at rate r,

$$(31.36) \qquad Y_{2t} = b(L_{2t}^0 e^{-st})e^{rt} = bL_{2t}^0 e^{(r-s)t}$$

Empirical Estimates of Local Public Service Growth

It seems plausible that society would want to split its real income gains across both sectors. In terms of demand elasticities, all this requires is that the demand for Y_1 be relatively price inelastic and relatively income elastic. According to Baumol and Oates, the demand elasticities for public services are likely to satisfy these conditions. They believe available empirical evidence suggests relatively low price elasticities, on the order of $-.3$, and relatively larger income elasticities, on the order of $+.7$. Using their own example,[18] suppose that the

---

[18] Baumol and Oates, *The Theory of Environmental Policy*, pp. 264–66.

aggregate demand for public service has a standard log-linear form:

(31.37) $$\log q_t = \log a + \alpha \log Y_t + \beta \log P_t$$

where:

> q_t = demand for public sector output.
> a = constant.
> Y_t = income.
> P_t = the price of public sector output, with private sector output as the numeraire.
> α, β = the income and price elasticities of demand, respectively.

The log-linear demand function implies:

(31.38) $$\frac{\dot q}{q} = \alpha \frac{\dot Y}{Y} + \beta \frac{\dot P}{P}$$

where:

> $\dot q = \dfrac{dq}{dt}$, and so forth.

Define:

(31.39) $$E_t = q_t \cdot p_t$$

where:

> E_t = total expenditures on public sector output.

Thus:

(31.40) $$\frac{\dot E}{E} = \frac{\dot q}{q} + \frac{\dot p}{p}$$

Substituting for $\dot q/q$ from (31.38) and rearranging terms, yields:

(31.41) $$\frac{\dot E}{E} = (1 + \beta)\frac{\dot p}{p} + \alpha\left(\frac{\dot Y}{Y}\right)$$

Suppose private sector productivity has been rising at 3 percent per year, a rate approximately equal to average U.S. productivity growth in this century. Assuming no growth in public sector productivity, and using the simple model presented above, the relative cost or price of public sector services would be rising at 3 percent per year. Hence $\dot p/p = 3$ percent. Finally, assume $\dot Y/Y = 2$ percent per year, the average annual rate of growth in real income from 1950–70. These results, combined with the estimates that $\alpha = .7$ and $\beta = -.3$, imply $\dot E/E = 3.5$ percent per year from equation (31.41). This was approximately the average annual rate of growth in state and local public sector expenditures from 1950–70.[19] According to their analysis, then, only $1/7$ ($=.5/3.5$) of this expenditure growth went to increased public sector outputs. The remaining $6/7$ ($=3.0/3.5$) simply financed relative price increases for public services.

Tax Pressures and Fiscal Illusion

If Baumol's and Oates's conjecture is correct that the demand for local public service output grew during the past 20–25 years, this may well provide the key to explaining why national grants-in-aid grew so rapidly during this same period. A growth rate of .5 percent per year may not seem large at first, but *any* growth in real output, coupled with the "cost-disease" phenomenon, puts significant pressure on local budgets.

This point can be demonstrated most easily with the Baumol-Oates model by assuming that state and local governments collect proportional income taxes rather than sales or property taxes.[20] Suppose, on the one hand, that the public wants only a constant level of public services, consistent with the *equal-expenditure-share* example above. In this case, a proportional income tax will automatically raise sufficient revenues to finance the required expenditures. Following Baumol and Oates, let V_t be the tax rate in time t. With V_t applied to all labor income and a constant labor supply, tax revenues in time t are:

$$(31.42) \qquad T_t = V_t W_t L_0$$

Total expenditures on Y_{1t}, the public services are:

$$(31.43) \qquad E_t = W_t L_{1t} = W_t L_{10}$$

(with Y_{1t} constant over time, $L_{1t} = L_{10}$, also constant). Setting $T_t = E_t$,

$$(31.44) \qquad V_t W_t L_0 = W_t L_{10}$$

$$(31.45) \qquad V_t = \frac{L_{10}}{L_0} = V$$

Hence, a constant tax rate equal to L_{10}/L_0 will raise the required revenues. Furthermore, this should not create any particular political pressures for the local governments. The electorate would probably not object to a constant income tax rate over time. Because total sales equal total income, it follows that a tax on total sales only requires a constant tax rate as well. The only possible problem would arise with property taxes in which the assessed tax

---

[19] Expenditures net of inflation. It should be understood that all of the above analysis is independent of any increase in the general price level. "Cost disease" is a relative price phenomenon, and applies equally to any good or service that experiences less than average productivity growth, for example, theater, dining in fine restaurants and the like.

[20] Property taxes are inappropriate for a model with labor as its only factor of production. Sales taxes are virtually identical to income taxes in this model, but income taxes involve less notation. Any conclusions with respect to income taxes generalize easily to sales taxes as well if one assumes competitive or markup pricing behavior. Refer to Baumol and Oates, *The Theory of Environmental Policy*, p. 260, for a complete analysis of the sales tax.

base is constant. Since the base is not growing, but required expenditures are, tax rates must be increased each year to raise sufficient revenues. This could create political pressures if people react more to changes in rates than to changes in collections caused by natural increases in the tax base. This same point applies if towns hold rates constant, but continually increase assessed values. The burdens are the same in any case, but people may perceive that rate or base changes involve an increased burden. Baumol and Oates refer to this false perception as "fiscal illusion."[21]

All these taxes suffer the possibility of "fiscal illusion" if the public demands an increasing level of public services. Required income taxes are still given by (31.42), but now *both* W_t and L_{1t} are growing. Since the tax base, L_0, is constant, V_t must increase over time as well. This can be illustrated by referring to the case analyzed above whereby the public demands a constant proportion of public to outputs, or $Y_{1t}/Y_{2t} = C$. We saw that

$$(31.46) \qquad L_{1t} = \frac{L_0 k e^{rt}}{1 + k e^{rt}} \to L_0 \text{ as } t \to \infty$$

Assume wages are growing at some rate u, so that

$$(31.47) \qquad W_t = W_0 e^{ut}$$

Thus, income tax collections grow according to the relationship

$$(31.48) \qquad T_t = V_t W_t L_0 = V_t W_0 e^{ut} L_0$$

But required revenues are:

$$(31.49) \qquad E_t = W_t L_{1t} = W_0 e^{ut} L_0 \left(\frac{k e^{rt}}{1 + k e^{rt}} \right)$$

Setting $T_t = E_t$,

$$(31.50) \qquad V_t W_0 e^{ut} L_0 = W_0 e^{ut} L_0 \left(\frac{k e^{rt}}{1 + k e^{rt}} \right)$$

Hence:

$$(31.51) \qquad V_t = \frac{k e^{rt}}{1 + k e^{rt}} = \frac{L_{1t}}{L_0} \to 1 \text{ as } t \to \infty$$

Notice that V_t is independent of u, the rate of growth in wages. Rather, V_t depends only upon r, the rate of growth in productivity, and approaches 100 percent over time. Given that society must devote 100 percent of its income to Y_{1t} in the limit, it follows that the tax rate must also approach 100 percent. Notice also that this result obtains for any steady growth rate s in Y_{1t}. V_t will still equal L_{1t}/L_0 and $L_{1t} \to L_0$ in the limit.

Despite ever increasing demands for public services, the public is likely to revolt long before $V_t \to 100$ percent, especially since tax payments are not

---

[21] Ibid., p. 256.

directly tied to public services as they would be under the benefits-received principle of taxation. Recent U.S. history is instructive on this point. Demand for state and local public services grew modestly over the past 30 years, only .5 percent per year, if the Baumol-Oates scenario can be believed. Nonetheless, state and local governments were forced to seek out new revenue sources, and/or increase rates on existing taxes. By the end of the 1970s at least some segments of the public had had enough. Proposition 13 became law in California, and as this is being written a number of other states are considering similar spending-tax caps on either state or local budgets. The predicted tax revolt has arrived, yet no state sales tax exceeds 10 percent, and state income tax rates tend to be modest by national standards. Some property tax rates exceed 10 percent, [22] but these are based on more or less constant assessed values. With constant assessments, property tax rates would soon exceed 100 percent even if public service output were held constant. The lessons are clear. People may want increased public services *and* constant tax rates, but if public services really do suffer from "cost-disease," these twin desires are simply not compatible, even abstracting from the problem of general price inflation.

Suppose, however, that the real issue behind a tax revolt is "fiscal illusion," that people will tolerate ever increasing taxes so long as the revenue increases result from growth in the tax base. If so, then a graduated income tax will solve the revenue expenditure dilemma. Designing the required progressive tax system in the simple Baumol-Oates model proceeds as follows. Let $W_t = W_0 e^{ut}$, define the growth in wages over time, as above. Define:

$$(31.52) \qquad \bar{W}_t = \frac{W_t}{W_0} = e^{ut}$$

Taking logarithms of both sides:

$$(31.53) \qquad \ln(\bar{W}_t) = ut$$

or

$$(31.54) \qquad \frac{\ln \bar{W}_t}{u} = t$$

Using this expression for t, e^{rt} can be rewritten as follows:

$$(31.55) \qquad e^{rt} = e^{(r/u)\ln(\bar{W}_t)} = e^{\ln(\bar{W}_t)^{r/u}} = \bar{W}_t^{r/u}$$

From the preceding analysis, we know that the income tax rate required to raise sufficient revenues to finance Y_{1t} at time t, for $Y_{1t}/Y_{2t} = C$, is:

$$(31.56) \qquad V_t = \frac{ke^{rt}}{1 + ke^{rt}}$$

---

[22] For instance, in 1975 the property tax rate in the City of Boston was 13.59 percent (estimated at 13.498 percent on full value). R. Eisenmenger, A. Munnell, and J. Poskanzer, *Options for Fiscal Reform in Massachusetts*, Research Report No. 57, Federal Reserve Bank of Boston, March 1975, appendix 14.1, p. 318, and appendix 4.1, p. 238, respectively.

Substituting for e^{rt} in (31.56) yields:

$$(31.57) \qquad V_t(\bar{W}_t) = \frac{k \cdot (\bar{W}_t)^{(r/u)}}{1 + k\bar{W}_t^{(r/u)}}$$

where V_t is the required average rate of tax over time.

The marginal tax rate is then computed by differentiating (31.57) with respect to W_t.

$$(31.58) \qquad \frac{dV_t}{d\bar{W}_t} = \frac{\left[\left(\frac{r}{u}\right)k \cdot \bar{W}_t^{(r/u)-1}\right](1 + k\bar{W}_t^{(r/u)}) - (k\bar{W}_t^{(r/u)})\left[k\left(\frac{r}{u}\right)\bar{W}_t^{(r/u)-1}\right]}{(1 + k\bar{W}_t^{r/u})^2}$$

Simplifying

$$(31.59) \qquad \frac{dV_t}{d\bar{W}_t} = \frac{\left(\frac{r}{u}\right)k\bar{W}_t^{(r/u-1)}}{(1 + k\bar{W}_t^{(r/u)})^2} > 0 \qquad u \le r$$

With $u \le r$, the average rate V_t rises steadily over time, as expected. Moreover, starting with a base year W_0 and a given k, estimates of r and u will be sufficient to design the required tax system. This is a tall order, all the more so when one considers the reality of numerous factors of production, but the point remains that a tax system can be designed once and for all that will generate the required tax revenues. No further changes in rates are necessary.

The conclusion from this analysis is clear. If "fiscal illusion" does exist, the national government, with its graduated personal income tax, has a natural political advantage in raising revenues. Consequently, the obvious method of supporting ever increasing demands for local public services is through ever-increasing grants-in-aid financed with the national tax. Of course, the existence of fiscal illusion remains an unanswered empirical question at this point, but there are two strong pieces of evidence arguing in support of this phenomenon. First, national grants-in-aid did increase rapidly over the past 25 years. It is inconceivable that state and local expenditures would have increased as rapidly without them. Second, the initial tax revolts in the 1970s were against state and local governments, not the national government, this despite the fact that growth in federal tax collections also exceeded the growth in personal incomes during this time period.[23] Neither of these facts is conclusive, but the entire Baumol-Oates analysis is at least highly plausible, enough so that continued growth in the ratio of national grants-in-aid to state and local tax revenues during the 1980s would hardly be surprising. The only foreseeable offsetting tendency, one that is not captured by their simple model, is the projected decline in the number of school-aged children. This will tend to place a natural ceiling on state and local expenditures and simultaneously ease fiscal pressures, since the income-earning taxpaying population will not decline concomitantly.

---

[23] From 1950–78 federal government receipts increased from $50.0 to $431.6 billions (preliminary), an 8.6-fold increase. Source: *Economic Report of the President, January 1979*, Table B–72, p. 183.

But once this smaller population cohort joins the labor force, and the current work force retires, the fiscal pressures predicted by Baumol and Oates will inevitably begin anew.

ADDITIONAL DESIGN CHARACTERISTICS OF GRANTS-IN-AID

Because they have attained such prominence in the U.S. fiscal system, grants-in-aid have been the subject of voluminous research by public sector economists over the past two decades. Broadly speaking, this research has focused on two main issues. The first concerns the practical problem of designing grants-in-aid that are at least roughly consistent with underlying theoretical concepts drawn from the literature on optimal federalism. A second large body of empirical research has addressed itself to both the expected and actual responses of state and local governments to the various national grant-in-aid programs.

Practical Issues in Grant Design

With respect to the first issue of grant design, it is clear that U.S. grants-in-aid bear, for the most part, only a distant relationship to the theory of optimal federalism. This is especially true of the more common first-best theoretical analysis. Recall that the theory of optimal federalism details exactly how grants-in-aid are to be used to promote society's distributional and allocational goals. If one believes the conventional analysis, grants-in-aid should be totally unrelated to distributional goals. These should be met entirely by means of national taxes and transfers directly among individuals. If one believes our alternative model, grants-in-aid are central to the resolution of distributional imbalances and should be employed by all but the lowest level governments within the fiscal hierarchy. Moreover, the grants should be lump-sum, meaning unconditional, and nonmatching. They should also be closed ended, with the amounts of aid determined solely by each government's social welfare function. With respect to the allocational question, both models suggest that grants-in-aid can be useful in resolving externality problems associated with imperfect correspondences. These grants should be conditional, matching, and open ended, strictly tied to activities generating the externality, with the matching rate(s) determined solely by the marginal benefit or harm arising from the externality, along the lines of the usual Pigovian taxes and subsidies. The matching rate should not be related to any distributional considerations in an otherwise first-best environment.

In point of fact, almost no significant U.S. grant program follows these guidelines. General Revenue Sharing is the only obvious exception. It does approximate the guidelines for redistributional grants under our alternative model. But the other major redistributional grants-in-aid, the Public Assistance programs, which include Supplemental Security Income (SSI), Aid for Dependent Children (AFDC), and medical vendor payments under Medicare and

Medicaid, are all matching grants in which explicit state by state redistribution is accomplished by varying the matching rate inversely with state income. Moreover, Medicaid is open ended.

With respect to society's allocational goals, all the major allocational grant programs are conditional, as required by the first-best model of federalism, but they are also closed ended, instead of open ended, and many are non-matching. Furthermore, if they happen to be matching grants, the matching rate bears little or no relationship to externality theory. Often it is just some arbitrarily determined number, equal to all recipients. For example, under the Federal Highway Aid programs, expenditures for the Interstate system received a 90 percent subsidy, other roads a 50 percent subsidy, in all states. The higher matching rate for the Interstate system makes some sense if one argues that it confers additional national defense externalities, but there is no reason to suppose that the 90 percent rate is an accurate reflection of the Interstate's marginal external economies.

Matching rates do vary across states and/or localities for some allocational grants,[24] but the rates are usually tied to income as in the Public Assistance programs, and not to varying degrees of externality. In grants of this kind the national government is obviously trying to pursue both distributional and allocational goals with one program. Such dual-purpose matching grants are consistent with second-best versions of our alternative model with a nonoptimal distribution of income. One could presumably describe an underlying social welfare function and a pattern of externalities that might justify a particular set of matching rates as a reasonable approximation to conditions such as (31.12)–(31.15), but the national government clearly had no such sophisticated model in mind when these grants were designed.

Alternative Design Criteria

It is hardly surprising, of course, that actual grants-in-aid bear little relationship to theoretical design criteria, simply because the theory is so difficult to apply in this instance. Distributional norms based on social welfare functions can never be more than suggestive, and it may be unconstitutional to vary matching formulas across states on the basis of marginal external benefit or harm. Faced with these realities, economists have resorted to developing practical design criteria that are at least roughly consistent with the underlying theory. For example, LeGrand, in "Fiscal Equity and Central Grants to Local Authorities," suggests three sensible practical guidelines for grant-in-aid programs whose goals are redistributional.[25] First, the grants must be a function of the income or wealth of the receiving government such that poorer than average jurisdictions receive aid and richer than average communities pay a

---

[24] For a listing of the allocation requirements and matching formulas for the major grant-in-aid programs as of 1971, see *Special Revenue Sharing: An Analyses of the Administration's Grant Consolidation Proposals*, appendix D.

[25] J. LeGrand, "Fiscal Equity and Central Government Grants to Local Authorities," *Economic Journal*, September 1975.

tax (receive a negative grant). By contrast, existing grants always give something to all governments. The political motivations behind this are clear, but such grants tend by their very nature to have limited redistributional power. Second, LeGrand suggests that the amount of aid received (tax paid) ought to be independent of any expenditure decisions made by the receiving government. This guideline recognizes two theoretical principles, that redistributional policy ought properly be concerned with each government's overall initial level of resources, and that, consistent with the federalist ideal, the grantor should not interfere with the decision-making process of any lower level government. LeGrand's third guideline states that grants should vary directly with the receiving government's fiscal effort, the idea being that governments with little interest in providing public services should receive correspondingly less aid. This criterion is somewhat troublesome since it tends to contradict the second guideline. It implies that the grantor will try to influence the overall level of public services, if not the composition of these services. In any case, it is a commonly accepted principle. The U.S. Congress has frequently incorporated effort parameters into aid formulas.[26]

The beauty of these three guidelines is that they imply a remarkably simple aid formula based on what LeGrand calls the Purchasing Power Effort (PPE) Ratio.

Let:

T_i = total taxes collected by government i.

P_i = a price index of public services provided by government i.

E_i = the tax rate in government i.

Y_i = the per capita tax base in government i.

The Purchasing Power Effort Ratio for government i is simply:

$$(31.60) \qquad PPE_i = \frac{T_i}{E_i P_i} = \frac{E_i Y_i}{E_i P_i} = \frac{Y_i}{P_i}$$

PPE is often referred to as the *fiscal capacity* of government i. In addition to computing the *PPE* for each lower level government, the grantor picks a target $PPE_T = Y_T/P_T$. The grant, G_i, is then designed to put all jurisdictions at that target PPE_T. Thus, G_i is such that

$$(31.61) \qquad \frac{T_i + G_i}{E_i P_i} = \frac{Y_i}{P_i} + \frac{G_i}{E_i P_i} = \frac{Y_T}{P_T}$$

Assuming $P_i = P_T$, all i, or that public service prices are constant across all jurisdictions,

$$(31.62) \qquad G_i = E_i(Y_T - Y_i)$$

---

[26] General Revenue Sharing is a recent example, in which aid received depends in part on the tax collections within the state and community. Maxwell and Aronson, *Financing State and Local Governments*, p. 72, fn. 24.

All three of LeGrand's criteria are satisfied by this simple formula, which is just a product of each jurisdictions fiscal effort, as embodied in the tax rate, and its fiscal capacity where fiscal capacity is defined as the per capita tax base. Redistribution would be significant, since richer than average towns would actually pay taxes. By including E_i the formula also addresses a problem that many people find particularly inequitable, namely that wealthy communities can offer better public services than the poorest communities even though their tax rates are only a fraction of the tax rates in the poorest communities. LeGrand's formula doubly rewards the poor, high tax rate communities. Finally, if one concedes that social welfare rankings may properly be functions of fiscal effort, among other things, this simple formula is reasonably consistent with the redistributional decision rules of our alternative model of fiscal federalism. It bears roughly the same relationship to these norms as the Haig-Simons ability-to-pay criterion does to the interpersonal equity conditions of single government social welfare maximization. Both substitute income for utility, although the Haig-Simons criterion contains nothing comparable to the fiscal effort term.

The literature on practical grant design has also addressed itself to goals that are not directly related to the normative neoclassical theory of fiscal federalism. For example, the national government may decide that each state should provide at least a minimum level of monthly income to all families qualifying for Aid for Dependent Children, where the income level is standardized by family size. Or a state may decide that each city and town should provide a minimum level of educational expenditures on each school-aged child. Legislators often support grant-in-aid programs with this goal in mind.

Minimum public assistance benefits can be thought of as arising from a particular social welfare function, but exhaustive public services invested with minimum service requirements are sometimes referred to as "merit goods." They fall between the standard neoclassical dichotomy of distributional versus allocational services in that they typically embody some in-kind distributional impact as well as certain externality elements. Public health care, education, and housing are the most common examples, minimum consumption of which comes to be viewed as a fundamental right.

The standard first-best neoclassical approach to inadequate consumption of these services would be two-pronged, consisting of Pigovian subsidies (taxes) to account for the externality component and direct cash transfers to the poor to capture the distributional component.[27] Many-person second-best decision

---

[27] Minimum provision of merit goods can be consistent with first-best neoclassical theory under special assumptions. For instance, the interpersonal equity conditions require lump-sum transfers of one good or factor. Special forms of the social welfare function could imply minimum service levels for one of these services, but, in general, not more than one. Given pareto optimality, all other interpersonal equity conditions are dependent on any one of them. Another instance of minimum service levels, this time based on the externality component, would occur if people's tastes were two-tiered, with an extremely high MRS for others' education at or below some given level, and a zero MRS above that level. Generally, however, merit goods are viewed as allocational and distributional hybrids as represented in the text.

rules do generally combine allocational and distributional goals, but in the form of price subsidies rather than minimum service provisions. Most often, however, governments have chosen to meet these deficiencies directly, and somewhat paternalistically, by in-kind provision of these basic services. Once minimum requirements have been established, the natural way to ensure that they are met in any of these areas is through conditional, nonmatching, closed-ended grants in each specific area, with the funding level equal to the minimum expenditure requirement.[28] The theory of optimal fiscal federalism has no use for grants of this type, but they are an obvious remedy for the in-between "merit" good.

As our final example of practical grant design criteria we will consider briefly the analysis of Martin Feldstein with respect to local public educational expenditures. [29] In the early and mid-1970s, a number of state supreme courts ruled that financing public educational expenditures entirely from local property taxes was inherently discriminatory, since wealthier communities could provide better education with less fiscal effort, that is, lower tax rates.[30] The states were required to design a more equitable state-wide financial arrangement, one which would somehow provide transfers from the wealthier to the poorer communities. Feldstein suggests using a matching grant for this purpose, in which the matching rate applied to any one community is inversely related to its wealth. He reasons that the courts' decisions imply a fiscal solution which sets the elasticity of educational output with respect to wealth equal to zero ($E_{ed,W=0}$). In order to achieve this, however, one needs reliable econometric estimates of the price and income (wealth) elasticities of educational expenditures independent of a new grant program. These estimates can then be used to design the required matching rates.

To see how this would work, suppose it were possible to estimate a constant elasticity demand-for-education equation across communities of the form

$$(31.63) \qquad\qquad Ed = C \cdot P^{\alpha} W^{\beta}$$

where:

> Ed = a measure of educational output per capita.
> P = the price of educational output.
> W = a measure of per capita community wealth.
> α, β = price and wealth elasticities, respectively.
> C = a constant term embodying all other factors influencing the demand for education.

Rewriting (31.63) in logarithms yields:

$$(31.64) \qquad\qquad \log Ed = C' + \alpha \log P + \beta \log W$$

---

[28] Oates analyzes the merit good case in *Fiscal Federalism*, pp. 85–94.

[29] M. Feldstein, "Wealth Neutrality and Local Choice in Public Education," *American Economic Review*, March 1975.

[30] *Serrano v. Priest* in California was the landmark decision. *Serrano v. Priest*, L. A. 29820, Superior Court No. 938254.

Next, posit a matching aid formula of the form:

(31.65) $$P = W^k$$

or

(31.66) $$\log P = k \log W$$

where:

k = the elasticity of price with respect to wealth.

Substituting (31.66) into (31.64) yields:

(31.67) $\log Ed = C' + \alpha(k \log W) + \beta \log W = C' + (\alpha k + \beta) \log W$

With this matching program:

(31.68) $$\frac{d \log Ed}{d \log W} = E_{ed,W} = \alpha k + \beta$$

Setting $E_{ed,W} = 0$ implies:

(31.69) $$k = -\frac{\beta}{\alpha}$$

Thus, the required matching rate elasticity just equals the ratio of the wealth and price elasticities of education within the state, at least for a log-linear demand for education function. In order to demonstrate his technique Feldstein estimated an education equation for a cross section of Massachusetts communities. The required matching rate elasticity for Massachusetts turned out to be between .33 and .37.[31]

It is worth repeating that matching grants for which the matching rate varies with respect to income or wealth have no role in the first-best theory of federalism and are, at best, only suggested by second-best considerations. Nonetheless, if the law requires neutralizing the effect of wealth on educational opportunity within states, then Feldstein's grant-in-aid formula provides a direct way of achieving this goal.

The preceding examples of grant design highlight an important point, that public sector economists have found the grant-in-aid to be an extremely useful practical policy tool, even though the first-best theory of optimal federalism assigns it a rather limited role. Since the prevailing first-best model of optimal federalism uses grants only for resolving highly specific externality problems, if at all, the theory of grant design has necessarily evolved independently from that model. Assigning distributional content to grant-in-aid formulas, which the LeGrand, merit goods and Feldstein analyses all do, can be justified in part by appealing to our alternative model or to second-best considerations, but our comments in this section are obviously only a beginning step in that direction. They hardly represent a comprehensive integrated theory of grant design. But unless the literature begins to move away from the prevailing

---

[31] Feldstein, "Wealth Neutrality and Local Choice in Public Education," p. 85.

model of federalism grant design will continue to be episodic, appealing to specific issues without giving much thought to the role of these grants in the overall schema of an optimal fiscal structure.

THE RESPONSE TO GRANTS-IN-AID

The final issue in our analysis of grants-in-aid concerns the response of receiving governments to existing grant-in-aid formulas. The literature in this area has been motivated by two factors, first that grants-in-aid have become so important to state and local governments, and second, that governments receive many different kinds of grants-in-aid. Recall that grant formulas vary across three dimensions: conditional-unconditional, matching-nonmatching, and closed ended–open ended. Public sector economists have had a natural theoretical interest in the expected responses to the various possible combinations of formula parameters. Should it matter, for example, whether governments receive conditional or unconditional grants, matching or nonmatching grants, and so forth? On an empirical level, econometric analysis has tried to pinpoint the actual response to existing grants, both for its own sake and as a test of the theoretical analysis. Taken together, this body of literature is as extensive as any in public sector analysis, yet both the theoretical and empirical analysis of grant response has been far from conclusive.

The Theory of Grant Response

Let us turn first to the theoretical issue of the expected response to grants-in-aid. The analysis of this question has usually employed a consumer-theoretic approach, in which the receiving government is viewed as a single utility-maximizing consumer subject to the balanced-budget constraint that total expenditures must equal total revenues. The grants literature has also characteristically equated expenditures with outputs, by implicitly or explicitly assuming that prices of all public services equal one (excluding any matching grants, which reduce prices below one). The standard analysis, then, proceeds along the following lines.

Assume for purposes of illustration that a typical receiving government has a utility function of this form

$$(31.70) \qquad\qquad U = U(E, O, Y - T)$$

where:

E = expenditures on education.
O = expenditures on all other public services.
Y = income (or wealth) within the jurisdiction.
T = taxes.

$(Y - T)$ measures the disposable income remaining in the private sector. The fact that it enters the utility function represents the disutility of raising taxes.

FIGURE 31–3

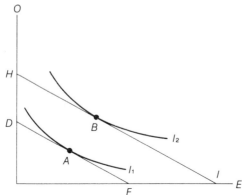

The balanced-budget constraint, net of grants-in-aid, is:

(31.71) $$E + O = T$$

In the usual manner, the receiving government is assumed to maximize utility with respect to E, O, and T, subject to its balanced-budget constraint.

The receipt of *any* grant-in-aid will have the effect of relaxing the budget constraint. However, the varying formula options change the budget constraint in quite different ways, so that different options may produce different effects both on the composition of expenditures and the public-private sector mix. In the following analysis we will focus only on the compositional expenditure effects by assuming that tax revenues are constant. This will permit a simple geometric representation of the various alternatives, which could be easily extended to the case of endogenous tax revenues.

Consider, first, the simplest case of the *unconditional, nonmatching, closed-ended* grant[32] in amount $\bar{G}$. The new budget constraint becomes:

(31.72) $$E + O = T + \bar{G}$$

representing a parallel shift in the budget line. Using indifference curve analysis, if the receiving government is originally at point A on budget line DF in Figure 31–3, the budget line will shift out to HI by amount $\bar{G}$, permitting the receiving government to reach a higher level of utility, say point B on indifference curve I_2. While B theoretically could be anywhere on HI depending on tastes, one would expect the government to move somewhere in the region north and east of A. Since the unconditional grant generates only an income effect, B would fall outside that region only if the income elasticity of either E or O were negative, that is, if one of the public services were an inferior good. This seems highly unlikely.

An *unconditional matching* grant, either closed or open ended is identical to the nonmatching grant in this analysis. Suppose the grantor matches some

---

[32] An open-ended nonmatching unconditional grant is obviously nonsensical.

proportion, α, of total taxes ("fiscal effort"). With taxes exogenous, total aid received is $\alpha \cdot \bar{T}$ and represents a parallel shift in the budget line DF. With $\alpha\bar{T} = \bar{G}$, the receiving government will once again move to point B on HI.[33]

In point of fact, the U.S. national government has strongly preferred conditional to unconditional grants on the grounds that the conditional grant provides accountability for the grant monies. The argument goes as follows: If the U.S. authorizes $1 million of aid to some state for educational expenditures, at least Congress knows that the $1 million is being spent on education. If Congress simply offers the state $1 million unconditionally, the money could be spent on anything, and perhaps foolishly.

This line of reasoning has been extremely persuasive. As noted earlier in the chapter, General Revenue Sharing was the first (virtually) unconditional grant program ever authorized by Congress, and this not until 1972. It remains to this day the only unconditional grant-in-aid.

It turns out, however, that the argument of accountability can be specious. The analysis is complicated by the fact that conditional grants may take one of three basic forms:

a.   Nonmatching, closed ended.[34]
b.   Matching, open ended.
c.   Matching, closed ended.

Let us consider each of these in turn.

With respect to the *conditional, nonmatching* grant, the key question is whether this grant will generate a different pattern of expenditures than an unconditional grant of equal dollar magnitude. The answer in most instances is no. Suppose the government depicted in Figure 31–3 receives a conditional grant for education in amount $\bar{E}_G$, such that $\bar{E}_G = \bar{G}$. The new budget constraint with this grant is:

$$(31.73) \qquad\qquad (E - \bar{E}_G) + O = T$$

or

$$(31.74) \qquad\qquad E + O = T + \bar{E}_G$$

The budget line again shifts out parallel to DF, to FKI in Figure 31–4, with $FK = \bar{E}_G$. The only difference relative to the unconditional grant is that the receiving government is restricted from points on the dotted line segment HK. Since $\bar{E}_G$ is earmarked for educational expenditures, the best the government can do in terms of all other goods and services, O, is spend all its own resources (T) on O, and accept the grant of $\bar{E}_G$ to finance expenditures on E. But this places the government at point K.

---

[33] Unconditional matching and nonmatching grants will have different effects if taxes are endogenous, however, since the matching grant introduces a price effect on $(Y - T)$. Refer to the analysis below on the conditional matching grant.

[34] A nonmatching, open-ended grant is unlikely for it allows the receiving government to consume the aided item until it reaches the point of satiation. No government is likely to authorize such a grant given that all funds have opportunity costs attached to them.

FIGURE 31–4

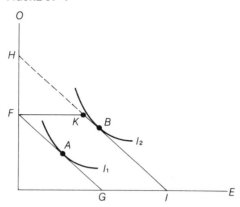

According to the diagram, the government will again select point B, so that adding the condition that the grant be spent on E is of absolutely no consequence. This will always be the case if the equilibrium with the unconditional grant lies on the line segment KI. Conversely, the condition will matter only if the grant is large relative to the government's expenditures on E, which will occur if the grant is especially large, or if the grant is relatively modest but the receiving government has little interest in E expenditures without the grant. This case is depicted in Figure 31–5.

With the unconditional grant $\bar{G}$ $(=\bar{E}_G)$, the government moves to point B on I_2. With the conditional grant, the government is forced to a nonoptimal corner solution K, because the grant exceeds the amount it would spent on E even with the unconditional grant. Notice, too, that K must lie on a lower indifference curve than I_2. In other words, if the condition matters, meaning that it distorts allocations relative to an equal dollar unconditional grant, the receiving government would always prefer the unconditional grant. The preferences of the grantor have been allowed to prevail in this case.

FIGURE 31–5

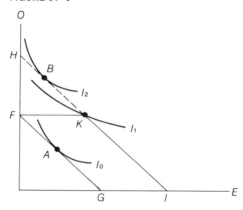

FIGURE 31–6

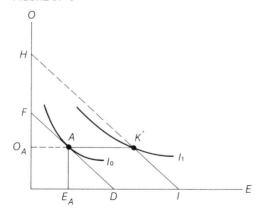

Given the national government's decided preference for conditional grants, one might infer that the distortion case is most often relevant, but this does not appear to be so. Receiving governments generally spend some of their own resources on aided items, which can happen only if the conditional grant is nondistorting. Receiving governments forced to a corner solution would never supplement the grant funds.

At some point during the 1960s Congress must have sensed that a conditional grant will not necessarily stimulate additional expenditures on the aided item because it began to add new conditions to its grant program. Presumably for every additional dollar of conditional aid Congress gives to a state or locality, it expects to generate at least a dollar of additional expenditure on the aided item. But as we have just seen, if the receiving government is not at a corner solution, and does not want to increase there expenditures, it can simply substitute grant funds for its own resources, thereby freeing resources to be spent on other items.

This turned out to be a particular problem with increases in the national contribution to public assitance payments in the early 1960s. Some states were not increasing benefits per welfare recipient dollar for dollar when the national contribution to average benefits was increased.[35] To ensure the appropriate stimulation, Congress specified that increased aid would only be forthcoming if the receiving government did not reduce its "own" expenditures (expenditures financed by its own revenue sources) on the aided item. This new condition became a common feature of many grant programs after the mid-1960s.

Specifying no reduction in "own" expenditures has the probable effect of forcing a corner solution on the receiving government. For suppose the government is originally at point A in Figure 31–6. The receipt of a conditional grant

---

[35] For detailed information and empirical analysis of the individual state welfare programs, see R. Tresch, "State Governments and the Welfare System: An Econometric Analysis," *Southern Economic Journal*, July 1975. Also, R. Tresch, "Estimation of State Expenditure Functions, 1954–1969" (Ph.D. diss., Department of Economics, Massachusetts Institute of Technology, February 1973).

$\bar{E}_G = AK'$, with the added condition that the receiving government must spend at least E_A from its own revenues, shifts the budget line rightward by $\bar{E}_G$ from point A, not point F as above. At a minimum, expenditures on E must now be $E_A + \bar{E}_G$, and the grantor has achieved dollar-for-dollar stimulation on E. A corner solution is a likely result, since if the receiving government moved to a position between K' and I on the new budget line, the added condition would not have been necessary. The grantor would have achieved stimulation in excess on $\bar{E}_G$ in any case, even with an unconditional grant. One can assume, however, that lack of stimulation induced the added condition in the first place.

Notice that the additional condition may tend to become inoperative over time. If the reference base, E_A, is not increased each year, the corner point K' will move proportionally closer to the O axis as the budget line moves out over time. At the point where the receiving government wants to spend at least $(E_A + \bar{E}_G)$ on E anyway, it will be in equilibrium on the interior of line segment $K'I$. To avoid this result, the grantor would have to build in some automatic growth rate to the base.

Our analysis has two important implications for the recent national interest in bloc grants, in which the national government consolidates a number of grants in a related area into one "bloc" grant, equal in dollar amount to the total of all the original more narrowly defined grants. (Community Development was the first such grant instituted in 1975.) In the first place, consolidation into bloc grants risks lowering state and local expenditures in the aided area if it has any effect at all. Some of the displaced, narrowly defined grants may have been distorting relative to an unconditional grant. If so, then total expenditures on community development can be expected to decline after consolidation, since the bloc grant will almost certainly not be distorting. For example, it is inconceivable that the amount of funds any state or locality will receive for community development, broadly defined, will equal or exceed the total amount these governments would have spent on all community development programs, combined, with an equal dollar unconditional grant. In other words, they will almost certainly supplement these bloc grant funds with their own resources. If, on the other hand, none of the original grants were distorting, consolidation into an equal-dollar bloc grant will have no effect whatsoever.

The second implication follows immediately from the first. Since the bloc grant is almost certainly not going to be distorting, there is no reason to use it. Simply give the funds unconditionally. Unconditional grants are much easier to administer and they can be expected to produce the same expenditure effects anyway. Taking both implications into consideration, it is hard to understand the attraction for broadly defined, conditional, nonmatching bloc grants.

The final point to make concerning conditional, nonmatching grants is a political one. Despite the previous analysis it is possible that even "small" conditional grants will distort expenditures relative to equal dollar unconditional grants if the political process reacts differently to the two types of grants. Local officials may rally support around programs with specific aid attached to them, a bias that would be missing with the unconditional grant. In terms of the above analysis the mere offer of a conditional grant for E changes preferences

FIGURE 31–7

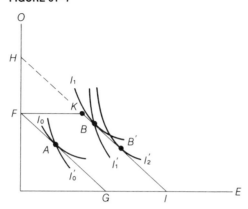

toward E-type projects. Indifference curves become steeper (higher MRS at any given O, E combination) with the conditional grant, so that the government moves to B' rather than B in Figure 31–7, its preferred solution with an equivalent unconditional grant. Whether or not such a "twist" in preferences is rational is impossible to determine, since the change in tastes render the two situations noncomparable. It is even ambiguous to speak of distortion relative to the unconditional grant in this case, but to the extent such twisting occurs, conditional grants will satisfy the paternalistic motives of the grantor.

The second type of conditional grant, a *matching open-ended* grant, can be expected to elicit a different response from the nonmatching grant even if preferences remain the same. The matching grant will generally distort expenditures in favor of the aided item relative to an equal dollar unconditional grant, because the matching formula introduces a substitution effect in favor of the aided item. Moreover, if the substitution effect does distort expenditures, then the receiving government would always prefer the equal dollar unconditional grant. In this sense, offering aid on a matching basis lowers the utility to the receiving government.

These two points can be demonstrated quite easily with the indifference curve analysis. Suppose the receiving government is originally at point A in Figure 31–8 without the grant. If the government now receives a matching grant at rate α, the new budget constraint is:

(31.75) $$(1 - \alpha)E + O = T$$

The budget line rotates around point F to FM, where the slope of FM equals $(1 - \alpha)$.

One unusual feature of the matching grant is that the grantor cannot determine in advance how much aid it will give, since aid is endogenous to the receiving government, dependent upon the new equilibrium it chooses. Suppose it selects point C in Figure 31–8. Once C is established, the point at which $MRS_{E,O} = (1 - \alpha)$, we know that the grantor offers NC dollars of aid for E, and that the receiving government spends NP dollars of its own resources on E. The matching grant, then, must be compared to an unconditional grant

FIGURE 31-8

of NC dollars, represented by the dotted line HI. Comparing C to B, the equilibrium on HI, C will generally lie to the southeast and on a lower indifference curve as drawn. In terms of the geometry, if indifference curve I_1 is tangent to budget line FM with slope $(1 - \alpha)$, it will generally not be tangent to HI, by the assumption of diminishing marginal rate of substitution. B is also revealed preferred to C, since the government purchased commodity bundle B when it could have bought C, and could not have purchased B when it bought C. Both the results derive solely from the substitution effect. Since the dollar amounts of aid are equal in this comparison, the two grants have the same income effects, by definition.

This analysis of the distorting effects of matching grants is exactly analogous to the analysis of distorting taxation in Chapter 15, in which it was shown that commodity taxes create a deadweight loss relative to equal revenue lump-sum taxes because they introduce a distorting substitution effect. The only substantive difference in the grants analysis is that the use of the word distortion is somewhat misleading in the case of the grant. The grantor presumably selects a matching grant because it wants to distort expenditures in favor of E. For instance, it may be reacting to an externality situation with an imperfect correspondence for which a matching grant is the appropriate response. Thus, the receiving government may suffer a deadweight loss relative to an equal dollar conditional grant, but society as a whole might gain. The grant improves resource allocation just as a Pigovian externality tax distorts behavior toward a preferred alternative. If it so happens that the particular matching grant is nonoptimal, then the issue of distortion is ambiguous, in general. The receiving government loses, and the grantor gains from the distortion, so that the net effect on society is ambiguous.

The final grant to be considered is the *conditional, matching, closed-ended* grant. This type of grant is especially important since the U.S. national government has chosen it for many of its largest programs. For instance, most transportation and public assistance grants (with the exception of Medicaid) use the closed-ended matching formula.

FIGURE 31-9

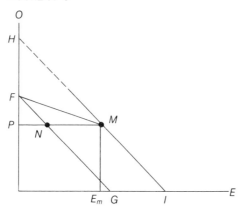

These grants are also intriguing in that they are matching grants which may not have significantly distorted state and local expenditures toward the aided categories. The reason is that they are also closed ended. That is, the receiving government is given a discount on expenditures only up to some predetermined maximum. Given this feature, the receiving government's budget line rotates only in part. Once the allowable maximum is reached, it becomes parallel to the original budget line. The situation is depicted in Figure 31-9.

Up to E_m, the government receives a matching grant on E expenditures, with the matching rate equal to MN/MP. The maximum amount of aid is MN dollars. Any expenditures beyond M must be financed entirely out of "own" funds. Thus, the new budget line, FMI, becomes parallel to the original budget line FG after point M.

Whether or not this type of grant distorts expenditures relative to an equal dollar unconditional grant depends on the position of the with-grant equilibrium. If the equilibrium occurs along the line segment FM, then the matching rate is relevant, and the analysis of the preceding section applies in toto. The grant creates a substitution effect that distorts expenditures and lowers the receiving government's utility relative to the unconditional grant. If, on the other hand, the receiving government moves to a new equilibrium on line segment MI, the grant is nondistorting, entirely equivalent to a nondistorting conditional, nonmatching grant. The aid of MN dollars is exogenous. The receiving government could not possibly care how it received MN, whether as a straight dollar grant or as a percentage of some base amount which is smaller than its total expenditures.

It is easy to determine whether or not a conditional closed-ended matching grant is distorting. If the receiving government takes the maximum allowable grant and adds some of its own resources to the aided category, the grant must be exogenous and nondistorting. If, however, the government receives less than the allowable maximum, the matching rate must be applicable along with its substitution effect. Actual U.S. aid programs fall into both categories. By this test, the ABC portion of the Federal Highway Act has almost always been exogenous for all states.[36] AFDC grants, on the other hand, are exogenous for some states, but endogenous (distorting) for others, although the majority of aid goes to large states for which the aid is exogenous (e.g., New York, California, and so forth).[37]

Empirical Evidence on U.S. Grants-in-Aid

What exactly has been the impact of U.S. grants-in-aid on state and local governments? Perhaps no other single question in public sector analysis has been researched as intensively, to the point where studies now exist in virtually every conceivable format. Data bases have varied from highly aggregated data on combined state and local budgets from the national accounts, to less aggregated data on a selection of state or local governments, to fairly disaggregated data by functional category (welfare, transportation, and so forth) either at the state or local or combined state and local level. Some of the studies use annual or quarterly time series data, other are cross sectional, and still others use pooled data sets. Estimation techniques vary considerably as well, from ordinary least squares to various kinds of simultaneous estimation techniques. Despite this mountain of evidence, however, it is still not clear what the effects of grants-in-aid have actually been.

In 1969 Gramlich reviewed 15 cross-section studies and 5 time-series for the National Tax Association,[38] trying to determine if a consensus had arisen on a single point, the marginal response of total state and/or local expenditures to grants-in-aid, $\partial TE/\partial G$. Instead of consensus, he discovered an uncomfortably wide range of estimates. The cross-section estimates ranged from 0 to 2.45, that is to say, from total substitution of grant funds for own resources to the rather remarkable conclusion that a dollar of additional aid elicits an additional $1.45 of tax revenues. Most estimates, however, were in the $[1-2]$ range, implying mild stimulation. The time-series estimates were lower overall, ranging from .32 to 1.12, with the majority of estimates less than 1. Since all but one of the time-series studies used quarterly data, the lower estimates are understandable. Even so, proponents of grants-in-aid have to be disturbed by the implication that states and localities substitute grant funds for own resources resources in the short run.

More recent work (e.g., O'Brien and Tresch)[39] has used larger micro data sets disaggregated by function to get at the compositional effects of grants-in-aid.

---

[36] On this point see L. Sherman, "The Impacts of the Federal Aid Highway Program on State and Local Highway Expenditures" (Ph.D. diss., Department of Civil Engineering, Massachusetts Institute of Technology, February 1975), chaps. II and III. These chapters contain a complete and detailed history of the Federal Highway Aid Program.

[37] Tresch, "State Governments and the Welfare System: An Econometric Analysis"; and Tresch, "Estimation of State Expenditure Functions, 1954–1969."

[38] E. Gramlich, "The Effects of Federal Grants on State-Local Expenditures: A Review of the Econometric Literature," S. Bowers, ed., 1969 *Proceedings of the Sixty-Second Annual Conference on Taxation at Boston, Massachusetts, September 29–October 3, 1969* (Columbus, Ohio: National Tax Association, 1970).

[39] T. O'Brien, "Grants-in-Aid: Some Further Answers," *National Tax Journal*, March 1971; and R. W. Tresch, "Estimating State Expenditure Functions: An Empirical Test of the Time Series Informational Content of Cross-Section Estimates," *Public Finance*, nos. 3-4, 1974.

To cite one example, Tresch analyzed state data on six functional categories from 1953–69 in an attempt to answer the following types of questions: Do individual year cross-section estimates of grant responses stand up over time? Is pooling the data set legitimate? Is a particular functional area more responsive to categorical grants specific to it than to grants in general? What were the separate substitution and income effects of the matching, closed-ended public assistance grants during this time period? The results were extremely mixed, and often discouraging. Tresch found that cross-section estimates are highly variable over time, and further statistical analysis showed that pooling data was not always legitimate. The attempt to separate out income and substitution effects for the welfare grants also ran into difficulties. The exogenous income effect came through strongly, but the estimates on the substitution effect were seldom significantly different from zero, and in some years even had incorrect positive signs. The clearest pattern emerging from his analysis was that functional categories are strikingly more responsive to categorical grants than to grants-in-aid generally. Since the major categorical grants in areas such as education, health, and transportation are closed ended, and pass the test for exogeneity, this result strongly suggests that categorical grants actually do change political tastes in favor of the aided categories. As indicated above, consumer theory would not predict different responses.

That empirical analysis on the response to grants-in-aid has produced such mixed and inconclusive results is obviously disheartening, but it is hardly surprising. Any attempt to analyze grant response will be faced with enormous difficulties. Two problems are especially ominous. In the first place, there are simply an enormous number of grants-in-aid, literally hundreds at last count. Moreover, many of the individual programs are exceedingly complex. AFDC, for example, has a matching rate that varies by average payment per recipient in each state, and by state income. In addition, some states require participation by localities, others do not. The problem, obviously, is that available data will seldom be sufficiently disaggregated to capture all relevant aspects of given aid formulas. Suppose, for example, one has data on educational expenditures for each state and total grants received for education. A regression of educational expenditures on grants aggregates over scores of separate educational grant programs, many of which are matching grants. Some of these matching programs are likely to be endogenous, even if all these grants were closed ended. But if this is so, a regression of educational expenditures on grants will be subject to simultaneous equation bias, and the extent of the bias is going to be virtually impossible to determine. The bias intensifies the more aggregated the data, yet some of the studies Gramlich reviewed regressed total state or state and local expenditures on total grants. The implicit or explicit assumption in these aggregated studies is that all grants are exogenous, but this is highly unlikely.

The second serious problem for empirical analysis is that no one is really sure how to model state or local behavior. The vast majority of our theoretical knowledge on the response to grants-in-aid, summarized above, derives from models that view the receiving government as a single utility maximizing consumer, the model presented above. Much of the latest theoretical literature has focused on the bureaucratic nature of governmental decision making, following Niskanen.[40] The fact that local governments *produce* many different kinds of services has also received a great deal of empirical attention, but to date this literature has had a relatively minor impact on the theory of grants-in-aid.[41] Rather than embark on a detailed review of these studies, we will simply note that until an underlying behavioral model is agreed upon, estimated grant responses will not be terribly useful for policy purposes.

A related problem concerns the obvious interdependent nature of a government's decision-making process, whatever that process may be. Decisions about some functional category, say education, will impact at least one other functional category, including the desired public-private sector resource mix. Thus, even if one had incredibly detailed data on grants and expenditures within one functional category, estimating a set of expenditure equations based on these data alone may not be very worthwile since they will inevitably fail to account for the impacts of this category on others and vice versa. These grants may really be financing increases in some other category, a phenomenon which a partial behavioral model cannot possibly capture. This merely underscores the point that our failure to understand state and local decision making processes is a formidable obstacle to determining the effects of grants-in-aid.

REFERENCES

Aronson, J., and Maxwell, J. *Financing State and Local Governments.* 3d ed. Washington, D.C.: The Brookings Institution, 1977.

Baumol, W. J., and Oates, W. *The Theory of Environmental Policy.* Englewood Cliffs, N.J.: Prentice-Hall, Inc., 1975.

Breton, A., and Wintrobe, R. "The Equilibrium Size of a Budget-Maximizing Bureau: A Note on Niskanen's Theory of Bureaucracy." *Journal of Political Economy,* February 1975.

Brown, S.; Fox, W.; Godsey, W.; and Stam, J. *Economics of Size in Local Government: An Annotated Bibliography.* Rural Development Research Report No. 9. Economic Development Division, Economics, Statistics, and Cooperatives Service, U.S. Department of Agriculture, April 1979.

Economic Report of the President, January 1979. Washington, D.C.: U.S. Government Printing Office, 1979.

Eisenmenger, R.; Munnell, A.; and Poskanzer, J. *Options for Fiscal Reform in Massachusetts.* Research Report No. 57. Federal Reserve Bank of Boston, March 1975.

----

[40] W. Niskanen, Jr., *Bureaucracy and Representative Government* (Chicago: Aldine-Atherton, 1971). See also A. Breton and R. Wintrobe, "The Equilibrium Size of a Budget-Maximizing Bureau: A Note on Niskanen's Theory of Bureaucracy," *Journal of Political Economy,* February 1975.

[41] See W. Fox, J. Stam, W. Godsey, and S. Brown, *Economics of Size in Local Government: An Annotated Bibliography,* Rural Development Research Report No. 9, Economic Development Division, Economics, Statistics, and Cooperatives Service, U.S. Department of Agriculture, April 1979.

Feldstein, M. "Wealth Neutrality and Local Choice in Public Education." *American Economic Review,* March 1975.

Gramlich, E. "The Effects of Federal Grants on State-Local Expenditures: A Review of the Econometric Literature." In *1969 Proceedings of the Sixty-Second Annual Conference on Taxation at Boston, Massachusetts, September 29–October 3, 1969,* edited by S. Bowers. Columbus, Ohio: National Tax Association, 1970.

LeGrand, J. "Fiscal Equity and Central Government Grants to Local Authorities." *Economic Journal,* September 1975.

Niskanen, Jr., W. *Bureaucracy and Representative Government.* Chicago: Aldine-Atherton, 1971.

Oates, W. *Fiscal Federalism.* New York: Harcourt Brace Jovanovich, Inc., 1972.

O'Brien, T. "Grants-in-Aid: Some Further Answers." *National Tax Journal,* March 1971.

Scott, A. "The Evaluation of Federal Grants." *Economica,* November 1952.

Serrano v. Priest. L.A. 29820, Superior Court No. 938254.

Sherman, L. *"The Impacts of the Federal Aid Highway Program on State and Local Highway Expenditures."* Ph.D. dissertation, Department of Civil Engineering, Massachusetts Institute of Technology, 1975.

Special Analyses: Budget of the United States Government, Fiscal Year 1980. Washington, D.C.: U.S. Government Printing Office, 1979.

Special Revenue Sharing: An Analysis of the Administration's Grant Consolidation Proposals. Information Report M-70. Advisory Commission on Intergovernmental Relations, Washington, D.C., December 1971.

The Role of Equalization in Federal Grants. A-19. Advisory Commission on Intergovernmental Relations, Washington, D.C., 1964.

Tresch, R. "Estimating State Expenditure Functions: An Empirical Test of the Time-Series Informational Content of Cross-Section Estimates." *Public Finance,* no. 3–4/1974.

———. *"Estimation of State Expenditure Functions, 1954–1969."* Ph.D. dissertation, Department of Economics, Massachusetts Institute of Technology, February 1973.

———. "State Governments and the Welfare System: An Econometric Analysis." *Southern Economic Journal,* July 1975.

Name Index

Subject Index

A

Aaron-McGuire incidence analysis, 419–22
Ability to pay principle, 115, 261–91, 320, 364, 591, 628
Ad valorem taxes, 54–55, 319–20, 364, 367, 387–91, 602
Aid for Dependent Children—U.S., 257–59, 599, 603, 628, 640, 641
Anti-pollution policies—U.S., 153–56, 163–76, 570
Arrow-Lind theorem, 480, 508–16, 562, 575
Arrow's impossibility theorem, 25
Atkinson-Feldstein social welfare function, 24n, 25
Automobile emissions standards—U.S., 154–55, 168–69, 570
Average cost pricing, 179, 202–18, 242, 262, 426–27, 443–44, 593
Averch-Johnson effect, 208–13, 216, 426

B

Baumol-Oates cost disease model, 604, 615–25
Bell Telephone, 213
Benefits received principle, 107, 115–21, 204–6, 252, 261–63, 419, 567, 581, 583, 591–593, 622–23
Bergson-Samuelson social welfare function, 22–25, 37, 41, 58, 79, 80, 87, 94, 301, 305, 351–52, 365, 467, 519, 545–48, 596–97
Bliss point (Bator), 23, 27, 45, 56, 89, 111, 252, 296, 542–45
Bloc grants, 603–4, 636
Boiteux problem, 209n, 298n, 302, 330n, 426–27, 443–52

C

California—Proposition 13, 623
Clarke taxes, 119–21, 419
Clean Air Acts—U.S., 154–55, 163–64, 169, 570
Club goods, 128–29, 570–74
Community Development Grant—U.S., 604, 636

Compensating surplus, 524–34
Competition problem in fiscal federalism, 565, 567, 590–600, 615
Conditional grants, 597–98, 602–11, 625–42
Consumer sovereignty, 5–6, 8, 13, 15, 25, 56–58, 108–9, 262, 301, 593
Consumer's surplus
  Hicksian, 67–69, 347, 462–64, 523–27, 531, 548, 562
  Marshallian, 68–69, 188, 194–98, 216, 238, 247, 306, 373–74, 523–27, 548–51
Corlett-Hague problem, 333–36, 370, 383
Cost benefit analysis
  common pitfalls, 483–84, 556–62
    double counting, 484, 561
    Keynesian multipliers, 484, 558–59
    miscounting profits, 484, 557–58
    public sector biases, 484, 525, 561–62
    wages as benefits, 484, 559–60
  definition, 427–28, 476, 483
  discount rate for public projects, 478–80, 486–506, 508, 512, 515–18, 537, 556, 561–62
    Bradford model, 487, 496–503
    Diamond-Mirrlees analysis, 460, 495, 501, 516
    externalities, 493–94, 504n, 562
    Harberger's weighted average rule, 479, 486, 491, 496, 500, 502–4
    opportunity cost, 479–80, 486–506, 516, 537, 561–62
    reinvestment of project benefits, 487, 492, 496–504, 562
    social rate of time preference, 479–80, 486–506, 516
    U.S. practice, 505–6
  distributional considerations, 477, 483, 493, 504–62
    new neoclassical position (Boadway), 545, 554–55
    social rate of time preference, 493, 504–6
    standard neoclassical position (Weisbrod), 26n, 545–53, 555
      Weisbrod's empirical analysis, 552–53

This book has been set Monophoto 400 in 10 and 9 point Times Roman, leaded 2 points. Part and chapter numbers are Times Roman Bold. Part titles are 16 point Roman Bold, and chapter titles are 14 point Times Roman. The size of the type page is 28 by 47½ picas.